# STATISTICAL HANDBOOK ON CONSUMPTION AND WEALTH IN THE UNITED STATES

Edited by
Chandrika Kaul
and Valerie Tomaselli-Moschovitis

Oryx Press
1999

*The rare Arabian Oryx is believed to have inspired the myth of the unicorn. This desert antelope became virtually extinct in the early 1960s. At that time, several groups of international conservationists arranged to have nine animals sent to the Phoenix Zoo to be the nucleus of a captive breeding herd. Today, the Oryx population is over 1,000, and over 500 have been returned to the Middle East.*

© 1999 by The Moschovitis Group
Published by The Oryx Press
4041 North Central at Indian School Road
Phoenix, Arizona 85012-3397
http://www.oryxpress.com

Published simultaneously in Canada
Printed and bound in the United States of America

∞ The paper used in this publication meets the minimum requirements of American National Standard for Information Science—Permanence of Paper for Printed Library Materials, ANSI Z39.48, 1984.

*Library of Congress Cataloging-in-Publication Data*

Statistical handbook on consumption and wealth in the United States.
    p. cm.
    Includes bibliographical references and index.
    ISBN 1-57356-251-3 (alk. paper)
    1. Consumption (Economics)—United States—Statistics.    2. Wealth—United States—Statistics.    I. Kaul, Chandrika.    II. Tomaselli-Moschovitis, Valerie
HC110.C6S73    2000
339.4'1'0973021—dc21                                              99-38530
                                                                              CIP

# Contents

Introduction   v

List of Tables and Charts   vii

**A. General Economic Data**   1
  A1. Gross Domestic Product (GDP) and Gross National Product (GNP)   2
  A2. Relation of National Product to Income and Saving   10
  A3. Net Stock of Fixed Reproducible Tangible Wealth   11
  A4. Foreign Direct Investment in the United States   14
  A5. Gross State Product   16

**B. Personal, Family, and Household Income and Wealth**   22
  B1. Personal Income Totals and Analysis of Personal Income, Seasonally Adjusted at Annual Rates   24
  B2. Households and Median Income, by Selected Characteristics   26
  B3. Analysis of Personal Income and Its Disposition   32
  B4. Personal Income, by State   34
  B5. Projections of Personal Income in Constant (1987) Dollars, by State   38
  B6. Personal Income and Expenditures, per Capita, in Current Dollars   39
  B7. Personal Income per Capita by State, in Current and Constant Dollars   40
  B8. Disposable Personal Income per Capita   44
  B9. Average Annual Pay and Personal Earnings   46
  B10. Personal Earnings by Highest Degree Earned   50
  B11. Median Income for 4-Person Families, by State   53
  B12. Money Income of Families—Median Income by Race and Hispanic Origin   60
  B13. Median Income of Families, by Type of Family   62
  B14. Median Income of Nonmarried-Couple Households and by Household Size   65
  B15. Money Income of Households and Families—Percent Distribution, by Income Level, Race, and Hispanic Origin   66
  B16. Selected Measures of Household Income, 1969–1996   68
  B17. Gross Saving and Investment   69
  B18. Flow of Funds Accounts—Individual Savings   71
  B19. IRAs and 401(k) Plans   73
  B20. Nonfinancial Assets Held by Families, by Type of Asset   75

**C. Business and Corporate Wealth**   77
  C1. Number of Business Tax Returns, Business Receipts, and Corporate Balance Sheet   78
  C2. Corporations—Selected Financial Items, by Industry   80
  C3. Corporations—Annual Percent Change in Receipts, by Industry   83
  C4. Corporations—Selected Financial Items, by Asset-Size Class and Industry   83
  C5. Corporations—Receipts, Percent Distribution by Asset-Size Class and Industry   84
  C6. Corporate Profits, by Industry   85
  C7. U.S. Largest Public Companies   87
  C8. 1000 Largest Industrial Corporations   89
  C9. U.S. Multinational Companies   90
  C10. Net Stock of Fixed Private Capital   94
  C11. Farms   94

**D. Overview of Consumption**   97
  D1. Personal Consumption Expenditures in Current and Constant Dollars   99
  D2. Average Annual Expenditures of All Consumer Units, by Year, 1989–1995   103
  D3. Average Annual Expenditures of All Consumer Units, by Region, 1995   106

D4. Average Annual Expenditures of All Consumer Units, by Size of Unit, 1995   109

D5. Average Annual Expenditures of All Consumer Units, by Type of Unit, 1995   111

D6. Average Annual Expenditures of All Consumer Units, by Type of Unit, Husband and Wife with Children, 1995   114

D7. Average Annual Expenditures of All Consumer Units, by Race and Hispanic Origin, 1995   116

D8. Average Annual Expenditures of All Consumer Units, by Age of Householder, 1995   118

D9. Annual Expenditure per Child, 1996   120

**E. Consumption—Material Goods   121**

E1. Per Capita Consumption of Major Food Commodities   123

E2. Food—Retail Prices of Selected Items   133

E3. Per Capita Consumption of Selected Beverages, by Type   135

E4. Macronutrients, Quantities Available for Consumption per Capita per Day   137

E5. Value of New Construction Put in Place   143

E6. New Privately Owned Housing Units Started, Total and by State   147

E7. Homeownership Rates, Total and by State   149

E8. Construction Contracts—Value of Construction and Floor Space of Buildings   151

E9. Energy Supply and Disposition   153

E10. Energy Consumption—Total and per Capita, by State   157

E11. Energy Consumption—by End-Use Sector and Selected Sources, by State   158

E12. Recent Trends in Apparel and Footwear   162

E13. Recent Trends in Household Appliances   168

E14. Microcomputer Software Sales   174

E15. Recent Trends in Soap, Cleaners, and Toilet Goods   175

**F. Consumption—Services   177**

F1. Selected Personal Services   179

F2. Business Services   181

F3. Public Elementary and Secondary Education   186

F4. Availability and Use of Selected Teaching Resources   190

F5. Institutions of Higher Education   193

F6. Internet Access and Usage   198

F7. Selected Health Services, Estimated Receipts and Growth in Receipts   205

F8. National Health Expenditures, by Object   208

F9. Health Services and Supplies—Per Capita Consumer Expenditures, by Object   210

F10. Life Insurance Purchases in the United States   212

F11. Automobile Insurance—Average Expenditures per Insured Vehicle   213

**G. Consumption—Travel, Leisure, and Other Non-Essentials   215**

G1. Travel by U.S. Residents   217

G2. Characteristics of Trips   219

G3. Domestic Travel Expenditures, by State   220

G4. Media Usage and Consumer Spending   221

G5. Books, Quantity Sold and Expenditure   224

G6. Book Purchasing by Adults—Total, Mass Market, Trade, and Hardcover   227

G7. Newspapers—Number and Circulation   229

G8. Expenditures per Consumer Unit for Entertainment and Reading   231

G9. Profile of Consumer Expenditures for Sound Recordings   234

G10. Recent Trends in Dolls, Toys, and Games   236

G11. Motion Pictures and Amusement and Recreation Services—Estimated Receipts   238

G12. Amusement Parks—Estimated Receipts by Source   241

G13. Selected Recreational Activities   242

G14. Selected Spectator Sports   244

G15. Participation in Selected Sports Activities   248

G16. Household Pet Ownership   251

G17. Charity and Philanthropy   251

**H. The Role of Government   254**

H1. Federal Budget   255

H2. Federal Receipts, by Source   258

H3. Federal Budget Outlays   259

H4. Gross Federal Debt   260

H5. Small Business Administration (SBA) Loans to Small Businesses   262

H6. Social Welfare Expenditures under Public Programs   263

H7. State Governments—Sources of General Revenue   268

**Appendix: International Perspective   273**

**Index   281**

# Introduction

## OVERVIEW

The United States is one of the wealthiest nations in the world. Its wealth can be measured not merely by examining data on the top economic "performers" of the country, but by examining the variety and amount of goods and services that all types of individuals and entities consume. Consumption and the habits of consumption "trickle down" to all levels of the economy. And what might be considered excessive consumption or, at least, a high level of spending on discretionary items—pets, sports, and recreation, for example—is a feature of many demographic and economic groups throughout the country.

Consumerism in the United States, and the wealth that undergirds it, has been a topic of much public attention and research in recent years. This *Statistical Handbook* provides users a systematic statistical portrait of wealth and consumption, two aspects of our economy that help to define economic, political, and cultural experiences in the United States.

Many of the data presented in this volume are explored across a wide range of economic, demographic, and geographic variables, allowing users a detailed depiction of wealth and spending in various individual and corporate populations. Researchers will be able to locate a wide variety of highly specific data, from the amount of money spent on particular cuts of meat to the amount spent on admission to sporting events, such as baseball games and greyhound races.

Most data are presented in short-term timeframes—within the last 10 years—or in snapshots of recent years. In some instances, when applicable and available, long- or mid-range timeframes are used to give a deeper historical context to key indicators.

## CONTENT AND ORGANIZATION

Organized into eight sections covering such topics as personal and business wealth, consumption of material goods, consumption of services, and the role of government in wealth and consumption, the volume offers a sampling of data in some of the most important topics of this broad-ranging subject. Section A presents an overview involving basic economic data that detail the structure and performance of the U.S. economy. From this background information, Section B covers personal and household income and wealth, presenting information on income, savings, and investment. Section C investigates business wealth—including its sources and uses, and how businesses create and use wealth.

Section D turns the discussion to consumption, presenting an overview of household spending in the United States. It includes data on basic expenditure categories—food, clothing, housing, etc.—broken out across such variables as household sizes and types, race and ethnicity, etc. Sections E through G explore consumption in more detail: Section E covers material goods, Section F covers services, and Section G covers travel, leisure, and other non-essentials.

The final section, Section H, explores government's role in generating wealth and consumption in the United States, at both the national and state level. This government role involves several important functions concerning income and expenditures, including both supporting income and wealth generation through policy initiatives and contributing to spending on its own in support of public interests.

## SOURCES, METHODOLOGY, AND PRESENTATION

The data in this volume are from several sources, predominantly from governmental agencies such as the U.S. Census Bureau and the Bureau of Economic Analysis. Often, the tables are reproduced exactly; however, in some instances, the tables are modified to make the information more understandable and readable for the user. Such modifications include breaking tables up into several different tables, re-labeling to ensure clarity and consistency between tables and charts, and taking out total columns and rows that are considered excessive, redundant, or inapplicable. If the user wishes to see the original table or chart, full source source information is provided with each table or chart.

Charts often present summary information, while tables separate the information into more detailed breakdowns. Frequently, charts show summary totals across time spans so that a broad-stroke historical picture is presented in an accessible, visual format. The user should examine such charts to gain an understanding of overriding trends in the data.

Occasionally, however, charts will be used to present variations between key variables other than time. For instance, Section E: Consumption of Material Goods opens with a series of charts detailing per capita food consumption, including charts on various types of food including red meat, poultry, fish, and dairy products.

Attempts have been made to include the most current information available from official sources. The various government agencies that process segments of statistical data do so on varying schedules, so that the most current information available for all types of information is not always from the same year. Roughly, the latest available data included in this volume come from 1995 to 1997. Future editions will offer regular updates.

When dealing with massive amounts of statistical data, it is possible that mistakes may occur. While the editors have tried to prevent such occurrences, they will appreciate being informed of any errors that readers detect.

# List of Tables and Charts

## A. GENERAL ECONOMIC DATA

### A1. Gross Domestic Product (GDP) and Gross National Product (GNP)

A1-1.  Gross Domestic Product and Gross National Product, per Capita, in Current Dollars: 1960–1997

A1-2.  GDP in Current Dollars: 1960–1997, in Billions of Dollars

A1-3.  GDP in Current Dollars: 1960–1980, in Billions of Dollars

A1-4.  GDP in Current Dollars: 1983–1985, in Billions of Dollars

A1-5.  GDP in Current Dollars: 1986–1988, in Billions of Dollars

A1-6.  GDP in Current Dollars: 1989–1991, in Billions of Dollars

A1-7.  GDP in Current Dollars: 1992–1994, in Billions of Dollars

A1-8.  GDP in Current Dollars: 1995–1997, in Billions of Dollars

A1-9.  GDP in Constant Dollars: 1960–1997, in Billions of Dollars

A1-10. GDP in Constant (1992) Dollars: 1960–1980, in Billions of Dollars

A1-11. GDP in Constant (1992) Dollars: 1983–1985, in Billions of Dollars

A1-12. GDP in Constant (1992) Dollars: 1986–1988, in Billions of Dollars

A1-13. GDP in Constant (1992) Dollars: 1989–1991, in Billions of Dollars

A1-14. GDP in Constant (1992) Dollars: 1992–1994, in Billions of Dollars

A1-15. GDP in Constant (1992) Dollars: 1995–1997, in Billions of Dollars

### A2. Relation of National Product to Income and Saving

A2-1.  Relation of GDP, GNP, Net National Product, National Income, Personal Income, Disposable Personal Income, and Personal Saving: 1990–1993, in Billions of Dollars

A2-2.  Relation of GDP, GNP, Net National Product, National Income, Personal Income, Disposable Personal Income, and Personal Saving: 1994–1997, in Billions of Dollars

### A3. Net Stock of Fixed Reproducible Tangible Wealth

A3-1.  Net Stock of Fixed Reproducible Tangible Wealth: 1980–1990, in Billions of Dollars, as of December 31

A3-2.  Net Stock of Fixed Reproducible Tangible Wealth: 1992–1995, in Billions of Dollars, as of December 31

A3-3.  Net Stock of Fixed Reproducible Tangible Wealth: 1980–1991, in Billions of Dollars, as of December 31

A3-4.  Net Stock of Fixed Reproducible Tangible Wealth: 1992–1996, in Billions of Dollars, as of December 31

### A4. Foreign Direct Investment in the United States

A4-1.  Foreign Direct Investment in the United States, Summary Totals—Gross Book Value of Property, Plant, and Equipment, U.S. Affiliates of Foreign Companies: 1981–1996, in Millions of Dollars

A4-2.  Foreign Direct Investment in the United States—Gross Book Value of Property, Plant, and Equipment, U.S. Affiliates of Foreign Companies, by State: 1981–1996, in Millions of Dollars

**A5. Gross State Product**

A5-1.    Gross State Product, in Millions of Dollars, with Resident Population, 1996

A5-2.    Projections of Gross State Product in Constant (1987) Dollars, by State: 1992–2010, in Billions of Dollars

A5-3.    Gross State Product in Current Dollars, Total: 1990–1996, in Billions of Dollars

A5-4.    Gross State Product in Constant (1992) Dollars, Total: 1990–1996, in Billions of Dollars

A5-5.    Gross State Product in Current Dollars: 1990–1996, in Billions of Dollars

A5-6.    Gross State Product in Constant (1992) Dollars: 1990–1996, in Billions of Dollars

# B. PERSONAL, FAMILY, AND HOUSEHOLD INCOME AND WEALTH

**B1. Personal Income Totals and Analysis of Personal Income, Seasonally Adjusted at Annual Rates**

B1-1.    Personal Income Totals, Seasonally Adjusted at Annual Rates, 1996-1998, in Billions of Dollars

B1-2.    Analysis of Personal Income, Seasonally Adjusted at Annual Rates, 1996–July 1998, in Billions of Dollars

B1-3.    Analysis of Personal Income, Seasonally Adjusted at Annual Rates, Aug. 1998–Nov. 1998, in Billions of Dollars

**B2. Households and Median Income, by Selected Characteristics**

B2-1.    Households and Median Income, by Selected Characteristics: 1989, 1996, and 1997

B2-2.    Households and Median Income Percent Changes, by Selected Characteristics: 1996–1997 and 1989–1997

**B3. Analysis of Personal Income and Its Disposition**

B3-1.    Personal Income and Its Disposition: 1990–1997, in Billions of Dollars (except as indicated)

B3-2.    Analysis of Personal Income and Its Disposition: 1990–1993, in Billions of Dollars (except as indicated)

B3-3.    Analysis of Personal Income and Its Disposition: 1994–1997, in Billions of Dollars (except as indicated)

**B4. Personal Income, by State**

B4-1.    Personal Income, by State, Current Dollars: 1990–1997, in Billions of Dollars

B4-2.    Personal Income, by State, Constant (1992) Dollars: 1990–1997, in Billions of Dollars

B4-3.    Percent Distribution and Average Annual Percent Change of Personal Income, by State, in Constant (1992) Dollars: 1990–1997, in Billions of Dollars

**B5. Projections of Personal Income in Constant (1987) Dollars, by State**

B5-1.    Projections of Personal Income in Constant (1987) Dollars, by State: 1993–2010, in Billions of Dollars

**B6. Personal Income and Expenditures, per Capita, in Current Dollars**

B6-1.    Personal Income and Expenditures, per Capita, in Current Dollars: 1960–1997

**B7. Personal Income per Capita by State, in Current and Constant Dollars**

B7-1.    Personal Income per Capita in Current Dollars, by State: 1997

B7-2.    Personal Income per Capita in Current Dollars, by State: 1990–1997

B7-3.    Personal Income per Capita in Constant (1992) Dollars[1], by State: 1997

B7-4.    Personal Income per Capita in Constant (1992) Dollars[1], by State: 1990–1997

**B8. Disposable Personal Income per Capita**

B8-1.    Disposable Personal Income per Capita in Current Dollars, by State: 1990 and 1997, in Dollars (1997 data preliminary)

B8-2.    Disposable Personal Income per Capita in Constant (1992) Dollars, by State: 1990 and 1997, in Dollars (1997 data preliminary)

**B9. Average Annual Pay and Personal Earnings**

B9-1.   Average Annual Pay[1], Totals, 1996 (preliminary)

B9-2.   Average Annual Pay[1], Private Industry Totals, 1996 (preliminary)

B9-3.   Average Annual Pay[1], Private Industry Breakdown, 1996 (preliminary)

B9-4.   Projections of Earnings in Constant (1987) Dollars, by State: 1993–2010, in Billions of Dollars

**B10. Personal Earnings by Highest Degree Earned**

B10-1.  Mean Personal Earnings, Totals, by Highest Degree Earned, with No College Degree: 1997

B10-2.  Mean Personal Earnings, by Highest Degree Earned, with No College Degree: 1997

B10-3.  Mean Personal Earnings, Totals, by Highest Degree Earned, with College Degree: 1997

B10-4.  Mean Personal Earnings, by Highest Degree Earned, with College Degree: 1997

**B11. Median Income for 4-Person Families, by State**

B11-1.  Median Income for 4-Person Families, by State: 1974–1977 Calendar Years

B11-2.  Median Income for 4-Person Families, by State: 1978–1981 Calendar Years

B11-3.  Median Income for 4-Person Families, by State: 1982–1985 Calendar Years

B11-4.  Median Income for 4-Person Families, by State: 1986–1989 Calendar Years

B11-5.  Median Income for 4-Person Families, by State: 1990–1992 Calendar Years

B11-6.  Median Income for 4-Person Families, by State: 1993–1996 Calendar Years

**B12. Money Income of Families—Median Income by Race and Hispanic Origin**

B12-1.  Money Income of Families—Median Income, by Race and Hispanic Origin, in Current Dollars: 1970–1996

B12-2.  Money Income of Families—Median Income, by Race and Hispanic Origin, in Constant (1996) Dollars: 1970–1996

**B13. Median Income of Families, by Type of Family**

B13-1.  Median Income of Families, Totals, in Current Dollars: 1970–1996

B13-2.  Median Income of Families, by Type of Family, in Current Dollars: 1970–1996

B13-3.  Median Income of Families, Totals, in Constant (1996) Dollars: 1970–1996

B13-4.  Median Income of Families, by Type of Family, in Constant (1996) Dollars: 1970–1996

**B14. Median Income of Nonmarried-Couple Households and by Household Size**

B14-1.  Median Income of Nonmarried-Couple Households: 1969–1996, in Constant (1996) Dollars

B14-2.  Median Income of Nonmarried-Couple Households, by Household Size: 1969–1996, in Constant (1996) Dollars

**B15. Money Income of Households and Families— Percent Distribution, by Income Level, Race, and Hispanic Origin**

B15-1.  Money Income of Households—Percent Distribution, by Income Level, Race, and Hispanic Origin, in Constant (1996) Dollars: 1970–1996

B15-2.  Money Income of Families—Percent Distribution, by Income Level, Race, and Hispanic Origin, in Constant (1996) Dollars: 1970–1996

**B16. Selected Measures of Household Income, 1969–1996**

B16-1.  Selected Measures of Household Income, 1969–1996: All Households

**B17. Gross Saving and Investment**

B17-1.  Gross Saving and Investment, Totals: 1990– 1997, in Billions of Dollars

B17-2.  Gross Saving and Investment: 1990–1993, in Billions of Dollars

B17-3.  Gross Saving and Investment: 1994–1997, in Billions of Dollars

**B18. Flow of Funds Accounts—Individual Savings**

B18-1.  Flow of Funds Accounts—Composition of Individuals' Savings: 1980–1990, in Billions of Dollars

B18-2.  Flow of Funds Accounts—Composition of Individuals' Savings: 1991–1996, in Billions of Dollars

**B19. IRAs and 401(k) Plans**

B19-1.  Individual Retirement Accounts (IRA) Plans—Value, by Type of Holder: 1985–1991, as of December 31, in Billions of Dollars, Estimated

B19-2.  Individual Retirement Accounts (IRA) Plans—Value, by Type of Holder: 1992–1996, as of December 31, in Billions of Dollars, Estimated

B19-3.  401(k) Plan Total Assets—1985–1996

B19-4.  401(k) Plan Assets—Type of Assets, 1997

B19-5.  401(k) Plan Assets—Type of Financial Institution Managing Assets, 1997

**B20. Nonfinancial Assets Held by Families, by Type of Asset**

B20-1.  Nonfinancial Assets Held by Families, Percent of Families Owning Assets, by Type of Asset: 1995

B20-2.  Nonfinancial Assets Held by Families, Median Value, by Type of Asset: 1995, in Thousands of Dollars

## C. BUSINESS AND CORPORATE WEALTH

**C1. Number of Business Tax Returns, Business Receipts, and Corporate Balance Sheet**

C1-1.  Number of Business Tax Returns, by Type of Enterprise: 1980–1995

C1-2.  Business Receipts, by Type of Enterprise: 1980–1995

C1-3.  Corporate Balance Sheet, Total of Nonfinancial Corporations: 1988–1996

**C2. Corporations—Selected Financial Items, by Industry**

C2-1.  Corporations—Selected Financial Items, by Industry: 1980–1990, in Billions of Dollars, (except as indicated).

C2-2.  Corporations—Selected Financial Items, by Industry: 1991–1994, in Billions of Dollars, (except as indicated).

**C3. Corporations—Annual Percent Change in Receipts, by Industry**

C3-1.  Corporations—Annual Percent Change in Receipts, by Industry: 1980–1994

**C4. Corporations—Selected Financial Items, by Asset-Size Class and Industry**

C4-1.  Corporations—Selected Financial Items, by Asset-Size Class and Industry: 1995, in Millions of Dollars, (except number of returns)

**C5. Corporations—Receipts, Percent Distribution by Asset-Size Class and Industry**

C5-1.  Corporations—Receipts, Percent Distribution by Asset-Size Class and Industry: 1995

**C6. Corporate Profits, by Industry**

C6-1.  Corporate Profits, Taxes, and Dividends: 1990–1996, in Billions of Dollars

C6-2.  Corporate Profits, Pre-Tax and After Tax, Totals: 1990–1996, in Millions of Dollars

C6-3.  Corporate Profits, Pre-Tax and After Tax, by Industry: 1990–1996, in Millions of Dollars

**C7. U.S. Largest Public Companies**

C7-1.  U.S. Largest Public Companies, Profitability: 1997, in Percents

C7-2.  U.S. Largest Public Companies, Growth in Sales: 1997, in Percents

C7-3.  U.S. Largest Public Companies, Growth in Earnings and Debt to Capital: 1997, in Percents

**C8. 1000 Largest Industrial Corporations**

C8-1.  1000 Largest Industrial Corporations—Profits, by Industry: 1997

C8-2.  1000 Largest Industrial Corporations—Earnings and Return to Investors, by Industry: 1987 and 1997

### C9. U.S. Multinational Companies

C9-1. U.S. Multinational Companies, Total Multinationals and only U.S. Parents—Gross Product: 1994 and 1995, in Millions of Dollars

C9-2. U.S. Multinational Companies, Foreign Affiliates—Gross Product: 1994 and 1995, in Millions of Dollars

C9-3. U.S. Multinational Companies, with U.S. Parents, Selected Characteristics: 1995, Preliminary, in Billions of Dollars, (except as indicated)

C9-4. U.S. Multinational Companies, Foreign Affiliates, Selected Characteristics: 1995, Preliminary, in Billions of Dollars, (except as indicated)

### C10. Net Stock of Fixed Private Capital

C10-1. Net Stock of Fixed Private Capital: 1990–1996 (as of Dec. 31)

### C11. Farms

C11-1. Farms—Number, Acreage, and Value, by Type of Organization: 1987 and 1992

C11-2. Farms—Number, Acreage, and Value, by Type of Organization, Percent Distribution: 1987 and 1992

C11-3. Farms—Number and Acreage, by Size of Farm: 1982–1992

C11-4. Farms—Acreage, by Size of Farm: 1982–1992

C11-5. Farms—Acreage, by Size of Farm, Percent Distribution: 1992

## D. OVERVIEW OF CONSUMPTION

### D1. Personal Consumption Expenditures in Current and Constant Dollars

D1-1. Personal Consumption Expenditures in Current Dollars, Totals: 1990–1996

D1-2. Personal Consumption Expenditures in Current Dollars, by Type: 1990–1996, in Billions of Dollars *(continued in D1-3 and D1-4)*

D1-3. Personal Consumption Expenditures in Current Dollars, by Type: 1990–1996, in Billions of Dollars *(continued from previous table)*

D1-4. Personal Consumption Expenditures in Current Dollars, by Type: 1990–1996, in Billions of Dollars *(continued from previous table)*

D1-5. Personal Consumption Expenditures in Chained, or Constant (1992), Dollars, Totals: 1990–1996

D1-6. Personal Consumption Expenditures in Chained, or Constant (1992), Dollars, by Type: 1990–1996, in Billions of Dollars *(continued in D1-7 and D1-8)*

D1-7. Personal Consumption Expenditures in Chained, or Constant (1992), Dollars, by Type: 1990–1996, in Billions of Dollars *(continued from previous table)*

D1-8. Personal Consumption Expenditures in Chained, or Constant (1992), Dollars, by Type: 1990–1996, in Billions of Dollars *(continued from previous table)*

### D2. Average Annual Expenditures of All Consumer Units, by Year, 1989–1995

D2-1. Average Annual Expenditures of All Consumer Units, Number of Units: 1989–1995

D2-2. Average Annual Expenditures of All Consumer Units, Total Expenditures: 1989–1995

D2-3. Average Annual Expenditures of All Consumer Units, by Type of Expenditure: 1989–1991, in Dollars

D2-4. Average Annual Expenditures of All Consumer Units, by Type of Expenditure: 1992–1995, in Dollars

### D3. Average Annual Expenditures of All Consumer Units, by Region, 1995

D3-1. Average Annual Expenditures of All Consumer Units, by Region, Totals: 1995

D3-2. Average Annual Expenditures of All Consumer Units, by Region: 1995 *(continued in D3-3 and D3-4)*

D3-3. Average Annual Expenditures of All Consumer Units, by Region: 1995 *(continued from previous table)*

D3-4. Average Annual Expenditures of All Consumer Units, by Region: 1995 *(continued from previous table)*

### D4. Average Annual Expenditures of All Consumer Units, by Size of Unit, 1995

D4-1. Average Annual Expenditures of All Consumer Units, by Size of Unit, Totals: 1995

D4-2. Average Annual Expenditures of All Consumer Units, by Size of Unit: 1995 *(continued in D4-3 and D4-4)*

D4-3. Average Annual Expenditures of All Consumer Units, by Size of Unit: 1995 *(continued from previous table)*

D4-4. Average Annual Expenditures of All Consumer Units, by Size of Unit: 1995 *(continued from previous table)*

**D5. Average Annual Expenditures of All Consumer Units, by Type of Unit, 1995**

D5-1. Average Annual Expenditures of All Consumer Units, by Type of Household Unit, Totals: 1995

D5-2. Average Annual Expenditures of All Consumer Units, by Type of Household Unit: 1995 *(continued in D5-3 and D5-4)*

D5-3. Average Annual Expenditures of All Consumer Units, by Type of Household Unit: 1995 *(continued from previous table)*

D5-4. Average Annual Expenditures of All Consumer Units, by Type of Household Unit: 1995 *(continued from previous table)*

**D6. Average Annual Expenditures of All Consumer Units, by Type of Unit, Husband and Wife with Children, 1995**

D6-1. Average Annual Expenditures of All Consumer Units, by Type of Household Unit, Husband and Wife with Children, Totals: 1995

D6-2. Average Annual Expenditures of All Consumer Units, by Type of Household Unit, Husband and Wife with Children: 1995 *(continued in D6-3)*

D6-3. Average Annual Expenditures of All Consumer Units, by Type of Household Unit, Husband and Wife with Children: 1995 *(continued from previous table)*

**D7. Average Annual Expenditures of All Consumer Units, by Race and Hispanic Origin, 1995**

D7-1. Average Annual Expenditures of All Consumer Units, by Race and Hispanic Origin: 1995, in Dollars

D7-2. Average Annual Expenditures of All Consumer Units, by Race and Hispanic Origin: 1995, in Dollars *(continued in D7-3)*

D7-3. Average Annual Expenditures of All Consumer Units, by Race and Hispanic Origin: 1995, in Dollars *(continued from previous table)*

**D8. Average Annual Expenditures of All Consumer Units, by Age of Householder, 1995**

D8-1. Average Annual Expenditures of All Consumer Units, by Age of Householder: 1995 *(continued in D8-2)*

D8-2. Average Annual Expenditures of All Consumer Units, by Age of Householder: 1995 *(continued from previous table)*

**D9. Annual Expenditure per Child, 1996**

D9-1. Annual Expenditure Per Child by Husband-Wife Families, by Family Income and Expenditure Type, 1996, in Dollars

**E. CONSUMPTION—MATERIAL GOODS**

**E1. Per Capita Consumption of Major Food Commodities**

E1-1. Per Capita Consumption of Major Food Commodities: 1980–1996, in Pounds, Retail Weight (except as indicated)

E1-2. Per Capita Consumption of Major Food Commodities: 1980–1992, in Pounds, Retail Weight (except as indicated) *(continued in E1-3 and E1-4)*

E1-3. Per Capita Consumption of Major Food Commodities: 1980–1992, in Pounds, Retail Weight (except as indicated) *(continued from previous table)*

E1-4. Per Capita Consumption of Major Food Commodities: 1980–1992, in Pounds, Retail Weight (except as indicated) *(continued from previous table)*

E1-5. Per Capita Consumption of Major Food Commodities: 1993–1996, in Pounds, Retail Weight *(except as indicated) (continued in E1-6 and E1-7)*

E1-6. Per Capita Consumption of Major Food Commodities: 1993–1996, in Pounds, Retail Weight (except as indicated) *(continued from previous table)*

E1-7.   Per Capita Consumption of Major Food Commodities: 1993–1996, in Pounds, Retail Weight (except as indicated) *(continued from previous table)*

**E2. Food—Retail Prices of Selected Items**

E2-1.   Food—Retail Prices of Selected Items: 1990–1993 (as of December), in Dollars per Pound, (except as indicated)

E2-2.   Food—Retail Prices of Selected Items: 1994–1997 (as of December), in Dollars per Pound, (except as indicated)

**E3. Per Capita Consumption of Selected Beverages, by Type**

E3-1.   Per Capita Consumption of Selected Beverages, by Type: 1980–1991, in Gallons, Retail Weight (except as indicated).

E3-2.   Per Capita Consumption of Selected Beverages, by Type: 1992–1996, in Gallons, Retail Weight (except as indicated)

**E4. Macronutrients, Quantities Available for Consumption per Capita per Day**

E4-1.   Macronutrients; Energy, Protein, Carbohydrates, Quantities Available for Consumption per Capita per Day: 1970–1994

E4-2.   Macronutrients, Fats and Cholesterol, Quantities Available for Consumption per Capita per Day: 1970–1994

E4-3.   Macronutrients, Vitamins and Minerals, Quantities Available for Consumption per Capita per Day: 1970–1994 *(continued in E4-4, E4-5, and E4-6)*

E4-4.   Macronutrients, Vitamins and Minerals, Quantities Available for Consumption per Capita per Day: 1970–1994 *(continued from previous table)*

E4-5.   Macronutrients, Vitamins and Minerals, Quantities Available for Consumption per Capita per Day: 1970–1994 *(continued from previous table)*

E4-6.   Macronutrients, Vitamins and Minerals, Quantities Available for Consumption per Capita per Day: 1970–1994 *(continued from previous table)*

**E5. Value of New Construction Put in Place**

E5-1.   Value of New Construction Put in Place, Current Dollars, Totals: 1990–1997, in Millions of Dollars

E5-2.   Value of New Construction Put in Place, Current Dollars: 1990–1997, in Millions of Dollars *(continued in E5-3)*

E5-3.   Value of New Construction Put in Place, Current Dollars: 1990–1997, in Millions of Dollars *(continued from previous table)*

E5-4.   Value of New Construction Put in Place, Constant (1992) Dollars, Totals: 1990–1997, in Millions of Dollars

E5-5.   Value of New Construction Put in Place, Constant (1992) Dollars: 1990–1997, in Millions of Dollars *(continued in E5-6)*

E5-6.   Value of New Construction Put in Place, Constant (1992) Dollars: 1990–1997, in Millions of Dollars *(continued from previous table)*

**E6. New Privately Owned Housing Units Started, Total and by State**

E6-1.   New Privately Owned Housing Units Started, Total: 1995–1998, in Thousands of Units

E6-2.   New Privately Owned Housing Units Started, by State: 1995–1998, in Thousands of Units

**E7. Homeownership Rates, Total and by State**

E7-1.   Homeownership Rates, Totals: 1985–1997, in Percent.

E7-2.   Homeownership Rates, by State: 1985–1997, in Percent

**E8. Construction Contracts—Value of Construction and Floor Space of Buildings**

E8-1.   Construction Contracts—Value of Construction and Floor Space of Buildings, by Class of Construction: 1980–1997 *(continued in E8-2)*

E8-2.   Construction Contracts—Value of Construction and Floor Space of Buildings, by Class of Construction: 1980–1997 *(continued from previous table)*

**E9. Energy Supply and Disposition**

E9-1.   Energy Supply and Disposition, Production and Consumption: 1990–1996, in Quadrillion Btu

E9-2.   Energy Supply and Disposition, Exports and Imports: 1990–1996, in Quadrillion Btu

E9-3.   Energy Supply and Disposition, by Type of Fuel: 1990–1992, in Quadrillion Btu

E9-4.   Energy Supply and Disposition, by Type of Fuel: 1993–1996, in Quadrillion Btu

**E10. Energy Consumption—Total and per Capita, by State**

E10-1.  Energy Consumption—Total and per Capita, by State: 1995, in Trillions of Btu (except as indicated)

**E11. Energy Consumption—by End-Use Sector and Selected Sources**

E11-1.  Energy Consumption—by End-Use Sector, Totals: 1995, in Trillions of Btu (except as indicated)

E11-2.  Energy Consumption—by End-Use Sector, by State: 1995, in Trillions of Btu (except as indicated)

E11-3.  Energy Consumption—by Selected Sources, Totals: 1995, in Trillions of Btu (except as indicated)

E11-4.  Energy Consumption—by Selected Sources, by State: 1995, in Trillions of Btu (except as indicated)

**E12. Recent Trends in Apparel and Footwear**

E12-1.  Recent Trends in Apparel and Other Textile Products (SIC 23), Current and Constant (1992) Dollars: 1991–1996

E12-2.  Recent Trends in Selected Women's Outerwear (SIC 2331, 2335, 2337): 1991–1993

E12-3.  Recent Trends in Selected Women's Outerwear (SIC 2331, 2335, 2337): 1994–1997

E12-4.  Recent Trends in Selected Men's and Boys' Apparel (SIC 2311, 2321, -3, -5, -6): 1991–1997

E12-5.  Recent Trends in Footwear, Except Rubber (SIC 314): 1991–1993

E12-6.  Recent Trends in Footwear, Except Rubber (SIC 314): 1994–1997

**E13. Recent Trends in Household Appliances**

E13-1.  Recent Trends in Household Appliances (SIC 363): 1991–1993

E13-2.  Recent Trends in Household Appliances (SIC 363): 1994–1997

E13-3.  Appliances and Office Equipment Used by Households, by Region: 1997

E13-4.  Appliances and Office Equipment Used by Households, by Family Income: 1997

E13-5.  Share of Households Using Appliances, Selected Household Efficiency Appliances, by Family Income: 1997

E13-6.  Share of Households Using Appliances, Selected Telecommunications and Media Equipment, by Family Income: 1997

**E14. Microcomputer Software Sales**

E14-1.  Microcomputer Software Sales: 1995, in Millions of Dollars

E14-2.  Microcomputer Software Sales: 1996, in Millions of Dollars

**E15. Recent Trends in Soap, Cleaners, and Toilet Goods**

E15-1.  Recent Trends in Soap, Cleaners, and Toilet Goods (SIC 284): 1991–1993

E15-2.  Recent Trends in Soap, Cleaners, and Toilet Goods (SIC 284): 1994–1997

**F. CONSUMPTION—SERVICES**

**F1. Selected Personal Services**

F1-1.   Selected Personal Services (SIC 72)—Estimated Receipts for Taxable Firms: 1989–1997, in Millions of Dollars

F1-2.   Selected Personal Services (SIC 72)—Estimated Receipts for Taxable Firms: 1988–1992, in Millions of Dollars

F1-3.   Selected Personal Services (SIC 72)—Estimated Receipts for Taxable Firms: 1993–1997, in Millions of Dollars

F1-4.   Selected Personal Services (SIC 72)—Estimated per Capita Receipts for Taxable Firms: 1988–1992

F1-5.   Selected Personal Services (SIC 72)—Estimated per Capita Receipts for Taxable Firms: 1993–1997

**F2. Business Services**

F2-1.   Business Services—Annual Receipts of Taxable Firms: 1985–1996, in Billions of Dollars, Estimated

**F3. Public Elementary and Secondary Education**

F3-1.   Public Elementary and Secondary Education Estimated Finances, Receipts, and Expenditures: 1980–1997, in Millions of Dollars

F3-2.   Public Elementary and Secondary Education Estimated Finances, Expenditures: 1980–1997, in Millions of Dollars (except as noted)

F3-3.   Public Elementary and Secondary Education Estimated Finances, Receipts: 1980–1997, in Millions of Dollars (except as noted)

F3-4.   Public Elementary and Secondary Education Estimated Finances, Expenditures, by State: 1997, in Millions of Dollars (except as noted)

F3-5.   Public Elementary and Secondary Education Estimated Finances, Receipts, by State: 1997, in Millions of Dollars (except as noted)

**F4. Availability and Use of Selected Teaching Resources**

F4-1.   Availability and Use of Selected Teaching Resources, by Gender of Teacher: 1996, in Percent

F4-2.   Availability and Use of Selected Teaching Resources, by Level of Education: 1996, in Percent

F4-3.   Availability and Use of Selected Teaching Resources, by Race: 1996, in Percent

F4-4.   Availability and Use of Selected Teaching Resources, by Size of School System: 1996, in Percent

**F5. Institutions of Higher Education**

F5-1.   Institutions of Higher Education, Tuition and Fees, Totals: 1985–1997, in Dollars

F5-2.   Institutions of Higher Education, Dormitory Charges, Totals: 1985–1997, in Dollars

F5-3.   Institutions of Higher Education, Board Rates, Totals: 1985–1997, in Dollars

F5-4.   Institutions of Higher Education, Tuition and Fees: 1985–1997, in Dollars

F5-5.   Institutions of Higher Education, Dormitory Charges: 1985–1997, in Dollars

F5-6.   Institutions of Higher Education, Board Rates: 1985–1997, in Dollars

**F6. Internet Access and Usage**

F6-1.   Internet Access and Usage, and Online Service Usage, Share of Population with Any Online Internet Usage: 1998, as of Spring

F6-2.   Internet Access and Usage, and Online Service Usage, Total and by Age, Sex, and Region: 1998, as of Spring (*continued in F6-3*)

F6-3.   Internet Access and Usage, and Online Service Usage, Total and by Age, Sex, and Region: 1998, as of Spring (*continued from previous table*)

F6-4.   Internet Access and Usage, and Online Service Usage, by Household, Marriage, and Employment Characteristics: 1998, as of Spring (*continued in F6-5*)

F6-5.   Internet Access and Usage, and Online Service Usage, by Household, Marriage, and Employment Characteristics: 1998, as of Spring (*continued from previous table*)

**F7. Selected Health Services, Estimated Receipts and Growth in Receipts**

F7-1.   Selected Health Services (SIC 80)—Estimated Receipts for Taxable Firms: 1988–1992, in Millions of Dollars

F7-2.   Selected Health Services (SIC 80)—Estimated Receipts for Taxable Firms: 1993–1997, in Millions of Dollars

F7-3.   Selected Health Services (SIC 80)—Estimated Year-to-Year Percent Change in Receipts for Taxable Firms: 1988–1992

F7-4.   Selected Health Services (SIC 80)—Estimated Year-to-Year Percent Change in Receipts for Taxable Firms: 1993–1997

**F8. National Health Expenditures, by Object**

F8-1.   National Health Expenditures, by Object, Totals: 1990–1996, in Billions of Dollars

F8-2.   National Health Expenditures, by Object: 1990–1996, in Billions of Dollars

**F9. Health Services and Supplies—Per Capita Consumer Expenditures, by Object**

F9-1.   Health Services and Supplies—Per Capita Consumer Expenditures, by Object, Totals: 1980 to 1996, in Dollars

F9-2.   Health Services and Supplies—Per Capita Consumer Expenditures, by Object: 1980–1991, in Dollars (except percent)

F9-3.   Health Services and Supplies—Per Capita Consumer Expenditures, by Object: 1992–1996, in Dollars (except percent)

**F10. Life Insurance Purchases in the United States**

F10-1.  Life Insurance Purchases in the United States—Number: 1980–1996

F10-2.  Life Insurance Purchases in the United States—Value of Amount Purchased: 1980–1996

**F11. Automobile Insurance—Average Expenditures per Insured Vehicle**

F11-1.  Automobile Insurance—Average Expenditures per Insured Vehicle, Totals: 1994–1996, in Dollars

F11-2.  Automobile Insurance—Average Expenditures per Insured Vehicle, by State: 1994–1996, in Dollars

**G. CONSUMPTION—TRAVEL, LEISURE, AND OTHER NON-ESSENTIALS**

**G1. Travel by U.S. Residents**

G1-1.   Travel by U.S. Residents—Summary: 1985–1997, in Millions

G1-2.   Travel by U.S. Residents—Summary: 1985–1992, in Millions (except party size)

G1-3.   Travel by U.S. Residents—Summary: 1993–1997, in Millions (except party size)

**G2. Characteristics of Trips**

G2-1.   Characteristics of Business Trips: 1985–1997

G2-2.   Characteristics of Pleasure Trips: 1985–1997

**G3. Domestic Travel Expenditures, by State**

G3-1.   Domestic Travel Expenditures, by State: 1995

**G4. Media Usage and Consumer Spending**

G4-1.   Media Usage: 1990–1998 (projected)

G4-2.   Media Usage: 1990–1994

G4-3.   Media Usage: 1995–1998 (projected)

G4-4.   Consumer Spending on Media: 1990–1998 (projected)

G4-5.   Consumer Spending on Media: 1990–1994

G4-6.   Consumer Spending on Media: 1995–1998 (projected)

**G5. Books, Quantity Sold and Expenditure**

G5-1.   Books, Quantity Sold, Totals: 1982–1996, in Millions of Units

G5-2.   Books, Quantity Sold: 1982–1996, in Millions of Units

G5-3.   Books, Consumer Expenditures, Totals: 1982–1996, in Millions of Dollars

G5-4.   Books, Consumer Expenditures: 1982–1996, in Millions of Dollars

**G6. Book Purchasing by Adults—Total, Mass Market, Trade, and Hardcover**

G6-1.   Book Purchasing by Adults, Total and Mass Market: 1991 and 1996, in Percent

G6-2.   Book Purchasing by Adults, Trade and Hardcover: 1991 and 1996, in Percent

**G7. Newspapers—Number and Circulation**

G7-1.   Daily Newspapers—Number and Circulation, by State: 1997

G7-2.   Sunday Newspapers—Number and Circulation, by State: 1997

## G8. Expenditures per Consumer Unit for Entertainment and Reading

G8-1. Expenditures per Consumer Unit for Entertainment and Reading, Average Annual Figures: 1985–1995, in Dollars (except as indicated)

G8-2. Expenditures per Consumer Unit for Entertainment and Reading, Percent of Total Expenditure: 1985–1995 (except as indicated)

G8-3. Expenditures per Consumer Unit for Entertainment and Reading: 1985–1995, in Dollars (except as indicated)

G8-4. Expenditures per Consumer Unit for Entertainment and Reading, by Characteristic: 1985–1995, in Dollars (except as indicated)

## G9. Profile of Consumer Expenditures for Sound Recordings

G9-1. Profile of Consumer Expenditures for Sound Recordings: 1990–1997, in Millions of Dollars

G9-2. Profile of Consumer Expenditures for Sound Recordings: 1990–1997, in Percent, (except total value)

## G10. Recent Trends in Dolls, Toys, and Games

G10-1. Recent Trends in Dolls, Toys, and Games (SIC 3942, 3944): 1991–1993

G10-2. Recent Trends in Dolls, Toys, and Games (SIC 3942, 3944): 1994–1997

## G11. Motion Pictures and Amusement and Recreation Services—Estimated Receipts

G11-1. Motion Pictures and Amusement and Recreation Services—Estimated Receipts, Totals: 1988–1997, in Millions of Dollars

G11-2. Motion Pictures (SIC 78) and Amusement and Recreation Services (SIC 79)—Estimated Receipts: 1988–1992, in Millions of Dollars

G11-3. Motion Pictures (SIC 78) and Amusement and Recreation Services (SIC 79)—Estimated Receipts: 1993–1997, in Millions of Dollars

G11-4. Selected Motion Pictures (SIC 78) and Amusement and Recreation Services (SIC 79)—Estimated Per Capita Receipts: 1988–1992, in Whole Dollars

G11-5. Selected Motion Pictures (SIC 78) and Amusement and Recreation Services (SIC 79)—Estimated per Capita Receipts: 1993–1997, in Whole Dollars

## G12. Amusement Parks—Estimated Receipts by Source

G12-1. Amusement Parks (SIC 7996)—Estimated Receipts, by Source: 1993–1997, in Millions of Dollars

G12-2. Amusement Parks (SIC 7996)—Estimated Sources of Receipts as a Percent of Total Dollar Volume: 1993–1997

## G13. Selected Recreational Activities

G13-1. Selected Recreational Activities: 1975–1990

G13-2. Selected Recreational Activities: 1993–1996

## G14. Selected Spectator Sports

G14-1. Selected Spectator Sports: 1985–1992

G14-2. Selected Spectator Sports: 1985–1992 (*continued from previous table*)

G14-3. Selected Spectator Sports: 1993–1996

G14-4. Selected Spectator Sports: 1993–1996 (*continued from previous table*)

## G15. Participation in Selected Sports Activities

G15-1. Participation in Selected Sports Activities, Total and by Gender: 1996, in Thousands except Rank

G15-2. Participation in Selected Sports Activities, by Age Category: 1996, in Thousands

G15-3. Participation in Selected Sports Activities, by Household Income: 1996, in Thousands

## G16. Household Pet Ownership

G16-1. Household Pet Ownership: 1996

## G17. Charity and Philanthropy

G17-1. Charity Contributions—Average Dollar Amount and Percent of Household Income, by Year (1991–1995) and by Age of Respondent

G17-2. Charity Contributions—Average Dollar Amount and Percent of Household Income, by Household Income, 1995

G17-3. Private Philanthropy Funds, by Source and Allocation: 1980–1990, in Billion of Dollars

G17-4. Private Philanthropy Funds, by Source and Allocation: 1991–1996, in Billion of Dollars

## H. THE ROLE OF GOVERNMENT

### H1. Federal Budget

H1-1. Federal Budget—Summary: 1945–1998, in Millions of Dollars, for Fiscal Years ending in Year Shown

H1-2. Federal Budget—Outlays as Percent of GDP: 1945–1998, in Millions of Dollars, for Fiscal Years ending in Year Shown

### H2. Federal Receipts, by Source

H2-1. Federal Receipts, by Source: 1980–1990, in Millions of Dollars, for Fiscal Years ending in Year Shown

H2-2. Federal Receipts, by Source: 1995–1998, in Millions of Dollars, for Fiscal Years ending in Year Shown

### H3. Federal Budget Outlays

H3-1. Federal Budget Outlays—Defense, Human and Physical Resources, and Net Interest Payments: 1980–1993, in Millions of Dollars, for Fiscal Years ending in Year Shown

H3-2. Federal Budget Outlays—Defense, Human and Physical Resources, and Net Interest Payments: 1994–1998, in Millions of Dollars, for Fiscal Years ending in Year Shown

### H4. Gross Federal Debt

H4-1. Federal Budget—Summary, Gross Federal Debt: 1945–1998, in Millions of Dollars, for Fiscal Years ending in Year Shown

H4-2. Federal Budget—Summary, Gross Federal Debt as Percent of GDP: 1945–1998, for Fiscal Years ending in Year Shown

### H5. Small Business Administration (SBA) Loans to Small Businesses

H5-1. Small Business Administration Loans to Small Businesses: 1980–1991, for Fiscal Years ending in Year Shown

H5-2. Small Business Administration Loans to Small Businesses: 1992–1996, for Fiscal Years ending in Year Shown

### H6. Social Welfare Expenditures under Public Programs

H6-1. Social Welfare Expenditures under Public Programs: 1980–1994, in Billions of Dollars, (except percent) for Fiscal Years ending in Year Shown

H6-2. Social Welfare Expenditures under Public Programs, Per Capita: 1980–1994, in Dollars, for Fiscal Years ending in Year Shown

H6-3. Social Welfare Expenditures under Public Programs: 1980–1994, in Billions of Dollars, (except percent), for Fiscal Years ending in Year Shown

H6-4. Social Welfare Expenditures under Public Programs: 1980–1994, in Dollars, for Fiscal Years ending in Year Shown

H6-5. Social Welfare Expenditures under Public Programs, Totals: 1980–1994, for Fiscal Years ending in Year Shown

### H7. State Governments—Sources of General Revenue

H7-1. State Governments—Revenue, by State: 1996, in Millions of Dollars (except as noted)

H7-2. State Governments—Sources of General Revenue, Taxation by State: 1996, in Millions of Dollars (except as noted)

H7-3. State Governments—Sources of General Revenue, Taxation by State: 1996, in Millions of Dollars (except as noted)

H7-4. State Governments—Sources of General Revenue, Intergovernmental and Miscellaneous, by State: 1996, in Millions of Dollars (except as noted)

H7-5. State Governments—Sources of General Revenue; Utility, Liquor, and Insurance Trust Revenue: 1996, in Millions of Dollars (except as noted)

# A. General Economic Data

## GENERAL OVERVIEW

The opening section presents basic economic information on the United States. It is intended to provide a backdrop for the specific investigation of wealth and consumption that follows. Measures such as Gross Domestic Product, Net Stock of Fixed Reproducible Tangible Wealth, and Foreign Direct Investment for the entire country outline the economic base from which the United States creates wealth and supports regional variations in consumption. Tables detailing state product information are also presented so that the user can see wealth and consumption throughout the United States.

## EXPLANATION OF INDICATORS

**A1. Gross Domestic Product (GDP) and Gross National Product (GNP):** These indicators represent the total material capacity of the U.S. economy since the 1960s. They measure the total goods and services produced by labor and capital within the country (GDP) and owned by residents of the U.S. in foreign countries as well as within the country's geographic borders (GNP). The first table below presents GDP and GNP across a time series; it represents the data in current dollars, which does not factor out the effects of inflation. (See Appendix: International Perspective to compare U.S. GDP with that of other countries of the world.)

The next several tables and graphs outline the general categories of outlays that comprise GDP, that is, the final uses of the country's total production. As such, they indicate the way in which GDP can be employed in the generation of wealth and consumption. The tables and graphs detail the components of GDP both in current and constant dollars from 1960 through 1997.

**A2. Relation of National Product to Income and Saving:** The next two tables represent how the national product accounts—GDP and GNP along with Net National Product—relate to national income and finally personal income and savings. The manner in which aggregate national product finally translates into personal income, disposable income, and then savings shows how personal wealth relies on the productive capacity of the economy.

**A3. Net Stock of Fixed Reproducible Tangible Wealth:** These tables and charts represent the disposition of tangible wealth (buildings, equipment, etc.) in the U.S. economy from 1980 through 1996. Each table breaks down the components of tangible wealth into private, government, and consumer-owned assets and presents the data in both current and chained, or constant, dollars.

**A4. Foreign Direct Investment in the United States:** These tables and charts detail the investment made by foreign entities in the United States both in the aggregate and on a state-by-state basis. They help to measure the extent to which the income-generating assets of the country derive from foreign-owned investment.

**A5. Gross State Product:** The several tables and charts concerning state product included in this chapter represent the economic capacity of individual states with the country. They help to signify the size of the economic base from which individuals within states generate wealth and consumption.

## A1. GROSS DOMESTIC PRODUCT (GDP) AND GROSS NATIONAL PRODUCT (GNP)

### A1-1. Gross Domestic Product and Gross National Product, per Capita, in Current Dollars: 1960–1997

| Year | Current Dollars, Gross Domestic Product | Current Dollars, Gross National Product |
|------|------------------------------------------|------------------------------------------|
| 1960 | 2,913 | 2,931 |
| 1965 | 3,700 | 3,728 |
| 1970 | 5,050 | 5,081 |
| 1971 | 5,419 | 5,456 |
| 1972 | 5,894 | 5,935 |
| 1973 | 6,524 | 6,584 |
| 1974 | 6,998 | 7,071 |
| 1975 | 7,550 | 7,611 |
| 1976 | 8,341 | 8,419 |
| 1977 | 9,201 | 9,295 |
| 1978 | 10,292 | 10,392 |
| 1979 | 11,361 | 11,507 |
| 1980 | 12,226 | 12,381 |
| 1981 | 13,547 | 13,698 |
| 1982 | 13,961 | 14,095 |
| 1983 | 14,998 | 15,135 |
| 1984 | 16,508 | 16,640 |
| 1985 | 17,529 | 17,614 |
| 1986 | 18,374 | 18,427 |
| 1987 | 19,323 | 19,359 |
| 1988 | 20,605 | 20,659 |
| 1989 | 21,984 | 22,042 |
| 1990 | 22,979 | 23,064 |
| 1991 | 23,416 | 23,478 |
| 1992 | 24,447 | 24,490 |
| 1993 | 25,403 | 25,476 |
| 1994 | 26,647 | 26,678 |
| 1995 | 27,605 | 27,625 |
| 1996 | 28,752 | 28,759 |
| 1997 | 30,161 | 30,088 |

*Note:*
Based on Bureau of the Census estimated population including Armed Forces abroad; based on quarterly averages.

*Source: Statistical Abstract of the United States 1998*, No. 730; <http://www.census.gov/prod/3/98pubs/98statab/sasec14.pdf>. Underlying data from U.S. Bureau of Economic Analysis, *National Income and Product Accounts of the United States, 1929-94,* Vol. 2; and *Survey of Current Business*, August 1997 and May 1998.

## A1-2. GDP in Current Dollars: 1960–1997, in Billions of Dollars

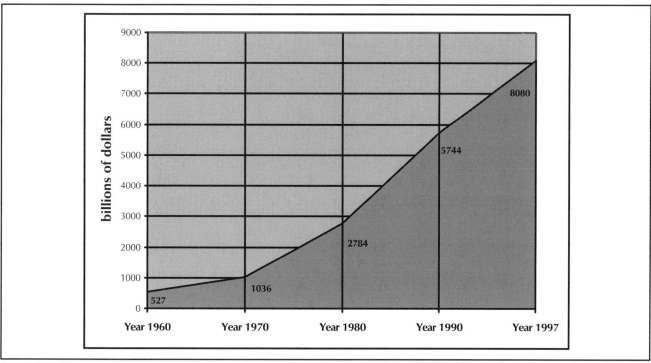

*Source: Statistical Abstract of the United States 1998,* No 715, <http://wwwcensusgov/prod/3/98pubs/98statab/sasec14pdf>. Underlying data from U.S. Bureau of Economic Analysis, *National Income and Product Accounts of the United States, 1929-94,*Vol. 1 and *Survey of Current Business,* August 1997 and May 1998.

## A1-3. GDP in Current Dollars: 1960–1980, in Billions of Dollars

|  | 1960 | 1970 | 1980 |
|---|---|---|---|
| Gross domestic product (GDP) | 526.6 | 1035.6 | 2784.2 |
| Personal consumption expenditures | 332.2 | 648.1 | 1760.4 |
| Durable goods | 43.3 | 85.0 | 213.5 |
| Nondurable goods | 152.9 | 272.0 | 695.5 |
| Services | 136.0 | 291.1 | 851.4 |
| Gross private domestic investment | 78.8 | 150.2 | 465.9 |
| Fixed investment | 75.5 | 148.1 | 473.5 |
| Change in business inventories | 3.2 | 2.2 | -7.6 |
| Net exports of goods and services | 2.4 | 1.2 | -14.9 |
| Exports | 25.3 | 57.0 | 278.9 |
| Imports | 22.8 | 55.8 | 293.8 |
| Government consumption expenditures and gross investment | 113.2 | 236.1 | 572.8 |
| Federal | 65.6 | 115.9 | 248.4 |
| National defense | 54.9 | 90.6 | 174.2 |
| State and local | 47.6 | 120.2 | 324.4 |

*Source: Statistical Abstract of the United States 1998,* No. 715, <http://wwwcensusgov/prod/3/98pubs/98statab/sasec14pdf>. Underlying data from U.S. Bureau of Economic Analysis, *National Income and Product Accounts of the United States, 1929-94,*Vol. 1 and *Survey of Current Business,* August 1997 and May 1998.

## A1-4. GDP in Current Dollars: 1983–1985, in Billions of Dollars

|  | 1983 | 1984 | 1985 |
|---|---|---|---|
| Gross domestic product (GDP) | 3514.5 | 3902.4 | 4180.7 |
| Personal consumption expenditures | 2283.4 | 2492.3 | 2704.8 |
| Durable goods | 279.8 | 325.1 | 361.1 |
| Nondurable goods | 830.3 | 883.6 | 927.6 |
| Services | 1173.3 | 1283.6 | 1416.1 |
| Gross private domestic investment | 547.1 | 715.6 | 715.1 |
| Fixed investment | 552.0 | 648.1 | 688.9 |
| Change in business inventories | -4.9 | 67.5 | 26.2 |
| Net exports of goods and services | -51.7 | -102.0 | -114.2 |
| Exports | 277.0 | 303.1 | 303.0 |
| Imports | 328.6 | 405.1 | 417.2 |
| Government consumption expenditures and gross investment | 735.7 | 796.6 | 875.0 |
| Federal | 344.5 | 372.6 | 410.1 |
| National defense | 255.0 | 282.7 | 312.4 |
| State and local | 391.2 | 424.0 | 464.9 |

*Source: Statistical Abstract of the United States 1998,* No. 715, <http://wwwcensusgov/prod/3/98pubs/98statab/sasec14pdf>. Underlying data from U.S. Bureau of Economic Analysis, *National Income and Product Accounts of the United States, 1929-94,* Vol. 1 and *Survey of Current Business,* August 1997 and May 1998.

## A1-5. GDP in Current Dollars: 1986–1988, in Billions of Dollars

|  | 1986 | 1987 | 1988 |
|---|---|---|---|
| Gross domestic product (GDP) | 4422.2 | 4692.3 | 5049.6 |
| Personal consumption expenditures | 2892.7 | 3094.5 | 3349.7 |
| Durable goods | 398.7 | 416.7 | 451.0 |
| Nondurable goods | 957.2 | 1014.0 | 1081.1 |
| Services | 1536.8 | 1663.8 | 1817.6 |
| Gross private domestic investment | 722.5 | 747.2 | 773.9 |
| Fixed investment | 712.9 | 722.9 | 763.1 |
| Change in business inventories | 9.6 | 24.2 | 10.9 |
| Net exports of goods and services | -131.5 | -142.1 | -106.1 |
| Exports | 320.7 | 365.7 | 447.2 |
| Imports | 452.2 | 507.9 | 553.2 |
| Government consumption expenditures and gross investment | 938.5 | 992.8 | 1032.0 |
| Federal | 435.2 | 455.7 | 457.3 |
| National defense | 332.4 | 350.4 | 354.0 |
| State and local | 503.3 | 537.2 | 574.7 |

*Source: Statistical Abstract of the United States 1998,* No. 715, <http://wwwcensusgov/prod/3/98pubs/98statab/sasec14pdf>. Underlying data from U.S. Bureau of Economic Analysis, *National Income and Product Accounts of the United States, 1929-94,*Vol. 1 and *Survey of Current Business*, August 1997 and May 1998.

## A1-6. GDP in Current Dollars: 1989–1991, in Billions of Dollars

|  | 1989 | 1990 | 1991 |
|---|---|---|---|
| Gross domestic product (GDP) | 5438.7 | 5743.8 | 5916.7 |
| Personal consumption expenditures | 3594.8 | 3839.3 | 3975.1 |
| Durable goods | 472.8 | 476.5 | 455.2 |
| Nondurable goods | 1163.8 | 1245.3 | 1277.6 |
| Services | 1958.1 | 2117.5 | 2242.3 |
| Gross private domestic investment | 829.2 | 799.7 | 736.2 |
| Fixed investment | 797.5 | 791.6 | 738.5 |
| Change in business inventories | 31.7 | 8.0 | -2.3 |
| Net exports of goods and services | -80.4 | -71.3 | -20.5 |
| Exports | 509.3 | 557.3 | 601.8 |
| Imports | 589.7 | 628.6 | 622.3 |
| Government consumption expenditures and gross investment | 1095.1 | 1176.1 | 1225.9 |
| Federal | 477.2 | 503.6 | 522.6 |
| National defense | 360.6 | 373.1 | 383.5 |
| State and local | 617.9 | 672.6 | 703.4 |

*Source: Statistical Abstract of the United States 1998,* No. 715, <http://wwwcensusgov/prod/3/98pubs/98statab/sasec14pdf>. Underlying data from U.S. Bureau of Economic Analysis, *National Income and Product Accounts of the United States, 1929-94,*Vol. 1 and *Survey of Current Business,* August 1997 and May 1998.

## A1-7. GDP in Current Dollars: 1992–1994, in Billions of Dollars

|  | 1992 | 1993 | 1994 |
|---|---|---|---|
| Gross domestic product (GDP) | 6244.4 | 6558.1 | 6947.0 |
| Personal consumption expenditures | 4219.8 | 4459.2 | 4717.0 |
| Durable goods | 488.5 | 530.2 | 579.5 |
| Nondurable goods | 1321.8 | 1370.7 | 1428.4 |
| Services | 2409.4 | 2558.4 | 2709.1 |
| Gross private domestic investment | 790.4 | 876.2 | 1007.9 |
| Fixed investment | 783.4 | 855.7 | 946.6 |
| Change in business inventories | 7.0 | 20.5 | 61.2 |
| Net exports of goods and services | -29.5 | -60.7 | -90.9 |
| Exports | 639.4 | 658.6 | 721.2 |
| Imports | 669.0 | 719.3 | 812.1 |
| Government consumption expenditures and gross investment | 1263.8 | 1283.4 | 1313.0 |
| Federal | 528.0 | 518.3 | 510.2 |
| National defense | 375.8 | 360.7 | 349.2 |
| State and local | 735.8 | 765.0 | 802.8 |

*Source: Statistical Abstract of the United States 1998,* No. 715, <http://wwwcensusgov/prod/3/98pubs/98statab/sasec14pdf>. Underlying data from U.S. Bureau of Economic Analysis, *National Income and Product Accounts of the United States, 1929-94,*Vol. 1 and *Survey of Current Business,* August 1997 and May 1998.

## A1-8. GDP in Current Dollars: 1995–1997, in Billions of Dollars

|  | 1995 | 1996 | 1997 |
|---|---|---|---|
| Gross domestic product (GDP) | 7265.4 | 7636.0 | 8079.9 |
| Personal consumption expenditures | 4957.7 | 5207.6 | 5485.8 |
| Durable goods | 608.5 | 634.5 | 659.3 |
| Nondurable goods | 1475.8 | 1534.7 | 1592.0 |
| Services | 2873.4 | 3038.4 | 3234.5 |
| Gross private domestic investment | 1038.2 | 1116.5 | 1242.5 |
| Fixed investment | 1008.1 | 1090.7 | 1174.1 |
| Change in business inventories | 30.1 | 25.9 | 68.4 |
| Net exports of goods and services | -86.0 | -94.8 | -101.1 |
| Exports | 818.4 | 870.9 | 957.1 |
| Imports | 904.5 | 965.7 | 1058.1 |
| Government consumption expenditures and gross investment | 1355.5 | 1406.7 | 1452.7 |
| Federal | 509.6 | 520.0 | 523.8 |
| National defense | 344.6 | 352.8 | 350.3 |
| State and local | 846.0 | 886.7 | 928.9 |

*Source: Statistical Abstract of the United States 1998,* No. 715, <http://wwwcensusgov/prod/3/98pubs/98statab/sasec14pdf>. Underlying data from U.S. Bureau of Economic Analysis, *National Income and Product Accounts of the United States, 1929-94,* Vol. 1 and *Survey of Current Business*, August 1997 and May 1998.

## A1-9. GDP in Constant Dollars: 1960–1997, in Billions of Dollars

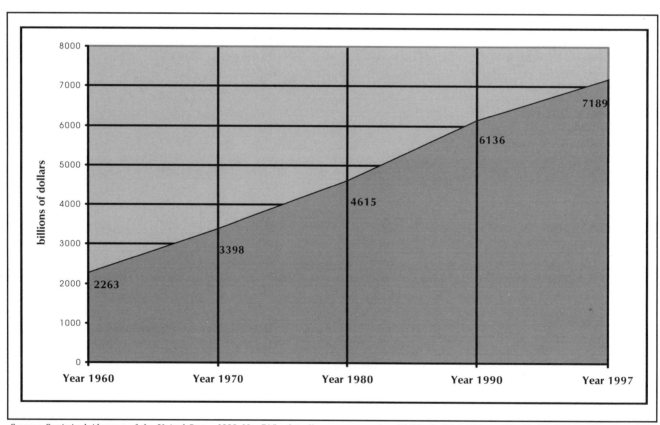

*Source: Statistical Abstract of the United States 1998,* No. 715, <http://wwwcensusgov/prod/3/98pubs/98statab/sasec14pdf>. Underlying data from U.S. Bureau of Economic Analysis, *National Income and Product Accounts of the United States, 1929-94,* Vol. 1 and *Survey of Current Business*, August 1997 and May 1998.

## A1-10. GDP in Constant (1992) Dollars: 1960–1980, in Billions of Dollars

|  | 1960 | 1970 | 1980 |
|---|---|---|---|
| Gross domestic product (GDP) | 2262.9 | 3397.6 | 4615.0 |
| Personal consumption expenditures | 1432.6 | 2197.8 | 3009.7 |
| Durable goods | 105.2 | 187.0 | 282.6 |
| Nondurable goods | 615.4 | 859.1 | 1065.1 |
| Services | 717.4 | 1155.4 | 1670.7 |
| Gross private domestic investment | 270.5 | 426.1 | 628.3 |
| Fixed investment | 269.2 | 432.1 | 648.4 |
| Change in business inventories | 10.5 | 5.4 | -10.2 |
| Net exports of goods and services | -21.3 | -65.0 | 10.1 |
| Exports | 86.8 | 158.1 | 331.4 |
| Imports | 108.1 | 223.1 | 321.3 |
| Government consumption expenditures and gross investment | 617.2 | 866.8 | 941.4 |
| Federal | 349.4 | 427.2 | 399.3 |
| National defense | 301.3 | 349.0 | 280.7 |
| State and local | 267.2 | 440.0 | 543.6 |

*Source: Statistical Abstract of the United States 1998,* No. 715, <http://wwwcensusgov/prod/3/98pubs/98statab/sasec14pdf>. Underlying data from U.S. Bureau of Economic Analysis, *National Income and Product Accounts of the United States, 1929-94,*Vol. 1 and *Survey of Current Business*, August 1997 and May 1998.

## A1-11. GDP in Constant (1992) Dollars: 1983–1985, in Billions of Dollars

|  | 1983 | 1984 | 1985 |
|---|---|---|---|
| Gross domestic product (GDP) | 4803.7 | 5140.1 | 5323.5 |
| Personal consumption expenditures | 3240.6 | 3407.6 | 3566.5 |
| Durable goods | 327.4 | 374.9 | 411.4 |
| Nondurable goods | 1112.4 | 1151.8 | 1178.3 |
| Services | 1809.0 | 1883.0 | 1977.3 |
| Gross private domestic investment | 642.1 | 833.4 | 823.8 |
| Fixed investment | 654.2 | 762.4 | 799.3 |
| Change in business inventories | -5.7 | 75.3 | 30.2 |
| Net exports of goods and services | -63.3 | -127.3 | -147.9 |
| Exports | 303.3 | 328.4 | 337.3 |
| Imports | 366.6 | 455.7 | 485.2 |
| Government consumption expenditures and gross investment | 987.3 | 1018.4 | 1080.1 |
| Federal | 452.7 | 463.7 | 495.6 |
| National defense | 334.6 | 348.1 | 374.1 |
| State and local | 534.9 | 555.0 | 584.7 |

*Source: Statistical Abstract of the United States 1998,* No. 715, <http://wwwcensusgov/prod/3/98pubs/98statab/sasec14pdf>. Underlying data from U.S. Bureau of Economic Analysis, *National Income and Product Accounts of the United States, 1929-94,*Vol. 1 and *Survey of Current Business*, August 1997 and May 1998.

## A1-12. GDP in Constant (1992) Dollars: 1986–1988, in Billions of Dollars

|  | 1986 | 1987 | 1988 |
|---|---|---|---|
| Gross domestic product (GDP) | 5487.7 | 5649.5 | 5865.2 |
| Personal consumption expenditures | 3708.7 | 3822.3 | 3972.7 |
| Durable goods | 448.4 | 454.9 | 483.5 |
| Nondurable goods | 1215.9 | 1239.3 | 1274.4 |
| Services | 2041.4 | 2126.9 | 2212.4 |
| Gross private domestic investment | 811.8 | 821.5 | 828.2 |
| Fixed investment | 805.0 | 799.4 | 818.3 |
| Change in business inventories | 11.1 | 26.4 | 11.7 |
| Net exports of goods and services | -163.9 | -156.2 | -114.4 |
| Exports | 362.2 | 402.0 | 465.8 |
| Imports | 526.1 | 558.2 | 580.2 |
| Government consumption expenditures and gross investment | 1135.0 | 1165.9 | 1180.9 |
| Federal | 518.4 | 534.4 | 524.6 |
| National defense | 393.4 | 409.2 | 405.5 |
| State and local | 616.9 | 631.8 | 656.6 |

*Source: Statistical Abstract of the United States 1998,* No. 715, <http://wwwcensusgov/prod/3/98pubs/98statab/sasec14pdf>. Underlying data from U.S. Bureau of Economic Analysis, *National Income and Product Accounts of the United States, 1929-94,*Vol. 1 and *Survey of Current Business,* August 1997 and May 1998.

## A1-13. GDP in Constant (1992) Dollars: 1989–1991, in Billions of Dollars

|  | 1989 | 1990 | 1991 |
|---|---|---|---|
| Gross domestic product (GDP) | 6062.0 | 6136.3 | 6079.4 |
| Personal consumption expenditures | 4064.6 | 4132.2 | 4105.8 |
| Durable goods | 496.2 | 493.3 | 462.0 |
| Nondurable goods | 1303.5 | 1316.1 | 1302.9 |
| Services | 2262.3 | 2321.3 | 2341.0 |
| Gross private domestic investment | 863.5 | 815.0 | 738.1 |
| Fixed investment | 832.0 | 805.8 | 741.3 |
| Change in business inventories | 33.3 | 10.4 | -3.0 |
| Net exports of goods and services | -82.7 | -61.9 | -22.3 |
| Exports | 520.2 | 564.4 | 599.9 |
| Imports | 603.0 | 626.3 | 622.2 |
| Government consumption expenditures and gross investment | 1213.9 | 1250.4 | 1258.0 |
| Federal | 531.5 | 541.9 | 539.4 |
| National defense | 401.6 | 401.5 | 397.5 |
| State and local | 682.6 | 708.6 | 718.7 |

*Source: Statistical Abstract of the United States 1998,* No. 715, <http://wwwcensusgov/prod/3/98pubs/98statab/sasec14pdf>. Underlying data from U.S. Bureau of Economic Analysis, *National Income and Product Accounts of the United States, 1929-94,*Vol. 1 and *Survey of Current Business,* August 1997 and May 1998.

## A1-14. GDP in Constant (1992) Dollars: 1992–1994, in Billions of Dollars

|  | 1992 | 1993 | 1994 |
|---|---|---|---|
| Gross domestic product (GDP) | 6244.4 | 6389.6 | 6610.7 |
| Personal consumption expenditures | 4219.8 | 4343.6 | 4486.0 |
| Durable goods | 488.5 | 523.8 | 561.2 |
| Nondurable goods | 1321.8 | 1351.0 | 1389.9 |
| Services | 2409.4 | 2468.9 | 2535.5 |
| Gross private domestic investment | 790.4 | 863.6 | 975.7 |
| Fixed investment | 783.4 | 842.8 | 915.5 |
| Change in business inventories | 7.0 | 22.1 | 60.6 |
| Net exports of goods and services | -29.5 | -70.2 | -104.6 |
| Exports | 639.4 | 658.2 | 712.4 |
| Imports | 669.0 | 728.4 | 817.0 |
| Government consumption expenditures and gross investment | 1263.8 | 1252.1 | 1252.3 |
| Federal | 528.0 | 505.7 | 486.6 |
| National defense | 375.8 | 354.4 | 336.9 |
| State and local | 735.8 | 746.4 | 765.7 |

*Source: Statistical Abstract of the United States 1998,* No. 715, <http://wwwcensusgov/prod/3/98pubs/98statab/sasec14pdf>. Underlying data from U.S. Bureau of Economic Analysis, *National Income and Product Accounts of the United States, 1929-94,* Vol. 1 and *Survey of Current Business,* August 1997 and May 1998.

## A1-15. GDP in Constant (1992) Dollars: 1995–1997, in Billions of Dollars

|  | 1995 | 1996 | 1997 |
|---|---|---|---|
| Gross domestic product (GDP) | 6742.1 | 6928.4 | 7188.8 |
| Personal consumption expenditures | 4595.3 | 4714.1 | 4867.5 |
| Durable goods | 583.6 | 611.1 | 645.5 |
| Nondurable goods | 1412.6 | 1432.3 | 1458.5 |
| Services | 2599.6 | 2671.0 | 2764.1 |
| Gross private domestic investment | 991.5 | 1069.1 | 1197.0 |
| Fixed investment | 962.1 | 1041.7 | 1123.6 |
| Change in business inventories | 27.3 | 25.0 | 65.7 |
| Net exports of goods and services | -98.8 | -114.4 | -146.5 |
| Exports | 791.2 | 857.0 | 962.7 |
| Imports | 890.1 | 971.5 | 1109.2 |
| Government consumption expenditures and gross investment | 1251.9 | 1257.9 | 1269.6 |
| Federal | 470.3 | 464.2 | 457.0 |
| National defense | 322.6 | 317.8 | 308.6 |
| State and local | 781.6 | 793.7 | 812.7 |

*Source: Statistical Abstract of the United States 1998,* No. 715, <http://wwwcensusgov/prod/3/98pubs/98statab/sasec14pdf>. Underlying data from U.S. Bureau of Economic Analysis, *National Income and Product Accounts of the United States, 1929-94,* Vol. 1 and *Survey of Current Business,* August 1997 and May 1998.

## A2. RELATION OF NATIONAL PRODUCT TO INCOME AND SAVING

### A2-1. Relation of GDP, GNP, Net National Product, National Income, Personal Income, Disposable Personal Income, and Personal Saving: 1990–1993, in Billions of Dollars

| ITEM | 1990 | 1991 | 1992 | 1993 |
|---|---|---|---|---|
| Gross domestic product | 5743.8 | 5916.7 | 6244.4 | 6558.1 |
| Plus: Receipts of factor income from the rest of the world[1] | 177.5 | 156.2 | 137.9 | 150.8 |
| Less: Payments of factor income to the rest of the world[2] | 156.4 | 140.5 | 126.8 | 132.1 |
| Equals: Gross national product | 5764.9 | 5932.4 | 6255.5 | 6576.8 |
| Less: Consumption of fixed capital | 651.5 | 679.9 | 713.5 | 727.9 |
| Equals: Net national product[3] | 5113.4 | 5252.5 | 5542.0 | 5848.9 |
| Less: Indirect business tax and nontax liability | 442.6 | 478.1 | 505.6 | 532.5 |
| Plus: Subsidies[4] | 25.3 | 23.6 | 27.1 | 31.1 |
| Equals: National income[3] | 4652.1 | 4761.6 | 4990.4 | 5266.8 |
| Less: Corporate profits[5] | 397.1 | 411.3 | 428.0 | 492.8 |
| Net interest | 467.3 | 448.0 | 414.3 | 402.5 |
| Contributions for social insurance | 518.5 | 543.5 | 571.4 | 596.0 |
| Wage accruals less disbursements | 0.1 | -0.1 | -15.8 | 4.4 |
| Plus: Personal interest income | 704.4 | 699.2 | 667.2 | 651.0 |
| Personal dividend income | 142.9 | 153.6 | 159.4 | 185.3 |
| Government transfer payments to persons | 666.5 | 749.1 | 835.7 | 889.8 |
| Business transfer payments to persons | 21.3 | 20.8 | 22.5 | 22.1 |
| Equals: Personal income | 4804.2 | 4981.6 | 5277.2 | 5519.2 |
| Less: Personal tax and nontax payments | 624.8 | 624.8 | 650.5 | 690.0 |
| Equals: Disposable personal income | 4179.4 | 4356.8 | 4626.7 | 4829.2 |
| Less: Personal outlays | 3958.1 | 4097.4 | 4341.0 | 4580.7 |
| Equals: Personal saving | 221.3 | 259.5 | 285.6 | 248.5 |

*Notes:*
1. Consists largely of receipts by U.S. residents of interest and dividends and reinvested earnings of foreign affiliates of U.S. corporations.
2. Consists largely of payments to foreign residents of interest and dividends and reinvested earnings of U.S. affiliates of foreign corporations.
3. Includes items not shown separately.
4. Less current surplus of government enterprises.
5. With inventory valuation and capital consumption adjustments.

*Source: Statistical Abstract of the United States*, No. 721; <http://www.census.gov/prod/3/98pubs/98statab/sasec14.pdf>. Underlying data from U.S. Bureau of Economic Analysis, *National Income and Product Accounts of the United States, 1929-94,* Vol. 1; and *Survey of Current Business*, August 1997 and May 1998.

### A2-2. Relation of GDP, GNP, Net National Product, National Income, Personal Income, Disposable Personal Income, and Personal Saving: 1994–1997, in Billions of Dollars

| ITEM | 1994 | 1995 | 1996 | 1997 |
|---|---|---|---|---|
| Gross domestic product | 6947.0 | 7265.4 | 7636.0 | 8079.9 |
| Plus: Receipts of factor income from the rest of the world[1] | 176.5 | 222.8 | 234.3 | 262.2 |
| Less: Payments of factor income to the rest of the world[2] | 168.3 | 217.5 | 232.6 | 282.0 |
| Equals: Gross national product | 6955.2 | 7270.6 | 7637.7 | 8060.1 |
| Less: Consumption of fixed capital | 777.5 | 796.8 | 830.1 | 867.9 |
| Equals: Net national product[3] | 6177.7 | 6473.9 | 6807.6 | 7192.2 |
| Less: Indirect business tax and nontax liability | 568.5 | 582.8 | 604.8 | 619.4 |
| Plus: Subsidies[4] | 26.6 | 25.2 | 25.4 | 26.1 |
| Equals: National income[3] | 5590.7 | 5912.3 | 6254.5 | 6649.7 |
| Less: Corporate profits[5] | 570.5 | 650.0 | 735.9 | 805.0 |
| Net interest | 412.3 | 425.1 | 425.1 | 448.7 |
| Contributions for social insurance | 630.5 | 659.1 | 692.0 | 732.1 |
| Wage accruals less disbursements | 13.3 | 13.1 | 1.1 | 1.2 |
| Plus: Personal interest income | 668.1 | 718.9 | 735.7 | 768.6 |
| Personal dividend income | 204.8 | 251.9 | 291.2 | 321.5 |
| Government transfer payments to persons | 930.9 | 990.0 | 1042.0 | 1094.1 |
| Business transfer payments to persons | 23.7 | 25.0 | 26.0 | 27.1 |
| Equals: Personal income | 5791.8 | 6150.8 | 6495.2 | 6873.9 |

**A2-2. Relation of GDP, GNP, Net National Product, National Income, Personal Income, Disposable Personal Income, and Personal Saving: 1994–1997, in Billions of Dollars** *(continued)*

| ITEM | 1994 | 1995 | 1996 | 1997 |
|---|---|---|---|---|
| Less: Personal tax and nontax payments | 739.1 | 795.1 | 886.9 | 988.7 |
| Equals: Disposable personal income | 5052.7 | 5355.7 | 5608.3 | 5885.2 |
| Less: Personal outlays | 4842.1 | 5101.1 | 5368.8 | 5658.5 |
| Equals: Personal saving | 210.6 | 254.6 | 239.6 | 226.7 |

*Notes:*
1. Consists largely of receipts by U.S. residents of interest and dividends and reinvested earnings of foreign affiliates of U.S. corporations.
2. Consists largely of payments to foreign residents of interest and dividends and reinvested earnings of U.S. affiliates of foreign corporations.
3. Includes items not shown separately.
4. Less current surplus of government enterprises.
5. With inventory valuation and capital consumption adjustments.

*Source: Statistical Abstract of the United States*, No. 721; <http://www.census.gov/prod/3/98pubs/98statab/sasec14.pdf>. Underlying data from U.S. Bureau of Economic Analysis, *National Income and Product Accounts of the United States, 1929-94,*Vol. 1; and *Survey of Current Business*, August 1997 and May 1998.

# A3. NET STOCK OF FIXED REPRODUCIBLE TANGIBLE WEALTH

**A3-1. Net Stock of Fixed Reproducible Tangible Wealth: 1980–1990, in Billions of Dollars, as of December 31**

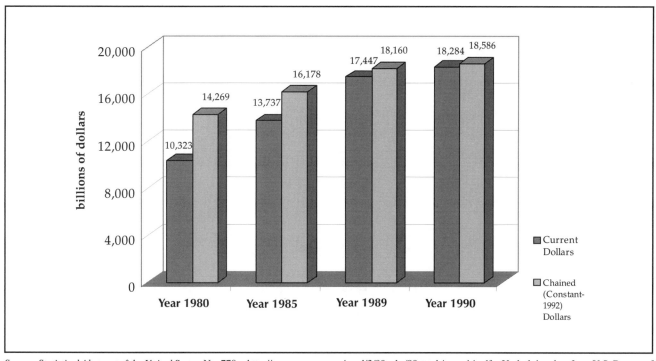

*Source: Statistical Abstract of the United States*, No. 770; <http://www.census.gov/prod/3/98pubs/98statab/sasec14.pdf>. Underlying data from U.S. Bureau of Economic Analysis, *Survey of Current Business*, May 1998, and previous issues.

## A3-2. Net Stock of Fixed Reproducible Tangible Wealth: 1992–1995, in Billions of Dollars, as of December 31

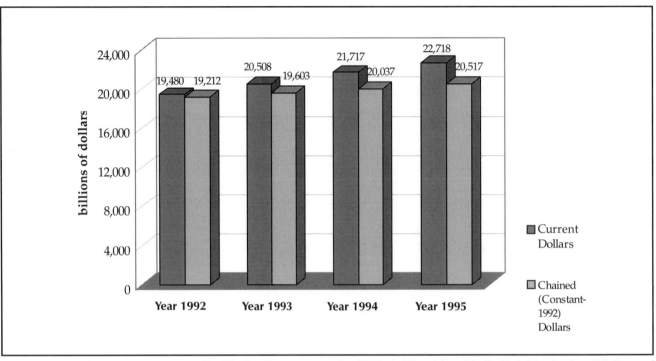

*Source: Statistical Abstract of the United States*, No. 770; <http://www.census.gov/prod/3/98pubs/98statab/sasec14.pdf>. Underlying data from U.S. Bureau of Economic Analysis, *Survey of Current Business*, May 1998, and previous issues.

## A3-3. Net Stock of Fixed Reproducible Tangible Wealth: 1980–1991, in Billions of Dollars, as of December 31

| ITEM | 1980 | 1985 | 1989 | 1990 | 1991 |
|---|---|---|---|---|---|
| CURRENT DOLLARS | | | | | |
| Private | 7,154 | 9,583 | 12,149 | 12,707 | 12,955 |
| Nonresidential equipment | 1,375 | 1,850 | 2,322 | 2,452 | 2,519 |
| Information processing and related equipment | 225 | 413 | 558 | 586 | 603 |
| Industrial equipment | 525 | 646 | 823 | 877 | 898 |
| Transportation equipment | 306 | 395 | 456 | 473 | 491 |
| Other equipment | 319 | 396 | 485 | 516 | 527 |
| Nonresidential structures | 2,266 | 3,155 | 3,916 | 4,107 | 4,177 |
| Nonresidential buildings, excluding farm | 1,169 | 1,787 | 2,372 | 2,518 | 2,594 |
| Utilities | 695 | 853 | 997 | 1,017 | 1,032 |
| Residential | 3,513 | 4,578 | 5,911 | 6,147 | 6,259 |
| Housing units | 2,898 | 3,730 | 4,808 | 4,984 | 5,057 |
| Government | 2,251 | 2,889 | 3,535 | 3,711 | 3,827 |
| Equipment | 300 | 425 | 511 | 552 | 577 |
| Structures | 1,952 | 2,464 | 3,024 | 3,159 | 3,250 |
| Federal | 698 | 889 | 1,042 | 1,090 | 1,127 |
| Defense | 483 | 613 | 712 | 744 | 768 |
| State and local | 1,554 | 2,000 | 2,493 | 2,621 | 2,701 |
| Consumer durable goods | 918 | 1,265 | 1,763 | 1,866 | 1,935 |
| Motor vehicles | 257 | 392 | 564 | 590 | 593 |
| Furniture and household equipment | 459 | 605 | 804 | 846 | 885 |
| Other | 203 | 268 | 396 | 429 | 457 |
| CHAINED (1992) DOLLARS | | | | | |
| Private | 9,950 | 11,346 | 12,617 | 12,890 | 13,078 |
| Nonresidential equipment | 1,855 | 2,178 | 2,451 | 2,507 | 2,537 |

**A3-3. Net Stock of Fixed Reproducible Tangible Wealth: 1980–1991, in Billions of Dollars, as of December 31** *(continued)*

| ITEM | 1980 | 1985 | 1989 | 1990 | 1991 |
|---|---|---|---|---|---|
| Nonresidential structures | 3,177 | 3,697 | 4,051 | 4,142 | 4,205 |
| Residential | 4,921 | 5,471 | 6,115 | 6,240 | 6,335 |
| Government | 3,127 | 3,382 | 3,697 | 3,782 | 3,860 |
| Federal | 969 | 1,022 | 1,109 | 1,126 | 1,139 |
| State and local | 2,156 | 2,357 | 2,584 | 2,652 | 2,717 |
| Consumer durable goods | 1,198 | 1,455 | 1,850 | 1,919 | 1,950 |

*Source: Statistical Abstract of the United States*, No. 770; <http://www.census.gov/prod/3/98pubs/98statab/sasec14.pdf>. Underlying data from U.S. Bureau of Economic Analysis, *Survey of Current Business*, May 1998, and previous issues.

**A3-4. Net Stock of Fixed Reproducible Tangible Wealth: 1992–1996, in Billions of Dollars, as of December 31**

| ITEM | 1992 | 1993 | 1994 | 1995 | 1996 |
|---|---|---|---|---|---|
| CURRENT DOLLARS | | | | | |
| Private | 13,484 | 14,199 | 15,064 | 15,739 | 16,503 |
| Nonresidential equipment | 2,590 | 2,687 | 2,823 | 2,989 | 3,169 |
| Information processing and related equipment | 629 | 650 | 674 | 704 | 785 |
| Industrial equipment | 917 | 946 | 991 | 1,050 | 1,084 |
| Transportation equipment | 510 | 539 | 581 | 627 | 660 |
| Other equipment | 534 | 552 | 577 | 608 | 639 |
| Nonresidential structures | 4,303 | 4,529 | 4,776 | 4,971 | 5,163 |
| Nonresidential buildings, excluding farm | 2,686 | 2,835 | 3,011 | 3,144 | 3,299 |
| Utilities | 1,062 | 1,120 | 1,160 | 1,200 | 1,236 |
| Residential | 6,591 | 6,983 | 7,466 | 7,779 | 8,171 |
| Housing units | 5,327 | 5,667 | 6,078 | 6,322 | 6,639 |
| Government | 3,991 | 4,201 | 4,426 | 4,656 | 4,855 |
| Equipment | 600 | 618 | 635 | 647 | 656 |
| Structures | 3,390 | 3,583 | 3,791 | 4,009 | 4,199 |
| Federal | 1,169 | 1,227 | 1,263 | 1,297 | 1,333 |
| Defense | 798 | 839 | 857 | 868 | 884 |
| State and local | 2,822 | 2,974 | 3,163 | 3,360 | 3,522 |
| Consumer durable goods | 2,005 | 2,108 | 2,226 | 2,323 | 2,415 |
| Motor vehicles | 607 | 629 | 659 | 679 | 702 |
| Furniture and household equipment | 926 | 985 | 1,046 | 1,102 | 1,154 |
| Other | 471 | 493 | 521 | 543 | 559 |
| CHAINED (1992) DOLLARS | | | | | |
| Private | 13,278 | 13,536 | 13,830 | 14,163 | 14,551 |
| Nonresidential equipment | 2,579 | 2,649 | 2,749 | 2,881 | 3,035 |
| Nonresidential structures | 4,251 | 4,300 | 4,345 | 4,404 | 4,482 |
| Residential | 6,448 | 6,587 | 6,738 | 6,886 | 7,048 |
| Government | 3,940 | 4,008 | 4,069 | 4,133 | 4,206 |
| Federal | 1,148 | 1,150 | 1,147 | 1,144 | 1,147 |
| State and local | 2,787 | 2,854 | 2,918 | 2,986 | 3,056 |
| Consumer durable goods | 1,998 | 2,064 | 2,144 | 2,229 | 2,323 |

*Source: Statistical Abstract of the United States*, No. 770; <http://www.census.gov/prod/3/98pubs/98statab/sasec14.pdf>. Underlying data from U.S. Bureau of Economic Analysis, *Survey of Current Business,* May 1998, and previous issues.

## A4. FOREIGN DIRECT INVESTMENT IN THE UNITED STATES

### A4-1. Foreign Direct Investment in the United States, Summary Totals—Gross Book Value of Property, Plant, and Equipment, U.S. Affiliates of Foreign Companies: 1981–1996, in Millions of Dollars

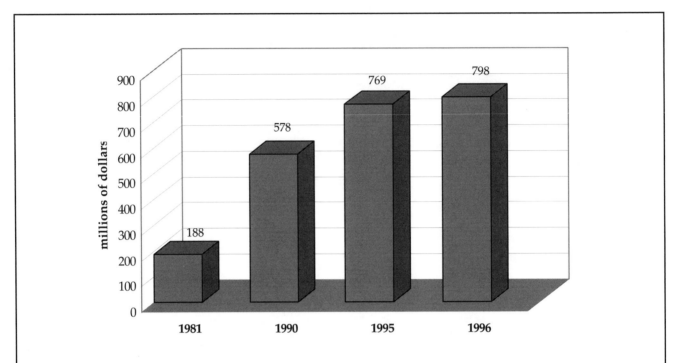

*General Note:* A U.S. affiliate is a U.S. business enterprise in which one foreign owner (individual, branch, partnership, association, trust corporation, or government) has a direct or indirect voting interest of 10 percent or more. Universe estimates based on a sample survey of nonbank affiliates with assets, sales, or net income of $10 million or more.

*Source: Statistical Abstract of the United States 1998,* No. 1309; <http://wwwcensusgov/prod/3/98pubs/98statab/sasec28pdf>. Underlying data from U.S. Bureau of Economic Analysis, *Survey of Current Business,* June 1998, and *Foreign Direct Investment in the United States, Operations of U.S. Affiliates of Foreign Companies,* annual.

### A4-2. Foreign Direct Investment in the United States—Gross Book Value of Property, Plant, and Equipment, U.S. Affiliates of Foreign Companies, by State: 1981–1996, in Millions of Dollars

| State and other area | 1981 | 1990 | 1995 | 1996 |
|---|---|---|---|---|
| Total | 187,956 | 578,355 | 769,491 | 797,647 |
| United States | 178,003 | 552,902 | 733,089 | 758,356 |
| Alabama | 2,776 | 7,300 | 10,598 | 11,635 |
| Alaska | (D) | 19,435 | 25,558 | 25,904 |
| Arizona | 2,949 | 7,234 | 6,699 | 9,101 |
| Arkansas | 636 | 2,344 | 3,666 | 3,657 |
| California | 20,404 | 75,768 | 96,576 | 100,718 |
| Colorado | 2,369 | 6,544 | 8,602 | 8,440 |
| Connecticut | 1,254 | 5,357 | 8,466 | 8,641 |
| Delaware | 1,869 | 5,818 | 2,919 | 3,103 |
| District of Columbia | 547 | 3,869 | 4,983 | 4,951 |
| Florida | 6,295 | 18,659 | 24,865 | 28,952 |
| Georgia | 4,558 | 16,729 | 22,432 | 22,491 |
| Hawaii | (D) | 11,830 | 15,972 | 15,547 |
| Idaho | 312 | 776 | 1,026 | 1,171 |
| Illinois | 5,646 | 23,420 | 34,305 | 33,687 |
| Indiana | 1,883 | 13,426 | 18,782 | 16,022 |

## A4-2. Foreign Direct Investment in the United States—Gross Book Value of Property, Plant, and Equipment, U.S. Affiliates of Foreign Companies, by State: 1981–1996, in Millions of Dollars *(continued)*

| State and other area | 1981 | 1990 | 1995 | 1996 |
|---|---|---|---|---|
| Iowa | 1,032 | 2,712 | 4,527 | 5,096 |
| Kansas | 877 | 5,134 | 3,233 | 4,680 |
| Kentucky | 1,848 | 9,229 | 15,136 | 14,785 |
| Louisiana | 7,872 | 17,432 | 20,543 | 21,774 |
| Maine | 1,637 | 2,080 | 3,885 | 3,846 |
| Maryland | 2,103 | 5,713 | 9,197 | 9,670 |
| Massachusetts | 1,712 | 8,890 | 12,707 | 13,749 |
| Michigan | 4,188 | 12,012 | 21,370 | 17,913 |
| Minnesota | 2,902 | 11,972 | 8,688 | 9,514 |
| Mississippi | 1,431 | 2,989 | 3,055 | 2,465 |
| Missouri | 1,894 | 5,757 | 8,327 | 10,016 |
| Montana | 1,235 | 2,181 | 1,938 | 1,865 |
| Nebraska | 241 | 776 | 1,320 | 1,645 |
| Nevada | 556 | 5,450 | 8,242 | 8,287 |
| New Hampshire | 409 | 1,446 | 2,212 | 2,141 |
| New Jersey | 6,552 | 18,608 | 26,175 | 26,688 |
| New Mexico | 997 | 4,312 | 4,363 | 4,451 |
| New York | 7,892 | 36,424 | 52,992 | 52,752 |
| North Carolina | 5,543 | 15,234 | 21,475 | 22,913 |
| North Dakota | 1,155 | 1,251 | 915 | 911 |
| Ohio | 5,178 | 20,549 | 29,932 | 32,617 |
| Oklahoma | 2,760 | 6,049 | 5,448 | 5,410 |
| Oregon | 845 | 3,427 | 5,807 | 5,349 |
| Pennsylvania | 5,772 | 16,587 | 24,432 | 24,448 |
| Rhode Island | 359 | 1,120 | 2,240 | 2,573 |
| South Carolina | 5,318 | 10,067 | 13,438 | 15,124 |
| South Dakota | 299 | 553 | 665 | 665 |
| Tennessee | 3,747 | 10,280 | 14,227 | 14,999 |
| Texas | 23,383 | 57,079 | 68,142 | 72,315 |
| Utah | 1,791 | 3,918 | 5,612 | 6,287 |
| Vermont | 315 | 631 | 1,037 | 1,017 |
| Virginia | 3,046 | 10,702 | 15,129 | 16,999 |
| Washington | 2,430 | 7,985 | 11,462 | 11,621 |
| West Virginia | 3,992 | 7,975 | 7,809 | 7,389 |
| Wisconsin | 2,320 | 5,088 | 7,415 | 7,792 |
| Wyoming | 2,144 | 2,782 | 4,544 | 4,569 |
| Puerto Rico | 413 | 1,499 | 2,174 | 1,763 |
| Other territories and offshore | 7,496 | 18,484 | 17,798 | 18,901 |
| Foreign | 2,044 | 5,470 | 16,430 | 18,627 |

*Notes:*

D   Withheld to avoid disclosure of data of individual companies.

*General Note:* A U.S. affiliate is a U.S. business enterprise in which one foreign owner (individual, branch, partnership, association, trust corporation, or government) has a direct or indirect voting interest of 10 percent or more. Universe estimates based on a sample survey of nonbank affiliates with assets, sales, or net income of $10 million or more.

*Source: Statistical Abstract of the United States 1998,* No. 1309; <http://wwwcensusgov/prod/3/98pubs/98statab/sasec28pdf>. Underlying data from U.S. Bureau of Economic Analysis, *Survey of Current Business,* June 1998, and *Foreign Direct Investment in the United States, Operations of U.S. Affiliates of Foreign Companies,* annual.

## A5. GROSS STATE PRODUCT

### A5-1. Gross State Product, in Millions of Dollars, with Resident Population, 1996

| State | Gross State Product | Resident Population, In Thousands |
|---|---|---|
| United States | 204,229 | 265,179 |
| Alabama | 99,190 | 4,287 |
| Alaska | 24,161 | 605 |
| Arizona | 111,520 | 4,434 |
| Arkansas | 56,417 | 2,506 |
| California | 962,696 | 31,858 |
| Colorado | 116,227 | 3,816 |
| Connecticut | 124,046 | 3,267 |
| Delaware | 28,331 | 723 |
| District of Columbia | 51,197 | 539 |
| Florida | 360,496 | 14,419 |
| Georgia | 216,033 | 7,334 |
| Hawaii | 36,317 | 1,183 |
| Idaho | 27,898 | 1,188 |
| Illinois | 370,778 | 11,845 |
| Indiana | 155,797 | 5,828 |
| Iowa | 76,315 | 2,848 |
| Kansas | 68,014 | 2,579 |
| Kentucky | 95,410 | 3,882 |
| Louisiana | 121,143 | 4,341 |
| Maine | 28,894 | 1,239 |
| Maryland | 143,190 | 5,060 |
| Massachusetts | 208,591 | 6,085 |
| Michigan | 263,336 | 9,731 |
| Minnesota | 141,573 | 4,649 |
| Mississippi | 56,406 | 2,711 |
| Missouri | 145,123 | 5,364 |
| Montana | 18,509 | 877 |
| Nebraska | 47,187 | 1,649 |
| Nevada | 53,687 | 1,601 |
| New Hampshire | 34,108 | 1,160 |
| New Jersey | 276,377 | 8,002 |
| New Mexico | 42,698 | 1,711 |
| New York | 613,287 | 18,134 |
| North Carolina | 204,229 | 7,309 |
| North Dakota | 15,701 | 643 |
| Ohio | 304,353 | 11,163 |
| Oklahoma | 72,767 | 3,295 |
| Oregon | 86,967 | 3,196 |
| Pennsylvania | 328,540 | 12,040 |
| Rhode Island | 25,629 | 988 |
| South Dakota | 20,289 | 3,717 |
| South Carolina | 89,476 | 738 |
| Tennessee | 140,750 | 5,307 |
| Texas | 551,830 | 19,091 |
| Utah | 50,352 | 2,018 |
| Vermont | 14,611 | 586 |
| Virginia | 197,809 | 6,666 |
| Washington | 159,602 | 5,520 |
| West Virginia | 37,160 | 1,820 |
| Wisconsin | 139,160 | 5,146 |
| Wyoming | 16,847 | 480 |

*Source:* For Gross State Product, Bureau of Economic Analysis, *Survey of Current Business*, <http://www.census.gov/>. For Resident Population, *Statistical Abstract of the United States 1998*, No. 26; underlying data from U.S. Bureau of the Census, *1990 Census of Population and Housing, Population and Housing Unit Counts* (CHP-2), *Current Population Reports*, P25-1106, and ST-97-1 *Estimates of the Population of the States: Annual Time Series*, July 1, 1990 to July 1, 1997.

## A5-2. Projections of Gross State Product in Constant (1987) Dollars, by State: 1992–2010, in Billions of Dollars

| | Gross State Product, 1992 | Gross State Product, 2000 | Gross State Product, 2010 |
|---|---|---|---|
| United States | 5001.4 | 6025.6 | 7219.4 |
| Alabama | 66.0 | 79.6 | 95.2 |
| Alaska | 23.0 | 26.8 | 30.9 |
| Arizona | 62.3 | 83.3 | 105.8 |
| Arkansas | 37.3 | 45.6 | 54.5 |
| California | 652.3 | 783.0 | 969.0 |
| Colorado | 69.0 | 88.8 | 110.5 |
| Connecticut | 82.5 | 97.0 | 115.1 |
| Delaware | 18.4 | 22.7 | 27.3 |
| District of Columbia | 32.0 | 34.2 | 37.7 |
| Florida | 222.6 | 288.4 | 364.2 |
| Georgia | 128.6 | 164.2 | 203.7 |
| Hawaii | 27.2 | 32.0 | 38.4 |
| Idaho | 17.7 | 22.9 | 28.4 |
| Illinois | 246.8 | 292.7 | 345.1 |
| Indiana | 103.3 | 126.8 | 150.5 |
| Iowa | 50.5 | 58.9 | 68.6 |
| Kansas | 47.1 | 56.6 | 67.2 |
| Kentucky | 63.7 | 76.9 | 90.9 |
| Louisiana | 79.9 | 92.5 | 106.8 |
| Maine | 20.1 | 23.8 | 28.3 |
| Maryland | 95.4 | 111.4 | 131.7 |
| Massachusetts | 135.1 | 160.0 | 187.6 |
| Michigan | 171.7 | 201.1 | 231.4 |
| Minnesota | 92.9 | 112.2 | 133.8 |
| Mississippi | 37.2 | 45.7 | 54.3 |
| Missouri | 93.6 | 111.3 | 131.8 |
| Montana | 13.0 | 16.2 | 19.6 |
| Nebraska | 31.6 | 37.9 | 45.2 |
| Nevada | 31.4 | 43.2 | 56.2 |
| New Hampshire | 21.6 | 26.8 | 32.4 |
| New Jersey | 184.1 | 215.9 | 253.4 |
| New Mexico | 27.3 | 35.4 | 43.7 |
| New York | 413.1 | 464.6 | 526.9 |
| North Carolina | 130.5 | 164.3 | 200.1 |
| North Dakota | 11.1 | 12.7 | 14.9 |
| Ohio | 203.2 | 240.4 | 279.7 |
| Oklahoma | 50.7 | 60.2 | 70.4 |
| Oregon | 52.5 | 65.2 | 79.3 |
| Pennsylvania | 222.1 | 255.7 | 294.5 |
| Rhode Island | 17.8 | 20.9 | 24.5 |
| South Carolina | 58.9 | 74.1 | 91.6 |
| South Dakota | 12.7 | 15.8 | 19.2 |
| Tennessee | 91.3 | 114.9 | 139.3 |
| Texas | 350.0 | 433.6 | 525.2 |
| Utah | 30.0 | 40.6 | 52.6 |
| Vermont | 10.0 | 12.2 | 14.6 |
| Virginia | 125.1 | 148.9 | 179.2 |
| Washington | 105.8 | 128.8 | 159.7 |
| West Virginia | 26.8 | 30.9 | 35.6 |
| Wisconsin | 92.8 | 113.2 | 135.1 |
| Wyoming | 12.0 | 14.7 | 17.6 |

*Source: Statistical Abstract of the United States 1998*, No. 730; <http://www.census.gov/prod/3/98pubs/98statab/sasec14.pdf>. Underlying data from U.S. Bureau of Economic Analysis, *BEA Regional Projections to 2045*: Volume 1, States.

## A5-3. Gross State Product in Current Dollars, Total: 1990–1996, in Billions of Dollars

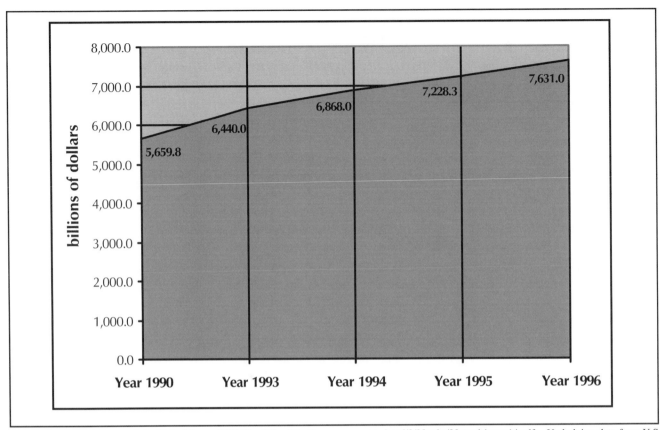

*Source: Statistical Abstract of the United States 1998*, No. 719, <http://www.census.gov/prod/3/98pubs/98statab/sasec14.pdf>. Underlying data from U.S. Bureau of Economic Analysis, *Survey of Current Business*, June 1998.

## A5-4. Gross State Product in Constant (1992) Dollars, Total: 1990–1996, in Billions of Dollars

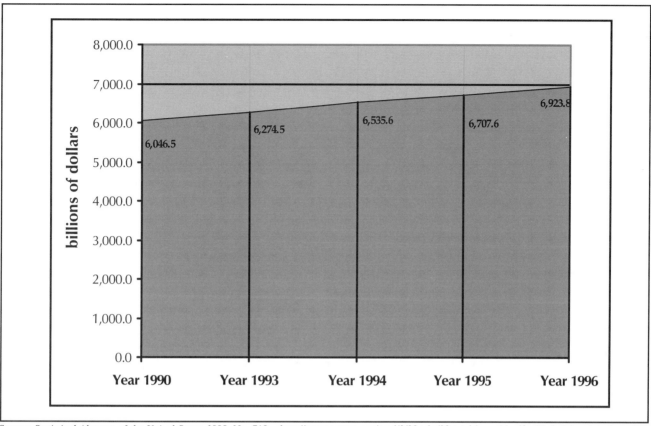

*Source: Statistical Abstract of the United States 1998,* No. 719, <http://www.census.gov/prod/3/98pubs/98statab/sasec14.pdf>. Underlying data from U.S. Bureau of Economic Analysis, *Survey of Current Business,* June 1998.

## A5-5. Gross State Product in Current Dollars: 1990–1996, in Billions of Dollars

|  | 1990 | 1993 | 1994 | 1995 | 1996 |
|---|---|---|---|---|---|
| Alabama | 71.1 | 83.0 | 89.3 | 95.0 | 99.2 |
| Alaska | 25.4 | 22.5 | 21.9 | 23.7 | 24.2 |
| Arizona | 68.5 | 85.0 | 95.4 | 104.0 | 111.5 |
| Arkansas | 37.9 | 46.5 | 50.4 | 53.4 | 56.4 |
| California | 792.7 | 843.1 | 876.0 | 913.5 | 962.7 |
| Colorado | 74.4 | 92.9 | 100.7 | 107.9 | 116.2 |
| Connecticut | 98.5 | 107.5 | 112.6 | 118.6 | 124.0 |
| Delaware | 21.0 | 23.7 | 24.1 | 26.9 | 28.3 |
| District of Columbia | 40.7 | 47.0 | 48.1 | 49.7 | 51.2 |
| Florida | 255.2 | 300.7 | 321.7 | 339.0 | 360.5 |
| Georgia | 140.5 | 170.9 | 186.0 | 200.8 | 216.0 |
| Hawaii | 32.4 | 35.2 | 35.2 | 36.0 | 36.3 |
| Idaho | 17.5 | 22.4 | 24.5 | 26.9 | 27.9 |
| Illinois | 273.4 | 312.3 | 336.9 | 352.9 | 370.8 |
| Indiana | 109.6 | 129.7 | 141.4 | 148.8 | 155.8 |
| Iowa | 55.0 | 62.0 | 68.7 | 71.4 | 76.3 |
| Kansas | 51.3 | 58.2 | 61.9 | 64.1 | 68.0 |
| Kentucky | 67.7 | 79.9 | 86.1 | 90.6 | 95.4 |
| Louisiana | 91.1 | 94.7 | 103.9 | 112.9 | 121.1 |
| Maine | 23.2 | 25.1 | 26.2 | 27.7 | 28.9 |
| Maryland | 113.7 | 124.6 | 132.9 | 137.4 | 143.2 |
| Massachusetts | 158.9 | 174.0 | 186.0 | 195.9 | 208.6 |
| Michigan | 188.0 | 217.3 | 240.6 | 251.8 | 263.3 |
| Minnesota | 99.5 | 114.6 | 124.6 | 131.4 | 141.6 |
| Mississippi | 38.7 | 46.6 | 50.8 | 53.6 | 56.4 |
| Missouri | 104.1 | 118.3 | 129.1 | 137.5 | 145.1 |
| Montana | 13.3 | 16.1 | 16.9 | 17.7 | 18.5 |
| Nebraska | 33.2 | 38.4 | 42.1 | 43.7 | 47.2 |
| Nevada | 31.3 | 39.5 | 44.5 | 48.7 | 53.7 |
| New Hampshire | 23.7 | 27.2 | 29.3 | 31.8 | 34.1 |
| New Jersey | 214.1 | 243.9 | 255.8 | 266.1 | 276.4 |
| New Mexico | 26.7 | 36.3 | 40.9 | 40.8 | 42.7 |
| New York | 498.3 | 541.1 | 565.2 | 587.7 | 613.3 |
| North Carolina | 142.5 | 168.6 | 182.3 | 192.2 | 204.2 |
| North Dakota | 11.4 | 12.7 | 13.7 | 14.5 | 15.7 |
| Ohio | 227.1 | 256.6 | 276.7 | 292.1 | 304.4 |
| Oklahoma | 56.9 | 64.0 | 66.0 | 68.6 | 72.8 |
| Oregon | 57.0 | 68.9 | 74.7 | 80.8 | 87.0 |
| Pennsylvania | 245.8 | 283.1 | 296.8 | 313.3 | 328.5 |
| Rhode Island | 21.5 | 23.3 | 23.9 | 25.0 | 25.6 |
| South Carolina | 65.4 | 75.2 | 80.7 | 85.3 | 89.5 |
| South Dakota | 12.9 | 16.3 | 17.5 | 18.7 | 20.3 |
| Tennessee | 94.2 | 116.7 | 127.9 | 134.9 | 140.8 |
| Texas | 388.9 | 453.0 | 484.1 | 514.2 | 551.8 |
| Utah | 31.1 | 38.1 | 42.0 | 45.6 | 50.4 |
| Vermont | 11.6 | 13.0 | 13.6 | 13.9 | 14.6 |
| Virginia | 148.1 | 170.0 | 178.8 | 187.0 | 197.8 |
| Washington | 114.1 | 136.4 | 144.7 | 150.0 | 159.6 |
| West Virginia | 28.0 | 31.9 | 34.5 | 36.0 | 37.2 |
| Wisconsin | 99.2 | 117.7 | 125.8 | 132.7 | 139.2 |
| Wyoming | 13.5 | 14.6 | 14.9 | 15.8 | 16.8 |

*Source: Statistical Abstract of the United States 1998*, No. 719, <http://www.census.gov/prod/3/98pubs/98statab/sasec14.pdf>. Underlying data from U.S. Bureau of Economic Analysis, *Survey of Current Business*, June 1998.

## A5-6. Gross State Product in Constant (1992) Dollars: 1990–1996, in Billions of Dollars

| | 1990 | 1993 | 1994 | 1995 | 1996 |
|---|---|---|---|---|---|
| Alabama | 75.5 | 80.9 | 85.5 | 88.4 | 90.7 |
| Alaska | 25.2 | 22.1 | 21.5 | 22.7 | 21.4 |
| Arizona | 72.9 | 82.8 | 91.2 | 97.3 | 102.6 |
| Arkansas | 40.0 | 45.3 | 48.2 | 49.9 | 51.5 |
| California | 845.2 | 819.1 | 835.5 | 855.1 | 880.1 |
| Colorado | 79.0 | 90.8 | 96.8 | 101.6 | 106.8 |
| Connecticut | 105.2 | 103.9 | 107.0 | 110.2 | 113.0 |
| Delaware | 23.2 | 26.0 | 26.2 | 27.1 | 28.9 |
| District of Columbia | 45.3 | 46.8 | 46.6 | 46.7 | 47.8 |
| Florida | 273.0 | 291.6 | 305.7 | 314.3 | 326.1 |
| Georgia | 150.0 | 166.4 | 178.2 | 187.4 | 197.1 |
| Hawaii | 34.9 | 36.3 | 35.6 | 34.9 | 34.9 |
| Idaho | 18.5 | 21.8 | 23.5 | 25.5 | 25.9 |
| Illinois | 290.8 | 306.8 | 325.6 | 333.8 | 345.5 |
| Indiana | 116.3 | 126.5 | 135.1 | 139.6 | 144.1 |
| Iowa | 58.0 | 60.4 | 66.0 | 67.5 | 70.3 |
| Kansas | 54.3 | 56.7 | 59.4 | 60.3 | 62.0 |
| Kentucky | 72.3 | 78.2 | 83.4 | 86.4 | 89.3 |
| Louisiana | 93.7 | 92.3 | 100.7 | 107.5 | 109.6 |
| Maine | 24.8 | 24.4 | 24.9 | 25.4 | 26.0 |
| Maryland | 122.3 | 121.4 | 126.5 | 127.6 | 130.2 |
| Massachusetts | 169.9 | 168.9 | 177.3 | 183.0 | 191.0 |
| Michigan | 202.1 | 211.2 | 228.9 | 234.9 | 241.0 |
| Minnesota | 105.1 | 110.9 | 118.4 | 122.0 | 128.7 |
| Mississippi | 40.8 | 45.2 | 48.4 | 50.2 | 51.7 |
| Missouri | 111.3 | 115.5 | 123.4 | 128.5 | 132.8 |
| Montana | 13.9 | 15.7 | 16.2 | 16.6 | 16.9 |
| Nebraska | 34.9 | 37.4 | 40.4 | 41.3 | 43.2 |
| Nevada | 33.1 | 38.6 | 42.3 | 44.8 | 48.3 |
| New Hampshire | 25.2 | 26.4 | 28.0 | 30.0 | 31.7 |
| New Jersey | 227.7 | 236.4 | 242.8 | 246.9 | 251.1 |
| New Mexico | 27.9 | 35.6 | 39.8 | 39.6 | 40.4 |
| New York | 535.6 | 527.6 | 543.7 | 549.6 | 563.3 |
| North Carolina | 154.5 | 165.2 | 177.9 | 183.9 | 190.9 |
| North Dakota | 11.9 | 12.4 | 13.2 | 13.7 | 14.3 |
| Ohio | 241.6 | 250.2 | 264.7 | 273.6 | 280.7 |
| Oklahoma | 59.5 | 62.3 | 63.6 | 65.0 | 66.7 |
| Oregon | 60.8 | 66.5 | 70.6 | 75.0 | 79.4 |
| Pennsylvania | 261.9 | 273.6 | 281.6 | 290.6 | 298.7 |
| Rhode Island | 23.1 | 22.6 | 22.8 | 23.3 | 23.3 |
| South Carolina | 69.5 | 73.6 | 77.7 | 80.1 | 82.7 |
| South Dakota | 13.7 | 15.9 | 16.8 | 17.5 | 18.4 |
| Tennessee | 100.5 | 113.4 | 121.9 | 125.8 | 128.7 |
| Texas | 404.1 | 438.9 | 465.5 | 486.1 | 502.9 |
| Utah | 32.9 | 37.1 | 40.2 | 42.4 | 45.9 |
| Vermont | 12.3 | 12.6 | 13.0 | 13.0 | 13.5 |
| Virginia | 160.6 | 167.1 | 173.4 | 177.0 | 183.2 |
| Washington | 122.2 | 132.1 | 137.2 | 138.7 | 143.8 |
| West Virginia | 29.3 | 31.5 | 33.5 | 34.3 | 35.0 |
| Wisconsin | 105.0 | 115.1 | 120.8 | 124.6 | 128.7 |
| Wyoming | 13.4 | 14.6 | 15.1 | 15.7 | 15.8 |

*Note:*
For constant, or chained, (1992) dollar estimates, states will not add to U.S. total.

*Source: Statistical Abstract of the United States 1998*, No. 719, <http://www.census.gov/prod/3/98pubs/98statab/sasec14.pdf>. Underlying data from U.S. Bureau of Economic Analysis, *Survey of Current Business*, June 1998.

# B. Personal, Family, and Household Income and Wealth

## GENERAL OVERVIEW

Section B makes the transition from Section A's broad-scale macroeconomic investigation to a more tightly focused portrait of personal wealth. The statistics in this section focus at the micro level on personal, family, and household data. The analysis includes information on income, salary, and earnings, on a personal and household basis, along with information on savings and investment. While many of the indicators are aggregated totals, the targeted analysis breaks into detailed categories, in many cases presenting subcategories of income and wealth based on both geographic and demographic variables. Examples of these variables are race and ethnicity, age of householder, size of household, and location of household.

## EXPLANATION OF INDICATORS

**B1. Personal Income Totals and Analysis of Personal Income, Seasonally Adjusted at Annual Rates:** The first chart and first two tables represent the total personal income in the United States and analyze the components that make up aggregate personal income from 1996 through 1998. Breaking the data down into such items as wages, rental income, and government transfer payments, the tables allow the user to understand the detailed sources of personal income. Government reporting systems, primarily the U.S. Bureau of the Census, from which much of this data is taken, define personal income as all income to persons less deductions for social insurance. "Persons" include individuals, non-profit organizations serving individuals, private trust funds, and private welfare funds.

**B2. Households and Median Income, by Selected Characteristics:** The next table and supporting charts represent current information on the median household income in 1997 and 1996, and a reference point in the past (1989). Median household income is the income that falls directly in the middle of the spread of household income data; in other words, it represents the mid-

point in the full range of reported household incomes. The table shows aggregate totals, along with detailed median information according to several variables, such as type of household, race or ethnic origin of householder, age of householder, and region of household. The supplemental charts show the percent change in real income for these variables over two time spans: 1996–1997 and 1989–1997, the latter giving a broader timeframe to measure the smaller incremental change (1996–1997) against.

**B3. Analysis of Personal Income and Its Disposition:** The next chart and two tables present data detailing the relationship between personal income and disposable income and consumption. On an aggregate basis, it shows both the sources of income and its uses. The tables span eight years, from 1990–1997, giving a picture of the most recent trends in personal income and consumption.

**B4. Personal Income, by State:** The next three tables present aggregate personal income data on a state-by-state basis from 1990 through 1997. The data in the first table are in current dollars, showing the full effects of inflation, and the data in the next table are in constant dollars, adjusting for the effects of inflation. The last of the three tables in this group shows the percent distribution and average annual change of each state's personal income.

**B5. Projections of Personal Income in Constant (1987) Dollars, by State:** This table projects personal income data to 2010, using a touchstone of 1993 to give a historical anchor to the projections. It uses constant dollars based on a 1987 valuation.

**B6. Personal Income and Expenditures, per Capita, in Current Dollars:** This table presents personal income, disposable income, and expenditures per capita, thereby relating total aggregate income and consumption figures to the total population. The per person figures cover the years from 1960 through 1997, providing a picture of long-term trends in the second half of the 20th century. The data are in current dollars and show the full effect of inflation across the decades.

**B7. Personal Income per Capita by State, in Current and Constant Dollars:** The next chart presents personal income per capita over the short-term, followed by a table presenting the personal income per capita over the same period on a state-by-state basis. The data are represented in current dollars. The next chart and table present the same data on a constant dollar basis, deflating the effects of inflation based on the 1992 dollar valuation.

**B8. Disposable Personal Income per Capita:** The next two tables present data on disposable personal income, first in terms of current dollars, then in terms of constant (1992) dollars. Disposable income, calculated by deducting tax and non-tax government payments (fees, licenses, etc.) from personal income figures, represents the moneys available to individuals for consumption and savings.

**B9. Average Annual Pay and Personal Earnings:** The next four tables represent data on earned income. This aspect of personal income relates to moneys received from outside parties for work performed (salaries, fees, etc.) or investment proceeds (stock dividends, interest, rental income, etc.). The first three tables, on average annual pay, present state-by-state averages for total pay and then pay broken down into private (non-government) sources. The fourth table represents earnings projections to 2010, from a starting point of 1993, to show past comparisons.

**B10. Personal Earnings by Highest Degree Earned:** The next two sets of charts and tables break down personal earnings by highest type of degree received, manifesting the relationship between income-earning potential and higher education. The data present a snapshot of a recent year, 1997. Other variables such as age, gender, and race of individual, are explored, offering the user measures to help analyze the personal economic effects of educational attainment over a wide range of individuals and groups.

**B11. Median Income for 4-Person Families, by State:** The next six tables represent the median income received by a family for over 20 years, from 1974 through 1996. This state-by-state presentation offers an opportunity to analyze long-term trends for a family of standardized size (4-person).

**B12. Money Income of Families—Median Income by Race and Hispanic Origin:** The next two tables present data on the money income of families, that is, income that families receive exclusive of non-cash payments such as health benefits, food stamps, and subsidized housing. The data cover long-term trends (1970–1996) and break out the median income into race

and Hispanic origin components. The first table presents data in current dollars, and the table that follows presents data in terms of constant (1996) dollars.

**B13. Median Income of Families, by Type of Family:** The next set of charts and tables presents median family income from 1970 through 1996 both on an aggregate level (the charts) and broken down by type of household: married couples, wife in labor force, no husband present, etc. Such details allow the user to see the effect that household characteristics have on income- and wealth-generating potential. Current figures are provided in the first set of tables, and data in constant terms in the next set.

**B14. Median Income of Nonmarried-Couple Households and by Household Size:** The next two tables represent long-term trends (1969–1996) in two other types of household categorizations not detailed on the previous table and charts: by nonmarried-couple households and by household size. Breakdowns within the categories are outlined, including male and female householders for nonmarried-couple households and one- and two-or-more-person households for the household size classification.

**B15. Money Income of Households and Families—Percent Distribution, by Income Level, Race, and Hispanic Origin:** The next two tables represent income distribution figures for households and for families in the U.S. The tables show how the total aggregate income to households and families is spread across the income-earning spectrum: from households earning less than $10,000 per year up to those earning over $75,000 per year. Also provided is the median household income figure for easy comparison.

**B16. Selected Measures of Household Income, 1969–1996:** This table outlines various features of household income across the long term (1969–1996) such as median income value, rate of poverty in householders, and share of households at low, medium, and high income levels.

**B17. Gross Saving and Investment:** The following chart and tables present aggregate data on savings and investment including moneys attributed to individual, corporate, and government savings and investment. The chart presents totals and the tables analyze the components of savings and investment over the short-term—1990 through 1997.

**B18. Flow of Funds Accounts—Individual Savings:** The next two tables analyze the composition of individual savings, breaking the totals into such assets as deposit accounts, securities, and tangible assets. The two tables extend across a short- to mid-term time frame:

from 1980 through 1996.

**B19. IRAs and 401(k) Plans:** The next group—a set of two tables and then a chart with two tables—presents data on the amount of savings placed in retirement instruments. The data analyze the amounts on a year-by-year basis and also break down yearly totals into types of accounts and the types of institutions managing the assets. Taken together, the chart and tables help to the portray the recent trends in the disposition and management of the most widespread types of retirement instru-

ments used in the country.

**B20. Nonfinancial Assets Held by Families, by Type of Asset:** The next two tables detail the nonfinancial aspects of investments owned by families, including such items as real estate, vehicles, etc. The variables covered include the amount of assets owned by different ages of heads of families, family income levels, work status, and tenure (owner or renter). This table presents a snapshot from the year 1995.

## B1. PERSONAL INCOME TOTALS AND ANALYSIS OF PERSONAL INCOME, SEASONALLY ADJUSTED AT ANNUAL RATES

**B1-1. Personal Income Totals, Seasonally Adjusted at Annual Rates, 1996–1998, in Billions of Dollars**

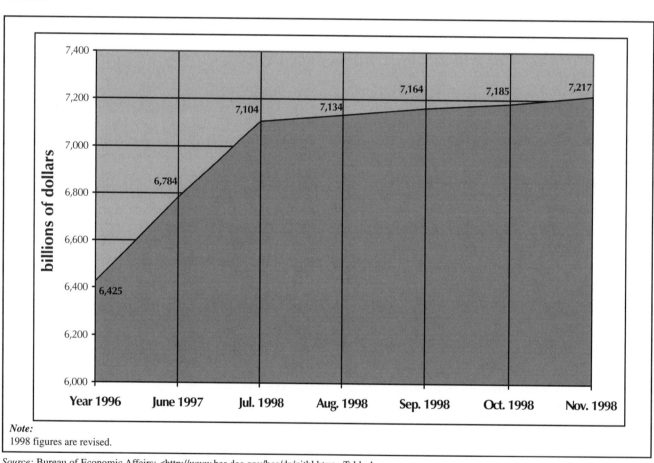

*Note:*
1998 figures are revised.

*Source:* Bureau of Economic Affairs; <http://www.bea.doc.gov/bea/dn/pitbl.htm>, Table 1.

## B1-2. Analysis of Personal Income, Seasonally Adjusted at Annual Rates, 1996–July 1998, in Billions of Dollars

|  | 1996 | 1997 June | 1998 July |
|---|---|---|---|
| Personal income | 6,425.20 | 6,784.00 | 7,104.40 |
| Wage and salary disbursements | 3,631.10 | 3,889.80 | 4,131.00 |
| Private industries | 2,990.20 | 3,225.70 | 3,442.80 |
| Goods-producing industries | 909 | 975 | 1,021.30 |
| Manufacturing | 674.6 | 719.5 | 748.3 |
| Distributive industries | 823.3 | 879.8 | 934.4 |
| Service industries | 1,257.90 | 1,370.80 | 1,487.10 |
| Government | 640.9 | 664.2 | 688.1 |
| Other labor income | 387 | 392.9 | 406.6 |
| Proprietors' income with IVA and CCAdj | 527.7 | 551.2 | 574.8 |
| Farm | 38.9 | 35.5 | 28.2 |
| Nonfarm | 488.8 | 515.8 | 546.6 |
| Rental income of persons with CCAdj | 150.2 | 158.2 | 162.6 |
| Personal dividend income | 248.2 | 260.3 | 262.3 |
| Personal interest income | 719.4 | 747.3 | 765 |
| Transfer payments to persons | 1,068.00 | 1,110.40 | 1,148.30 |
| Old-age, survivors, disability, and health insurance benefits | 538.0 | 565.9 | 586.2 |
| Government unemployment: |  |  |  |
| Insurance benefits | 21.9 | 19.9 | 19.6 |
| Other | 508.0 | 524.6 | 542.5 |
| Less: Personal contributions for social insurance | 306.3 | 326.2 | 346.2 |

*Notes:*
CCAdj indicates Capital consumption adjustment.
IVA indicates Inventory valuation adjustment.

*Source:* Bureau of Economic Affairs; <http://www.bea.doc.gov/bea/dn/pitbl.htm>, Table 1.

## B1-3. Analysis of Personal Income, Seasonally Adjusted at Annual Rates, Aug. 1998–Nov. 1998, in Billions of Dollars

|  | 1998** Aug. | 1998** Sep. | 1998** Oct. | 1998** Nov. |
|---|---|---|---|---|
| Personal income | 7,133.70 | 7,164.10 | 7,184.60 | 7,216.60 |
| Wage and salary disbursements | 4,153.60 | 4,183.40 | 4,194.30 | 4,216.70 |
| Private industries | 3,463.40 | 3,490.60 | 3,499.20 | 3,518.70 |
| Goods-producing industries | 1,020.90 | 1,030.60 | 1,032.70 | 1,034.10 |
| Manufacturing | 743.8 | 752.4 | 756.4 | 754.4 |
| Distributive industries | 941.5 | 946.3 | 949.6 | 951.4 |
| Service industries | 1,501.00 | 1,513.80 | 1,516.90 | 1,533.10 |
| Government | 690.2 | 692.8 | 695.1 | 698 |
| Other labor income | 407.5 | 408.3 | 409.2 | 410.1 |
| Proprietors' income with IVA and CCAdj | 577.2 | 574.7 | 576.4 | 585.4 |
| Farm | 26.8 | 25.2 | 23.5 | 26.6 |
| Nonfarm | 550.5 | 549.5 | 552.9 | 558.8 |
| Rental income of persons with CCAdj | 163 | 163.5 | 164.4 | 165.8 |
| Personal dividend income | 262.4 | 262.8 | 263.7 | 264.7 |
| Personal interest income | 767.3 | 769.4 | 770.7 | 771 |
| Transfer payments to persons | 1,150.40 | 1,151.80 | 1,156.60 | 1,155.50 |
| Old-age, survivors, disability, and health insurance benefits | 588.0 | 588.5 | 590.4 | 588.7 |
| Government unemployment: |  |  |  |  |
| Insurance benefits | 19.5 | 19.4 | 19.6 | 19.4 |
| Other | 542.9 | 544.0 | 546.6 | 547.4 |
| Less: Personal contributions for social insurance | 347.7 | 349.9 | 350.8 | 352.5 |

*Notes:*
** Revised
CCAdj indicates Capital consumption adjustment.
IVA indicates Inventory valuation adjustment.

*Source:* Bureau of Economic Affairs; <http://www.bea.doc.gov/bea/dn/pitbl.htm>, Table 1.

## B2. HOUSEHOLDS AND MEDIAN INCOME, BY SELECTED CHARACTERISTICS

### B2-1. Households and Median Income, by Selected Characteristics: 1989, 1996, and 1997

| Characteristics | 1997 Number (1000s) | 1997 Median Income (dollars) | Median Income (in 1997 dollars) 1996 | Median Income (in 1997 dollars) 1989[r] |
|---|---|---|---|---|
| **HOUSEHOLDS** | | | | |
| All households | 102,528 | 37,005 | 36,306 | 37,303 |
| **Type of Household** | | | | |
| Family households | 70,880 | 45,347 | 44,071 | 44,647 |
| Married-couple families | 54,317 | 51,681 | 51,002 | 49,925 |
| Female householder, no husband present | 12,652 | 23,040 | 22,059 | 22,315 |
| Male householder, no wife present | 3,911 | 36,634 | 36,476 | 39,108 |
| Nonfamily households | 31,648 | 21,705 | 21,454 | 22,221 |
| Female householder | 17,516 | 17,613 | 16,774 | 17,865 |
| Male householder | 14,133 | 27,592 | 27,892 | 29,036 |
| **Race and Hispanic Origin of Householder** | | | | |
| White | 86,106 | 38,972 | 38,014 | 39,241 |
| White, not Hispanic | 77,936 | 40,577 | 39,677 | 40,166 |
| Black | 12,474 | 25,050 | 24,021 | 23,583 |
| Asian and Pacific Islander | 3,125 | 45,249 | 44,269 | 46,611 |
| Hispanic origin[1] | 8,590 | 26,628 | 25,477 | 28,192 |
| **Age of Householder** | | | | |
| 15 to 24 years | 5,435 | 22,583 | 21,930 | 24,027 |
| 25 to 34 years | 19,033 | 38,174 | 36,711 | 38,442 |
| 35 to 44 years | 23,943 | 46,359 | 45,439 | 48,554 |
| 45 to 54 years | 19,547 | 51,875 | 51,630 | 53,738 |
| 55 to 64 years | 13,072 | 41,356 | 40,729 | 39,946 |
| 65 years and over | 21,497 | 20,761 | 19,894 | 20,402 |
| **Nativity of the householder** | | | | |
| Native born | 91,713 | 37,643 | 36,920 | (NA) |
| Foreign born | 10,818 | 31,318 | 30,697 | (NA) |
| Not a citizen | 5,946 | 26,959 | 26,239 | (NA) |
| **Region** | | | | |
| Northeast | 19,810 | 38,929 | 38,264 | 42,123 |
| Midwest | 24,236 | 38,316 | 37,418 | 37,107 |
| South | 36,578 | 34,345 | 33,166 | 33,412 |
| West | 21,905 | 39,162 | 37,977 | 40,081 |
| **Residence** | | | | |
| Inside metropolitan areas | 82,122 | 39,381 | 38,504 | 40,151 |
| Inside central cities | 31,907 | 31,548 | 31,058 | (NA) |
| Outside central cities | 50,215 | 44,668 | 43,429 | (NA) |
| Outside metropolitan areas | 20,406 | 30,057 | 28,734 | 28,942 |
| **EARNINGS OF FULL-TIME, YEAR-ROUND WORKERS** | | | | |
| Male | 54,909 | 33,674 | 32,882 | 35,179 |
| Female | 37,683 | 24,973 | 24,254 | 24,237 |
| **PER CAPITA INCOME** | | | | |
| All races[2] | 269,094 | 19,241 | 18,552 | 17,999 |
| White | 221,650 | 20,425 | 19,621 | 19,088 |
| White, not Hispanic | 192,178 | 21,905 | 20,991 | (NA) |
| Black | 34,598 | 12,351 | 12,172 | 11,231 |
| Asian and Pacific Islander | 10,492 | 18,226 | 18,332 | (NA) |
| Hispanic origin[1] | 30,773 | 10,773 | 10,279 | 10,605 |

*Notes:*

1. People of Hispanic origin may be of any race.

2. Data for American Indians, Eskimos, and Aleuts are not shown separately. Data for this population group are not tabulated from the CPS because of its small size.

(r) Revised to reflect implementation of 1990 census adjusted population controls.

X indicates not applicable.

NA indicates not available.

*General Note:* Households and people as of March of the following year.

*Source:* U.S. Bureau of the Census, *Current Population Reports, P 60-200, Money Income in the United States: 1997*, Table A; U.S. Census Bureau, *The Official Statistics* TM Sep. 8, 1998; <http://www.census.gov/prod/3/98pubs/p60-200.pdf>.

**B2-2. Households and Median Income Percent Changes, by Selected Characteristics: 1996–1997 and 1989–1997**

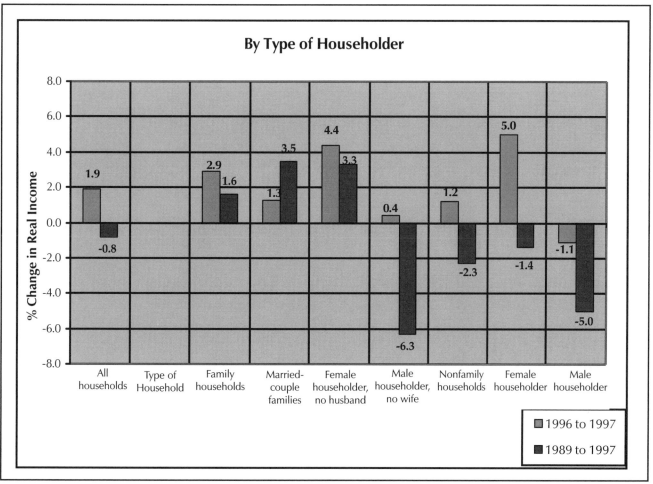

*Source:* U.S. Bureau of the Census, *Current Population Reports, P 60-200, Money Income in the United States: 1997*, Table A; U.S. Census Bureau, *The Official Statistics* TM Sep. 8, 1998; <http://www.census.gov/prod/3/98pubs/p60-200.pdf>.

**B2-2. Households and Median Income Percent Changes, by Selected Characteristics: 1996–1997 and 1989–1997** *(continued)*

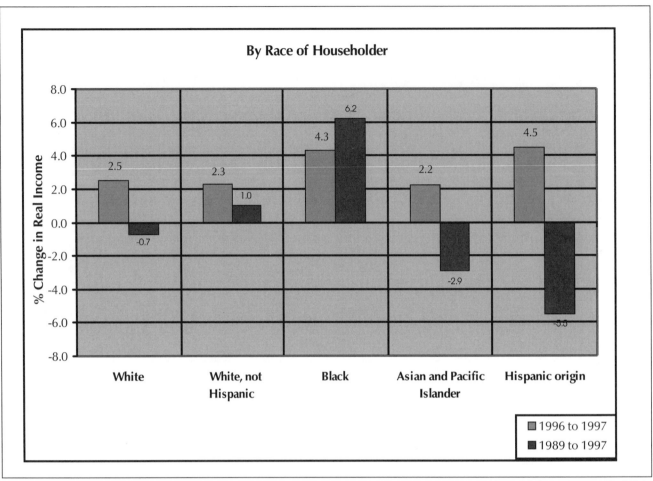

*Source:* U.S. Bureau of the Census, *Current Population Reports, P 60-200, Money Income in the United States: 1997,* Table A; U.S. Census Bureau, *The Official Statistics* TM Sep. 8, 1998; <http://www.census.gov/prod/3/98pubs/p60-200.pdf>.

**B2-2. Households and Median Income Percent Changes, by Selected Characteristics: 1996–1997 and 1989–1997** *(continued)*

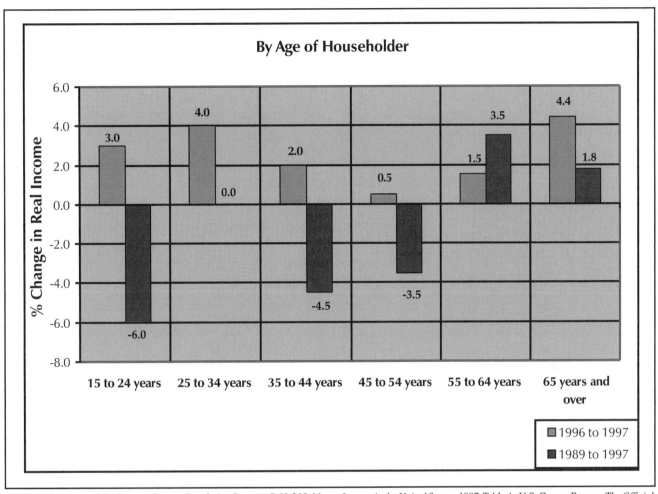

*Source:* U.S. Bureau of the Census, *Current Population Reports, P 60-200, Money Income in the United States: 1997,* Table A; U.S. Census Bureau, *The Official Statistics* TM Sep. 8, 1998; <http://www.census.gov/prod/3/98pubs/p60-200.pdf/>.

**B2-2. Households and Median Income Percent Changes, by Selected Characteristics: 1996–1997 and 1989–1997** *(continued)*

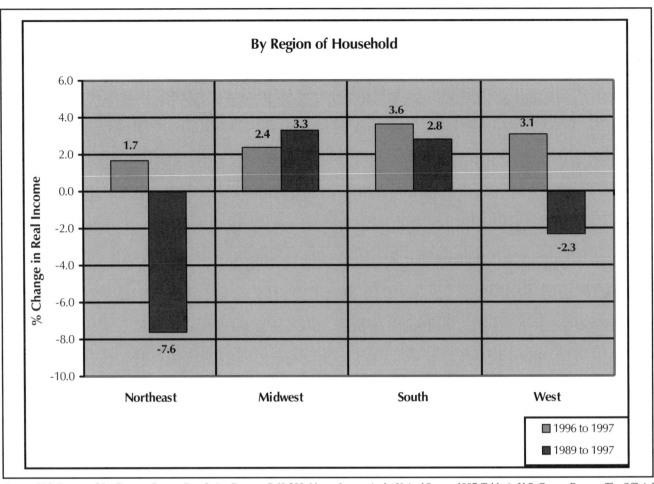

*Source:* U.S. Bureau of the Census, *Current Population Reports, P 60-200, Money Income in the United States: 1997*, Table A; U.S. Census Bureau, *The Official Statistics* TM Sep. 8, 1998; <http://www.census.gov/prod/3/98pubs/p60-200.pdf/>.

**B2-2. Households and Median Income Percent Changes, by Selected Characteristics: 1996–1997 and 1989–1997** *(continued)*

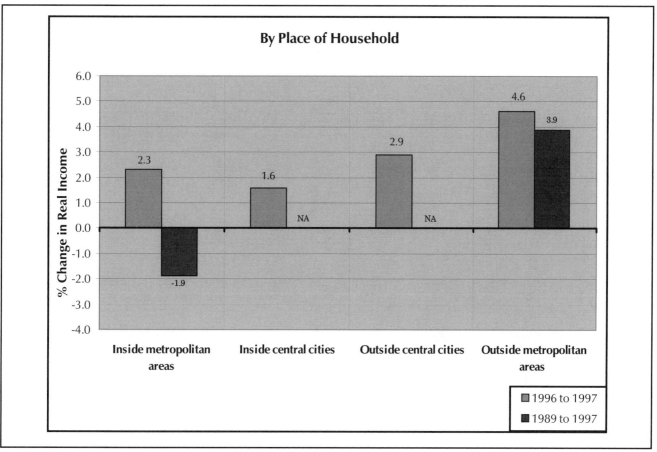

*Source:* U.S. Bureau of the Census, *Current Population Reports, P 60-200, Money Income in the United States: 1997*, Table A; U.S. Census Bureau, *The Official Statistics* TM Sep. 8, 1998; <http://www.census.gov/prod/3/98pubs/p60-200.pdf/>.

## B3. ANALYSIS OF PERSONAL INCOME AND ITS DISPOSITION

### B3-1. Personal Income and Its Disposition: 1990–1997, in Billions of Dollars (except as indicated)

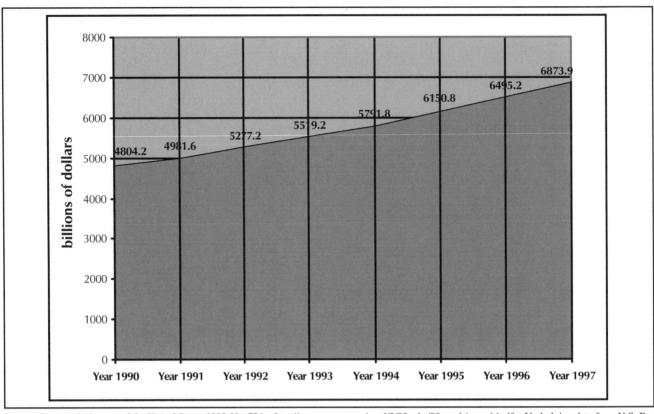

*Source: Statistical Abstract of the United States 1998,* No. 724, <http://wwwcensusgov/prod/3/98pubs/98statab/sasec14pdf>. Underlying data from U.S. Bureau of Economic Analysis, *National Income and Product Accounts of the United States, 1929-94,* Vol. 1; and *Survey of Current Business*, August 1997 and May 1998.

### B3-2. Analysis of Personal Income and Its Disposition: 1990–1993, in Billions of Dollars (except as indicated)

| ITEM | 1990 | 1991 | 1992 | 1993 |
|---|---|---|---|---|
| Personal income | 4804.2 | 4981.6 | 5277.2 | 5519.2 |
| Wage and salary disbursements | 2757.5 | 2827.6 | 2986.4 | 3089.6 |
| Commodity-producing industries[1] | 754.2 | 746.3 | 765.7 | 781.2 |
| Manufacturing | 561.2 | 562.5 | 583.5 | 592.9 |
| Distributive industries[2] | 634.1 | 646.6 | 680.3 | 699.4 |
| Service industries[3] | 852.1 | 888.7 | 972.6 | 1024.7 |
| Government | 517.2 | 546.1 | 567.8 | 584.3 |
| Other labor income | 300.6 | 322.7 | 351.3 | 385.1 |
| Proprietors' income[4] | 374.0 | 376.5 | 423.8 | 450.8 |
| Rental income of persons[5] | 61.0 | 67.9 | 79.4 | 105.7 |
| Personal dividend income | 142.9 | 153.6 | 159.4 | 185.3 |
| Personal interest income | 704.4 | 699.3 | 667.2 | 651.0 |
| Transfer payments to persons | 687.8 | 769.9 | 858.2 | 912.0 |
| Less: Personal contributions for social insurance | 223.9 | 235.8 | 248.4 | 260.3 |
| Less: Personal tax and nontax payments | 624.8 | 624.8 | 650.6 | 690.0 |

## B3-2. Analysis of Personal Income and Its Disposition: 1990–1993, in Billions of Dollars (except as indicated) *(continued)*

| ITEM | 1990 | 1991 | 1992 | 1993 |
|---|---|---|---|---|
| Equals: Disposable personal income | 4179.4 | 4356.8 | 4626.7 | 4829.2 |
| Less: Personal outlays | 3958.1 | 4097.4 | 4341.0 | 4580.7 |
| Personal consumption expenditures | 3839.3 | 3975.1 | 4219.8 | 4459.2 |
| Interest paid by persons | 108.9 | 111.9 | 111.7 | 108.2 |
| Personal transfer payments to the rest of the world (net) | 9.9 | 10.4 | 9.6 | 13.3 |
| | | | | |
| Equals: Personal saving | 221.3 | 259.5 | 285.7 | 248.5 |
| Addenda: | | | | |
| Disposable personal income: | | | | |
| Total, billions of chained (1992) dollars | 4498.2 | 4500.0 | 4626.7 | 4703.9 |
| Per capita (dollars): | | | | |
| Current dollars | 16720.0 | 17241.8 | 18112.2 | 18706.0 |
| Chained (1992) dollars | 17996.1 | 17808.9 | 18112.8 | 18221.0 |
| Personal saving as percentage of disposable personal income | 5.3 | 6.0 | 6.2 | 5.1 |

*Notes:*
1. Comprises agriculture, forestry, fishing, mining, construction, and manufacturing.
2. Comprises transportation, communication, public utilities, and trade.
3. Comprises finance, insurance, real estate, services, and rest of world.
4. With capital consumption and inventory valuation adjustments.
5. With capital consumption adjustment.

*Source: Statistical Abstract of the United States 1998*, No. 724, <http://wwwcensusgov/prod/3/98pubs/98statab/sasec14pdf>. Underlying data from U.S. Bureau of Economic Analysis, *National Income and Product Accounts of the United States, 1929-94*, Vol. 1; and *Survey of Current Business*, August 1997 and May 1998.

## B3-3. Analysis of Personal Income and Its Disposition: 1994–1997, in Billions of Dollars (except as indicated)

| ITEM | 1994 | 1995 | 1996 | 1997 |
|---|---|---|---|---|
| Personal income | 5791.8 | 6150.8 | 6495.2 | 6873.9 |
| Wage and salary disbursements | 3240.7 | 3429.5 | 3632.5 | 3877.4 |
| Commodity-producing industries[1] | 824.4 | 864.4 | 909.1 | 960.3 |
| Manufacturing | 620.8 | 648.4 | 674.7 | 706.0 |
| Distributive industries[2] | 741.4 | 783.1 | 823.3 | 876.3 |
| Service industries[3] | 1072.7 | 1159.0 | 1257.5 | 1375.5 |
| Government | 602.2 | 623.0 | 642.6 | 665.3 |
| Other labor income | 405.0 | 406.8 | 407.6 | 416.6 |
| Proprietors' income[4] | 471.6 | 489.0 | 520.3 | 544.5 |
| Rental income of persons[5] | 124.4 | 132.8 | 146.3 | 147.9 |
| Personal dividend income | 204.8 | 251.9 | 291.2 | 321.5 |
| Personal interest income | 668.1 | 718.9 | 735.7 | 768.6 |
| Transfer payments to persons | 954.7 | 1015.0 | 1068.0 | 1121.1 |
| Less: Personal contributions for social insurance | 277.5 | 293.1 | 306.3 | 323.7 |
| Less: Personal tax and nontax payments | 739.1 | 795.1 | 886.9 | 988.7 |
| | | | | |
| Equals: Disposable personal income | 5052.7 | 5355.7 | 5608.3 | 5885.2 |
| Less: Personal outlays | 4842.1 | 5101.1 | 5368.8 | 5658.5 |
| Personal consumption expenditures | 4717.0 | 4957.7 | 5207.6 | 5485.8 |
| Interest paid by persons | 110.9 | 128.5 | 145.2 | 154.8 |
| Personal transfer payments to the rest of the world (net) | 14.2 | 14.8 | 15.9 | 17.9 |

## B3-3. Analysis of Personal Income and Its Disposition: 1994–1997, in Billions of Dollars (except as indicated) *(continued)*

| ITEM | 1994 | 1995 | 1996 | 1997 |
|---|---|---|---|---|
| Equals: Personal saving | 210.6 | 254.6 | 239.6 | 226.7 |
| Addenda: | | | | |
| Disposable personal income: | | | | |
| Total, billions of chained (1992) dollars | 4805.1 | 4964.2 | 5076.9 | 5221.9 |
| Per capita (dollars): | | | | |
| Current dollars | 19381.0 | 20349.0 | 21117.0 | 21969.0 |
| Chained (1992) dollars | 18431.0 | 18861.0 | 19116.0 | 19493.0 |
| Personal saving as percentage of disposable personal income | 4.2 | 4.8 | 4.3 | 3.9 |

*Notes:*
1. Comprises agriculture, forestry, fishing, mining, construction, and manufacturing.
2. Comprises transportation, communication, public utilities, and trade.
3. Comprises finance, insurance, real estate, services, and rest of world.
4. With capital consumption and inventory valuation adjustments.
5. With capital consumption adjustment.

*Source: Statistical Abstract of the United States 1998*, No. 724; <http://wwwcensusgov/prod/3/98pubs/98statab/sasec14pdf>. Underlying data from U.S. Bureau of Economic Analysis, *National Income and Product Accounts of the United States*, *1929-94,*Vol. 1; and *Survey of Current Business*, August 1997 and May 1998.

## B4. PERSONAL INCOME, BY STATE

## B4-1. Personal Income, by State, Current Dollars: 1990–1997, in Billions of Dollars

| | 1990 | 1995 | 1996 | 1997 |
|---|---|---|---|---|
| United States | 4786.3 | 6137.9 | 6480.0 | 6851.1 |
| Alabama | 61.7 | 82.1 | 86.0 | 90.0 |
| Alaska | 11.7 | 14.6 | 14.9 | 15.4 |
| Arizona | 61.2 | 87.5 | 94.6 | 101.9 |
| Arkansas | 33.1 | 45.0 | 47.5 | 49.4 |
| California | 640.3 | 764.6 | 808.2 | 857.4 |
| Colorado | 63.8 | 91.7 | 98.2 | 105.3 |
| Connecticut | 87.2 | 106.5 | 111.7 | 118.6 |
| Delaware | 14.5 | 18.8 | 20.1 | 21.2 |
| District of Columbia | 15.5 | 18.0 | 18.4 | 19.0 |
| Florida | 249.7 | 328.1 | 348.9 | 370.1 |
| Georgia | 113.3 | 157.8 | 168.9 | 180.1 |
| Hawaii | 24.0 | 29.6 | 30.1 | 30.9 |
| Idaho | 15.6 | 22.4 | 23.6 | 24.8 |
| Illinois | 235.0 | 301.7 | 318.1 | 335.5 |
| Indiana | 95.5 | 125.7 | 131.9 | 138.4 |
| Iowa | 47.0 | 59.2 | 63.6 | 65.9 |
| Kansas | 44.6 | 56.2 | 59.7 | 63.3 |
| Kentucky | 55.8 | 72.7 | 76.8 | 80.7 |
| Louisiana | 62.4 | 82.2 | 85.6 | 90.0 |
| Maine | 21.2 | 25.0 | 26.1 | 27.4 |
| Maryland | 108.0 | 133.6 | 140.0 | 147.6 |
| Massachusetts | 139.9 | 172.1 | 181.4 | 192.8 |
| Michigan | 174.4 | 229.5 | 239.3 | 249.8 |
| Minnesota | 85.0 | 111.0 | 119.5 | 125.6 |
| Mississippi | 32.8 | 45.0 | 47.6 | 49.9 |
| Missouri | 90.6 | 116.8 | 123.3 | 129.7 |
| Montana | 12.1 | 16.2 | 16.9 | 17.6 |
| Nebraska | 27.8 | 35.1 | 37.9 | 39.4 |
| Nevada | 24.7 | 37.9 | 41.7 | 44.9 |
| New Hampshire | 23.1 | 29.5 | 31.1 | 32.9 |

## B4-1. Personal Income, by State, Current Dollars: 1990–1997, in Billions of Dollars *(continued)*

|  | 1990 | 1995 | 1996 | 1997 |
|---|---|---|---|---|
| New Jersey | 193.4 | 238.5 | 250.2 | 263.0 |
| New Mexico | 22.0 | 30.8 | 32.2 | 33.9 |
| New York | 416.7 | 505.4 | 529.9 | 557.8 |
| North Carolina | 111.0 | 152.6 | 162.6 | 173.3 |
| North Dakota | 9.7 | 11.9 | 13.2 | 13.0 |
| Ohio | 197.1 | 251.1 | 262.2 | 275.9 |
| Oklahoma | 49.2 | 61.3 | 64.5 | 68.2 |
| Oregon | 49.9 | 68.9 | 73.9 | 79.1 |
| Pennsylvania | 230.9 | 285.2 | 299.2 | 313.2 |
| Rhode Island | 19.8 | 23.5 | 24.3 | 25.4 |
| South Carolina | 54.1 | 70.3 | 74.0 | 78.0 |
| South Dakota | 10.8 | 14.0 | 15.3 | 15.8 |
| Tennessee | 79.9 | 111.8 | 116.9 | 123.6 |
| Texas | 295.1 | 400.6 | 426.2 | 459.9 |
| Utah | 24.6 | 36.2 | 39.1 | 42.1 |
| Vermont | 10.0 | 12.6 | 13.2 | 13.8 |
| Virginia | 124.6 | 160.3 | 168.4 | 178.0 |
| Washington | 96.2 | 130.3 | 139.5 | 149.9 |
| West Virginia | 25.4 | 32.0 | 33.2 | 34.4 |
| Wisconsin | 86.9 | 114.6 | 120.4 | 126.5 |
| Wyoming | 7.8 | 10.0 | 10.4 | 10.9 |

*Notes:*
1997 data are preliminary. Represents a measure of income received from all sources during the calendar year by residents of each state. Data exclude federal employees overseas and U.S. residents employed by private U.S. firms on temporary foreign assignment.

*Source: Statistical Abstract of the United States 1998*, No. 727; <http://www.census.gov/prod/3/98pubs/98statab/sasec14.pdf>. Underlying data from U.S. Bureau of Economic Analysis, *Survey of Current Business*, May 1998, and unpublished data.

## B4-2. Personal Income, by State, Constant (1992) Dollars: 1990–1997, in Billions of Dollars

|  | 1990 | 1995 | 1996 | 1997 |
|---|---|---|---|---|
| United States | 5151.5 | 5689.0 | 5865.9 | 6079.0 |
| Alabama | 66.4 | 76.1 | 77.8 | 79.9 |
| Alaska | 12.6 | 13.5 | 13.5 | 13.7 |
| Arizona | 65.9 | 81.1 | 85.6 | 90.4 |
| Arkansas | 35.6 | 41.7 | 43.0 | 43.8 |
| California | 689.1 | 708.7 | 731.6 | 760.7 |
| Colorado | 68.7 | 85.0 | 88.9 | 93.4 |
| Connecticut | 93.8 | 98.7 | 101.1 | 105.2 |
| Delaware | 15.6 | 17.4 | 18.2 | 18.8 |
| District of Columbia | 16.7 | 16.7 | 16.7 | 16.8 |
| Florida | 268.8 | 304.1 | 315.8 | 328.4 |
| Georgia | 121.9 | 146.3 | 152.9 | 159.8 |
| Hawaii | 25.8 | 27.4 | 27.2 | 27.4 |
| Idaho | 16.7 | 20.7 | 21.4 | 22.0 |
| Illinois | 253.0 | 279.6 | 288.0 | 297.7 |
| Indiana | 102.8 | 116.5 | 119.4 | 122.8 |
| Iowa | 50.6 | 54.8 | 57.6 | 58.5 |
| Kansas | 48.0 | 52.1 | 54.0 | 56.1 |
| Kentucky | 60.0 | 67.4 | 69.5 | 71.6 |
| Louisiana | 67.2 | 76.2 | 77.4 | 79.9 |
| Maine | 22.8 | 23.1 | 23.6 | 24.3 |
| Maryland | 116.3 | 123.8 | 126.8 | 130.9 |
| Massachusetts | 150.6 | 159.5 | 164.2 | 171.1 |
| Michigan | 187.7 | 212.7 | 216.6 | 221.7 |
| Minnesota | 91.5 | 102.9 | 108.1 | 111.4 |
| Mississippi | 35.3 | 41.8 | 43.1 | 44.3 |

**B4-2. Personal Income, by State, Constant (1992) Dollars: 1990–1997, in Billions of Dollars** *(continued)*

| | 1990 | 1995 | 1996 | 1997 |
|---|---|---|---|---|
| Missouri | 97.5 | 108.2 | 111.6 | 115.0 |
| Montana | 13.0 | 15.0 | 15.3 | 15.6 |
| Nebraska | 29.9 | 32.5 | 34.3 | 35.0 |
| Nevada | 26.5 | 35.2 | 37.8 | 39.9 |
| New Hampshire | 24.9 | 27.3 | 28.1 | 29.2 |
| New Jersey | 208.1 | 221.1 | 226.5 | 233.3 |
| New Mexico | 23.7 | 28.5 | 29.1 | 30.1 |
| New York | 448.5 | 468.4 | 479.7 | 494.9 |
| North Carolina | 119.5 | 141.4 | 147.2 | 153.8 |
| North Dakota | 10.5 | 11.0 | 11.9 | 11.5 |
| Ohio | 212.1 | 232.8 | 237.4 | 244.8 |
| Oklahoma | 53.0 | 56.8 | 58.4 | 60.5 |
| Oregon | 53.7 | 63.8 | 66.9 | 70.2 |
| Pennsylvania | 248.5 | 264.3 | 270.9 | 277.9 |
| Rhode Island | 21.3 | 21.8 | 22.0 | 22.6 |
| South Carolina | 58.2 | 65.1 | 66.9 | 69.2 |
| South Dakota | 11.6 | 13.0 | 13.9 | 14.0 |
| Tennessee | 85.9 | 103.6 | 105.9 | 109.6 |
| Texas | 317.6 | 371.3 | 385.8 | 408.0 |
| Utah | 26.5 | 33.5 | 35.4 | 37.3 |
| Vermont | 10.8 | 11.7 | 12.0 | 12.2 |
| Virginia | 134.1 | 148.6 | 152.4 | 158.0 |
| Washington | 103.6 | 120.8 | 126.3 | 133.0 |
| West Virginia | 27.4 | 29.7 | 30.0 | 30.5 |
| Wisconsin | 93.5 | 106.2 | 109.0 | 112.3 |
| Wyoming | 8.4 | 9.3 | 9.4 | 9.6 |

*Notes:*
Implicit price deflator for personal consumption expenditures is used as a deflator.
1997 data are preliminary. Represents a measure of income received from all sources during the calendar year by residents of each state. Data exclude federal employees overseas and U.S. residents employed by private U.S. firms on temporary foreign assignment.

*Source: Statistical Abstract of the United States 1998*, No. 727; <http://www.census.gov/prod/3/98pubs/98statab/sasec14.pdf>. Underlying data from U.S. Bureau of Economic Analysis, *Survey of Current Business*, May 1998, and unpublished data.

**B4-3. Percent Distribution and Average Annual Percent Change of Personal Income, by State, in Constant (1992) Dollars: 1990–1997, in Billions of Dollars**

| | Percent distribution | | Average annual percentage change | |
|---|---|---|---|---|
| | 1990 | 1997 | 1990–96 | 1996–97 |
| **United States** | 100.0 | 100.0 | 2.2 | 3.6 |
| Alabama | 1.3 | 1.3 | 2.7 | 2.7 |
| Alaska | 0.2 | 0.2 | 1.2 | 1.5 |
| Arizona | 1.3 | 1.5 | 4.5 | 5.6 |
| Arkansas | 0.7 | 0.7 | 3.2 | 1.9 |
| California | 13.4 | 12.5 | 1.0 | 4.0 |
| Colorado | 1.3 | 1.5 | 4.4 | 5.1 |
| Connecticut | 1.8 | 1.7 | 1.3 | 4.1 |
| Delaware | 0.3 | 0.3 | 2.6 | 3.3 |
| District of Columbia | 0.3 | 0.3 | 0.0 | 0.6 |
| Florida | 5.2 | 5.4 | 2.7 | 4.0 |
| Georgia | 2.4 | 2.6 | 3.8 | 4.5 |
| Hawaii | 0.5 | 0.5 | 0.9 | 0.7 |
| Idaho | 0.3 | 0.4 | 4.2 | 2.8 |
| Illinois | 4.9 | 4.9 | 2.2 | 3.4 |
| Indiana | 2.0 | 2.0 | 2.5 | 2.8 |

**B4-3. Percent Distribution and Average Annual Percent Change of Personal Income, by State, in Constant (1992) Dollars: 1990–1997, in Billions of Dollars *(continued)***

| | Percent distribution | | Average annual percentage change | |
|---|---|---|---|---|
| | **1990** | **1997** | **1990–96** | **1996–97** |
| Iowa | 1.0 | 1.0 | 2.2 | 1.6 |
| Kansas | 0.9 | 0.9 | 2.0 | 3.9 |
| Kentucky | 1.2 | 1.2 | 2.5 | 3.0 |
| Louisiana | 1.3 | 1.3 | 2.4 | 3.2 |
| Maine | 0.4 | 0.4 | 0.6 | 3.0 |
| Maryland | 2.3 | 2.2 | 1.5 | 3.2 |
| Massachusetts | 2.9 | 2.8 | 1.5 | 4.2 |
| Michigan | 3.6 | 3.6 | 2.4 | 2.4 |
| Minnesota | 1.8 | 1.8 | 2.8 | 3.1 |
| Mississippi | 0.7 | 0.7 | 3.4 | 2.8 |
| Missouri | 1.9 | 1.9 | 2.3 | 3.0 |
| Montana | 0.3 | 0.3 | 2.8 | 2.0 |
| Nebraska | 0.6 | 0.6 | 2.3 | 2.0 |
| Nevada | 0.5 | 0.7 | 6.1 | 5.6 |
| New Hampshire | 0.5 | 0.5 | 2.0 | 3.9 |
| New Jersey | 4.0 | 3.8 | 1.4 | 3.0 |
| New Mexico | 0.5 | 0.5 | 3.5 | 3.4 |
| New York | 8.7 | 8.1 | 1.1 | 3.2 |
| North Carolina | 2.3 | 2.5 | 3.5 | 4.5 |
| North Dakota | 0.2 | .2 | 2.1 | -3.4 |
| Ohio | 4.1 | 4.0 | 1.9 | 3.1 |
| Oklahoma | 1.0 | 1.0 | 1.6 | 3.6 |
| Oregon | 1.0 | 1.2 | 3.7 | 4.9 |
| Pennsylvania | 4.8 | 4.6 | 1.4 | 2.6 |
| Rhode Island | 0.4 | 0.4 | 0.5 | 2.7 |
| South Carolina | 1.1 | 1.1 | 2.3 | 3.4 |
| South Dakota | 0.2 | 0.2 | 3.1 | 0.7 |
| Tennessee | 1.7 | 1.8 | 3.6 | 3.5 |
| Texas | 6.2 | 6.7 | 3.3 | 5.8 |
| Utah | 0.5 | 0.6 | 4.9 | 5.4 |
| Vermont | 0.2 | 0.2 | 1.8 | 1.7 |
| Virginia | 2.6 | 2.6 | 2.2 | 3.7 |
| Washington | 2.0 | 2.2 | 3.4 | 5.3 |
| West Virginia | 0.5 | 0.5 | 1.5 | 1.7 |
| Wisconsin | 1.8 | 1.8 | 2.6 | 3.0 |
| Wyoming | 0.2 | 0.2 | 1.9 | 2.1 |

*Notes:*
Implicit price deflator for personal consumption expenditures is used as a deflator.
1997 data are preliminary. Represents a measure of income received from all sources during the calendar year by residents of each state. Data exclude federal employees overseas and U.S. residents employed by private U.S. firms on temporary foreign assignment.

*Source: Statistical Abstract of the United States 1998*, No. 726; <http://www.census.gov/prod/3/98pubs/98statab/sasec14.pdf>. Underlying data from U.S. Bureau of Economic Analysis, *Survey of Current Business*, May 1998, and unpublished data.

## B5. PROJECTIONS OF PERSONAL INCOME IN CONSTANT (1987) DOLLARS, BY STATE

### B5-1. Projections of Personal Income in Constant (1987) Dollars, by State: 1993–2010, in Billions of Dollars

|  | Personal Income 1993 | Personal Income 2000 | Personal Income 2010 |
|---|---|---|---|
| **United States** | 4183.9 | 4894.5 | 5917.2 |
| Alabama | 55.9 | 64.6 | 77.5 |
| Alaska | 10.8 | 12.6 | 15.3 |
| Arizona | 55.7 | 70.4 | 91.0 |
| Arkansas | 30.3 | 35.2 | 42.0 |
| California | 533.3 | 638.3 | 795.5 |
| Colorado | 59.8 | 73.3 | 92.5 |
| Connecticut | 71.5 | 81.8 | 97.5 |
| Delaware | 11.9 | 14.0 | 17.0 |
| District of Columbia | 13.5 | 14.3 | 15.5 |
| Florida | 221.2 | 276.7 | 357.2 |
| Georgia | 103.7 | 126.2 | 157.9 |
| Hawaii | 21.4 | 25.4 | 31.0 |
| Idaho | 15.0 | 18.2 | 22.4 |
| Illinois | 205.8 | 234.7 | 277.7 |
| Indiana | 85.5 | 98.4 | 116.8 |
| Iowa | 40.3 | 46.3 | 54.1 |
| Kansas | 39.3 | 45.9 | 54.8 |
| Kentucky | 50.1 | 57.8 | 68.6 |
| Louisiana | 55.6 | 63.8 | 75.8 |
| Maine | 18.2 | 20.9 | 25.2 |
| Maryland | 92.7 | 108.3 | 130.4 |
| Massachusetts | 114.9 | 130.8 | 154.8 |
| Michigan | 152.0 | 170.6 | 197.5 |
| Minnesota | 74.1 | 86.8 | 103.6 |
| Mississippi | 30.3 | 35.0 | 41.6 |
| Missouri | 79.9 | 92.5 | 110.4 |
| Montana | 11.4 | 13.6 | 16.6 |
| Nebraska | 24.8 | 28.9 | 34.4 |
| Nevada | 24.7 | 32.1 | 42.6 |
| New Hampshire | 19.5 | 23.1 | 28.0 |
| New Jersey | 164.4 | 189.0 | 223.1 |
| New Mexico | 20.6 | 25.0 | 31.4 |
| New York | 351.9 | 387.6 | 439.6 |
| North Carolina | 101.3 | 122.6 | 151.4 |
| North Dakota | 8.5 | 9.8 | 11.4 |
| Ohio | 169.9 | 192.6 | 225.0 |
| Oklahoma | 43.0 | 49.6 | 58.9 |
| Oregon | 46.0 | 55.3 | 68.1 |
| Pennsylvania | 199.8 | 223.9 | 260.5 |
| Rhode Island | 16.6 | 18.8 | 22.2 |
| South Carolina | 47.8 | 57.1 | 70.7 |
| South Dakota | 10.0 | 11.9 | 14.4 |
| Tennessee | 73.3 | 87.8 | 107.4 |
| Texas | 269.3 | 323.9 | 398.5 |
| Utah | 23.4 | 29.9 | 39.3 |
| Vermont | 8.6 | 10.2 | 12.4 |
| Virginia | 109.2 | 127.0 | 154.3 |
| Washington | 89.3 | 107.3 | 134.7 |
| West Virginia | 22.9 | 25.6 | 29.6 |
| Wisconsin | 78.0 | 90.8 | 108.8 |
| Wyoming | 7.2 | 8.5 | 10.2 |

*Source: Statistical Abstract of the United States 1998*, No. 730; <http://www.census.gov/prod/3/98pubs/98statab/sasec14.pdf>. Underlying data from U.S. Bureau of Economic Analysis, *BEA Regional Projections to 2045*, Volume 1: States.

## B6. PERSONAL INCOME AND EXPENDITURES, PER CAPITA, IN CURRENT DOLLARS

### B6-1. Personal Income and Expenditures, per Capita, in Current Dollars: 1960–1997

| Year | Current dollars personal income | Current dollars disposable personal income | Current dollars personal consumption expenditures |
|---|---|---|---|
| 1960 | 2,277 | 2,008 | 1,838 |
| 1965 | 2,860 | 2,541 | 2,286 |
| 1970 | 4,077 | 3,545 | 3,160 |
| 1971 | 4,328 | 3,805 | 3,383 |
| 1972 | 4,703 | 4,074 | 3,671 |
| 1973 | 5,217 | 4,553 | 4,018 |
| 1974 | 5,672 | 4,928 | 4,353 |
| 1975 | 6,091 | 5,367 | 4,765 |
| 1976 | 6,673 | 5,837 | 5,268 |
| 1977 | 7,315 | 6,362 | 5,797 |
| 1978 | 8,176 | 7,097 | 6,418 |
| 1979 | 9,105 | 7,861 | 7,079 |
| 1980 | 10,037 | 8,665 | 7,730 |
| 1981 | 11,132 | 9,566 | 8,440 |
| 1982 | 11,744 | 10,145 | 8,943 |
| 1983 | 12,379 | 10,803 | 9,744 |
| 1984 | 13,602 | 11,929 | 10,543 |
| 1985 | 14,464 | 12,629 | 11,341 |
| 1986 | 15,200 | 13,289 | 12,019 |
| 1987 | 16,013 | 13,896 | 12,743 |
| 1988 | 17,076 | 14,905 | 13,669 |
| 1989 | 18,194 | 15,790 | 14,531 |
| 1990 | 19,220 | 16,721 | 15,360 |
| 1991 | 19,715 | 17,242 | 15,732 |
| 1992 | 20,660 | 18,113 | 16,520 |
| 1993 | 21,379 | 18,706 | 17,273 |
| 1994 | 22,216 | 19,381 | 18,093 |
| 1995 | 23,370 | 20,349 | 18,837 |
| 1996 | 24,457 | 21,117 | 19,608 |
| 1997 | 25,660 | 21,969 | 20,478 |

*Note:*
Based on Bureau of the Census estimated population including Armed Forces abroad; based on quarterly averages.

*Source: Statistical Abstract of the United States 1998,* No. 730; <http://www.census.gov/prod/3/98pubs/98statab/sasec14.pdf>. Underlying data from U.S. Bureau of Economic Analysis, *National Income and Product Accounts of the United States, 1929-94,* Vol. 2; and *Survey of Current Business,* August 1997 and May 1998.

# B7. PERSONAL INCOME PER CAPITA BY STATE, IN CURRENT AND CONSTANT DOLLARS

## B7-1. Personal Income per Capita in Current Dollars, by State: 1997

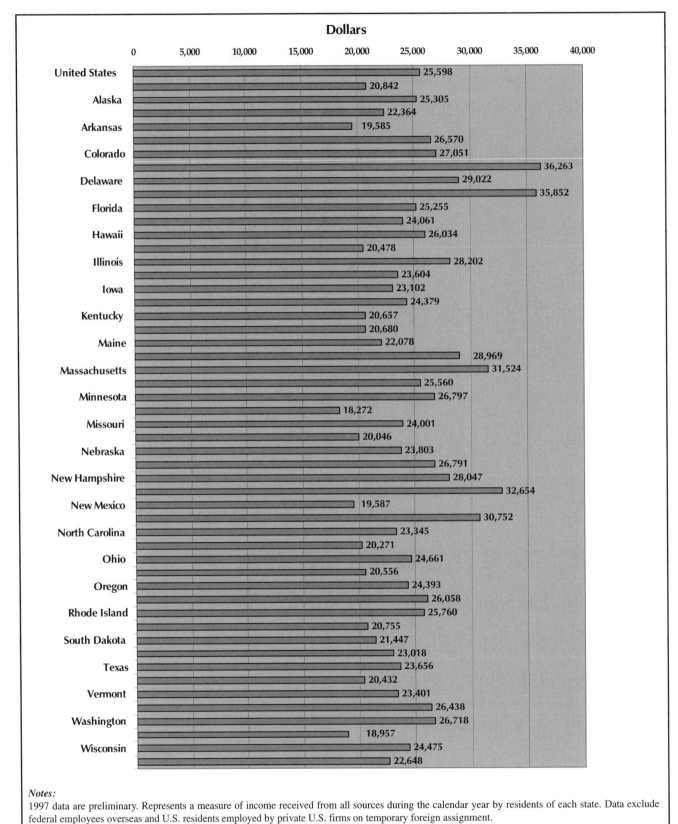

*Notes:*
1997 data are preliminary. Represents a measure of income received from all sources during the calendar year by residents of each state. Data exclude federal employees overseas and U.S. residents employed by private U.S. firms on temporary foreign assignment.

*Source: Statistical Abstract of the United States 1998*, No. 727; <http://www.census.gov/prod/3/98pubs/98statab/sasec14.pdf>. Underlying data from U.S. Bureau of Economic Analysis, *Survey of Current Business*, May 1998, and unpublished data.

## B7-2. Personal Income per Capita in Current Dollars, by State: 1990–1997

|  | 1990 | 1995 | 1996 | 1997 |
|---|---|---|---|---|
| United States | 19,188 | 23,359 | 24,436 | 25,598 |
| Alabama | 15,231 | 19,254 | 20,056 | 20,842 |
| Alaska | 21,097 | 24,214 | 24,597 | 25,305 |
| Arizona | 16,640 | 20,316 | 21,335 | 22,364 |
| Arkansas | 14,042 | 18,144 | 18,967 | 19,585 |
| California | 21,393 | 24,229 | 25,368 | 26,570 |
| Colorado | 19,322 | 24,517 | 25,740 | 27,051 |
| Connecticut | 26,507 | 32,603 | 34,174 | 36,263 |
| Delaware | 21,648 | 26,235 | 27,782 | 29,022 |
| District of Columbia | 25,701 | 32,609 | 34,172 | 35,852 |
| Florida | 19,185 | 23,139 | 24,198 | 25,255 |
| Georgia | 17,407 | 21,940 | 23,028 | 24,061 |
| Hawaii | 21,564 | 25,103 | 25,421 | 26,034 |
| Idaho | 15,368 | 19,199 | 19,865 | 20,478 |
| Illinois | 20,534 | 25,580 | 26,855 | 28,202 |
| Indiana | 17,191 | 21,716 | 22,633 | 23,604 |
| Iowa | 16,911 | 20,826 | 22,330 | 23,102 |
| Kansas | 17,968 | 21,886 | 23,133 | 24,379 |
| Kentucky | 15,106 | 18,847 | 19,773 | 20,657 |
| Louisiana | 14,790 | 18,999 | 19,709 | 20,680 |
| Maine | 17,190 | 20,227 | 21,087 | 22,078 |
| Maryland | 22,517 | 26,567 | 27,676 | 28,969 |
| Massachusetts | 23,249 | 28,397 | 29,808 | 31,524 |
| Michigan | 18,730 | 23,767 | 24,588 | 25,560 |
| Minnesota | 19,378 | 24,097 | 25,699 | 26,797 |
| Mississippi | 12,719 | 16,743 | 17,561 | 18,272 |
| Missouri | 17,672 | 21,927 | 22,984 | 24,001 |
| Montana | 15,067 | 18,602 | 19,278 | 20,046 |
| Nebraska | 17,562 | 21,424 | 22,975 | 23,803 |
| Nevada | 20,241 | 24,809 | 26,059 | 26,791 |
| New Hampshire | 20,767 | 25,726 | 26,772 | 28,047 |
| New Jersey | 24,930 | 29,982 | 31,265 | 32,654 |
| New Mexico | 14,502 | 18,246 | 18,814 | 19,587 |
| New York | 23,147 | 27,850 | 29,221 | 30,752 |
| North Carolina | 16,674 | 21,233 | 22,244 | 23,345 |
| North Dakota | 15,281 | 18,504 | 20,479 | 20,271 |
| Ohio | 18,147 | 22,560 | 23,493 | 24,661 |
| Oklahoma | 15,633 | 18,748 | 19,574 | 20,556 |
| Oregon | 17,452 | 21,915 | 23,111 | 24,393 |
| Pennsylvania | 19,410 | 23,673 | 24,851 | 26,058 |
| Rhode Island | 19,729 | 23,783 | 24,613 | 25,760 |
| South Carolina | 15,448 | 19,073 | 19,898 | 20,755 |
| South Dakota | 15,510 | 19,032 | 20,749 | 21,447 |
| Tennessee | 16,328 | 21,350 | 22,032 | 23,018 |
| Texas | 17,310 | 21,381 | 22,324 | 23,656 |
| Utah | 14,231 | 18,317 | 19,384 | 20,432 |
| Vermont | 17,721 | 21,609 | 22,545 | 23,401 |
| Virginia | 20,054 | 24,284 | 25,255 | 26,438 |
| Washington | 19,637 | 23,974 | 25,277 | 26,718 |
| West Virginia | 14,197 | 17,576 | 18,225 | 18,957 |
| Wisconsin | 17,722 | 22,416 | 23,390 | 24,475 |
| Wyoming | 17,213 | 20,954 | 21,587 | 22,648 |

*Notes:*
1997 data are preliminary. Represents a measure of income received from all sources during the calendar year by residents of each state. Data exclude federal employees overseas and U.S. residents employed by private U.S. firms on temporary foreign assignment.

*Source: Statistical Abstract of the United States 1998*, No. 727; <http://www.census.gov/prod/3/98pubs/98statab/sasec14.pdf>. Underlying data from U.S. Bureau of Economic Analysis, *Survey of Current Business*, May 1998, and unpublished data.

## B7-3. Personal Income per Capita in Constant (1992) Dollars[1], by State: 1997

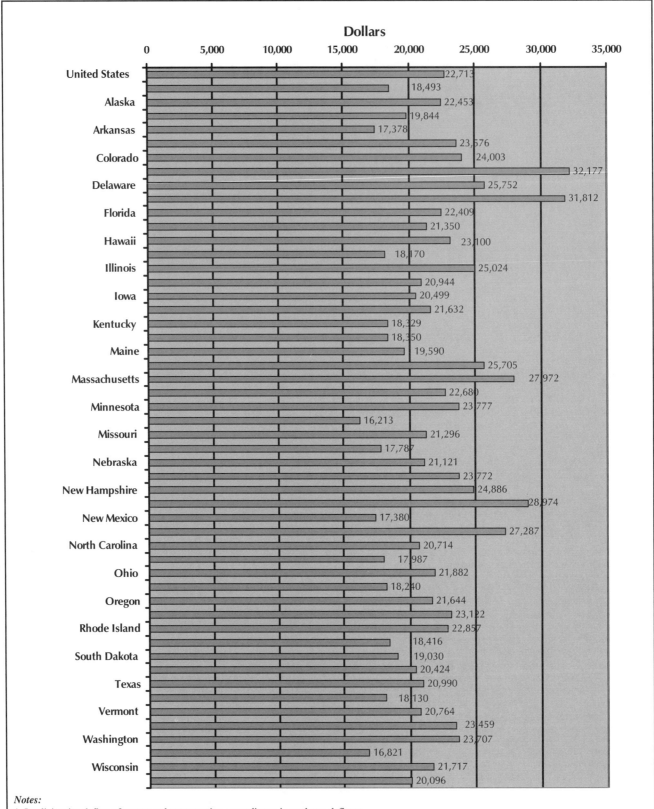

*Notes:*

1. Implicit price deflator for personal consumption expenditures is used as a deflator.

*General note:* 1997 data are preliminary. Represents a measure of income received from all sources during the calendar year by residents of each state. Data exclude federal employees overseas and U.S. residents employed by private U.S. firms on temporary foreign assignment.

*Source: Statistical Abstract of the United States 1998*, No. 727; <http://www.census.gov/prod/3/98pubs/98statab/sasec14.pdf>. Underlying data from U.S. Bureau of Economic Analysis, *Survey of Current Business*, May 1998, and unpublished data.

## B7-4. Personal Income per Capita in Constant (1992) Dollars[1], by State: 1990–1997

| | 1990 | 1995 | 1996 | 1997 | Rank 1990 | Rank 1997 |
|---|---|---|---|---|---|---|
| United States | 20,652 | 21,651 | 22,120 | 22,713 | X | X |
| Alabama | 16,393 | 17,846 | 18,155 | 18,493 | 42 | 38 |
| Alaska | 22,707 | 22,443 | 22,266 | 22,453 | 9 | 19 |
| Arizona | 17,910 | 18,830 | 19,313 | 19,844 | 35 | 35 |
| Arkansas | 15,114 | 16,817 | 17,169 | 17,378 | 49 | 48 |
| California | 23,026 | 22,457 | 22,964 | 23,576 | 8 | 13 |
| Colorado | 20,796 | 22,724 | 23,300 | 24,003 | 18 | 9 |
| Connecticut | 28,530 | 30,219 | 30,935 | 32,177 | 1 | 1 |
| Delaware | 23,300 | 24,316 | 25,149 | 25,752 | 6 | 5 |
| District of Columbia | 27,662 | 30,224 | 30,933 | 31,812 | X | X |
| Florida | 20,649 | 21,447 | 21,905 | 22,409 | 19 | 20 |
| Georgia | 18,735 | 20,336 | 20,845 | 21,350 | 28 | 25 |
| Hawaii | 23,210 | 23,267 | 23,012 | 23,100 | 7 | 16 |
| Idaho | 16,541 | 17,795 | 17,982 | 18,170 | 41 | 43 |
| Illinois | 22,101 | 23,709 | 24,310 | 25,024 | 11 | 7 |
| Indiana | 18,503 | 20,128 | 20,488 | 20,944 | 30 | 29 |
| Iowa | 18,201 | 19,303 | 20,214 | 20,499 | 33 | 32 |
| Kansas | 19,339 | 20,285 | 20,941 | 21,632 | 22 | 24 |
| Kentucky | 16,259 | 17,469 | 17,899 | 18,329 | 43 | 41 |
| Louisiana | 15,919 | 17,610 | 17,841 | 18,350 | 45 | 40 |
| Maine | 18,502 | 18,748 | 19,088 | 19,590 | 31 | 36 |
| Maryland | 24,235 | 24,624 | 25,053 | 25,705 | 5 | 6 |
| Massachusetts | 25,023 | 26,320 | 26,983 | 27,972 | 3 | 3 |
| Michigan | 20,159 | 22,029 | 22,258 | 22,680 | 20 | 18 |
| Minnesota | 20,857 | 22,335 | 23,263 | 23,777 | 16 | 10 |
| Mississippi | 13,690 | 15,519 | 15,897 | 16,213 | 50 | 50 |
| Missouri | 19,021 | 20,323 | 20,806 | 21,296 | 25 | 26 |
| Montana | 16,217 | 17,242 | 17,451 | 17,787 | 44 | 46 |
| Nebraska | 18,902 | 19,857 | 20,798 | 21,121 | 26 | 27 |
| Nevada | 21,786 | 22,995 | 23,589 | 23,772 | 12 | 11 |
| New Hampshire | 22,352 | 23,845 | 24,235 | 24,886 | 10 | 8 |
| New Jersey | 26,832 | 27,789 | 28,302 | 28,974 | 2 | 2 |
| New Mexico | 15,609 | 16,912 | 17,031 | 17,380 | 46 | 47 |
| New York | 24,913 | 25,813 | 26,452 | 27,287 | 4 | 4 |
| North Carolina | 17,946 | 19,680 | 20,136 | 20,714 | 34 | 31 |
| North Dakota | 16,447 | 17,151 | 18,538 | 17,987 | 40 | 45 |
| Ohio | 19,532 | 20,910 | 21,266 | 21,882 | 21 | 21 |
| Oklahoma | 16,826 | 17,377 | 17,719 | 18,240 | 37 | 42 |
| Oregon | 18,784 | 20,312 | 20,921 | 21,644 | 27 | 23 |
| Pennsylvania | 20,891 | 21,942 | 22,496 | 23,122 | 17 | 15 |
| Rhode Island | 21,235 | 22,044 | 22,280 | 22,857 | 14 | 17 |
| South Carolina | 16,627 | 17,678 | 18,012 | 18,416 | 39 | 39 |
| South Dakota | 16,694 | 17,640 | 18,782 | 19,030 | 38 | 37 |
| Tennessee | 17,574 | 19,789 | 19,944 | 20,424 | 36 | 33 |
| Texas | 18,631 | 19,817 | 20,208 | 20,990 | 29 | 28 |
| Utah | 15,317 | 16,977 | 17,547 | 18,130 | 47 | 44 |
| Vermont | 19,073 | 20,029 | 20,408 | 20,764 | 24 | 30 |
| Virginia | 21,584 | 22,508 | 22,861 | 23,459 | 13 | 14 |
| Washington | 21,136 | 22,221 | 22,881 | 23,707 | 15 | 12 |
| West Virginia | 15,280 | 16,291 | 16,498 | 16,821 | 48 | 49 |
| Wisconsin | 19,074 | 20,777 | 21,173 | 21,717 | 23 | 22 |
| Wyoming | 18,527 | 19,422 | 19,541 | 20,096 | 32 | 34 |

*Notes:*
1. Implicit price deflator for personal consumption expenditures is used as a deflator.
X indicates not applicable.
*General note:* 1997 data are preliminary. Represents a measure of income received from all sources during the calendar year by residents of each state. Data exclude federal employees overseas and U.S. residents employed by private U.S. firms on temporary foreign assignment.

*Source: Statistical Abstract of the United States 1998*, No. 727; <http://www.census.gov/prod/3/98pubs/98statab/sasec14.pdf>. Underlying data from U.S. Bureau of Economic Analysis, *Survey of Current Business*, May 1998, and unpublished data.

## B8. DISPOSABLE PERSONAL INCOME PER CAPITA

### B8-1. Disposable Personal Income per Capita in Current Dollars, by State: 1990 and 1997, in Dollars (1997 data preliminary)

| | Current Dollars 1990 | Current Dollars 1997 |
|---|---|---|
| United States | 16,689 | 21,908 |
| Alabama | 13,572 | 18,334 |
| Alaska | 18,148 | 21,707 |
| Arizona | 14,663 | 19,345 |
| Arkansas | 12,559 | 17,304 |
| California | 18,421 | 22,674 |
| Colorado | 16,790 | 22,751 |
| Connecticut | 22,847 | 29,598 |
| Delaware | 18,544 | 24,430 |
| District of Columbia | 21,807 | 30,372 |
| Florida | 16,959 | 21,894 |
| Georgia | 15,236 | 20,620 |
| Hawaii | 18,375 | 22,531 |
| Idaho | 13,492 | 17,687 |
| Illinois | 17,727 | 23,855 |
| Indiana | 14,987 | 20,166 |
| Iowa | 14,708 | 20,014 |
| Kansas | 15,680 | 20,879 |
| Kentucky | 13,247 | 17,918 |
| Louisiana | 13,289 | 18,384 |
| Maine | 15,090 | 19,256 |
| Maryland | 19,184 | 24,386 |
| Massachusetts | 19,853 | 25,990 |
| Michigan | 16,297 | 21,794 |
| Minnesota | 16,571 | 22,205 |
| Mississippi | 11,587 | 16,532 |
| Missouri | 15,476 | 20,706 |
| Montana | 13,165 | 17,465 |
| Nebraska | 15,428 | 20,503 |
| Nevada | 17,560 | 22,742 |
| New Hampshire | 18,494 | 24,438 |
| New Jersey | 21,547 | 27,422 |
| New Mexico | 12,960 | 17,327 |
| New York | 19,608 | 25,713 |
| North Carolina | 14,578 | 20,099 |
| North Dakota | 13,598 | 17,837 |
| Ohio | 15,817 | 21,093 |
| Oklahoma | 13,620 | 18,006 |
| Oregon | 15,128 | 20,517 |
| Pennsylvania | 16,925 | 22,434 |
| Rhode Island | 17,315 | 22,297 |
| South Carolina | 13,671 | 18,147 |
| South Dakota | 13,952 | 19,195 |
| Tennessee | 14,712 | 20,390 |
| Texas | 15,399 | 20,868 |
| Utah | 12,422 | 17,370 |
| Vermont | 15,477 | 20,401 |
| Virginia | 17,362 | 22,388 |
| Washington | 17,233 | 23,154 |
| West Virginia | 12,673 | 16,803 |
| Wisconsin | 15,306 | 20,634 |
| Wyoming | 15,207 | 19,801 |

*Source: Statistical Abstract of the United States 1998, No. 728; <http://www.census.gov/prod/3/98pubs/98statab/sasec14.pdf>. Underlying data from U.S. Bureau of Economic Analysis, Survey of Current Business, May 1998, and unpublished data.*

**B8-2. Disposable Personal Income per Capita in Constant (1992) Dollars, by State: 1990 and 1997, in Dollars (1997 data preliminary)**

| | Constant (1992) Dollars, 1990 | Constant (1992) Dollars, 1997 |
|---|---|---|
| United States | 17,963 | 19,439 |
| Alabama | 14,608 | 16,268 |
| Alaska | 19,533 | 19,261 |
| Arizona | 15,782 | 17,165 |
| Arkansas | 13,517 | 15,354 |
| California | 19,827 | 20,119 |
| Colorado | 18,071 | 20,187 |
| Connecticut | 24,590 | 26,263 |
| Delaware | 19,959 | 21,677 |
| District of Columbia | 23,471 | 26,949 |
| Florida | 18,253 | 19,427 |
| Georgia | 16,399 | 18,296 |
| Hawaii | 19,777 | 19,992 |
| Idaho | 14,522 | 15,694 |
| Illinois | 19,080 | 21,167 |
| Indiana | 16,131 | 17,894 |
| Iowa | 15,830 | 17,759 |
| Kansas | 16,877 | 18,526 |
| Kentucky | 14,258 | 15,899 |
| Louisiana | 14,303 | 16,312 |
| Maine | 16,242 | 17,086 |
| Maryland | 20,648 | 21,638 |
| Massachusetts | 21,368 | 23,061 |
| Michigan | 17,541 | 19,338 |
| Minnesota | 17,836 | 19,703 |
| Mississippi | 12,471 | 14,669 |
| Missouri | 16,657 | 18,373 |
| Montana | 14,170 | 15,497 |
| Nebraska | 16,605 | 18,193 |
| Nevada | 18,900 | 20,179 |
| New Hampshire | 19,905 | 21,684 |
| New Jersey | 23,191 | 24,332 |
| New Mexico | 13,949 | 15,374 |
| New York | 21,104 | 22,815 |
| North Carolina | 15,690 | 17,834 |
| North Dakota | 14,636 | 15,827 |
| Ohio | 17,024 | 18,716 |
| Oklahoma | 14,659 | 15,977 |
| Oregon | 16,282 | 18,205 |
| Pennsylvania | 18,217 | 19,906 |
| Rhode Island | 18,636 | 19,784 |
| South Carolina | 14,714 | 16,102 |
| South Dakota | 15,017 | 17,032 |
| Tennessee | 15,835 | 18,092 |
| Texas | 16,574 | 18,516 |
| Utah | 13,370 | 15,413 |
| Vermont | 16,658 | 18,102 |
| Virginia | 18,687 | 19,865 |
| Washington | 18,548 | 20,545 |
| West Virginia | 13,640 | 14,909 |
| Wisconsin | 16,474 | 18,309 |
| Wyoming | 16,367 | 17,570 |

*Source: Statistical Abstract of the United States 1998*, No. 728; <http://www.census.gov/prod/3/98pubs/98statab/sasec14.pdf>. Underlying data from U.S. Bureau of Economic Analysis, *Survey of Current Business*, May 1998, and unpublished data.

## B9. AVERAGE ANNUAL PAY AND PERSONAL EARNINGS

### B9-1. Average Annual Pay[1], Totals, 1996 (preliminary)

| | Total Dollars | Rank |
|---|---|---|
| United States | 28,945 | X |
| Alabama | 25,180 | 31 |
| Alaska | 32,461 | 5 |
| Arizona | 26,387 | 26 |
| Arkansas | 22,294 | 46 |
| California | 31,773 | 6 |
| Colorado | 28,520 | 14 |
| Connecticut | 36,579 | 2 |
| Delaware | 30,711 | 9 |
| District of Columbia | 44,458 | X |
| Florida | 25,640 | 29 |
| Georgia | 27,488 | 20 |
| Hawaii | 27,363 | 21 |
| Idaho | 23,353 | 42 |
| Illinois | 31,285 | 8 |
| Indiana | 26,477 | 25 |
| Iowa | 23,679 | 41 |
| Kansas | 24,609 | 32 |
| Kentucky | 24,462 | 36 |
| Louisiana | 24,528 | 34 |
| Maine | 23,850 | 39 |
| Maryland | 30,293 | 10 |
| Massachusetts | 33,940 | 4 |
| Michigan | 31,522 | 7 |
| Minnesota | 28,869 | 13 |
| Mississippi | 21,822 | 47 |
| Missouri | 26,608 | 24 |
| Montana | 21,146 | 49 |
| Nebraska | 23,291 | 44 |
| Nevada | 27,788 | 17 |
| New Hampshire | 27,691 | 19 |
| New Jersey | 35,928 | 3 |
| New Mexico | 23,716 | 40 |
| New York | 36,831 | 1 |
| North Carolina | 25,408 | 30 |
| North Dakota | 21,242 | 48 |
| Ohio | 27,775 | 18 |
| Oklahoma | 23,329 | 43 |
| Oregon | 27,027 | 23 |
| Pennsylvania | 28,973 | 11 |
| Rhode Island | 27,194 | 22 |
| South Carolina | 24,039 | 38 |
| South Dakota | 20,724 | 50 |
| Tennessee | 25,963 | 28 |
| Texas | 28,129 | 15 |
| Utah | 24,572 | 33 |
| Vermont | 24,480 | 35 |
| Virginia | 28,001 | 16 |
| Washington | 28,881 | 12 |
| West Virginia | 24,075 | 37 |
| Wisconsin | 26,021 | 27 |
| Wyoming | 22,870 | 45 |

*Notes:*

1. For workers covered by state unemployment insurance laws and for federal workers covered by unemployment compensation for federal workers.
Re state rankings: When states share the same rank, the next lower rank is omitted. States may share the same value but have different ranks due to rounding. X indicates not applicable.

*Source:* U.S. Bureau of the Census, *State and Metropolitan Area Data Book 1997-98*, table A-21 and A-22, <http://www.census.gov/Press-Release/state11.prn>.

## B9-2. Average Annual Pay[1], Private Industry Totals,[2] 1996 (preliminary)

|  | Total Dollars | Rank |
|---|---|---|
| United States | 28,581 | X |
| Alabama | 24,592 | 32 |
| Alaska | 30,548 | 9 |
| Arizona | 25,923 | 26 |
| Arkansas | 21,832 | 46 |
| California | 31,183 | 6 |
| Colorado | 28,182 | 15 |
| Connecticut | 36,439 | 2 |
| Delaware | 30,592 | 8 |
| District of Columbia | 40,195 | X |
| Florida | 25,045 | 30 |
| Georgia | 27,611 | 17 |
| Hawaii | 26,371 | 24 |
| Idaho | 23,047 | 41 |
| Illinois | 31,130 | 7 |
| Indiana | 26,379 | 23 |
| Iowa | 23,160 | 40 |
| Kansas | 24,574 | 33 |
| Kentucky | 24,130 | 34 |
| Louisiana | 24,732 | 31 |
| Maine | 23,288 | 39 |
| Maryland | 28,945 | 10 |
| Massachusetts | 33,765 | 4 |
| Michigan | 31,406 | 5 |
| Minnesota | 28,554 | 11 |
| Mississippi | 21,461 | 47 |
| Missouri | 26,551 | 21 |
| Montana | 20,082 | 50 |
| Nebraska | 22,823 | 43 |
| Nevada | 26,931 | 20 |
| New Hampshire | 27,648 | 16 |
| New Jersey | 35,351 | 3 |
| New Mexico | 22,604 | 44 |
| New York | 36,714 | 1 |
| North Carolina | 25,168 | 29 |
| North Dakota | 20,754 | 48 |
| Ohio | 27,448 | 18 |
| Oklahoma | 22,901 | 42 |
| Oregon | 26,434 | 22 |
| Pennsylvania | 28,369 | 13 |
| Rhode Island | 26,129 | 25 |
| South Carolina | 23,637 | 38 |
| South Dakota | 20,111 | 49 |
| Tennessee | 25,724 | 27 |
| Texas | 28,421 | 12 |
| Utah | 24,103 | 35 |
| Vermont | 24,040 | 36 |
| Virginia | 27,315 | 19 |
| Washington | 28,217 | 14 |
| West Virginia | 23,724 | 37 |
| Wisconsin | 25,505 | 28 |
| Wyoming | 22,264 | 45 |

*Notes:*
1. For workers covered by state unemployment insurance laws and for federal workers covered by unemployment compensation for federal workers.
2. Excludes government.
Re state rankings: When states share the same rank, the next lower rank is omitted. States may share the same value but have different ranks due to rounding. X indicates not applicable.

*Source:* U.S. Bureau of the Census, *State and Metropolitan Area Data Book 1997-98,* table A-21 and A-22, <http://www.census.gov/Press-Release/state11.prn>.

## B9-3. Average Annual Pay[1], Private Industry Breakdown, 1996 (preliminary)

| | Manufacturing | | Retail trade | |
|---|---|---|---|---|
| | Dollars | Rank | Dollars | Rank |
| United States | 36,235 | X | 15,215 | X |
| Alabama | 28,705 | 45 | 13,663 | 36 |
| Alaska | 29,205 | 42 | 18,325 | 2 |
| Arizona | 37,168 | 13 | 16,075 | 11 |
| Arkansas | 24,811 | 49 | 13,828 | 33 |
| California | 39,810 | 7 | 17,276 | 5 |
| Colorado | 37,080 | 14 | 15,528 | 16 |
| Connecticut | 47,045 | 2 | 17,806 | 3 |
| Delaware | 50,692 | 1 | 14,993 | 19 |
| District of Columbia | 52,970 | X | 16,260 | X |
| Florida | 31,946 | 28 | 15,621 | 14 |
| Georgia | 30,595 | 34 | 14,848 | 20 |
| Hawaii | 29,884 | 38 | 16,849 | 8 |
| Idaho | 32,274 | 26 | 13,783 | 34 |
| Illinois | 38,343 | 10 | 15,668 | 13 |
| Indiana | 36,328 | 16 | 13,394 | 38 |
| Iowa | 31,707 | 30 | 12,422 | 45 |
| Kansas | 32,967 | 25 | 13,396 | 37 |
| Kentucky | 31,631 | 31 | 13,190 | 39 |
| Louisiana | 35,137 | 19 | 13,168 | 40 |
| Maine | 30,521 | 35 | 14,126 | 29 |
| Maryland | 38,074 | 11 | 16,365 | 9 |
| Massachusetts | 42,635 | 5 | 16,853 | 7 |
| Michigan | 46,739 | 3 | 14,560 | 23 |
| Minnesota | 37,250 | 12 | 14,497 | 25 |
| Mississippi | 24,334 | 50 | 12,747 | 43 |
| Missouri | 34,315 | 21 | 14,243 | 27 |
| Montana | 26,856 | 46 | 12,382 | 46 |
| Nebraska | 28,857 | 44 | 12,627 | 44 |
| Nevada | 31,905 | 29 | 17,574 | 4 |
| New Hampshire | 36,378 | 15 | 15,535 | 15 |
| New Jersey | 44,126 | 4 | 18,366 | 1 |
| New Mexico | 29,630 | 40 | 13,884 | 32 |
| New York | 41,843 | 6 | 16,890 | 6 |
| North Carolina | 29,110 | 43 | 14,352 | 26 |
| North Dakota | 26,569 | 47 | 11,859 | 50 |
| Ohio | 38,356 | 9 | 14,126 | 29 |
| Oklahoma | 29,740 | 39 | 13,012 | 41 |
| Oregon | 34,870 | 20 | 15,857 | 12 |
| Pennsylvania | 36,328 | 16 | 14,515 | 24 |
| Rhode Island | 31,250 | 32 | 14,665 | 22 |
| South Carolina | 30,085 | 37 | 13,725 | 35 |
| South Dakota | 24,882 | 48 | 11,942 | 49 |
| Tennessee | 30,790 | 33 | 15,018 | 18 |
| Texas | 36,163 | 18 | 15,341 | 17 |
| Utah | 30,196 | 36 | 14,237 | 28 |
| Vermont | 33,019 | 24 | 13,998 | 31 |
| Virginia | 31,999 | 27 | 14,746 | 21 |
| Washington | 39,086 | 8 | 16,083 | 10 |
| West Virginia | 33,678 | 22 | 12,295 | 48 |
| Wisconsin | 33,464 | 23 | 12,916 | 42 |
| Wyoming | 29,486 | 41 | 12,372 | 47 |

*Notes:*

1. For workers covered by state unemployment insurance laws and for federal workers covered by unemployment compensation for federal workers.
Re state rankings: When states share the same rank, the next lower rank is omitted. States may share the same value but have different ranks due to rounding.
X indicates not applicable.

*Soruce:* U.S. Bureau of the Census, *State and Metropolitan Area Data Book 1997-98*, table A-21 and A-22, <http://www.census.gov/Press-Release/state11.prn>.

## B9-4. Projections of Earnings in Constant (1987) Dollars, by State: 1993–2010, in Billions of Dollars

|  | Earnings, 1993 | Earnings, 2000 | Earnings, 2010 |
|---|---|---|---|
| United States | 3017.5 | 3532.7 | 4207.5 |
| Alabama | 40.0 | 46.3 | 54.7 |
| Alaska | 9.0 | 10.4 | 12.4 |
| Arizona | 38.5 | 48.7 | 61.6 |
| Arkansas | 21.6 | 25.3 | 29.6 |
| California | 390.6 | 468.0 | 577.1 |
| Colorado | 45.0 | 55.2 | 68.7 |
| Connecticut | 50.8 | 58.3 | 68.7 |
| Delaware | 9.4 | 11.0 | 13.1 |
| District of Columbia | 25.1 | 27.6 | 30.9 |
| Florida | 136.2 | 170.1 | 215.3 |
| Georgia | 79.0 | 96.1 | 118.3 |
| Hawaii | 16.4 | 19.4 | 23.3 |
| Idaho | 11.2 | 13.5 | 16.4 |
| Illinois | 151.4 | 173.1 | 202.1 |
| Indiana | 62.4 | 71.9 | 83.8 |
| Iowa | 27.8 | 32.3 | 37.0 |
| Kansas | 27.5 | 32.2 | 37.8 |
| Kentucky | 35.6 | 41.0 | 47.9 |
| Louisiana | 39.0 | 44.9 | 52.4 |
| Maine | 12.3 | 14.2 | 16.8 |
| Maryland | 59.7 | 69.3 | 82.0 |
| Massachusetts | 84.8 | 97.6 | 114.3 |
| Michigan | 109.8 | 123.2 | 140.1 |
| Minnesota | 56.2 | 65.8 | 77.5 |
| Mississippi | 20.7 | 24.1 | 28.1 |
| Missouri | 57.6 | 66.5 | 77.9 |
| Montana | 7.6 | 9.0 | 10.8 |
| Nebraska | 18.3 | 21.2 | 24.8 |
| Nevada | 18.5 | 24.0 | 31.2 |
| New Hampshire | 12.7 | 15.2 | 18.2 |
| New Jersey | 111.3 | 128.4 | 150.1 |
| New Mexico | 14.6 | 17.7 | 21.9 |
| New York | 256.5 | 285.1 | 321.6 |
| North Carolina | 76.7 | 92.3 | 111.2 |
| North Dakota | 6.0 | 7.0 | 8.0 |
| Ohio | 123.1 | 140.0 | 161.3 |
| Oklahoma | 29.7 | 34.1 | 39.7 |
| Oregon | 33.2 | 39.9 | 48.3 |
| Pennsylvania | 137.3 | 154.6 | 177.3 |
| Rhode Island | 10.8 | 12.4 | 14.5 |
| South Carolina | 34.7 | 41.6 | 50.7 |
| South Dakota | 7.2 | 8.5 | 10.1 |
| Tennessee | 55.5 | 66.5 | 79.9 |
| Texas | 205.3 | 245.7 | 297.4 |
| Utah | 18.2 | 23.2 | 30.2 |
| Vermont | 6.1 | 7.3 | 8.7 |
| Virginia | 77.0 | 89.5 | 107.3 |
| Washington | 64.5 | 77.1 | 95.3 |
| West Virginia | 14.5 | 16.1 | 18.3 |
| Wisconsin | 55.5 | 64.5 | 75.8 |
| Wyoming | 5.1 | 5.9 | 6.9 |

*Source: Statistical Abstract of the United States 1998*, No. 730; <http://www.census.gov/prod/3/98pubs/98statab/sasec14.pdf>. Underlying data from U.S. Bureau of Economic Analysis, *BEA Regional Projections to 2045*, Volume 1: States.

## B10. PERSONAL EARNINGS BY HIGHEST DEGREE EARNED

### B10-1. Mean Personal Earnings, Totals, by Highest Degree Earned, with No College Degree: 1997

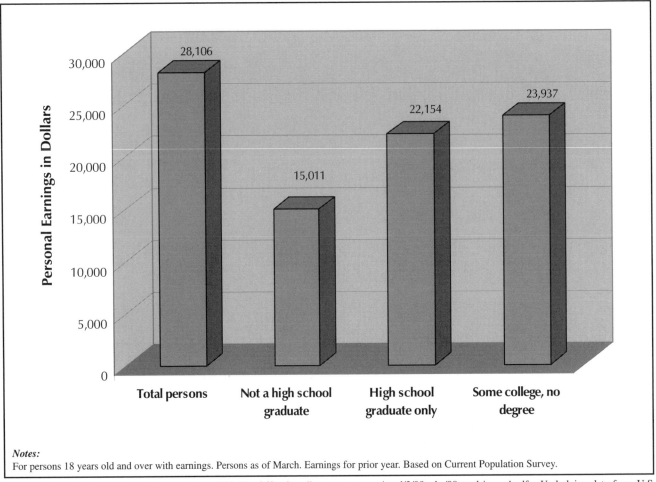

*Notes:*
For persons 18 years old and over with earnings. Persons as of March. Earnings for prior year. Based on Current Population Survey.

*Source: Statistical Abstract of the United States 1998*, No. 263; <http://www.census.gov/prod/3/98pubs/98statab/sasec4.pdf>. Underlying data from U.S. Bureau of the Census, *Current Population Reports*, P20-505.

## B10-2. Mean Personal Earnings, by Highest Degree Earned, with No College Degree: 1997

| Characteristics | Total persons | Level of highest degree | | |
| --- | --- | --- | --- | --- |
| | | Not a high school graduate | High school graduate only | Some college no degree |
| MEAN EARNINGS | | | | |
| (dol) | | | | |
| All persons[1] | 28,106 | 15,011 | 22,154 | 23,937 |
| Age: | | | | |
| 18 to 24 years old | 10,394 | 6,950 | 11,221 | 9,125 |
| 25 to 34 years old | 25,010 | 14,692 | 20,373 | 23,608 |
| 35 to 44 years old | 33,451 | 17,975 | 25,613 | 29,640 |
| 45 to 54 years old | 36,720 | 19,865 | 27,133 | 34,141 |
| 55 to 64 years old | 32,152 | 19,098 | 24,829 | 34,178 |
| 65 years old plus | 20,256 | 12,051 | 14,536 | 15,771 |
| Sex: | | | | |
| Male | 34,705 | 17,826 | 27,642 | 30,057 |
| Female | 20,570 | 10,421 | 16,161 | 17,475 |
| White | 28,844 | 15,358 | 22,782 | 24,229 |
| Male | 35,821 | 18,246 | 28,591 | 30,847 |
| Female | 20,590 | 10,290 | 16,270 | 16,959 |
| Black | 21,978 | 13,110 | 18,722 | 23,148 |
| Male | 25,067 | 15,461 | 22,267 | 25,594 |
| Female | 19,271 | 10,337 | 15,379 | 21,155 |
| Hispanic[2] | 19,439 | 13,287 | 18,528 | 21,303 |
| Male | 21,870 | 14,986 | 21,593 | 25,795 |
| Female | 15,841 | 9,867 | 14,635 | 15,659 |

*Notes:*
1. Includes other races, not shown separately.
2. Persons of Hispanic origin may be of any race.
For persons 18 years old and over with earnings. Persons as of March. Earnings for prior year. Based on Current Population Survey.

*Source: Statistical Abstract of the United States 1998*, No. 263; <http://www.census.gov/prod/3/98pubs/98statab/sasec4.pdf>. Underlying data from U.S. Bureau of the *Census, Current Population Reports*, P20-505.

**B10-3. Mean Personal Earnings, Totals, by Highest Degree Earned, with College Degree: 1997**

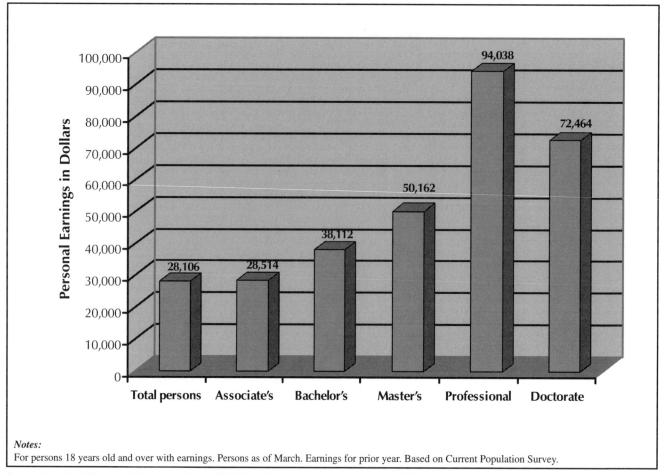

*Notes:*
For persons 18 years old and over with earnings. Persons as of March. Earnings for prior year. Based on Current Population Survey.

*Source: Statistical Abstract of the United States 1998*, No. 263; <http://www.census.gov/prod/3/98pubs/98statab/sasec4.pdf>. Underlying data from U.S. Bureau of the Census, *Current Population Reports*, P20-505.

## B10-4. Mean Personal Earnings, by Highest Degree Earned, with College Degree: 1997

| Characteristics | Total persons | Associate's | Bachelor's | Level of highest degree Master's | Professional | Doctorate |
|---|---|---|---|---|---|---|
| MEAN EARNINGS (dol ) | | | | | | |
| All persons[1] | 28,106 | 28,514 | 38,112 | 50,162 | 94,038 | 72,464 |
| **Age:** | | | | | | |
| 18 to 24 years old | 10,394 | 14,277 | 18,026 | 26,621 | 5,000 | (B) |
| 25 to 34 years old | 25,010 | 26,770 | 32,431 | 35,626 | 52,476 | 44,282 |
| 35 to 44 years old | 33,451 | 30,438 | 43,830 | 58,624 | 109,588 | 81,400 |
| 45 to 54 years old | 36,720 | 33,086 | 44,523 | 56,022 | 115,498 | 75,426 |
| 55 to 64 years old | 32,152 | 32,570 | 41,874 | 45,391 | 95,146 | 79,498 |
| 65 years old plus | 20,256 | 15,694 | 32,272 | 29,689 | 68,056 | 75,976 |
| **Sex:** | | | | | | |
| Male | 34,705 | 35,484 | 46,702 | 62,145 | 102,913 | 81,492 |
| Female | 20,570 | 22,480 | 28,701 | 36,483 | 72,015 | 51,865 |
| White | 28,844 | 28,867 | 38,936 | 50,813 | 92,612 | 73,647 |
| Male | 35,821 | 36,222 | 48,014 | 63,113 | 103,490 | 82,615 |
| Female | 20,590 | 22,122 | 28,667 | 36,687 | 64,618 | 53,862 |
| Black | 21,978 | 25,220 | 31,955 | 37,592 | (B) | (B) |
| Male | 25,067 | 29,561 | 35,558 | 40,313 | (B) | (B) |
| Female | 19,271 | 22,793 | 29,311 | 35,909 | (B) | (B) |
| Hispanic[2] | 19,439 | 25,014 | 32,955 | 36,827 | (B) | (B) |
| Male | 21,870 | 29,693 | 38,130 | 36,370 | (B) | (B) |
| Female | 15,841 | 20,192 | 27,407 | 37,660 | (B) | (B) |

*Notes*:
(B)  Base figure too small to meet statistical standards for reliability of a derived figure.
1. Includes other races, not shown separately.
2.Persons of Hispanic origin may be of any race.
For persons 18 years old and over with earnings. Persons as of March. Earnings for prior year. Based on Current Population Survey.

*Source: Statistical Abstract of the United States 1998*, No. 263; <http://www.census.gov/prod/3/98pubs/98statab/sasec4.pdf>. Underlying data from U.S. Bureau of the Census, *Current Population Reports*, P20-505.

## B11. MEDIAN INCOME FOR 4-PERSON FAMILIES, BY STATE

### B11-1. Median Income for 4-Person Families, by State: 1974–1977 Calendar Years

| Calendar year[1] Fiscal year[2] | 1974[4] 1977[3] | 1975[5] 1978[3] | 1976[6] 1979[3] | 1977 1980[3] |
|---|---|---|---|---|
| United States | $14,747 | $15,848 | $17,315 | $18,723 |
| Alabama | 12,805 | 14,018 | 15,346 | 16,629 |
| Alaska | 19,368 | 25,638 | 28,571 | 32,119 |
| Arizona | 15,230 | 15,829 | 17,131 | 19,101 |
| Arkansas | 11,890 | 12,969 | 13,679 | 15,068 |
| California | 15,931 | 17,393 | 18,931 | 20,858 |
| Colorado | 15,629 | 16,928 | 18,244 | 20,181 |
| Connecticut | 16,476 | 17,781 | 18,789 | 20,469 |
| Delaware | 15,231 | 16,243 | 16,859 | 18,245 |
| District of Columbia | 15,093 | 16,554 | 17,201 | 19,047 |
| Florida | 14,788 | 15,303 | 16,278 | 17,874 |
| Georgia | 13,666 | 14,538 | 15,799 | 16,835 |
| Hawaii | 17,069 | 18,825 | 20,113 | 21,718 |
| Idaho | 14,075 | 14,664 | 15,982 | 16,601 |
| Illinois | 16,350 | 17,793 | 19,336 | 20,243 |
| Indiana | 14,478 | 15,731 | 17,329 | 19,131 |
| Iowa | 14,371 | 16,536 | 16,919 | 18,441 |
| Kansas | 14,395 | 15,709 | 16,840 | 18,379 |
| Kentucky | 12,514 | 13,625 | 14,964 | 16,264 |
| Louisiana | 12,600 | 13,992 | 15,354 | 16,511 |
| Maine | 12,552 | 12,948 | 14,429 | 15,025 |
| Maryland | 16,650 | 18,132 | 19,331 | 21,193 |

## B11-1. Median Income for 4-Person Families, by State: 1974–1977 Calendar Years *(continued)*

| Calendar year[1]<br>Fiscal year[2] | 1974[4]<br>1977[3] | 1975[5]<br>1978[3] | 1976[6]<br>1979[3] | 1977<br>1980[3] |
|---|---|---|---|---|
| Massachusetts | 15,630 | 16,546 | 17,842 | 19,508 |
| Michigan | 16,174 | 16,919 | 18,572 | 20,908 |
| Minnesota | 15,792 | 16,871 | 17,970 | 20,715 |
| Mississippi | 11,562 | 12,174 | 13,475 | 14,635 |
| Missouri | 13,770 | 14,996 | 16,177 | 17,862 |
| Montana | 13,686 | 14,900 | 15,522 | 16,389 |
| Nebraska | 13,364 | 15,381 | 15,205 | 16,523 |
| Nevada | 15,357 | 16,945 | 18,290 | 20,308 |
| New Hampshire | 13,986 | 14,954 | 16,937 | 18,190 |
| New Jersey | 16,727 | 17,984 | 19,865 | 21,409 |
| New Mexico | 12,143 | 13,954 | 15,504 | 16,801 |
| New York | 15,169 | 16,105 | 17,200 | 18,216 |
| North Carolina | 13,183 | 13,883 | 15,214 | 16,252 |
| North Dakota | 15,005 | 15,321 | 15,469 | 16,008 |
| Ohio | 15,121 | 15,848 | 17,515 | 19,195 |
| Oklahoma | 12,645 | 14,436 | 15,621 | 17,144 |
| Oregon | 15,013 | 16,349 | 17,761 | 19,771 |
| Pennsylvania | 14,489 | 15,753 | 17,054 | 18,348 |
| Rhode Island | 14,404 | 15,691 | 16,991 | 17,910 |
| South Carolina | 13,055 | 13,879 | 15,416 | 16,573 |
| South Dakota | 12,824 | 13,351 | 13,684 | 15,733 |
| Tennessee | 12,788 | 13,646 | 14,859 | 15,677 |
| Texas | 13,924 | 15,802 | 17,420 | 18,930 |
| Utah | 14,003 | 15,352 | 16,656 | 18,250 |
| Vermont | 13,145 | 14,294 | 15,523 | 16,381 |
| Virginia | 15,130 | 16,348 | 17,955 | 19,244 |
| Washington | 15,401 | 16,818 | 18,359 | 20,207 |
| West Virginia | 12,569 | 14,064 | 15,564 | 16,793 |
| Wisconsin | 15,398 | 16,593 | 17,923 | 20,109 |
| Wyoming | 14,833 | 16,818 | 18,256 | 20,755 |

*Notes:*
1. The term "calendar year" refers to the year the money income was received by the Current Population Survey respondents.
2. The term "fiscal year" refers to the time period used for eligibility for the Department of Health and Human Services's Low Income Home Energy Assistance Program (LIHEAP).
3. As published in the *Federal Register.*
4. Implementation of a new March CPS processing system.
5. March CPS estimates were derived using pareto interpolation and may differ from published data which were derived using linear interpolation.
6. First year medians derived from the March CPS using both pareto and linear interpolation. Prior to this year all medians were derived using linear interpolation.

*Source:* U.S. Bureau of the Census, Income Statistics Branch/HHES Division; <http://www.census.gov/hhes/income/4person.html>.

## B11-2. Median Income for 4-Person Families, by State: 1978–1981 Calendar Years

| Calendar year[1]<br>Fiscal year[2] | 1978<br>1981[3] | 1979[7]<br>1982[3] | 1980[8]<br>1983[3] | 1981<br>1984[3] |
|---|---|---|---|---|
| United States | $20,428 | $22,395 | $24,332 | $26,274 |
| Alabama | 18,352 | 18,613 | 22,026 | 22,443 |
| Alaska | 27,572 | 31,037 | 32,745 | 35,834 |
| Arizona | 20,863 | 23,000 | 23,832 | 25,163 |
| Arkansas | 15,669 | 18,493 | 19,448 | 20,583 |
| California | 22,294 | 25,109 | 26,070 | 27,763 |
| Colorado | 21,778 | 25,228 | 25,943 | 28,756 |
| Connecticut | 22,278 | 24,410 | 28,376 | 31,108 |
| Delaware | 21,194 | 21,184 | 25,479 | 27,174 |

## B11-2. Median Income for 4-Person Families, by State: 1978–1981 Calendar Years *(continued)*

| Calendar year[1]<br>Fiscal Year[2] | 1978<br>1981[3] | 1979[7]<br>1982[3] | 1980[8]<br>1983[3] | 1981<br>1984[3] |
|---|---|---|---|---|
| District of Columbia | 16,769 | 21,310 | 25,476 | 28,312 |
| Florida | 18,118 | 20,757 | 21,355 | 23,504 |
| Georgia | 19,676 | 21,578 | 25,290 | 25,131 |
| Hawaii | 22,475 | 24,582 | 27,514 | 29,295 |
| Idaho | 19,042 | 20,429 | 21,251 | 22,821 |
| Illinois | 22,081 | 24,265 | 26,202 | 29,403 |
| Indiana | 20,566 | 22,614 | 24,043 | 24,832 |
| Iowa | 20,800 | 22,567 | 24,244 | 26,678 |
| Kansas | 19,792 | 22,848 | 23,334 | 24,842 |
| Kentucky | 17,924 | 19,138 | 20,960 | 22,409 |
| Louisiana | 18,691 | 20,166 | 23,711 | 26,144 |
| Maine | 16,885 | 18,074 | 21,207 | 22,201 |
| Maryland | 23,461 | 24,686 | 27,394 | 30,019 |
| Massachusetts | 20,512 | 23,786 | 26,381 | 28,839 |
| Michigan | 22,063 | 24,422 | 25,342 | 27,976 |
| Minnesota | 21,455 | 24,409 | 25,394 | 29,261 |
| Mississippi | 16,586 | 17,672 | 20,765 | 22,509 |
| Missouri | 19,268 | 21,294 | 23,488 | 25,339 |
| Montana | 17,878 | 20,051 | 23,449 | 24,953 |
| Nebraska | 19,319 | 20,749 | 22,941 | 24,835 |
| Nevada | 21,106 | 25,457 | 25,208 | 28,829 |
| New Hampshire | 20,247 | 22,335 | 23,554 | 25,332 |
| New Jersey | 22,189 | 24,640 | 27,772 | 30,793 |
| New Mexico | 18,738 | 21,032 | 20,453 | 21,488 |
| New York | 19,660 | 21,082 | 24,465 | 26,030 |
| North Carolina | 18,058 | 19,648 | 22,399 | 23,625 |
| North Dakota | 18,789 | 19,520 | 22,436 | 25,364 |
| Ohio | 20,950 | 22,528 | 24,898 | 26,851 |
| Oklahoma | 19,064 | 20,852 | 22,563 | 24,701 |
| Oregon | 21,534 | 24,031 | 23,208 | 24,516 |
| Pennsylvania | 19,753 | 22,314 | 24,814 | 26,519 |
| Rhode Island | 21,093 | 21,636 | 24,132 | 25,625 |
| South Carolina | 18,468 | 20,154 | 19,427 | 22,060 |
| South Dakota | 16,897 | 19,209 | 20,729 | 21,708 |
| Tennessee | 17,916 | 19,437 | 20,700 | 22,336 |
| Texas | 20,455 | 23,416 | 24,059 | 26,492 |
| Utah | 20,202 | 21,250 | 22,711 | 24,171 |
| Vermont | 18,458 | 19,314 | 21,773 | 23,551 |
| Virginia | 20,729 | 22,976 | 25,331 | 28,850 |
| Washington | 21,494 | 24,410 | 25,993 | 28,254 |
| West Virginia | 18,493 | 18,876 | 21,244 | 22,842 |
| Wisconsin | 21,034 | 23,518 | 25,050 | 27,232 |
| Wyoming | 22,452 | 22,673 | 25,853 | 27,553 |

*Notes:*
1. The term "calendar year" refers to the year the money income was received by the Current Population Survey respondents.
2. The term "fiscal year" refers to the time period used for eligibility for the Department of Health and Human Services's Low Income Home Energy Assistance Program (LIHEAP).
3. As published in the *Federal Register.*
7. CPS questionnaire expanded to record 27 possible values from 51 possible sources of income.
8. Implementation of 1980 census population controls in CPS estimates.
*Only notes that apply to this table are cited.

*Source:* U.S. Bureau of the Census, Income Statistics Branch/HHES Division; <http://www.census.gov/hhes/income/4person.html>.

## B11-3. Median Income for 4-Person Families, by State: 1982–1985 Calendar Years

| Calendar year[1]<br>Fiscal year[2] | 1982<br>1985[3] | 1983<br>1986[3] | 1984[9]<br>1987[3] | 1985[10]<br>1988[3] |
|---|---|---|---|---|
| United States | $27,619 | $29,184 | $31,097 | $32,777 |
| Alabama | 24,181 | 25,117 | 26,595 | 28,407 |
| Alaska | 31,823 | 38,238 | 44,017 | 42,897 |
| Arizona | 29,835 | 27,551 | 29,431 | 32,129 |
| Arkansas | 20,710 | 21,524 | 23,075 | 26,255 |
| California | 29,885 | 31,967 | 33,711 | 36,223 |
| Colorado | 30,663 | 32,294 | 34,154 | 35,214 |
| Connecticut | 35,361 | 37,703 | 39,070 | 40,677 |
| Delaware | 30,798 | 31,676 | 33,809 | 34,104 |
| District of Columbia | 26,897 | 28,701 | 31,104 | 32,610 |
| Florida | 25,745 | 25,455 | 28,858 | 31,364 |
| Georgia | 36,935 | 27,463 | 29,623 | 31,907 |
| Hawaii | 30,019 | 31,614 | 33,445 | 34,636 |
| Idaho | 23,529 | 24,009 | 25,499 | 27,383 |
| Illinois | 29,758 | 30,736 | 33,126 | 34,374 |
| Indiana | 26,123 | 26,924 | 30,302 | 31,369 |
| Iowa | 26,129 | 25,800 | 28,650 | 29,425 |
| Kansas | 23,596 | 27,569 | 30,330 | 31,114 |
| Kentucky | 23,732 | 24,096 | 25,815 | 27,307 |
| Louisiana | 27,165 | 27,953 | 28,430 | 29,910 |
| Maine | 23,036 | 24,178 | 26,237 | 28,537 |
| Maryland | 32,456 | 35,475 | 38,132 | 40,055 |
| Massachusetts | 30,327 | 33,990 | 36,731 | 39,079 |
| Michigan | 28,125 | 29,472 | 32,365 | 33,908 |
| Minnesota | 28,666 | 30,785 | 33,807 | 34,376 |
| Mississippi | 22,247 | 21,957 | 23,660 | 25,716 |
| Missouri | 26,035 | 27,789 | 30,050 | 31,414 |
| Montana | 24,965 | 25,278 | 26,072 | 27,999 |
| Nebraska | 25,372 | 26,100 | 28,752 | 30,655 |
| Nevada | 28,411 | 34,504 | 31,059 | 32,314 |
| New Hampshire | 28,810 | 30,414 | 33,255 | 35,702 |
| New Jersey | 32,781 | 36,448 | 39,096 | 40,800 |
| New Mexico | 23,642 | 23,906 | 25,468 | 27,127 |
| New York | 28,730 | 30,539 | 32,665 | 34,478 |
| North Carolina | 24,085 | 25,363 | 27,995 | 30,290 |
| North Dakota | 26,361 | 26,327 | 28,901 | 28,993 |
| Ohio | 27,100 | 28,305 | 30,779 | 33,478 |
| Oklahoma | 27,461 | 27,169 | 28,856 | 29,050 |
| Oregon | 25,988 | 26,404 | 28,633 | 30,741 |
| Pennsylvania | 27,209 | 28,274 | 29,573 | 32,265 |
| Rhode Island | 28,170 | 29,167 | 32,066 | 34,154 |
| South Carolina | 23,490 | 25,756 | 27,810 | 29,417 |
| South Dakota | 22,009 | 23,998 | 25,391 | 26,153 |
| Tennessee | 23,875 | 24,081 | 26,603 | 27,917 |
| Texas | 28,581 | 29,290 | 31,031 | 32,189 |
| Utah | 25,877 | 25,678 | 27,497 | 29,634 |
| Vermont | 23,797 | 25,441 | 26,645 | 30,019 |
| Virginia | 28,528 | 31,451 | 33,480 | 35,353 |
| Washington | 29,972 | 30,185 | 31,585 | 32,791 |
| West Virginia | 22,425 | 22,153 | 25,316 | 26,170 |
| Wisconsin | 27,873 | 28,979 | 30,622 | 32,007 |
| Wyoming | 29,582 | 28,480 | 29,752 | 30,741 |

*Notes:*

1. The term "calendar year" refers to the year the money income was received by the Current Population Survey respondents.

2. The term "fiscal year" refers to the time period used for eligibility for the Department of Health and Human Services's Low Income Home Energy Assistance Program (LIHEAP).

3. As published in the *Federal Register.*

9. Implementation of a new modeling technique and Hispanic population weighting controls.

10. Recording of amounts for earnings from longest job on the March CPS was increased to $299,999. Return to exclusive use of linear interpolation of model estimates.

*Only notes that apply to this table are cited.

*Source:* U.S. Bureau of the Census, Income Statistics Branch/HHES Division; <http://www.census.gov/hhes/income/4person.html>.

## B11-4. Median Income for 4-Person Families, by State: 1986–1989 Calendar Years

| Calendar year[1]<br>Fiscal year[2] | 1986<br>1989[3] | 1987[11]<br>1990[3] | 1988<br>1991[3] | 1989<br>1992[3] |
|---|---|---|---|---|
| United States | $34,716 | $36,812 | $39,051 | $40,763 |
| Alabama | 29,799 | 31,221 | 33,022 | 34,930 |
| Alaska | 41,292 | 47,106 | 47,247 | 48,411 |
| Arizona | 33,477 | 35,711 | 36,892 | 38,347 |
| Arkansas | 27,157 | 27,415 | 28,665 | 31,853 |
| California | 37,655 | 40,218 | 41,425 | 42,813 |
| Colorado | 36,026 | 37,778 | 39,095 | 40,265 |
| Connecticut | 44,330 | 47,195 | 50,720 | 53,313 |
| Delaware | 35,766 | 39,794 | 41,742 | 42,790 |
| District of Columbia | 35,424 | 36,523 | 38,562 | 40,574 |
| Florida | 33,368 | 35,247 | 37,280 | 37,399 |
| Georgia | 34,602 | 35,529 | 38,208 | 40,019 |
| Hawaii | 36,618 | 40,878 | 42,353 | 44,988 |
| Idaho | 27,075 | 29,701 | 31,454 | 33,633 |
| Illinois | 36,163 | 39,891 | 41,635 | 42,609 |
| Indiana | 32,026 | 35,016 | 37,939 | 38,201 |
| Iowa | 30,556 | 34,094 | 34,804 | 36,736 |
| Kansas | 32,512 | 34,474 | 35,796 | 37,938 |
| Kentucky | 28,464 | 30,257 | 32,088 | 34,390 |
| Louisiana | 29,614 | 31,964 | 32,514 | 34,406 |
| Maine | 31,297 | 31,957 | 35,385 | 38,336 |
| Maryland | 42,250 | 46,384 | 49,105 | 50,145 |
| Massachusetts | 42,295 | 44,329 | 48,296 | 51,799 |
| Michigan | 36,088 | 40,105 | 41,044 | 42,825 |
| Minnesota | 36,746 | 39,775 | 41,076 | 42,365 |
| Mississippi | 26,763 | 27,416 | 29,624 | 32,300 |
| Missouri | 33,149 | 35,437 | 37,187 | 38,478 |
| Montana | 29,190 | 31,015 | 32,333 | 33,882 |
| Nebraska | 31,484 | 32,969 | 34,287 | 37,902 |
| Nevada | 33,604 | 37,810 | 39,148 | 39,737 |
| New Hampshire | 39,503 | 40,833 | 45,619 | 47,983 |
| New Jersey | 44,591 | 47,846 | 52,305 | 53,229 |
| New Mexico | 27,474 | 27,675 | 29,350 | 31,156 |
| New York | 36,796 | 38,992 | 41,700 | 43,693 |
| North Carolina | 31,787 | 33,253 | 35,678 | 38,068 |
| North Dakota | 29,424 | 31,152 | 31,346 | 34,806 |
| Ohio | 34,038 | 36,344 | 38,145 | 41,469 |
| Oklahoma | 29,071 | 30,772 | 31,905 | 34,470 |
| Oregon | 31,392 | 34,555 | 36,623 | 38,723 |
| Pennsylvania | 32,700 | 35,638 | 37,855 | 40,404 |
| Rhode Island | 35,837 | 37,814 | 41,377 | 43,278 |
| South Carolina | 31,025 | 32,417 | 34,915 | 36,113 |
| South Dakota | 27,008 | 29,142 | 30,503 | 32,829 |
| Tennessee | 29,568 | 31,916 | 34,160 | 34,882 |
| Texas | 32,442 | 35,656 | 35,280 | 34,978 |
| Utah | 30,635 | 32,980 | 34,410 | 36,562 |
| Vermont | 32,490 | 33,983 | 36,467 | 40,397 |
| Virginia | 37,885 | 39,913 | 42,587 | 45,090 |
| Washington | 35,071 | 38,308 | 39,327 | 41,728 |
| West Virginia | 27,094 | 28,711 | 29,743 | 31,811 |
| Wisconsin | 33,739 | 36,674 | 38,662 | 40,557 |
| Wyoming | 28,742 | 33,692 | 33,667 | 35,620 |

*Notes:
1. The term "calendar year" refers to the year the money income was received by the Current Population Survey respondents.
2. The term "fiscal year" refers to the time period used for eligibility for the Department of Health and Human Services's Low Income Home Energy Assistance Program (LIHEAP).
3. As published in the *Federal Register.*
11. Implementation of a new March CPS processing system.
*Only notes that apply to this table are cited.

*Source:* U.S. Bureau of the Census, Income Statistics Branch/HHES Division; <http://www.census.gov/hhes/income/4person.html>.

## B11-5. Median Income for 4-Person Families, by State: 1990–1992 Calendar Years

| Calendar year[1]<br>Fiscal year[2] | 1990<br>1993[3] | 1991<br>1994[3] | 1992<br>1995[3] | 1992[12]<br>1995 |
|---|---|---|---|---|
| United States | $41,451 | $43,056 | $44,615 | $44,251 |
| Alabama | 35,937 | 37,638 | 39,659 | 39,438 |
| Alaska | 51,538 | 49,721 | 49,632 | 48,924 |
| Arizona | 38,799 | 39,364 | 39,900 | 39,288 |
| Arkansas | 31,913 | 34,566 | 36,682 | 36,388 |
| California | 45,184 | 46,643 | 46,774 | 46,230 |
| Colorado | 41,803 | 43,136 | 45,021 | 44,858 |
| Connecticut | 53,931 | 54,479 | 55,061 | 54,812 |
| Delaware | 46,524 | 48,531 | 50,999 | 51,139 |
| District of Columbia | 38,824 | 43,994 | 45,782 | 45,441 |
| Florida | 38,438 | 40,484 | 40,925 | 40,369 |
| Georgia | 41,184 | 41,274 | 42,696 | 42,366 |
| Hawaii | 50,234 | 49,367 | 50,821 | 50,856 |
| Idaho | 34,091 | 36,789 | 38,844 | 38,578 |
| Illinois | 44,220 | 45,707 | 47,474 | 47,354 |
| Indiana | 39,700 | 41,850 | 43,674 | 43,431 |
| Iowa | 38,090 | 39,763 | 41,827 | 41,633 |
| Kansas | 40,576 | 40,682 | 42,285 | 42,022 |
| Kentucky | 36,348 | 36,255 | 38,512 | 38,297 |
| Louisiana | 36,510 | 36,105 | 38,061 | 37,837 |
| Maine | 38,848 | 40,251 | 40,924 | 40,404 |
| Maryland | 53,385 | 51,103 | 51,864 | 51,577 |
| Massachusetts | 52,171 | 51,135 | 51,172 | 50,699 |
| Michigan | 43,545 | 44,605 | 45,704 | 45,364 |
| Minnesota | 43,031 | 44,785 | 46,518 | 46,322 |
| Mississippi | 30,242 | 33,941 | 35,731 | 35,355 |
| Missouri | 39,766 | 40,285 | 41,926 | 41,642 |
| Montana | 35,105 | 36,094 | 37,174 | 36,696 |
| Nebraska | 39,664 | 39,845 | 42,207 | 42,134 |
| Nevada | 41,629 | 42,418 | 43,472 | 42,976 |
| New Hampshire | 49,088 | 47,646 | 48,385 | 48,055 |
| New Jersey | 56,436 | 54,374 | 55,634 | 55,590 |
| New Mexico | 32,941 | 34,736 | 36,299 | 35,882 |
| New York | 44,200 | 46,649 | 48,039 | 47,776 |
| North Carolina | 39,718 | 39,934 | 41,766 | 41,525 |
| North Dakota | 36,127 | 37,186 | 40,179 | 40,155 |
| Ohio | 42,821 | 42,201 | 43,636 | 43,335 |
| Oklahoma | 34,141 | 36,285 | 37,704 | 37,264 |
| Oregon | 39,653 | 40,272 | 41,558 | 41,216 |
| Pennsylvania | 40,892 | 43,213 | 45,015 | 44,869 |
| Rhode Island | 44,598 | 46,190 | 46,797 | 46,397 |
| South Carolina | 38,797 | 39,134 | 40,753 | 40,495 |
| South Dakota | 34,632 | 36,406 | 38,703 | 38,562 |
| Tennessee | 34,279 | 38,552 | 40,549 | 40,325 |
| Texas | 37,789 | 39,204 | 40,695 | 40,342 |
| Utah | 38,632 | 39,526 | 41,505 | 41,295 |
| Vermont | 41,312 | 41,940 | 43,167 | 42,848 |
| Virginia | 44,597 | 44,488 | 45,492 | 45,105 |
| Washington | 44,306 | 43,982 | 46,327 | 46,282 |
| West Virginia | 33,666 | 35,163 | 37,437 | 37,229 |
| Wisconsin | 43,182 | 42,746 | 44,444 | 44,219 |
| Wyoming | 36,796 | 40,175 | 43,126 | 43,209 |

*Notes:
1. The term "calendar year" refers to the year the money income was received by the Current Population Survey respondents.
2. The term "fiscal year" refers to the time period used for eligibility for the Department of Health and Human Services's Low Income Home Energy Assistance Program (LIHEAP).
3. As published in the *Federal Register.*
12. Implementation of 1990 census population controls in CPS estimates.
*Only notes that apply to this table are cited.

*Source*: U.S. Bureau of the Census, Income Statistics Branch/HHES Division; <http://www.census.gov/hhes/income/4person.html>.

## B11-6. Median Income for 4-Person Families, by State: 1993–1996 Calendar Years

| Calendar year[1]<br>Fiscal year[2] | 1993[13]<br>1996[3] | 1994[14]<br>1997[3] | 1995[15]<br>1998 | 1996<br>1999 |
|---|---|---|---|---|
| United States | $45,161 | $47,012 | $49,687 | $51,518 |
| Alabama | 37,975 | 41,730 | 42,617 | 44,879 |
| Alaska | 51,181 | 53,555 | 56,045 | 62,078 |
| Arizona | 39,679 | 41,599 | 44,526 | 45,032 |
| Arkansas | 32,594 | 36,510 | 38,520 | 36,828 |
| California | 44,643 | 48,755 | 51,519 | 53,807 |
| Colorado | 47,112 | 48,801 | 50,941 | 53,632 |
| Connecticut | 59,288 | 62,107 | 62,157 | 67,380 |
| Delaware | 50,228 | 55,049 | 54,519 | 56,662 |
| District of Columbia | 46,943 | 52,015 | 49,837 | 53,256 |
| Florida | 40,405 | 43,374 | 44,626 | 44,829 |
| Georgia | 44,120 | 45,093 | 48,850 | 48,920 |
| Hawaii | 54,856 | 56,992 | 54,749 | 57,909 |
| Idaho | 39,851 | 41,208 | 42,142 | 44,133 |
| Illinois | 47,975 | 51,951 | 53,807 | 55,372 |
| Indiana | 44,274 | 47,212 | 47,465 | 52,962 |
| Iowa | 42,772 | 45,062 | 47,314 | 48,167 |
| Kansas | 43,155 | 44,409 | 46,611 | 49,034 |
| Kentucky | 36,291 | 37,984 | 40,587 | 44,932 |
| Louisiana | 35,177 | 39,734 | 41,442 | 41,851 |
| Maine | 41,513 | 42,647 | 45,507 | 48,632 |
| Maryland | 53,717 | 57,951 | 60,239 | 61,860 |
| Massachusetts | 55,120 | 58,695 | 59,191 | 62,385 |
| Michigan | 46,633 | 51,342 | 52,955 | 56,174 |
| Minnesota | 48,817 | 51,996 | 54,396 | 56,200 |
| Mississippi | 34,001 | 37,003 | 37,328 | 38,748 |
| Missouri | 42,162 | 44,266 | 45,795 | 50,015 |
| Montana | 38,157 | 39,219 | 42,987 | 41,462 |
| Nebraska | 42,262 | 45,497 | 44,886 | 46,726 |
| Nevada | 46,137 | 47,929 | 50,064 | 50,946 |
| New Hampshire | 49,452 | 51,491 | 54,492 | 56,497 |
| New Jersey | 57,916 | 60,697 | 61,409 | 65,586 |
| New Mexico | 35,560 | 37,170 | 37,365 | 38,143 |
| New York | 47,570 | 50,964 | 50,672 | 52,799 |
| North Carolina | 42,691 | 44,582 | 47,367 | 49,272 |
| North Dakota | 41,084 | 42,222 | 43,483 | 45,480 |
| Ohio | 46,116 | 46,848 | 50,893 | 51,835 |
| Oklahoma | 35,133 | 38,787 | 42,124 | 43,138 |
| Oregon | 42,745 | 44,432 | 46,229 | 46,245 |
| Pennsylvania | 47,109 | 49,120 | 50,884 | 53,814 |
| Rhode Island | 47,908 | 51,709 | 51,362 | 53,967 |
| South Carolina | 40,163 | 43,556 | 44,048 | 46,973 |
| South Dakota | 38,067 | 42,964 | 42,269 | 45,043 |
| Tennessee | 38,341 | 42,132 | 44,312 | 45,245 |
| Texas | 40,688 | 42,570 | 43,977 | 46,757 |
| Utah | 42,630 | 44,871 | 45,611 | 45,775 |
| Vermont | 44,184 | 46,320 | 47,376 | 49,401 |
| Virginia | 47,732 | 49,453 | 50,032 | 53,394 |
| Washington | 50,557 | 48,932 | 51,415 | 53,153 |
| West Virginia | 34,189 | 38,357 | 39,731 | 41,293 |
| Wisconsin | 46,363 | 48,982 | 50,628 | 52,986 |
| Wyoming | 45,414 | 47,961 | 45,925 | 46,830 |

*Notes:*
1. The term "calendar year" refers to the year the money income was received by the Current Population Survey respondents.
2. The term "fiscal year" refers to the time period used for eligibility for the Department of Health and Human Services's Low Income Home Energy Assistance Program (LIHEAP).
3. As published in the *Federal Register.*
13. Data collection method changed in the CPS from paper and pencil to computer-assisted interviewing. In addition, the March 1994 CPS income supplement was revised to allow for the coding of different income amounts on selected questionnaire items. Limits either increased or decreased in the following categories: earnings increased to $999,999; Social Security increased to $49,999; Supplemental Security Income and Public Assistance increased to $24,999; Veterans' Benefits increased to $99,999; Child Support and Alimony decreased to $49,999.
14. Introduction of new 1990 census-based sample design to the March CPS.
15. Full implementation of the 1990 census-based sample design and revised race edits to the March CPS.
*Only notes that apply to this table are cited.

*Source:* U.S. Bureau of the Census, Income Statistics Branch/HHES Division; <http://www.census.gov/hhes/income/4person.html>.

## B12. MONEY INCOME OF FAMILIES—MEDIAN INCOME BY RACE AND HISPANIC ORIGIN

### B12-1. Money Income of Families—Median Income, by Race and Hispanic Origin, in Current Dollars: 1970–1996

| Year | Median income in current dollars All families[1] | Median income in current dollars White | Median income in current dollars Black | Median income in current dollars Asian Pacific Islanders | Median income in current dollars Hispanic[2] |
|---|---|---|---|---|---|
| 1970 | 9,867 | 10,236 | 6,279 | (NA) | (NA) |
| 1980 | 21,023 | 21,904 | 12,674 | (NA) | 14,716 |
| 1981 | 22,388 | 23,517 | 13,266 | (NA) | 16,401 |
| 1982 | 23,433 | 24,603 | 13,598 | (NA) | 16,227 |
| 1983 | 24,580 | 25,757 | 14,506 | (NA) | 16,956 |
| 1984[3] | 26,433 | 27,686 | 15,431 | (NA) | 18,832 |
| 1985[4] | 27,735 | 29,152 | 16,786 | (NA) | 19,027 |
| 1986 | 29,458 | 30,809 | 17,604 | (NA) | 19,995 |
| 1987[5] | 30,970 | 32,385 | 18,406 | (NA) | 20,300 |
| 1988 | 32,191 | 33,915 | 19,329 | 36,560 | 21,769 |
| 1989 | 34,213 | 35,975 | 20,209 | 40,351 | 23,446 |
| 1990 | 35,353 | 36,915 | 21,423 | 42,246 | 23,431 |
| 1991 | 35,939 | 37,783 | 21,548 | 40,974 | 23,895 |
| 1992[6] | 36,573 | 38,670 | 21,103 | 42,255 | 23,555 |
| 1993[7] | 36,959 | 39,300 | 21,542 | 44,456 | 23,654 |
| 1994[8] | 38,782 | 40,884 | 24,698 | 46,122 | 24,318 |
| 1995[9] | 40,611 | 42,646 | 25,970 | 46,356 | 24,570 |
| 1996 | 42,300 | 44,756 | 26,522 | 49,105 | 26,179 |

*Notes:*
(NA) Not available.
1. Includes other races not shown separately.
2. Persons of Hispanic origin may be of any race.
3. Implementation of Hispanic population weighting controls.
4. Recording of amounts for earnings from longest job increased to $299,999.
5. Implementation of a new March CPS processing system.
6. Implementation of 1990 census population controls.
7. See text, Section 14, for information on data collection change.
8. Introduction of 1990 census sample design.
9. Full implementation of the 1990 census-based sample design and metropolitan definitions, 7,000 household sample reduction, and revised race edits.
*General Note:* Constant dollars based on CPI-U-X1 deflator. Households as of March of following year.

*Source: Statistical Abstract of the United States*, No. 746, <http://www.census.gov/prod/3/98pubs/98statab/sasec14.pdf>. Underlying data from U.S. Bureau of the Census, *Current Population Reports, P60-197.*

## B12-2. Money Income of Families—Median Income, by Race and Hispanic Origin, in Constant (1996) Dollars: 1970–1996

| Year | Median income in constant (1996) dollars All families[1] | Median income in constant (1996) dollars White | Median income in constant (1996) dollars Black | Median income in constant (1996) dollars Asian Pacific Islanders | Median income in constant (1996) dollars Hispanic[2] |
|---|---|---|---|---|---|
| 1970 | 37,485 | 38,887 | 23,854 | (NA) | (NA) |
| 1980 | 40,079 | 41,759 | 24,162 | (NA) | 28,055 |
| 1981 | 38,986 | 40,952 | 23,101 | (NA) | 28,561 |
| 1982 | 38,459 | 40,379 | 22,317 | (NA) | 26,632 |
| 1983 | 38,721 | 40,575 | 22,851 | (NA) | 26,711 |
| 1984[3] | 39,917 | 41,809 | 23,302 | (NA) | 28,438 |
| 1985[4] | 40,443 | 42,509 | 24,477 | (NA) | 27,745 |
| 1986 | 42,171 | 44,105 | 25,201 | (NA) | 28,624 |
| 1987[5] | 42,775 | 44,729 | 25,422 | (NA) | 28,038 |
| 1988 | 42,695 | 44,981 | 25,636 | 48,489 | 28,872 |
| 1989 | 43,290 | 45,520 | 25,571 | 51,057 | 29,667 |
| 1990 | 42,440 | 44,315 | 25,717 | 50,715 | 28,128 |
| 1991 | 41,401 | 43,525 | 24,823 | 47,201 | 27,527 |
| 1992[6] | 40,900 | 43,245 | 23,600 | 47,255 | 26,342 |
| 1993[7] | 40,131 | 42,672 | 23,391 | 48,271 | 25,684 |
| 1994[8] | 41,059 | 43,284 | 26,148 | 48,830 | 25,746 |
| 1995[9] | 41,810 | 43,905 | 26,737 | 47,725 | 25,296 |
| 1996 | 42,300 | 44,756 | 26,522 | 49,105 | 26,179 |

*Notes:*
(NA) Not available
1. Includes other races not shown separately.
2. Persons of Hispanic origin may be of any race.
3. Implementation of Hispanic population weighting controls.
4. Recording of amounts for earnings from longest job increased to $299,999.
5. Implementation of a new March CPS processing system.
6. Implementation of 1990 census population controls.
7. See text, Section 14, for information on data collection change.
8. Introduction of 1990 census sample design.
9. Full implementation of the 1990 census-based sample design and metropolitan definitions, 7,000 household sample reduction, and revised race edits.
*General Note:* Constant dollars based on CPI-U-X1 deflator. Households as of March of following year.

*Source: Statistical Abstract of the United States,* No. 746, <http://www.census.gov/prod/3/98pubs/98statab/sasec14.pdf>. Underlying data from U.S. Bureau of the Census, *Current Population Reports, P60-197.*

## B13. MEDIAN INCOME OF FAMILIES, BY TYPE OF FAMILY

### B13-1. Median Income of Families, Totals, in Current Dollars: 1970–1996

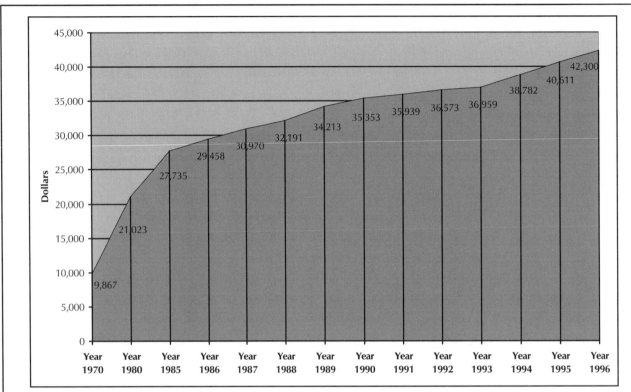

*Notes:*

Beginning in 1987, data based on revised processing procedures and not directly comparable with prior years.

1992 data based on 1990 census population controls.

For 1994 data, see text, Section 14, for information on data collection change.

For 1995 data, introduction of 1990 census sample design.

*General Notes:* Families as of March of following year. Beginning with 1980, based on householder concept and restricted to primary families. Based on Current Population Survey.

*Source:* U.S. Bureau of the Census, *Current Population Reports, P60-197;* and Internet site, <http://www.census.gov/hhes/income/histinc/index.html> (accessed 25 March 1998).

## B13-2. Median Income of Families, by Type of Family, in Current Dollars: 1970–1996

| Year | Median | Married Couple Families | | | Male householder, no wife present | Female householder, no husband present |
|------|--------|--------|----------------------|--------------------------|-----------------------------------|-----------------------------------------|
| | | Median | Wife in paid labor force | Wife not in paid labor force | | |
| 1970 | 9,867 | 10,516 | 12,276 | 9,304 | 9,012 | 5,093 |
| 1980 | 21,023 | 23,141 | 26,879 | 18,972 | 17,519 | 10,408 |
| 1985 | 27,735 | 31,100 | 36,431 | 24,556 | 22,622 | 13,660 |
| 1986 | 29,458 | 32,805 | 38,346 | 25,803 | 24,962 | 13,647 |
| 1987[1] | 30,970 | 34,879 | 40,751 | 26,640 | 25,208 | 14,683 |
| 1988 | 32,191 | 36,389 | 42,709 | 27,220 | 26,827 | 15,346 |
| 1989 | 34,213 | 38,547 | 45,266 | 28,747 | 27,847 | 16,442 |
| 1990 | 35,353 | 39,895 | 46,777 | 30,265 | 29,046 | 16,932 |
| 1991 | 35,939 | 40,995 | 48,169 | 30,075 | 28,351 | 16,692 |
| 1992[2] | 36,573 | 41,890 | 49,775 | 30,174 | 27,576 | 17,025 |
| 1993 | 36,959 | 43,005 | 51,204 | 30,218 | 26,467 | 17,443 |
| 1994[3] | 38,782 | 44,959 | 53,309 | 31,176 | 27,751 | 18,236 |
| 1995[4] | 40,611 | 47,062 | 55,823 | 32,375 | 30,358 | 19,691 |
| 1996 | 42,300 | 49,707 | 58,381 | 33,748 | 31,600 | 19,911 |

**Notes:**
1. Beginning in 1987, data based on revised processing procedures and not directly comparable with prior years.
2. Based on 1990 census population controls.
3. See text, Section 14, for information on data collection change.
4. Introduction of 1990 census sample design.
*General Notes:* Families as of March of following year. Beginning with 1980, based on householder concept and restricted to primary families. Based on Current Population Survey.

*Source:* U.S. Bureau of the Census, *Current Population Reports, P60-197;* Internet site, <http://www.census.gov/hhes/income/histinc/index.html> (accessed 25 March 1998).

## B13-3. Median Income of Families, Totals, in Constant (1996) Dollars: 1970–1996

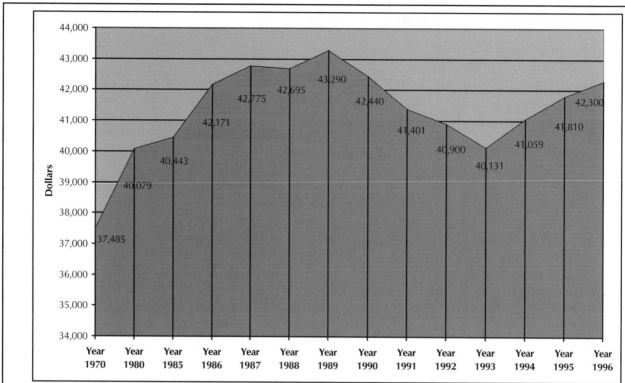

*Notes:*

Beginning in 1987, data based on revised processing procedures and not directly comparable with prior years.

1992 data based on 1990 census population controls.

For 1994 data, see text, Section 14, for information on data collection change.

For 1995 data, introduction of 1990 census sample design.

*General Notes:* Families as of March of following year. Beginning with 1980, based on householder concept and restricted to primary families. Based on Current Population Survey.

*Source:* U.S. Bureau of the Census, *Current Population Reports, P60-197;* Internet site, <http://www.census.gov/hhes/income/histinc/index.html> (accessed 25 March 1998).

## B13-4. Median Income of Families, by Type of Family, in Constant (1996) Dollars: 1970–1996

| Year | Median | Married Couple Families | | | Male householder, no wife present | Female householder, no husband present |
|---|---|---|---|---|---|---|
| | | Median | Wife in paid labor force | Wife not in paid labor force | | |
| 1970 | 37,485 | 39,951 | 46,637 | 35,346 | 34,237 | 19,348 |
| 1980 | 40,079 | 44,117 | 51,243 | 36,169 | 33,399 | 19,842 |
| 1985 | 40,443 | 45,349 | 53,123 | 35,807 | 32,987 | 19,919 |
| 1986 | 42,171 | 46,963 | 54,895 | 36,939 | 35,735 | 19,537 |
| 1987[1] | 42,775 | 48,174 | 56,284 | 36,794 | 34,816 | 20,280 |
| 1988 | 42,695 | 48,262 | 56,644 | 36,102 | 35,580 | 20,353 |
| 1989 | 43,290 | 48,774 | 57,276 | 36,374 | 35,235 | 20,804 |
| 1990 | 42,440 | 47,892 | 56,154 | 36,332 | 34,869 | 20,326 |
| 1991 | 41,401 | 47,226 | 55,490 | 34,646 | 32,660 | 19,229 |
| 1992[2] | 40,900 | 46,846 | 55,664 | 33,744 | 30,839 | 19,039 |
| 1993 | 40,131 | 46,695 | 55,598 | 32,811 | 28,738 | 18,940 |
| 1994[3] | 41,059 | 47,598 | 56,438 | 33,006 | 29,380 | 19,307 |
| 1995[4] | 41,810 | 48,452 | 57,471 | 33,331 | 31,254 | 20,272 |
| 1996 | 42,300 | 49,707 | 58,381 | 33,748 | 31,600 | 19,911 |

*Notes:*
1. Beginning in 1987, data based on revised processing procedures and not directly comparable with prior years.
2. Based on 1990 census population controls.
3. See text, Section 14, for information on data collection change.
4. Introduction of 1990 census sample design.
*General Note:* Constant dollars based on CPI-U-X1 deflator. Families as of March of following year. Beginning with 1980, based on householder concept and restricted to primary families. Based on *Current Population Survey.*

*Source:* U.S. Bureau of the Census, *Current Population Reports, P60-197;* Internet site, <http://www.census.gov/hhes/income/histinc/index.html> (accessed 25 March 1998).

## B14. MEDIAN INCOME OF NONMARRIED-COUPLE HOUSEHOLDS AND BY HOUSEHOLD SIZE

### B14-1. Median Income of Nonmarried-Couple Households: 1969–1996, in Constant (1996) Dollars

| Year | All households | Nonmarried-Couple Households with Related Children Under 18 Years Old | |
|---|---|---|---|
| | | Male householder | Female householder |
| 1969 | $33,072 | $33,749 | $16,327 |
| 1970 | $33,025 | $33,572 | $16,716 |
| 1971 | $32,763 | $33,855 | $16,181 |
| 1972 | $34,094 | $36,523 | $16,277 |
| 1973 | $34,674 | $35,568 | $16,295 |
| 1974 | $33,557 | $33,076 | $16,636 |
| 1975 | $32,779 | $33,549 | $16,114 |
| 1976 | $33,440 | $35,078 | $16,482 |
| 1977 | $33,671 | $35,084 | $17,130 |
| 1978 | $34,867 | $37,575 | $17,433 |
| 1979 | $34,666 | $36,619 | $18,468 |
| 1980 | $33,754 | $32,299 | $17,349 |
| 1981 | $33,087 | $35,357 | $17,069 |
| 1982 | $32,847 | $32,824 | $15,920 |
| 1983 | $32,941 | $33,496 | $15,618 |
| 1984 | $33,781 | $36,002 | $16,368 |
| 1985 | $34,413 | $33,411 | $16,431 |
| 1986 | $35,574 | $33,745 | $16,320 |
| 1987 | $35,910 | $34,747 | $16,693 |
| 1988 | $35,982 | $33,820 | $16,579 |
| 1989 | $36,598 | $34,646 | $17,651 |
| 1990 | $35,894 | $33,769 | $16,942 |
| 1991 | $34,559 | $32,267 | $16,589 |
| 1992 | $33,897 | $29,076 | $16,412 |
| 1993 | $33,660 | $29,520 | $15,951 |
| 1994 | $34,027 | $29,348 | $17,230 |
| 1995 | $35,004 | $32,224 | $18,449 |
| 1996 | $35,172 | $31,020 | $18,000 |

*Source:* U.S. Bureau of the Census, *March Current Population Surveys,* Table A2; <http://www.census.gov/hhes/income/mednhhld/ta2.html>.

## B14-2. Median Income of Nonmarried-Couple Households, by Household Size: 1969 to 1996, in Constant (1996) Dollars

| Year | One-person households Less than 65 years old, Male | One-person households Less than 65 years old, Female | One-person households 65 years Male | One-person households 65 years Female | Two or more persons, no rel. under 18 Male householder | Two or more persons, no rel. under 18 Female householder |
|------|------|------|------|------|------|------|
| 1969 | $23,893 | $15,929 | $8,936 | $7,025 | $34,060 | $26,796 |
| 1970 | $24,694 | $15,800 | $8,707 | $7,138 | $37,291 | $26,643 |
| 1971 | $24,755 | $16,120 | $9,421 | $7,539 | $32,250 | $27,303 |
| 1972 | $24,736 | $16,683 | $10,559 | $8,114 | $36,398 | $27,924 |
| 1973 | $25,928 | $17,296 | $10,059 | $8,603 | $39,115 | $28,255 |
| 1974 | $23,656 | $17,368 | $10,569 | $8,785 | $37,487 | $29,188 |
| 1975 | $23,730 | $16,751 | $10,397 | $8,990 | $37,773 | $28,086 |
| 1976 | $24,037 | $17,230 | $10,685 | $9,020 | $37,651 | $27,225 |
| 1977 | $25,322 | $17,564 | $10,558 | $9,320 | $38,458 | $29,543 |
| 1978 | $26,499 | $18,503 | $11,206 | $9,574 | $39,516 | $30,892 |
| 1979 | $26,514 | $18,366 | $11,227 | $9,382 | $39,916 | $31,140 |
| 1980 | $25,361 | $19,064 | $11,326 | $9,437 | $39,845 | $31,227 |
| 1981 | $25,874 | $18,683 | $11,901 | $9,602 | $38,542 | $29,517 |
| 1982 | $26,035 | $19,695 | $12,688 | $10,039 | $38,897 | $30,044 |
| 1983 | $24,732 | $20,440 | $13,615 | $10,926 | $38,614 | $29,439 |
| 1984 | $25,990 | $20,293 | $12,700 | $10,865 | $40,018 | $31,738 |
| 1985 | $26,820 | $20,473 | $13,526 | $10,508 | $41,351 | $33,297 |
| 1986 | $27,200 | $20,774 | $13,706 | $10,648 | $42,442 | $32,963 |
| 1987 | $27,623 | $21,289 | $13,812 | $10,922 | $41,509 | $33,964 |
| 1988 | $27,603 | $22,878 | $13,573 | $10,858 | $42,707 | $35,392 |
| 1989 | $27,854 | $22,776 | $14,288 | $11,388 | $43,770 | $35,454 |
| 1990 | $26,410 | $23,409 | $15,389 | $11,257 | $42,631 | $35,504 |
| 1991 | $25,920 | $21,921 | $14,113 | $11,068 | $41,057 | $33,292 |
| 1992 | $25,721 | $21,701 | $13,701 | $10,924 | $39,141 | $33,798 |
| 1993 | $25,908 | $21,550 | $14,821 | $10,823 | $40,175 | $33,172 |
| 1994 | $25,419 | $21,177 | $14,624 | $11,145 | $39,457 | $32,820 |
| 1995 | $25,880 | $21,426 | $15,048 | $11,304 | $39,329 | $32,463 |
| 1996 | $26,898 | $21,432 | $14,586 | $11,454 | $41,792 | $33,566 |

*Source:* U.S. Bureau of the Census, *March Current Population Surveys,* Table A2; <http://www.census.gov/hhes/income/mednhhld/ta2.html>.

## B15. MONEY INCOME OF HOUSEHOLDS AND FAMILIES—PERCENT DISTRIBUTION, BY INCOME LEVEL, RACE, AND HISPANIC ORIGIN

### B15-1. Money Income of Households—Percent Distribution, by Income Level, Race, and Hispanic Origin, in Constant (1996) Dollars: 1970–1996

| | Number households (1,000) | Percent under $10,000 | Percent $10,000 to $14,999 | Percent $15,000 to $24,999 | Percent $25,000 to $34,999 | Percent $35,000 to $49,999 | Percent $50,000 to $74,999 | Percent Distribution $75,000 and up | Median income dollars |
|------|------|------|------|------|------|------|------|------|------|
| **ALL HOUSE-HOLDS**[1] | | | | | | | | | |
| 1970 | 64,778 | 13.7 | 7.7 | 15.6 | 16.4 | 21.3 | 16.8 | 8.5 | 33,181 |
| 1975 | 72,867 | 13.0 | 8.8 | 16.2 | 15.6 | 19.4 | 17.8 | 9.2 | 32,943 |
| 1980 | 82,368 | 12.9 | 8.2 | 16.4 | 14.3 | 19.1 | 17.9 | 11.2 | 33,763 |
| 1985 | 88,458 | 12.7 | 8.3 | 15.6 | 14.2 | 17.8 | 17.8 | 13.5 | 34,439 |
| 1990 | 94,312 | 12.0 | 7.9 | 15.0 | 14.1 | 17.8 | 17.9 | 15.2 | 35,945 |
| 1994 | 98,990 | 12.6 | 8.7 | 15.8 | 14.1 | 16.3 | 16.9 | 15.5 | 34,158 |
| 1995 | 99,627 | 11.8 | 8.5 | 15.6 | 13.9 | 16.9 | 17.4 | 15.7 | 35,082 |
| 1996 | 101,018 | 11.8 | 8.6 | 15.4 | 13.7 | 16.3 | 18.0 | 16.4 | 35,492 |
| **WHITE** | | | | | | | | | |
| 1970 | 57,575 | 12.5 | 7.2 | 14.9 | 16.5 | 22.0 | 17.7 | 9.0 | 34,560 |
| 1975 | 64,392 | 11.6 | 8.4 | 15.9 | 15.5 | 20.0 | 18.8 | 9.9 | 34,451 |

**B15-1. Money Income of Households—Percent Distribution, by Income Level, Race, and Hispanic Origin, in Constant (1996) Dollars: 1970–1996** *(continued)*

| Year | Number of households (1,000s) | Percent under $10,000 | Percent $10,000 to $14,999 | Percent $15,000 to $24,999 | Percent $25,000 to $34,999 | Percent $35,000 to $49,999 | Percent $50,000 to $74,999 | Percent Distribution $75,000 and up | Median income dollars |
|---|---|---|---|---|---|---|---|---|---|
| 1980 | 71,872 | 11.3 | 7.7 | 16.0 | 14.5 | 19.7 | 18.9 | 12.1 | 35,620 |
| 1985 | 76,576 | 11.1 | 7.8 | 15.2 | 14.3 | 18.4 | 18.6 | 14.5 | 36,320 |
| 1990 | 80,968 | 10.2 | 7.6 | 14.8 | 14.3 | 18.3 | 18.8 | 16.2 | 37,492 |
| 1994 | 83,737 | 10.8 | 8.4 | 15.5 | 14.2 | 16.8 | 17.7 | 16.5 | 36,026 |
| 1995 | 84,511 | 10.2 | 8.2 | 15.4 | 14.0 | 17.3 | 18.1 | 16.8 | 36,822 |
| 1996 | 85,059 | 10.0 | 8.2 | 15.1 | 13.7 | 16.7 | 18.8 | 17.4 | 37,161 |
| **BLACK** | | | | | | | | | |
| 1970 | 6,180 | 25.0 | 12.1 | 21.5 | 15.2 | 14.5 | 8.7 | 2.8 | 21,035 |
| 1975 | 7,489 | 25.4 | 13.3 | 19.0 | 16.0 | 14.1 | 9.4 | 2.8 | 20,682 |
| 1980 | 8,847 | 25.9 | 12.9 | 19.8 | 13.2 | 14.4 | 10.0 | 3.8 | 20,521 |
| 1985 | 9,797 | 25.8 | 11.9 | 19.1 | 13.1 | 13.9 | 11.0 | 5.2 | 21,609 |
| 1990 | 10,671 | 26.3 | 11.1 | 17.0 | 13.3 | 14.5 | 11.2 | 6.5 | 22,420 |
| 1994 | 11,655 | 25.2 | 11.1 | 18.3 | 13.4 | 13.1 | 11.7 | 7.2 | 22,261 |
| 1995 | 11,577 | 23.5 | 11.3 | 18.5 | 13.7 | 14.7 | 11.5 | 6.7 | 23,054 |
| 1996 | 12,109 | 23.1 | 11.6 | 17.7 | 13.9 | 14.0 | 12.4 | 7.4 | 23,482 |
| **HISPANIC[2]** | | | | | | | | | |
| 1975 | 2,948 | 16.8 | 11.7 | 22.1 | 17.5 | 18.1 | 10.3 | 3.5 | 24,749 |
| 1980 | 3,906 | 16.7 | 10.7 | 21.2 | 16.2 | 16.9 | 12.8 | 5.5 | 26,025 |
| 1985 | 5,213 | 17.9 | 12.0 | 19.5 | 15.2 | 16.4 | 12.3 | 6.6 | 25,467 |
| 1990 | 6,220 | 16.7 | 11.6 | 18.6 | 15.8 | 17.0 | 12.8 | 7.5 | 26,806 |
| 1994 | 7,735 | 19.2 | 12.1 | 19.1 | 15.2 | 15.0 | 11.8 | 7.6 | 24,796 |
| 1995 | 7,939 | 19.2 | 12.3 | 21.0 | 15.2 | 14.0 | 11.8 | 6.5 | 23,535 |
| 1996 | 8,225 | 17.2 | 11.9 | 21.0 | 15.0 | 15.0 | 12.3 | 7.7 | 24,906 |

*Notes:*
1. Includes other races not shown separately.
2. Persons of Hispanic origin may be of any race. Income data for Hispanic origin households are not available prior to 1972.
*General Note:* Constant dollars based on CPI-U-X1 deflator Households as of March of following year. Based on *Current Population Survey*

*Source: Statistical Abstract of the United States 1998*, No. 738; <http://www.census.gov/prod/3/98pubs/98statab/sasec14.pdf>. Underlying data from U.S. Bureau of the Census, *Current Population Reports*, P60-197; and Internet site <http://www.census.gov/hhes/income/histinc/inchhdet.html> (accessed 25 March 1998).

**B15-2. Money Income of Families—Percent Distribution, by Income Level, Race, and Hispanic Origin, in Constant (1996) Dollars: 1970–1996**

| Year | Number of families (1,000s) | Percent under $10,000 | Percent $10,000 to $14,999 | Percent $15,000 to $24,999 | Percent $25,000 to $34,999 | Percent $35,000 to $49,999 | Percent $50,000 to $74,999 | Percent $75,000 and over | Median income (dollars) |
|---|---|---|---|---|---|---|---|---|---|
| **ALL FAMILIES[1]** | | | | | | | | | |
| 1970 | 52,227 | 7.3 | 6.4 | 15.1 | 17.4 | 24.4 | 19.6 | 9.9 | 37,485 |
| 1975 | 56,245 | 6.6 | 7.0 | 15.4 | 16.2 | 22.3 | 21.5 | 11.2 | 38,301 |
| 1980 | 60,309 | 6.9 | 6.3 | 14.8 | 14.6 | 21.5 | 21.8 | 14.0 | 40,079 |
| 1985 | 63,558 | 7.8 | 6.3 | 14.3 | 14.2 | 19.4 | 21.3 | 16.7 | 40,443 |
| 1990 | 66,322 | 7.4 | 5.9 | 13.2 | 13.8 | 19.3 | 21.3 | 19.2 | 42,440 |
| 1994 | 69,313 | 8.1 | 6.4 | 14.1 | 14.0 | 17.8 | 20.2 | 19.4 | 41,059 |
| 1995 | 69,597 | 7.2 | 6.3 | 13.9 | 13.8 | 18.3 | 20.7 | 19.7 | 41,810 |
| 1996 | 70,241 | 7.6 | 6.1 | 13.5 | 13.5 | 17.7 | 21.3 | 20.3 | 42,300 |
| **WHITE** | | | | | | | | | |
| 1970 | 46,535 | 6.1 | 5.8 | 14.3 | 17.4 | 25.2 | 20.6 | 10.6 | 38,887 |
| 1975 | 49,873 | 5.4 | 6.3 | 14.8 | 16.1 | 22.9 | 22.6 | 11.9 | 39,834 |
| 1980 | 52,710 | 5.5 | 5.5 | 14.1 | 14.6 | 22.2 | 23.0 | 15.0 | 41,759 |
| 1985 | 54,991 | 6.2 | 5.6 | 13.7 | 14.3 | 20.0 | 22.2 | 18.1 | 42,509 |
| 1990 | 56,803 | 5.5 | 5.2 | 12.7 | 13.9 | 19.8 | 22.4 | 20.5 | 44,315 |
| 1994 | 58,444 | 6.3 | 5.7 | 13.6 | 14.1 | 18.4 | 21.2 | 20.9 | 43,284 |

**B15-2. Money Income of Families—Percent Distribution, by Income Level, Race, and Hispanic Origin, in Constant (1996) Dollars: 1970–1996 *(continued)***

| Year | Number of families (1,000s) | Percent under $10,000 | Percent $10,000-$14,999 | Percent $15,000-$24,999 | Percent $25,000-$34,999 | Percent $35,000-$49,999 | Percent $50,000-$74,999 | Percent $75,000 and over | Median income (dollars) |
|------|------|------|------|------|------|------|------|------|------|
| 1995 | 58,872 | 5.5 | 5.7 | 13.4 | 13.8 | 18.7 | 21.7 | 21.2 | 43,905 |
| 1996 | 58,934 | 5.9 | 5.4 | 13.0 | 13.5 | 18.3 | 22.3 | 21.7 | 44,756 |
| **BLACK** | | | | | | | | | |
| 1970 | 4,928 | 17.9 | 12.3 | 22.8 | 16.8 | 16.8 | 10.3 | 3.2 | 23,854 |
| 1975 | 5,586 | 17.1 | 13.6 | 20.3 | 17.5 | 16.4 | 11.7 | 3.5 | 24,509 |
| 1980 | 6,317 | 18.3 | 13.1 | 20.5 | 14.3 | 16.4 | 12.6 | 4.9 | 24,162 |
| 1985 | 6,921 | 20.4 | 11.6 | 19.5 | 13.9 | 15.4 | 13.1 | 6.3 | 24,477 |
| 1990 | 7,471 | 20.8 | 11.2 | 17.0 | 13.5 | 15.8 | 13.3 | 8.3 | 25,717 |
| 1994 | 8,093 | 20.0 | 10.9 | 17.7 | 14.0 | 14.4 | 14.1 | 9.0 | 26,148 |
| 1995 | 8,055 | 18.8 | 10.6 | 18.0 | 14.3 | 16.1 | 13.4 | 8.6 | 26,737 |
| 1996 | 8,455 | 18.9 | 10.7 | 17.6 | 14.3 | 15.1 | 14.4 | 9.0 | 26,522 |
| **HISPANIC ORIGIN[2]** | | | | | | | | | |
| 1975 | 2,499 | 13.1 | 11.6 | 22.3 | 18.3 | 19.7 | 11.2 | 3.7 | 26,665 |
| 1980 | 3,235 | 12.8 | 10.7 | 21.2 | 17.2 | 18.4 | 14.0 | 5.7 | 28,055 |
| 1985 | 4,206 | 14.3 | 12.1 | 19.6 | 15.8 | 17.0 | 13.8 | 7.5 | 27,745 |
| 1990 | 4,981 | 14.1 | 11.6 | 19.1 | 15.6 | 17.6 | 13.8 | 8.2 | 28,128 |
| 1994 | 6,202 | 16.4 | 12.8 | 19.4 | 15.3 | 15.6 | 12.4 | 8.3 | 25,746 |
| 1995 | 6,287 | 15.5 | 11.9 | 22.3 | 15.8 | 14.4 | 12.8 | 7.2 | 25,295 |
| 1996 | 6,631 | 14.6 | 11.6 | 21.5 | 15.6 | 15.2 | 13.0 | 8.5 | 26,179 |

*Notes:*
1. Includes other races not shown separately.
2. Persons of Hispanic origin may be of any race.
*General Note:* Constant dollars based on CPI-U-X1 deflator. Families as of March of following year. Beginning with 1980, based on householder concept and restricted to primary families. Based on *Current Population Survey.*

*Source: Statistical Abstract of the United States 1998,* No. 745; <http://www.census.gov/prod/3/98pubs/98statab/sasec14.pdf>. Underlying data from U.S. Bureau of the *Census, Current Population Reports,* P60-197.

## B16. SELECTED MEASURES OF HOUSEHOLD INCOME, 1969—1996

### B16-1. Selected Measures of Household Income, 1969–1996: All Households

| Year | Number of households (1,000s) | Percent of all Households | Median income-value | Householder Poverty rate | Percent with specified level of relative income Low | Middle | High |
|------|------|------|------|------|------|------|------|
| 1969 | 63,406 | 100 | $33,072 | 13.9 | 20.7 | 67.2 | 12.1 |
| 1970 | 64,385 | 100 | $33,025 | 14.2 | 20.7 | 66.8 | 12.6 |
| 1971 | 66,679 | 100 | $32,763 | 14.0 | 20.7 | 66.3 | 12.9 |
| 1972 | 68,253 | 100 | $34,094 | 12.8 | 21.0 | 66.2 | 12.9 |
| 1973 | 69,805 | 100 | $34,674 | 11.9 | 20.9 | 66.1 | 13.0 |
| 1974 | 71,163 | 100 | $33,557 | 11.7 | 20.5 | 67.2 | 12.4 |
| 1975 | 72,867 | 100 | $32,779 | 12.7 | 20.9 | 66.3 | 12.9 |
| 1976 | 74,142 | 100 | $33,440 | 12.4 | 20.9 | 66.5 | 12.6 |
| 1977 | 76,030 | 100 | $33,671 | 12.0 | 21.2 | 66.0 | 12.9 |
| 1978 | 77,330 | 100 | $34,867 | 11.8 | 21.0 | 65.9 | 13.1 |
| 1979 | 80,776 | 100 | $34,666 | 12.1 | 21.2 | 65.7 | 13.1 |
| 1980 | 82,368 | 100 | $33,754 | 13.3 | 21.2 | 65.2 | 13.6 |
| 1981 | 83,527 | 100 | $33,087 | 14.0 | 21.6 | 64.1 | 14.3 |
| 1982 | 83,918 | 100 | $32,847 | 14.5 | 22.0 | 63.4 | 14.6 |
| 1983 | 85,290 | 100 | $32,941 | 14.5 | 22.1 | 63.1 | 14.8 |
| 1984 | 86,789 | 100 | $33,781 | 13.7 | 22.1 | 63.0 | 14.9 |
| 1985 | 88,458 | 100 | $34,413 | 13.6 | 22.2 | 62.6 | 15.2 |

## B16-1. Selected Measures of Household Income, 1969–1996: All Households *(continued)*

| Year | Number of households (1,000s) | Percent of all Households | Median income-value | Householder Poverty rate | Percent with specified level of relative income | | |
|------|------|------|------|------|------|------|------|
| | | | | | Low | Middle | High |
| 1986 | 89,479 | 100 | $35,574 | 13.3 | 22.3 | 62.3 | 15.4 |
| 1987 | 91,124 | 100 | $35,910 | 13.0 | 22.5 | 62.4 | 15.1 |
| 1988 | 92,830 | 100 | $35,982 | 12.7 | 22.5 | 62.1 | 15.4 |
| 1989 | 93,347 | 100 | $36,598 | 12.2 | 22.4 | 62.3 | 15.3 |
| 1990 | 94,312 | 100 | $35,894 | 13.0 | 22.0 | 62.7 | 15.3 |
| 1991 | 95,676 | 100 | $34,559 | 13.5 | 22.2 | 62.2 | 15.7 |
| 1992 | 96,426 | 100 | $33,897 | 14.1 | 22.7 | 61.5 | 15.9 |
| 1993 | 97,262 | 100 | $33,660 | 14.2 | 22.7 | 60.5 | 16.8 |
| 1994 | 99,087 | 100 | $34,027 | 13.8 | 22.3 | 60.8 | 16.9 |
| 1995 | 99,683 | 100 | $35,004 | 13.0 | 22.1 | 61.3 | 16.6 |
| 1996 | 101,081 | 100 | $35,172 | 13.0 | 22.2 | 61.2 | 16.6 |

*Source:* U.S. Bureau of the Census, *March Current Population Surveys,* Table A5; <http://www.census.gov/hhes/income/mednhhld/ta5.html>.

## B17. GROSS SAVING AND INVESTMENT

### B17-1. Gross Saving and Investment, Totals: 1990–1997, in Billions of Dollars

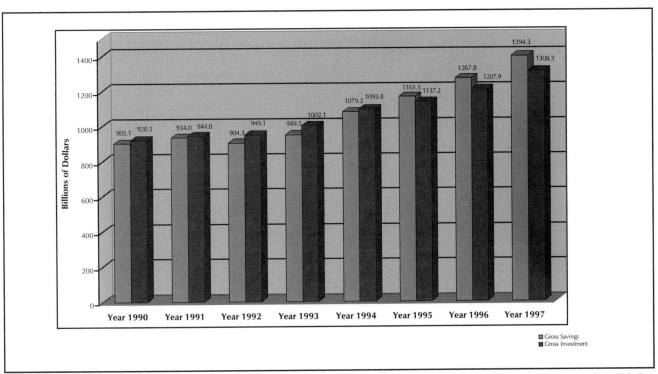

*Source: Statistical Abstract of the United States 1998,* No. 725; <http://wwwcensusgov/prod/3/98pubs/98statab/sasec14pdf>. Underlying data from U.S. Bureau of Economic Analysis, *National Income and Product Accounts of the United States, 1929-94,* Vol. 1; and *Survey of Current Business,* August 1997 and May 1998

## B17-2. Gross Saving and Investment: 1990–1993, in Billions of Dollars

| ITEM | 1990 | 1991 | 1992 | 1993 |
|---|---|---|---|---|
| Gross saving | 903.1 | 934.0 | 904.3 | 949.5 |
| Gross private saving | 860.3 | 930.6 | 970.7 | 979.3 |
| Personal saving | 221.3 | 259.5 | 285.6 | 248.5 |
| Undistributed corporate profits[1] | 104.7 | 114.8 | 115.5 | 131.9 |
| Undistributed profits | 79.4 | 77.7 | 93.9 | 104.5 |
| Inventory valuation adjustment | -13.5 | 4.0 | -7.5 | -8.5 |
| Capital consumption adjustment | 38.9 | 33.1 | 29.1 | 36.0 |
| Corporate consumption of fixed capital | 350.3 | 364.5 | 376.4 | 388.4 |
| Noncorporate consumption of fixed capital | 184.0 | 191.9 | 209.0 | 206.1 |
| Wage accruals less disbursements | (-) | (-) | -15.8 | 4.4 |
| Gross government saving | 42.7 | 3.3 | -66.5 | -29.8 |
| Federal | -94.0 | -132.2 | -215.0 | -182.7 |
| State and local | 136.7 | 135.5 | 148.6 | 152.9 |
| Capital grants received by the US (net) | (-) | (-) | (-) | (-) |
| Gross investment | 920.5 | 944.0 | 949.1 | 1002.1 |
| Gross private domestic investment | 799.7 | 736.2 | 790.4 | 876.2 |
| Gross government investment | 199.4 | 200.5 | 209.1 | 204.5 |
| Net foreign investment | -78.5 | 7.3 | -50.5 | -78.6 |
| Statistical discrepancy | 17.4 | 10.1 | 44.8 | 52.6 |

*Notes:*
(-) Represents or rounds to zero
1. With inventory valuation and capital consumption adjustments

*Source: Statistical Abstract of the United States 1998*, No. 725; <http://wwwcensusgov/prod/3/98pubs/98statab/sasec14pdf>. Underlying data from U.S. Bureau of Economic Analysis, *National Income and Product Accounts of the United States, 1929-94,* Vol. 1; and *Survey of Current Business*, August 1997 and May 1998

## B17-3. Gross Saving and Investment: 1994–1997, in Billions of Dollars

| ITEM | 1994 | 1995 | 1996 | 1997 |
|---|---|---|---|---|
| Gross saving | 1079.2 | 1165.5 | 1267.8 | 1394.3 |
| Gross private saving | 1030.2 | 1093.1 | 1125.5 | 1164.2 |
| Personal saving | 210.6 | 254.6 | 239.6 | 226.7 |
| Undistributed corporate profits[1] | 167.6 | 172.4 | 202.1 | 219.5 |
| Undistributed profits | 132.3 | 145.0 | 142.8 | 144.2 |
| Inventory valuation adjustment | -16.1 | -24.3 | -2.5 | 5.5 |
| Capital consumption adjustment | 51.4 | 51.6 | 61.8 | 69.7 |
| Corporate consumption of fixed capital | 412.3 | 428.9 | 452.3 | 475.6 |
| Noncorporate consumption of fixed capital | 226.3 | 224.1 | 230.5 | 241.2 |
| Wage accruals less disbursements | 13.3 | 13.1 | 1.1 | 1.2 |
| Gross government saving | 49.0 | 72.4 | 142.3 | 230.0 |
| Federal | -117.2 | -103.6 | -39.2 | 42.8 |
| State and local | 166.2 | 176.0 | 181.5 | 187.3 |
| Capital grants received by the US (net) | (-) | (-) | (-) | (-) |
| Gross investment | 1093.8 | 1137.2 | 1207.9 | 1308.3 |
| Gross private domestic investment | 1007.9 | 1038.2 | 1116.5 | 1242.5 |
| Gross government investment | 205.9 | 213.4 | 224.3 | 226.0 |
| Net foreign investment | -120.0 | -114.4 | -132.9 | -160.2 |
| Statistical discrepancy | 14.6 | -28.2 | -52.9 | -86.0 |

*Notes:*
(-) Represents or rounds to zero
1. With inventory valuation and capital consumption adjustments

*Source: Statistical Abstract of the United States 1998*, No. 725; <http://wwwcensusgov/prod/3/98pubs/98statab/sasec14pdf>. Underlying data from US Bureau of Economic Analysis, *National Income and Product Accounts of the United States, 1929-94,* Vol. 1; and *Survey of Current Business*, August 1997 and May 1998

## B18. FLOW OF FUNDS ACCOUNTS—INDIVIDUAL SAVINGS

### B18-1. Flow of Funds Accounts—Composition of Individuals' Savings: 1980–1990, in Billions of Dollars.

| COMPOSITION OF SAVINGS | 1980 | 1985 | 1990 |
|---|---|---|---|
| Increase in financial assets | 323.2 | 622.5 | 590.8 |
| Checkable deposits and currency | 9.2 | 41.8 | -19.0 |
| Time and savings deposits | 125.5 | 119.7 | 48.7 |
| Money market fund shares | 23.9 | 2.3 | 26.9 |
| Securities | 3.1 | 81.6 | 198.1 |
| Open market paper | -5.0 | -7.0 | 6.2 |
| US savings bonds | -7.3 | 5.3 | 8.5 |
| Other Treasury securities | 19.6 | 3.7 | 61.3 |
| Agency securities | 4.8 | 12.2 | 41.5 |
| Municipal securities | 8.3 | 94.9 | 27.7 |
| Corporate and foreign bonds | -14.6 | 2.6 | 45.1 |
| Corporate equities | -4.3 | -111.2 | -28.8 |
| Mutual fund shares | 1.8 | 81.2 | 36.6 |
| Private life insurance reserves | 9.7 | 10.4 | 25.3 |
| Private insured pension reserves | 22.3 | 55.6 | 95.9 |
| Private noninsured pension reserves | 60.2 | 126.6 | 64.1 |
| Govt insurance and pension reserves | 35.8 | 69.0 | 85.7 |
| Investment in tangible assets | 4.1 | 11.2 | 32.9 |
| Miscellaneous assets | 29.2 | 103.5 | 30.8 |
| Gross investment in tangible assets | 407.5 | 661.1 | 815.8 |
| Consumption of fixed capital | 296.0 | 409.8 | 577.9 |
| Net investment in tangible assets | 111.4 | 251.3 | 237.9 |
| Residential structures | 58.8 | 105.2 | 113.3 |
| Other fixed assets[1] | 31.5 | 35.4 | 23.3 |
| Consumer durables | 27.3 | 103.9 | 98.4 |
| Inventories[1] | -6.2 | 6.8 | 2.9 |
| Net increase in liabilities | 196.6 | 435.5 | 267.3 |
| Mortgage debt on nonfarm homes | 94.1 | 174.7 | 226.2 |
| Other mortgage debt[1] | 50.9 | 98.1 | 16.9 |
| Consumer credit | 2.3 | 73.9 | 16.1 |
| Policy loans | 6.7 | -0.1 | 4.1 |
| Security credit | 7.3 | 18.9 | -3.7 |
| Other liabilities[1] | 35.3 | 70.1 | 7.7 |
| Personal saving (Flow of Funds measure)[2] | 238.0 | 438.3 | 561.4 |
| Personal saving as a percentage of disposable personal income | 12.1 | 14.6 | 13.5 |

*Notes:*
1. Includes corporate farms.
2. Net acquisition of financial assets plus net investment in tangible assets minus net increase in liabilities.
Minus sign (-) indicates decrease.

*General Note:* Combined statement for households, farm business, and nonfarm noncorporate business.

*Source: Statistical Abstract of the United States 1998,* No. 731; <http://wwwcensusgov/prod/3/98pubs/98statab/sasec14pdf>. Underlying data from Board of Governors of the Federal Reserve System, *Flow of Funds Accounts,* quarterly.

## B18-2. Flow of Funds Accounts—Composition of Individuals' Savings: 1991–1996, in Billions of Dollars.

**COMPOSITION OF SAVINGS**

| Increase in financial assets | 1991 | 1992 | 1993 | 1994 | 1995 | 1996 |
|---|---|---|---|---|---|---|
| Checkable deposits and currency | 418.1 | 529.8 | 512.4 | 542.8 | 492.7 | 541.5 |
| Time and savings deposits | 43.2 | 98.9 | 54.5 | -8.9 | -38.2 | -47.7 |
| Money market fund shares | -54.2 | -76.5 | -106.9 | -5.8 | 152.6 | 144.4 |
| Securities | 9.1 | -41.3 | 5.9 | 13.7 | 95.5 | 90.8 |
| Open market paper | 127.4 | 252.3 | 194.3 | 205.7 | -56.5 | -35.7 |
| US savings bonds | -29.9 | -3.3 | 15.6 | -10.5 | 0.3 | 11.4 |
| Other Treasury securities | 11.9 | 19.1 | 14.7 | 8.0 | 5.1 | 2.0 |
| Agency securities | -22.0 | 59.6 | 11.8 | 153.2 | 5.0 | -62.1 |
| Municipal securities | 12.3 | 36.8 | -31.4 | 149.4 | -31.9 | 54.8 |
| Corporate and foreign bonds | 40.2 | -27.2 | -27.2 | -51.9 | -50.7 | -21.4 |
| Corporate equities | 29.6 | -8.5 | 37.3 | 2.1 | 51.4 | 27.7 |
| Mutual fund shares | -23.6 | 33.1 | -57.7 | -138.1 | -176.1 | -245.5 |
| Private life insurance reserves | 109.0 | 142.8 | 231.3 | 93.7 | 140.4 | 197.4 |
| Private insured pension reserves | 25.6 | 27.7 | 35.7 | 34.3 | 44.8 | 35.2 |
| Private noninsured pension reserves | 46.4 | 76.7 | 86.3 | 71.2 | 66.7 | 69.2 |
| Govt insurance and pension reserves | 72.5 | 81.8 | 82.7 | 87.1 | 98.3 | 85.2 |
| Investment in tangible assets | 83.0 | 83.7 | 81.8 | 93.7 | 75.4 | 97.4 |
| Miscellaneous assets | 17.5 | -7.1 | 0.9 | 17.8 | -49.7 | -25.0 |
| Gross investment in tangible assets | 46.4 | 32.4 | 76.9 | 30.8 | 101.9 | 123.5 |
| Consumption of fixed capital | 758.3 | 823.0 | 897.9 | 1021.5 | 1050.9 | 1107.4 |
| Net investment in tangible assets | 612.4 | 633.9 | 674.2 | 716.3 | 724.5 | 756.2 |
| Residential structures | 145.8 | 189.1 | 223.7 | 305.2 | 326.4 | 351.2 |
| Other fixed assets[1] | 92.0 | 114.5 | 142.3 | 164.7 | 164.0 | 178.9 |
| Consumer durables | 4.1 | -10.1 | 4.8 | 22.2 | 53.8 | 60.5 |
| Inventories[1] | 50.9 | 79.6 | 81.5 | 104.3 | 109.1 | 112.8 |
| Net increase in liabilities | -1.1 | 5.1 | -4.8 | 13.9 | -0.5 | -1.0 |
| Mortgage debt on nonfarm homes | 217.4 | 204.0 | 297.1 | 401.6 | 441.9 | 478.0 |
| Other mortgage debt[1] | 177.7 | 188.9 | 186.6 | 203.4 | 195.7 | 277.4 |
| Consumer credit | 5.3 | -28.8 | -17.8 | 3.7 | 21.5 | 45.7 |
| Policy loans | -13.7 | 5.0 | 61.5 | 126.3 | 141.6 | 94.4 |
| Security credit | 4.8 | 5.7 | 5.6 | 7.8 | 10.5 | 7.1 |
| Other liabilities[1] | 16.3 | -1.6 | 22.6 | -1.1 | 3.5 | 14.5 |
| Personal saving (Flow of Funds measure)[2] | 27.1 | 34.8 | 38.5 | 61.5 | 69.1 | 38.8 |
| Personal saving as a percentage of disposable | 346.5 | 514.9 | 439.0 | 446.4 | 377.2 | 414.7 |
| personal income | 8.0 | 11.2 | 9.2 | 8.9 | 7.1 | 7.4 |

*Notes:*
1. Includes corporate farms.
2. Net acquisition of financial assets plus net investment in tangible assets minus net increase in liabilities.
Minus sign (-) indicates decrease.
*General Note:* Combined statement for households, farm business, and nonfarm noncorporate business.

*Source: Statistical Abstract of the United States 1998*, No. 731; <http://wwwcensusgov/prod/3/98pubs/98statab/sasec14pdf>. Underlying data from Board of Governors of the Federal Reserve System, *Flow of Funds Accounts*, quarterly.

## B19. IRAS AND 401(K) PLANS

### B19-1. Individual Retirement Accounts (IRA) Plans—Value, by Type of Holder: 1985–1991, as of December 31, in Billions of Dollars, Estimated

| Type of holder | 1985 | 1989 | 1990 | 1991 |
|---|---|---|---|---|
| Total | 200 | 455 | 529 | 657 |
| Savings institutions | 56 | 98 | 95 | 91 |
| Commercial banks | 52 | 99 | 119 | 134 |
| Mutual funds | 32 | 112 | 127 | 169 |
| Self directed | 29 | 82 | 117 | 181 |
| Life insurance companies | 17 | 38 | 42 | 50 |
| Credit unions | 14 | 26 | 29 | 32 |

*Source: Statistical Abstract of the United States 1998*, No. 845; <http://wwwcensusgov/prod/3/98pubs/98statab/sasec16pdf>. Underlying data from Investment Company Institute, Washington, DC, *Mutual Fund Fact Book*, annual (copyright).

### B19-2. Individual Retirement Accounts (IRA) Plans—Value, by Type of Holder: 1992–1996, as of December 31, in Billions of Dollars, Estimated

| Type of holder | 1992 | 1993 | 1994 | 1995 | 1996 |
|---|---|---|---|---|---|
| Total | 746 | 868 | 941 | 1,170 | 1,347 |
| Savings institutions | 85 | 76 | 72 | 73 | 72 |
| Commercial banks | 137 | 134 | 136 | 143 | 144 |
| Mutual funds | 211 | 284 | 305 | 411 | 511 |
| Self directed | 225 | 271 | 318 | 415 | 483 |
| Life insurance companies | 56 | 70 | 79 | 94 | 106 |
| Credit unions | 32 | 32 | 32 | 34 | 33 |

*Source: Statistical Abstract of the United States 1998*, No. 845; <http://wwwcensusgov/prod/3/98pubs/98statab/sasec16pdf>. Underlying data from Investment Company Institute, Washington, DC, *Mutual Fund Fact Book*, annual (copyright).

### B19-3. 401(k) Plan Total Assets—1985–1996

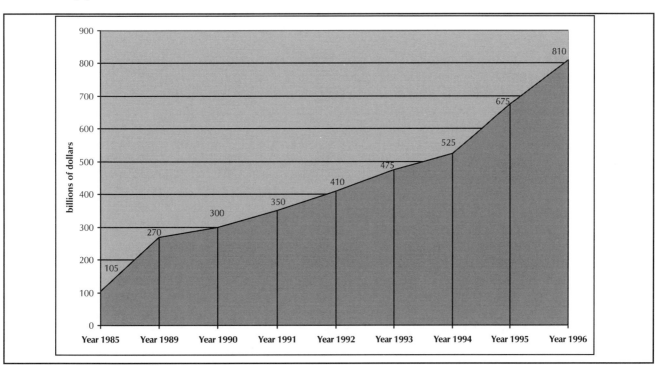

*Source:* Spectrum Group, Windsor, CT, *1997 Marketplace Update,* 1997 (copyright).

## B19-4. 401(k) Plan Assets—Type of Assets, 1997

| Type of Asset | Percent of companies offering investment option, 1997 | Assets, 1997 Amount in billion dollars | Assets 1997, Percent distribution |
|---|---|---|---|
| **Total** | (X) | 985 | 100 |
| Guaranteed investment account[1] | 52 | 177 | 18 |
| Equity | 96 | 325 | 33 |
| Money market | 55 | 30 | 3 |
| Balanced account | 64 | 108 | 11 |
| Bond fund | 69 | 69 | 7 |
| Company stock | 22 | 207 | 21 |
| Other | (NA) | (NA) | (NA) |

*Notes for Tables B19-4 and B19-5:*
NA Not available.
X Not applicable.
1. Covers bank certificate of deposits, guaranteed investment contracts (GIC's), GIC alternatives, and insurance company participating contracts.
2. Includes 401(k) plans

*Source:* Spectrum Group, Windsor, CT, *1997 Marketplace Update,* 1997 (copyright).

## B19-5. 401(k) Plan Assets—Type of Financial Institution Managing Assets, 1997

| Financial institution managing assets | Assets, 1997, Amount in billion dollars | Assets 1997, Percent distribution |
|---|---|---|
| All defined contribution plans[2] | 1,730 | 100 |
| Insurance companies | 450 | 26 |
| Banks | 433 | 25 |
| Mutual fund groups | 588 | 34 |
| Other | 260 | 15 |
| 401(k) plans | 985 | 100 |
| Insurance companies | 217 | 22 |
| Banks | 207 | 21 |
| Mutual fund groups | 414 | 42 |
| Other | 148 | 15 |

*Notes for Tables B19-4 and B19-5:*
1. Covers bank certificate of deposits, guaranteed investment contracts (GIC's), GIC alternatives, and insurance company participating contracts.
2. Includes 401(k) plans

*Source:* Spectrum Group, Windsor, CT, *1997 Marketplace Update,* 1997 (copyright).

# B20. NONFINANCIAL ASSETS HELD BY FAMILIES, BY TYPE OF ASSET

## B20-1. Nonfinancial Assets Held by Families, Percent of Families Owning Assets, by Type of Asset: 1995

| Age of family head and family income | Total | Vehicles | Primary residence | Investment real estate | Business | Other nonfinancial |
|---|---|---|---|---|---|---|
| **All families, total** | **91.1** | **84.2** | **64.7** | **18.0** | **11.1** | **9.0** |
| Age of family head: | | | | | | |
| Under 35 years old | 87.4 | 84.1 | 37.9 | 7.0 | 8.4 | 7.3 |
| 35 to 44 years old | 91.0 | 85.0 | 64.7 | 14.7 | 14.4 | 10.1 |
| 45 to 54 years old | 93.8 | 88.3 | 75.4 | 25.0 | 15.4 | 11.3 |
| 55 to 64 years old | 94.1 | 88.4 | 82.3 | 27.3 | 12.6 | 10.2 |
| 65 to 74 years old | 92.7 | 82.4 | 79.4 | 27.9 | 8.7 | 9.0 |
| 75 years old and over | 89.9 | 72.2 | 72.5 | 16.3 | 3.8 | 5.6 |
| Family income: | | | | | | |
| Less than $10,000 | 68.6 | 56.6 | 37.5 | 7.2 | 4.8 | 3.7 |
| $10,000 to $24,999 | 90.2 | 83.3 | 56.2 | 11.3 | 7.0 | 6.3 |
| $25,000 to $49,999 | 96.8 | 92.3 | 68.0 | 16.6 | 9.8 | 9.7 |
| $50,000 to $99,999 | 99.0 | 93.4 | 84.7 | 26.9 | 16.8 | 11.3 |
| $100,000 and more | 99.4 | 90.8 | 90.9 | 51.6 | 32.6 | 23.9 |
| Current work status of householder: | | | | | | |
| Professional, managerial | 96.6 | 91.1 | 70.5 | 24.8 | 9.7 | 14.5 |
| Technical, sales, clerical | 93.0 | 88.0 | 63.4 | 11.4 | 6.4 | 10.9 |
| Precision production | 97.1 | 93.2 | 67.0 | 16.1 | 7.4 | 8.8 |
| Machine operators and laborers | 93.8 | 92.1 | 61.0 | 14.1 | 5.6 | 6.8 |
| Service occupations | 86.9 | 83.7 | 50.4 | 9.0 | 3.7 | 2.1 |
| Self-employed | 96.1 | 86.1 | 74.2 | 33.1 | 58.2 | 15.5 |
| Retired | 88.2 | 76.3 | 70.5 | 18.9 | 3.3 | 5.8 |
| Other not working | 67.3 | 59.7 | 35.3 | 8.5 | 4.1 | 6.0 |
| Tenure: | | | | | | |
| Owner occupied | 100.0 | 90.8 | 100.0 | 22.8 | 13.7 | 10.5 |
| Renter occupied or other | 74.8 | 72.2 | (-) | 9.0 | 6.5 | 6.5 |

*Notes:*
(-) represents zero.
*General Notes:* Families include one-person units and, as used in this table, are comparable to the Bureau of Census household concept. Based on *Survey of Consumer Finance.*

*Source: Statistical Abstract of the United States 1998,* No. 768; <http://wwwcensusgov/prod/3/98pubs/98statab/sasec14pdf>. Underlying data from Board of Governors of the Federal Reserve System, *Federal Reserve Bulletin,* January 1997, and unpublished revisions.

## B20-2. Nonfinancial Assets Held by Families, Median Value[1], by Type of Asset: 1995, in Thousands of Dollars

| Age of family head and family income | Total | Vehicles | Primary residence | Investment real estate | Business | Other nonfinancial |
|---|---|---|---|---|---|---|
| **All families, total** | **82.8** | **9.9** | **89.0** | **50.0** | **45.0** | **8.8** |
| **Age of family head:** | | | | | | |
| Under 35 years old | 21.7 | 8.9 | 76.0 | 30.0 | 22.0 | 5.0 |
| 35 to 44 years old | 95.9 | 10.7 | 95.0 | 47.0 | 35.0 | 10.0 |
| 45 to 54 years old | 113.0 | 12.6 | 100.0 | 59.0 | 70.0 | 10.0 |
| 55 to 64 years old | 108.0 | 11.3 | 85.0 | 75.0 | 65.0 | 10.0 |
| 65 to 74 years old | 94.6 | 8.2 | 82.5 | 57.0 | 100.5 | 14.0 |
| 75 years old and over | 79.0 | 5.3 | 80.0 | 22.4 | 37.5 | 8.0 |
| **Family income:** | | | | | | |
| Less than $10,000 | 14.0 | 3.6 | 38.5 | 16.2 | 50.0 | 5.2 |
| $10,000 to $24,999 | 44.7 | 6.1 | 65.0 | 26.4 | 30.0 | 7.5 |
| $25,000 to $49,999 | 81.9 | 11.0 | 80.0 | 45.0 | 25.0 | 5.8 |
| $50,000 to $99,999 | 145.7 | 16.2 | 120.0 | 60.0 | 33.0 | 15.0 |
| $100,000 and more | 304.5 | 23.8 | 200.0 | 130.0 | 320.0 | 18.0 |

**B20-2. Nonfinancial Assets Held by Families, Median Value[1], by Type of Asset: 1995, in Thousands of Dollars** *(continued)*

| Age of family head and family income | Total | Vehicles | Primary residence | Investment real estate | Business | Other nonfinancial |
|---|---|---|---|---|---|---|
| **Current work status of householder:** | | | | | | |
| Professional, managerial | 129.1 | 12.5 | 130.0 | 55.5 | 18.0 | 10.6 |
| Technical, sales, clerical | 82.5 | 10.3 | 90.0 | 44.5 | 24.0 | 9.0 |
| Precision production | 72.7 | 12.1 | 80.0 | 37.5 | 20.0 | 5.0 |
| Machine operators and laborers | 56.3 | 10.8 | 65.0 | 30.0 | 20.0 | 8.0 |
| Service occupations | 36.3 | 7.0 | 70.0 | 30.0 | 80.2 | 10.0 |
| Self-employed | 180.1 | 12.7 | 120.0 | 100.0 | 75.0 | 8.0 |
| Retired | 78.0 | 7.4 | 75.0 | 45.0 | 100.0 | 10.0 |
| Other not working | 22.0 | 6.4 | 60.0 | 50.0 | 21.0 | 7.0 |
| **Tenure:** | | | | | | |
| Owner occupied | 115.8 | 11.9 | 89.0 | 50.0 | 55.0 | 10.0 |
| Renter occupied or other | 7.5 | 6.4 | (B) | 35.0 | 22.0 | 5.0 |

*Notes:*
(-) represents zero.
B Base figure too small to meet statistical standards for reliability of derived figure.
1. Median value of financial asset for families holding such assets.
*General Notes:* Families include one-person units and, as used in this table, are comparable to the Bureau of Census household concept. Based on *Survey of Consumer Finance.*

*Source: Statistical Abstract of the United States 1998*, No. 768; <http://wwwcensusgov/prod/3/98pubs/98statab/sasec14pdf>. Underlying data from Board of Governors of the Federal Reserve System, *Federal Reserve Bulletin*, January 1997, and unpublished revisions.

# C. Business and Corporate Wealth

## GENERAL OVERVIEW

Section C examines wealth in the business and corporate environment. The indicators presented—such as gross product, assets and liabilities, and income and expenses—examine the sources of corporate and business wealth, along with its disposition and uses. The data will help users to see how businesses create wealth and use it to their advantage—for growth, for further investment, and to generate income and wealth for individual investors. (Information on consumption of business services can be found in Section F.)

## EXPLANATION OF INDICATORS

**C1. Number of Business Tax Returns, Business Receipts, and Corporate Balance Sheet:** These first three charts offer basic background information on the business scene in the United States. Including the number of tax returns filed, receipts reported, and summarized balance sheet information, the data provide information on scope of business activity, breadth of income generated, and the wealth generated by business activity.

**C2. Corporations—Selected Financial Items, by Industry:** The next two tables offer information on business activity broken down by type of industry. This helps the user to investigate the income and wealth-generating capacity of the various sectors in the U.S. economy.

**C3. Corporations—Annual Percent Change in Receipts, by Industry:** This next table charts the annual change (growth, in most cases) in corporate income across various sectors. Starting in 1980, it presents a midrange timeframe, rooting the more current data in prior performance.

**C4. Corporations—Selected Financial Items, by Asset-Size Class and Industry:** This table shows the number of enterprises (by tax returns) and amount of assets, receipts, deductions, and net income by industry and by asset class size. Also, broken down by industry, it helps the user to investigate the income and wealth-

generating performance of companies of various sizes and in various sectors.

**C5. Corporations—Receipts, Percent Distribution by Asset-Size Class and Industry:** This table and chart show the percentage of total corporate receipts reported by corporations of various sizes, classified by amount of assets and industry. It offers a sectoral breakdown and presents a snapshot from the mid-decade, 1995. The chart offers a visual representation of the data, helping the user to visualize the performance of various sectors and size-classes of companies.

**C6. Corporate Profits, by Industry:** The next chart and two tables present information on corporate profits. The first analyzes corporate profits across a short-term timeframe (1990–1996), breaking corporate profits up into such items as pre-tax profits, taxes paid, and dividends. The next chart summarizes and compares pre-tax profits and profits after tax, helping the user to understand the share of wealth generated by corporations but consumed by public needs and interests. The following table shows the distribution of total pre-tax and after-tax corporate profits across the various industries in the U.S. economy.

**C7. U.S. Largest Public Companies:** The next three tables show the activity of the largest publicly held corporations, by industry, in terms of profitability, growth in sales, growth in earnings, and debt to capital ratio. These indicators represent hallmarks of corporate success. The data allow users to compare the performance of various industries in terms of their capacity to generate wealth.

**C8. 1000 Largest Industrial Corporations:** The next two tables present profits, earnings, and return information, for the 1000 largest companies in the U.S., broken down by industry. As with the previous set of tables, these allow a comparison of various industries in the economy and their capacity to generate income and wealth, not just for corporate reinvestment but for individual investment purposes as well.

**C9. U.S. Multinational Companies:** The next four tables present various data on the productive and income-generating capacity of multinational companies in the United States. The data categorize multinationals into those with U.S.-parent ownership and majority foreign-owned affiliates.

**C10. Net Stock of Fixed Private Capital:** This chart presents the total of privately owned capital from 1990 through 1996 in the U.S.. The data represent the total value of durable and non-durable income-generating

goods in stock as of the end of each of the years reported.

**C11. Farms:** The next five tables detail the amount of farm wealth in the United States, including such indicators as acreage, land value, value of products. The data are presented in terms of type of ownership (individual, family, partnership, and corporation) and size (acreage) of farms.

## C1. NUMBER OF BUSINESS TAX RETURNS, BUSINESS RECEIPTS, AND CORPORATE BALANCE SHEET

### C1-1. Number of Business Tax Returns, by Type of Enterprise: 1980–1995

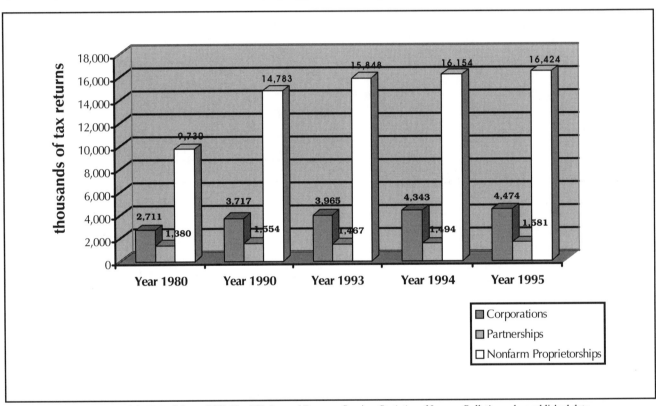

*Source: Statistical Abstract of the United States 1998, No. 855; Internal Revenue Service, Statistics of Income Bulletin; and unpublished data*

## C1-2. Business Receipts, by Type of Enterprise: 1980–1995

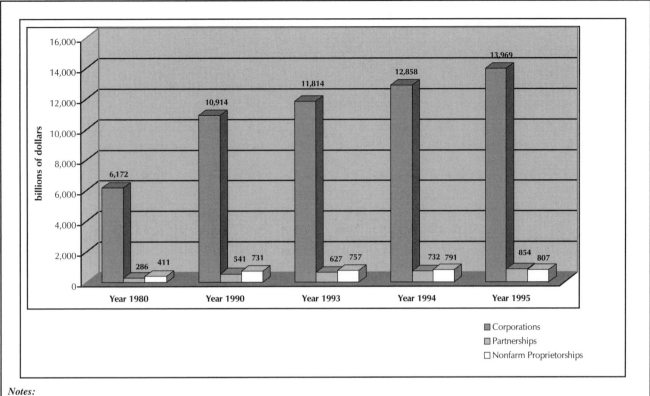

**Notes:**
Excludes investment income except for partnerships and corporations in finance, insurance, and real estate. Starting in 1990, investment income no longer included for S corporations.

*Source: Statistical Abstract of the United States 1998*, No. 855; Internal Revenue Service, *Statistics of Income Bulletin*; and unpublished data

## C1-3. Corporate Balance Sheet, Total of Nonfinancial Corporations: 1988–1996

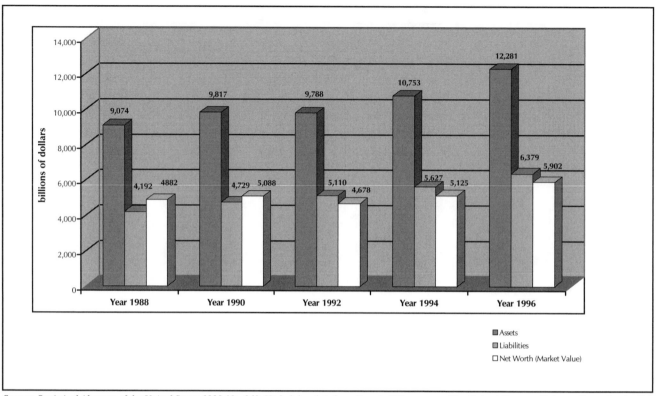

*Source: Statistical Abstract of the United States 1998*, No. 862. Underlying data from Board of Governors of the Federal Reserve, *Balance Sheets for the U.S. Economy.*

## C2. CORPORATIONS—SELECTED FINANCIAL ITEMS, BY INDUSTRY

### C2-1. Corporations—Selected Financial Items, by Industry: 1980–1990, in Billions of Dollars (except as indicated)

| INDUSTRY | 1980 | 1985 | 1989 | 1990 |
|---|---|---|---|---|
| **Agriculture, forestry, and fishing:** | | | | |
| Returns (1,000) | 81 | 103 | 123 | 126 |
| Assets | 40.7 | 52.7 | 63.4 | 68.3 |
| Liabilities[1] | 29.3 | 37.2 | 42.3 | 45.0 |
| Receipts[2] | 52.1 | 70.5 | 86.6 | 88.1 |
| Deductions[2] | 51.4 | 70.6 | 85.1 | 86.9 |
| Net income (less loss)[2] | 0.7 | -0.1 | 1.6 | 1.2 |
| **Mining:** | | | | |
| Returns (1,000) | 26 | 41 | 42 | 40 |
| Assets | 126.9 | 240.8 | 236.3 | 219.2 |
| Liabilities[1] | 72.9 | 136 | 109.9 | 108.9 |
| Receipts[2] | 176.7 | 142 | 102.4 | 111.4 |
| Deductions[2] | 169.1 | 145.4 | 99.5 | 106.5 |
| Net income (less loss)[2] | 7.8 | -2.5 | 3.1 | 5.3 |
| **Construction:** | | | | |
| Returns (1,000) | 272 | 318 | 393 | 407 |
| Assets | 132.9 | 215.3 | 249.7 | 243.8 |
| Liabilities[1] | 100.1 | 160.6 | 183 | 180 |
| Receipts[2] | 267.2 | 387.2 | 517.5 | 534.7 |
| Deductions[2] | 262.1 | 382.8 | 508.8 | 527.8 |
| Net income (less loss)[2] | 5.3 | 4.4 | 8.7 | 6.8 |

## C2-1. Corporations—Selected Financial Items, by Industry: 1980–1990, in Billions of Dollars (except as indicated) *(continued)*

| INDUSTRY | 1980 | 1985 | 1989 | 1990 |
|---|---|---|---|---|
| **Manufacturing:** | | | | |
| Returns (1,000) | 243 | 277 | 301 | 302 |
| Assets | 1,709.50 | 2,644.40 | 3,721.20 | 3,921.30 |
| Liabilities[1] | 960.3 | 1,544.70 | 2,347.70 | 2,529.10 |
| Receipts[2] | 2,404.30 | 2,831.10 | 3,531.20 | 3,688.70 |
| Deductions[2] | 2,290.60 | 2,733.10 | 3,377.10 | 3,545.10 |
| Net income (less loss)[2] | 125.7 | 113.8 | 180.5 | 171.4 |
| Transportation and public utilities: | | | | |
| Returns (1,000) | 111 | 138 | 156 | 160 |
| Assets | 758.4 | 1,246.40 | 1,474.40 | 1,522.00 |
| Liabilities[1] | 467.7 | 755.9 | 963.1 | 1,013.40 |
| Receipts[2] | 523.8 | 772.4 | 906.5 | 936.3 |
| Deductions[2] | 504 | 747.8 | 867.6 | 901 |
| Net income (less loss)[2] | 20 | 25.1 | 39.1 | 35.4 |
| Wholesale and retail trade: | | | | |
| Returns (1,000) | 800 | 917 | 1,013 | 1,023 |
| Assets | 646.9 | 1,010.00 | 1,390.60 | 1,447.30 |
| Liabilities[1] | 424.6 | 723.7 | 1,047.80 | 1,092.50 |
| Receipts[2] | 1,955.50 | 2,473.90 | 3,184.90 | 3,309.00 |
| Deductions[2] | 1,919.50 | 2,440.40 | 3,148.80 | 3,279.10 |
| Net income (less loss)[2] | 38.3 | 33.1 | 36.2 | 30.1 |
| Finance, insurance, and real estate: | | | | |
| Returns (1,000) | 493 | 518 | 593 | 609 |
| Assets | 4,022.20 | 7,029.50 | 9,957.50 | 10,193.30 |
| Liabilities[1] | 3,491.70 | 5,867.50 | 7,929.30 | 8,051.30 |
| Receipts[2, 3] | 697.5 | 1,182.00 | 1,868.00 | 1,954.70 |
| Deductions[2] | 652.6 | 1,104.60 | 1,730.50 | 1,809.90 |
| Net income (less loss)[2] | 33.1 | 60.7 | 108.9 | 109.9 |
| Services: | | | | |
| Returns (1,000) | 671 | 939 | 990 | 1,029 |
| Assets | 178.2 | 331 | 552.1 | 572.8 |
| Liabilities[1] | 125.3 | 241.1 | 419.8 | 429.7 |
| Receipts[2] | 279.9 | 534.6 | 735.5 | 779.3 |
| Deductions[2] | 271.8 | 528.7 | 724.9 | 769 |
| Net income (less loss)[2] | 8.2 | 5.9 | 11.0 | 10.6 |

*Notes:*
1. Liabilities does not include net worth.
2. Beginning in 1989, receipts, deductions, and net income of S corporations are limited to those from trade or business; those from investments are generally excluded. S corporations are certain small corporations with up to 35 shareholders (15 in 1980), mostly individuals, electing to be taxed at the shareholder level.
3. Beginning in 1989, includes gross sales (previously net sales) of securities, commodities, and real estate by exchanges, brokers, or dealers selling on their own account.
*General Note:* Covers active corporations only. Industrial distribution based on data collected from companies. Excludes corporations not allocable by industry.

*Source: Statistical Abstract of the United States 1998*, No. 864; <http://www.census.gov/prod/3/98pubs/98statab/sasec17.pdf>. Underlying data from U.S. Internal Revenue Service, *Statistics of Income, Corporation Income Tax Returns*, annual.

## C2-2. Corporations—Selected Financial Items, by Industry: 1991–1994, in Billions of Dollars (except as indicated)

| INDUSTRY | 1991 | 1992 | 1993 | 1994 |
|---|---|---|---|---|
| **Agriculture, forestry, and fishing:** | | | | |
| Returns (1,000) | 130 | 138 | 141 | 147 |
| Assets | 67.8 | 71.8 | 74.6 | 79.9 |
| Liabilities[1] | 45.0 | 46.7 | 46.9 | 50.6 |
| Receipts[2] | 85.9 | 95.6 | 98.3 | 100.9 |
| Deductions[2] | 85.3 | 94.0 | 96.7 | 99.6 |
| Net income (less loss)[2] | 0.6 | 1.6 | 1.6 | 1.3 |
| **Mining:** | | | | |
| Returns /(1,000) | 39 | 37 | 35 | 35 |
| Assets | 213 | 218.2 | 224 | 239.7 |
| Liabilities[1] | 106.4 | 112.1 | 112.6 | 121.1 |
| Receipts[2] | 103.3 | 112.8 | 112.1 | 115.7 |
| Deductions[2] | 99.5 | 110.3 | 109.6 | 112.3 |
| Net income (less loss)[2] | 4.0 | 2.7 | 2.6 | 3.6 |
| **Construction:** | | | | |
| Returns /(1,000) | 417 | 408 | 417 | 433 |
| Assets | 243 | 231.1 | 240.4 | 249.1 |
| Liabilities[1] | 172.4 | 159.5 | 164.6 | 170.9 |
| Receipts[2] | 515.1 | 499.4 | 538.3 | 592.8 |
| Deductions[2] | 509.2 | 493.9 | 530.7 | 581.2 |
| Net income (less loss)[2] | 6.1 | 5.5 | 7.5 | 11.6 |
| **Manufacturing:** | | | | |
| Returns /(1,000) | 300 | 300 | 307 | 312 |
| Assets | 4,028.40 | 4,113.10 | 4,225.10 | 4,525.50 |
| Liabilities[1] | 2,547.20 | 2,701.20 | 2,784.40 | 2,936.60 |
| Receipts[2] | 3,658.50 | 3,760.30 | 3,890.70 | 4,218.80 |
| Deductions[2] | 3,548.70 | 3,633.80 | 3,741.60 | 4,024.30 |
| Net income (less loss)[2] | 132.3 | 143.6 | 173.2 | 219.1 |
| **Transportation and public utilities:** | | | | |
| Returns(1,000) | 165 | 178 | 176 | 187 |
| Assets | 1,573.80 | 1,642.00 | 1,770.70 | 1,826.30 |
| Liabilities[1] | 1,044.90 | 1,106.30 | 1,190.90 | 1,207.20 |
| Receipts[2] | 954.9 | 997.6 | 1,037.20 | 1,103.20 |
| Deductions[2] | 917.8 | 956.5 | 984.9 | 1,036.10 |
| Net income (less loss)[2] | 37.7 | 41.8 | 52.9 | 68.3 |
| **Wholesale and retail trade:** | | | | |
| Returns (1,000) | 1,044 | 1,053 | 1,073 | 1,106 |
| Assets | 1,483.40 | 1,581.90 | 1,702.80 | 1,795.20 |
| Liabilities[1] | 1,108.60 | 1,177.70 | 1,254.20 | 1,303.10 |
| Receipts[2] | 3,380.60 | 3,503.90 | 3,709.50 | 4,052.20 |
| Deductions[2] | 3,350.90 | 3,463.40 | 3,659.80 | 3,984.00 |
| Net income (less loss)[2] | 30.0 | 41.3 | 49.7 | 68.5 |
| **Finance, insurance, and real estate:** | | | | |
| Returns (1,000) | 618 | 635 | 641 | 682 |
| Assets | 10,780.70 | 11,480.50 | 12,831.70 | 13895.3 |
| Liabilities[1] | 8,267.10 | 8,531.30 | 9,288.50 | 10053.1 |
| Receipts[2, 3] | 1,924.30 | 1,900.40 | 1,940.30 | 1976.5 |
| Deductions[2] | 1,771.20 | 1,724.30 | 1,723.30 | 1773.1 |
| Net income (less loss)[2] | 124.5 | 147.0 | 185.2 | 169.3 |
| **Services:** | | | | |
| Returns (1,000) | 1,062 | 1,100 | 1,158 | 1,424 |
| Assets | 636.8 | 661.6 | 744.8 | 833.9 |
| Liabilities[1] | 459.1 | 465 | 508.6 | 570.3 |
| Receipts[2] | 809.7 | 869.5 | 941.6 | 1198.0 |
| Deductions[2] | 800.2 | 851.1 | 916.5 | 1162.5 |
| Net income (less loss)[2] | 9.8 | 18.5 | 25.4 | 35.6 |

*Notes:*

1. Liabilities does not include net worth.

2. Beginning in 1989, receipts, deductions, and net income of S corporations are limited to those from trade or business; those from investments are generally excluded S corporations are certain small corporations with up to 35 shareholders (15 in 1980), mostly individuals, electing to be taxed at the shareholder level.

3. Beginning in 1989, includes gross sales (previously net sales) of securities, commodities, and real estate by exchanges, brokers, or dealers selling on their own account

*General Note:* Covers active corporations only. Industrial distribution based on data collected from companies. Excludes corporations not allocable by industry.

*Source: Statistical Abstract of the United States 1998*, No. 864; <http://www.census.gov/prod/3/98pubs/98statab/sasec17.pdf>. Underlying data from U.S. Internal Revenue *Service, Statistics of Income, Corporation Income Tax Returns*, annual.

## C3. CORPORATIONS—ANNUAL PERCENT CHANGE IN RECEIPTS, BY INDUSTRY

### C3-1. Corporations—Annual Percent Change in Receipts, by Industry: 1980–1994

|  | 1980 | 1985 | 1989 | 1990 | 1991 | 1992 | 1993 | 1994 |
|---|---|---|---|---|---|---|---|---|
| Agriculture, forestry, and fishing | -2.4 | 5.9 | 0.3 | 1.7 | -2.5 | 11.3 | 2.8 | 2.6 |
| Mining | 33.3 | 15.0 | 2.0 | 8.8 | -7.3 | 9.2 | -0.6 | 3.1 |
| Construction | 5.7 | 14.4 | 3.6 | 3.3 | -3.7 | -3.0 | 7.8 | 10.1 |
| Manufacturing | 11.7 | 2.3 | 5.4 | 4.5 | -0.8 | 2.8 | 3.5 | 8.4 |
| Transportation and public utilities | 17.5 | 6.4 | 8.1 | 3.3 | 2.0 | 4.5 | 4.0 | 6.3 |
| Wholesale and retail trade | 11.6 | 7.2 | 6.9 | 3.9 | 2.2 | 3.6 | 5.9 | 9.2 |
| Finance, insurance, and real estate | 24.3 | 14.4 | 9.0 | 4.6 | -1.6 | -1.2 | 2.1 | 1.8 |
| Services | 14.2 | 9.0 | 5.8 | 6.0 | 3.9 | 7.4 | 8.3 | 27.2 |

*Notes:*
Percents indicate change from preceding year. Covers active corporations only. Industrial distribution based on data collected from companies. Excludes corporations not allocable by industry.

*Source: Statistical Abstract of the United States 1998,* No. 864; http://www.census.gov/prod/3/98pubs/98statab/sasec17.pdf. Underlying data from US Internal Revenue Service, *Statistics of Income, Corporation Income Tax Returns,* annual.

## C4. CORPORATIONS—SELECTED FINANCIAL ITEMS, BY ASSET-SIZE CLASS AND INDUSTRY

### C4-1. Corporations—Selected Financial Items, by Asset-Size Class and Industry: 1995, in Millions of Dollars (except number of returns)

| Industry | Total | Asset-size Class under $10 million[1] | Asset-size Class $10-$24.9 million | Asset-size Class $25-$49.9 million | Asset-size Class $50-$99.9 million | Asset-size Class $100-$249.9 million | Asset-size Class $250 million million |
|---|---|---|---|---|---|---|---|
| **Agriculture, forestry, and fishing:** | | | | | | | |
| Returns | 147,527 | 146,887 | 387 | 136 | 55 | 41 | 21 |
| Assets | 86,299 | 55,560 | 5,642 | 4,725 | 3,824 | 5,660 | 10,888 |
| Receipts | 107,582 | 75,205 | 5,747 | 5,945 | 5,031 | 7,223 | 8,432 |
| Deductions | 105,967 | 74,533 | 5,596 | 5,781 | 4,915 | 7,079 | 8,063 |
| Net income (less loss) | 1,604 | 650 | 145 | 158 | 117 | 143 | 392 |
| **Mining:** | | | | | | | |
| Returns | 35,123 | 34,138 | 467 | 183 | 120 | 100 | 115 |
| Assets | 268,690 | 18,211 | 7,230 | 6,507 | 8,485 | 16,194 | 212,063 |
| Receipts | 126,760 | 23,521 | 5,339 | 4,317 | 4,763 | 11,239 | 77,581 |
| Deductions | 121,397 | 23,152 | 5,276 | 4,294 | 4,752 | 10,903 | 73,020 |
| Net income (less loss) | 5,531 | 360 | 58 | 22 | 10 | 336 | 4,746 |
| **Construction:** | | | | | | | |
| Returns | 449,882 | 447,264 | 1,906 | 427 | 169 | 73 | 43 |
| Assets | 265,813 | 156,343 | 27,700 | 14,806 | 12,293 | 10,992 | 43,677 |
| Receipts | 637,090 | 454,344 | 59,058 | 30,389 | 23,003 | 19,692 | 50,605 |
| Deductions | 622,622 | 444,031 | 57,573 | 29,734 | 22,562 | 19,434 | 49,289 |
| Net income (less loss) | 14,458 | 10,274 | 1,460 | 637 | 431 | 251 | 1,406 |
| **Manufacturing:** | | | | | | | |
| Returns | 319,699 | 306,004 | 6,727 | 2,855 | 1,595 | 1,194 | 1,324 |
| Assets | 4,941,073 | 218,050 | 103,637 | 100,292 | 113,422 | 190,677 | 4,214,995 |
| Receipts | 4,585,550 | 547,130 | 196,088 | 163,540 | 169,611 | 250,203 | 3,258,977 |
| Deductions | 4,354,564 | 534,475 | 189,322 | 157,593 | 162,665 | 237,581 | 3,072,927 |
| Net income (less loss) | 260,910 | 12,710 | 6,724 | 5,944 | 6,956 | 12,790 | 215,786 |
| **Transportation and public utilities:** | | | | | | | |
| Returns | 194,456 | 191,553 | 1,389 | 525 | 316 | 254 | 419 |
| Assets | 1,903,214 | 67,715 | 21,130 | 18,096 | 22,379 | 40,655 | 1,733,237 |
| Receipts | 1,156,710 | 185,736 | 28,891 | 20,008 | 21,793 | 32,642 | 867,640 |
| Deductions | 1,084,677 | 184,226 | 28,073 | 19,515 | 21,359 | 31,627 | 799,877 |
| Net income (less loss) | 72,911 | 1,495 | 794 | 493 | 437 | 1,021 | 68,670 |
| **Wholesale and retail trade:** | | | | | | | |
| Returns | 1,132,409 | 1,120,014 | 8,006 | 2,212 | 994 | 648 | 536 |
| Assets | 1,919,718 | 469,419 | 120,773 | 76,514 | 70,203 | 101,492 | 1,081,317 |
| Receipts | 4,310,347 | 1,731,685 | 394,155 | 222,410 | 174,214 | 237,623 | 1,550,260 |

## C4-1. Corporations—Selected Financial Items, by Asset-Size Class and Industry: 1995, In Millions of Dollars (except number of returns)

| Industry | Total | Asset-size Class under $10 million[1] | Asset-size Class $10-$24.9 million | Asset-size Class $25-$49.9 million | Asset-size Class $50-$99.9 million | Asset-size Class $100-$249.9 million | Asset-size Class $250 million million |
|---|---|---|---|---|---|---|---|
| Deductions | 4,247,561 | 1,714,987 | 388,541 | 218,984 | 171,397 | 233,806 | 1,519,846 |
| Net income (less loss) | 63,567 | 16,621 | 5,600 | 3,427 | 2,807 | 3,798 | 31,314 |
| **Finance, insurance, and real estate:** | | | | | | | |
| Returns | 683,211 | 657,531 | 6,961 | 4,958 | 4,537 | 4,483 | 4,740 |
| Assets | 15,677,287 | 279,073 | 111,614 | 179,546 | 324,948 | 708,041 | 14,074,066 |
| Receipts[2] | 2,278,104 | 237,842 | 27,614 | 29,957 | 41,127 | 86,944 | 1,854,620 |
| Deductions | 1,985,796 | 228,923 | 27,546 | 28,185 | 35,635 | 69,995 | 1,595,512 |
| Net income (less loss) | 256,811 | 8,389 | -213 | 1,233 | 3,961 | 13,017 | 230,424 |
| **Services:** | | | | | | | |
| Returns | 1,504,230 | 1,498,591 | 3,240 | 1,065 | 574 | 422 | 339 |
| Assets | 950,737 | 250,133 | 49,105 | 37,215 | 41,887 | 69,641 | 502,757 |
| Receipts | 1,335,695 | 796,771 | 70,318 | 46,706 | 42,696 | 63,114 | 316,089 |
| Deductions | 1,297,475 | 778,225 | 69,553 | 45,535 | 41,953 | 61,450 | 300,760 |
| Net income (less loss) | 38,408 | 18,452 | 751 | 1,150 | 727 | 1,685 | 15,642 |

*Notes:*
Covers active corporations only. Excludes corporations not allocable by industry.
The industrial distribution is based on data collected from companies; see text of *Statistical Abstract of the United States 1998*, Section 17.
Detail may not add to total because of rounding.
1. Includes returns with zero assets.
2. Includes investment income.

*Source: Statistical Abstract of the United States 1998*, No. 865; <http://wwwcensusgov/prod/3/98pubs/98statab/sasec17pdf>. Underlying data from U.S. Internal Revenue Service, *Statistics of Income, Corporation Income Tax Returns*, annual. Corporations, by Asset-Size Class and Industry: 1995

## C5. CORPORATIONS—RECEIPTS, PERCENT DISTRIBUTION BY ASSET-SIZE CLASS AND INDUSTRY

### C5-1. Corporations—Receipts, Percent Distribution by Asset-Size Class and Industry: 1995

| Industry | Total | Asset-size Class under $10 million[1] | Asset-size Class $10-$24.9 million | Asset-size Class $25-$49.9 million | Asset-size Class $50-$99.9 million | Asset-size Class $100-$249.9 million | Asset-size Class $250 million million |
|---|---|---|---|---|---|---|---|
| **RECEIPTS** | | | | | | | |
| Agriculture, forestry, and fishing | 100 | 70 | 5 | 6 | 5 | 7 | 8 |
| Mining | 100 | 19 | 4 | 3 | 4 | 9 | 61 |
| Construction | 100 | 71 | 9 | 5 | 4 | 3 | 8 |
| Manufacturing | 100 | 12 | 4 | 4 | 4 | 5 | 71 |
| Transportation and public utilities | 100 | 16 | 2 | 2 | 2 | 3 | 75 |
| Wholesale and retail trade | 100 | 40 | 9 | 5 | 4 | 6 | 36 |
| Finance, insurance, and real estate[1] | 100 | 10 | 1 | 1 | 2 | 4 | 81 |
| Services | 100 | 60 | 5 | 3 | 3 | 5 | 24 |

*Note:*
1. Includes returns with zero assets.

*Source: Statistical Abstract of the United States 1998*, No. 865. Underlying data from U.S. Internal Revenue Service, *Statistics of Income, Corporation Tax Returns*, annual.

## C5-1. Corporations—Receipts, Percent Distribution by Asset-Size Class and Industry: 1995 *(continued)*

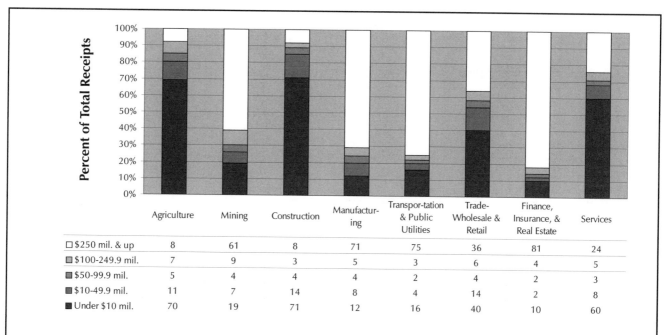

| | Agriculture | Mining | Construction | Manufacturing | Transportation & Public Utilities | Trade- Wholesale & Retail | Finance, Insurance, & Real Estate | Services |
|---|---|---|---|---|---|---|---|---|
| ☐ $250 mil. & up | 8 | 61 | 8 | 71 | 75 | 36 | 81 | 24 |
| ▨ $100-249.9 mil. | 7 | 9 | 3 | 5 | 3 | 6 | 4 | 5 |
| ■ $50-99.9 mil. | 5 | 4 | 4 | 4 | 2 | 4 | 2 | 3 |
| ■ $10-49.9 mil. | 11 | 7 | 14 | 8 | 4 | 14 | 2 | 8 |
| ■ Under $10 mil. | 70 | 19 | 71 | 12 | 16 | 40 | 10 | 60 |

*Notes:*

1. Includes investment income

*General notes:* Covers active corporations only. Excludes corporations not allocable by industry. The industrial distribution is based on data collected from companies; see text, Section 17. Detail may not add to total because of rounding.

*Source: Statistical Abstract of the United States 1998*, No. 865. Underlying data from U.S. Internal Revenue Service, *Statistics of Income, Corporation Tax Returns*, annual.

## C6. CORPORATE PROFITS, BY INDUSTRY

### C6-1. Corporate Profits, Taxes, and Dividends: 1990–1996, in Billions of Dollars

| ITEM | 1990 | 1991 | 1992 | 1993 | 1994 | 1995 | 1996 |
|---|---|---|---|---|---|---|---|
| Profits before tax | 372 | 374 | 406 | 464 | 531 | 599 | 640 |
| Profits tax liability | 141 | 133 | 143 | 164 | 195 | 219 | 233 |
| Profits after tax | 231 | 241 | 263 | 301 | 336 | 380 | 407 |
| Dividends | 152 | 163 | 170 | 197 | 211 | 227 | 244 |
| Undistributed profits | 79 | 78 | 94 | 103 | 125 | 153 | 163 |
| Inventory valuation adjustment (IVA) | -14 | 4 | -8 | -7 | -13 | -28 | -9 |
| Capital consumption adjustment | 39 | 33 | 29 | 34 | 36 | 34 | 39 |
| Net interest | 467 | 448 | 414 | 399 | 395 | 404 | 403 |
| Addenda: | | | | | | | |
| Corporate profits after tax with IVA/CCA[1] | 257 | 278 | 285 | 328 | 359 | 386 | 437 |
| Net cash flow with inventory IVA/CCA[1] | 455 | 479 | 492 | 520 | 564 | 595 | 651 |
| Undistributed profits with IVA/CCA[1] | 105 | 115 | 116 | 131 | 148 | 159 | 193 |
| Consumption of fixed capital | 350 | 365 | 376 | 389 | 416 | 436 | 458 |
| Less: Inventory valuation adjustment (IVA) | -14 | 4 | -8 | -7 | -13 | -28 | -9 |
| Equals: Net cash flow | 469 | 475 | 499 | 527 | 577 | 623 | 660 |

*Notes:*

1. Inventory valuation adjustment/capital consumption adjustment.

*General Note:* Covers corporations organized for profit and other entities treated as corporations. Represents profits to U.S. residents, without deduction of depletion charges and exclusive of capital gains and losses; inter-corporate dividends from profits of domestic corporations are eliminated; net receipts of dividends, reinvested earnings of incorporated foreign affiliates, and earnings of unincorporated foreign affiliates are added.

*Source: Statistical Abstract of the United States 1998*, No. 902; <http://www.census.gov/prod/3/98pubs/98statab/sasec17.pdf>. Underlying data from U.S. Bureau of Economic Analysis, *National Income and Product Accounts of the United States,* and *Survey of Current Business,* August 1997.

## C6-2. Corporate Profits, Pre-Tax and After Tax, Totals: 1990–1996, in Millions of Dollars

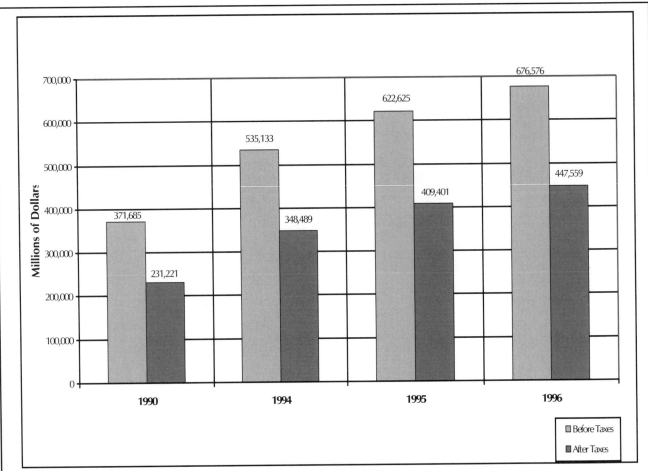

*Notes:*
Consists of receipts by all U.S. residents, including both corporations and persons, of earnings of unincorporated foreign affiliates, dividends from their incorporated foreign affiliates, and their share of their incorporated foreign affiliates, net of corresponding outflows.
Profits are without inventory valuation and capital consumption adjustments. Covers corporations organized for profit and other entities treated as corporations. Represents profits to U.S. residents, without deduction of depletion charges and exclusive of capital gains and losses; inter-corporate dividends from profits of domestic corporations are eliminated; net receipts of dividends, reinvested earnings of incorporated foreign affiliates, and earnings of unincorporated foreign affiliates are added.

*Source: Statistical Abstract of the United States 1998*, No. 903; <http://wwwcensusgov/prod/3/98pubs/98statab/sasec17pdf>.

## C6-3. Corporate Profits, Pre-Tax and After Tax, by Industry: 1990–1996, in Millions of Dollars

| | Before Taxes | | | | After Taxes | | | |
|---|---|---|---|---|---|---|---|---|
| | 1990 | 1994 | 1995 | 1996 | 1990 | 1994 | 1995 | 1996 |
| Corporate profits | 371,685 | 535,133 | 622,625 | 676,576 | 231,221 | 348,489 | 409,401 | 447,559 |
| Domestic industries | 305,945 | 461,754 | 535,918 | 580,659 | 165,481 | 275,110 | 322,694 | 351,642 |
| Agriculture, forestry, and fishing | 1,619 | 1,384 | 1,852 | 2,038 | 993 | 681 | 1,102 | 1,219 |
| Mining | 2,459 | 3,416 | 4,492 | 6,508 | 876 | 2,509 | 3,073 | 4,366 |
| Construction | 10,999 | 13,756 | 17,789 | (NA) | 8,781 | 11,447 | 14,885 | 15,791 |
| Manufacturing | 115,543 | 158,788 | 193,432 | 204,520 | 67,503 | 97,992 | 127,143 | 131,815 |
| Transportation | 934 | 10,408 | 11,632 | 12,332 | -1,993 | 6,222 | 7,238 | (NA) |
| Communications | 20,014 | 36,821 | 33,448 | 35,859 | 11,831 | 24,758 | 20,760 | 21,992 |
| Wholesale trade | 19,839 | 33,311 | 32,797 | (NA) | 13,695 | 24,485 | 23,181 | 26,534 |
| Retail trade | 24,382 | 48,803 | 45,114 | (NA) | 15,426 | 35,439 | 32,603 | 36,712 |
| Finance, insurance, and real estate | 65,354 | 72,341 | 101,771 | 108,550 | 17,873 | 11,507 | 24,312 | 30,667 |
| Services | 20,241 | 46,817 | 52,194 | 59,031 | 14,901 | 36,231 | 41,710 | 46,627 |
| Rest of the world | 65,740 | 73,379 | 86,707 | 95,917 | 65,740 | 73,379 | 86,707 | 95,917 |

*Notes:*

(NA) indicates not available

Consists of receipts by all U.S. residents, including both corporations and persons, of earnings of unincorporated foreign affiliates, dividends from their incorporated foreign affiliates, and their share of their incorporated foreign affiliates, net of corresponding outflows.

Profits are without inventory valuation and capital consumption adjustments. Covers corporations organized for profit and other entities treated as corporations. Represents profits to U.S. residents, without deduction of depletion charges and exclusive of capital gains and losses; inter-corporate dividends from profits of domestic corporations are eliminated; net receipts of dividends, reinvested earnings of incorporated foreign affiliates, and earnings of unincorporated foreign affiliates are added.

*Source: Statistical Abstract of the United States 1998*, No. 903; <http://wwwcensusgov/prod/3/98pubs/98statab/sasec17pdf>.

## C7. U.S. LARGEST PUBLIC COMPANIES

## C7-1. U.S. Largest Public Companies, Profitability: 1997, in Percents

| Industry | Profitability return on capital[1], 5-year average | Profitability return on capital[1], latest 12 months |
|---|---|---|
| All industries, median | 10.5 | 10.3 |
| Aerospace and defense | 13.4 | 12.6 |
| Business services and supplies | 12.4 | 10.9 |
| Capital goods | 13.1 | 14.7 |
| Chemicals | 13.2 | 11.6 |
| Computers and software | 15.1 | 14.4 |
| Construction | 10.1 | 12.4 |
| Consumer durables | 10.0 | 11.1 |
| Energy distributors | 6.6 | 6.5 |
| Energy extractors | 8.7 | 11.4 |
| Entertainment and information | 10.5 | 8.7 |
| Financial services | 12.2 | 11.7 |
| Food distributors | 10.1 | 9.1 |
| Food, drink and tobacco | 10.1 | 10.4 |
| Forest products and packaging | 7.6 | 4.8 |
| Health care products | 14.6 | 12.7 |
| Health care services | 10.4 | 7.4 |
| Household and personal products | 9.4 | 11.7 |
| Insurance | 11.7 | 12.3 |
| Metals | 9.7 | 7.8 |
| Retailing | 9.5 | 9.0 |
| Telecommunications | 10.2 | 11.3 |
| Travel and transport | 8.9 | 9.6 |

*Notes:*

1. After-tax profits, the amount remaining if the interest paid on long-term debt was taxed, and minority interest divided by a firm's total capitalization. Total capitalization is long-term debt, common and preferred equity, deferred taxes, investment tax credits, and minority interest in consolidated subsidiaries.

*General Note:* For fiscal years ending in the 12-month period, ending September 30.

*Source: Statistical Abstract of the United States 1998*, No. 898; <http://www.census.gov/prod/3/98pubs/98statab/sasec17.pdf>. Underlying data from Forbes, Inc., New York, NY, *Forbes Annual Report on American Industry* (copyright).

## C7-2. U.S. Largest Public Companies, Growth in Sales: 1997, in Percents

| Industry | Growth in Sales[1] 5-year average | Growth in Sales[1] Latest 12 months |
|---|---|---|
| All industries, median | 8.9 | 7.9 |
| Aerospace and defense | 4.0 | 8.9 |
| Business services and supplies | 14.9 | 13.3 |
| Capital goods | 10.4 | 7.6 |
| Chemicals | 6.5 | 2.0 |
| Computers and software | 26.0 | 10.6 |
| Construction | 11.7 | 9.9 |
| Consumer durables | 10.4 | 6.4 |
| Energy distributors | 4.6 | 6.6 |
| Energy extractors | 4.7 | 9.8 |
| Entertainment and information | 7.8 | 9.5 |
| Financial services | 10.2 | 11.4 |
| Food distributors | 7.3 | 4.7 |
| Food, drink and tobacco | 6.2 | 4.0 |
| Forest products and packaging | 7.2 | -0.9 |
| Health care products | 11.1 | 8.8 |
| Health care services | 24.9 | 22.3 |
| Household and personal products | 7.8 | 7.0 |
| Insurance | 6.2 | 8.4 |
| Metals | 7.6 | 3.8 |
| Retailing | 11.2 | 9.5 |
| Telecommunications | 15.1 | 11.5 |
| Travel and transport | 10.4 | 8.9 |

*Notes:*
Minus sign (-) indicates decrease.
1. Net sales plus other operating revenue
*General Note:* For fiscal years ending in the 12-month period, ending September 30.

*Source: Statistical Abstract of the United States 1998*, No. 898; <http://www.census.gov/prod/3/98pubs/98statab/sasec17.pdf>. Underlying data from Forbes, Inc., New York, NY, *Forbes Annual Report on American Industry* (copyright).

## C7-3. U.S. Largest Public Companies, Growth in Earnings and Debt to Capital: 1997, in Percents

| Industry | Growth in Earnings per Share 5-year average | Growth in Earnings per Share Latest 12 months | Debt/Capital, latest 12 months (percent) |
|---|---|---|---|
| All industries, median | 6.7 | 14.9 | 32.8 |
| Aerospace and defense | 7.2 | 10.7 | 32.1 |
| Business services and supplies | 9.2 | 19.8 | 28.7 |
| Capital goods | 14.0 | 15.7 | 30.7 |
| Chemicals | 11.2 | 12.2 | 32.0 |
| Computers and software | 16.5 | 19.6 | 15.4 |
| Construction | 22.7 | 25.6 | 39.9 |
| Consumer durables | 8.0 | 13.1 | 33.6 |
| Energy distributors | 3.3 | -0.3 | 36.8 |
| Energy extractors | -20.7 | 33.3 | 30.3 |
| Entertainment and information | 9.0 | 40.0 | 40.9 |
| Financial services | 14.4 | 20.8 | 41.8 |
| Food distributors | -17.3 | 10.4 | 46.5 |
| Food, drink and tobacco | -7.3 | 18.6 | 40.9 |
| Forest products and packaging | (NS) | -44.8 | 39.6 |
| Health care products | 8.6 | 15.5 | 19.4 |
| Health care services | 6.0 | 23.5 | 35.4 |
| Household and personal products | -11.3 | 28.8 | 36.0 |
| Insurance | 7.6 | 14.9 | 15.8 |
| Metals | (NS) | -13.7 | 30.1 |

## C7-3. U.S. Largest Public Companies, Growth in Earnings and Debt to Capital: 1997, in Percents *(continued)*

| Industry | Growth in Earnings per Share | | Debt/Capital, latest 12 months (percent) |
|---|---|---|---|
| | 5-year average | Latest 12 months | |
| Retailing | -13.0 | 16.8 | 27.9 |
| Telecommunications | 9.3 | 12.8 | 28.9 |
| Travel and transport | -3.0 | 16.4 | 38.9 |

*Notes:*
(NS) indicates not significant.
Minus sign (-) indicates decrease.
*General Note:* For fiscal years ending in the 12-month period ending September 30.

*Source: Statistical Abstract of the United States 1998*, No. 898; <http://www.census.gov/prod/3/98pubs/98statab/sasec17.pdf>. Underlying data from Forbes, Inc., New York, NY, *Forbes Annual Report on American Industry* (copyright).

## C8. 1000 LARGEST INDUSTRIAL CORPORATIONS

## C8-1. 1000 Largest Industrial Corporations—Profits, by Industry: 1997

| | Revenue percent change from 1996 | Profits percent change from 1996 | Profits as percent of revenue | Profits as percent of assets | Profits as percent of stockholder's equity |
|---|---|---|---|---|---|
| Aerospace | 13 | 18 | 5 | 6 | 21 |
| Apparel | 7 | 24 | 7 | 9 | 19 |
| Beverages | 4 | 17 | 6 | 8 | 17 |
| Building materials, glass | 9 | 66 | 7 | 8 | 23 |
| Chemicals | 2 | 3 | 6 | 6 | 17 |
| Computer and data services | 11 | 15 | 5 | 7 | 14 |
| Computer peripherals | 13 | 70 | 7 | 12 | 22 |
| Computers, office equipment | 12 | 21 | 5 | 5 | 16 |
| Diversified outsourcing services | 15 | 21 | 2 | 6 | 21 |
| Electronics, electrical equip | 10 | 11 | 5 | 7 | 15 |
| Electronics, network communications | 33 | 25 | 14 | 17 | 22 |
| Electronics, semiconductors | 4 | 6 | 12 | 10 | 16 |
| Food | 4 | 18 | 3 | 7 | 17 |
| Food services | 7 | 12 | 2 | 4 | 12 |
| Forest and paper products | 1 | -59 | 2 | 2 | 4 |
| Industrial and farm equipment | 10 | 17 | 5 | 6 | 16 |
| Insurance: Life, health (stock) | 9 | 36 | 8 | 1 | 11 |
| Insurance: Property and casualty (stock) | 7 | 28 | 9 | 3 | 12 |
| Metal products | 8 | 20 | 8 | 7 | 17 |
| Metals | 3 | 19 | 4 | 5 | 13 |
| Motor vehicles and parts | 6 | 36 | 4 | 4 | 17 |
| Petroleum refining | (-) | 6 | 5 | 6 | 14 |
| Pharmaceuticals | 8 | 12 | 14 | 13 | 27 |
| Pipelines | 37 | -19 | 3 | 2 | 8 |
| Publishing, printing | 8 | (-) | 7 | 7 | 15 |
| Savings institutions | 10 | 20 | 10 | 1 | 11 |
| Scientific, photo, and control equip | 8 | (-) | 7 | 7 | 14 |
| Securities | 22 | 25 | 10 | 1 | 19 |
| Soaps, cosmetics | 6 | 17 | 7 | 10 | 27 |
| Utilities, gas and electric | 6 | (-) | 8 | 3 | 11 |
| Wholesalers | 11 | 14 | 1 | 3 | 11 |

*Notes:*
Minus sign (-) indicates decrease.
(-) Represents or rounds to zero
*General Note:* Data are medians.

*Source: Statistical Abstract of the United States 1998*, No. 901; <http://www.census.gov/prod/3/98pubs/98statab/sasec17.pdf>. Underlying data from Time Warner, New York, NY, *The Fortune Directories* (copyright).

**C8-2. 1000 Largest Industrial Corporations—Earnings and Return to Investors, by Industry: 1987 and 1997**

| | Earnings per share, 1987–97 annual rate | Total return to investors (percent), 1987–97 annual rate | Total return to investors (percent), 1997 |
|---|---|---|---|
| Aerospace | 7 | 21 | 20 |
| Apparel | 6 | 12 | -1 |
| Beverages | 9 | 21 | 32 |
| Building materials, glass | -2 | 14 | 3 |
| Chemicals | 7 | 14 | 19 |
| Computer and data services | 14 | 17 | 35 |
| Computer peripherals | 13 | 22 | 33 |
| Computers, office equipment | 10 | 12 | 24 |
| Diversified outsourcing services | 14 | 19 | 64 |
| Electronics, electrical equip | 9 | 17 | 20 |
| Electronics, network communications | 27 | 21 | -15 |
| Electronics, semiconductors | 23 | 15 | 7 |
| Food | 10 | 18 | 43 |
| Food services | 15 | 18 | 19 |
| Forest and paper products | -4 | 10 | 6 |
| Industrial and farm equipment | 9 | 15 | 31 |
| Insurance: Life, health (stock) | 12 | 23 | 42 |
| Insurance: Property and casualty (stock) | 9 | 20 | 41 |
| Metal products | 12 | 17 | 36 |
| Metals | 8 | 14 | -5 |
| Motor vehicles and parts | 6 | 14 | 37 |
| Petroleum refining | 7 | 14 | 22 |
| Pharmaceuticals | 14 | 23 | 34 |
| Pipelines | 6 | 20 | 16 |
| Publishing, printing | 8 | 14 | 38 |
| Savings institutions | 5 | 22 | 61 |
| Scientific, photo, and control equip | 10 | 14 | 13 |
| Securities | 15 | 29 | 81 |
| Soaps, cosmetics | 13 | 23 | 32 |
| Utilities, gas and electric | 1 | 14 | 27 |
| Wholesalers | 9 | 15 | 18 |

*Notes:*
Minus sign (-) indicates decrease.
*General Note:* Data are medians.

*Source: Statistical Abstract of the United States 1998*, No. 901; <http://www.census.gov/prod/3/98pubs/98statab/sasec17.pdf>. Underlying data from Time Warner, New York, NY, *The Fortune Directories* (copyright).

## C9. U.S. MULTINATIONAL COMPANIES

**C9-1. U.S. Multinational Companies, Total Multinationals and only U.S. Parents—Gross Product: 1994 and 1995, in Millions of Dollars**

| | Total U.S. Multinationals, 1994 | Total U.S. Multinationals, 1995 | U.S. Parents, 1994 | U.S. Parents, 1995 |
|---|---|---|---|---|
| All industries | 1,717,488 | 1,820,641 | 1,313,792 | 1,357,682 |
| Petroleum | 200,882 | 213,794 | 106,877 | 113,431 |
| Manufacturing | 902,871 | 945,908 | 697,663 | 713,144 |
| Food and kindred products | 107,043 | 108,219 | 82,293 | 83,060 |
| Chemical and allied products | 156,356 | 168,657 | 115,386 | 120,553 |
| Primary and fabricated metals | 43,661 | 51,148 | 35,610 | 41,961 |
| Industrial machinery and equipment[1] | 103,526 | 108,956 | 76,036 | 74,512 |
| Electronic and other electric equipment[1] | 90,457 | 102,028 | 70,591 | 77,059 |
| Transportation equipment | 190,124 | 190,518 | 154,238 | 153,613 |
| Other | 211,704 | 216,383 | 163,509 | 162,386 |
| Wholesale trade | 77,796 | 87,233 | 30,490 | 31,448 |

## C9-1. U.S. Multinational Companies, Total Multinationals and only U.S. Parents—Gross Product: 1994 and 1995, in Millions of Dollars *(continued)*

| | Total U.S. Multinationals, 1994 | Total U.S. Multinationals, 1995 | U.S. Parents, 1994 | U.S. Parents, 1995 |
|---|---|---|---|---|
| Finance (exc dep inst), insurance and real estate[1] | 66,138 | 71,630 | 57,652 | 56,804 |
| Finance, except depository institutions | 24,792 | 16,135 | 21,138 | 5,123 |
| Insurance | 41,399 | 57,988 | 35,251 | 49,928 |
| Real estate | (D) | (D) | 1,366 | 1,665 |
| Holding companies | -1,959 | -4,392 | -103 | 87 |
| Services | 118,022 | 129,870 | 89,822 | 96,175 |
| Hotels and other lodging places | 7,061 | 8,974 | 5,956 | 7,773 |
| Business services | 55,112 | 58,628 | 37,630 | 37,446 |
| Advertising | 5,147 | 5,945 | 2,467 | 2,823 |
| Equipment rental (exc auto, computers) | 1,908 | 2,524 | 1,037 | 1,200 |
| Computer and data processing | 25,308 | 28,919 | 15,963 | 18,068 |
| Business services, nec | 22,750 | 21,241 | 18,163 | 15,355 |
| Automotive rental and leasing | 4,346 | 4,670 | 3,188 | 3,346 |
| Motion pictures, television tape and film | 11,191 | 12,028 | 10,066 | 10,421 |
| Health services | 13,374 | 15,907 | 13,064 | 15,627 |
| Engineering and architectural services[1] | 6,350 | 8,219 | 4,646 | 6,167 |
| Management and public relations | 6,480 | 6,127 | 4,492 | 3,620 |
| Other | 14,105 | 15,316 | 10,777 | 11,775 |
| Other industries | 351,780 | 372,207 | 331,289 | 346,680 |

*Notes:*
(D) Figure withheld to avoid disclosure pertaining to a specific organization or individual.
1. For changes in industry definition, see text.
*General Notes:* Gross product measures valued added by a firm.
Consists of nonbank U.S. parent companies and their nonbank foreign affiliates.
A U.S. parent comprises the domestic operations of a multinational and is a U.S. person that owns or controls 10 percent or more of the voting securities, or the equivalent, of a foreign business enterprise. A U.S. person can be an incorporated business enterprise.
A majority-owned foreign affiliate is a foreign business enterprise in which a U.S. parent company owns or controls 50 percent or more of the voting securities.

*Source: Statistical Abstract of the United States 1998*, No. 907; <http://www.census.gov/prod/3/98pubs/98statab/sasec17.pdf>. Underlying data from U.S. Bureau of Economic Analysis, *Survey of Current Business*, October 1997.

## C9-2. U.S. Multinational Companies, Foreign Affiliates—Gross Product: 1994 and 1995, in Millions of Dollars

| | Majority-owned Foreign Affiliates, 1994 | Majority-owned Foreign Affiliates, 1995 |
|---|---|---|
| All industries | 403,696 | 462,959 |
| Petroleum | 94,005 | 100,363 |
| Manufacturing | 205,208 | 232,764 |
| Food and kindred products | 24,750 | 25,159 |
| Chemical and allied products | 40,970 | 48,104 |
| Primary and fabricated metals | 8,051 | 9,187 |
| Industrial machinery and equipment[1] | 27,490 | 34,444 |
| Electronic and other electric equipment[1] | 19,866 | 24,969 |
| Transportation equipment | 35,886 | 36,905 |
| Other | 48,195 | 53,997 |
| Wholesale trade | 47,306 | 55,785 |
| Finance (exc dep inst), insurance and real estate[1] | 8,486 | 14,826 |
| Finance, except depository institutions | 3,654 | 11,012 |
| Insurance | 6,148 | 8,060 |
| Real estate | 541 | 233 |
| Holding companies | -1,856 | -4,479 |
| Services | 28,200 | 33,695 |
| Hotels and other lodging places | 1,105 | 1,201 |

## C9-2. U.S. Multinational Companies, Foreign Affiliates—Gross Product: 1994 and 1995, in Millions of Dollars *(continued)*

| | Majority-owned Foreign Affiliates, 1994 | Majority-owned Foreign Affiliates, 1995 |
|---|---|---|
| Business services | 17,482 | 21,182 |
|   Advertising | 2,680 | 3,122 |
|   Equipment rental (exc auto, computers) | 871 | 1,324 |
|   Computer and data processing | 9,345 | 10,851 |
|   Business services, nec | 4,587 | 5,886 |
|  Automotive rental and leasing | 1,158 | 1,324 |
|  Motion pictures, television tape and film | 1,125 | 1,607 |
|  Health services | 310 | 280 |
|  Engineering and architectural services[1] | 1,704 | 2,052 |
|  Management and public relations | 1,988 | 2,507 |
|  Other | 3,328 | 3,541 |
| Other industries | 20,491 | 25,527 |

*Notes:*
1. For changes in industry definition, see text.
*General Notes:* Gross product measures valued added by a firm.
Consists of nonbank U.S. parent companies and their nonbank foreign affiliates.
A U.S. parent comprises the domestic operations of a multinational and is a U.S. person that owns or controls 10 percent or more of the voting securities, or the equivalent, of a foreign business enterprise. A U.S. person can be an incorporated business enterprise.
A majority-owned foreign affiliate is a foreign business enterprise in which a U.S. parent company owns or controls 50 percent or more of the voting securities.

*Source: Statistical Abstract of the United States 1998*, No. 907; <http://www.census.gov/prod/3/98pubs/98statab/sasec17.pdf>. Underlying data from U.S. Bureau of Economic Analysis, *Survey of Current Business*, October 1997.

## C9-3. U.S. Multinational Companies, with U.S. Parents, Selected Characteristics: 1995, Preliminary, in Billions of Dollars (except as indicated)

| | U.S. Parents Total Assets | U.S. Parents Sales | Employment (1,000) | Employee Compensation |
|---|---|---|---|---|
| All industries | 7230.0 | 4236.9 | 18569.1 | 815.8 |
| Petroleum | 527.0 | 392.6 | 472.6 | 30.4 |
| Manufacturing | 2439.0 | 2009.3 | 9045.2 | 446.9 |
|  Food and kindred products | 259.4 | 262.6 | 1153.9 | 38.9 |
|  Chemical and allied products | 441.4 | 317.9 | 1072.6 | 64.5 |
|  Primary and fabricated metals | 115.7 | 121.7 | 565.3 | 26.1 |
|  Industrial machinery and equipment | 243.1 | 241.6 | 1040.9 | 52.1 |
|  Electronic and electric equipment | 338.3 | 224.7 | 1037.4 | 48.4 |
|  Transportation equipment | 594.3 | 444.2 | 1735.0 | 111.3 |
|  Other manufacturing | 447.0 | 396.6 | 2440.1 | 105.4 |
| Wholesale trade | 138.2 | 284.2 | 510.2 | 20.4 |
| Finance (deposit institutions), insurance, real estate | 2837.1 | 509.9 | 1035.0 | 65.3 |
| Services | 247.2 | 192.6 | 2192.0 | 70.4 |
| Other | 1041.5 | 848.4 | 5314.1 | 182.3 |

*Notes:*
(-) Represents zero
*General Notes:* Consists of nonbank U.S. parent companies and their nonbank foreign affiliates.
U.S. parent is a U.S. person that owns or controls directly or indirectly, 10 percent or more of the voting securities of an incorporated foreign business enterprise, or an equivalent interest in an unincorporated foreign business enterprise. A U.S. person can be an incorporated business enterprise.
A foreign affiliate is a foreign business enterprise owned or controlled by a U.S. parent company.

*Source: Statistical Abstract of the United States 1998*, No. 908; <http://www.census.gov/prod/3/98pubs/98statab/sasec17.pdf>. Underlying data from U.S. Bureau of Economic Analysis, *Survey of Current Business*, October, 1997.

## C9-4. U.S. Multinational Companies, Foreign Affiliates, Selected Characteristics: 1995, Preliminary, in Billions of Dollars (except as indicated)

| | **Foreign Affiliates** | | | | | |
| --- | --- | --- | --- | --- | --- | --- |
| | **Total assets** | **Sales** | **Employment (1,000)** | **Employee compensation** | **U.S. exports shipped to foreign affiliates** | **U.S. imports shipped to foreign affiliates** |
| All industries | 2815.1 | 2140.4 | 7377.0 | 239.7 | 174.8 | 153.1 |
| Petroleum | 272.1 | 428.0 | 230.9 | 11.7 | 3.0 | 11.1 |
| Manufacturing | 779.3 | 984.9 | 4376.6 | 136.5 | 111.0 | 126.1 |
| Food and kindred products | 99.6 | 113.2 | 554.4 | 13.5 | 3.4 | 2.7 |
| Chemical and allied products | 181.0 | 189.1 | 591.9 | 24.6 | 12.7 | 7.4 |
| Primary and fabricated metals | 35.3 | 36.9 | 195.7 | 6.2 | 2.6 | 2.9 |
| Industrial machinery and equipment | 112.9 | 159.2 | 529.4 | 20.8 | 19.6 | 30.1 |
| Electronic and electric equipment | 71.5 | 95.4 | 846.0 | 14.9 | 19.5 | 20.0 |
| Transportation equipment | 124.7 | 218.3 | 697.6 | 26.5 | 39.0 | 49.2 |
| Other manufacturing | 154.4 | 172.8 | 961.5 | 30.0 | 14.2 | 13.8 |
| Wholesale trade | 206.0 | 367.5 | 538.3 | 26.7 | 55.5 | 13.2 |
| Finance (deposit institutions), insurance, real estate | 1229.6 | 108.4 | 191.0 | 10.3 | (-) | (-) |
| Services | 115.0 | 100.0 | 779.8 | 29.4 | 2.0 | 0.4 |
| Other | 213.1 | 151.6 | 1260.4 | 25.0 | 3.3 | 2.2 |

*Notes:*
(-) Represents zero
*General Notes:* Consists of nonbank U.S. parent companies and their nonbank foreign affiliates.
A foreign affiliate is a foreign business enterprise owned or controlled by a U.S. parent company.
A U.S. parent is a U.S. person that owns or controls directly or indirectly, 10 percent or more of the voting securities of an incorporated foreign business enterprise, or an equivalent interest in an unincorporated foreign business enterprise. A U.S. person can be an incorporated business enterprise.

*Source: Statistical Abstract of the United States 1998*, No. 908; <http://www.census.gov/prod/3/98pubs/98statab/sasec17.pdf>. Underlying data from U.S. Bureau of Economic Analysis, *Survey of Current Business*, October, 1997.

## C10. NET STOCK OF FIXED PRIVATE CAPITAL

### C10-1. Net Stock of Fixed Private Capital: 1990–1996 (as of Dec. 31)

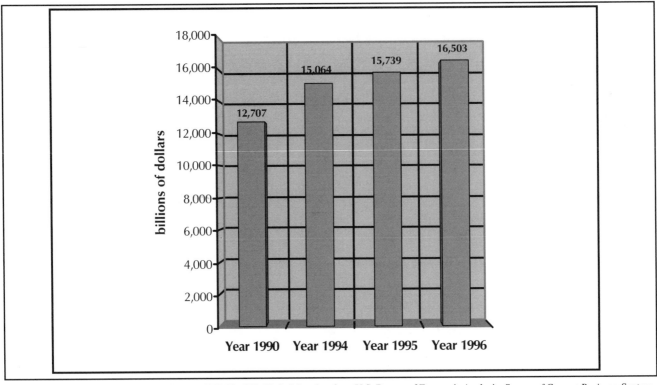

*Source: Statistical Abstract of the United States 1998*, No. 890. Underlying data from U.S. Bureau of Economic Analysis, *Survey of Current Business*, September, 1997.

## C11. FARMS

### C11-1. Farms—Number, Acreage, and Value, by Type of Organization: 1987 and 1992

| Item | Unit | Total[1] | Individual or family | Partnership | Corporation |
|---|---|---|---|---|---|
| **ALL FARMS** | | | | | |
| Number of farms: 1987 | 1,000 | 2,088 | 1,809 | 200 | 67 |
| Number of farms: 1992 | 1,000 | 1,925 | 1,653 | 187 | 73 |
| Land in farms: 1987 | Million acres | 964 | 628 | 153 | 119 |
| Land in farms: 1992 | Million acres | 946 | 604 | 153 | 123 |
| Value of land and buildings:[2] 1987 | Bil dol | 604 | 424 | 95 | 69 |
| Value of land and buildings:[2] 1992 | Bil dol | 687 | 474 | 109 | 85 |
| Value of farm products sold: 1987 | Bil dol | 136 | 77 | 23 | 35 |
| Value of farm products sold: 1992 | Bil dol | 163 | 88 | 29 | 44 |
| **FARMS WITH SALES OF $10,000 AND OVER** | | | | | |
| Number of farms: 1987 | 1,000 | 1,060 | 861 | 136 | 56 |
| Number of farms: 1992 | 1,000 | 1,019 | 820 | 131 | 61 |
| Land in farms: 1987 | Million acres | 829 | 525 | 143 | 116 |
| Land in farms: 1992 | Million acres | 822 | 512 | 143 | 119 |

*Notes:*
1. Includes other types, not shown separately.
2. Based on a sample of farms.

*Source: Statistical Abstract of the United States 1998*, No. 1103; <http://www.census.gov/prod/3/98pubs/98statab/sasec23.pdf>. Underlying data from U.S. Bureau of the Census, *1992 Census of Agriculture*, Vol. 1.

## C11-2. Farms—Number, Acreage, and Value, by Type of Organization, Percent Distribution: 1987 and 1992

| Item | Percent Distribution Total[1] | Percent Distribution Individual or Family | Percent Distribution Partnership | Percent Distribution Corporation |
|---|---|---|---|---|
| **ALL FARMS** | | | | |
| Number of farms: 1987 | 100 | 86.7 | 9.6 | 3.2 |
| Number of farms: 1992 | 100 | 85.9 | 9.7 | 3.8 |
| | | | | |
| Land in farms: 1987 | 100 | 65.1 | 15.9 | 12.4 |
| Land in farms: 1992 | 100 | 63.9 | 16.2 | 13.0 |
| | | | | |
| Value of land and buildings:[2] 1987 | 100 | 70.1 | 15.7 | 11.4 |
| Value of land and buildings:[2] 1992 | 100 | 69.0 | 15.8 | 12.4 |
| | | | | |
| Value of farm products sold: 1987 | 100 | 56.3 | 17.1 | 25.6 |
| Value of farm products sold: 1992 | 100 | 54.1 | 18.0 | 27.2 |
| | | | | |
| **FARMS WITH SALES OF $10,000 AND OVER** | | | | |
| Number of farms: 1987 | 100 | 81.3 | 12.8 | 5.3 |
| Number of farms: 1992 | 100 | 80.5 | 12.8 | 6.0 |
| | | | | |
| Land in farms: 1987 | 100 | 63.3 | 17.3 | 14.0 |
| Land in farms: 1992 | 100 | 62.2 | 17.4 | 14.4 |

*Notes:*
1. Includes other types, not shown separately.
2. Based on a sample of farms.

*Source: Statistical Abstract of the United States 1998*, No. 1103; <http://www.census.gov/prod/3/98pubs/98statab/sasec23.pdf>. Underlying data from U.S. Bureau of the Census, *1992 Census of Agriculture*, Vol. 1.

## C11-3. Farms—Number and Acreage, by Size of Farm: 1982–1992

| | Number of Farms (1,000) | | | Land in Farms  (million acres) | | |
|---|---|---|---|---|---|---|
| | 1982 | 1987 | 1992 | 1982 | 1987 | 1992 |
| Total | 2,241 | 2,088 | 1,925 | 986.8 | 964.5 | 945.5 |
| Under 10 acres | 188 | 183 | 166 | 0.7 | 0.7 | 0.7 |
| 10 to 49 acres | 449 | 412 | 388 | 12.1 | 11.1 | 10.3 |
| 50 to 99 acres | 344 | 311 | 283 | 24.8 | 22.5 | 20.4 |
| 100 to 179 acres | 368 | 334 | 301 | 49.9 | 45.3 | 40.7 |
| 180 to 259 acres | 211 | 192 | 172 | 45.7 | 41.5 | 37.2 |
| 260 to 499 acres | 315 | 286 | 255 | 113.0 | 103.0 | 91.7 |
| 500 to 999 acres | 204 | 200 | 186 | 140.5 | 138.5 | 129.3 |
| 1,000 to 1,999 acres | 97 | 102 | 102 | 132.4 | 138.8 | 139.0 |
| 2,000 acres and over | 65 | 67 | 71 | 467.5 | 463.2 | 476.3 |

*Source: Statistical Abstract of the United States 1998*, No. 1100; <http://www.census.gov/prod/3/98pubs/98statab/sasec23.pdf>.

## C11-4. Farms—Acreage, by Size of Farm: 1982–1992

| | Cropland harvested (million acres) 1982 | Cropland harvested (million acres) 1987 | Cropland harvested (million acres) 1992 |
|---|---|---|---|
| Total | 326.3 | 282.2 | 295.9 |
| Under 10 acres | 0.3 | 0.2 | 0.2 |
| 10 to 49 acres | 4.5 | 3.9 | 3.5 |
| 50 to 99 acres | 9.5 | 7.9 | 7.2 |
| 100 to 179 acres | 21.2 | 17.1 | 15.4 |
| 180 to 259 acres | 21.7 | 17.2 | 15.5 |
| 260 to 499 acres | 60.5 | 47.3 | 43.6 |
| 500 to 999 acres | 77.6 | 67.4 | 68.6 |
| 1,000 to 1,999 acres | 64.5 | 61.1 | 69.3 |
| 2,000 acres and over | 66.6 | 60.2 | 72.5 |

*Source: Statistical Abstract of the United States 1998*, No. 1100; <http://www.census.gov/prod/3/98pubs/98statab/sasec23.pdf>.

## C11-5. Farms—Acreage, by Size of Farm, Percent Distribution: 1992

| | Percent Distribution, 1992 Number of Farms | Percent Distribution, 1992 All Land in Farms | Percent Distribution, 1992 Cropland Harvested |
|---|---|---|---|
| Total | 100 | 100 | 100 |
| Under 10 acres | 8.6 | 0.1 | 0.1 |
| 10 to 49 acres | 20.1 | 1.1 | 1.2 |
| 50 to 99 acres | 14.7 | 2.2 | 2.4 |
| 100 to 179 acres | 15.6 | 4.3 | 5.2 |
| 180 to 259 acres | 8.9 | 3.9 | 5.2 |
| 260 to 499 acres | 13.3 | 9.7 | 14.7 |
| 500 to 999 acres | 9.7 | 13.7 | 23.2 |
| 1,000 to 1,999 acres | 5.3 | 14.7 | 23.4 |
| 2,000 acres and over | 3.7 | 50.4 | 24.5 |

*Source: Statistical Abstract of the United States 1998*, No. 1100; <http://www.census.gov/prod/3/98pubs/98statab/sasec23.pdf>.

# D. Overview of Consumption

## GENERAL OVERVIEW

This section presents an overview of household consumption in the United States. It analyzes consumption data from a variety of perspectives. Nearly all tables present detailed categories of consumption (food, housing, apparel, transportation, etc.), while exploring diverse variables, such as consumption across a time series, across household sizes and types, and across race and ethnicity. This multilayered portrait functions as a broad-based backdrop for the more detailed analyses of consumption in later sections.

## EXPLANATION OF INDICATORS

**D1. Personal Consumption Expenditures in Current and Constant Dollars:** The first set of charts and tables examines personal consumption over the course of the current decade, from 1990 through 1996. The data presented include both current expenditure totals, with the effects of inflation factored in (the first chart and next three tables), and constant dollar totals (chained to 1992 dollar valuations), muting the effects of inflation (the following chart and three tables). The charts show summary totals over the time period, while the tables break the totals out into many categories covering such personal expenditures as food, clothing, and housing.

**D2. Average Annual Expenditures of All Consumer Units, by Year, 1989–1995:** The next set of charts and tables presents detailed data on consumption broken down by year. The first two charts in this grouping present the total number of household units surveyed and the average annual amount of expenditures for those household units. The remaining two tables show the yearly totals, from 1989 to 1991 and from 1992 to 1995.

**D3. Average Annual Expenditures of All Consumer Units, by Region, 1995:** The next grouping (one chart and three tables) presents a snapshot in time: 1995,

mid-decade. It shows average annual household expenditures by regions within the United States. The chart, coming first, shows summary averages for each region, and the tables present averages of all types of expenses. The first table shows detail on food expenses, including such items as cereals, meats, and dairy products; the second table shows detail on household expenses including such items as housing, utilities, and furnishings; the final table shows other types of personal and household expenses, including such items as apparel, transportation, health care, and entertainment.

**D4. Average Annual Expenditures of All Consumer Units, by Size of Unit, 1995:** The next grouping (one chart and three tables) presents a snapshot in time: 1995, mid-decade. It shows average annual household expenditures, by size of household unit, including one-, two-, three-, four-, and over-five-person households. The organization is similar to the previous set. The chart, coming first, shows summary averages for each size of household unit, and the tables present averages of all types of expenses. The first table shows detail on food expenses, including such items as cereals, meats, and dairy products; the second table shows detail on household expenses including such items as housing, utilities, and furnishings; the final table shows other types of personal and household expenses, including such items as apparel, transportation, health care, and entertainment.

**D5. Average Annual Expenditures of All Consumer Units, by Type of Unit, 1995:** The next grouping (one chart and three tables) presents a snapshot in time: 1995, mid-decade. It shows average annual household expenditures, by the kind of household unit covered, including households with husband and wife only, husband and wife with children, single parents with children, etc. The organization is similar to the previous set. The chart, coming first, shows summary averages for each kind of household unit, and the tables present averages of all types of expenses. The first table shows detail on food expenses, including such items as cereals, meats, and dairy products; the second table shows detail on household expenses, including such items as housing, utilities, and furnishings; the final table shows other types of personal and household expenses, including such items as apparel, transportation, health care, and entertainment.

**D6. Average Annual Expenditures of All Consumer Units, by Type of Unit, Husband and Wife with Children, 1995:** The next grouping (one chart and two tables) presents a snapshot in time: 1995, mid-decade. It shows average annual household expenditures, by the kind of husband-wife-child unit, including households with oldest child under six, oldest child six to 17, etc. The organization is similar to the previous set. The chart, coming first, shows summary averages for each husband-wife-child, and the tables present averages of all types of expenses. The first table shows details on food expenses, including such items as cereals, meats, and dairy products; the second table shows details on household expenses, including such items as housing, utilities, and furnishings and other types of personal and household expenses, including such items as apparel, transportation, health care, and entertainment.

**D7. Average Annual Expenditures of All Consumer Units, by Race and Hispanic Origin, 1995:** The next grouping (one chart and two tables) presents a snapshot in time: 1995, mid-decade. It shows average annual household expenditures, by race and Hispanic origins.

The organization is similar to the previous set. The chart, coming first, shows summary averages for each race, and the tables present averages of all types of expenses. The first table shows detail on food expenses, including such items as cereals, meats, and dairy products and household expenses, including such items as housing, utilities, furnishings, and medical care. The second table shows other types of personal expenses, including such items as transportation, health care, entertainment, and education.

**D8. Average Annual Expenditures of All Consumer Units, by Age of Householder, 1995:** The next grouping (two tables) again presents a snapshot in time: 1995, mid-decade. It shows average annual household expenditures, by the age of the person recognized as householder. The first table shows detail on food expenses, including such items as cereals, meats, and dairy products; the second table shows detail on household expenses, including such items as housing, utilities, furnishings, and shows other types of personal and household expenses, including such items as apparel, transportation, health care, and entertainment.

**D9. Annual Expenditure per Child, 1996:** The final table presents another snapshot in time, specifically, 1996. It details the annual expenditure per child by amounts of various types of expenditures, by income level, and by the age of child.

## D1. PERSONAL CONSUMPTION EXPENDITURES IN CURRENT AND CONSTANT DOLLARS

### D1-1. Personal Consumption Expenditures in Current Dollars, Totals: 1990–1996

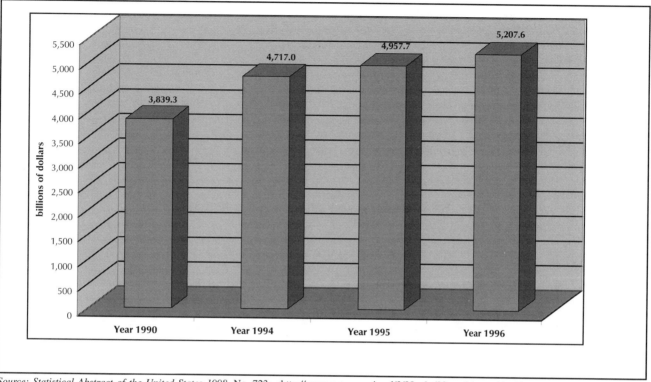

*Source: Statistical Abstract of the United States 1998*, No. 723; <http://wwwcensusgov/prod/3/98pubs/98statab/sasec14.pdf>. Underlying data from U.S. Bureau of Economic Analysis, *National Income and Product Accounts of the United States, 1929-94*, Vol. 1; and *Survey of Current Business*, August 1997.

### D1-2. Personal Consumption Expenditures in Current Dollars, by Type: 1990–1996, in Billions of Dollars *(continued in D1-3 and D1-4)*

| Expenditure | 1990 | 1994 | 1995 | 1996 |
|---|---|---|---|---|
| Food and tobacco[1] | 672.5 | 761.7 | 783.8 | 805.7 |
|   Food purchased for off-premise consumption | 404.8 | 451.6 | 462.2 | 478.4 |
|   Purchased meals and beverages[2] | 218.0 | 254.3 | 264.1 | 268.7 |
|   Tobacco products | 42.0 | 47.3 | 48.7 | 49.6 |
| Clothing, accessories, and jewelry[1] | 262.7 | 312.7 | 323.4 | 336.3 |
|   Shoes | 31.9 | 36.0 | 36.8 | 38.1 |
|   Clothing | 173.8 | 211.6 | 217.7 | 226.0 |
|   Jewelry and watches | 31.2 | 37.7 | 39.3 | 41.6 |
| Personal care | 57.3 | 68.4 | 71.9 | 75.7 |
| Housing[1] | 586.3 | 712.7 | 750.3 | 787.2 |
|   Owner-occupied nonfarm dwellings-space rent | 410.7 | 507.0 | 532.2 | 558.3 |
|   Tenant-occupied nonfarm dwellings-space rent | 150.1 | 174.0 | 184.6 | 193.6 |
| Household operation[1] | 436.2 | 535.0 | 562.8 | 591.9 |
|   Furniture[3] | 39.0 | 45.9 | 48.0 | 49.6 |
|   Semidurable house furnishings[4] | 21.2 | 27.2 | 28.9 | 30.1 |
|   Cleaning and polishing preparations | 41.9 | 50.8 | 52.3 | 54.5 |
|   Household utilities | 138.3 | 163.8 | 168.5 | 177.9 |
|     Electricity | 71.9 | 84.2 | 88.0 | 90.3 |
|     Gas | 26.8 | 32.4 | 31.5 | 34.9 |
|     Water and other sanitary services | 27.5 | 36.6 | 38.8 | 41.1 |
|     Fuel oil and coal | 12.0 | 10.5 | 10.2 | 11.6 |
|     Telephone and telegraph | 60.4 | 82.6 | 90.2 | 96.9 |

*Notes:*
1. Includes other expenditures not shown separately.
2. Consists of purchases (including tips) of meals and beverages from retail, service, and amusement establishments; hotels; dining and buffet cars; schools; school fraternities; institutions; clubs; and industrial lunch rooms. Includes meals and beverages consumed both on and off-premise.
3. Includes mattresses and bedsprings.
4. Consists largely of textile house furnishings including piece goods allocated to house furnishing use. Also includes lamp shades, brooms, and brushes.

*Source: Statistical Abstract of the United States 1998*, No. 723; <http://wwwcensusgov/prod/3/98pubs/98statab/sasec14.pdf>. Underlying data from U.S. Bureau of Economic Analysis, *National Income and Product Accounts of the United States, 1929-94*, Vol. 1; and *Survey of Current Business*, August 1997

**D1-3. Personal Consumption Expenditures in Current Dollars, by Type: 1990–1996, in Billions of Dollars** *(continued from previous table)*

| Expenditure | 1990 | 1994 | 1995 | 1996 |
|---|---|---|---|---|
| Medical care[1] | 615.6 | 826.1 | 871.6 | 912.8 |
| Drug preparations and sundries[5] | 65.1 | 81.6 | 85.7 | 90.9 |
| Physicians | 140.8 | 180.0 | 191.4 | 196.5 |
| Dentists | 32.9 | 43.9 | 47.6 | 50.9 |
| Hospitals and nursing homes[6] | 265.7 | 357.0 | 375.9 | 394.2 |
| Health insurance | 37.4 | 55.0 | 53.6 | 56.3 |
| Medical care[7] | 31.3 | 42.9 | 40.7 | 41.8 |
| Personal business[1] | 290.1 | 370.4 | 389.1 | 421.1 |
| Expense of handling life insurance[8] | 56.4 | 72.6 | 75.4 | 79.9 |
| Legal services | 41.8 | 48.8 | 49.1 | 52.2 |
| Funeral and burial expenses | 9.0 | 11.1 | 12.2 | 12.8 |

*Notes:*
1. Includes other expenditures not shown separately.
5. Excludes drug preparations and related products dispensed by physicians, hospitals, and other medical services.
6. Consists of (1) current expenditures (including consumption of fixed capital) of nonprofit hospitals and nursing homes and (2) payments by patients to proprietary and government hospitals and nursing homes.
7. Consists of (1) premiums, less benefits and dividends, for health hospitalization and accidental death and dismemberment insurance provided by commercial insurance carriers and (2) administrative expenses (including consumption of fixed capital) of Blue Cross and Blue Shield plans and of other independent prepaid and self-insured health plans.
8. Consists of (1) operating expenses of life insurance carriers and private noninsured pension plans and (2) premiums less benefits and dividends of fraternal benefit societies Excludes expenses allocated by commercial carriers to accident and health insurance.
*Only notes that apply to this table are cited.

*Source: Statistical Abstract of the United States 1998*, No. 723; <http://wwwcensusgov/prod/3/98pubs/98statab/sasec14.pdf>. Underlying data from U.S. Bureau of Economic Analysis, *National Income and Product Accounts of the United States, 1929-94*,Vol. 1; and *Survey of Current Business*, August 1997.

**D1-4. Personal Consumption Expenditures in Current Dollars, by Type: 1990–1996, in Billions of Dollars** *(continued from previous table)*

| Expenditure | 1990 | 1994 | 1995 | 1996 |
|---|---|---|---|---|
| Transportation | 463.3 | 542.2 | 572.3 | 602.2 |
| User-operated transportation[1] | 426.9 | 502.6 | 530.1 | 557.7 |
| New autos | 92.4 | 91.2 | 87.1 | 86.1 |
| Net purchases of used autos | 31.6 | 44.1 | 52.4 | 55.3 |
| Tires, tubes, accessories, etc | 29.4 | 34.5 | 35.8 | 37.9 |
| Repair, greasing, washing, parking, storage, rental, and leasing | 84.1 | 116.4 | 128.7 | 140.1 |
| Gasoline and oil | 96.6 | 109.4 | 114.4 | 122.6 |
| Purchased local transportation | 7.8 | 8.9 | 9.2 | 10.1 |
| Mass transit systems | 5.2 | 5.9 | 6.0 | 6.6 |
| Taxicab | 2.6 | 3.0 | 3.2 | 3.5 |
| Purchased intercity transportation[1] | 28.5 | 30.7 | 33.0 | 34.4 |
| Railway (commutation) | 0.8 | 0.7 | 0.8 | 0.8 |
| Bus | 1.0 | 1.1 | 1.3 | 1.3 |
| Airline | 23.9 | 25.8 | 27.7 | 28.2 |
| Recreation[1] | 281.6 | 370.2 | 402.5 | 431.1 |
| Magazines, newspapers, and sheet music | 21.5 | 24.5 | 25.5 | 26.5 |
| Nondurable toys and sport supplies | 31.6 | 39.7 | 42.2 | 45.4 |
| Video/audio products, computing equip., musical instruments | 53.8 | 78.5 | 85.2 | 89.7 |
| Education and research | 80.7 | 104.7 | 112.2 | 119.6 |
| Higher education | 44.0 | 59.0 | 62.2 | 65.2 |
| Religious and welfare activities | 100.4 | 131.2 | 139.8 | 150.5 |
| Foreign travel and other, net | -7.4 | -18.3 | -22.1 | -26.5 |
| Foreign travel by US residents | 41.2 | 50.1 | 51.9 | 54.9 |
| Less: Expenditures in the United States by nonresidents | 51.6 | 69.7 | 75.2 | 82.7 |

*Notes:*
1. Includes other expenditures not shown separately.

*Source: Statistical Abstract of the United States 1998*, No. 723; <http://wwwcensusgov/prod/3/98pubs/98statab/sasec14.pdf>. Underlying data from U.S. Bureau of Economic Analysis, *National Income and Product Accounts of the United States, 1929-94*,Vol. 1;and *Survey of Current Business*, August 1997.

## D1-5. Personal Consumption Expenditures in Chained, or Constant (1992), Dollars, Totals: 1990–1996

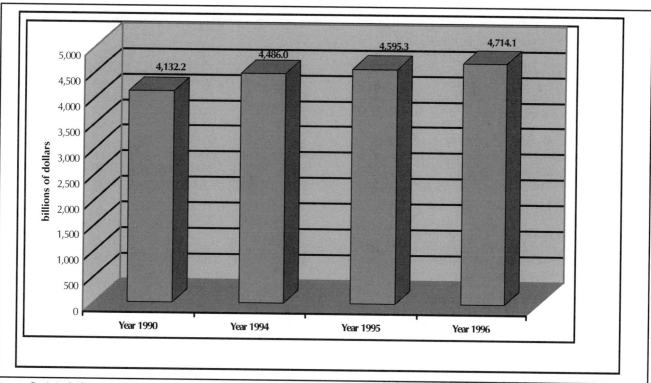

*Source: Statistical Abstract of the United States 1998*, No. 723; <http://wwwcensusgov/prod/3/98pubs/98statab/sasec14.pdf>. Underlying data from U.S. Bureau of Economic Analysis, *National Income and Product Accounts of the United States, 1929-94*, Vol. 1; and *Survey of Current Business*, August 1997.

## D1-6. Personal Consumption Expenditures in Chained, or Constant (1992), Dollars, by Type: 1990–1996, in Billions of Dollars (continued in D1-7 and D1-8)

| Expenditure | 1990 | 1994 | 1995 | 1996 |
|---|---|---|---|---|
| Food and tobacco[1] | 713.5 | 735.0 | 737.9 | 736.5 |
| Food purchased for off-premise consumption | 423.3 | 434.5 | 433.4 | 434.7 |
| Purchased meals and beverages[2] | 231.6 | 245.1 | 248.7 | 246.6 |
| Tobacco products | 50.9 | 47.2 | 47.4 | 46.8 |
| Clothing, accessories, and jewelry[1] | 279.4 | 308.5 | 321.8 | 335.3 |
| Shoes | 34.0 | 35.7 | 36.6 | 37.6 |
| Clothing | 183.7 | 211.2 | 220.6 | 229.9 |
| Jewelry and watches | 34.0 | 35.6 | 36.8 | 39.7 |
| Personal care | 60.6 | 65.5 | 67.9 | 70.1 |
| Housing[1] | 627.2 | 674.3 | 688.2 | 700.2 |
| Owner-occupied nonfarm dwellings-space rent | 437.6 | 479.6 | 487.2 | 495.3 |
| Tenant-occupied nonfarm dwellings-space rent | 160.0 | 165.2 | 171.1 | 174.9 |
| Household operation[1] | 457.0 | 514.5 | 533.6 | 548.4 |
| Furniture[3] | 40.6 | 43.2 | 44.2 | 44.6 |
| Semidurable house furnishings[4] | 22.0 | 25.7 | 26.9 | 28.2 |
| Cleaning and polishing preparations | 43.7 | 50.2 | 50.0 | 50.6 |
| Household utilities | 146.7 | 156.3 | 159.4 | 163.1 |
| Electricity | 76.1 | 82.6 | 84.3 | 85.2 |
| Gas | 27.7 | 30.0 | 30.7 | 32.7 |
| Water and other sanitary services | 31.9 | 33.0 | 33.8 | 34.6 |
| Fuel oil and coal | 11.2 | 10.7 | 10.5 | 10.6 |
| Telephone and telegraph | 61.3 | 79.6 | 86.6 | 91.1 |

*Notes:*
1. Includes other expenditures not shown separately.
2. Consists of purchases (including tips) of meals and beverages from retail, service, and amusement establishments; hotels; dining and buffet cars; schools; school fraternities; institutions; clubs; and industrial lunch rooms Includes meals and beverages consumed both on and off-premise.
3. Includes mattresses and bedsprings.
4. Consists largely of textile house furnishings including piece goods allocated to house furnishing use. Also includes lamp shades, brooms, and brushes.

*Source: Statistical Abstract of the United States 1998*, No. 723; <http://wwwcensusgov/prod/3/98pubs/98statab/sasec14.pdf>. Underlying data from U.S. Bureau of Economic Analysis, *National Income and Product Accounts of the United States, 1929-94*, Vol. 1; and *Survey of Current Business*, August 1997.

## D1-7. Personal Consumption Expenditures in Chained, or Constant (1992), Dollars, by Type: 1990–1996, in Billions of Dollars *(continued from previous table)*

| Expenditure | 1990 | 1994 | 1995 | 1996 |
|---|---|---|---|---|
| Medical care[1] | 691.1 | 751.0 | 766.2 | 782.4 |
| Drug preparations and sundries[5] | 74.5 | 76.7 | 79.1 | 81.7 |
| Physicians | 158.5 | 162.4 | 166.1 | 169.3 |
| Dentists | 37.7 | 39.8 | 41.1 | 42.0 |
| Hospitals and nursing homes[6] | 299.0 | 331.5 | 336.6 | 343.1 |
| Health insurance | 41.3 | 40.0 | 37.5 | 36.9 |
| Medical care[7] | 35.3 | 36.6 | 35.2 | 34.7 |
| Personal business[1] | 331.3 | 352.1 | 350.7 | 363.6 |
| Expense of handling life insurance[8] | 61.2 | 68.1 | 67.9 | 68.5 |
| Legal services | 46.4 | 45.3 | 44.0 | 45.2 |
| Funeral and burial expenses | 10.1 | 10.1 | 10.5 | 10.4 |

*Notes:
1. Includes other expenditures not shown separately.
5. Excludes drug preparations and related products dispensed by physicians, hospitals, and other medical services.
6. Consists of (1) current expenditures (including consumption of fixed capital) of nonprofit hospitals and nursing homes and (2) payments by patients to proprietary and government hospitals and nursing homes.
7. Consists of (1) premiums, less benefits and dividends, for health hospitalization and accidental death and dismemberment insurance provided by commercial insurance carriers and (2) administrative expenses (including consumption of fixed capital) of Blue Cross and Blue Shield plans and of other independent prepaid and self-insured health plans.
8. Consists of (1) operating expenses of life insurance carriers and private noninsured pension plans and (2) premiums less benefits and dividends of fraternal benefit societies Excludes expenses allocated by commercial carriers to accident and health insurance.
*Only notes that apply to this table are cited.

*Source: Statistical Abstract of the United States 1998*, No. 723; <http://wwwcensusgov/prod/3/98pubs/98statab/sasec14.pdf>. Underlying data from U.S. Bureau of Economic Analysis, *National Income and Product Accounts of the United States, 1929-94*, Vol. 1; and *Survey of Current Business*, August 1997.

## D1-8. Personal Consumption Expenditures in Chained, or Constant (1992), Dollars, by Type: 1990–1996, in Billions of Dollars *(continued from previous table)*

| Expenditure | 1990 | 1994 | 1995 | 1996 |
|---|---|---|---|---|
| Transportation | 491.3 | 515.3 | 528.0 | 540.3 |
| User-operated transportation[1] | 454.2 | 476.6 | 487.8 | 497.7 |
| New autos | 98.1 | 86.2 | 80.6 | 78.2 |
| Net purchases of used autos | 35.0 | 37.5 | 40.8 | 42.1 |
| Tires, tubes, accessories, etc | 30.0 | 35.1 | 36.2 | 38.3 |
| Repair, greasing, washing, parking, storage, rental, and leasing | 94.7 | 108.5 | 116.5 | 123.3 |
| Gasoline and oil | 108.1 | 109.8 | 113.1 | 114.1 |
| Purchased local transportation | 8.6 | 8.6 | 8.5 | 8.5 |
| Mass transit systems | 5.7 | 5.7 | 5.5 | 5.6 |
| Taxicab | 2.9 | 2.9 | 3.0 | 3.0 |
| Purchased intercity transportation[1] | 28.6 | 30.1 | 31.7 | 34.2 |
| Railway (commutation) | 0.8 | 0.7 | 0.7 | 0.7 |
| Bus | 1.1 | 1.1 | 1.4 | 1.4 |
| Airline | 23.7 | 25.5 | 26.8 | 28.8 |
| Recreation[1] | 291.8 | 365.2 | 395.7 | 424.4 |
| Magazines, newspapers, and sheet music | 23.8 | 22.9 | 22.9 | 22.7 |
| Nondurable toys and sport supplies | 32.6 | 38.9 | 41.4 | 43.9 |
| Video/audio products, computing equip., musical instruments | 47.9 | 87.4 | 101.8 | 119.5 |
| Education and research | 89.3 | 96.8 | 99.4 | 102.7 |
| Higher education | 50.2 | 53.1 | 53.7 | 54.0 |
| Religious and welfare activities | 106.6 | 125.6 | 128.6 | 136.6 |
| Foreign travel and other, net | -8.2 | -16.2 | -19.5 | -21.5 |
| Foreign travel by US residents | 46.1 | 48.8 | 48.9 | 50.8 |
| Less: Expenditures in the United States by nonresidents | 57.7 | 66.4 | 69.5 | 73.5 |

Notes:
1. Includes other expenditures not shown separately.

*Source: Statistical Abstract of the United States 1998*, No. 723; <http://wwwcensusgov/prod/3/98pubs/98statab/sasec14.pdf>. Underlying data from U.S. Bureau of Economic Analysis, *National Income and Product Accounts of the United States, 1929-94*, Vol. 1; and *Survey of Current Business*, August 1997.

## D2. AVERAGE ANNUAL EXPENDITURES OF ALL CONSUMER UNITS, BY YEAR, 1989–1995

### D2-1. Average Annual Expenditures of All Consumer Units, Number of Units: 1989–1995

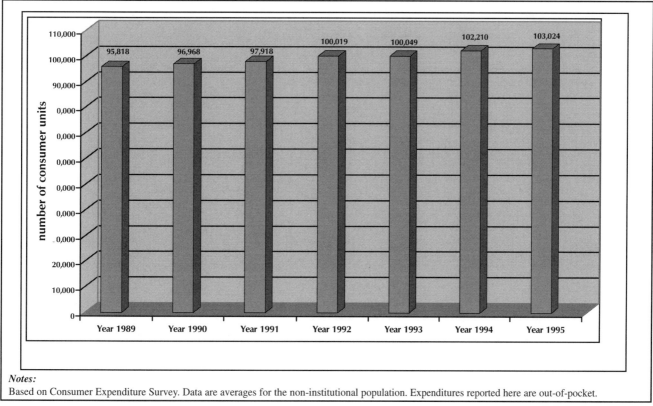

*Notes:*
Based on Consumer Expenditure Survey. Data are averages for the non-institutional population. Expenditures reported here are out-of-pocket.

*Source: Statistical Abstract of the United States 1998*, No. 736; <http://www.census.gov/prod/3/98pubs/98statab/sasec14.pdf>. Underlying data from U.S. Bureau of Labor Statistics, *Consumer Expenditures in 1995*; and earlier reports.

## D2-2. Average Annual Expenditures of All Consumer Units, Total Expenditures: 1989–1995

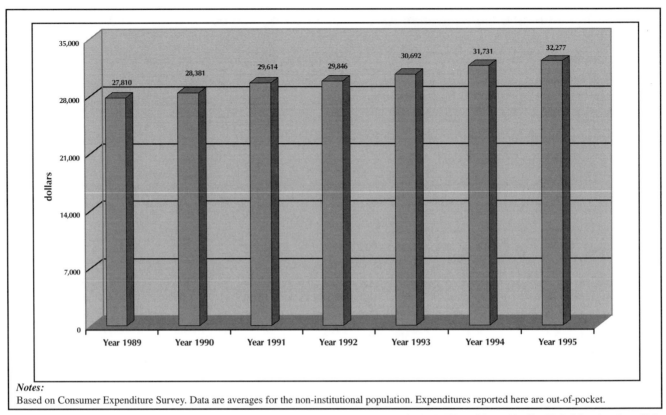

*Notes:*
Based on Consumer Expenditure Survey. Data are averages for the non-institutional population. Expenditures reported here are out-of-pocket.

*Source: Statistical Abstract of the United States 1998*, No. 736; <http://www.census.gov/prod/3/98pubs/98statab/sasec14.pdf>. Underlying data from U.S. Bureau of Labor Statistics, *Consumer Expenditures in 1995*; and earlier reports.

## D2-3. Average Annual Expenditures of All Consumer Units, by Type of Expenditure: 1989–1991, in Dollars

| TYPE | 1989 | 1990 | 1991 |
|---|---|---|---|
| Food | 4,152 | 4,296 | 4,271 |
| Food at home | 2,390 | 2,485 | 2,651 |
| Cereal and bakery products | 359 | 368 | 404 |
| Meats, poultry, fish, and eggs | 611 | 668 | 709 |
| Dairy products | 304 | 295 | 294 |
| Fruits and vegetables | 408 | 408 | 429 |
| Other food at home | 708 | 746 | 815 |
| Food away from home | 1,762 | 1,811 | 1,620 |
| Alcoholic beverages | 284 | 293 | 297 |
| Housing | 8,434 | 8,703 | 9,252 |
| Shelter | 4,660 | 4,836 | 5,191 |
| Fuels, utilities, public services | 1,835 | 1,890 | 1,990 |
| Household operations, furnishings | 1,546 | 1,571 | 1,648 |
| Housekeeping supplies | 394 | 406 | 424 |
| Apparel and services | 1,582 | 1,618 | 1,735 |
| Transportation | 5,187 | 5,120 | 5,151 |
| Vehicle purchase | 2,291 | 2,129 | 2,111 |
| Gasoline and motor oil | 985 | 1,047 | 995 |
| Other transportation | 1,911 | 1,944 | 2,045 |
| Health care | 1,407 | 1,480 | 1,554 |
| Tobacco products, smoking supplies | 261 | 274 | 276 |
| Life and other personal insurance | 346 | 345 | 356 |
| Pensions and Social Security | 2,125 | 2,248 | 2,431 |
| Other expenditures | 4,030 | 4,003 | 4,291 |

*Notes:*
Based on Consumer Expenditure Survey. Data are averages for the non-institutional population. Expenditures reported here are out-of-pocket.

*Source: Statistical Abstract of the United States 1998*, No. 736; <http://www.census.gov/prod/3/98pubs/98statab/sasec14.pdf>. Underlying data from U.S. Bureau of Labor Statistics, *Consumer Expenditures in 1995*; and earlier reports.

## D2-4. Average Annual Expenditures of All Consumer Units, by Type of Expenditure: 1992–1995, in Dollars

| TYPE | 1992 | 1993 | 1994 | 1995 |
|---|---|---|---|---|
| Food | 4,273 | 4,399 | 4,411 | 4,505 |
| Food at home | 2,643 | 2,735 | 2,712 | 2,803 |
| Cereal and bakery products | 411 | 434 | 429 | 441 |
| Meats, poultry, fish, and eggs | 687 | 734 | 732 | 752 |
| Dairy products | 302 | 295 | 289 | 297 |
| Fruits and vegetables | 428 | 444 | 437 | 457 |
| Other food at home | 814 | 827 | 825 | 856 |
| Food away from home | 1,631 | 1,664 | 1,698 | 1,702 |
| Alcoholic beverages | 301 | 268 | 278 | 277 |
| Housing | 9,477 | 9,636 | 10,106 | 10,465 |
| Shelter | 5,411 | 5,415 | 5,686 | 5,932 |
| Fuels, utilities, public services | 1,984 | 2,112 | 2,189 | 2,193 |
| Household operations, furnishings | 1,649 | 1,699 | 1,838 | 1,911 |
| Housekeeping supplies | 433 | 410 | 393 | 430 |
| Apparel and services | 1,710 | 1,676 | 1,644 | 1,704 |
| Transportation | 5,228 | 5,453 | 6,044 | 6,016 |
| Vehicle purchase | 2,189 | 2,319 | 2,725 | 2,639 |
| Gasoline and motor oil | 973 | 977 | 986 | 1,006 |
| Other transportation | 2,066 | 2,157 | 2,334 | 2,371 |
| Health care | 1,634 | 1,776 | 1,755 | 1,732 |

## D2-4. Average Annual Expenditures of All Consumer Units, by Type of Expenditure: 1992–1995, in Dollars *(continued)*

| TYPE | 1992 | 1993 | 1994 | 1995 |
|---|---|---|---|---|
| Tobacco products, smoking supplies | 275 | 268 | 259 | 269 |
| Life and other personal insurance | 353 | 399 | 398 | 374 |
| Pensions and Social Security | 2,397 | 2,509 | 2,540 | 2,593 |
| Other expenditures | 4,198 | 4,308 | 4,297 | 4,340 |

*Notes:*
Based on Consumer Expenditure Survey. Data are averages for the non-institutional population. Expenditures reported here are out-of-pocket.

*Source: Statistical Abstract of the United States 1998*, No. 736; <http://www.census.gov/prod/3/98pubs/98statab/sasec14.pdf>. Underlying data from U.S. Bureau of Labor Statistics, *Consumer Expenditures in 1995;* and earlier reports.

## D3. AVERAGE ANNUAL EXPENDITURES OF ALL CONSUMER UNITS, BY REGION, 1995

## D3-1. Average Annual Expenditures of All Consumer Units, by Region, Totals: 1995

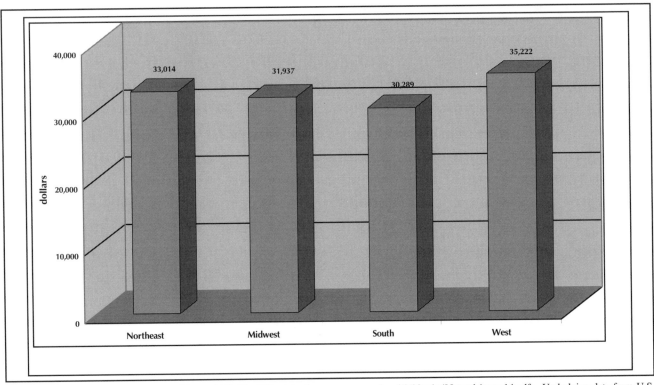

*Source: Statistical Abstract of the United States 1998*, No. 734; <http://www.census.gov/prod/3/98pubs/98statab/sasec14.pdf>. Underlying data from U.S. Bureau of Labor Statistics, *Consumer Expenditures in 1995;* and unpublished data.

## D3-2. Average Annual Expenditures of All Consumer Units, by Region: 1995 *(continued in D3-3 and D3-4)*

| | Northeast | Midwest | South | West |
|---|---|---|---|---|
| Food | 4,870 | 4,348 | 4,272 | 4,726 |
| Food at home | 3,122 | 2,626 | 2,626 | 2,998 |
| Cereals and bakery products | 528 | 411 | 404 | 454 |
| Cereals and cereal products | 195 | 152 | 153 | 171 |
| Bakery products | 333 | 259 | 251 | 282 |
| Meats, poultry, fish, and eggs | 866 | 669 | 746 | 754 |
| Beef | 232 | 221 | 233 | 223 |
| Pork | 156 | 137 | 172 | 153 |
| Other meats | 131 | 101 | 93 | 97 |
| Poultry | 182 | 116 | 131 | 132 |
| Fish and seafood | 129 | 70 | 88 | 116 |
| Eggs | 36 | 24 | 29 | 34 |
| Dairy products | 328 | 279 | 270 | 331 |
| Fresh milk and cream | 132 | 118 | 116 | 132 |
| Other dairy products | 196 | 161 | 154 | 199 |
| Fruits and vegetables | 552 | 412 | 419 | 480 |
| Fresh fruits | 175 | 136 | 126 | 154 |
| Fresh vegetables | 176 | 114 | 127 | 145 |
| Processed fruits | 120 | 87 | 83 | 104 |
| Processed vegetables | 81 | 75 | 84 | 77 |
| Other food at home | 847 | 855 | 787 | 979 |
| Nonalcoholic beverages | 250 | 244 | 226 | 250 |
| Food away from home | 1,748 | 1,722 | 1,646 | 1,728 |
| Alcoholic beverages | 327 | 261 | 242 | 307 |

*Source: Statistical Abstract of the United States 1998*, No. 734; <http://www.census.gov/prod/3/98pubs/98statab/sasec14.pdf>. Underlying data from U.S. Bureau of Labor Statistics, *Consumer Expenditures in 1995*; and unpublished data.

## D3-3. Average Annual Expenditures of All Consumer Units, by Region: 1995 *(continued from previous table)*

| | Northeast | Midwest | South | West |
|---|---|---|---|---|
| Housing | 11,485 | 9,754 | 9,287 | 12,265 |
| Shelter | 6,993 | 5,198 | 4,859 | 7,550 |
| Owned dwellings | 4,311 | 3,521 | 3,026 | 4,691 |
| Mortgage interest and charges | 2,212 | 1,903 | 1,634 | 3,026 |
| Property taxes | 1,439 | 955 | 693 | 807 |
| Maintenance, repair, insurance, other | 659 | 663 | 700 | 859 |
| Rented dwellings | 2,164 | 1,316 | 1,524 | 2,416 |
| Other lodging | 518 | 361 | 309 | 443 |
| Utilities, fuels, and public services | 2,297 | 2,184 | 2,266 | 1,982 |
| Natural gas | 332 | 395 | 159 | 234 |
| Electricity | 810 | 783 | 1,065 | 713 |
| Fuel oil and other fuels | 223 | 77 | 47 | 33 |
| Telephone | 718 | 706 | 715 | 692 |
| Water and other public services | 214 | 224 | 281 | 311 |
| Household operations | 482 | 451 | 544 | 545 |
| Personal services | 238 | 270 | 261 | 258 |
| Other household expenses | 244 | 180 | 283 | 286 |
| Housekeeping supplies | 467 | 418 | 393 | 467 |
| Household furnishings and equipment | 1,245 | 1,504 | 1,225 | 1,721 |
| Household textiles | 122 | 109 | 100 | 70 |
| Furniture | 304 | 313 | 327 | 368 |
| Floor coverings | 54 | 221 | 50 | 450 |
| Major appliances | 132 | 167 | 166 | 145 |
| Small appliances, misc housewares | 84 | 91 | 82 | 85 |
| Miscellaneous household equipment | 548 | 603 | 501 | 604 |

*Source: Statistical Abstract of the United States 1998*, No. 734; <http://www.census.gov/prod/3/98pubs/98statab/sasec14.pdf>. Underlying data from U.S. Bureau of Labor Statistics, *Consumer Expenditures in 1995*; and unpublished data.

**D3-4. Average Annual Expenditures of All Consumer Units, by Region: 1995** *(continued from previous table)*

| | Northeast | Midwest | South | West |
|---|---|---|---|---|
| Apparel and services | 1,751 | 1,721 | 1,667 | 1,697 |
|   Men and boys | 421 | 418 | 414 | 457 |
|   Women and girls | 695 | 713 | 622 | 628 |
|   Children under 2 years old | 87 | 75 | 81 | 80 |
|   Footwear | 278 | 277 | 289 | 262 |
|   Other apparel products and services | 270 | 237 | 261 | 271 |
| Transportation | 5,468 | 6,378 | 6,039 | 6,069 |
|   Vehicle purchases (net outlay) | 2,145 | 2,954 | 2,856 | 2,380 |
|     Cars and trucks, new | 1,111 | 1,212 | 1,327 | 1,036 |
|     Cars and trucks, used | 975 | 1,696 | 1,505 | 1,332 |
|   Gasoline and motor oil | 877 | 1,043 | 1,031 | 1,045 |
|   Other vehicle expenses | 1,960 | 2,078 | 1,881 | 2,214 |
|     Vehicle finance charges | 182 | 278 | 305 | 244 |
|     Maintenance and repair | 584 | 643 | 632 | 764 |
|     Vehicle insurance | 767 | 689 | 682 | 739 |
|     Rent, lease, licenses, other | 427 | 468 | 262 | 467 |
|   Public transportation | 486 | 302 | 271 | 429 |
| Health care | 1,757 | 1,759 | 1,790 | 1,584 |
| Entertainment | 1,544 | 1,602 | 1,459 | 1,939 |
| Personal care products and services | 438 | 373 | 386 | 435 |
| Reading | 186 | 170 | 135 | 177 |
| Education | 576 | 492 | 436 | 403 |
| Tobacco products and smoking supplies | 260 | 299 | 283 | 217 |
| Miscellaneous | 708 | 794 | 722 | 860 |
| Cash contributions | 724 | 962 | 902 | 1,113 |
| Personal insurance and pensions | 2,920 | 3,022 | 2,670 | 3,432 |
|   Life and other personal insurance | 353 | 403 | 392 | 330 |
|   Pensions and Social Security | 2,567 | 2,619 | 2,277 | 3,102 |
|     Personal taxes | 3,215 | 2,837 | 2,438 | 4,101 |

*Source: Statistical Abstract of the United States 1998,* No. 734; <http://www.census.gov/prod/3/98pubs/98statab/sasec14.pdf>. Underlying data from U.S. Bureau of Labor Statistics, *Consumer Expenditures in 1995;* and unpublished data.

## D4. AVERAGE ANNUAL EXPENDITURES OF ALL CONSUMER UNITS, BY SIZE OF UNIT, 1995

### D4-1. Average Annual Expenditures of All Consumer Units, by Size of Unit, Totals: 1995

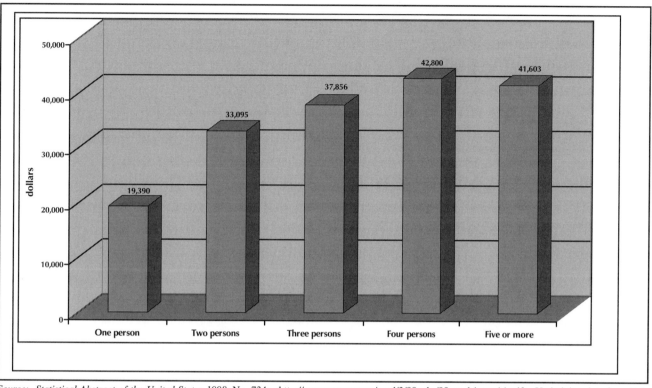

Source: *Statistical Abstract of the United States 1998,* No. 734; <http://www.census.gov/prod/3/98pubs/98statab/sasec14.pdf>. Underlying data from U.S. Bureau of Labor Statistics, *Consumer Expenditures in 1995*; and unpublished data.

### D4-2. Average Annual Expenditures of All Consumer Units, by Size of Unit: 1995 *(continued in D4-3 and D4-4)*

|  | One person | Two persons | Three persons | Four persons | Five or more persons |
|---|---|---|---|---|---|
| Food | 2,500 | 4,366 | 5,228 | 6,280 | 6,805 |
| Food at home | 1,401 | 2,587 | 3,276 | 4,085 | 4,761 |
| Cereals and bakery products | 221 | 402 | 504 | 667 | 747 |
| Cereals and cereal products | 76 | 146 | 190 | 251 | 310 |
| Bakery products | 145 | 256 | 314 | 416 | 437 |
| Meats, poultry, fish, and eggs | 343 | 678 | 900 | 1,118 | 1,359 |
| Beef | 97 | 200 | 280 | 360 | 401 |
| Pork | 67 | 143 | 179 | 240 | 286 |
| Other meats | 49 | 89 | 129 | 157 | 182 |
| Poultry | 64 | 121 | 171 | 191 | 263 |
| Fish and seafood | 50 | 97 | 110 | 131 | 162 |
| Eggs | 15 | 27 | 32 | 39 | 65 |
| Dairy products | 148 | 271 | 339 | 436 | 520 |
| Fresh milk and cream | 60 | 104 | 140 | 184 | 242 |
| Other dairy products | 88 | 166 | 199 | 253 | 278 |
| Fruits and vegetables | 250 | 451 | 518 | 607 | 735 |
| Fresh fruits | 84 | 146 | 157 | 182 | 232 |
| Fresh vegetables | 76 | 141 | 156 | 172 | 215 |
| Processed fruits | 50 | 88 | 113 | 142 | 154 |
| Processed vegetables | 40 | 77 | 92 | 111 | 135 |
| Other food at home | 439 | 786 | 1,015 | 1,258 | 1,400 |
| Nonalcoholic beverages | 127 | 219 | 290 | 348 | 386 |
| Food away from home | 1,098 | 1,778 | 1,951 | 2,195 | 2,043 |
| Alcoholic beverages | 248 | 309 | 265 | 296 | 253 |

Source: *Statistical Abstract of the United States 1998,* No. 734; <http://www.census.gov/prod/3/98pubs/98statab/sasec14.pdf>. Underlying data from U.S. Bureau of Labor Statistics, *Consumer Expenditures in 1995*; and unpublished data.

## D4-3. Average Annual Expenditures of All Consumer Units, by Size of Unit: 1995 *(continued from previous table)*

| | One person | Two persons | Three persons | Four persons | Five or more persons |
|---|---|---|---|---|---|
| Housing | 7,036 | 10,581 | 11,768 | 13,577 | 13,085 |
| Shelter | 4,359 | 5,760 | 6,563 | 7,717 | 7,256 |
| Owned dwellings | 1,850 | 3,901 | 4,376 | 5,613 | 4,935 |
| Mortgage interest and charges | 823 | 1,857 | 2,726 | 3,639 | 3,253 |
| Property taxes | 496 | 1,172 | 954 | 1,209 | 971 |
| Maintenance, repair, insurance, other | 531 | 872 | 696 | 764 | 711 |
| Rented dwellings | 2,283 | 1,360 | 1,770 | 1,613 | 1,982 |
| Other lodging | 226 | 499 | 416 | 492 | 339 |
| Utilities, fuels, and public services | 1,423 | 2,265 | 2,505 | 2,734 | 2,839 |
| Natural gas | 170 | 286 | 291 | 337 | 352 |
| Electricity | 532 | 895 | 1,017 | 1,119 | 1,141 |
| Fuel oil and other fuels | 65 | 99 | 88 | 96 | 95 |
| Telephone | 507 | 714 | 816 | 839 | 894 |
| Water and other public services | 149 | 272 | 293 | 344 | 357 |
| Household operations | 250 | 429 | 646 | 1,006 | 525 |
| Personal services | 61 | 129 | 414 | 673 | 351 |
| Other household expenses | 189 | 301 | 232 | 334 | 173 |
| Housekeeping supplies | 235 | 476 | 490 | 530 | 586 |
| Household furnishings and equipment | 768 | 1,651 | 1,565 | 1,589 | 1,879 |
| Household textiles | 58 | 130 | 108 | 103 | 111 |
| Furniture | 167 | 320 | 460 | 438 | 428 |
| Floor coverings | 96 | 332 | 79 | 119 | 165 |
| Major appliances | 79 | 168 | 174 | 179 | 263 |
| Small appliances, misc housewares | 58 | 98 | 85 | 100 | 99 |
| Miscellaneous household equipment | 311 | 602 | 658 | 650 | 814 |

*Source: Statistical Abstract of the United States 1998, No. 734; <http://www.census.gov/prod/3/98pubs/98statab/sasec14.pdf>. Underlying data from U.S. Bureau of Labor Statistics, Consumer Expenditures in 1995; and unpublished data.*

## D4-4. Average Annual Expenditures of All Consumer Units, by Size of Unit: 1995 *(continued from previous table)*

| | One person | Two persons | Three persons | Four persons | Five or more persons |
|---|---|---|---|---|---|
| Apparel and services | 991 | 1,524 | 2,097 | 2,479 | 2,499 |
| Men and boys | 235 | 353 | 512 | 648 | 720 |
| Women and girls | 391 | 642 | 820 | 910 | 853 |
| Children under 2 years old | 16 | 43 | 142 | 151 | 178 |
| Footwear | 176 | 201 | 322 | 483 | 437 |
| Other apparel products and services | 173 | 285 | 301 | 288 | 311 |
| Transportation | 2,916 | 6,158 | 7,852 | 8,156 | 8,222 |
| Vehicle purchases (net outlay) | 1,036 | 2,563 | 3,718 | 3,789 | 3,975 |
| Cars and trucks, new | 551 | 1,293 | 1,613 | 1,533 | 1,530 |
| Cars and trucks, used | 461 | 1,226 | 2,071 | 2,206 | 2,434 |
| Gasoline and motor oil | 531 | 1,016 | 1,248 | 1,376 | 1,382 |
| Other vehicle expenses | 1,111 | 2,146 | 2,552 | 2,567 | 2,493 |
| Vehicle finance charges | 92 | 277 | 342 | 377 | 382 |
| Maintenance and repair | 393 | 702 | 833 | 791 | 742 |
| Vehicle insurance | 411 | 752 | 886 | 908 | 878 |
| Rent, lease, licenses, other | 214 | 415 | 492 | 491 | 491 |
| Public transportation | 239 | 433 | 334 | 423 | 372 |
| Health care | 1,109 | 2,126 | 1,775 | 1,969 | 1,856 |
| Entertainment | 992 | 1,667 | 1,834 | 2,187 | 1,986 |
| Personal care products and services | 236 | 433 | 470 | 533 | 488 |
| Reading | 120 | 187 | 176 | 189 | 146 |
| Education | 293 | 360 | 616 | 759 | 665 |

**D4-4. Average Annual Expenditures of All Consumer Units, by Size of Unit: 1995 *(continued from previous table)***

|  | One person | Two persons | Three persons | Four persons | Five or more persons |
|---|---|---|---|---|---|
| Tobacco products and smoking supplies | 172 | 272 | 325 | 323 | 362 |
| Miscellaneous | 654 | 822 | 768 | 843 | 797 |
| Cash contributions | 621 | 1,213 | 933 | 926 | 883 |
| Personal insurance and pensions | 1,502 | 3,079 | 3,751 | 4,281 | 3,556 |
| Life and other personal insurance | 140 | 422 | 434 | 565 | 508 |
| Pensions and Social Security | 1,363 | 2,657 | 3,317 | 3,716 | 3,048 |
| Personal taxes | 2,016 | 3,214 | 3,610 | 4,033 | 3,278 |

*Source: Statistical Abstract of the United States 1998,* No. 734; <http://www.census.gov/prod/3/98pubs/98statab/sasec14.pdf>. Underlying data from U.S. Bureau of Labor Statistics, *Consumer Expenditures in 1995*; and unpublished data.

# D5. AVERAGE ANNUAL EXPENDITURES OF ALL CONSUMER UNITS, BY TYPE OF UNIT, 1995

## D5-1. Average Annual Expenditures of All Consumer Units, by Type of Household Unit, Totals: 1995

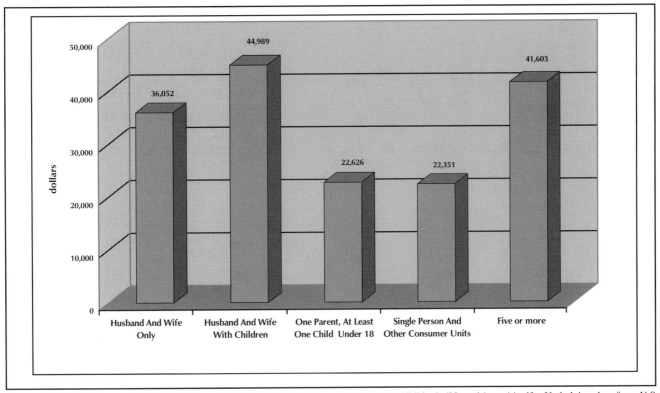

*Source: Statistical Abstract of the United States 1998,* No. 735; <http://www.census.gov/prod/3/98pubs/98statab/sasec14.pdf>. Underlying data from U.S. Bureau of Labor Statistics, *Consumer Expenditures in 1995*; and unpublished data.

## D5-2. Average Annual Expenditures of All Consumer Units, by Type of Household Unit: 1995 *(continued in D5-3 and D5-4)*

|  | Husband and Wife Only | Husband and Wife with Children | One Parent, at Least One Child under 18 | Single Person and Other Consumer Unit |
|---|---|---|---|---|
| Food | 4,722 | 6,368 | 3,586 | 3,017 |
| Food at home | 2,772 | 4,041 | 2,529 | 1,830 |
| Cereals and bakery products | 430 | 649 | 406 | 284 |
| Cereals and cereal products | 151 | 249 | 172 | 105 |
| Bakery products | 279 | 400 | 234 | 180 |
| Meats, poultry, fish, and eggs | 717 | 1,078 | 752 | 490 |
| Beef | 214 | 322 | 241 | 145 |
| Pork | 148 | 218 | 164 | 106 |
| Other meats | 93 | 159 | 105 | 66 |
| Poultry | 126 | 201 | 134 | 91 |
| Fish and seafood | 109 | 135 | 79 | 61 |
| Eggs | 28 | 42 | 29 | 21 |
| Dairy products | 285 | 437 | 273 | 193 |
| Fresh milk and cream | 107 | 185 | 128 | 80 |
| Other dairy products | 179 | 252 | 146 | 112 |
| Fruits and vegetables | 490 | 621 | 372 | 307 |
| Fresh fruits | 161 | 189 | 115 | 98 |
| Fresh vegetables | 153 | 179 | 90 | 96 |
| Processed fruits | 93 | 142 | 90 | 62 |
| Processed vegetables | 82 | 112 | 77 | 51 |
| Other food at home | 849 | 1,256 | 726 | 555 |
| Nonalcoholic beverages | 230 | 343 | 202 | 166 |
| Food away from home | 1,950 | 2,327 | 1,057 | 1,187 |
| Alcoholic beverages | 338 | 303 | 95 | 251 |

*Source: Statistical Abstract of the United States 1998*, No. 735; <http://www.census.gov/prod/3/98pubs/98statab/sasec14.pdf>. Underlying data from U.S. Bureau of Labor Statistics, *Consumer Expenditures in 1995*; and unpublished data.

## D5-3. Average Annual Expenditures of All Consumer Units, by Type of Household Unit: 1995 *(continued from previous table)*

|  | Husband and Wife Only | Husband and Wife with Children | One Parent, at Least One Child under 18 | Single Person and Other Consumer Unit |
|---|---|---|---|---|
| Housing | 11,512 | 13,997 | 8,171 | 7,643 |
| Shelter | 6,176 | 7,863 | 4,710 | 4,577 |
| Owned dwellings | 4,637 | 5,963 | 1,788 | 2,022 |
| Mortgage interest and charges | 2,190 | 3,857 | 1,176 | 941 |
| Property taxes | 1,419 | 1,263 | 404 | 537 |
| Maintenance, repair, insurance, other | 1,029 | 843 | 208 | 545 |
| Rented dwellings | 909 | 1,376 | 2,808 | 2,341 |
| Other lodging | 630 | 524 | 114 | 215 |
| Utilities, fuels, and public services | 2,396 | 2,751 | 1,880 | 1,685 |
| Natural gas | 304 | 328 | 238 | 208 |
| Electricity | 956 | 1,128 | 761 | 637 |
| Fuel oil and other fuels | 112 | 99 | 42 | 70 |
| Telephone | 723 | 845 | 658 | 592 |
| Water and other public services | 301 | 351 | 180 | 178 |
| Household operations | 451 | 888 | 589 | 276 |
| Personal services | 93 | 586 | 468 | 94 |
| Other household expenses | 358 | 302 | 121 | 182 |
| Housekeeping supplies | 548 | 584 | 270 | 266 |
| Household furnishings and equipment | 1,941 | 1,911 | 722 | 839 |
| Household textiles | 144 | 115 | 54 | 70 |
| Furniture | 367 | 520 | 236 | 183 |
| Floor coverings | 437 | 145 | 24 | 91 |
| Major appliances | 194 | 207 | 92 | 99 |
| Small appliances, misc housewares | 109 | 106 | 51 | 63 |
| Miscellaneous household equipment | 689 | 818 | 265 | 333 |

*Source: Statistical Abstract of the United States 1998*, No. 735; <http://www.census.gov/prod/3/98pubs/98statab/sasec14.pdf>. Underlying data from U.S. Bureau of Labor Statistics, *Consumer Expenditures in 1995*; and unpublished data.

## D5-4. Average Annual Expenditures of All Consumer Units, by Type of Household Unit: 1995
**(continued from previous table)**

| | Husband and Wife Only | Husband and Wife with Children | One Parent, at Least One Child under 18 | Single Person and Other Consumer Unit |
|---|---|---|---|---|
| Apparel and services | 1,588 | 2,477 | 1,655 | 1,188 |
| Men and boys | 380 | 647 | 441 | 282 |
| Women and girls | 666 | 914 | 624 | 471 |
| Children under 2 years old | 41 | 159 | 120 | 33 |
| Footwear | 199 | 431 | 286 | 202 |
| Other apparel products and services | 301 | 326 | 184 | 199 |
| Transportation | 6,535 | 8,936 | 3,919 | 3,887 |
| Vehicle purchases (net outlay) | 2,584 | 4,169 | 1,913 | 1,635 |
| Cars and trucks, new | 1,417 | 1,776 | 617 | 742 |
| Cars and trucks, used | 1,128 | 2,343 | 1,274 | 867 |
| Gasoline and motor oil | 1,096 | 1,463 | 642 | 669 |
| Other vehicle expenses | 2,337 | 2,899 | 1,151 | 1,337 |
| Vehicle finance charges | 286 | 408 | 167 | 148 |
| Maintenance and repair | 759 | 888 | 406 | 461 |
| Vehicle insurance | 797 | 1,002 | 450 | 496 |
| Rent, lease, licenses, other | 494 | 601 | 128 | 232 |
| Public transportation | 518 | 404 | 213 | 246 |
| Health care | 2,438 | 2,102 | 803 | 1,225 |
| Entertainment | 1,830 | 2,319 | 1,082 | 1,099 |
| Personal care products and services | 451 | 530 | 305 | 294 |
| Reading | 211 | 206 | 77 | 122 |
| Education | 391 | 847 | 264 | 299 |
| Tobacco products and smoking supplies | 242 | 312 | 234 | 239 |
| Miscellaneous | 798 | 822 | 514 | 741 |
| Cash contributions | 1,457 | 1,033 | 550 | 646 |
| Personal insurance and pensions | 3,541 | 4,738 | 1,372 | 1,699 |
| Life and other personal insurance | 505 | 598 | 194 | 176 |
| Pensions and Social Security | 3,035 | 4,140 | 1,177 | 1,523 |
| Personal taxes | 3,717 | 4,635 | 830 | 2,039 |

*Source: Statistical Abstract of the United States 1998*, No. 735; <http://www.census.gov/prod/3/98pubs/98statab/sasec14.pdf>. Underlying data from U.S. Bureau of Labor Statistics, *Consumer Expenditures in 1995*; and unpublished data.

## D6. AVERAGE ANNUAL EXPENDITURES OF ALL CONSUMER UNITS, BY TYPE OF UNIT, HUSBAND AND WIFE WITH CHILDREN, 1995

### D6-1. Average Annual Expenditures of All Consumer Units, by Type of Household Unit, Husband and Wife with Children, Totals: 1995

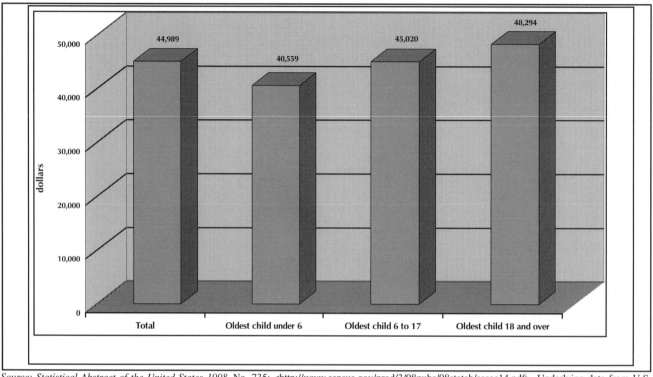

*Source: Statistical Abstract of the United States 1998*, No. 735; <http://www.census.gov/prod/3/98pubs/98statab/sasec14.pdf>. Underlying data from U.S. Bureau of Labor Statistics, *Consumer Expenditures in 1995*; and unpublished data.

### D6-2. Average Annual Expenditures of All Consumer Units, by Type of Household Unit, Husband and Wife with Children: 1995 *(continued in D6-3)*

| | Total | Oldest child under 6 | Oldest child 6–17 | Oldest child 18 and over |
|---|---|---|---|---|
| Expenditures, total | 44,989 | 40,559 | 45,020 | 48,294 |
| Food | 6,368 | 5,129 | 6,592 | 6,944 |
| Food at home | 4,041 | 3,455 | 4,181 | 4,264 |
| Cereals and bakery products | 649 | 533 | 688 | 670 |
| Cereals and cereal products | 249 | 199 | 273 | 243 |
| Bakery products | 400 | 334 | 415 | 427 |
| Meats, poultry, fish, and eggs | 1,078 | 849 | 1,115 | 1,207 |
| Beef | 322 | 248 | 337 | 357 |
| Pork | 218 | 179 | 221 | 248 |
| Other meats | 159 | 115 | 165 | 187 |
| Poultry | 201 | 155 | 212 | 222 |
| Fish and seafood | 135 | 119 | 135 | 150 |
| Eggs | 42 | 33 | 45 | 44 |
| Dairy products | 437 | 378 | 454 | 455 |
| Fresh milk and cream | 185 | 164 | 194 | 185 |
| Other dairy products | 252 | 214 | 260 | 270 |
| Fruits and vegetables | 621 | 549 | 635 | 655 |
| Fresh fruits | 189 | 164 | 194 | 200 |
| Fresh vegetables | 179 | 153 | 179 | 201 |
| Processed fruits | 142 | 140 | 143 | 141 |
| Processed vegetables | 112 | 92 | 119 | 113 |
| Other food at home | 1,256 | 1,145 | 1,290 | 1,276 |
| Nonalcoholic beverages | 343 | 264 | 362 | 375 |
| Food away from home | 2,327 | 1,675 | 2,411 | 2,680 |
| Alcoholic beverages | 303 | 250 | 304 | 350 |

*Source: Statistical Abstract of the United States 1998*, No. 735; <http://www.census.gov/prod/3/98pubs/98statab/sasec14.pdf>. Underlying data from U.S. Bureau of Labor Statistics, *Consumer Expenditures in 1995*; and unpublished data.

## D6-3. Average Annual Expenditures of All Consumer Units, by Type of Household Unit, Husband and Wife with Children: 1995 *(continued from previous table)*

|  | Total | Oldest child under 6 | Oldest child 6–17 | Oldest child 18 and over |
|---|---|---|---|---|
| Housing | 13,997 | 14,527 | 14,318 | 13,002 |
| Shelter | 7,863 | 8,030 | 8,201 | 7,101 |
| Owned dwellings | 5,963 | 5,806 | 6,199 | 5,629 |
| Mortgage interest and charges | 3,857 | 4,133 | 4,179 | 3,047 |
| Property taxes | 1,263 | 1,016 | 1,234 | 1,495 |
| Maintenance, repair, insurance, other | 843 | 657 | 786 | 1,087 |
| Rented dwellings | 1,376 | 1,963 | 1,484 | 747 |
| Other lodging | 524 | 262 | 518 | 725 |
| Utilities, fuels, and public services | 2,751 | 2,346 | 2,709 | 3,121 |
| Natural gas | 328 | 259 | 320 | 395 |
| Electricity | 1,128 | 941 | 1,139 | 1,241 |
| Fuel oil and other fuels | 99 | 88 | 89 | 127 |
| Telephone | 845 | 777 | 808 | 965 |
| Water and other public services | 351 | 281 | 354 | 395 |
| Household operations | 888 | 1,919 | 767 | 376 |
| Personal services | 586 | 1,632 | 464 | 66 |
| Other household expenses | 302 | 287 | 303 | 311 |
| Housekeeping supplies | 584 | 541 | 587 | 615 |
| Household furnishings and equipment | 1,911 | 1,691 | 2,054 | 1,788 |
| Household textiles | 115 | 112 | 110 | 129 |
| Furniture | 520 | 599 | 531 | 442 |
| Floor coverings | 145 | 51 | 199 | 107 |
| Major appliances | 207 | 179 | 198 | 244 |
| Small appliances, misc housewares | 106 | 63 | 100 | 157 |
| Miscellaneous household equipment | 818 | 687 | 916 | 709 |
| Expenditures, total | 44,989 | 40,559 | 45,020 | 48,294 |
| Apparel and services | 2,477 | 2,471 | 2,453 | 2,534 |
| Men and boys | 647 | 536 | 678 | 671 |
| Women and girls | 914 | 699 | 953 | 1,029 |
| Children under 2 years old | 159 | 470 | 86 | 50 |
| Footwear | 431 | 465 | 428 | 404 |
| Other apparel products and services | 326 | 301 | 308 | 380 |
| Transportation | 8,936 | 7,707 | 8,435 | 10,798 |
| Vehicle purchases (net outlay) | 4,169 | 3,584 | 4,060 | 4,798 |
| Cars and trucks, new | 1,776 | 1,281 | 1,947 | 1,808 |
| Cars and trucks, used | 2,343 | 2,266 | 2,078 | 2,901 |
| Gasoline and motor oil | 1,463 | 1,221 | 1,397 | 1,764 |
| Other vehicle expenses | 2,899 | 2,587 | 2,572 | 3,771 |
| Vehicle finance charges | 408 | 414 | 400 | 418 |
| Maintenance and repair | 888 | 693 | 769 | 1,282 |
| Vehicle insurance | 1,002 | 756 | 896 | 1,379 |
| Rent, lease, licenses, other | 601 | 724 | 507 | 692 |
| Public transportation | 404 | 315 | 406 | 465 |
| Health care | 2,102 | 1,746 | 2,026 | 2,509 |
| Entertainment | 2,319 | 1,980 | 2,501 | 2,222 |
| Personal care products and services | 530 | 401 | 561 | 573 |
| Reading | 206 | 182 | 199 | 235 |
| Education | 847 | 192 | 773 | 1,457 |
| Tobacco products and smoking supplies | 312 | 248 | 316 | 352 |
| Miscellaneous | 822 | 800 | 804 | 874 |
| Cash contributions | 1,033 | 500 | 1,091 | 1,306 |
| Personal insurance and pensions | 4,738 | 4,425 | 4,646 | 5,137 |
| Life and other personal insurance | 598 | 444 | 628 | 652 |
| Pensions and Social Security | 4,140 | 3,980 | 4,018 | 4,486 |
| Personal taxes | 4,635 | 4,287 | 4,577 | 5,006 |

*Source: Statistical Abstract of the United States 1998*, No. 735; <http://www.census.gov/prod/3/98pubs/98statab/sasec14.pdf>. Underlying data from U.S. Bureau of Labor Statistics, *Consumer Expenditures in 1995*; and unpublished data.

## D7. AVERAGE ANNUAL EXPENDITURES OF ALL CONSUMER UNITS, BY RACE AND HISPANIC ORIGIN, 1995

### D7-1. Average Annual Expenditures of All Consumer Units, by Race and Hispanic Origin: 1995, in Dollars

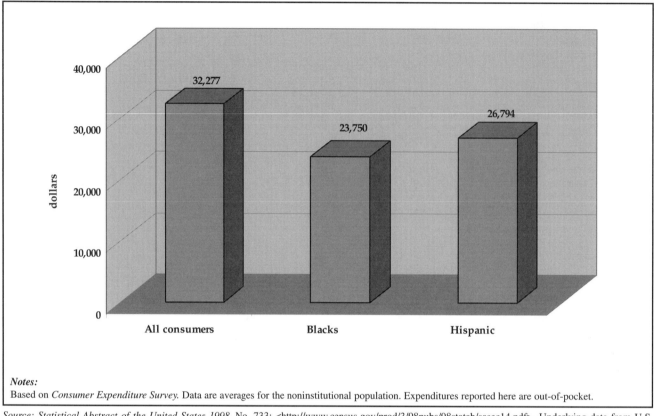

*Notes:*
Based on *Consumer Expenditure Survey*. Data are averages for the noninstitutional population. Expenditures reported here are out-of-pocket.

*Source: Statistical Abstract of the United States 1998*, No. 733; <http://www.census.gov/prod/3/98pubs/98statab/sasec14.pdf>. Underlying data from U.S. Bureau of Labor Statistics, *Consumer Expenditures in 1995*; and unpublished data.

## D7-2. Average Annual Expenditures of All Consumer Units, by Race and Hispanic Origin: 1995, in Dollars *(continued in D7-3)*

| | All Consumers | Blacks | Hispanic |
|---|---|---|---|
| **Expenditures, total** | 32,277 | 23,750 | 26,794 |
| Food | 4,505 | 3,446 | 4,678 |
| Food at home | 2,803 | 2,442 | 3,370 |
| Cereals and bakery products | 441 | 371 | 454 |
| Cereals and cereal products | 165 | 163 | 203 |
| Bakery products | 276 | 208 | 251 |
| Meats, poultry, fish, and eggs | 752 | 866 | 1,097 |
| Beef | 228 | 221 | 331 |
| Pork | 156 | 207 | 229 |
| Other meats | 104 | 107 | 121 |
| Poultry | 138 | 172 | 205 |
| Fish and seafood | 97 | 120 | 148 |
| Eggs | 30 | 39 | 62 |
| Dairy products | 297 | 209 | 347 |
| Fresh milk and cream | 123 | 92 | 179 |
| Other dairy products | 174 | 117 | 168 |
| Fruits and vegetables | 457 | 388 | 593 |
| Fresh fruits | 144 | 117 | 202 |
| Fresh vegetables | 137 | 108 | 185 |
| Processed fruits | 96 | 94 | 117 |
| Processed vegetables | 80 | 69 | 89 |
| Other food at home | 856 | 609 | 879 |
| Nonalcoholic beverages | 240 | 184 | 258 |
| Food away from home | 1,702 | 1,004 | 1,309 |
| Alcoholic beverages | 277 | 157 | 197 |
| Housing | 10,465 | 8,144 | 9,223 |
| Shelter | 5,932 | 4,502 | 5,572 |
| Owned dwellings | 3,754 | 1,922 | 2,354 |
| Mortgage interest and charges | 2,107 | 1,097 | 1,521 |
| Property taxes | 932 | 425 | 466 |
| Maintenance, repair, insurance, other | 716 | 400 | 367 |
| Rented dwellings | 1,786 | 2,433 | 3,102 |
| Other lodging | 392 | 147 | 115 |
| Utilities, fuels, and public services | 2,193 | 2,206 | 1,958 |
| Natural gas | 268 | 315 | 223 |
| Electricity | 870 | 840 | 693 |
| Fuel oil and other fuels | 87 | 48 | 19 |
| Telephone | 708 | 781 | 796 |
| Water and other public services | 260 | 222 | 226 |
| Household operations | 508 | 318 | 316 |
| Personal services | 258 | 226 | 211 |
| Other household expenses | 250 | 92 | 104 |
| Housekeeping supplies | 430 | 255 | 387 |
| Household furnishings and equipment | 1,403 | 862 | 991 |
| Household textiles | 100 | 46 | 59 |
| Furniture | 327 | 319 | 278 |
| Floor coverings | 177 | 34 | 122 |
| Major appliances | 155 | 170 | 118 |
| Small appliances, misc housewares | 85 | 41 | 50 |
| Miscellaneous household equipment | 557 | 252 | 364 |
| Apparel and services | 1,704 | 1,765 | 1,719 |
| Men and boys | 425 | 366 | 422 |
| Women and girls | 660 | 655 | 507 |
| Children under 2 years old | 81 | 92 | 158 |
| Footwear | 278 | 405 | 334 |
| Other apparel products and services | 259 | 247 | 298 |

*Notes:*
Based on *Consumer Expenditure Survey.* Data are averages for the noninstitutional population. Expenditures reported here are out-of-pocket.

*Source: Statistical Abstract of the United States 1998*, No. 733; <http://www.census.gov/prod/3/98pubs/98statab/sasec14.pdf>. Underlying data from U.S. Bureau of Labor Statistics, *Consumer Expenditures in 1995*; and unpublished data.

**D7-3. Average Annual Expenditures of All Consumer Units, by Race and Hispanic Origin: 1995, in dollars** *(continued from previous table)*

| | All Consumers | Blacks | Hispanic |
|---|---|---|---|
| Transportation | 6,016 | 4,515 | 5,145 |
| Vehicle purchases (net outlay) | 2,639 | 2,077 | 2,497 |
| Cars and trucks, new | 1,194 | 927 | 861 |
| Cars and trucks, used | 1,411 | 1,111 | 1,636 |
| Gasoline and motor oil | 1,006 | 713 | 891 |
| Other vehicle expenses | 2,016 | 1,453 | 1,438 |
| Vehicle finance charges | 261 | 245 | 172 |
| Maintenance and repair | 653 | 507 | 477 |
| Vehicle insurance | 713 | 503 | 528 |
| Rent, lease, licenses, other | 390 | 198 | 261 |
| Public transportation | 355 | 273 | 319 |
| Health care | 1,732 | 1,059 | 1,055 |
| Entertainment | 1,612 | 925 | 1,060 |
| Personal care products and services | 403 | 370 | 369 |
| Reading | 163 | 75 | 74 |
| Education | 471 | 256 | 293 |
| Tobacco products and smoking supplies | 269 | 176 | 142 |
| Miscellaneous | 766 | 456 | 526 |
| Cash contributions | 925 | 564 | 378 |
| Personal insurance and pensions | 2,967 | 1,842 | 1,936 |
| Life and other personal insurance | 374 | 345 | 190 |
| Pensions and Social Security | 2,593 | 1,498 | 1,746 |
| Personal taxes | 3,055 | 1,484 | 1,640 |

*Notes:*
Based on *Consumer Expenditure Survey*. Data are averages for the noninstitutional population. Expenditures reported here are out-of-pocket.

*Source: Statistical Abstract of the United States 1998*, No. 733; <http://www.census.gov/prod/3/98pubs/98statab/sasec14.pdf>. Underlying data from U.S. Bureau of Labor Statistics, *Consumer Expenditures in 1995*; and unpublished data.

## D8. AVERAGE ANNUAL EXPENDITURES OF ALL CONSUMER UNITS, BY AGE OF HOUSEHOLDER, 1995

### D8-1. Average Annual Expenditures of All Consumer Units, by Age of Householder: 1995 *(continued in D8-2)*

| | Under 25 yrs. | 25–34 yrs | 35–44 yrs. | 45–54 yrs. | 55–64 yrs. | 65 yrs. and over |
|---|---|---|---|---|---|---|
| **Expenditures, total** | 18,429 | 31,488 | 38,425 | 42,181 | 32,604 | 22,265 |
| Food | 2,690 | 4,470 | 5,367 | 5,469 | 4,539 | 3,388 |
| Food at home | 1,407 | 2,759 | 3,345 | 3,223 | 2,832 | 2,367 |
| Cereals and bakery products | 227 | 422 | 539 | 501 | 425 | 385 |
| Cereals and cereal products | 95 | 172 | 208 | 183 | 151 | 130 |
| Bakery products | 133 | 251 | 331 | 318 | 274 | 255 |
| Meats, poultry, fish, and eggs | 331 | 724 | 900 | 899 | 807 | 610 |
| Beef | 108 | 217 | 273 | 274 | 253 | 175 |
| Pork | 61 | 159 | 181 | 184 | 169 | 127 |
| Other meats | 52 | 99 | 129 | 114 | 111 | 86 |
| Poultry | 66 | 132 | 170 | 169 | 127 | 113 |
| Fish and seafood | 27 | 90 | 111 | 125 | 114 | 81 |
| Eggs | 16 | 28 | 36 | 32 | 33 | 28 |
| Dairy products | 155 | 301 | 352 | 338 | 293 | 248 |
| Fresh milk and cream | 66 | 135 | 147 | 134 | 121 | 98 |
| Other dairy products | 89 | 167 | 206 | 204 | 171 | 150 |
| Fruits and vegetables | 213 | 433 | 509 | 513 | 496 | 437 |
| Fresh fruits | 61 | 137 | 157 | 157 | 153 | 151 |
| Fresh vegetables | 57 | 122 | 148 | 166 | 157 | 132 |
| Processed fruits | 55 | 96 | 110 | 100 | 102 | 87 |
| Processed vegetables | 40 | 78 | 94 | 90 | 84 | 67 |
| Other food at home | 482 | 878 | 1,044 | 973 | 811 | 687 |
| Nonalcoholic beverages | 155 | 246 | 289 | 283 | 230 | 182 |
| Food away from home | 1,283 | 1,711 | 2,022 | 2,246 | 1,707 | 1,021 |
| Alcoholic beverages | 277 | 299 | 314 | 348 | 253 | 171 |

*Notes:*
Based on *Consumer Expenditure Survey*. Data are averages for the noninstitutional population. Expenditures reported here are out-of-pocket.

*Source: Statistical Abstract of the United States 1998*, No. 733; <http://www.census.gov/prod/3/98pubs/98statab/sasec14.pdf>. Underlying data from U.S. Bureau of Labor Statistics, *Consumer Expenditures in 1995*; and unpublished data.

## D8-2. Average Annual Expenditures of All Consumer Units, by Age of Householder: 1995
**(continued from previous table)**

| | Under 25 yrs. | 25–34 yrs | 35–44 yrs. | 45–54 yrs. | 55–64 yrs. | 65 yrs. and over |
|---|---|---|---|---|---|---|
| **Expenditures, total** | 18,429 | 31,488 | 38,425 | 42,181 | 32,604 | 22,265 |
| Housing | 5,908 | 10,541 | 12,631 | 12,894 | 10,291 | 7,590 |
| Shelter | 3,625 | 6,162 | 7,552 | 7,560 | 5,358 | 3,668 |
| Owned dwellings | 485 | 3,104 | 5,066 | 5,576 | 3,799 | 2,401 |
| Mortgage interest and charges | 306 | 2,211 | 3,385 | 3,201 | 1,719 | 511 |
| Property taxes | 86 | 546 | 986 | 1,414 | 1,117 | 973 |
| Maintenance, repair, insurance, other | 93 | 347 | 695 | 961 | 963 | 917 |
| Rented dwellings | 2,985 | 2,873 | 2,102 | 1,334 | 986 | 931 |
| Other lodging | 155 | 185 | 384 | 650 | 572 | 335 |
| Utilities, fuels, and public services | 1,159 | 1,989 | 2,388 | 2,628 | 2,442 | 1,982 |
| Natural gas | 95 | 222 | 279 | 314 | 322 | 284 |
| Electricity | 436 | 762 | 962 | 1,034 | 984 | 801 |
| Fuel oil and other fuels | 17 | 49 | 86 | 92 | 105 | 129 |
| Telephone | 541 | 745 | 778 | 859 | 723 | 517 |
| Water and other public services | 69 | 211 | 284 | 329 | 308 | 251 |
| Household operations | 199 | 701 | 604 | 445 | 374 | 466 |
| Personal services | 155 | 559 | 378 | 115 | 65 | 127 |
| Other household expenses | 44 | 141 | 226 | 330 | 309 | 339 |
| Housekeeping supplies | 135 | 360 | 490 | 501 | 514 | 423 |
| Household furnishings and equipment | 790 | 1,329 | 1,597 | 1,760 | 1,603 | 1,051 |
| Household textiles | 24 | 83 | 112 | 158 | 126 | 67 |
| Furniture | 271 | 391 | 434 | 397 | 279 | 143 |
| Floor coverings | 38 | 85 | 142 | 165 | 167 | 366 |
| Major appliances | 93 | 137 | 171 | 189 | 176 | 132 |
| Small appliances, misc housewares | 63 | 71 | 85 | 101 | 143 | 58 |
| Miscellaneous household equipment | 301 | 561 | 653 | 750 | 712 | 284 |
| Apparel and services | 1,206 | 1,904 | 2,079 | 2,090 | 1,833 | 876 |
| Men and boys | 279 | 511 | 536 | 519 | 431 | 191 |
| Women and girls | 383 | 611 | 774 | 868 | 830 | 407 |
| Children under 2 years old | 95 | 154 | 106 | 59 | 45 | 18 |
| Footwear | 230 | 334 | 380 | 311 | 207 | 145 |
| Other apparel products and services | 219 | 294 | 284 | 333 | 320 | 115 |
| Transportation | 4,033 | 6,188 | 7,488 | 8,017 | 5,726 | 3,377 |
| Vehicle purchases (net outlay) | 1,913 | 2,846 | 3,643 | 3,516 | 2,108 | 1,166 |
| Cars and trucks, new | 555 | 1,273 | 1,730 | 1,332 | 1,118 | 680 |
| Cars and trucks, used | 1,322 | 1,531 | 1,873 | 2,129 | 953 | 485 |
| Gasoline and motor oil | 701 | 1,014 | 1,182 | 1,324 | 1,063 | 604 |
| Other vehicle expenses | 1,236 | 2,029 | 2,289 | 2,725 | 2,142 | 1,285 |
| Vehicle finance charges | 179 | 347 | 322 | 361 | 223 | 78 |
| Maintenance and repair | 379 | 579 | 720 | 923 | 709 | 474 |
| Vehicle insurance | 455 | 668 | 781 | 930 | 792 | 531 |
| Rent, lease, licenses, other | 222 | 435 | 465 | 510 | 419 | 201 |
| Public transportation | 184 | 299 | 374 | 452 | 413 | 323 |
| Health care | 465 | 1,096 | 1,609 | 1,850 | 1,909 | 2,647 |
| Entertainment | 1,081 | 1,682 | 1,951 | 2,138 | 1,577 | 929 |
| Personal care products and services | 243 | 387 | 450 | 517 | 407 | 326 |
| Reading | 71 | 134 | 173 | 199 | 188 | 161 |
| Education | 667 | 335 | 436 | 1,028 | 366 | 155 |
| Tobacco products and smoking supplies | 245 | 270 | 310 | 347 | 314 | 139 |
| Miscellaneous | 347 | 687 | 815 | 1,018 | 948 | 603 |
| Cash contributions | 114 | 455 | 908 | 1,463 | 1,043 | 1,101 |
| Personal insurance and pensions | 1,081 | 3,040 | 3,894 | 4,803 | 3,211 | 802 |
| Life and other personal insurance | 69 | 251 | 440 | 563 | 555 | 245 |
| Pensions and Social Security | 1,012 | 2,788 | 3,453 | 4,240 | 2,656 | 558 |
| Personal taxes | 1,075 | 3,299 | 3,794 | 4,916 | 3,128 | 1,083 |

*Notes:*
Based on *Consumer Expenditure Survey.* Data are averages for the noninstitutional population Expenditures reported here are out-of-pocket.

*Source: Statistical Abstract of the United States 1998,* No. 733; <http://www.census.gov/prod/3/98pubs/98statab/sasec14.pdf>. Underlying data from U.S. Bureau of Labor Statistics, *Consumer Expenditures in 1995;* and unpublished data.

## D9. ANNUAL EXPENDITURE PER CHILD, 1996

### D9-1. Annual Expenditure per Child by Husband-Wife Families, by Family Income and Expenditure Type, 1996, in Dollars

| AGE OF CHILD | Total | Housing | Food | Transportation | Clothing | Health care | Child care & education | Misc.[1] |
|---|---|---|---|---|---|---|---|---|
| **INCOME: LESS THAN $34,700** | | | | | | | | |
| Less than 2 yrs old | 5,670 | 2,160 | 810 | 720 | 370 | 390 | 660 | 560 |
| 3–5 yrs old | 5,780 | 2,140 | 900 | 700 | 360 | 370 | 740 | 570 |
| 6–8 yrs old | 5,900 | 2,060 | 1,160 | 810 | 400 | 420 | 440 | 610 |
| 9–11 yrs old | 5,940 | 1,860 | 1,380 | 880 | 450 | 460 | 270 | 640 |
| 12–14 yrs old | 6,740 | 2,080 | 1,450 | 1,000 | 750 | 470 | 190 | 800 |
| 15–17 yrs old | 6,650 | 1,680 | 1,570 | 1,340 | 670 | 500 | 310 | 580 |
| **INCOME: $34,700-$58,300** | | | | | | | | |
| Less than 2 yrs old | 7,860 | 2,930 | 960 | 1,080 | 440 | 510 | 1,080 | 860 |
| 3–5 yrs old | 8,060 | 2,900 | 1,110 | 1,050 | 430 | 490 | 1,200 | 880 |
| 6–8 yrs old | 8,130 | 2,830 | 1,420 | 1,170 | 470 | 560 | 770 | 910 |
| 9–11 yrs old | 8,100 | 2,630 | 1,670 | 1,240 | 520 | 600 | 500 | 940 |
| 12–14 yrs old | 8,830 | 2,840 | 1,680 | 1,350 | 880 | 610 | 370 | 1,100 |
| 15–17 yrs old | 8,960 | 2,440 | 1,870 | 1,710 | 780 | 640 | 630 | 890 |
| **INCOME: MORE THAN $58,300** | | | | | | | | |
| Less than 2 yrs old | 11,680 | 4,650 | 1,280 | 1,510 | 580 | 580 | 1,630 | 1,450 |
| 3–5 yrs old | 11,910 | 4,620 | 1,450 | 1,480 | 560 | 560 | 1,780 | 1,460 |
| 6–8 yrs old | 11,870 | 4,550 | 1,740 | 1,600 | 620 | 640 | 1,220 | 1,500 |
| 9–11 yrs old | 11,790 | 4,350 | 2,030 | 1,670 | 670 | 690 | 850 | 1,530 |
| 12–14 yrs old | 12,620 | 4,570 | 2,130 | 1,780 | 1,110 | 690 | 650 | 1,690 |
| 15–17 yrs old | 12,930 | 4,160 | 2,240 | 2,160 | 1,010 | 730 | 1,150 | 1,480 |

*Notes:*

1. Expenses include personal care items, entertainment, and reading materials.

*General Note:* Expenditures based on data from the 1990-92 *Consumer Expenditure Survey* updated to 1996 dollars using the Consumer Price Index.

*Source: Statistical Abstract of the United States 1998*, No. 732; <http://www.census.gov/prod/3/98pubs/98statab/sasec14.pdf>. Underlying data from Dept. of Agriculture, Center for Nutrition Policy and Promotion, *Expenditures on Children by Families, 1996 Annual Report.* No. 732.

# E. Consumption—Material Goods

## GENERAL OVERVIEW

The data in Section E begin to describe consumption habits in the United States in detail. Whereas the previous section presented basic overview information on consumption in the United States, the tables and charts here cover one aspect of consumption—material goods—in great depth. The next two sections—F and G—cover other specific areas of consumption in great detail as well: Services (Section F), and Travel, Leisure, and Other Non-Essentials (Section G).

Data on several basic categories of material goods are presented here, such as food, housing, clothing, and appliances. The examination of these categories reaches deeply into highly specific subcategories; for example, the food category covers not just meat but the kind and cut of meat as well. The data also present information on several variables including year-by-year and state-by-state analyses. The section also examines, in some instances where applicable and appropriate, not just total consumption, but prices as well.

## EXPLANATION OF INDICATORS

**E1. Per Capita Consumption of Major Food Commodities:** The first set of tables and charts presents data on a vast variety of foods consumed on a per capita basis over the course of a 16-year period (1980 to 1996). The eight charts at the beginning show the per capita consumption of major food groups, without specific totals of the subcategories within each food group, to help the user develop a broad-stroke view of the current trends in food consumption. The following six tables present detailed information on each of those subcategories spread across the 16-year period.

**E2. Food—Retail Prices of Selected Items:** The next two tables present detailed information on the price of specific food products. Broken down into five general categories—cereals and bakery products, meats,

dairy products, fresh fruit and vegetables, and processed fruits and vegetables—the data on prices are extended over a time period from 1990 to 1997. This helps the viewer put a dollar figure on the consumption levels presented in the above set of tables and charts.

**E3. Per Capita Consumption of Selected Beverages, by Type:** The next two tables present data on beverages consumed on a per capita basis over the course of a 16-year period (1980 to 1996). The data are broken down into detailed subcategories within two general beverage types: alcoholic and non-alcoholic.

**E4. Macronutrients, Quantities Available for Consumption per Capita per Day:** The next six tables present data on trends, over a 24-year time frame (1970 to 1994), concerning all types of nutrients consumed by the U.S. public. In terms of per capita/per day intake, they give the user an understanding of the amount of nutritional value available to the U.S. consumer.

**E5. Value of New Construction Put in Place:** The next group (two sets of one chart and two tables) presents data on new construction values within the current decade (1990 to 1997). The first set (a chart and two tables) presents construction values put in place in current dollars. The lead chart presents total figures and the two tables present data on construction values broken down by private, then public, construction. The remaining set (a chart and two tables) presents the same data in constant dollars, with the effects of inflation muted, based on 1992 dollar valuations.

**E6. New Privately Owned Housing Units Started, Total and by State:** The next chart and table present data on the building of new private housing on a state-by-state basis. They cover the last half of the current decade, exposing the most recent trends in new residential construction. The last column in each table separates out single-family units from all of the other residences.

**E7. Homeownership Rates, Total and by State:** The next chart and table outline rates of individual home ownership throughout the period from 1985 to 1997. The chart shows totals for the U.S. and the table shows rates for individual states across the country. The rates represent the percentage of individual householders who own the residences they occupy.

**E8. Construction Contracts—Value of Construction and Floor Space of Buildings:** The next two tables present data on the value of real estate in various categories from 1980 to 1997, including residential and non-residential, and all of their subcategories. They include both money value information along with square footage, allowing the user to analyze the amount of value and space available in various categories of building and construction.

**E9. Energy Supply and Disposition:** The next two charts and two tables outline the amount of energy produced, traded (imports and exports), and consumed—in terms of type of fuel—from 1990 to 1996. It presents an overall view of the relationship between consumption and production of energy. The charts present summary totals of production and consumption, followed by exports and imports, to allow the user a broad-based view of energy supply and use in the U.S.

**E10. Energy Consumption—Total and per Capita, by State:** The table provides a snapshot of energy consumption in 1995. It presents the total for each state and the per capita amount consumed, bringing the total energy consumed into relation to the population.

**E11. Energy Consumption—by End-Use Sector and Selected Sources:** The next group—two charts and two tables—detail the state-by-state snapshot of energy consumption in 1995 presented above. The first chart and table show consumption broken down into economic sectors—residential, commercial, industrial, and transportation; the chart shows totals and the table details state-by-state consumption. The next chart and table show consumption broken down into sources of energy: petroleum, natural gas, coal, hydroelectric power, and nuclear electric power; again the chart shows totals, and the table details state-by-state consumption.

**E12. Recent Trends in Apparel and Footwear:** The next grouping (one chart and five tables) presents detailed information about the amount of consumption, in terms of total sales, in a wide variety of categories of clothing and footwear. The chart presents sales breakdowns in both current and constant (1992) dollar values so that the user can investigate the amount of consumption with and without the effects of inflation factored in.

**E13. Recent Trends in Household Appliances:** The next group of four tables and two charts presents data on trends in household appliances. The first two tables are similar in format to the tables above concerning apparel: they detail various categories of household appliances and report the total value of sales in those categories. Separate data are given for both current and constant (1992) dollar values so that the user can evaluate the effects of inflation in this category of consumption. The next two tables show the percentage of households that own a wide variety of appliances. The first table presents the data according to regional breakdowns and the second according to family income level, allowing the user to analyze patterns of consumption across regional and economic variables.

The two charts following the tables graph the share of households using selected appliances and equipment by family income. The first chart features appliances used for household efficiency and the next chart features telecommunications and media equipment. These charts help the user to investigate the effect of family income on the capacity to purchase capital goods that make household living more convenient and perhaps more enjoyable.

**E14. Microcomputer Software Sales:** The next two tables present a snapshot of home PC software sales in 1995 and 1996. Each table breaks sales into a wide variety of software applications such as entertainment, home creativity, and desktop publishing, and report the category sales according to the type of operating system the applications are bought for: DOS, Windows, Macintosh, etc.

**E15. Recent Trends in Soap, Cleaners, and Toilet Goods:** A last category of material goods—cleaning products—is presented in the remaining two tables. In a layout similar to the above tables on apparel and household appliances, showing a variety of subcategories in both current and constant (1992) dollar values, the data cover the current decade, from 1991 to 1997.

## E1. PER CAPITA CONSUMPTION OF MAJOR FOOD COMMODITIES

### E1-1. Per Capita Consumption of Major Food Commodities: 1980–1996, in Pounds, Retail Weight (except as indicated)

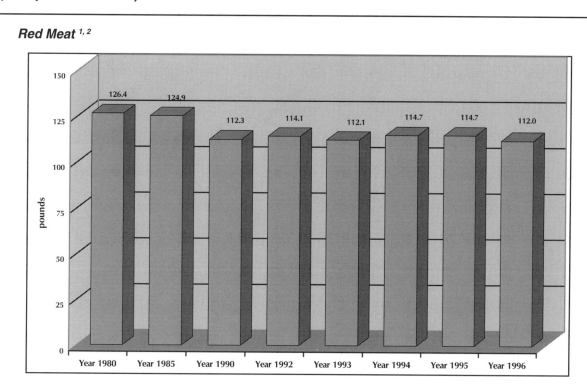

*Red Meat* [1, 2]

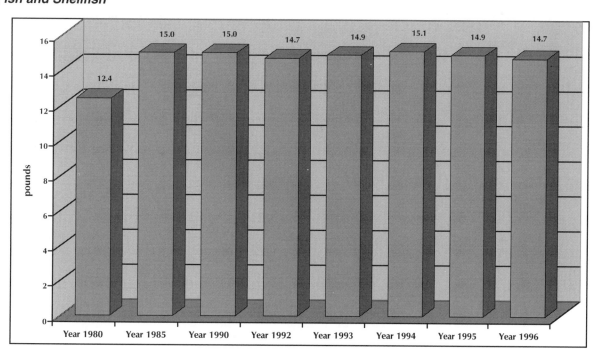

*Fish and Shellfish* [3]

## E1-1. Per Capita Consumption of Major Food Commodities: 1980–1996, in Pounds, Retail Weight (except as indicated) *(continued)*

*Poultry Products* [2, 4]

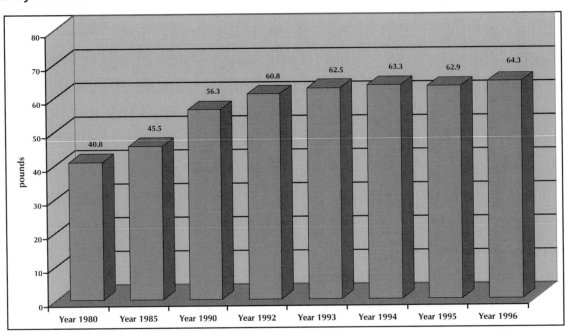

*Dairy Products*

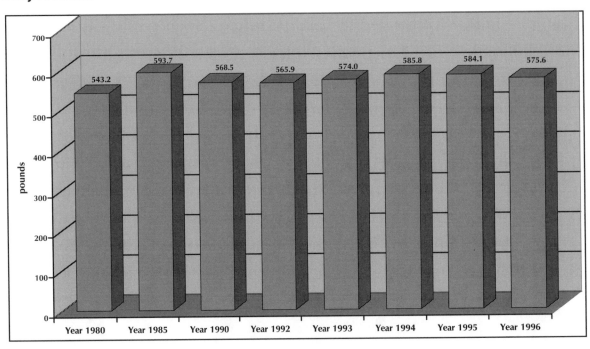

**E1-1. Per Capita Consumption of Major Food Commodities: 1980–1996, in Pounds, Retail Weight (except as indicated)** *(continued)*

### Fats and Oils

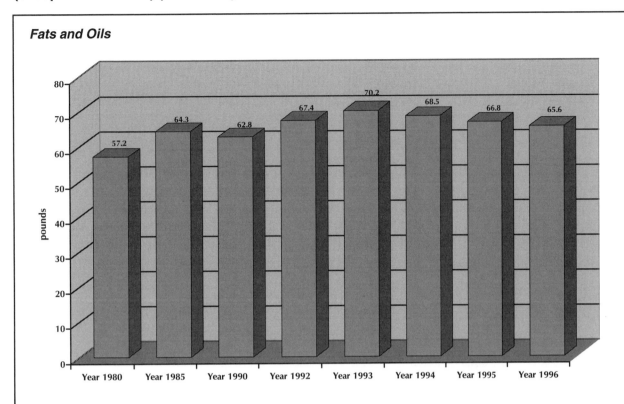

### Flour and Cereal Products

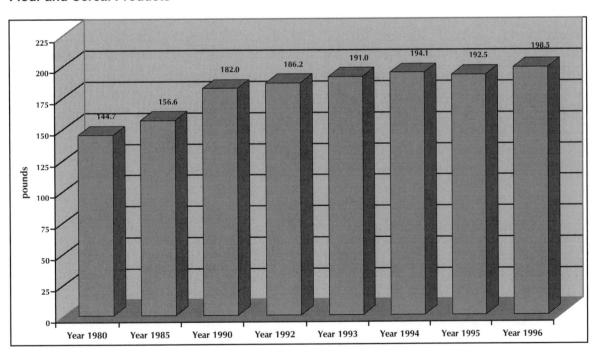

## E1-1. Per Capita Consumption of Major Food Commodities: 1980–1996, in Pounds, Retail Weight (except as indicated) *(continued)*

### *Breakfast Cereals*

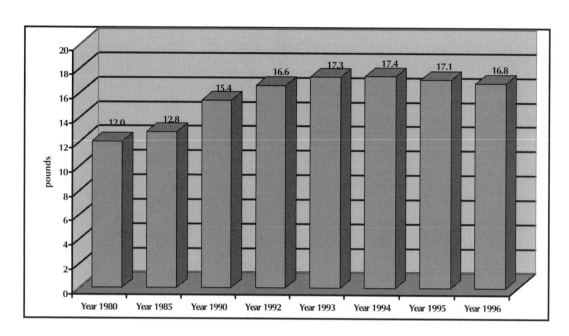

### *Caloric Sweets* [5]

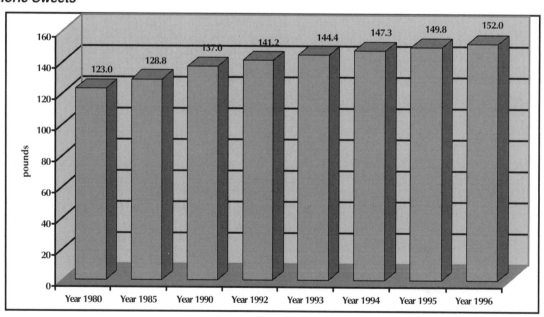

*Notes:*
1. Excludes edible offals.
2. Excludes shipments to Puerto Rico and the other U.S. possessions.
3. Excludes game fish consumption.
4. Includes skin, neck meat, and giblets.
5. Dry weight. Includes edible syrups (maple, molasses, etc.) and honey not shown separately.

*General Notes:* Consumption represents the residual after exports, nonfood use and ending stocks are subtracted from the sum of beginning stocks, domestic production, and imports. Based on Bureau of the Census estimated population. Estimates reflect revisions based on the 1990 Census of Population.

*Source: Statistical Abstract of the United States 1998,* No. 247; <http://www.census.gov/prod/3/98pubs/98statab/sasec3.pdf>. Underlying data from U.S. Department of Agriculture, Economic Research Service, *Food Consumption, Prices, and Expenditures, 1997; Annual Data, 1970-1995;* and *Agricultural Outlook,* monthly.

**E1-2. Per Capita Consumption of Major Food Commodities: 1980–1992, in Pounds, Retail Weight (except as indicated)** *(continued in E1-3 and E1-4)*

|  | 1980 | 1985 | 1990 | 1992 |
|---|---|---|---|---|
| Red meat, total (boneless, trimmed weight) [1,2] | 126.4 | 124.9 | 112.3 | 114.1 |
| Beef | 72.1 | 74.6 | 64.0 | 62.8 |
| Veal | 1.3 | 1.5 | 0.9 | 0.8 |
| Lamb and mutton | 1.0 | 1.1 | 1.0 | 1.0 |
| Pork (excluding lard) | 52.1 | 47.7 | 46.4 | 49.5 |
| Fish and shellfish (edible weight) [3] | 12.4 | 15.0 | 15.0 | 14.7 |
| Fresh and frozen | 7.8 | 9.7 | 9.6 | 9.8 |
| Canned | 4.3 | 5.0 | 5.1 | 4.6 |
| Tuna | 3.0 | 3.3 | 3.7 | 3.5 |
| Cured | 0.3 | 0.3 | 0.3 | 0.3 |
| Poultry products: (boneless weight) [2,4] | 40.8 | 45.5 | 56.3 | 60.8 |
| Chicken | 32.7 | 36.4 | 42.5 | 46.7 |
| Turkey | 8.1 | 9.1 | 13.8 | 14.1 |
| Eggs (number) | 271.1 | 254.7 | 234.3 | 235.0 |
| Shell | 236.2 | 216.5 | 186.3 | 180.7 |
| Processed | 34.9 | 38.2 | 48.0 | 54.3 |

*Notes:*
1. Excludes edible offals.
2. Excludes shipments to Puerto Rico and the other U.S. possessions.
3. Excludes game fish consumption.
4. Includes skin, neck meat, and giblets.
*General Notes:* Consumption represents the residual after exports, nonfood use and ending stocks are subtracted from the sum of beginning stocks, domestic production, and imports. Based on Bureau of the Census estimated population. Estimates reflect revisions based on the 1990 Census of Population.

*Source: Statistical Abstract of the United States 1998,* No. 247; <http://www.census.gov/prod/3/98pubs/98statab/sasec3.pdf>. Underlying data from U.S. Department of Agriculture, Economic Research Service, *Food Consumption, Prices, and Expenditures, 1997; Annual Data, 1970-1995;* and *Agricultural Outlook,* monthly.

## E1-3. Per Capita Consumption of Major Food Commodities: 1980–1992, in Pounds, Retail Weight (except as indicated) *(continued from previous table)*

| | 1980 | 1985 | 1990 | 1992 |
|---|---|---|---|---|
| **Dairy products:** | | | | |
| Total (milk equivalent, milkfat basis) [5] | 543.2 | 593.7 | 568.5 | 565.9 |
| Fluid milk and cream [6] | 245.5 | 240.8 | 233.4 | 230.5 |
| Beverage milks | 237.4 | 229.7 | 221.8 | 218.3 |
| Plain whole milk | 141.7 | 119.7 | 87.7 | 81.2 |
| Plain reduced-fat milk (2%) | 54.7 | 68.5 | 78.4 | 78.1 |
| Plain light and skim milks | 26.9 | 27.4 | 42.8 | 46.2 |
| Flavored whole milk | 4.7 | 3.7 | 2.8 | 2.7 |
| Flavored reduced-fat, light, and skim milks | 5.3 | 6.0 | 6.6 | 6.9 |
| Buttermilk | 4.1 | 4.4 | 3.5 | 3.2 |
| Yogurt (excl. frozen) | 2.5 | 4.0 | 4.0 | 4.2 |
| Cream [7] | 3.4 | 4.4 | 4.6 | 4.8 |
| Sour cream and dips | 1.8 | 2.3 | 2.5 | 2.7 |
| Condensed and evaporated milks: | | | | |
| Whole milk | 3.8 | 3.6 | 3.2 | 3.2 |
| Skim milk | 3.3 | 3.8 | 4.8 | 5.2 |
| Cheese [8] | 17.5 | 22.5 | 24.6 | 26.0 |
| American | 9.6 | 12.2 | 11.1 | 11.3 |
| Cheddar | 6.9 | 9.8 | 9.0 | 9.2 |
| Italian. | 4.4 | 6.5 | 9.0 | 10.0 |
| Mozzarella | 3.0 | 4.6 | 6.9 | 7.7 |
| Other [9] | 3.4 | 3.9 | 4.5 | 4.7 |
| Swiss | 1.3 | 1.3 | 1.4 | 1.2 |
| Cream and Neufchatel | 1.0 | 1.2 | 1.7 | 2.0 |
| Cottage cheese | 4.5 | 4.1 | 3.4 | 3.1 |
| Ice cream | 17.5 | 18.1 | 15.8 | 16.3 |
| Ice milk | 7.1 | 6.9 | 7.7 | 7.1 |
| Frozen yogurt | (NA) | (NA) | 2.8 | 3.1 |
| **Fats and oils:** | | | | |
| Total fat content only | 57.2 | 64.3 | 62.8 | 67.4 |
| Butter (product weight) | 4.5 | 4.9 | 4.4 | 4.4 |
| Margarine (product weight) | 11.3 | 10.8 | 10.9 | 11.0 |
| Lard (direct use) | 2.6 | 1.8 | 1.9 | 1.7 |
| Edible tallow (direct use) | 1.1 | 1.9 | 0.5 | 2.4 |
| Shortening | 18.2 | 22.9 | 22.2 | 22.4 |
| Salad and cooking oils | 21.2 | 23.6 | 24.8 | 27.2 |
| Other edible fats and oils | 1.5 | 1.6 | 1.2 | 1.4 |

*Notes:*

NA Not available

5. Includes other products, not shown separately.

6. Fluid milk figures are aggregates of commercial sales and milk produced and consumed on farms.

7. Heavy cream, light cream, and half and half.

8. Excludes cottage, pot, and baker's cheese.

9. Includes other cheeses not shown separately.

*Only notes that apply to this table are cited.

*General Notes:* Consumption represents the residual after exports, nonfood use and ending stocks are subtracted from the sum of beginning stocks, domestic production, and imports. Based on Bureau of the Census estimated population. Estimates reflect revisions based on the 1990 Census of Population.

*Source: Statistical Abstract of the United States 1998,* No. 247; <http://www.census.gov/prod/3/98pubs/98statab/sasec3.pdf>. Underlying data from U.S. Department of Agriculture, Economic Research Service, *Food Consumption, Prices, and Expenditures, 1997; Annual Data, 1970-1995;* and *Agricultural Outlook,* monthly.

## E1-4. Per Capita Consumption of Major Food Commodities: 1980–1992, in Pounds, Retail Weight (except as indicated) *(continued from previous table)*

|  | 1980 | 1985 | 1990 | 1992 |
|---|---|---|---|---|
| Flour and cereal products | 144.7 | 156.6 | 182.0 | 186.2 |
| Wheat flour | 116.9 | 124.6 | 136.0 | 138.8 |
| Rye flour | 0.7 | 0.7 | 0.6 | 0.6 |
| Rice, milled | 9.4 | 9.1 | 16.2 | 17.5 |
| Corn products | 12.9 | 17.2 | 21.9 | 22.1 |
| Oat products | 3.9 | 4.0 | 6.5 | 6.5 |
| Barley products | 1.0 | 1.0 | 0.8 | 0.7 |
| Breakfast cereals | 12.0 | 12.8 | 15.4 | 16.6 |
| Ready-to-eat | 9.7 | 10.5 | 12.6 | 13.9 |
| Ready-to-cook | 2.3 | 2.3 | 2.9 | 2.6 |
| Caloric sweeteners, total [10] | 123.0 | 128.8 | 137.0 | 141.2 |
| Sugar, refined cane and beet | 83.6 | 62.7 | 64.4 | 64.6 |
| Corn sweeteners (dry weight) | 38.2 | 64.8 | 71.1 | 75.2 |
| Other: |  |  |  |  |
| Cocoa beans | 3.4 | 4.6 | 5.4 | 5.7 |
| Coffee(green beans) | 10.3 | 10.5 | 10.3 | 10.0 |
| Peanuts (shelled) | 4.8 | 6.3 | 6.0 | 6.2 |
| Tree nuts (shelled) | 1.8 | 2.5 | 2.4 | 2.2 |

*Notes:*
10. Dry weight. Includes edible syrups (maple, molasses, etc.) and honey not shown separately.
*Only notes that apply to this table are cited.
*General Notes:* Consumption represents the residual after exports, nonfood use and ending stocks are subtracted from the sum of beginning stocks, domestic production, and imports. Based on Bureau of the Census estimated population. Estimates reflect revisions based on the 1990 Census of Population.

*Source: Statistical Abstract of the United States 1998,* No. 247; <http://www.census.gov/prod/3/98pubs/98statab/sasec3.pdf>. Underlying data from U.S. Department of Agriculture, Economic Research Service, *Food Consumption, Prices, and Expenditures, 1997; Annual Data, 1970-1995;* and *Agricultural Outlook*, monthly.

## E1-5. Per Capita Consumption of Major Food Commodities: 1993–1996, in Pounds, Retail Weight (except as indicated) *(continued in E1-6 and E1-7)*

|  | 1993 | 1994 | 1995 | 1996 |
|---|---|---|---|---|
| Red meat, total (boneless, trimmed weight) [1,2] | 112.1 | 114.7 | 114.7 | 112.0 |
| Beef | 61.5 | 63.6 | 64.0 | 64.2 |
| Veal | 0.8 | 0.8 | 0.8 | 1.0 |
| Lamb and mutton | 1.0 | 0.9 | 0.9 | 0.8 |
| Pork (excluding lard) | 48.9 | 49.5 | 49.0 | 46.0 |
| Fish and shellfish (edible weight) [3] | 14.9 | 15.1 | 14.9 | 14.7 |
| Fresh and frozen | 10.1 | 10.3 | 9.9 | 9.9 |
| Canned | 4.5 | 4.5 | 4.7 | 4.5 |
| Tuna | 3.5 | 3.3 | 3.4 | 3.2 |
| Cured. | 0.3 | 0.3 | 0.3 | 0.3 |
| Poultry products: (boneless weight) [2,4] | 62.5 | 63.3 | 62.9 | 64.3 |
| Chicken | 48.5 | 49.3 | 48.8 | 49.8 |
| Turkey | 14.0 | 14.1 | 14.1 | 14.6 |
| Eggs (number) | 235.6 | 237.6 | 234.6 | 236.2 |
| Shell | 179.1 | 176.9 | 173.8 | 174.1 |
| Processed | 56.5 | 60.6 | 60.8 | 62.1 |

*Notes:*

1. Excludes edible offals.
2. Excludes shipments to Puerto Rico and the other U.S. possessions.
3. Excludes game fish consumption.
4. Includes skin, neck meat, and giblets.

*General Notes:* Consumption represents the residual after exports, nonfood use and ending stocks are subtracted from the sum of beginning stocks, domestic production, and imports. Based on Bureau of the Census estimated population. Estimates reflect revisions based on the 1990 Census of Population.

*Source: Statistical Abstract of the United States 1998,* No. 247; <http://www.census.gov/prod/3/98pubs/98statab/sasec3.pdf>. Underlying data from U.S. Department of Agriculture, Economic Research Service, *Food Consumption, Prices, and Expenditures,* 1997; *Annual Data, 1970-1995;* and *Agricultural Outlook,* monthly.

## E1-6. Per Capita Consumption of Major Food Commodities: 1993–1996, in Pounds, Retail Weight (except as indicated) *(continued from previous table)*

| | 1993 | 1994 | 1995 | 1996 |
|---|---|---|---|---|
| **Dairy products:** | | | | |
| Total (milk equivalent, milkfat basis) [5] | 574.0 | 585.8 | 584.1 | 575.6 |
| Fluid milk and cream [6] | 225.7 | 226.3 | 223.2 | 223.5 |
| Beverage milks | 213.4 | 213.5 | 209.7 | 210.0 |
| Plain whole milk . | 77.4 | 76.0 | 72.6 | 72.1 |
| Plain reduced-fat milk (2%) | 76.0 | 74.9 | 70.4 | 69.1 |
| Plain light and skim milks | 47.3 | 49.7 | 53.9 | 55.7 |
| Flavored whole milk | 2.7 | 2.7 | 2.7 | 2.7 |
| Flavored reduced-fat, light, and skim milks | 6.9 | 7.1 | 7.3 | 7.7 |
| Buttermilk | 3.0 | 2.9 | 2.8 | 2.7 |
| Yogurt (excl. frozen) | 4.3 | 4.7 | 5.1 | 4.8 |
| Cream [7] | 4.9 | 4.9 | 5.1 | 5.4 |
| Sour cream and dips | 2.7 | 2.8 | 2.9 | 2.9 |
| Condensed and evaporated milks: | | | | |
| Whole milk | 3.0 | 2.6 | 2.3 | 2.3 |
| Skim milk | 5.2 | 5.5 | 4.5 | 4.1 |
| Cheese [8] | 26.2 | 26.8 | 27.3 | 27.7 |
| American | 11.4 | 11.5 | 11.8 | 12.0 |
| Cheddar | 9.1 | 9.1 | 9.1 | 9.2 |
| Italian. | 9.8 | 10.3 | 10.4 | 10.8 |
| Mozzarella | 7.6 | 7.9 | 8.0 | 8.5 |
| Other [9] | 5.0 | 5.0 | 5.0 | 5.0 |
| Swiss | 1.2 | 1.2 | 1.1 | 1.1 |
| Cream and Neufchatel | 2.1 | 2.2 | 2.1 | 2.2 |
| Cottage cheese | 2.9 | 2.8 | 2.7 | 2.6 |
| Ice cream | 16.1 | 16.1 | 15.7 | 15.9 |
| Ice milk | 6.9 | 7.6 | 7.5 | 7.6 |
| Frozen yogurt | 3.5 | 3.5 | 3.5 | 2.7 |
| **Fats and oils:** | | | | |
| Total fat content only | 70.2 | 68.5 | 66.8 | 65.6 |
| Butter (product weight) | 4.7 | 4.8 | 4.5 | 4.3 |
| Margarine (product weight) | 11.1 | 9.9 | 9.2 | 9.1 |
| Lard (direct use) | 1.7 | 2.3 | 2.2 | 2.3 |
| Edible tallow (direct use) | 2.2 | 2.4 | 2.7 | 3.0 |
| Shortening | 25.1 | 24.1 | 22.5 | 22.2 |
| Salad and cooking oils | 26.8 | 26.2 | 26.8 | 26.0 |
| Other edible fats and oils | 1.7 | 1.6 | 1.6 | 1.4 |

*Notes:*

5. Includes other products, not shown separately.

6. Fluid milk figures are aggregates of commercial sales and milk produced and consumed on farms.

7. Heavy cream, light cream, and half and half.

8. Excludes cottage, pot, and baker's cheese.

9. Includes other cheeses not shown separately.

*Only notes that apply to this table are cited.

*General Notes:* Consumption represents the residual after exports, nonfood use and ending stocks are subtracted from the sum of beginning stocks, domestic production, and imports. Based on Bureau of the Census estimated population. Estimates reflect revisions based on the 1990 Census of Population.

*Source: Statistical Abstract of the United States 1998,* No. 247; <http://www.census.gov/prod/3/98pubs/98statab/sasec3.pdf>. Underlying data from U.S. Department of Agriculture, Economic Research Service, *Food Consumption, Prices, and Expenditures, 1997; Annual Data, 1970-1995;* and *Agricultural Outlook,* monthly.

## E1-7. Per Capita Consumption of Major Food Commodities: 1993–1996, in Pounds, Retail Weight (except as indicated) *(continued from previous table)*

| | 1993 | 1994 | 1995 | 1996 |
|---|---|---|---|---|
| **Flour and cereal products** | **191.0** | **194.1** | **192.5** | **198.5** |
| Wheat flour | 143.3 | 144.5 | 141.8 | 148.8 |
| Rye flour | 0.6 | 0.6 | 0.6 | 0.6 |
| Rice, milled | 17.6 | 19.3 | 20.1 | 18.9 |
| Corn products | 22.3 | 22.5 | 22.7 | 22.9 |
| Oat products | 6.5 | 6.5 | 6.5 | 6.6 |
| Barley products | 0.7 | 0.7 | 0.7 | 0.7 |
| **Breakfast cereals** | **17.3** | **17.4** | **17.1** | **16.8** |
| Ready-to-eat | 14.6 | 14.8 | 14.6 | 14.3 |
| Ready-to-cook | 2.7 | 2.6 | 2.5 | 2.5 |
| Caloric sweeteners, total [10] | 144.4 | 147.3 | 149.8 | 152.0 |
| Sugar, refined cane and beet | 64.3 | 65.0 | 65.5 | 66.2 |
| Corn sweeteners (dry weight) | 78.7 | 81.0 | 83.0 | 84.5 |
| **Other:** | | | | |
| Cocoa beans | 5.4 | 4.8 | 4.6 | 4.6 |
| Coffee(green beans) | 9.1 | 8.2 | 8.0 | 9.0 |
| Peanuts (shelled) | 6.0 | 5.8 | 5.7 | 5.7 |
| Tree nuts (shelled) | 2.2 | 2.3 | 1.9 | 2.1 |

*Notes:*

10. Dry weight. Includes edible syrups (maple, molasses, etc.) and honey not shown separately.

*Only notes that apply to this table are cited.

*General Notes:* Consumption represents the residual after exports, nonfood use and ending stocks are subtracted from the sum of beginning stocks, domestic production, and imports. Based on Bureau of the Census estimated population. Estimates reflect revisions based on the 1990 Census of Population.

*Source: Statistical Abstract of the United States 1998,* No. 247; <http://www.census.gov/prod/3/98pubs/98statab/sasec3.pdf>. Underlying data from U.S. Department of Agriculture, Economic Research Service, *Food Consumption, Prices, and Expenditures, 1997; Annual Data, 1970-1995;* and *Agricultural Outlook,* monthly.

## E2. FOOD—RETAIL PRICES OF SELECTED ITEMS

### E2-1. Food—Retail Prices of Selected Items: 1990–1993 (as of December), in Dollars per Pound (except as indicated)

| FOOD | 1990 | 1992 | 1993 |
|---|---|---|---|
| Cereals and bakery products: | | | |
| Flour, white, all purpose | 0.24 | 0.23 | 0.22 |
| Rice, white, large grain, raw | 0.49 | 0.53 | 0.50 |
| Spaghetti and macaroni | 0.85 | 0.86 | 0.84 |
| Bread, white, pan | 0.70 | 0.74 | 0.76 |
| Meats, poultry, fish and eggs: | | | |
| Ground chuck, 100% beef | 2.02 | 1.91 | 1.91 |
| Rib roast, USDA Choice | 4.54 | 4.69 | 4.73 |
| Round steak, USDA Choice | 3.42 | 3.34 | 3.32 |
| Sirloin steak, bone-in | 3.65 | 3.75 | 3.69 |
| T-bone steak | 5.45 | 5.39 | 5.77 |
| Pork: | | | |
| Bacon, sliced | 2.28 | 1.86 | 2.02 |
| Chops, center cut, bone-in | 3.32 | 3.15 | 3.24 |
| Shoulder picnic, bone-in, smoked | 1.41 | 1.18 | 1.19 |
| Sausage | 2.42 | 2.14 | 1.99 |
| Poultry: | | | |
| Chicken, fresh, whole | 0.86 | 0.88 | 0.91 |
| Chicken breast, bone-in | 2.00 | 2.08 | 2.17 |
| Chicken legs, bone-in | 1.17 | 1.14 | 1.13 |
| Turkey, frozen, whole | 0.96 | 0.93 | 0.95 |
| Eggs, grade A, large, (dozen) | 1.00 | 0.93 | 0.87 |
| Dairy products: | | | |
| Milk, fresh, whole, fortified (1/2 gal) | 1.39 | 1.39 | 1.43 |
| Butter, salted, grade AA, stick | 1.92 | 1.64 | 1.61 |
| Ice cream, prepack, bulk,reg(1/2 gal) | 2.54 | 2.49 | 2.59 |
| Fresh fruits and vegetables: | | | |
| Apples, red delicious | 0.77 | 0.76 | 0.78 |
| Bananas | 0.43 | 0.40 | 0.41 |
| Oranges, navel | 0.56 | 0.52 | 0.56 |
| Grapefruit | 0.56 | 0.52 | 0.50 |
| Lemons | 0.97 | 0.90 | 1.05 |
| Pears, Anjou | 0.79 | 0.80 | 0.89 |
| Potatoes, white | 0.32 | 0.31 | 0.36 |
| Lettuce, iceberg | 0.58 | 0.66 | 0.53 |
| Tomatoes, field grown | 0.86 | 1.23 | 1.31 |
| Cabbage | 0.39 | 0.38 | 0.37 |
| Carrots, short trimmed and topped | 0.44 | 0.44 | 0.41 |
| Celery | 0.49 | 0.48 | 0.49 |
| Cucumbers | 0.56 | 0.51 | 0.93 |
| Processed fruits and vegetables: | | | |
| Orange juice, frozen concentrate, 12 oz can, per 16 oz | 2.02 | 1.70 | 1.67 |
| Potatoes, frozen, french fried | 0.85 | 0.86 | 0.87 |

*Source: Statistical Abstract of the United States 1998,* No. 787; <http://wwwcensusgov/prod/3/98pubs/98statab/sasec15pdf>. Underlying data from U.S. Bureau of Labor Statistics, *CPI Detailed Report,* January issues.

## E2-2. Food—Retail Prices of Selected Items: 1994–1997 (as of December), in Dollars per Pound (except as indicated)

| FOOD | 1994 | 1995 | 1996 | 1997 |
|---|---|---|---|---|
| Cereals and bakery products: | | | | |
| Flour, white, all purpose | 0.23 | 0.24 | 0.30 | 0.28 |
| Rice, white, large grain, raw | 0.53 | 0.55 | 0.55 | 0.58 |
| Spaghetti and macaroni | 0.87 | 0.88 | 0.84 | 0.88 |
| Bread, white, pan | 0.75 | 0.84 | 0.87 | 0.88 |
| Meats, poultry, fish and eggs: | | | | |
| Ground chuck, 100% beef | 1.84 | 1.85 | 1.85 | 1.81 |
| Rib roast, USDA Choice | 4.88 | 4.81 | 5.09 | 5.21 |
| Round steak, USDA Choice | 3.24 | 3.20 | 3.22 | 3.09 |
| Sirloin steak, bone-in | (NA) | (NA) | (NA) | (NA) |
| T-bone steak | 5.86 | 5.92 | 5.87 | 6.07 |
| Pork: | | | | |
| Bacon, sliced | 1.89 | 2.17 | 2.64 | 2.61 |
| Chops, center cut, bone-in | 3.03 | 3.29 | 3.44 | 3.39 |
| Shoulder picnic, bone-in, smoked | 1.13 | 1.17 | 1.31 | 1.29 |
| Sausage | 1.85 | 1.92 | 2.15 | 2.08 |
| Poultry: | | | | |
| Chicken, fresh, whole | 0.90 | 0.94 | 1.00 | 1.00 |
| Chicken breast, bone-in | 1.91 | 1.95 | 2.09 | 1.99 |
| Chicken legs, bone-in | 1.12 | 1.20 | 1.26 | 1.22 |
| Turkey, frozen, whole | 0.98 | 0.99 | 1.02 | 0.98 |
| Eggs, grade A, large, (dozen) | 0.87 | 1.16 | 1.31 | 1.17 |
| Dairy products: | | | | |
| Milk, fresh, whole, fortified (1/2 gal) | 1.44 | 1.48 | 1.65 | 1.61 |
| Butter, salted, grade AA, stick | 1.54 | 1.73 | 2.17 | 2.46 |
| Ice cream, prepack, bulk,reg(1/2 gal) | 2.62 | 2.68 | 2.94 | 3.02 |
| Fresh fruits and vegetables: | | | | |
| Apples, red delicious | 0.72 | 0.83 | 0.89 | 0.90 |
| Bananas | 0.46 | 0.45 | 0.48 | 0.46 |
| Oranges, navel | 0.55 | 0.64 | 0.59 | 0.58 |
| Grapefruit | 0.47 | 0.49 | 0.55 | 0.53 |
| Lemons | 1.04 | 1.12 | 1.14 | 1.06 |
| Pears, Anjou | (NA) | (NA) | 1.06 | 0.85 |
| Potatoes, white | 0.34 | 0.38 | 0.33 | 0.37 |
| Lettuce, iceberg | 0.91 | 0.61 | 0.62 | 0.70 |
| Tomatoes, field grown | 1.43 | 1.51 | 1.21 | 1.62 |
| Cabbage | 0.45 | 0.41 | 0.40 | 0.46 |
| Carrots, short trimmed and topped | 0.48 | 0.53 | 0.54 | 0.50 |
| Celery | 0.52 | 0.54 | 0.44 | 0.57 |
| Cucumbers | 0.69 | 0.53 | 0.60 | 0.58 |
| Processed fruits and vegetables: | | | | |
| Orange juice, frozen concentrate, 12 oz can, per 16 oz | 1.55 | 1.57 | 1.73 | 1.67 |
| Potatoes, frozen, french fried | 0.84 | 0.86 | 0.90 | 0.95 |

*Notes:*
NA Not available

*Source: Statistical Abstract of the United States 1998*, No. 787; <http://wwwcensusgov/prod/3/98pubs/98statab/sasec15pdf>. Underlying data from U.S. Bureau of Labor Statistics, *CPI Detailed Report,* January issues.

## E3. PER CAPITA CONSUMPTION OF SELECTED BEVERAGES, BY TYPE

### E3-1. Per Capita Consumption of Selected Beverages, by Type: 1980–1991, in Gallons, Retail Weight (except as indicated)

| COMMODITY | 1980 | 1985 | 1990 | 1991 |
|---|---|---|---|---|
| Nonalcoholic | (NA) | (NA) | 128.6 | 130.8 |
| Milk (plain and flavored) | 27.6 | 26.7 | 25.7 | 25.7 |
| Whole | 17.0 | 14.3 | 10.5 | 10.2 |
| Reduced-fat, light, and skim | 10.5 | 12.3 | 15.2 | 15.5 |
| Tea | 7.3 | 7.1 | 6.9 | 7.4 |
| Coffee | 26.7 | 27.4 | 26.9 | 26.8 |
| Bottled water | 2.4 | 4.5 | 8.0 | 8.0 |
| Soft drinks | 35.1 | 35.7 | 46.3 | 47.9 |
| Diet | 5.1 | 7.1 | 10.7 | 11.7 |
| Regular | 29.9 | 28.7 | 35.6 | 36.3 |
| Selected fruit juices | 6.8 | 7.4 | 8.1 | 7.6 |
| Fruit drinks, cocktails, and ades | (NA) | (NA) | 6.3 | 6.9 |
| Canned iced tea | (NA) | (NA) | 0.1 | 0.2 |
| Vegetable juices | (NA) | (NA) | 0.3 | 0.3 |
| Alcoholic (adult population) | 42.8 | 40.7 | 39.5 | 37.8 |
| Beer | 36.6 | 34.6 | 34.4 | 33.2 |
| Wine[1] | 3.2 | 3.5 | 2.9 | 2.7 |
| Distilled spirits | 3.0 | 2.6 | 2.2 | 2.0 |

*Notes:*
(NA) Not available
1. Beginning in 1985, includes wine coolers.
*General Notes:* Consumption represents the residual after exports, nonfood use and ending stocks are subtracted from the sum of beginning stocks, domestic production, and imports. Based on Bureau of the Census estimated population. Estimates reflect revisions based on the 1990 Census of Population.

*Source: Statistical Abstract of the United States 1998,* No. 249; <http://www.census.gov/prod/3/98pubs/98statab/sasec3.pdf>. Underlying data from U.S. Dept of Agriculture, Economic Research Service, *Food Consumption, Prices, and Expenditures*, annual; and *Agricultural Outlook*, monthly.

## E3-2. Per Capita Consumption of Selected Beverages, by Type: 1992–1996, in Gallons, Retail Weight (except as indicated)

| COMMODITY | 1992 | 1993 | 1994 | 1995 | 1996 |
|---|---|---|---|---|---|
| Nonalcoholic | 130.6 | 131.0 | 133.0 | 133.0 | 136.9 |
| Milk (plain and flavored) | 25.3 | 24.7 | 24.8 | 24.3 | 24.3 |
| Whole | 9.8 | 9.3 | 9.2 | 8.8 | 8.7 |
| Reduced-fat, light, and skim | 15.6 | 15.4 | 15.6 | 15.6 | 15.7 |
| Tea | 8.1 | 8.4 | 8.2 | 8.0 | 8.0 |
| Coffee | 25.9 | 23.4 | 21.1 | 20.5 | 23.1 |
| Bottled water | 8.2 | 9.4 | 10.7 | 11.6 | 12.4 |
| Soft drinks | 48.5 | 50.1 | 51.3 | 51.6 | 51.9 |
| Diet | 11.6 | 11.7 | 11.8 | 11.8 | 11.7 |
| Regular | 36.9 | 38.4 | 39.5 | 39.8 | 40.2 |
| Selected fruit juices | 7.6 | 7.3 | 8.6 | 8.2 | 8.7 |
| Fruit drinks, cocktails, and ades | 6.5 | 7.0 | 7.4 | 7.8 | 7.4 |
| Canned iced tea | 0.2 | 0.4 | 0.6 | 0.7 | 0.8 |
| Vegetable juices | 0.3 | 0.3 | 0.3 | 0.3 | 0.3 |
| Alcoholic (adult population) | 37.3 | 36.7 | 36.6 | 35.9 | 36.1 |
| Beer | 32.7 | 32.4 | 32.2 | 31.6 | 31.6 |
| Wine[1] | 2.7 | 2.5 | 2.5 | 2.6 | 2.7 |
| Distilled spirits | 2.0 | 1.9 | 1.8 | 1.8 | 1.8 |

*Notes:*
(NA) Not available
1. Beginning in 1985, includes wine coolers.
*General Notes:* Consumption represents the residual after exports, nonfood use and ending stocks are subtracted from the sum of beginning stocks, domestic production, and imports. Based on Bureau of the Census estimated population. Estimates reflect revisions based on the 1990 Census of Population.

*Source: Statistical Abstract of the United States 1998,* No. 249; <http://www.census.gov/prod/3/98pubs/98statab/sasec3.pdf>. Underlying data from U.S. Dept of Agriculture, Economic Research Service, *Food Consumption, Prices, and Expenditures,* annual; and *Agricultural Outlook,* monthly.

# E4. MACRONUTRIENTS, QUANTITIES AVAILABLE FOR CONSUMPTION PER CAPITA PER DAY

## E4-1. Macronutrients; Energy, Protein, Carbohydrates, Quantities Available for Consumption per Capita per Day: 1970–1994[1]

| Year | Food Energy Kilocalories | Protein Grams | Carbohydrate Grams |
|------|--------------------------|---------------|--------------------|
| 1970 | 3,300 | 386 | 470 |
| 1971 | 3,300 | 387 | 470 |
| 1972 | 3,300 | 386 | 460 |
| 1973 | 3,200 | 390 | 440 |
| 1974 | 3,200 | 383 | 440 |
| 1975 | 3,200 | 385 | 430 |
| 1976 | 3,300 | 399 | 430 |
| 1977 | 3,300 | 398 | 430 |
| 1978 | 3,200 | 392 | 430 |
| 1979 | 3,300 | 400 | 430 |
| 1980 | 3,300 | 406 | 430 |
| 1981 | 3,300 | 394 | 430 |
| 1982 | 3,300 | 396 | 420 |
| 1983 | 3,300 | 400 | 430 |
| 1984 | 3,400 | 404 | 430 |
| 1985 | 3,500 | 420 | 430 |
| 1986 | 3,500 | 425 | 420 |
| 1987 | 3,500 | 436 | 420 |
| 1988 | 3,600 | 443 | 420 |
| 1989 | 3,500 | 445 | 410 |
| 1990 | 3,600 | 458 | 400 |
| 1991 | 3,600 | 464 | 400 |
| 1992 | 3,700 | 473 | 410 |
| 1993 | 3,700 | 482 | 410 |
| 1994 | 3,800 | 491 | 410 |

*Notes:*
1. Computed by Center for Nutrition Policy and Promotion (CNPP), USDA. Based on Economic Research Service estimates of per capita quantities of food available for consumption (retail weight) and on CNPP estimates of quantities of produce from home gardens and certain other foods. No deduction is made in food supply estimates for loss of food or nutrients in further processing, in marketing, or in the home. Data include iron, thiamin, riboflavin, niacin, vitamin A, vitamin B6, vitamin B12 and ascorbic acid added by enrichment and fortification.

*Source:* U.S. Department of Agriculture, *Agricultural Statistics 1998*, Table 13-2; <http://www.usda.gov>.

## E4-2. Macronutrients, Fats and Cholesterol, Quantities Available for Consumption per Capita per Day: 1970–1994[1]

| Year | Fat, Total Fat, Grams | Fat, Saturated, Grams | Fat, Mono-unsaturated, Grams | Fat, Polyunsaturated, Grams | Cholesterol, Milligrams |
|---|---|---|---|---|---|
| 1970 | 95 | 154 | 54 | 63 | 26 |
| 1971 | 96 | 154 | 55 | 63 | 26 |
| 1972 | 95 | 155 | 54 | 63 | 27 |
| 1973 | 94 | 150 | 52 | 61 | 27 |
| 1974 | 94 | 151 | 52 | 62 | 27 |
| 1975 | 93 | 146 | 50 | 59 | 27 |
| 1976 | 97 | 152 | 51 | 60 | 29 |
| 1977 | 96 | 149 | 51 | 59 | 28 |
| 1978 | 95 | 150 | 51 | 59 | 29 |
| 1979 | 96 | 151 | 51 | 60 | 30 |
| 1980 | 96 | 153 | 52 | 60 | 30 |
| 1981 | 96 | 153 | 51 | 61 | 30 |
| 1982 | 96 | 152 | 51 | 60 | 30 |
| 1983 | 97 | 157 | 53 | 62 | 31 |
| 1984 | 98 | 155 | 53 | 62 | 29 |
| 1985 | 101 | 163 | 55 | 65 | 32 |
| 1986 | 102 | 162 | 54 | 65 | 32 |
| 1987 | 103 | 160 | 53 | 64 | 32 |
| 1988 | 105 | 161 | 53 | 64 | 33 |
| 1989 | 104 | 156 | 51 | 63 | 32 |
| 1990 | 105 | 156 | 51 | 63 | 32 |
| 1991 | 107 | 155 | 50 | 63 | 32 |
| 1992 | 108 | 158 | 52 | 64 | 32 |
| 1993 | 108 | 161 | 52 | 66 | 32 |
| 1994 | 110 | 159 | 52 | 65 | 31 |

*Notes:*

1. Computed by Center for Nutrition Policy and Promotion (CNPP), USDA. Based on Economic Research Service estimates of per capita quantities of food available for consumption (retail weight) and on CNPP estimates of quantities of produce from home gardens and certain other foods. No deduction is made in food supply estimates for loss of food or nutrients in further processing, in marketing, or in the home. Data include iron, thiamin, riboflavin, niacin, vitamin A, vitamin B6, vitamin B12 and ascorbic acid added by enrichment and fortification.

*Source:* U.S. Department of Agriculture, *Agricultural Statistics 1998*, Table 13-2; <http://www.usda.gov>.

## E4-3. Macronutrients, Vitamins and Minerals, Quantities Available for Consumption per Capita per Day: 1970–1994[1] *(continued in E4-4, E4-5, and E4-6)*

| Year | Vitamin A Micrograms retinol equivalent | Carotenes Micrograms retinol equivalent | Vitamin E Milligrams alpha-tocopherol | Vitamin C Milligrams |
|---|---|---|---|---|
| 1970 | 1,500 | 510 | 13.7 | 107 |
| 1971 | 1,510 | 520 | 13.5 | 108 |
| 1972 | 1,530 | 550 | 13.9 | 108 |
| 1973 | 1,520 | 580 | 14.4 | 106 |
| 1974 | 1,560 | 600 | 14.2 | 108 |
| 1975 | 1,550 | 620 | 14.4 | 112 |
| 1976 | 1,580 | 620 | 14.7 | 113 |
| 1977 | 1,530 | 580 | 14.2 | 112 |
| 1978 | 1,510 | 580 | 14.5 | 108 |
| 1979 | 1,530 | 610 | 14.6 | 109 |
| 1980 | 1,520 | 600 | 14.6 | 112 |
| 1981 | 1,510 | 600 | 14.7 | 109 |
| 1982 | 1,510 | 620 | 15.0 | 110 |
| 1983 | 1,500 | 600 | 15.4 | 115 |
| 1984 | 1,530 | 640 | 14.9 | 112 |
| 1985 | 1,520 | 630 | 16.2 | 114 |
| 1986 | 1,500 | 610 | 16.3 | 118 |
| 1987 | 1,530 | 640 | 16.4 | 115 |
| 1988 | 1,470 | 610 | 16.9 | 116 |
| 1989 | 1,500 | 640 | 16.5 | 115 |
| 1990 | 1,530 | 670 | 16.6 | 111 |
| 1991 | 1,500 | 640 | 17.0 | 115 |
| 1992 | 1,540 | 670 | 17.1 | 117 |
| 1993 | 1,530 | 670 | 17.6 | 122 |
| 1994 | 1,520 | 660 | 16.9 | 124 |

*Notes:*

1. Computed by Center for Nutrition Policy and Promotion (CNPP), USDA. Based on Economic Research Service estimates of per capita quantities of food available for consumption (retail weight) and on CNPP estimates of quantities of produce from home gardens and certain other foods. No deduction is made in food supply estimates for loss of food or nutrients in further processing, in marketing, or in the home. Data include iron, thiamin, riboflavin, niacin, vitamin A, vitamin B6, vitamin B12 and ascorbic acid added by enrichment and fortification.

*Source:* U.S. Department of Agriculture, *Agricultural Statistics 1998,* Table 13-2; <http://www.usda.gov>.

## E4-4. Macronutrients, Vitamins and Minerals, Quantities Available for Consumption per Capita per Day: 1970–1994[1] *(continued from previous table)*

| Year | Thiamin Milligrams | Riboflavin Milligrams | Niacin Milligrams | Vitamin B6 Milligrams | Folate Micrograms | Vitamin B12 Micrograms |
|---|---|---|---|---|---|---|
| 1970 | 2.0 | 2.3 | 22 | 2.0 | 279 | 9.5 |
| 1971 | 2.0 | 2.3 | 22 | 2.0 | 280 | 9.5 |
| 1972 | 2.0 | 2.3 | 22 | 2.0 | 279 | 9.4 |
| 1973 | 2.0 | 2.3 | 22 | 1.9 | 284 | 8.9 |
| 1974 | 2.1 | 2.3 | 23 | 2.0 | 276 | 9.2 |
| 1975 | 2.2 | 2.3 | 24 | 1.9 | 298 | 8.8 |
| 1976 | 2.3 | 2.5 | 26 | 2.0 | 303 | 9.1 |
| 1977 | 2.3 | 2.4 | 25 | 2.0 | 302 | 9.0 |
| 1978 | 2.2 | 2.4 | 25 | 1.9 | 291 | 8.7 |
| 1979 | 2.3 | 2.4 | 25 | 2.0 | 299 | 8.5 |
| 1980 | 2.3 | 2.4 | 25 | 2.0 | 292 | 8.4 |
| 1981 | 2.3 | 2.4 | 26 | 2.0 | 292 | 8.5 |
| 1982 | 2.3 | 2.4 | 25 | 2.0 | 298 | 8.2 |
| 1983 | 2.3 | 2.4 | 26 | 2.0 | 301 | 8.4 |
| 1984 | 2.3 | 2.5 | 26 | 2.0 | 295 | 8.5 |
| 1985 | 2.4 | 2.5 | 27 | 2.1 | 310 | 8.5 |
| 1986 | 2.4 | 2.5 | 27 | 2.1 | 313 | 8.4 |
| 1987 | 2.5 | 2.5 | 27 | 2.1 | 304 | 8.5 |
| 1988 | 2.5 | 2.5 | 28 | 2.1 | 316 | 8.3 |
| 1989 | 2.6 | 2.5 | 28 | 2.2 | 308 | 8.2 |
| 1990 | 2.6 | 2.5 | 28 | 2.2 | 311 | 8.2 |
| 1991 | 2.6 | 2.5 | 28 | 2.2 | 321 | 8.2 |
| 1992 | 2.7 | 2.6 | 29 | 2.3 | 326 | 8.3 |
| 1993 | 2.7 | 2.6 | 29 | 2.3 | 329 | 8.0 |
| 1994 | 2.7 | 2.6 | 29 | 2.3 | 331 | 8.1 |

*Notes:*
1. Computed by Center for Nutrition Policy and Promotion (CNPP), USDA. Based on Economic Research Service estimates of per capita quantities of food available for consumption (retail weight) and on CNPP estimates of quantities of produce from home gardens and certain other foods. No deduction is made in food supply estimates for loss of food or nutrients in further processing, in marketing, or in the home. Data include iron, thiamin, riboflavin, niacin, vitamin A, vitamin B6, vitamin B12 and ascorbic acid added by enrichment and fortification.

*Source:* U.S. Department of Agriculture, *Agricultural Statistics 1998*, Table 13-2; <http://www.usda.gov>.

## E4-5. Macronutrients, Vitamins and Minerals, Quantities Available for Consumption per Capita per Day: 1970–1994[1] *(continued from previous table)*

| Year | Minerals, Calcium Milligrams | Minerals, Phosphorus Milligrams | Minerals, Magnesium Milligrams |
|------|------|------|------|
| 1970 | 890 | 1,460 | 320 |
| 1971 | 890 | 1,470 | 320 |
| 1972 | 890 | 1,470 | 330 |
| 1973 | 880 | 1,440 | 330 |
| 1974 | 850 | 1,430 | 320 |
| 1975 | 840 | 1,430 | 320 |
| 1976 | 890 | 1,480 | 330 |
| 1977 | 880 | 1,470 | 320 |
| 1978 | 880 | 1,460 | 320 |
| 1979 | 890 | 1,480 | 330 |
| 1980 | 870 | 1,460 | 320 |
| 1981 | 860 | 1,460 | 320 |
| 1982 | 870 | 1,460 | 330 |
| 1983 | 890 | 1,490 | 330 |
| 1984 | 900 | 1,500 | 330 |
| 1985 | 920 | 1,540 | 350 |
| 1986 | 930 | 1,570 | 350 |
| 1987 | 930 | 1,580 | 350 |
| 1988 | 930 | 1,600 | 360 |
| 1989 | 920 | 1,600 | 360 |
| 1990 | 940 | 1,620 | 370 |
| 1991 | 940 | 1,630 | 380 |
| 1992 | 950 | 1,660 | 380 |
| 1993 | 950 | 1,650 | 380 |
| 1994 | 960 | 1,680 | 380 |

*Notes:*

1. Computed by Center for Nutrition Policy and Promotion (CNPP), USDA. Based on Economic Research Service estimates of per capita quantities of food available for consumption (retail weight) and on CNPP estimates of quantities of produce from home gardens and certain other foods. No deduction is made in food supply estimates for loss of food or nutrients in further processing, in marketing, or in the home. Data include iron, thiamin, riboflavin, niacin, vitamin A, vitamin B6, vitamin B12 and ascorbic acid added by enrichment and fortification.

*Source:* U.S. Department of Agriculture, *Agricultural Statistics 1998*, Table 13-2; <http://www.usda.gov>.

## E4-6. Macronutrients, Vitamins and Minerals, Quantities Available for Consumption per Capita per Day: 1970–1994[1] *(continued from previous table)*

| Year | Mineral, Iron Milligrams | Minerals, Zinc Milligrams | Minerals, Copper Milligrams | Minerals, Potassium Milligrams |
|------|-----|-----|-----|-----|
| 1970 | 15.4 | 12.2 | 1.6 | 3,510 |
| 1971 | 15.6 | 12.3 | 1.6 | 3,500 |
| 1972 | 15.6 | 12.2 | 1.6 | 3,490 |
| 1973 | 15.8 | 11.8 | 1.6 | 3,460 |
| 1974 | 18.1 | 12.0 | 1.6 | 3,410 |
| 1975 | 19.8 | 11.8 | 1.7 | 3,440 |
| 1976 | 23.8 | 12.3 | 1.7 | 3,530 |
| 1977 | 23.3 | 12.2 | 1.7 | 3,460 |
| 1978 | 23.0 | 12.0 | 1.6 | 3,410 |
| 1979 | 16.1 | 11.9 | 1.7 | 3,480 |
| 1980 | 16.0 | 11.8 | 1.7 | 3,440 |
| 1981 | 16.2 | 11.9 | 1.7 | 3,400 |
| 1982 | 16.4 | 11.9 | 1.7 | 3,430 |
| 1983 | 17.4 | 12.1 | 1.7 | 3,490 |
| 1984 | 18.4 | 12.1 | 1.7 | 3,500 |
| 1985 | 19.1 | 12.5 | 1.8 | 3,590 |
| 1986 | 19.2 | 12.6 | 1.8 | 3,650 |
| 1987 | 19.3 | 12.5 | 1.8 | 3,590 |
| 1988 | 19.8 | 12.7 | 1.8 | 3,630 |
| 1989 | 19.8 | 12.6 | 1.8 | 3,630 |
| 1990 | 20.2 | 12.7 | 1.8 | 3,650 |
| 1991 | 20.5 | 12.8 | 1.9 | 3,690 |
| 1992 | 20.8 | 13.0 | 1.9 | 3,750 |
| 1993 | 20.9 | 13.0 | 1.9 | 3,750 |
| 1994 | 21.2 | 13.2 | 1.9 | 3,780 |

*Notes:*

1. Computed by Center for Nutrition Policy and Promotion (CNPP), USDA. Based on Economic Research Service estimates of per capita quantities of food available for consumption (retail weight) and on CNPP estimates of quantities of produce from home gardens and certain other foods. No deduction is made in food supply estimates for loss of food or nutrients in further processing, in marketing, or in the home. Data include iron, thiamin, riboflavin, niacin, vitamin A, vitamin B6, vitamin B12 and ascorbic acid added by enrichment and fortification.

*Source:* U.S. Department of Agriculture, *Agricultural Statistics 1998*, Table 13-2; <http://www.usda.gov>.

## E5. VALUE OF NEW CONSTRUCTION PUT IN PLACE

### E5-1. Value of New Construction Put in Place, Current Dollars, Totals: 1990–1997, in Millions of Dollars

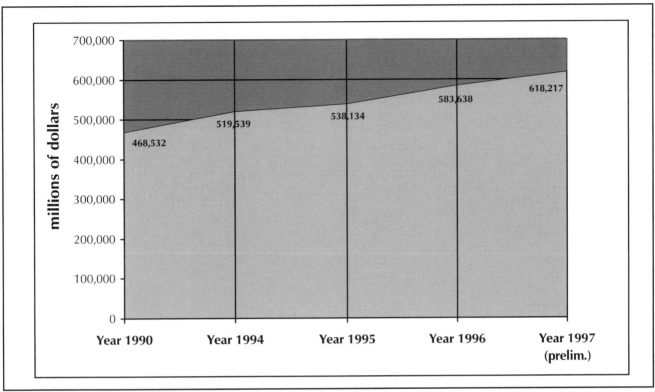

*Source: Statistical Abstract of the United States 1998*, No. 1194 at <http://www.census.gov/prod/3/98pubs/98statab/sasec25.pdf>. Underlying data from U.S. Bureau of the Census, *Current Construction Reports*, Series C30, *Value of Construction*, monthly.

## E5-2. Value of New Construction Put in Place, Current Dollars: 1990–1997, in Millions of Dollars *(continued in E5-3)*

| | 1990 | 1994 | 1995 | 1996 | 1997 (prelim.) |
|---|---|---|---|---|---|
| **Private construction** | **370,102** | **367,247** | **360,040** | **385,967** | **395,321** |
| Residential buildings | 188,045 | 218,005 | 201,677 | 220,017 | 221,546 |
| New housing units | 131,632 | 153,250 | 142,413 | 153,966 | 156,038 |
| One unit | 111,832 | 140,416 | 126,773 | 136,516 | 137,156 |
| Two or more units | 19,800 | 12,833 | 15,640 | 17,450 | 18,882 |
| Improvements | 56,414 | 64,755 | 59,264 | 66,052 | 65,508 |
| Nonresidential buildings | 146,661 | 111,416 | 120,627 | 131,188 | 139,067 |
| Industrial | 34,373 | 26,803 | 29,043 | 28,503 | 26,440 |
| Office | 35,838 | 20,553 | 22,891 | 24,329 | 27,631 |
| Hotels, motels | 10,917 | 4,308 | 6,351 | 9,521 | 10,741 |
| Other commercial | 40,922 | 34,756 | 38,098 | 42,042 | 42,748 |
| Religious | 3,642 | 3,584 | 3,864 | 3,955 | 4,951 |
| Educational | 4,715 | 4,471 | 4,908 | 5,880 | 7,101 |
| Hospital and institutional | 11,103 | 11,377 | 10,051 | 10,280 | 11,576 |
| Miscellaneous [2] | 5,151 | 5,565 | 5,421 | 6,677 | 7,880 |
| Farm nonresidential | 2,862 | 2,990 | 2,692 | 3,319 | 3,329 |
| Public utilities | 29,537 | 32,074 | 32,401 | 29,286 | 29,448 |
| Telecommunications | 9,891 | 9,785 | 10,073 | 10,245 | 9,918 |
| Other public utilities | 19,646 | 22,289 | 22,328 | 19,041 | 19,529 |
| Railroads | 2,633 | 3,186 | 3,201 | 3,894 | 4,321 |
| Electric light and power | 11,572 | 13,877 | 12,656 | 9,914 | 10,545 |
| Gas | 5,013 | 4,308 | 5,637 | 4,330 | 3,820 |
| Petroleum pipelines | 428 | 918 | 834 | 903 | 843 |
| All other private [3] | 2,997 | 2,763 | 2,643 | 2,156 | 1,931 |

*\*Notes:*

2. Includes amusement and recreational buildings, bus and airline terminals, animal hospitals and shelters, etc.

3. Includes privately owned streets and bridges, parking areas, sewer and water facilities, parks and playgrounds, golf courses, airfields, etc.

\*Only notes that apply to this table are cited.

*Source: Statistical Abstract of the United States 1998*, No. 1194 at <http://www.census.gov/prod/3/98pubs/98statab/sasec25.pdf>. Underlying data from U.S. Bureau of the Census, *Current Construction Reports*, Series C30, *Value of Construction*, monthly.

## E5-3. Value of New Construction Put in Place, Current Dollars: 1990–1997, in Millions of Dollars *(continued from previous table)*

|  | 1990 | 1994 | 1995 | 1996 | 1997 (prelim.) |
|---|---|---|---|---|---|
| **Public construction** | **107,478** | **120,193** | **130,657** | **137,333** | **147,058** |
| Buildings | 43,615 | 49,446 | 55,700 | 58,659 | 63,603 |
|   Housing and redevelopment | 3,808 | 3,835 | 4,491 | 4,614 | 4,861 |
|   Industrial | 1,434 | 1,465 | 1,508 | 1,389 | 998 |
|   Educational | 16,055 | 20,361 | 23,278 | 24,112 | 27,065 |
|   Hospital | 2,860 | 3,951 | 4,332 | 4,638 | 5,042 |
|   Other[4] | 19,458 | 19,834 | 22,089 | 23,907 | 25,637 |
| Highways and streets | 32,105 | 37,419 | 38,498 | 41,243 | 45,197 |
| Military facilities | 2,665 | 2,318 | 3,011 | 2,634 | 2,620 |
| Conservation and development | 4,686 | 6,363 | 6,368 | 6,011 | 5,658 |
| Sewer systems | 10,276 | 8,700 | 9,435 | 10,433 | 10,463 |
| Water supply facilities | 4,909 | 4,647 | 5,283 | 5,964 | 6,339 |
| Miscellaneous public[5] | 9,223 | 11,301 | 12,362 | 12,388 | 13,177 |

*\*Notes:*
4. Includes federal administrative buildings, prisons, police and fire stations, courthouses, civic centers, passenger terminals, space facilities, postal facilities, etc.
5. Includes open amusement and recreational facilities, power generating facilities, transit systems, airfields, open parking facilities, etc.
\*Only notes that apply to this table are cited.

*Source: Statistical Abstract of the United States 1998*, No. 1194 at <http://www.census.gov/prod/3/98pubs/98statab/sasec25>.pdf. Underlying data from U.S. Bureau of the Census, *Current Construction Reports*, Series C30, *Value of Construction*, monthly.

## E5-4. Value of New Construction Put in Place, Constant (1992) Dollars, Totals: 1990 to 1997, in Millions of Dollars

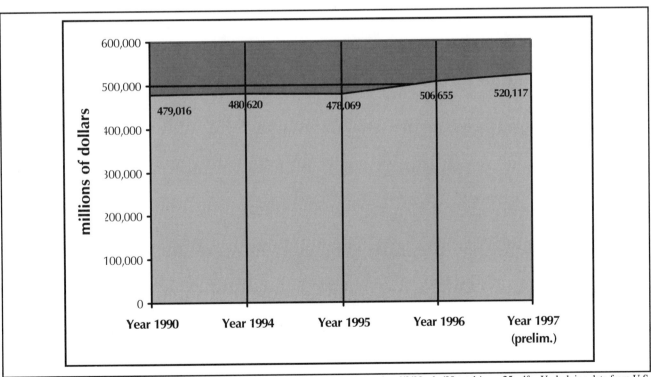

*Source: Statistical Abstract of the United States 1998*, No. 1194 at <http://www.census.gov/prod/3/98pubs/98statab/sasec25.pdf>. Underlying data from U.S. Bureau of the Census, *Current Construction Reports*, Series C30, *Value of Construction*, monthly.

**E5-5. Value of New Construction Put in Place, Constant (1992) Dollars: 1990–1997, in Millions of Dollars (continued in E5-6)**

| | 1990 | 1994 | 1995 | 1996 | 1997 (prelim.) |
|---|---|---|---|---|---|
| **Private construction** | **370,102** | **367,247** | **360,040** | **385,967** | **395,321** |
| Residential buildings | 188,045 | 218,005 | 201,677 | 220,017 | 221,546 |
| New housing units | 131,632 | 153,250 | 142,413 | 153,966 | 156,038 |
| One unit | 111,832 | 140,416 | 126,773 | 136,516 | 137,156 |
| Two or more units | 19,800 | 12,833 | 15,640 | 17,450 | 18,882 |
| Improvements | 56,414 | 64,755 | 59,264 | 66,052 | 65,508 |
| Nonresidential buildings | 146,661 | 111,416 | 120,627 | 131,188 | 139,067 |
| Industrial | 34,373 | 26,803 | 29,043 | 28,503 | 26,440 |
| Office | 35,838 | 20,553 | 22,891 | 24,329 | 27,631 |
| Hotels, motels | 10,917 | 4,308 | 6,351 | 9,521 | 10,741 |
| Other commercial | 40,922 | 34,756 | 38,098 | 42,042 | 42,748 |
| Religious | 3,642 | 3,584 | 3,864 | 3,955 | 4,951 |
| Educational | 4,715 | 4,471 | 4,908 | 5,880 | 7,101 |
| Hospital and institutional | 11,103 | 11,377 | 10,051 | 10,280 | 11,576 |
| Miscellaneous [2] | 5,151 | 5,565 | 5,421 | 6,677 | 7,880 |
| Farm nonresidential | 2,862 | 2,990 | 2,692 | 3,319 | 3,329 |
| Public utilities | 29,537 | 32,074 | 32,401 | 29,286 | 29,448 |
| Telecommunications | 9,891 | 9,785 | 10,073 | 10,245 | 9,918 |
| Other public utilities | 19,646 | 22,289 | 22,328 | 19,041 | 19,529 |
| Railroads | 2,633 | 3,186 | 3,201 | 3,894 | 4,321 |
| Electric light and power | 11,572 | 13,877 | 12,656 | 9,914 | 10,545 |
| Gas | 5,013 | 4,308 | 5,637 | 4,330 | 3,820 |
| Petroleum pipelines | 428 | 918 | 834 | 903 | 843 |
| All other private [3] | 2,997 | 2,763 | 2,643 | 2,156 | 1,931 |

*Notes:

2. Includes amusement and recreational buildings, bus and airline terminals, animal hospitals and shelters, etc.

3. Includes privately owned streets and bridges, parking areas, sewer and water facilities, parks and playgrounds, golf courses, airfields, etc.

*Only notes that apply to this table are cited.

Source: Statistical Abstract of the United States 1998, No. 1194 at <http://www.census.gov/prod/3/98pubs/98statab/sasec25.pdf>. Underlying data from U.S. Bureau of the Census, Current Construction Reports, Series C30, Value of Construction, monthly.

## E5-6. Value of New Construction Put in Place, Constant (1992) Dollars: 1990–1997, in Millions of Dollars *(continued from previous table)*

| | 1990 | 1994 | 1995 | 1996 | 1997 (prelim.) |
|---|---|---|---|---|---|
| **Public construction** | **108,914** | **113,373** | **118,029** | **120,688** | **124,796** |
| Buildings | 44,583 | 45,728 | 49,683 | 51,119 | 53,515 |
|   Housing and redevelopment | 3,914 | 3,495 | 3,928 | 3,958 | 4,055 |
|   Industrial | 1,465 | 1,358 | 1,348 | 1,214 | 842 |
|   Educational | 16,398 | 18,838 | 20,800 | 21,035 | 22,786 |
|   Hospital | 2,924 | 3,663 | 3,871 | 4,050 | 4,247 |
|   Other [4] | 19,882 | 18,373 | 19,737 | 20,863 | 21,585 |
| Highways and streets | 31,777 | 36,219 | 35,303 | 36,483 | 38,605 |
| Military facilities | 2,683 | 2,196 | 2,728 | 2,317 | 2,223 |
| Conservation and development | 4,870 | 5,996 | 5,779 | 5,335 | 4,841 |
| Sewer systems | 10,670 | 8,199 | 8,557 | 9,260 | 8,951 |
| Water supply facilities | 4,987 | 4,237 | 4,695 | 5,187 | 5,393 |
| Miscellaneous public [5] | 9,344 | 10,799 | 11,284 | 10,987 | 11,267 |

*\*Notes:*

4. Includes federal administrative buildings, prisons, police and fire stations, courthouses, civic centers, passenger terminals, space facilities, postal facilities, etc.

5. Includes open amusement and recreational facilities, power generating facilities, transit systems, airfields, open parking facilities, etc.

*\*Only notes that apply to this table are cited.*

*Source: Statistical Abstract of the United States 1998*, No. 1194 at <http://www.census.gov/prod/3/98pubs/98statab/sasec25.pdf>. Underlying data from U.S. Bureau of the Census, *Current Construction Reports*, Series C30, *Value of Construction*, monthly.

## E6. NEW PRIVATELY OWNED HOUSING UNITS STARTED, TOTAL AND BY STATE

### E6-1. New Privately Owned Housing Units Started, Total: 1995–1998, in Thousands of Units

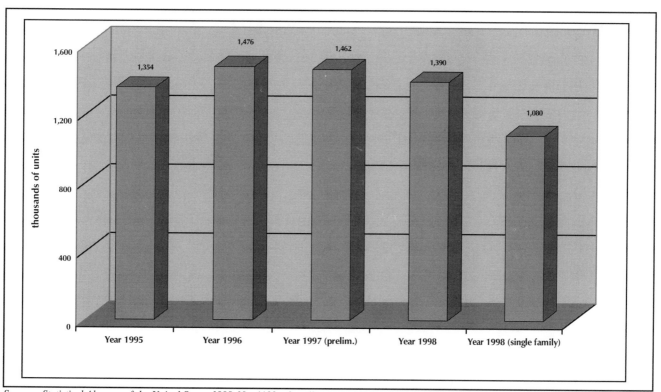

*Source: Statistical Abstract of the United States 1998*, No. 1199; <http://www.census.gov/prod/3/98pubs/98statab/sasec25.pdf>. Underlying data from National Association of Home Builders, Economics Division, Washington, DC. Data provided by the Econometric Forecasting Service.

## E6-2. New Privately Owned Housing Units Started, by State: 1995–1998, in Thousands of Units

| | 1995 | 1996 | 1997 | 1998 est; total units | 1998 est; single family units |
|---|---|---|---|---|---|
| Alabama | 21.2 | 20.3 | 18.7 | 17.3 | 13.8 |
| Alaska | 2.5 | 2.2 | 2.2 | 2.0 | 1.5 |
| Arizona | 53.5 | 58.3 | 58.2 | 53.9 | 42.2 |
| Arkansas | 12.2 | 11.5 | 10.5 | 9.8 | 7.0 |
| California | 86.9 | 97.7 | 113.3 | 121.6 | 95.5 |
| Colorado | 39.7 | 42.5 | 43.1 | 36.6 | 27.2 |
| Connecticut | 9.1 | 9.8 | 10.9 | 10.8 | 9.5 |
| Delaware | 5.3 | 5.5 | 5.6 | 5.3 | 5.0 |
| District of Columbia | 0.1 | (-) | (-) | (-) | (-) |
| Florida | 123.4 | 140.1 | 145.1 | 138.1 | 100.9 |
| Georgia | 77.2 | 78.4 | 72.2 | 66.7 | 53.4 |
| Hawaii | 6.9 | 4.0 | 3.9 | 3.7 | 2.3 |
| Idaho | 9.5 | 9.5 | 8.9 | 7.9 | 6.6 |
| Illinois | 48.8 | 51.8 | 48.5 | 46.2 | 35.7 |
| Indiana | 36.8 | 39.7 | 37.0 | 34.1 | 28.4 |
| Iowa | 9.4 | 9.9 | 9.7 | 9.4 | 6.0 |
| Kansas | 11.0 | 14.0 | 11.6 | 11.6 | 8.9 |
| Kentucky | 18.9 | 19.1 | 19.3 | 18.2 | 14.7 |
| Louisiana | 14.4 | 16.5 | 16.1 | 14.9 | 12.3 |
| Maine | 4.2 | 4.6 | 4.3 | 4.4 | 4.1 |
| Maryland | 28.9 | 28.3 | 27.0 | 25.7 | 22.7 |
| Massachusetts | 16.3 | 18.2 | 19.3 | 19.6 | 17.4 |
| Michigan | 47.6 | 54.5 | 51.6 | 48.3 | 40.0 |
| Minnesota | 25.0 | 26.7 | 24.2 | 23.6 | 20.0 |
| Mississippi | 12.2 | 11.2 | 10.5 | 9.5 | 7.5 |
| Missouri | 25.6 | 27.4 | 25.5 | 24.1 | 19.7 |
| Montana | 3.1 | 2.8 | 2.4 | 2.4 | 1.5 |
| Nebraska | 8.0 | 10.2 | 9.7 | 9.5 | 5.5 |
| Nevada | 33.8 | 39.5 | 35.9 | 32.4 | 23.0 |
| New Hampshire | 4.3 | 4.9 | 5.3 | 5.4 | 4.7 |
| New Jersey | 25.3 | 26.0 | 29.4 | 27.4 | 24.3 |
| New Mexico | 9.7 | 9.7 | 9.5 | 8.8 | 6.6 |
| New York | 23.4 | 28.7 | 27.6 | 28.1 | 18.8 |
| North Carolina | 64.4 | 70.6 | 75.9 | 70.7 | 57.0 |
| North Dakota | 3.2 | 2.4 | 2.4 | 2.3 | 1.2 |
| Ohio | 43.6 | 50.5 | 46.3 | 43.3 | 32.3 |
| Oklahoma | 11.8 | 11.7 | 12.0 | 11.6 | 9.3 |
| Oregon | 25.0 | 28.0 | 26.8 | 25.4 | 16.5 |
| Pennsylvania | 31.1 | 34.8 | 36.0 | 35.9 | 31.3 |
| Rhode Island | 2.5 | 2.7 | 2.9 | 2.8 | 2.5 |
| South Carolina | 26.1 | 32.2 | 34.2 | 31.4 | 25.2 |
| South Dakota | 3.9 | 3.8 | 3.1 | 3.0 | 2.2 |
| Tennessee | 36.4 | 40.9 | 35.8 | 33.3 | 27.2 |
| Texas | 112.5 | 124.5 | 130.2 | 116.4 | 85.7 |
| Utah | 20.7 | 22.4 | 17.9 | 17.3 | 13.4 |
| Vermont | 2.0 | 2.3 | 2.1 | 2.0 | 1.7 |
| Virginia | 45.2 | 47.2 | 45.9 | 44.9 | 36.9 |
| Washington | 37.9 | 42.4 | 42.1 | 42.2 | 29.2 |
| West Virginia | 4.8 | 4.0 | 4.3 | 4.0 | 3.3 |
| Wisconsin | 27.1 | 30.0 | 25.5 | 24.8 | 17.4 |
| Wyoming | 1.9 | 2 | 1.6 | 1.4 | 1.2 |

*Notes:*
(-) represents or rounds to zero

*Source: Statistical Abstract of the United States 1998,* No. 1199; <http://www.census.gov/prod/3/98pubs/98statab/sasec25.pdf>. Underlying data from National Association of Home Builders, Economics Division, Washington, DC. Data provided by the Econometric Forecasting Service.

## E7. HOMEOWNERSHIP RATES, TOTAL AND BY STATE

### E7-1. Homeownership Rates, Totals: 1985–1997, in Percent

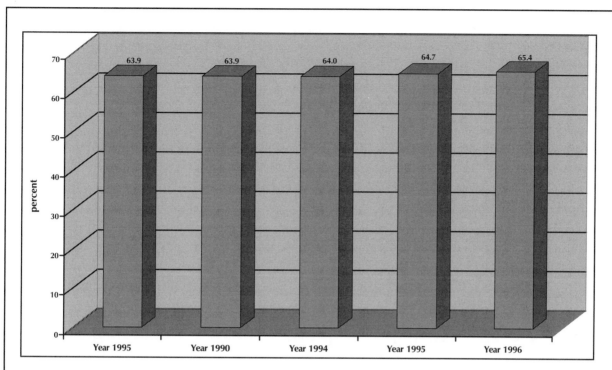

*General Notes:* Represents the proportion of owner households to the total number of occupied households. Based on the Current Population Survey/ Housing Vacancy Survey.

*Source:* U.S. Bureau of the Census, Internet site <http://wwwcensusgov/ftp/pub/hhes/www/hvshtml>. *Statistical Abstract of the United States 1998*, No. 1216; <http://www.census.gov/prod/3/98pubs/98statab/sasec25.pdf>.

## E7-2. Homeownership Rates, by State: 1985–1997, in Percent

| STATE | 1985 | 1990 | 1994 | 1995 | 1996 | 1997 |
|---|---|---|---|---|---|---|
| Alabama | 70.4 | 68.4 | 68.5 | 70.1 | 71.0 | 71.3 |
| Alaska | 61.2 | 58.4 | 58.8 | 60.9 | 62.9 | 67.2 |
| Arizona | 64.7 | 64.5 | 67.7 | 62.9 | 62.0 | 63.0 |
| Arkansas | 66.6 | 67.8 | 68.1 | 67.2 | 66.6 | 66.7 |
| California | 54.2 | 53.8 | 55.5 | 55.4 | 55.0 | 55.7 |
| Colorado | 63.6 | 59.0 | 62.9 | 64.6 | 64.5 | 64.1 |
| Connecticut | 69.0 | 67.9 | 63.8 | 68.2 | 69.0 | 68.1 |
| Delaware | 70.3 | 67.7 | 70.5 | 71.7 | 71.5 | 69.2 |
| Dist of Columbia | 37.4 | 36.4 | 37.8 | 39.2 | 40.4 | 42.5 |
| Florida | 67.2 | 65.1 | 65.7 | 66.6 | 67.1 | 66.9 |
| Georgia | 62.7 | 64.3 | 63.4 | 66.6 | 69.3 | 70.9 |
| Hawaii | 51.0 | 55.5 | 52.3 | 50.2 | 50.6 | 50.2 |
| Idaho | 71.0 | 69.4 | 70.7 | 72.0 | 71.4 | 72.3 |
| Illinois | 60.6 | 63.0 | 64.2 | 66.4 | 68.2 | 68.1 |
| Indiana | 67.6 | 67.0 | 68.4 | 71.0 | 74.2 | 74.1 |
| Iowa | 69.9 | 70.7 | 70.1 | 71.4 | 72.8 | 72.7 |
| Kansas | 68.3 | 69.0 | 69.0 | 67.5 | 67.5 | 66.5 |
| Kentucky | 68.5 | 65.8 | 70.6 | 71.2 | 73.2 | 75.0 |
| Louisiana | 70.2 | 67.8 | 65.8 | 65.3 | 64.9 | 66.4 |
| Maine | 73.7 | 74.2 | 72.6 | 76.7 | 76.5 | 74.9 |
| Maryland | 65.6 | 64.9 | 64.1 | 65.8 | 66.9 | 70.5 |
| Massachusetts | 60.5 | 58.6 | 60.6 | 60.2 | 61.7 | 62.3 |
| Michigan | 70.7 | 72.3 | 72.0 | 72.2 | 73.3 | 73.3 |
| Minnesota | 70.0 | 68.0 | 68.9 | 73.3 | 75.4 | 75.4 |
| Mississippi | 69.6 | 69.4 | 69.2 | 71.1 | 73.0 | 73.7 |
| Missouri | 69.2 | 64.0 | 68.4 | 69.4 | 70.2 | 70.5 |
| Montana | 66.5 | 69.1 | 68.8 | 68.7 | 68.6 | 67.5 |
| Nebraska | 68.5 | 67.3 | 68.0 | 67.1 | 66.8 | 66.7 |
| Nevada | 57.0 | 55.8 | 55.8 | 58.6 | 61.1 | 61.2 |
| New Hampshire | 65.5 | 65.0 | 65.1 | 66.0 | 65.0 | 66.8 |
| New Jersey | 62.3 | 65.0 | 64.1 | 64.9 | 64.6 | 63.1 |
| New Mexico | 68.2 | 68.6 | 66.8 | 67.0 | 67.1 | 69.6 |
| New York | 50.3 | 53.3 | 52.5 | 52.7 | 52.7 | 52.6 |
| North Carolina | 68.0 | 69.0 | 68.7 | 70.1 | 70.4 | 70.2 |
| North Dakota | 69.9 | 67.2 | 63.3 | 67.3 | 68.2 | 68.1 |
| Ohio | 67.9 | 68.7 | 67.4 | 67.9 | 69.2 | 69.0 |
| Oklahoma | 70.5 | 70.3 | 68.5 | 69.8 | 68.4 | 68.5 |
| Oregon | 61.5 | 64.4 | 63.9 | 63.2 | 63.1 | 61.0 |
| Pennsylvania | 71.6 | 73.8 | 71.8 | 71.5 | 71.7 | 73.3 |
| Rhode Island | 61.4 | 58.5 | 56.5 | 57.9 | 56.6 | 58.7 |
| South Carolina | 72.0 | 71.4 | 72.0 | 71.3 | 72.9 | 74.1 |
| South Dakota | 67.6 | 66.2 | 66.4 | 67.5 | 67.8 | 67.6 |
| Tennessee | 67.6 | 68.3 | 65.2 | 67.0 | 68.8 | 70.2 |
| Texas | 60.5 | 59.7 | 59.7 | 61.4 | 61.8 | 61.5 |
| Utah | 71.5 | 70.1 | 69.3 | 71.5 | 72.7 | 72.5 |
| Vermont | 69.5 | 72.6 | 69.4 | 70.4 | 70.3 | 69.1 |
| Virginia | 68.5 | 69.8 | 69.3 | 68.1 | 68.5 | 68.4 |
| Washington | 66.8 | 61.8 | 62.4 | 61.6 | 63.1 | 62.9 |
| West Virginia | 75.9 | 72.0 | 73.7 | 73.1 | 74.3 | 74.6 |
| Wisconsin | 63.8 | 68.3 | 64.2 | 67.5 | 68.2 | 68.3 |
| Wyoming | 73.2 | 68.9 | 65.8 | 69.0 | 68.0 | 67.6 |

*General Notes:* Represents the proportion of owner households to the total number of occupied households. Based on the Current Population Survey/ Housing Vacancy Survey.

*Source:* U.S. Bureau of the Census, Internet site <http://wwwcensusgov/ftp/pub/hhes/www/hvshtml>. *Statistical Abstract of the United States 1998*, No. 1216; <http://www.census.gov/prod/3/98pubs/98statab/sasec25.pdf>.

# E8. CONSTRUCTION CONTRACTS—VALUE OF CONSTRUCTION AND FLOOR SPACE OF BUILD-INGS

## E8-1. Construction Contracts—Value of Construction and Floor Space of Buildings, by Class of Construction: 1980–1997 *(continued in E8-2)*

| | Total | Residential | Total | Nonresidential Buildings Commercial[1] | Manufacturing | Educa-tional[2] |
|---|---|---|---|---|---|---|
| **VALUE (bil. dol.)** | | | | | | |
| 1980 | 151.8 | 60.4 | 56.9 | 27.7 | 9.2 | 7.4 |
| 1985 | 235.6 | 102.1 | 92.1 | 54.6 | 8.1 | 10.0 |
| 1987 | 259.0 | 114.1 | 98.8 | 53.7 | 8.6 | 13.2 |
| 1988 | 262.2 | 116.2 | 97.9 | 51.6 | 9.5 | 14.1 |
| 1989 | 271.3 | 116.2 | 106.1 | 53.6 | 12.7 | 15.9 |
| 1990 | 246.0 | 100.9 | 95.4 | 44.8 | 8.4 | 16.6 |
| 1991 | 230.8 | 94.4 | 86.2 | 32.7 | 8.3 | 19.0 |
| 1992 | 252.2 | 110.6 | 87.0 | 32.8 | 8.9 | 17.6 |
| 1993 | 271.5 | 123.9 | 88.8 | 34.2 | 9.0 | 19.3 |
| 1994 | 296.7 | 133.6 | 101.5 | 40.8 | 11.2 | 21.0 |
| 1995 | 306.4 | 127.8 | 114.1 | 46.6 | 13.8 | 22.9 |
| 1996 | 331.2 | 146.3 | 120.0 | 51.7 | 13.1 | 22.9 |
| 1997 | 352.4 | 151.5 | 132.8 | 57.0 | 13.3 | 27.3 |
| **FLOOR SPACE (mil. sq. ft.)** | | | | | | |
| 1980 | 3,102 | 1,839 | 1,263 | 738 | 220 | 103 |
| 1985 | 3,853 | 2,324 | 1,529 | 1,039 | 165 | 111 |
| 1987 | 3,756 | 2,288 | 1,469 | 933 | 160 | 139 |
| 1988 | 3,594 | 2,181 | 1,413 | 883 | 162 | 142 |
| 1989 | 3,516 | 2,115 | 1,400 | 867 | 158 | 151 |
| 1990 | 3,020 | 1,817 | 1,203 | 694 | 128 | 152 |
| 1991 | 2,634 | 1,653 | 981 | 476 | 100 | 177 |
| 1992 | 2,799 | 1,864 | 936 | 462 | 95 | 156 |
| 1993 | 3,062 | 2,091 | 971 | 481 | 110 | 165 |
| 1994 | 3,410 | 2,267 | 1,144 | 600 | 143 | 172 |
| 1995 | 3,452 | 2,172 | 1,280 | 700 | 163 | 186 |
| 1996 | 3,769 | 2,476 | 1,293 | 721 | 155 | 176 |
| 1997 | 4,058 | 2,574 | 1,484 | 827 | 182 | 195 |

*Notes:*
1. Includes nonindustrial warehouses.
2. Includes science.
*General Notes:* Building construction includes new structures and additions; nonbuilding construction includes major alterations to existing structures which affect only valuation, since no additional floor area is created by "alteration."

*Source: Statistical Abstract of the United States 1998,* No. 1195; <http://www.census.gov/prod/3/98pubs/98statab/sasec25.pdf>. Underlying data from F.W. Dodge, a Division of the McGraw-Hill Companies, New York, NY (copyright).

## E8-2. Construction Contracts—Value of Construction and Floor Space of Buildings, by Class of Construction: 1980–1997 *(continued from previous table)*

| | Nonresidential Buildings | | | | | |
|---|---|---|---|---|---|---|
| **VALUE (bil. dol.)** | **Hospital** | **Public buildings** | **Religious** | **Social and Recreational** | **Miscellaneous** | **Non-building construction** |
| 1980 | 5.4 | 1.6 | 1.2 | 2.7 | 1.7 | 34.5 |
| 1985 | 7.8 | 3.1 | 2.0 | 4.0 | 2.5 | 41.4 |
| 1987 | 9.0 | 4.7 | 2.1 | 4.3 | 3.2 | 46.1 |
| 1988 | 8.2 | 4.4 | 2.2 | 4.7 | 3.2 | 48.1 |
| 1989 | 8.8 | 5.2 | 2.0 | 5.0 | 2.9 | 49.0 |
| 1990 | 9.2 | 5.7 | 2.2 | 5.3 | 3.1 | 49.7 |
| 1991 | 9.6 | 6.2 | 2.4 | 5.1 | 3.0 | 50.2 |
| 1992 | 10.9 | 5.8 | 2.5 | 5.5 | 3.1 | 54.6 |
| 1993 | 10.5 | 3.9 | 2.4 | 6.8 | 2.6 | 58.9 |
| 1994 | 10.5 | 6.1 | 2.5 | 6.5 | 3.0 | 61.6 |
| 1995 | 10.8 | 6.2 | 2.8 | 7.1 | 3.8 | 64.4 |
| 1996 | 11.0 | 6.3 | 2.9 | 8.1 | 4.0 | 64.9 |
| 1997 | 11.4 | 6.7 | 3.7 | 9.6 | 3.9 | 68.1 |
| **FLOOR SPACE (mil. sq. ft.)** | | | | | | |
| 1980 | 55 | 18 | 28 | 49 | 52 | (X) |
| 1985 | 73 | 28 | 32 | 44 | 38 | (X) |
| 1987 | 78 | 42 | 32 | 46 | 38 | (X) |
| 1988 | 71 | 38 | 32 | 49 | 37 | (X) |
| 1989 | 72 | 41 | 27 | 48 | 35 | (X) |
| 1990 | 69 | 47 | 29 | 51 | 32 | (X) |
| 1991 | 72 | 50 | 29 | 45 | 33 | (X) |
| 1992 | 77 | 41 | 30 | 42 | 32 | (X) |
| 1993 | 75 | 30 | 30 | 51 | 29 | (X) |
| 1994 | 72 | 45 | 30 | 51 | 31 | (X) |
| 1995 | 70 | 39 | 33 | 56 | 33 | (X) |
| 1996 | 76 | 41 | 32 | 60 | 32 | (X) |
| 1997 | 85 | 46 | 41 | 75 | 34 | (X) |

*Notes:*
(X) indicates not applicable.
*General Notes:* Building construction includes new structures and additions; nonbuilding construction includes major alterations to existing structures which affect only valuation, since no additional floor area is created by "alteration."

*Source: Statistical Abstract of the United States 1998*, No. 1195; <http://www.census.gov/prod/3/98pubs/98statab/sasec25.pdf>. Underlying data from F.W. Dodge, a Division of the McGraw-Hill Companies, New York, NY (copyright).

## E9. ENERGY SUPPLY AND DISPOSITION

### E9-1. Energy Supply and Disposition, Production and Consumption: 1990–1996, in Quadrillion Btu

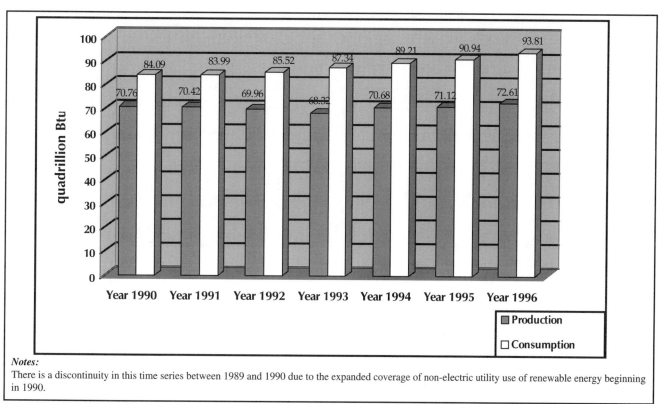

*Notes:*
There is a discontinuity in this time series between 1989 and 1990 due to the expanded coverage of non-electric utility use of renewable energy beginning in 1990.

*Source: Statistical Abstract of the United States 1998*, No. 948; <http://www.census.gov/statab/freq/98s0948.txt>. Underlying data from U.S. Energy Information Administration, *Annual Energy Review*.

**E9-2. Energy Supply and Disposition, Exports and Imports: 1990–1996, in Quadrillion Btu**

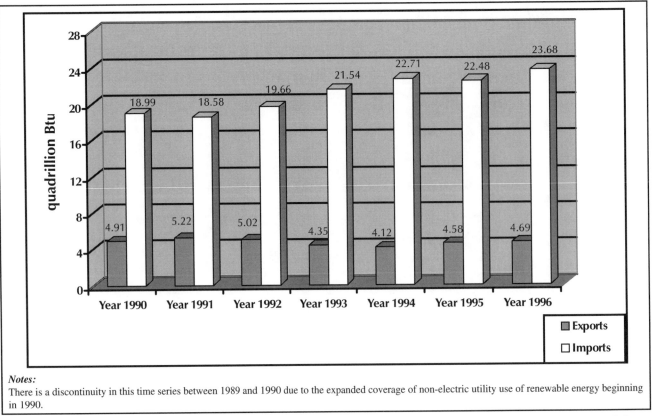

*Notes:*
There is a discontinuity in this time series between 1989 and 1990 due to the expanded coverage of non-electric utility use of renewable energy beginning in 1990.

*Source: Statistical Abstract of the United States 1998*, No. 948; <http://www.census.gov/statab/freq/98s0948.txt>. Underlying data from U.S. Energy Information Administration, *Annual Energy Review*.

## E9-3. Energy Supply and Disposition, by Type of Fuel: 1990–1992, in Quadrillion Btu

| TYPE OF FUEL | 1990 | 1991 | 1992 |
|---|---|---|---|
| Production[1] | 70.76 | 70.42 | 69.96 |
| Crude oil[2] | 15.57 | 15.70 | 15.22 |
| Natural gas liquids | 2.17 | 2.31 | 2.36 |
| Natural gas | 18.36 | 18.23 | 18.38 |
| Coal | 22.46 | 21.59 | 21.59 |
| Nuclear electric power | 6.16 | 6.58 | 6.61 |
| Renewable energy[1] | 6.07 | 6.06 | 5.84 |
| Hydroelectric power[3] | 3.01 | 2.98 | 2.61 |
| Geothermal[1] | 0.33 | 0.34 | 0.35 |
| Biofuels[1,4] | 2.63 | 2.64 | 2.79 |
| Net trade[5] | -14.08 | -13.36 | -14.64 |
| Exports | 4.91 | 5.22 | 5.02 |
| Coal | 2.77 | 2.85 | 2.68 |
| Natural gas | 0.09 | 0.13 | 0.22 |
| Petroleum | 1.82 | 2.13 | 2.01 |
| Imports | 18.99 | 18.58 | 19.66 |
| Coal | 0.07 | 0.08 | 0.10 |
| Natural gas | 1.55 | 1.80 | 2.16 |
| Petroleum[6] | 12.77 | 12.55 | 13.25 |
| Consumption | 84.09 | 83.99 | 85.52 |
| Petroleum[7] | 33.55 | 32.85 | 33.53 |
| Natural gas[8] | 19.30 | 19.61 | 20.13 |
| Coal | 19.10 | 18.77 | 19.21 |
| Nuclear electric power | 6.16 | 6.58 | 6.61 |
| Renewable energy[1] | 6.17 | 6.27 | 6.11 |
| Hydroelectric power[3,9] | 3.10 | 3.18 | 2.85 |
| Geothermal[1] | 0.35 | 0.35 | 0.37 |
| Biofuels[1,4] | 2.63 | 2.64 | 2.79 |

*Notes:*
1. There is a discontinuity in this time series between 1989 and 1990 due to the expanded coverage of non-electric utility use of renewable energy beginning in 1990.
2. Includes lease condensate.
3. There is a discontinuity in this time series between 1989 and 1990; beginning in 1990, pumped storage is removed and expanded coverage of industrial use of hydroelectric power is included.
4. Includes wood, wood waste, peat, wood liquors, railroad ties, pitch, wood sludge, municipal solid waste, agricultural waste, straw, tires, landfill gases, fish oils, and/or other waste.
5. Exports minus imports.
6. Includes imports of crude oil for the Strategic Petroleum Reserve, which began in 1977. Includes imports of unfinished oils and natural gas plant liquids.
7. Petroleum products supplied, including natural gas plant liquids and crude oil burned as fuel.
8. Includes supplemental gaseous fuels.
9. Includes net imports of electricity.

*Source: Statistical Abstract of the United States 1998,* No. 948; <http://www.census.gov/statab/freq/98s0948.txt>. Underlying data from U.S. Energy Information Administration, *Annual Energy Review.*

## E9-4. Energy Supply and Disposition, by Type of Fuel: 1993–1996, in Quadrillion Btu

| TYPE OF FUEL | 1993 | 1994 | 1995 | 1996 |
|---|---|---|---|---|
| Production[1] | 68.32 | 70.68 | 71.12 | 72.61 |
| Crude oil[2] | 14.49 | 14.10 | 13.89 | 13.74 |
| Natural gas liquids | 2.41 | 2.39 | 2.44 | 2.53 |
| Natural gas | 18.58 | 19.35 | 19.10 | 19.53 |
| Coal | 20.22 | 22.07 | 21.98 | 22.61 |
| Nuclear electric power | 6.52 | 6.84 | 7.18 | 7.17 |
| Renewable energy[1] | 6.13 | 5.97 | 6.56 | 7.06 |
| Hydroelectric power[3] | 2.88 | 2.67 | 3.21 | 3.59 |
| Geothermal[1] | 0.36 | 0.36 | 0.31 | 0.34 |
| Biofuels[1,4] | 2.78 | 2.84 | 2.95 | 3.02 |
| Net trade[5] | -17.18 | -18.58 | -17.86 | -18.99 |
| Exports | 4.35 | 4.12 | 4.58 | 4.69 |
| Coal | 1.96 | 1.88 | 2.32 | 2.37 |
| Natural gas | 0.14 | 0.16 | 0.16 | 0.16 |
| Petroleum | 2.12 | 1.99 | 1.99 | 2.06 |
| Imports | 21.54 | 22.71 | 22.48 | 23.68 |
| Coal | 0.18 | 0.19 | 0.18 | 0.18 |
| Natural gas | 2.40 | 2.68 | 2.90 | 2.90 |
| Petroleum[6] | 14.75 | 15.34 | 15.63 | 16.24 |
| Consumption | 87.34 | 89.21 | 90.94 | 93.81 |
| Petroleum[7] | 33.84 | 34.73 | 34.66 | 35.72 |
| Natural gas[8] | 20.83 | 21.29 | 22.16 | 22.59 |
| Coal | 19.83 | 20.02 | 20.08 | 20.99 |
| Nuclear electric power | 6.52 | 6.84 | 7.18 | 7.17 |
| Renewable energy[1] | 6.40 | 6.28 | 6.85 | 7.39 |
| Hydroelectric power[3,9] | 3.14 | 2.96 | 3.47 | 3.91 |
| Geothermal[1] | 0.38 | 0.38 | 0.33 | 0.35 |
| Biofuels[1,4] | 2.78 | 2.84 | 2.95 | 3.02 |

*Notes:*

1. There is a discontinuity in this time series between 1989 and 1990 due to the expanded coverage of non-electric utility use of renewable energy beginning in 1990.

2. Includes lease condensate.

3. There is a discontinuity in this time series between 1989 and 1990; beginning in 1990, pumped storage is removed and expanded coverage of industrial use of hydroelectric power is included.

4. Includes wood, wood waste, peat, wood liquors, railroad ties, pitch, wood sludge, municipal solid waste, agricultural waste, straw, tires, landfill gases, fish oils, and/or other waste.

5. Exports minus imports.

6. Includes imports of crude oil for the Strategic Petroleum Reserve, which began in 1977. Includes imports of unfinished oils and natural gas plant liquids.

7. Petroleum products supplied, including natural gas plant liquids and crude oil burned as fuel.

8. Includes supplemental gaseous fuels.

9. Includes net imports of electricity.

*Source: Statistical Abstract of the United States 1998*, No. 948; <http://www.census.gov/statab/freq/98s0948.txt>. Underlying data from U.S. Energy Information Administration, *Annual Energy Review.*

# E10. ENERGY CONSUMPTION—TOTAL AND PER CAPITA, BY STATE

## E10-1. Energy Consumption—Total and per Capita, by State: 1995, in Trillions of Btu (except as indicated)

| State | Total* | Per capital (mil BTU) |
|---|---|---|
| United States | 90,547.40 | 344.4 |
| Alabama | 1,933.30 | 455.3 |
| Alaska | 686.3 | 1,139.1 |
| Arizona | 1,058.90 | 246 |
| Arkansas | 997.9 | 401.6 |
| California | 7,577.00 | 240 |
| Colorado | 1,075.20 | 286.9 |
| Connecticut | 786.3 | 240.4 |
| Delaware | 264 | 368.1 |
| Dist. of Columbia | 177.8 | 320.7 |
| Florida | 3,518.60 | 248.1 |
| Georgia | 2,512.10 | 348.5 |
| Hawaii | 254.8 | 216.1 |
| Idaho | 456.2 | 391.2 |
| Illinois | 3,804.30 | 322.7 |
| Indiana | 2,592.10 | 447.2 |
| Iowa | 1,067.30 | 375.4 |
| Kansas | 1,040.60 | 405.9 |
| Kentucky | 1,770.40 | 459 |
| Louisiana | 3,813.60 | 879.1 |
| Maine | 513.3 | 414.4 |
| Maryland | 1,311.90 | 260.4 |
| Massachusetts | 1,493.80 | 246.1 |
| Michigan | 3,157.00 | 331 |
| Minnesota | 1,622.10 | 351.5 |
| Mississippi | 1,058.80 | 392.7 |
| Missouri | 1,662.80 | 312.6 |
| Montana | 378.9 | 435.4 |
| Nebraska | 580.3 | 354 |
| Nevada | 537.2 | 350.3 |
| New Hampshire | 284.5 | 247.8 |
| New Jersey | 2,542.90 | 319.9 |
| New Mexico | 575 | 340.3 |
| New York | 3,913.40 | 215.1 |
| North Carolina | 2,328.10 | 323.2 |
| North Dakota | 350.1 | 545.8 |
| Ohio | 4,038.00 | 362.7 |
| Oklahoma | 1,359.60 | 415.2 |
| Oregon | 1,048.20 | 332.9 |
| Pennsylvania | 3,885.70 | 322.2 |
| Rhode Island | 235.1 | 237 |
| South Carolina | 1,400.70 | 382 |
| South Dakota | 235.8 | 323.2 |
| Tennessee | 1,975.20 | 376.5 |
| Texas | 10,511.50 | 559.1 |
| Utah | 638.4 | 326 |
| Vermont | 149.9 | 256.3 |
| Virginia | 2,056.00 | 310.8 |
| Washington | 2,158.60 | 396.2 |
| West Virginia | 818.9 | 448.7 |
| Wisconsin | 1,749.10 | 341.5 |
| Wyoming | 405.2 | 845.6 |

*Notes:*
*Sources of energy includes geothermal, wood and waste, and net interstate sales of electricity, including losses, not shown separately

*Source: Statistical Abstract of the United States 1998*, No. 952. Underlying data from U.S. Energy Information Administration, *State Energy Data Report*, annual.

## E11. ENERGY CONSUMPTION—BY END-USE SECTOR AND SELECTED SOURCES

### E11-1. Energy Consumption—by End-Use Sector, Totals: 1995, in Trillions of Btu (except as indicated)

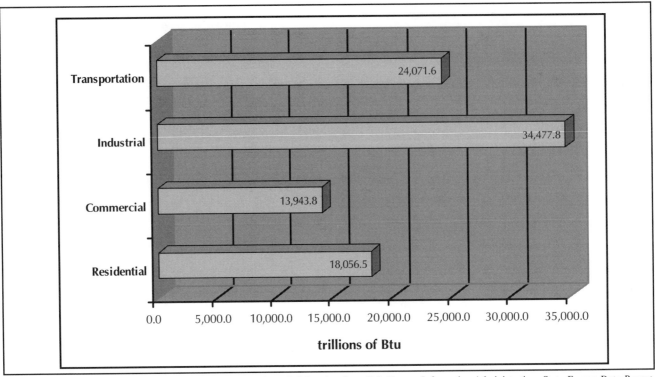

Source: Statistical Abstract of the United States 1998, No. 952. Underlying data from U.S. Energy Information Administration, *State Energy Data Report*, annual.

## E11-2. Energy Consumption—by End-Use Sector, by State: 1995, in Trillions of Btu (except as indicated)

| State | Residential | Commercial | Industrial | Transportation |
|---|---|---|---|---|
| Alabama | 331.5 | 167.4 | 974.8 | 459.5 |
| Alaska | 49.5 | 62.7 | 404.9 | 169.3 |
| Arizona | 234.2 | 226.9 | 223.2 | 378 |
| Arkansas | 187.1 | 114 | 433.1 | 263.7 |
| California | 1,310.30 | 1,206.60 | 2,237.70 | 2,833.40 |
| Colorado | 242 | 225 | 282.8 | 325.4 |
| Connecticut | 242.1 | 180.1 | 165.3 | 204.5 |
| Delaware | 54.3 | 39.5 | 109.3 | 60.9 |
| Dist. of Columbia | 36.3 | 111.4 | 3.3 | 26.8 |
| Florida | 973 | 750.3 | 570 | 1,225.30 |
| Georgia | 530.1 | 373.4 | 807.2 | 801.4 |
| Hawaii | 20.8 | 24.4 | 73.7 | 135.8 |
| Idaho | 85.6 | 73.1 | 184.8 | 112.8 |
| Illinois | 955.5 | 703.3 | 1,333.60 | 811.9 |
| Indiana | 478.8 | 295 | 1,185.00 | 633.4 |
| Iowa | 232.2 | 150.9 | 422.3 | 262 |
| Kansas | 197.7 | 171.7 | 391 | 280.2 |
| Kentucky | 317.2 | 196 | 826.4 | 430.8 |
| Louisiana | 319.3 | 216.1 | 2,520.00 | 758.2 |
| Maine | 97.9 | 50.7 | 278.3 | 103.4 |
| Maryland | 365.3 | 323.3 | 270.3 | 353 |
| Massachusetts | 418.9 | 356.4 | 318.7 | 405.5 |
| Michigan | 770.9 | 561 | 1,073.90 | 771.9 |
| Minnesota | 358.4 | 214.2 | 623.6 | 440.1 |
| Mississippi | 192 | 109.7 | 418.2 | 338.9 |
| Missouri | 432.6 | 317.3 | 363.5 | 549.3 |
| Montana | 63.8 | 51 | 162.5 | 101.7 |
| Nebraska | 133 | 120.1 | 159.6 | 167.6 |
| Nevada | 97.4 | 81.3 | 196.1 | 162.5 |
| New Hampshire | 79.7 | 52.5 | 76.3 | 81.7 |
| New Jersey | 529.5 | 493.5 | 655.4 | 864.5 |
| New Mexico | 80 | 96.2 | 202.4 | 196.3 |
| New York | 1,053.10 | 1,088.10 | 883.8 | 916.4 |
| North Carolina | 544.8 | 388.7 | 784.5 | 610.1 |
| North Dakota | 57 | 43.6 | 175.9 | 74.6 |
| Ohio | 904.5 | 626.9 | 1,639.30 | 867.3 |
| Oklahoma | 253.3 | 183.6 | 556.3 | 366.3 |
| Oregon | 220.1 | 171.8 | 365 | 297.3 |
| Pennsylvania | 901.6 | 585.7 | 1,484.50 | 913.9 |
| Rhode Island | 68.4 | 49.5 | 64.3 | 58.6 |
| South Carolina | 275.5 | 183.5 | 617.9 | 323.7 |
| South Dakota | 57.2 | 39.3 | 58.1 | 81.2 |
| Tennessee | 417.3 | 127.6 | 896.5 | 533.8 |
| Texas | 1,220.00 | 1,079.80 | 6,032.90 | 2,169.30 |
| Utah | 110.4 | 100.6 | 245.8 | 184.5 |
| Vermont | 44.1 | 25.3 | 34.7 | 50.6 |
| Virginia | 489.8 | 431.6 | 530.3 | 604.3 |
| Washington | 406 | 304.3 | 786.7 | 635.5 |
| West Virginia | 145.9 | 93.6 | 399.5 | 179.9 |
| Wisconsin | 387.4 | 263.2 | 720.8 | 394.6 |
| Wyoming | 37.8 | 40.1 | 227.2 | 100 |

*Notes:*
* Includes net imports of coal coke not allocated by state.

*Source: Statistical Abstract of the United States 1998,* No. 952. Underlying data from U.S. Energy Information Administration, *State Energy Data Report,* annual.

**E11-3. Energy Consumption—by Selected Sources, Totals: 1995, in Trillions of Btu (except as indicated)**

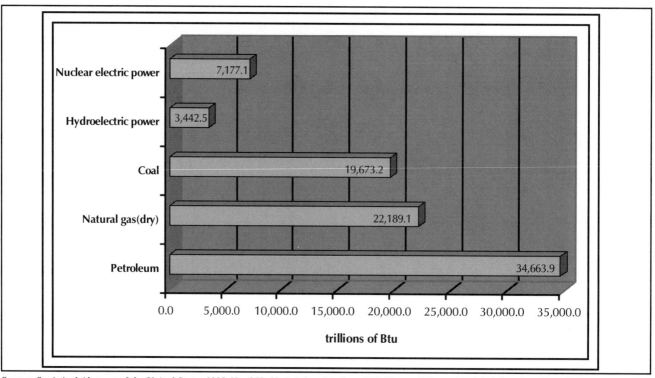

*Source: Statistical Abstract of the United States 1998*, No. 952. Underlying data from U.S. Energy Information Administration, *State Energy Data Report*, annual.

## E11-4. Energy Consumption—by Selected Sources, by State: 1995, in Trillions of Btu (except as indicated)

| State | Petroleum | Natural gas (dry) | Coal | Hydroelectric power | Nuclear electric power |
|---|---|---|---|---|---|
| Alabama | 559.6 | 330.9 | 826.9 | 97.9 | 221.2 |
| Alaska | 222.2 | 432.8 | 12.9 | 14.1 | (-) |
| Arizona | 409.1 | 124.3 | 342.4 | 87.3 | 287.6 |
| Arkansas | 308.8 | 276.6 | 237.4 | 33.1 | 124.2 |
| California | 3,293.90 | 1,955.90 | 61 | 529.6 | 322.4 |
| Colorado | 390.5 | 288.7 | 337.3 | 22.9 | (-) |
| Connecticut | 370.4 | 136 | 23.7 | 14 | 199.8 |
| Delaware | 122.9 | 62.7 | 52.4 | (-) | (-) |
| Dist. of Columbia | 37.1 | 33.2 | 0.1 | (-) | (-) |
| Florida | 1,620.20 | 532.6 | 653 | 2.4 | 306.3 |
| Georgia | 963.6 | 380 | 728.5 | 48.8 | 326.8 |
| Hawaii | 234.8 | 2.9 | 2.6 | 1 | (-) |
| Idaho | 146 | 65.7 | 8.9 | 113.6 | (-) |
| Illinois | 1,236.60 | 1,100.10 | 816.9 | 1.3 | 836.4 |
| Indiana | 864.2 | 541.7 | 1,341.90 | 4.8 | (-) |
| Iowa | 378.1 | 263.6 | 368.8 | 10.3 | 39.8 |
| Kansas | 367.8 | 369.1 | 290.9 | 0.1 | 107.2 |
| Kentucky | 620.4 | 245.6 | 927.6 | 35.3 | (-) |
| Louisiana | 1,476.50 | 1,778.00 | 217.5 | 9.9 | 167.2 |
| Maine | 243 | 5.5 | 7.1 | 66.4 | 2.1 |
| Maryland | 496.1 | 199.1 | 289.6 | 14.9 | 137.9 |
| Massachusetts | 682.7 | 371.7 | 104.4 | 11 | 47.8 |
| Michigan | 991 | 987.4 | 775.8 | 47.8 | 260.6 |
| Minnesota | 615.8 | 357.7 | 337.2 | 46 | 141.1 |
| Mississippi | 399.6 | 295.6 | 103.8 | (-) | 85.4 |
| Missouri | 700.1 | 281 | 591.4 | 19.1 | 87.8 |
| Montana | 159.6 | 59.6 | 171.2 | 111 | (-) |
| Nebraska | 218.5 | 133.7 | 179.5 | 14.7 | 79.8 |
| Nevada | 202.6 | 114.7 | 162.7 | 20.3 | (-) |
| New Hampshire | 151 | 20.1 | 35.5 | 24.7 | 89.3 |
| New Jersey | 1,238.40 | 610.9 | 55.1 | *-0.9 | 179.1 |
| New Mexico | 208.2 | 219.4 | 275.3 | 2.7 | (-) |
| New York | 1,491.10 | 1,172.40 | 287.1 | 319.3 | 280.7 |
| North Carolina | 845.8 | 209.4 | 601.1 | 59.8 | 382.7 |
| North Dakota | 118 | 47.6 | 399.8 | 28.5 | (-) |
| Ohio | 1,190.00 | 930.1 | 1,379.80 | 2.4 | 178.7 |
| Oklahoma | 446.2 | 579.5 | 343.5 | 28 | (-) |
| Oregon | 361.2 | 151.7 | 20.2 | 431.1 | (-) |
| Pennsylvania | 1,330.50 | 746.7 | 1,386.50 | 8.2 | 708.3 |
| Rhode Island | 98.7 | 72 | 0.1 | 10.5 | (-) |
| South Carolina | 435.5 | 156 | 314.5 | 28.8 | 524.1 |
| South Dakota | 114.5 | 34.8 | 36.7 | 61.9 | (-) |
| Tennessee | 678.5 | 264.8 | 668.2 | 92.9 | 167.4 |
| Texas | 4,746.30 | 3,943.20 | 1,361.70 | 17.5 | 385.3 |
| Utah | 234.2 | 166.7 | 357.2 | 10 | (-) |
| Vermont | 80.5 | 7.2 | 0.1 | 27.6 | 41.1 |
| Virginia | 771.9 | 254.9 | 342.2 | 2.3 | 267.9 |
| Washington | 846.9 | 229.2 | 69.8 | 833.2 | 74 |
| West Virginia | 272.6 | 157.4 | 860.3 | 12.4 | (-) |
| Wisconsin | 535.7 | 384.7 | 443 | 55.6 | 116.9 |
| Wyoming | 136.8 | 103.9 | 461.9 | 8.2 | (-) |

*Notes:*
(-) Represents zero.
* A negative number occurs when more electricity is expended than is created to provide electricity during peak demand periods.

*Source: Statistical Abstract of the United States 1998*, No. 952. Underlying data from US Energy Information Administration, *State Energy Data Report,* annual.

## E12. RECENT TRENDS IN APPAREL AND FOOTWEAR

### E12-1. Recent Trends in Apparel and Other Textile Products (SIC 23), Current and Constant (1992) Dollars: 1991–1996

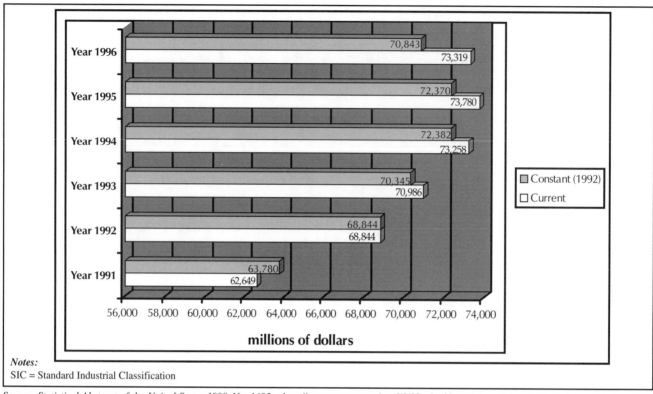

*Notes:*
SIC = Standard Industrial Classification

*Source: Statistical Abstract of the United States 1998,* No. 1405; <http://www.census.gov/prod/3/98pubs/98statab/sasec31.pdf>. Underlying data from U.S. Department of Commerce, Bureau of the Census, International Trade Administration (ITA).

## E12-2. Recent Trends in Selected Women's Outerwear (SIC 2331, 2335, 2337): 1991–1993

| ITEM | Unit | 1991 | 1992 | 1993 |
|---|---|---|---|---|
| **INDUSTRY DATA** | | | | |
| Value of shipments[1] | Million dollars | 14,415 | 13,733 | 14,123 |
| 2331 Women's/misses' blouses | Million dollars | 3,973 | 3,970 | 4,012 |
| 2335 Women's/misses' dresses | Million dollars | 5,922 | 5,366 | 5,602 |
| 2337 Women's suits and coats | Million dollars | 4,520 | 4,397 | 4,509 |
| Value of shipments (1992 dollars) | Million dollars | 14,610 | 13,733 | 14,063 |
| 2331 Women's/misses' blouses | Million dollars | 4,096 | 3,970 | 3,976 |
| 2335 Women's/misses' dresses | Million dollars | 5,957 | 5,366 | 5,597 |
| 2337 Women's suits and coats | Million dollars | 4,556 | 4,397 | 4,491 |
| **PRODUCT DATA** | | | | |
| Value of shipments[2] | Million dollars | 12,805 | 13,581 | 14,275 |
| 2331 Women's/misses' blouses | Million dollars | 3,618 | 4,195 | 4,580 |
| 2335 Women's/misses' dresses | Million dollars | 5,443 | 5,278 | 5,431 |
| 2337 Women's suits and coats | Million dollars | 3,745 | 4,108 | 4,264 |
| Value of shipments (1992 dollars) | Million dollars | 12,980 | 13,581 | 14,211 |
| 2331 Women's/misses' blouses | Million dollars | 3,730 | 4,195 | 4,539 |
| 2335 Women's/misses' dresses | Million dollars | 5,475 | 5,278 | 5,426 |
| 2337 Women's suits and coats | Million dollars | 3,775 | 4,108 | 4,247 |
| **TRADE DATA** | | | | |
| Value of imports | Million dollars | 6,119 | 7,073 | 7,718 |
| 2331 Women's/misses' blouses | Million dollars | 2,923 | 3,501 | 3,864 |
| 2335 Women's/misses' dresses | Million dollars | 981 | 1,054 | 1,130 |
| 2337 Women's suits and coats | Million dollars | 2,215 | 2,518 | 2,724 |
| Value of exports | Million dollars | 362 | 519 | 590 |
| 2331 Women's/misses' blouses | Million dollars | 101 | 171 | 213 |
| 2335 Women's/misses' dresses | Million dollars | 65 | 98 | 105 |
| 2337 Women's suits and coats | Million dollars | 197 | 250 | 272 |

*Notes:*
SIC = Standard Industrial Classification
1. Value of all products and services sold by establishments in the selected women's outerwear industry.
2. Value of products classified in the selected women's outerwear industry produced by all industries.

*Source: Statistical Abstract of the United States 1998,* No. 1408; <http://www.census.gov/prod/3/98pubs/98statab/sasec31.pdf>. Underlying data from U.S. Department of Commerce, Bureau of the Census, International Trade Administration (ITA).

## E12-3. Recent Trends in Selected Women's Outerwear (SIC 2331, 2335, 2337): 1994–1997

| ITEM | Unit | 1994 | 1995 | 1996 | 1997 |
|---|---|---|---|---|---|
| **INDUSTRY DATA** | | | | | |
| Value of shipments[1] | Million dollars | 14,598 | 14,413 | 13,851 | (NA) |
| 2331 Women's/misses' blouses | Million dollars | 4,147 | 3,797 | 3,649 | (NA) |
| 2335 Women's/misses' dresses | Million dollars | 6,396 | 6,928 | 6,606 | (NA) |
| 2337 Women's suits and coats | Million dollars | 4,055 | 3,688 | 3,596 | (NA) |
| Value of shipments (1992 dollars) | Million dollars | 14,644 | 14,604 | 14,248 | (NA) |
| 2331 Women's/misses' blouses | Million dollars | 4,053 | 3,686 | 3,563 | (NA) |
| 2335 Women's/misses' dresses | Million dollars | 6,507 | 7,128 | 6,896 | (NA) |
| 2337 Women's suits and coats | Million dollars | 4,084 | 3,790 | 3,789 | (NA) |
| **PRODUCT DATA** | | | | | |
| Value of shipments[2] | Million dollars | 14,400 | 14,083 | 13,734 | (NA) |
| 2331 Women's/misses' blouses | Million dollars | 4,425 | 4,012 | 3,752 | (NA) |
| 2335 Women's/misses' dresses | Million dollars | 6,042 | 6,397 | 6,336 | (NA) |
| 2337 Women's suits and coats | Million dollars | 3,933 | 3,674 | 3,646 | (NA) |
| Value of shipments (1992 dollars) | Million dollars | 14,433 | 14,253 | 14,119 | (NA) |
| 2331 Women's/misses' blouses | Million dollars | 4,325 | 3,896 | 3,664 | (NA) |
| 2335 Women's/misses' dresses | Million dollars | 6,146 | 6,582 | 6,614 | (NA) |
| 2337 Women's suits and coats | Million dollars | 3,961 | 3,775 | 3,842 | (NA) |
| **TRADE DATA** | | | | | |
| Value of imports | Million dollars | 7,960 | 8,430 | 8,943 | 9,768 |
| 2331 Women's/misses' blouses | Million dollars | 3,948 | 3,906 | 3,980 | 4,658 |
| 2335 Women's/misses' dresses | Million dollars | 1,339 | 1,688 | 1,870 | 1,930 |
| 2337 Women's suits and coats | Million dollars | 2,673 | 2,836 | 3,093 | 3,180 |
| Value of exports | Million dollars | 591 | 714 | 725 | 820 |
| 2331 Women's/misses' blouses | Million dollars | 243 | 342 | 339 | 376 |
| 2335 Women's/misses' dresses | Million dollars | 103 | 113 | 115 | 148 |
| 2337 Women's suits and coats | Million dollars | 245 | 259 | 272 | 297 |

*Notes:*
SIC = Standard Industrial Classification
(NA) Not available
1. Value of all products and services sold by establishments in the selected women's outerwear industry.
2. Value of products classified in the selected women's outerwear industry produced by all industries.

*Source: Statistical Abstract of the United States 1998,* No. 1408; <http://www.census.gov/prod/3/98pubs/98statab/sasec31.pdf>. Underlying data from U.S. Department of Commerce, Bureau of the Census, International Trade Administration (ITA).

## E12-4. Recent Trends in Selected Men's and Boys' Apparel (SIC 2311, 2321, -3, -5, -6): 1991–1997

| ITEM | Unit | 1991 | 1992 | 1993 | 1994 | 1995 | 1996 | 1997 |
|------|------|------|------|------|------|------|------|------|
| **INDUSTRY DATA** | | | | | | | | |
| Value of shipments[1] | Million dollars | 16,083 | 16,991 | 16,819 | 17,088 | 17,246 | 17,208 | (NA) |
| 2311 Men's/boys suits/ coats | Million dollars | 2,579 | 2,430 | 2,463 | 2,362 | 2,078 | 1,968 | (NA) |
| 2321 Men's/boys shirts | Million dollars | 4,698 | 5,921 | 5,012 | 5,082 | 5,186 | 4,939 | (NA) |
| 2323 Men's/boys neckwear | Million dollars | 556 | 618 | 619 | 705 | 792 | 652 | (NA) |
| 2325 Men's/boys trousers | Million dollars | 6,760 | 6,519 | 7,055 | 7,226 | 7,506 | 7,658 | (NA) |
| 2326 Men's/boys work clothing | Million dollars | 1,491 | 1,503 | 1,670 | 1,714 | 1,863 | 1,991 | (NA) |
| Value of shipments (1992 dollars) | Million dollars | 16,640 | 16,991 | 16,538 | 16,669 | 16,837 | 16,437 | (NA) |
| 2311 Men's/boys suits/ coats | Million dollars | 2,639 | 2,430 | 2,471 | 2,338 | 2,044 | 1,915 | (NA) |
| 2321 Men's/boys shirts | Million dollars | 4,888 | 5,921 | 4,938 | 5,017 | 5,104 | 4,880 | (NA) |
| 2323 Men's/boys neckwear | Million dollars | 565 | 618 | 611 | 695 | 772 | 628 | (NA) |
| 2325 Men's/boys trousers | Million dollars | 7,042 | 6,519 | 6,889 | 6,975 | 7,169 | 7,190 | (NA) |
| 2326 Men's/boys work clothing | Million dollars | 1,506 | 1,503 | 1,629 | 1,644 | 1,748 | 1,823 | (NA) |
| **PRODUCT DATA** | | | | | | | | |
| Value of shipments[2] | Million dollars | 14,143 | 15,810 | 15,405 | 16,129 | 16,096 | 15,441 | (NA) |
| 2311 Men's/boys suits/ coats | Million dollars | 2,450 | 2,387 | 2,257 | 2,417 | 2,020 | 1,913 | (NA) |
| 2321 Men's/boys shirts | Million dollars | 3,915 | 5,318 | 4,632 | 4,709 | 4,792 | 4,303 | (NA) |
| 2323 Men's/boys neckwear | Million dollars | 525 | 544 | 529 | 594 | 618 | 574 | (NA) |
| 2325 Men's/boys trousers | Million dollars | 5,911 | 6,065 | 6,338 | 6,636 | 6,771 | 6,757 | (NA) |
| 2326 Men's/boys work clothing | Million dollars | 1,341 | 1,495 | 1,650 | 1,773 | 1,895 | 1,894 | (NA) |
| Value of shipments (1992 dollars) | Million dollars | 14,628 | 15,810 | 15,147 | 15,733 | 15,550 | 14,744 | (NA) |
| 2311 Men's/boys suits/ coats | Million dollars | 2,508 | 2,387 | 2,263 | 2,393 | 1,986 | 1,861 | (NA) |
| 2321 Men's/boys shirts | Million dollars | 4,074 | 5,318 | 4,563 | 4,649 | 4,717 | 4,252 | (NA) |
| 2323 Men's/boys neckwear | Million dollars | 533 | 544 | 521 | 586 | 602 | 553 | (NA) |
| 2325 Men's/boys trousers | Million dollars | 6,158 | 6,065 | 6,190 | 6,405 | 6,467 | 6,344 | (NA) |
| 2326 Men's/boys work clothing | Million dollars | 1,355 | 1,495 | 1,609 | 1,700 | 1,777 | 1,734 | (NA) |
| **TRADE DATA** | | | | | | | | |
| Value of imports | Million dollars | 6,168 | 7,624 | 8,281 | 9,178 | 10,873 | 11,426 | 13,282 |
| 2311 Men's/boys suits/ coats | Million dollars | 678 | 789 | 824 | 954 | 1,042 | 1,134 | 1,317 |
| 2321 Men's/boys shirts | Million dollars | 3,039 | 4,028 | 4,519 | 4,917 | 5,875 | 6,006 | 6,810 |
| 2323 Men's/boys neckwear | Million dollars | 140 | 151 | 158 | 156 | 167 | 174 | 184 |
| 2325 Men's/boys trousers | Million dollars | 2,310 | 2,657 | 2,780 | 3,151 | 3,789 | 4,113 | 4,972 |
| 2326 Men's/boys work clothing | Million dollars | (NA) | (NA) | (NA) | (NA) | (NA) | (NA) | (NA) |
| Value of exports | Million dollars | 1,140 | 1,478 | 1,795 | 2,036 | 2,158 | 2,374 | 2,661 |
| 2311 Men's/boys suits/ coats | Million dollars | 161 | 197 | 237 | 292 | 269 | 264 | 251 |
| 2321 Men's/boys shirts | Million dollars | 333 | 457 | 595 | 721 | 842 | 919 | 1,091 |
| 2323 Men's/boys neckwear | Million dollars | 14.5 | 15.5 | 21.1 | 17.9 | 18.4 | 21.1 | 20.6 |
| 2325 Men's/boys trousers | Million dollars | 631 | 809 | 942 | 1,005 | 1,029 | 1,170 | 1,298 |
| 2326 Men's/boys work clothing | Million dollars | (NA) | (NA) | (NA) | (NA) | (NA) | (NA) | (NA) |

*Notes:*
SIC = Standard Industrial Classification
(NA) not available
1. Value of all products and services sold by establishments in the selected men's and boys apparel industry.
2. Value of products classified in the selected men's and boys apparel industry produced by all industries.

*Source: Statistical Abstract of the United States 1998*, No. 1406. Underlying data from U.S. Department of Commerce, Bureau of the Census, International Trade Administration (ITA).

## E12-5. Recent Trends in Footwear, Except Rubber (SIC 314): 1991–1993

| ITEM | Unit | 1991 | 1992 | 1993 |
|---|---|---|---|---|
| **INDUSTRY DATA** | | | | |
| Value of shipments[1] | Million dollars | 3,588 | 3,898 | 3,974 |
| 3142 House slippers | Million dollars | 264 | 285 | 302 |
| 3143 Men's footwear | Million dollars | 1,962 | 2,210 | 2,351 |
| 3144 Women's footwear | Million dollars | 1,097 | 1,095 | 1,010 |
| 3149 Footwear nec | Million dollars | 266 | 309 | 310 |
| Value of shipments (1992 dollars) | Million dollars | 3,680 | 3,898 | 3,907 |
| 3142 House slippers | Million dollars | 258 | 285 | 310 |
| 3143 Men's footwear | Million dollars | 2,016 | 2,210 | 2,305 |
| 3144 Women's footwear | Million dollars | 1,135 | 1,095 | 987 |
| 3149 Footwear nec | Million dollars | 271 | 309 | 305 |
| Total employment | 1,000 | 51.1 | 48.8 | 48.5 |
| Production workers | 1,000 | 44 | 41.4 | 41.3 |
| Average hourly earnings | Dollars | 7.14 | 7.33 | 7.43 |
| Capital expenditures | Million dollars | 28.1 | 51.2 | 40.3 |
| 3142 House slippers | Million dollars | 2.1 | 2.1 | 2.5 |
| 3143 Men's footwear | Million dollars | 16.2 | 32.8 | 26.1 |
| 3144 Women's footwear | Million dollars | 8.1 | 10.5 | 6.8 |
| 3149 Footwear nec | Million dollars | 1.7 | 5.8 | 4.9 |
| **PRODUCT DATA** | | | | |
| Value of shipments[2] | Million dollars | 3,495 | 3,608 | 3,707 |
| 3142 House slippers | Million dollars | 256 | 259 | 256 |
| 3143 Men's footwear | Million dollars | 1,763 | 1,807 | 1,970 |
| 3144 Women's footwear | Million dollars | 1,186 | 1,229 | 1,188 |
| 3149 Footwear nec | Million dollars | 289 | 314 | 293 |
| Value of shipments (1992 dollars) | Million dollars | 3,586 | 3,608 | 3,643 |
| 3142 House slippers | Million dollars | 251 | 259 | 263 |
| 3143 Men's footwear | Million dollars | 1,812 | 1,807 | 1,931 |
| 3144 Women's footwear | Million dollars | 1,228 | 1,229 | 1,160 |
| 3149 Footwear nec | Million dollars | 295 | 314 | 289 |
| **TRADE DATA** | | | | |
| Value of imports | Million dollars | 8,336 | 8,616 | 9,290 |
| Value of exports | Million dollars | 307 | 343 | 332 |

*Notes:*
SIC = Standard Industrial Classification
The symbol "nec" indicates not included in other categories.
1. Value of all products and services sold by establishments in the footwear, except rubber industry.
2. Value of products classified in the footwear, except rubber industry produced by all industries.

*Source: Statistical Abstract of the United States 1998*, No. 1438; <http://www.census.gov/prod/3/98pubs/98statab/sasec31.pdf>. Underlying data from U.S. Department of Commerce, Bureau of the Census, International Trade Administration (ITA).

## E12-6. Recent Trends in Footwear, Except Rubber (SIC 314): 1994–1997

| ITEM | Unit | 1994 | 1995 | 1996 | 1997 |
|---|---|---|---|---|---|
| **INDUSTRY DATA** | | | | | |
| Value of shipments[1] | Million dollars | 3,923 | 3,688 | 3,605 | (NA) |
| 3142 House slippers | Million dollars | 204 | 113 | 128 | (NA) |
| 3143 Men's footwear | Million dollars | 2,461 | 2,420 | 2,413 | (NA) |
| 3144 Women's footwear | Million dollars | 950 | 758 | 555 | (NA) |
| 3149 Footwear nec | Million dollars | 309 | 397 | 509 | (NA) |
| Value of shipments (1992 dollars) | Million dollars | 3,816 | 3,477 | 3,345 | (NA) |
| 3142 House slippers | Million dollars | 205 | 109 | 122 | (NA) |
| 3143 Men's footwear | Million dollars | 2,382 | 2,257 | 2,218 | (NA) |
| 3144 Women's footwear | Million dollars | 927 | 730 | 522 | (NA) |
| 3149 Footwear nec | Million dollars | 302 | 381 | 483 | (NA) |
| Total employment | 1,000 | 46.8 | 44.4 | 36.7 | (NA) |
| Production workers | 1,000 | 40.3 | 37.7 | 31.1 | (NA) |
| Average hourly earnings | Dollars | 7.44 | 7.85 | 8.32 | (NA) |
| Capital expenditures | Million dollars | 58.8 | 34.1 | 34.5 | (NA) |
| 3142 House slippers | Million dollars | 4.8 | 1.5 | 1.2 | (NA) |
| 3143 Men's footwear | Million dollars | 43.3 | 23.6 | 25.8 | (NA) |
| 3144 Women's footwear | Million dollars | 7.6 | 4.3 | 2.4 | (NA) |
| 3149 Footwear nec | Million dollars | 3.1 | 4.7 | 5.1 | (NA) |
| **PRODUCT DATA** | | | | | |
| Value of shipments[2] | Million dollars | 3,739 | 3,402 | 3,128 | (NA) |
| 3142 House slippers | Million dollars | 208 | 122 | 116 | (NA) |
| 3143 Men's footwear | Million dollars | 2,040 | 1,926 | 1,924 | (NA) |
| 3144 Women's footwear | Million dollars | 1,190 | 959 | 735 | (NA) |
| 3149 Footwear nec | Million dollars | 301 | 394 | 354 | (NA) |
| Value of shipments (1992 dollars) | Million dollars | 3,639 | 3,217 | 2,906 | (NA) |
| 3142 House slippers | Million dollars | 209 | 118 | 110 | (NA) |
| 3143 Men's footwear | Million dollars | 1,975 | 1,797 | 1,768 | (NA) |
| 3144 Women's footwear | Million dollars | 1,161 | 924 | 692 | (NA) |
| 3149 Footwear nec | Million dollars | 294 | 378 | 336 | (NA) |
| **TRADE DATA** | | | | | |
| Value of imports | Million dollars | 9,698 | 9,984 | 10,478 | 11,544 |
| Value of exports | Million dollars | 382 | 370 | 385 | 378 |

*Notes:*
SIC = Standard Industrial Classification
The symbol "nec" indicates not included in other categories.
(NA) Not available.
1. Value of all products and services sold by establishments in the footwear, except rubber industry.
2. Value of products classified in the footwear, except rubber industry produced by all industries.

*Source: Statistical Abstract of the United States 1998*, No. 1438; <http://www.census.gov/prod/3/98pubs/98statab/sasec31.pdf>. Underlying data from U.S. Department of Commerce, Bureau of the Census, International Trade Administration (ITA).

# E13. RECENT TRENDS IN HOUSEHOLD APPLIANCES

## E13-1. Recent Trends in Household Appliances (SIC 363): 1991–1993

| ITEM | Unit | 1991 | 1992 | 1993 |
|---|---|---|---|---|
| **INDUSTRY DATA** | | | | |
| Value of shipments[1] | Million dollars | 17,175 | 18,633 | 20,435 |
| 3631 Household cooking equipment | Million dollars | 2,806 | 2,950 | 3,010 |
| 3632 Household refrigerators | Million dollars | 3,613 | 4,232 | 4,463 |
| 3633 Household laundry equipment | Million dollars | 3,112 | 3,329 | 3,871 |
| 3634 Electric housewares and fans | Million dollars | 3,021 | 2,897 | 3,106 |
| 3635 Household vacuums | Million dollars | 1,752 | 1,905 | 2,096 |
| 3639 Home appliances, nec | Million dollars | 2,872 | 3,320 | 3,889 |
| Value of shipments (1992 dollars) | Million dollars | 17,246 | 18,633 | 20,179 |
| 3631 Household cooking equipment | Million dollars | 2,806 | 2,950 | 2,911 |
| 3632 Household refrigerators | Million dollars | 3,616 | 4,232 | 4,436 |
| 3633 Household laundry equipment | Million dollars | 3,075 | 3,329 | 3,887 |
| 3634 Electric housewares and fans | Million dollars | 3,061 | 2,897 | 3,087 |
| 3635 Household vacuums | Million dollars | 1,743 | 1,905 | 2,037 |
| 3639 Home appliances, nec | Million dollars | 2,945 | 3,320 | 3,820 |
| **PRODUCT DATA** | | | | |
| Value of shipments[2] | Million dollars | 16,089 | 16,789 | 18,027 |
| 3631 Household cooking equipment | Million dollars | 2,942 | 3,007 | 3,162 |
| 3632 Household refrigerators | Million dollars | 3,621 | 4,048 | 4,309 |
| 3633 Household laundry equipment | Million dollars | 2,860 | 2,995 | 3,299 |
| 3634 Electric housewares and fans | Million dollars | 2,608 | 2,653 | 2,710 |
| 3635 Household vacuums | Million dollars | 1,834 | 1,809 | 2,015 |
| 3639 Home appliances, nec | Million dollars | 2,224 | 2,279 | 2,531 |
| Value of shipments (1992 dollars) | Million dollars | 16,141 | 16,789 | 17,792 |
| 3631 Household cooking equipment | Million dollars | 2,942 | 3,007 | 3,058 |
| 3632 Household refrigerators | Million dollars | 3,625 | 4,048 | 4,283 |
| 3633 Household laundry equipment | Million dollars | 2,826 | 2,995 | 3,312 |
| 3634 Electric housewares and fans | Million dollars | 2,642 | 2,653 | 2,694 |
| 3635 Household vacuums | Million dollars | 1,825 | 1,809 | 1,958 |
| 3639 Home appliances, nec | Million dollars | 2,281 | 2,279 | 2,486 |
| **TRADE DATA** | | | | |
| Value of imports | Million dollars | 3,675 | 4,322 | 4,535 |
| Value of exports | Million dollars | 2,066 | 2,307 | 2,482 |

*Notes:*
SIC = Standard Industrial Classification
The symbol "nec" indicates not included in other categories.
1. Value of all products and services sold by establishments in the household appliances industry
2. Value of products classified in the household appliances industry produced by all industries.

*Source: Statistical Abstract of the United States 1998*, No. 1459; <http://www.census.gov/prod/3/98pubs/98statab/sasec31.pdf>. Underlying data from U.S. Department of Commerce, Bureau of the Census, International Trade Administration (ITA).

## E13-2. Recent Trends in Household Appliances (SIC 363): 1994–1997

| ITEM | Unit | 1994 | 1995 | 1996 | 1997 |
|---|---|---|---|---|---|
| **INDUSTRY DATA** | | | | | |
| Value of shipments[1] | Million dollars | 22,829 | 21,776 | 22,157 | (NA) |
| 3631 Household cooking equipment | Million dollars | 3,849 | 3,918 | 3,565 | (NA) |
| 3632 Household refrigerators | Million dollars | 5,149 | 5,200 | 5,605 | (NA) |
| 3633 Household laundry equipment | Million dollars | 4,612 | 4,133 | 4,233 | (NA) |
| 3634 Electric housewares and fans | Million dollars | 3,053 | 3,298 | 3,032 | (NA) |
| 3635 Household vacuums | Million dollars | 1,933 | 2,045 | 2,425 | (NA) |
| 3639 Home appliances, nec | Million dollars | 4,233 | 3,183 | 3,297 | (NA) |
| Value of shipments (1992 dollars) | Million dollars | 22,512 | 21,498 | 21,717 | (NA) |
| 3631 Household cooking equipment | Million dollars | 3,755 | 3,856 | 3,481 | (NA) |
| 3632 Household refrigerators | Million dollars | 5,068 | 5,154 | 5,538 | (NA) |
| 3633 Household laundry equipment | Million dollars | 4,668 | 4,191 | 4,258 | (NA) |
| 3634 Electric housewares and fans | Million dollars | 3,065 | 3,328 | 3,066 | (NA) |
| 3635 Household vacuums | Million dollars | 1,843 | 1,941 | 2,303 | (NA) |
| 3639 Home appliances, nec | Million dollars | 4,114 | 3,028 | 3,070 | (NA) |
| Total employment | 1,000 | 111 | 110 | 108 | (NA) |
| Production workers | 1,000 | 90.6 | 87.7 | 87 | (NA) |
| Average hourly earnings | Dollars | 11.74 | 12.23 | 12.81 | (NA) |
| Capital expenditures | Million dollars | 517 | 630 | 721 | (NA) |
| **PRODUCT DATA** | | | | | |
| Value of shipments[2] | Million dollars | 19,841 | 20,095 | 20,581 | (NA) |
| 3631 Household cooking equipment | Million dollars | 3,821 | 3,904 | 3,766 | (NA) |
| 3632 Household refrigerators | Million dollars | 4,995 | 5,121 | 5,356 | (NA) |
| 3633 Household laundry equipment | Million dollars | 3,671 | 3,541 | 3,699 | (NA) |
| 3634 Electric housewares and fans | Million dollars | 2,651 | 2,875 | 2,501 | (NA) |
| 3635 Household vacuums | Million dollars | 1,788 | 1,907 | 2,341 | (NA) |
| 3639 Home appliances, nec | Million dollars | 2,916 | 2,748 | 2,919 | (NA) |
| Value of shipments (1992 dollars) | Million dollars | 19,559 | 19,834 | 20,160 | (NA) |
| 3631 Household cooking equipment | Million dollars | 3,727 | 3,842 | 3,677 | (NA) |
| 3632 Household refrigerators | Million dollars | 4,916 | 5,075 | 5,292 | (NA) |
| 3633 Household laundry equipment | Million dollars | 3,715 | 3,592 | 3,721 | (NA) |
| 3634 Electric housewares and fans | Million dollars | 2,662 | 2,902 | 2,529 | (NA) |
| 3635 Household vacuums | Million dollars | 1,705 | 1,809 | 2,223 | (NA) |
| 3639 Home appliances, nec | Million dollars | 2,834 | 2,614 | 2,717 | (NA) |
| **TRADE DATA** | | | | | |
| Value of imports | Million dollars | 4,915 | 5,131 | 5,444 | 5,764 |
| Value of exports | Million dollars | 2,568 | 2,621 | 2,791 | 2,958 |

*Notes:*
SIC = Standard Industrial Classification
The symbol "nec" indicates not included in other categories.
(NA) indicates not available.
1. Value of all products and services sold by establishments in the household appliances industry.
2. Value of products classified in the household appliances industry produced by all industries.

*Source: Statistical Abstract of the United States 1998,* No. 1459; <http://www.census.gov/prod/3/98pubs/98statab/sasec31.pdf>. Underlying data from U.S. Department of Commerce, Bureau of the Census, International Trade Administration (ITA).

# E13-3. Appliances and Office Equipment Used by Households, by Region: 1997

| Type of appliance | Households using appliance | Region, Northeast | Region, Midwest | Region, South | Region, West |
|---|---|---|---|---|---|
| Total households (mil) | 101.5 | 19.7 | 24.1 | 35.9 | 21.8 |
| PERCENT WITH— | | | | | |
| Air conditioner: | | | | | |
|   Central system | 47.1 | 22.3 | 51.4 | 69.7 | 27.6 |
|   Room | 26.1 | 41.4 | 27.4 | 24.3 | 13.9 |
| Clothes washer | 77.4 | 76.0 | 78.9 | 81.9 | 69.6 |
|   Clothes dryer[1] | 71.1 | 66.7 | 75.7 | 74.2 | 65.1 |
|   Electric | 55.0 | 48.2 | 50.1 | 66.3 | 48.2 |
|   Natural gas | 15.3 | 17.9 | 23.9 | 7.4 | 16.6 |
| Dishwasher | 50.2 | 48.5 | 46.9 | 51.5 | 53.1 |
| Ceiling fan | 60.1 | 51.3 | 63.6 | 71.2 | 46.0 |
| Freezer | 33.2 | 25.7 | 41.8 | 36.9 | 24.2 |
|   One | 30.2 | 24.2 | 38.4 | 33.1 | 22.0 |
|   Two or more | 2.9 | 1.5 | 3.4 | 3.8 | 2.2 |
| Microwave oven | 83.0 | 78.7 | 86.9 | 82.4 | 83.3 |
| Oven | 98.8 | 99.3 | 99.1 | 98.6 | 98.2 |
|   Electric | 61.5 | 49.7 | 56.6 | 72.0 | 60.1 |
|   Natural gas | 33.2 | 44.8 | 38.1 | 22.1 | 35.7 |
| Self cleaning oven | 44.0 | 48.5 | 45.0 | 41.8 | 42.7 |
| Range | 99.2 | 99.6 | 99.4 | 99.0 | 98.8 |
|   Electric | 60.3 | 48.8 | 55.6 | 70.9 | 58.4 |
|   Natural gas | 34.6 | 45.5 | 39.4 | 23.5 | 37.7 |
| Refrigerator | 99.9 | 99.9 | 99.9 | 99.9 | 99.7 |
|   Frost free | 86.8 | 85.2 | 85.1 | 90.0 | 84.7 |
| Water heater[1] | 100.0 | 100.0 | 100.0 | 100.0 | 100.0 |
|   Electric | 39.5 | 26.5 | 27.6 | 58.3 | 33.3 |
|   Natural gas | 51.7 | 46.8 | 66.4 | 37.4 | 63.2 |
| Stereo equipment | 68.8 | 66.7 | 67.0 | 67.8 | 74.4 |
| Color TV | 98.7 | 98.8 | 99.0 | 98.7 | 98.2 |
|   One | 31.9 | 31.8 | 32.1 | 29.1 | 36.1 |
|   Two | 37.4 | 36.1 | 36.2 | 38.9 | 37.2 |
|   Three | 19.1 | 20.8 | 20.4 | 18.4 | 17.3 |
|   Four | 7.6 | 7.5 | 7.8 | 8.9 | 5.5 |
|   Five or more | 2.8 | 2.6 | 2.5 | 3.4 | 2.2 |
| VCR | 87.6 | 86.1 | 89.7 | 86.0 | 89.0 |
| Personal computers | 35.0 | 31.9 | 38.0 | 31.0 | 41.3 |
|   One | 29.2 | 27.2 | 32.4 | 25.9 | 32.8 |
|   Two or more | 5.9 | 4.7 | 5.6 | 5.1 | 8.5 |
|   With modem | 20.4 | 17.8 | 21.7 | 18.2 | 24.9 |
|   With laser printer | 12.4 | 11.3 | 12.9 | 11.7 | 14.2 |
|   Used 15 hrs per week or less | 25.2 | 21.5 | 27.7 | 23.0 | 29.2 |
|   Used 16 hrs per week or more | 9.9 | 10.4 | 10.2 | 8.0 | 12.1 |
|     Personal use only | 4.7 | 4.5 | 5.2 | 4.2 | 5.3 |
|     Business use only | 2.1 | 2.3 | 2.5 | 1.1 | 3.1 |
|     Both | 3.1 | 3.6 | 2.6 | 2.7 | 3.7 |
| Cordless phone | 61.4 | 59.6 | 63.8 | 61.4 | 60.2 |
| Facsimile machine | 6.2 | 6.5 | 5.3 | 5.6 | 8.1 |
| Photocopier | 3.7 | 3.8 | 3.9 | 3.5 | 3.9 |
| Answering machine | 58.4 | 62.2 | 61.0 | 54.2 | 59.1 |

*Notes:*
1. Includes other types, not shown separately.
*General Notes:* Preliminary data. Represents appliances possessed and generally used by the household. Based on *Residential Energy Consumption Survey.*

*Source: Statistical Abstract of the United States 1998,* No. 1223; <http://www.census.gov/prod/3/98pubs/98statab/sasec25.pdf>. Underlying data from US Energy Information Administration, Internet site <http://wwweiadoe/emeu/consumption>

## E13-4. Appliances and Office Equipment Used by Households, by Family Income: 1997

| Type of appliance | Family income under $10,000 | Family income $10,000 to $24,999 | Family income $25,000 to $49,000 | Family income $50,000 and over |
|---|---|---|---|---|
| Total households (mil) | 13.3 | 29.1 | 31.1 | 27.9 |
| PERCENT WITH— | | | | |
| Air conditioner: | | | | |
| Central system | 27.7 | 37.7 | 50.7 | 62.2 |
| Room | 33.9 | 29.8 | 25.4 | 19.2 |
| Clothes washer | 52.7 | 69.0 | 81.5 | 93.4 |
| Clothes dryer[1] | 36.2 | 61.0 | 77.1 | 91.8 |
| Electric | 31.0 | 49.0 | 59.9 | 67.5 |
| Natural gas | 4.8 | 11.1 | 16.4 | 23.6 |
| Dishwasher | 15.7 | 35.5 | 53.6 | 78.2 |
| Ceiling fan | 39.3 | 55.2 | 64.4 | 70.3 |
| Freezer | 25.7 | 30.0 | 35.1 | 37.9 |
| One | 23.6 | 27.5 | 32.2 | 34.1 |
| Two or more | 2.0 | 2.5 | 2.9 | 3.8 |
| Microwave oven | 60.3 | 81.1 | 86.7 | 91.5 |
| Oven | 96.4 | 98.7 | 99.4 | 99.3 |
| Electric | 49.2 | 58.7 | 63.9 | 67.5 |
| Natural gas | 41.8 | 34.8 | 31.5 | 29.5 |
| Self cleaning oven | 18.1 | 31.1 | 47.0 | 66.6 |
| Range | 96.8 | 99.1 | 99.8 | 99.6 |
| Electric | 49.2 | 58.4 | 62.9 | 64.6 |
| Natural gas | 42.0 | 35.5 | 32.8 | 32.1 |
| Refrigerator | 99.3 | 99.9 | 99.9 | 100.0 |
| Frost free | 73.0 | 83.1 | 88.5 | 95.2 |
| Water heater[1] | 100.0 | 100.0 | 100.0 | 100.0 |
| Electric | 41.9 | 43.9 | 39.9 | 33.1 |
| Natural gas | 46.3 | 48.0 | 51.7 | 58.0 |
| Stereo equipment | 45.2 | 60.1 | 73.7 | 83.7 |
| Color TV | 96.1 | 98.4 | 99.2 | 99.6 |
| One | 55.6 | 40.5 | 27.3 | 16.6 |
| Two | 30.9 | 37.7 | 41.6 | 35.4 |
| Three | 7.5 | 15.5 | 20.4 | 26.8 |
| Four | 1.7 | 3.6 | 8.2 | 14.0 |
| Five or more | (S) | 1.1 | 1.7 | 6.8 |
| VCR | 66.8 | 84.0 | 91.6 | 96.6 |
| Personal computers | 9.7 | 16.5 | 36.9 | 64.5 |
| One | 7.9 | 14.5 | 32.8 | 50.6 |
| Two or more | (S) | 2.0 | 4.1 | 13.8 |
| With modem | 5.2 | 8.6 | 19.7 | 40.7 |
| With laser printer | 2.5 | 4.4 | 12.8 | 25.1 |
| Used 15 hrs per week or less | 6.3 | 12.2 | 28.2 | 44.4 |
| Used 16 hrs per week or more | 3.4 | 4.2 | 8.7 | 20.0 |
| Personal use only | 2.3 | 2.3 | 4.1 | 9.1 |
| Business use only | (S) | (S) | 1.4 | 5.0 |
| Both | (S) | 1.2 | 3.3 | 6.0 |
| Cordless phone | 35.3 | 51.5 | 66.9 | 77.9 |
| Facsimile machine | (S) | 2.5 | 5.3 | 13.3 |
| Photocopier | (S) | 1.5 | 3.9 | 7.3 |
| Answering machine | 30.2 | 49.1 | 62.3 | 77.2 |

*Notes:*
(S) Figure does not meet publication standards.
1. Includes other types, not shown separately.
*General Notes:* Preliminary data. Represents appliances possessed and generally used by the household. Based on *Residential Energy Consumption Survey.*

*Source: Statistical Abstract of the United States 1998,* No. 1223; <http://www.census.gov/prod/3/98pubs/98statab/sasec25.pdf>. Underlying data from U.S. Energy Information Administration, Internet site <http://wwweiadoe/emeu/consumption> .

**E13-5. Share of Households Using Appliances, Selected Household Efficiency Appliances, by Family Income: 1997**

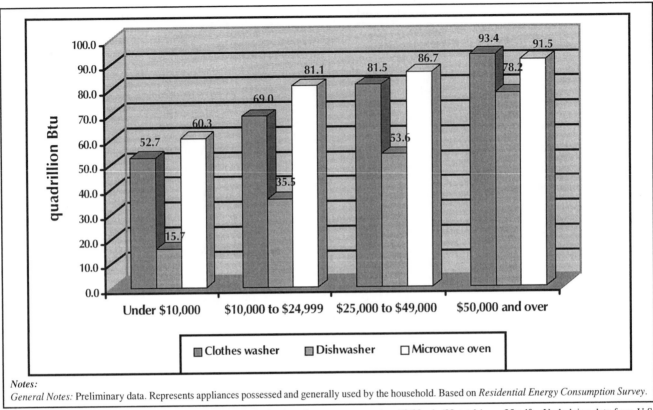

Notes:
*General Notes:* Preliminary data. Represents appliances possessed and generally used by the household. Based on *Residential Energy Consumption Survey*.

*Source: Statistical Abstract of the United States 1998,* No. 1223; <http://www.census.gov/prod/3/98pubs/98statab/sasec25.pdf>. Underlying data from U.S. Energy Information Administration, Internet site <http://wwweiadoe/emeu/consumption>.

**E13-6. Share of Households Using Appliances, Selected Telecommunications and Media Equipment, by Family Income: 1997**

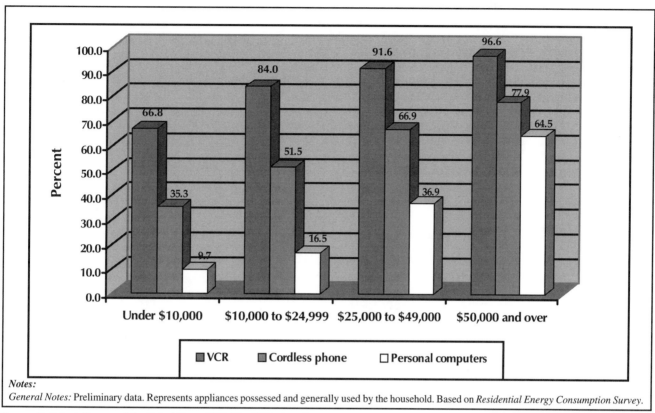

Notes:

*General Notes:* Preliminary data. Represents appliances possessed and generally used by the household. Based on *Residential Energy Consumption Survey.*

*Source: Statistical Abstract of the United States 1998,* No. 1223; <http://www.census.gov/prod/3/98pubs/98statab/sasec25.pdf>. Underlying data from U.S. Energy Information Administration, Internet site <http://wwweiadoe/emeu/consumption>.

# E14. MICROCOMPUTER SOFTWARE SALES

## E14-1. Microcomputer Software Sales: 1995, in Millions of Dollars

| APPLICATION | Total | PC/ MS-DOS | Windows[1] | Macintosh |
|---|---|---|---|---|
| Total[2] | 9772.0 | 1041.2 | 7333.4 | 1520.8 |
| Entertainment. | 826.2 | 403.5 | 317.4 | 105.3 |
| Home creativity | 300.8 | 2.9 | 253.8 | 44.0 |
| Home education | 939.7 | 32.5 | 728.2 | 185.1 |
| Finance | 397.4 | 80.7 | 270.6 | 46.2 |
| Word processors | 1085.0 | 25.0 | 987.2 | 63.5 |
| Spreadsheets | 865.2 | 12.3 | 803.4 | 46.8 |
| Databases | 336.6 | 8.7 | 302.9 | 24.2 |
| Integrated | 133.5 | 2.1 | 86.9 | 43.9 |
| Utilities | 621.0 | 110.9 | 371.2 | 101.9 |
| Presentation graphic | 462.9 | (B) | 427.5 | 30.4 |
| Drawing and painting | 461.9 | (B) | 146.7 | 309.9 |
| Desktop publishing | 357.2 | (B) | 244.6 | 112.6 |
| Other graphics | 313.8 | 22.4 | 216.1 | 76.1 |
| Project management | 164.2 | 6.7 | 142.9 | 14.6 |
| Personal info. manager. | 395.2 | 1.9 | 343.3 | 49.7 |
| Languages and tools | 361.3 | 11.8 | 337.2 | 8.8 |
| Other productivity | 1624.7 | 184.3 | 1069.5 | 279.7 |

*Notes:*
(B) Base figure too small to meet statistical standards for reliability of a derived figure.
1. 16- and 32-bit.
2. Includes other software platforms, not shown separately.
*General Note:* Estimated North American retail sales.

*Source: Statistical Abstract of the United States 1998,* No. 930; <http://www.census.gov/prod/3/98pubs/98statab/sasec18.pdf>. Underlying data from Software Publishers Association (now Software and Information Industry Association), Washington, DC, *SPA Software Sales Report* (News Release), March 31, 1997 (copyright).

## E14-2. Microcomputer Software Sales: 1996, in Millions of Dollars

| APPLICATION | Total | PC/ MS-DOS | Windows 32-bit | Windows 16-bit | Macintosh |
|---|---|---|---|---|---|
| Total[1] | 10580.4 | 558.2 | 3199.6 | 5327.5 | 1170.8 |
| Entertainment. | 861.9 | 303.4 | 343.3 | 169.6 | 45.5 |
| Home creativity | 337.7 | 3.4 | 118.6 | 190.5 | 25.3 |
| Home education | 958.3 | 22.9 | 102.0 | 658.2 | 174.4 |
| Finance | 467.8 | 34.2 | 8.8 | 388.7 | 36.2 |
| Word processors | 976.3 | 2.1 | 373.4 | 556.7 | 43.4 |
| Spreadsheets | 881.6 | 2.4 | 295.9 | 547.4 | 35.2 |
| Databases | 429.8 | 4.7 | 174.1 | 210.1 | 40.0 |
| Integrated | 107.1 | (B) | 29.2 | 48.6 | 28.5 |
| Utilities | 773.9 | 30.7 | 288.5 | 147.0 | 114.5 |
| Presentation graphic | 548.8 | (B) | 175.2 | 349.4 | 24.4 |
| Drawing and painting | 343.4 | (B) | 14.4 | 153.3 | 168.7 |
| Desktop publishing | 357.9 | (B) | 95.4 | 183.5 | 79.1 |
| Other graphics | 275.3 | 13.5 | 54.5 | 138.6 | 54.3 |
| Project management | 171.9 | 5.4 | 47.5 | 112.1 | 6.9 |
| Personal info. manager. | 348.8 | 2.0 | 86.7 | 210.4 | 39.1 |
| Languages and tools | 418.0 | 6.7 | 135.2 | 271.2 | 3.6 |
| Other productivity | 2321.8 | 126.3 | 857.1 | 992.1 | 251.8 |

*Notes:*
(B) Base figure too small to meet statistical standards for reliability of a derived figure.
1. Includes other software platforms, not shown separately.
*General Note:* Estimated North American retail sales.

*Source: Statistical Abstract of the United States 1998*, No. 930; <http://www.census.gov/prod/3/98pubs/98statab/sasec18.pdf>. Underlying data from Software Publishers Association (now Software and Information Industry Association), Washington, DC, *SPA Software Sales Report* (News Release), March 31, 1997 (copyright).

## E15. RECENT TRENDS IN SOAP, CLEANERS, AND TOILET GOODS

### E15-1. Recent Trends in Soap, Cleaners, and Toilet Goods (SIC 284): 1991–1993

| ITEM | Unit | 1991 | 1992 | 1993 |
|---|---|---|---|---|
| INDUSTRY DATA | | | | |
| Value of shipments[1] | Million dollars | 42,245 | 42,875 | 46,903 |
|   2841 Soap and other detergents | Million dollars | 15,442 | 14,729 | 15,458 |
|   2842 Polishes/sanitation goods | Million dollars | 6,229 | 6,659 | 8,079 |
|   2843 Surface active agents | Million dollars | 3,330 | 2,859 | 3,661 |
|   2844 Toilet preparations | Million dollars | 17,245 | 18,629 | 19,706 |
| Value of shipments (1992 Dollars) | Million dollars | 43,103 | 42,875 | 46,174 |
|   2841 Soap and other detergents | Million dollars | 15,854 | 14,729 | 15,259 |
|   2842 Polishes/sanitation goods | Million dollars | 6,324 | 6,659 | 8,014 |
|   2843 Surface active agents | Million dollars | 3,346 | 2,859 | 3,599 |
|   2844 Toilet preparations | Million dollars | 17,579 | 18,629 | 19,301 |
| Total employment | 1,000 | 123 | 123 | 124 |
|   2841 Soap and other detergents | 1,000 | 36.7 | 32.8 | 31.2 |
|   2842 Polishes/sanitation goods | 1,000 | 19.6 | 22 | 22.8 |
|   2843 Surface active agents | 1,000 | 9.3 | 8.2 | 8.6 |
|   2844 Toilet preparations | 1,000 | 57.5 | 59.8 | 61.7 |
| Production workers | 1,000 | 75.7 | 74.5 | 74.6 |
|   2841 Soap and other detergents | 1,000 | 23.1 | 19.9 | 17.9 |
|   2842 Polishes/sanitation goods | 1,000 | 12.2 | 13.4 | 13.8 |
|   2843 Surface active agents | 1,000 | 4.8 | 4.2 | 4.3 |
|   2844 Toilet preparations | 1,000 | 35.6 | 37 | 38.6 |
| Average hourly earnings | Dollars | 12.28 | 12.32 | 12.26 |
|   2841 Soap and other detergents | Dollars | 14.7 | 14.86 | 15.06 |
|   2842 Polishes/sanitation goods | Dollars | 11.13 | 11.84 | 11.94 |
|   2843 Surface active agents | Dollars | 14.33 | 15.09 | 15.95 |
|   2844 Toilet preparations | Dollars | 10.83 | 10.8 | 10.59 |
| Capital expenditures | Million dollars | 1,245 | 1,290 | 1,320 |
|   2841 Soap and other detergents | Million dollars | 641 | 571 | 514 |
|   2842 Polishes/sanitation goods | Million dollars | 139 | 121 | 130 |
|   2843 Surface active agents | Million dollars | 160 | 92 | 203 |
|   2844 Toilet preparations | Million dollars | 304 | 506 | 473 |
| PRODUCT DATA | | | | |
| Value of shipments[2] | Million dollars | 38,695 | 39,999 | 43,293 |
|   2841 Soap and other detergents | Million dollars | 11,785 | 11,022 | 11,594 |
|   2842 Polishes/sanitation goods | Million dollars | 5,546 | 6,477 | 7,492 |
|   2843 Surface active agents | Million dollars | 3,975 | 3,776 | 4,032 |
|   2844 Toilet preparations | Million dollars | 17,390 | 18,724 | 20,175 |
| Value of shipments (1992 Dollars) | Million dollars | 39,450 | 39,999 | 42,603 |
|   2841 Soap and other detergents | Million dollars | 12,099 | 11,022 | 11,445 |
|   2842 Polishes/sanitation goods | Million dollars | 5,630 | 6,477 | 7,433 |
|   2843 Surface active agents | Million dollars | 3,995 | 3,776 | 3,965 |
|   2844 Toilet preparations | Million dollars | 17,726 | 18,724 | 19,760 |
|   TRADE DATA | | | | |
| Value of imports | Million dollars | 1,076 | 1,308 | 1,463 |
|   2841 Soap and other detergents | Million dollars | 179 | 213 | 254 |
|   2842 Polishes/sanitation goods | Million dollars | 33.5 | 46 | 49.8 |
|   2843 Surface active agents | Million dollars | 152 | 158 | 204 |
|   2844 Toilet preparations | Million dollars | 712 | 892 | 956 |
| Value of exports | Million dollars | 2,235 | 2,529 | 2,853 |
|   2841 Soap and other detergents | Million dollars | 511 | 583 | 644 |
|   2842 Polishes/sanitation goods | Million dollars | 130 | 144 | 170 |
|   2843 Surface active agents | Million dollars | 477 | 548 | 604 |
|   2844 Toilet preparations | Million dollars | 1,118 | 1,254 | 1,437 |

*Notes:*
SIC = Standard Industrial Classification
1. Value of all products and services sold by establishments in the soap, cleaners, and toilet goods industry.
2. Value of products classified in the soap, cleaners, and toilet goods industry produced by all industries.

*Source: Statistical Abstract of the United States 1998*, No. 1428; <http://wwwcensusgov/prod/3/98pubs/98statab/sasec31pdf>. Underlying data from U.S. Department of Commerce, Bureau of the Census, International Trade Administration (ITA).

## E15-2. Recent Trends in Soap, Cleaners, and Toilet Goods (SIC 284): 1994–1997

| ITEM | Unit | 1994 | 1995 | 1996 | 1997 |
|---|---|---|---|---|---|
| INDUSTRY DATA | | | | | |
| Value of shipments[1] | Million dollars | 46,548 | 49,795 | 51,809 | (NA) |
| 2841 Soap and other detergents | Million dollars | 14,603 | 15,735 | 15,779 | (NA) |
| 2842 Polishes/sanitation goods | Million dollars | 8,405 | 8,679 | 8,602 | (NA) |
| 2843 Surface active agents | Million dollars | 3,721 | 4,860 | 4,741 | (NA) |
| 2844 Toilet preparations | Million dollars | 19,820 | 20,522 | 22,688 | (NA) |
| Value of shipments (1992 Dollars) | Million dollars | 45,873 | 48,469 | 49,766 | (NA) |
| 2841 Soap and other detergents | Million dollars | 14,530 | 15,487 | 15,230 | (NA) |
| 2842 Polishes/sanitation goods | Million dollars | 8,264 | 8,353 | 8,239 | (NA) |
| 2843 Surface active agents | Million dollars | 3,609 | 4,529 | 4,248 | (NA) |
| 2844 Toilet preparations | Million dollars | 19,469 | 20,100 | 22,048 | (NA) |
| Total employment | 1,000 | 119 | 123 | 126 | (NA) |
| 2841 Soap and other detergents | 1,000 | 31.3 | 31.6 | 30.3 | (NA) |
| 2842 Polishes/sanitation goods | 1,000 | 21.4 | 23.1 | 24.2 | (NA) |
| 2843 Surface active agents | 1,000 | 8.1 | 7.9 | 8.8 | (NA) |
| 2844 Toilet preparations | 1,000 | 58.1 | 60.2 | 62.9 | (NA) |
| Production workers | 1,000 | 71.1 | 73.8 | 74.6 | (NA) |
| 2841 Soap and other detergents | 1,000 | 18.6 | 18 | 16.8 | (NA) |
| 2842 Polishes/sanitation goods | 1,000 | 13.1 | 14 | 14.2 | (NA) |
| 2843 Surface active agents | 1,000 | 3.9 | 3.9 | 4.5 | (NA) |
| 2844 Toilet preparations | 1,000 | 35.5 | 37.9 | 39.1 | (NA) |
| Average hourly earnings | Dollars | 12.36 | 12.75 | 13.02 | (NA) |
| 2841 Soap and other detergents | Dollars | 14.89 | 15.4 | 15.68 | (NA) |
| 2842 Polishes/sanitation goods | Dollars | 11.12 | 11.49 | 11.49 | (NA) |
| 2843 Surface active agents | Dollars | 16.8 | 16.2 | 16.55 | (NA) |
| 2844 Toilet preparations | Dollars | 10.93 | 11.44 | 11.89 | (NA) |
| Capital expenditures | Million dollars | 1,334 | 1,041 | 1,304 | (NA) |
| 2841 Soap and other detergents | Million dollars | 494 | 356 | 427 | (NA) |
| 2842 Polishes/sanitation goods | Million dollars | 124 | 154 | 173 | (NA) |
| 2843 Surface active agents | Million dollars | 225 | 120 | 161 | (NA) |
| 2844 Toilet preparations | Million dollars | 491 | 411 | 543 | (NA) |
| PRODUCT DATA | | | | | |
| Value of shipments[2] | Million dollars | 42,622 | 45,775 | 47,797 | (NA) |
| 2841 Soap and other detergents | Million dollars | 11,089 | 12,205 | 12,467 | (NA) |
| 2842 Polishes/sanitation goods | Million dollars | 7,601 | 7,755 | 7,327 | (NA) |
| 2843 Surface active agents | Million dollars | 3,648 | 4,703 | 4,836 | (NA) |
| 2844 Toilet preparations | Million dollars | 20,284 | 21,112 | 23,168 | (NA) |
| Value of shipments (1992 Dollars) | Million dollars | 41,971 | 44,538 | 45,900 | (NA) |
| 2841 Soap and other detergents | Million dollars | 11,033 | 12,013 | 12,033 | (NA) |
| 2842 Polishes/sanitation goods | Million dollars | 7,474 | 7,464 | 7,018 | (NA) |
| 2843 Surface active agents | Million dollars | 3,538 | 4,383 | 4,333 | (NA) |
| 2844 Toilet preparations | Million dollars | 19,926 | 20,678 | 22,515 | (NA) |
| TRADE DATA | | | | | |
| Value of imports | Million dollars | 1,689 | 1,936 | 2,100 | 2,318 |
| 2841 Soap and other detergents | Million dollars | 335 | 421 | 486 | 510 |
| 2842 Polishes/sanitation goods | Million dollars | 56.3 | 61.6 | 69.4 | 92.7 |
| 2843 Surface active agents | Million dollars | 263 | 296 | 288 | 305 |
| 2844 Toilet preparations | Million dollars | 1,035 | 1,157 | 1,257 | 1,410 |
| Value of exports | Million dollars | 3,358 | 3,710 | 4,132 | 4,759 |
| 2841 Soap and other detergents | Million dollars | 716 | 828 | 899 | 975 |
| 2842 Polishes/sanitation goods | Million dollars | 174 | 205 | 212 | 216 |
| 2843 Surface active agents | Million dollars | 734 | 790 | 826 | 940 |
| 2844 Toilet preparations | Million dollars | 1,733 | 1,887 | 2,195 | 2,628 |

*Notes:*
(SIC = Standard Industrial Classification
NA) Not available
1. Value of all products and services sold by establishments in the soap, cleaners, and toilet goods industry.
2. Value of products classified in the soap, cleaners, and toilet goods industry produced by all industries.

*Source:  Statistical Abstract of the United States 1998*, No. 1428; <http://wwwcensusgov/prod/3/98pubs/98statab/sasec31pdf>. Underlying data from U.S. Department of Commerce, Bureau of the Census, International Trade Administration (ITA).

# F. Consumption—Services

## GENERAL OVERVIEW

This section explores the consumption of services in the United States on a broad basis. It includes such categories as personal services, business services, education, health care, and insurance. Some of the data are presented in time series and some in state-by-state breakdowns. A wide course of variables is explored in reference to the above categories, including such demographic and economic features as age, family income, and educational level. The intent is to show as much pertinent detail as is possible and available in order to give the user a full sense of the scope of services consumed in the United States.

## EXPLANATION OF INDICATORS

**F1. Selected Personal Services:** The first grouping presents data on personal services across a 10-year time span from 1988 to 1997. The first chart and two tables present data on aggregate sales receipts for personal services, and the second set of tables presents per capita sales figures for the same indicators, allowing the user to relate total sales to number of purchasers in the marketplace. The chart presents summary totals so that the user may see the general growth patterns in spending on personal services, and the tables present detailed breakdowns, including such subcategories as laundry, dry cleaning, beauty salons, barber shops, and funeral services.

**F2. Business Services:** The next grouping—nine charts—presents data on business services (Standard Industrial Classification, or SIC, code 73) from 1985 to 1996. The data represent total sales receipts to taxable firms and serve as an indication of the level of consumption of business services—both by individuals and other businesses. The first chart shows the total of all subcategories and therefore offers the user the most general picture of spending on business services over the 12-year period. Legal services are included at the end of this series even though they occupy their own SIC code (81).

**F3. Public Elementary and Secondary Education:** The next grouping (one chart followed by four tables) presents information on education—both money spent on education and receipts used to cover those expenditures. The data are presented both in a mid-range time series (1980 to 1997) and on a state-by-state basis; the state-by-state info presents a snapshot of 1997.

The expenditure data show totals, per capita, and per pupil, on an average daily attendance (ADA) basis; these various permutations help the user understand how the total spent spreads out across the student population and how the total distributes across the number of pupils on a daily basis. The data on receipts break down into types of sources, including federal, state, local, and other.

**F4. Availability and Use of Selected Teaching Resources:** The next set of four tables analyzes the share of teaching resources available and used across several variables, including gender of teacher, level of education, race, and size of school system. These tables help users to analyze educational resources used according to these key variables. They also invite comparisons between availability and use of various resources, thereby allowing users to begin to analyze the functionality and, perhaps, the productivity of resources.

**F5. Institutions of Higher Education:** The next set (three charts and three tables) shows expenditures on higher education, including tuition, room, and board. The opening charts compare the average cost per pupil of tuition and fees, room (dormitory), and board between public and private institutions across a 13-year period (1985 to 1997). The tables detail the average cost of tuition, room, and board across types of institution, including the general breakdown between private and public, with further detail covering two-year, four-year, and over four-year institutions.

**F6. Internet Access and Usage:** The next group (seven charts and four tables) presents estimated data on the share of the adult population who have access to and who use the Internet. The charts show the share of the population who have any access whatsoever to the Internet across a wide scope of variables, including such features as age, gender, marital status, and household income. The tables present the same variety of variables, while examining other, more specific data such as access at home, at office, use at any time, and use within the last 30 days. Taken together, these charts and tables allow the user to examine the scope of "consumption" of Internet services and in what areas of the population its use is more prevalent.

**F7. Selected Health Services, Estimated Receipts and Growth in Receipts:** The next four tables present data on the amount of sales for various types of health care-related businesses (physicians' offices, clinics, hospitals, etc.) over the course of a 10-year period (1988 to 1997). The first two tables show total receipts in terms of dollars and the next two tables present percentage annual growth figures, allowing users to analyze the increase, or less frequently, decrease, in amount of health services consumed.

**F8. National Health Expenditures, by Object:** The next chart and table cover all expenditures relating to health, according to object of expense, from 1990 to 1996. Two broad categories are tracked in the table: spent by (consumers, insurance companies, government, etc.) and spent for (health services, medical research, and facilities construction), thereby expanding the investigation beyond basic healthcare services for the consumer. The chart covers aggregate expenditures, and the table presents detailed categories.

**F9. Health Services and Supplies—Per Capita Consumer Expenditures, by Object:** The next chart and following two tables present per capita figures on consumer health care services across a longer time frame: 1980 to 1996. The chart presents summary totals for each year, and the tables break out the totals according to object of expense, such as hospital care, physicians' care, home health care, nursing homes, etc.

**F10. Life Insurance Purchases in the United States:** The next two tables present information on life insurance from 1980 to 1996. The first table includes the number of policies broken down by type of policy purchased (ordinary, group, and industrial) and the second table presents data on the value of the policies purchased according to the same variables.

**F11. Automobile Insurance—Average Expenditures per Insured Vehicle:** The final chart and table in the section present the average cost for auto insurance, from 1994 to 1996. The chart presents the totals for the United States and the table presents the state-by-state averages.

# F1. SELECTED PERSONAL SERVICES

## F1-1. Selected Personal Services (SIC 72)—Estimated Receipts for Taxable Firms: 1989–1997, in Millions of Dollars

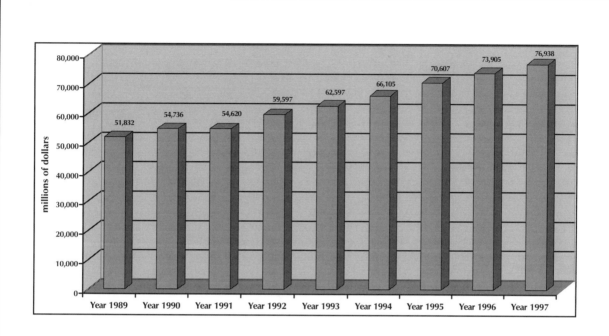

*Notes:*

SIC = Standard Industrial Classification

*General Notes:* Dollar volume estimates are in millions of dollars. Data for 1996 have been revised to reflect the use of 1996 administrative receipts for nonemployer firms. Estimates are for employer and nonemployer firms. Estimates are not adjusted for price changes. Group totals may include kinds of business not shown separately.

*Source:* U.S. Department of Commerce, Bureau of the Census, *Service Annual Survey: 1997* and *Current Population Reports,* Series P25-1127 and 1095; Table 3.1; <http://www.census.gov/svsd/sasann/view/alltab.pdf>.

## F1-2. Selected Personal Services (SIC 72)—Estimated Receipts for Taxable Firms: 1988–1992, in Millions of Dollars

| code | 1987 SIC kind of business | 1988 | 1989 | 1990 | 1991 | 1992 |
|------|---------------------------|------|------|------|------|------|
| 721 | Laundry, cleaning, and garment services | 15,700 | 16,616 | 17,347 | 17,579 | 18,805 |
| 7211 | Power laundries, family and commercial | 875 | 824 | 818 | 830 | 898 |
| 7212 | Garment pressing and agents for laundries and drycleaners | (NA) | (NA) | (NA) | (NA) | (NA) |
| 7213 | Linen supply | 2,277 | 2,283 | 2,387 | 2,496 | 2,672 |
| 7215 | Coin-operated laundries and dry cleaning | 2,506 | 2,927 | 3,214 | 3,072 | 2,931 |
| 7216 | Dry cleaning plants, except rug cleaning | 4,656 | 4,758 | 4,412 | 4,538 | 5,467 |
| 7217 | Carpet and upholstery cleaning | 1,326 | 1,410 | 1,692 | 1,764 | 1,946 |
| 7218 | Industrial launderers | 3,084 | 3,237 | 3,311 | 3,487 | 3,656 |
| 7221 | Photographic studios, portrait | 3,261 | 3,412 | 3,749 | 3,922 | 4,280 |
| 7231 | Beauty shops | 11,521 | 12,527 | 12,841 | 13,138 | 14,436 |
| 7241 | Barber shops | 1,434 | 1,390 | 1,439 | 1,466 | 1,515 |
| 7261 | Funeral service and crematories | 6,198 | 6,396 | 6,825 | 7,119 | 7,588 |
| 7291 | Tax return preparation services | (NA) | (NA) | 1,455 | 1,643 | 1,838 |

*Notes:*

(NA) Not available.

SIC = Standard Industrial Classification

*General Notes:* Dollar volume estimates are in millions of dollars. Data for 1996 have been revised to reflect the use of 1996 administrative receipts for nonemployer firms. Estimates are for employer and nonemployer firms. Estimates are not adjusted for price changes. Group totals may include kinds of business not shown separately.

*Source:* U.S. Department of Commerce, Bureau of the Census, *Service Annual Survey: 1997* and *Current Population Reports,* Series P25-1127 and 1095; Table 3.1; <http://www.census.gov/svsd/sasann/view/alltab.pdf>.

## F1-3. Selected Personal Services (SIC 72)—Estimated Receipts for Taxable Firms: 1993–1997, in Millions of Dollars

| code | 1987 SIC kind of business | 1993 | 1994 | 1995 | 1996 | 1997 |
|------|---------------------------|------|------|------|------|------|
| 721 | Laundry, cleaning, and garment services | 19,075 | 19,741 | 20,709 | 21,533 | 22,855 |
| 7211 | Power laundries, family and commercial | 913 | 906 | 932 | 875 | 817 |
| 7212 | Garment pressing and agents for laundries and drycleaners | (NA) | (NA) | 585 | 605 | 761 |
| 7213 | Linen supply | 2,570 | 2,573 | 2,576 | 2,601 | 2,815 |
| 7215 | Coin-operated laundries and dry cleaning | 2,949 | 3,074 | 3,352 | 3,468 | 3,671 |
| 7216 | Dry cleaning plants, except rug cleaning | 5,354 | 5,432 | 5,493 | 5,477 | 5,646 |
| 7217 | Carpet and upholstery cleaning | 2,200 | 2,292 | 2,353 | 2,544 | 2,771 |
| 7218 | Industrial launderers | 3,780 | 4,110 | 4,492 | 4,977 | 5,217 |
| 7221 | Photographic studios, portrait | 4,734 | 5,093 | 5,692 | 5,814 | 5,946 |
| 7231 | Beauty shops | 14,608 | 15,152 | 16,382 | 16,986 | 18,321 |
| 7241 | Barber shops | 1,514 | 1,558 | 1,609 | 1,639 | 1,814 |
| 7261 | Funeral service and crematories | 8,193 | 8,571 | 9,437 | 10,034 | 10,634 |
| 7291 | Tax return preparation services | 2,239 | 2,732 | 2,608 | 2,947 | 3181 |

*Notes:*
(NA) Not available.
SIC = Standard Industrial Classification
*General Notes:* Dollar volume estimates are in millions of dollars. Data for 1996 have been revised to reflect the use of 1996 administrative receipts for nonemployer firms. Estimates are for employer and nonemployer firms. Estimates are not adjusted for price changes.  Group totals may include kinds of business not shown separately.

*Source:* U.S. Department of Commerce, Bureau of the Census, *Service Annual Survey: 1997* and *Current Population Reports*, Series P25-1127 and 1095; Table 3.1; <http://www.census.gov/svsd/sasann/view/alltab.pdf>.

## F1-4. Selected Personal Services (SIC 72)—Estimated per Capita Receipts for Taxable Firms: 1988–1992

| code | 1987 SIC kind of business | 1988 | 1989 | 1990 | 1991 | 1992 |
|------|---------------------------|------|------|------|------|------|
| 72 | Personal services | 199 | 211 | 221 | 218 | 235 |
| 721 | Laundry, cleaning, and garment services | 65 | 68 | 70 | 70 | 74 |
| 7211 | Power laundries, family and commercial | 4 | 3 | 3 | 3 | 4 |
| 7212 | Garment pressing and agents for laundries and drycleaners | (NA) | (NA) | (NA) | (NA) | (NA) |
| 7213 | Linen supply | 9 | 9 | 10 | 10 | 11 |
| 7215 | Coin-operated laundries and dry cleaning | 10 | 12 | 13 | 12 | 12 |
| 7216 | Dry cleaning plants, except rug cleaning | 19 | 19 | 18 | 18 | 22 |
| 7217 | Carpet and upholstery cleaning | 5 | 6 | 7 | 7 | 8 |
| 7218 | Industrial launderers | 13 | 13 | 13 | 14 | 14 |
| 7221 | Photographic studios, portrait | 13 | 14 | 15 | 16 | 17 |
| 7231 | Beauty shops | 47 | 51 | 52 | 52 | 57 |
| 7241 | Barber shops | 6 | 6 | 6 | 6 | 6 |
| 7261 | Funeral service and crematories | 26 | 26 | 28 | 28 | 30 |
| 7291 | Tax return preparation services | (NA) | (NA) | 6 | 7 | 7 |

*Notes:*
(NA) Not available.
SIC = Standard Industrial Classification
*General Notes:* Estimates are in whole dollars. Data for 1996 have been revised to reflect the use of 1996 administrative receipts for nonemployer firms. Estimates are for employer and nonemployer firms. Estimates are not adjusted for price changes.

*Source:* U.S. Department of Commerce, Bureau of the Census, *Service Annual Survey: 1997* and *Current Population Reports,* Series P25-1127 and 1095; Table 3.3; <http://www.census.gov/svsd/sasann/view/alltab.pdf>.

## F1-5. Selected Personal Services (SIC 72)—Estimated per Capita Receipts for Taxable Firms: 1993–1997

| code | 1987 SIC kind of business | 1993 | 1994 | 1995 | 1996 | 1997 |
|---|---|---|---|---|---|---|
| 72 | Personal services | 244 | 255 | 270 | 280 | 289 |
| 721 | Laundry, cleaning, and garment services | 74 | 76 | 79 | 82 | 86 |
| 7211 | Power laundries, family and commercial | 4 | 3 | 4 | 3 | 3 |
| 7212 | Garment pressing and agents for laundries and drycleaners | (NA) | (NA) | 2 | 2 | 3 |
| 7213 | Linen supply | 10 | 10 | 10 | 10 | 11 |
| 7215 | Coin-operated laundries and dry cleaning | 12 | 12 | 13 | 13 | 14 |
| 7216 | Dry cleaning plants, except rug cleaning | 21 | 21 | 21 | 21 | 21 |
| 7217 | Carpet and upholstery cleaning | 9 | 9 | 9 | 10 | 10 |
| 7218 | Industrial launderers | 15 | 16 | 17 | 19 | 20 |
| 7221 | Photographic studios, portrait | 18 | 20 | 22 | 22 | 22 |
| 7231 | Beauty shops | 57 | 59 | 63 | 64 | 69 |
| 7241 | Barber shops | 6 | 6 | 6 | 6 | 7 |
| 7261 | Funeral service and crematories | 32 | 33 | 36 | 38 | 40 |
| 7291 | Tax return preparation services | 9 | 11 | 10 | 11 | 12 |

*Notes:*
(NA) Not available.
SIC = Standard Industrial Classification
*General Notes:* Estimates are in whole dollars. Data for 1996 have been revised to reflect the use of 1996 administrative receipts for nonemployer firms. Estimates are for employer and nonemployer firms. Estimates are not adjusted for price changes.

*Source:* U.S. Department of Commerce, Bureau of the Census, *Service Annual Survey: 1997* and *Current Population Reports*, Series P25-1127 and 1095; Table 3.3; <http://www.census.gov/svsd/sasann/view/alltab.pdf>.

## F2. BUSINESS SERVICES

## F2-1. Business Services—Annual Receipts of Taxable Firms: 1985–1996, in Billions of Dollars, Estimated

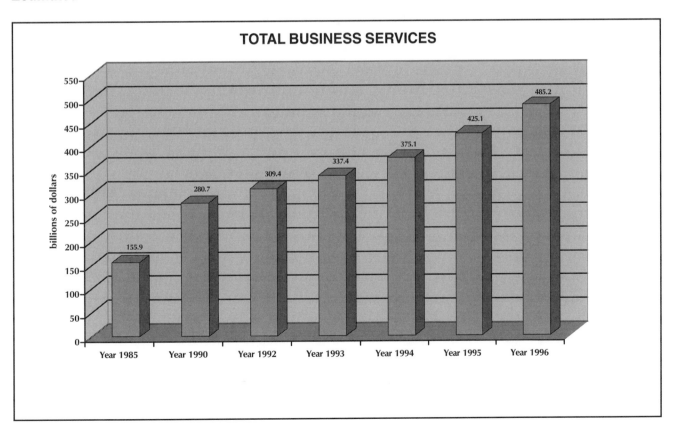

**F2-1. Business Services—Annual Receipts of Taxable Firms: 1985–1996, in Billions of Dollars, Estimated** *(continued)*

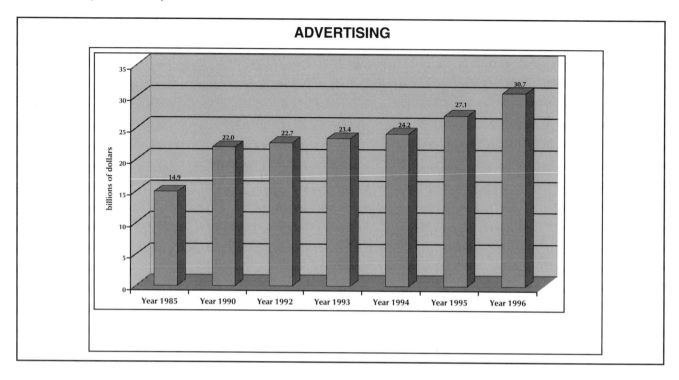

**F2-1. Business Services—Annual Receipts of Taxable Firms: 1985–1996, in Billions of Dollars, Estimated** *(continued)*

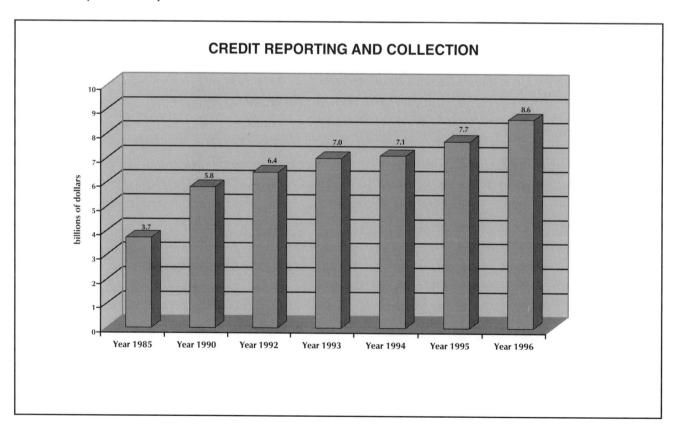

**F2-1. Business Services—Annual Receipts of Taxable Firms: 1985–1996, in Billions of Dollars, Estimated** *(continued)*

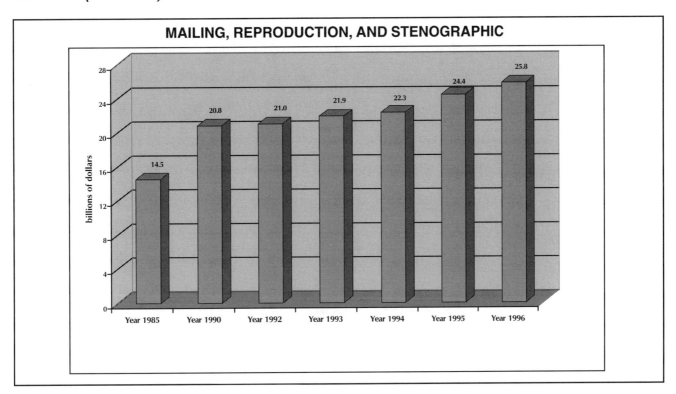

**F2-1. Business Services—Annual Receipts of Taxable Firms: 1985–1996, in Billions of Dollars, Estimated** *(continued)*

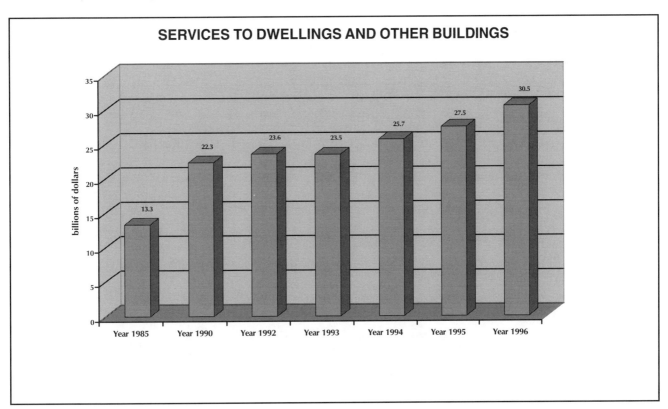

**F2-1. Business Services—Annual Receipts of Taxable Firms: 1985–1996, in Billions of Dollars, Estimated** *(continued)*

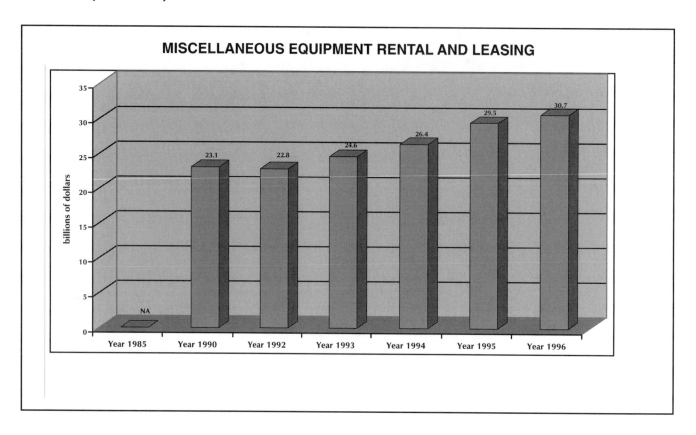

**MISCELLANEOUS EQUIPMENT RENTAL AND LEASING**

**F2-1. Business Services—Annual Receipts of Taxable Firms: 1985–1996, in Billions of Dollars, Estimated** *(continued)*

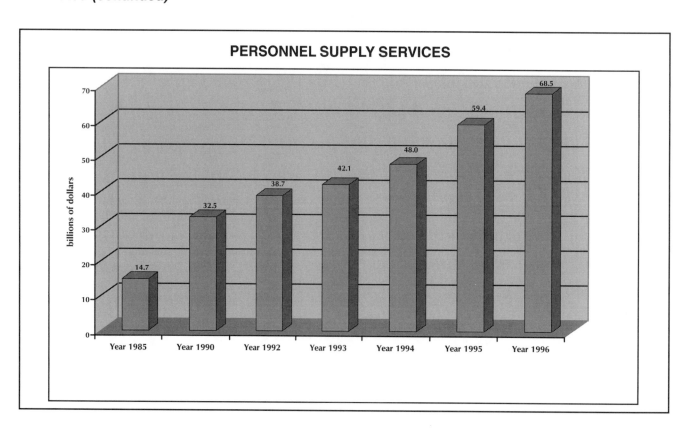

**PERSONNEL SUPPLY SERVICES**

**F2-1. Business Services—Annual Receipts of Taxable Firms: 1985–1996, in Billions of Dollars, Estimated** *(continued)*

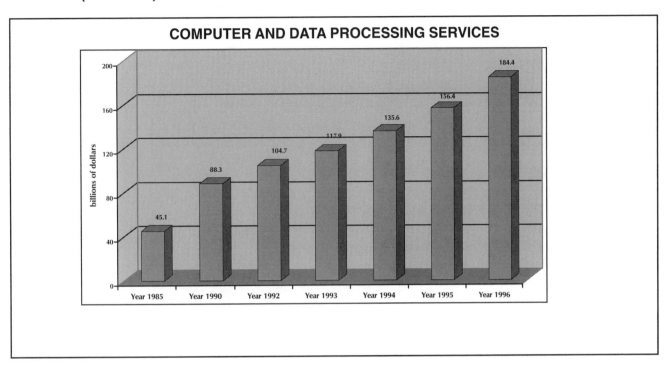

**F2-1. Business Services—Annual Receipts of Taxable Firms: 1985–1996, in Billions of Dollars, Estimated** *(continued)*

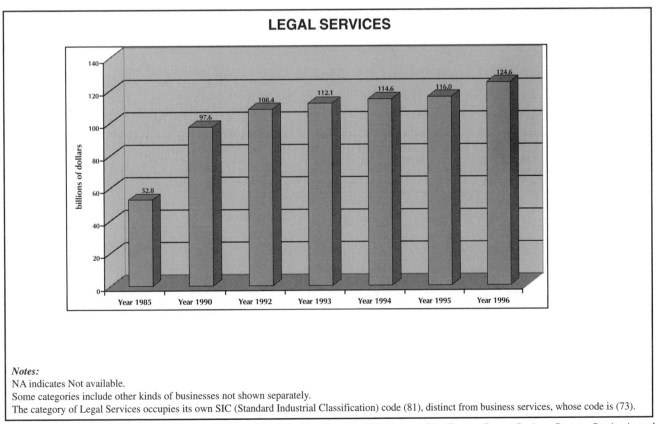

*Notes:*
NA indicates Not available.
Some categories include other kinds of businesses not shown separately.
The category of Legal Services occupies its own SIC (Standard Industrial Classification) code (81), distinct from business services, whose code is (73).

*Source: Statistical Abstract of the United States 1998*, No. 1298. Underlying data from U.S. Bureau of the Census, *Current Business Reports, Service Annual Survey: 1996* (BS/96) and unpublished data.

## F3. PUBLIC ELEMENTARY AND SECONDARY EDUCATION

### F3-1. Public Elementary and Secondary Education Estimated Finances, Receipts, and Expenditures: 1980–1997, in Millions of Dollars

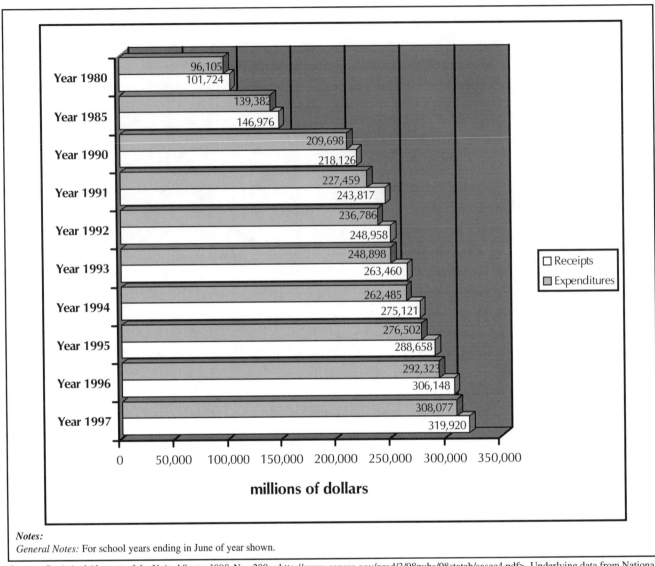

**millions of dollars**

*Notes:*
*General Notes:* For school years ending in June of year shown.

*Source: Statistical Abstract of the United States 1998*, No. 280; <http://www census gov/prod/3/98pubs/98statab/sasec4 pdf>. Underlying data from National Education Association, Washington, DC, *Estimates of School Statistics Database* (copyright).

## F3-2. Public Elementary and Secondary Education Estimated Finances, Expenditures: 1980–1997, in Millions of Dollars (except as noted)

| Year | Total[1] | Per capita (doll.) | Current expenditures, elementary and secondary day schools | Current expenditures, average per pupil in ADA[3], amount (doll.) |
|------|------|------|------|------|
| 1980 | 96,105  | 428   | 85,661  | 2,230 |
| 1985 | 139,382 | 591   | 127,230 | 3,483 |
| 1990 | 209,698 | 850   | 186,583 | 4,966 |
| 1991 | 227,459 | 915   | 200,911 | 5,262 |
| 1992 | 236,786 | 939   | 208,512 | 5,357 |
| 1993 | 248,898 | 976   | 219,297 | 5,538 |
| 1994 | 262,485 | 1,018 | 230,773 | 5,749 |
| 1995 | 276,502 | 1,062 | 242,729 | 5,950 |
| 1996 | 292,323 | 1,113 | 254,254 | 6,134 |
| 1997 | 308,077 | 1,162 | 268,026 | 6,360 |

*Notes:*

1. Includes interest on school debt and other current expenditures not shown separately.
2 Based on Bureau of the Census estimated resident population, as of July 1, the previous year.  Estimates reflect revisions based on the 1990 Census of Population.
3. Average daily attendance.
*General Notes:* For school years ending in June of year shown.

*Source: Statistical Abstract of the United States 1998*, No. 280; <http://www census gov/prod/3/98pubs/98statab/sasec4 pdf>. Underlying data from National Education Association, Washington, DC, *Estimates of School Statistics Database* (copyright).

## F3-3. Public Elementary and Secondary Education Estimated Finances, Receipts: 1980–1997, in Millions of Dollars (except as noted)

| Year | Total | Revenue receipts, total | Source, Federal | Source, State | Source, Local | Nonrevenue receipts[1] |
|------|------|------|------|------|------|------|
| 1980 | 101,724 | 97,635  | 9,020  | 47,929  | 40,686  | 4,089  |
| 1985 | 146,976 | 141,013 | 9,533  | 69,107  | 62,373  | 5,963  |
| 1990 | 218,126 | 208,656 | 13,184 | 100,787 | 94,685  | 9,469  |
| 1991 | 243,817 | 223,896 | 14,178 | 108,021 | 101,697 | 19,921 |
| 1992 | 248,958 | 235,122 | 15,707 | 111,530 | 107,885 | 13,836 |
| 1993 | 263,460 | 247,912 | 17,381 | 115,924 | 114,606 | 15,548 |
| 1994 | 275,121 | 259,587 | 18,434 | 119,443 | 121,710 | 15,534 |
| 1995 | 288,658 | 273,364 | 18,766 | 130,139 | 124,459 | 15,294 |
| 1996 | 306,148 | 286,927 | 19,323 | 138,045 | 129,560 | 19,221 |
| 1997 | 319,920 | 301,404 | 20,387 | 147,396 | 133,621 | 18,516 |

*Notes:*

1. Amount received by local education agencies from the sales of bonds and real property and equipment, loans, and proceeds from insurance adjustments.
*General Notes:* For school years ending in June of year shown.

*Source: Statistical Abstract of the United States 1998*, No. 280; <http://www census gov/prod/3/98pubs/98statab/sasec4 pdf>. Underlying data from National Education Association, Washington, DC, *Estimates of School Statistics Database* (copyright).

## F3-4. Public Elementary and Secondary Education Estimated Finances, Expenditures, by State: 1997, in Millions of Dollars (except as noted)

| State | Total[1] | Per capita[2] (doll.) | Current expenditures, elementary and secondary day schools | Current expenditures, average per pupil in ADA[3], amount (doll.) | Current expenditures, average per pupil in ADA[3], rank |
|---|---|---|---|---|---|
| Alabama | 4,558 | 1,063 | 3,895 | 5,478 | 36 |
| Alaska | 1,257 | 2,078 | 1,156 | 10,393 | 1 |
| Arizona | 4,493 | 1,013 | 3,556 | 4,777 | 47 |
| Arkansas | 2,206 | 880 | 1,904 | 4,498 | 48 |
| California | 34,137 | 1,072 | 29,657 | 5,327 | 41 |
| Colorado | 4,225 | 1,107 | 3,466 | 5,550 | 34 |
| Connecticut | 4,798 | 1,468 | 4,417 | 8,845 | 4 |
| Delaware | 902 | 1,246 | 818 | 8,098 | 6 |
| District of Columbia | 608 | 1,127 | 573 | 8,167 | 5 |
| Florida | 14,873 | 1,031 | 12,023 | 5,988 | 30 |
| Georgia | 9,328 | 1,272 | 7,904 | 6,459 | 20 |
| Hawaii | 1,273 | 1,076 | 1,054 | 6,066 | 26 |
| Idaho | 1,265 | 1,065 | 1,104 | 4,794 | 46 |
| Illinois | 12,754 | 1,077 | 10,699 | 6,048 | 27 |
| Indiana | 6,885 | 1,181 | 5,784 | 6,411 | 21 |
| Iowa | 2,988 | 1,049 | 2,632 | 5,546 | 35 |
| Kansas | 2,874 | 1,114 | 2,572 | 6,157 | 23 |
| Kentucky | 3,669 | 945 | 3,399 | 5,959 | 31 |
| Louisiana | 4,027 | 928 | 3,661 | 5,092 | 43 |
| Maine | 1,494 | 1,206 | 1,395 | 6,775 | 14 |
| Maryland | 5,988 | 1,183 | 5,360 | 7,052 | 12 |
| Massachusetts | 6,948 | 1,142 | 6,573 | 7,628 | 8 |
| Michigan | 12,722 | 1,307 | 11,207 | 7,318 | 11 |
| Minnesota | 6,739 | 1,450 | 5,110 | 6,529 | 19 |
| Mississippi | 2,347 | 866 | 2,059 | 4,351 | 50 |
| Missouri | 5,183 | 966 | 4,401 | 5,375 | 39 |
| Montana | 986 | 1,125 | 891 | 6,006 | 29 |
| Nebraska | 1,737 | 1,053 | 1,527 | 5,636 | 32 |
| Nevada | 1,955 | 1,221 | 1,413 | 5,384 | 38 |
| New Hampshire | 1,295 | 1,117 | 1,183 | 6,557 | 17 |
| New Jersey | 12,240 | 1,530 | 11,657 | 10,284 | 2 |
| New Mexico | 2,152 | 1,257 | 1,628 | 5,457 | 37 |
| New York | 27,621 | 1,523 | 24,346 | 9,628 | 3 |
| North Carolina | 7,094 | 971 | 6,311 | 5,623 | 33 |
| North Dakota | 615 | 958 | 567 | 5,016 | 44 |
| Ohio | 12,432 | 1,114 | 10,384 | 6,132 | 24 |
| Oklahoma | 3,033 | 920 | 2,600 | 4,486 | 49 |
| Oregon | 3,769 | 1,179 | 3,216 | 6,602 | 16 |
| Pennsylvania | 13,265 | 1,102 | 12,570 | 7,568 | 9 |
| Rhode Island | 1,150 | 1,164 | 1,113 | 8,030 | 7 |
| South Carolina | 3,876 | 1,043 | 3,288 | 5,357 | 40 |
| South Dakota | 730 | 989 | 632 | 4,990 | 45 |
| Tennessee | 4,541 | 856 | 4,367 | 5,286 | 42 |
| Texas | 24,481 | 1,282 | 21,255 | 6,041 | 28 |
| Utah | 2,133 | 1,057 | 1,719 | 3,822 | 51 |
| Vermont | 775 | 1,321 | 702 | 7,561 | 10 |
| Virginia | 7,196 | 1,079 | 6,489 | 6,370 | 22 |
| Washington | 6,936 | 1,257 | 5,543 | 6,084 | 25 |
| West Virginia | 2,135 | 1,173 | 1,914 | 6,769 | 15 |
| Wisconsin | 6,696 | 1,301 | 5,733 | 6,999 | 13 |
| Wyoming | 695 | 1,448 | 600 | 6,541 | 18 |

*Notes:*

1. Includes interest on school debt and other current expenditures not shown separately.

2 Based on Bureau of the Census estimated resident population, as of July 1, the previous year. Estimates reflect revisions based on the 1990 Census of Population.

3. Average daily attendance.

*General Notes:* For school years ending in June of year shown.

*Source: Statistical Abstract of the United States 1998*, No. 280; <http://www census gov/prod/3/98pubs/98statab/sasec4 pdf. Underlying data from National Education Association, Washington, DC, *Estimates of School Statistics Database* (copyright).

## F3-5. Public Elementary and Secondary Education Estimated Finances, Receipts, by State: 1997, in Millions of Dollars (except as noted)

| State | Total | Revenue receipts, total | Source, Federal | Source, State | Source, Local | Nonrevenue receipts[1] |
|---|---|---|---|---|---|---|
| Alabama | 4,147 | 3,883 | 397 | 2,517 | 969 | 264 |
| Alaska | 1,279 | 1,143 | 144 | 726 | 273 | 136 |
| Arizona | 4,574 | 4,057 | 292 | 1,976 | 1,789 | 517 |
| Arkansas | 2,429 | 2,267 | 189 | 1,495 | 583 | 162 |
| California | 35,528 | 34,780 | 2,909 | 20,832 | 11,038 | 748 |
| Colorado | 4,490 | 4,022 | 226 | 1,774 | 2,022 | 468 |
| Connecticut | 4,798 | 4,794 | 202 | 1,886 | 2,706 | 4 |
| Delaware | 917 | 900 | 69 | 594 | 238 | 17 |
| District of Columbia | 533 | 496 | 70 | (-) | 425 | 38 |
| Florida | 15,138 | 13,864 | 1,022 | 6,768 | 6,074 | 1,274 |
| Georgia | 9,456 | 8,260 | 545 | 4,343 | 3,372 | 1,196 |
| Hawaii | 1,325 | 1,325 | 98 | 1,198 | 30 | (-) |
| Idaho | 1,346 | 1,240 | 85 | 792 | 363 | 106 |
| Illinois | 14,150 | 12,997 | 973 | 3,513 | 8,512 | 1,153 |
| Indiana | 7,095 | 6,851 | 341 | 3,603 | 2,906 | 245 |
| Iowa | 3,289 | 3,090 | 117 | 1,657 | 1,316 | 199 |
| Kansas | 3,257 | 3,001 | 164 | 1,730 | 1,107 | 256 |
| Kentucky | 3,740 | 3,697 | 295 | 2,460 | 943 | 43 |
| Louisiana | 4,547 | 4,109 | 485 | 2,088 | 1,535 | 439 |
| Maine | 1,494 | 1,454 | 95 | 669 | 690 | 40 |
| Maryland | 6,044 | 5,783 | 324 | 2,315 | 3,144 | 261 |
| Massachusetts | 7,145 | 7,145 | 383 | 2,571 | 4,192 | (-) |
| Michigan | 13,454 | 12,806 | 848 | 8,685 | 3,273 | 648 |
| Minnesota | 6,690 | 5,937 | 237 | 3,260 | 2,440 | 753 |
| Mississippi | 2,423 | 2,311 | 325 | 1,272 | 714 | 112 |
| Missouri | 5,926 | 5,500 | 327 | 2,178 | 2,995 | 426 |
| Montana | 980 | 965 | 95 | 469 | 401 | 15 |
| Nebraska | 1,621 | 1,606 | 66 | 604 | 936 | 14 |
| Nevada | 1,805 | 1,639 | 72 | 550 | 1,017 | 166 |
| New Hampshire | 1,387 | 1,304 | 39 | 87 | 1,178 | 84 |
| New Jersey | 12,392 | 12,296 | 422 | 4,815 | 7,059 | 96 |
| New Mexico | 2,338 | 2,022 | 197 | 1,326 | 499 | 316 |
| New York | 28,871 | 26,754 | 1,624 | 10,471 | 14,659 | 2,116 |
| North Carolina | 7,121 | 6,740 | 500 | 4,424 | 1,817 | 381 |
| North Dakota | 659 | 645 | 76 | 272 | 298 | 14 |
| Ohio | 13,099 | 12,159 | 771 | 5,141 | 6,247 | 940 |
| Oklahoma | 3,257 | 3,007 | 269 | 1,880 | 858 | 250 |
| Oregon | 3,773 | 3,376 | 241 | 1,871 | 1,264 | 398 |
| Pennsylvania | 14,795 | 14,775 | 824 | 6,114 | 7,837 | 20 |
| Rhode Island | 1,202 | 1,202 | 71 | 477 | 654 | (-) |
| South Carolina | 4,261 | 3,918 | 310 | 2,063 | 1,545 | 344 |
| South Dakota | 767 | 747 | 74 | 239 | 435 | 19 |
| Tennessee | 4,441 | 4,240 | 357 | 2,153 | 1,731 | 201 |
| Texas | 25,188 | 22,958 | 1,789 | 9,839 | 11,330 | 2,229 |
| Utah | 2,185 | 2,183 | 137 | 1,368 | 678 | 1 |
| Vermont | 814 | 788 | 40 | 228 | 521 | 26 |
| Virginia | 6,477 | 6,410 | 346 | 2,358 | 3,706 | 67 |
| Washington | 7,253 | 6,523 | 389 | 4,473 | 1,661 | 730 |
| West Virginia | 2,140 | 2,093 | 180 | 1,315 | 598 | 47 |
| Wisconsin | 7,155 | 6,682 | 293 | 3,643 | 2,747 | 473 |
| Wyoming | 725 | 659 | 43 | 319 | 298 | 65 |

*Notes:*

1. Amount received by local education agencies from the sales of bonds and real property and equipment, loans, and proceeds from insurance adjustments.
*General Notes:* For school years ending in June of year shown.

*Source: Statistical Abstract of the United States 1998*, No. 280; <http://www.census gov/prod/3/98pubs/98statab/sasec4 pdf>. Underlying data from National Education Association, Washington, DC, *Estimates of School Statistics Database* (copyright).

## F4. AVAILABILITY AND USE OF SELECTED TEACHING RESOURCES

### F4-1. Availability and Use of Selected Teaching Resources, by Gender of Teacher: 1996, in Percent

| Resources | All Teachers | Teachers, Male | Teachers, Female |
|---|---|---|---|
| **RESOURCE AVAILABLE** | | | |
| Personal computers | 83.7 | 81.6 | 84.4 |
| Computers with CD-ROM drive | 58.2 | 62.8 | 56.6 |
| Networked computers | 45.0 | 50.5 | 43.1 |
| Computers with modems | 37.5 | 43.7 | 35.4 |
| VCR | 92.9 | 93.4 | 92.7 |
| Television monitor | 85.4 | 87.4 | 84.6 |
| Hypermedia or multimedia soft-ware | 39.9 | 43.6 | 38.6 |
| Standard software | 71.3 | 76.8 | 69.4 |
| Specialized instructional software | 56.3 | 52.4 | 57.6 |
| Online services/networks | 35.3 | 42.8 | 32.6 |
| Instructional laser/video disks | 37.3 | 41.2 | 36.0 |
| Instructional videotapes | 79.7 | 77.6 | 80.4 |
| Distance learning/video conferencing | 11.2 | 13.9 | 10.2 |
| **RESOURCE USED** | | | |
| Personal computers | 60.8 | 58.8 | 61.5 |
| Computers with CD-ROM drive | 29.4 | 34.0 | 27.8 |
| Networked computers | 23.9 | 28.4 | 22.3 |
| Computers with modems | 12.8 | 18.2 | 10.9 |
| VCR | 72.3 | 72.7 | 72.2 |
| Television monitor | 63.6 | 66.0 | 62.8 |
| Hypermedia or multimedia soft-ware | 20.0 | 20.3 | 19.9 |
| Standard software | 44.3 | 51.7 | 41.6 |
| Specialized instructional software | 38.3 | 32.4 | 40.4 |
| Online services/networks | 8.9 | 13.4 | 7.3 |
| Instructional laser/video disks | 16.1 | 17.5 | 15.7 |
| Instructional videotapes | 62.7 | 59.7 | 63.7 |
| Distance learning/video conferencing | 2.7 | 3.7 | 2.4 |

*Notes:*
*General Notes:* For resources available at the worksite or used for instructional purposes. Based on a sample survey conducted in the spring of 1996.

*Source: Statistical Abstract of the United States 1998*, No. 284; <http://wwwcensusgov/prod/3/98pubs/98statab/sasec4pdf>. Underlying data from National Education Association, Washington, DC, *Status of the American Public School Teacher, 1995-1996* (copyright).

### F4-2. Availability and Use of Selected Teaching Resources, by Level of Education: 1996, in Percent

| Resources | Level[1], Elementary | Level[1], Secondary |
|---|---|---|
| **RESOURCE AVAILABLE** | | |
| Personal computers | 86.9 | 80.9 |
| Computers with CD-ROM drive | 58.9 | 57.6 |
| Networked computers | 41.2 | 48.4 |
| Computers with modems | 35.8 | 39.0 |
| VCR | 93.3 | 92.9 |
| Television monitor | 82.0 | 88.9 |
| Hypermedia or multimedia soft-ware | 41.3 | 38.8 |
| Standard software | 68.3 | 74.3 |
| Specialized instructional software | 62.7 | 50.6 |
| Online services/networks | 29.3 | 40.7 |
| Instructional laser/video disks | 34.9 | 39.8 |
| Instructional videotapes | 78.5 | 80.7 |
| Distance learning/video conferencing | 7.9 | 14.2 |
| **RESOURCE USED** | | |
| Personal computers | 68.8 | 53.7 |
| Computers with CD-ROM drive | 32.0 | 26.8 |

**F4-2. Availability and Use of Selected Teaching Resources, by Level of Education: 1996, in Percent (continued)**

| Resources | Level[1], Elementary | Level[1], Secondary |
|---|---|---|
| Networked computers | 23.6 | 24.1 |
| Computers with modems | 13.3 | 12.6 |
| VCR | 72.2 | 72.7 |
| Television monitor | 58.3 | 68.9 |
| Hypermedia or multimedia soft-ware | 23.5 | 16.8 |
| Standard software | 40.6 | 47.9 |
| Specialized instructional software | 47.2 | 30.4 |
| Online services/networks | 7.9 | 9.8 |
| Instructional laser/video disks | 16.4 | 16.0 |
| Instructional videotapes | 63.7 | 62.2 |
| Distance learning/video conferencing | 1.9 | 3.6 |

*Notes:*
1. Level as determined by respondent.
*General Notes:* For resources available at the worksite or used for instructional purposes. Based on a sample survey conducted in the spring of 1996.

*Source: Statistical Abstract of the United States 1998*, No. 284; <http://wwwcensusgov/prod/3/98pubs/98statab/sasec4pdf>. Underlying data from National Education Association, Washington, DC, *Status of the American Public School Teacher, 1995-1996* (copyright).

**F4-3. Availability and Use of Selected Teaching Resources, by Race: 1996, in Percent**

| Resources | Race, White | Race, Minority |
|---|---|---|
| **RESOURCE AVAILABLE** | | |
| Personal computers | 84.7 | 77.1 |
| Computers with CD-ROM drive | 59.7 | 44.4 |
| Networked computers | 45.5 | 41.6 |
| Computers with modems | 38.4 | 30.8 |
| VCR | 93.6 | 85.3 |
| Television monitor | 86.0 | 78.0 |
| Hypermedia or multimedia soft-ware | 40.7 | 33.7 |
| Standard software | 73.1 | 55.9 |
| Specialized instructional software | 57.2 | 50.5 |
| Online services/networks | 36.7 | 24.5 |
| Instructional laser/video disks | 38.0 | 32.7 |
| Instructional videotapes | 80.8 | 70.8 |
| Distance learning/video conferencing | 10.9 | 14.2 |
| **RESOURCE USED** | | |
| Personal computers | 61.7 | 52.7 |
| Computers with CD-ROM drive | 30.5 | 17.0 |
| Networked computers | 24.5 | 19.6 |
| Computers with modems | 13.2 | 8.7 |
| VCR | 73.3 | 61.1 |
| Television monitor | 64.5 | 52.0 |
| Hypermedia or multimedia soft-ware | 20.5 | 15.0 |
| Standard software | 45.6 | 34.3 |
| Specialized instructional software | 39.5 | 31.4 |
| Online services/networks | 9.6 | 3.8 |
| Instructional laser/video disks | 16.4 | 12.7 |
| Instructional videotapes | 63.6 | 54.3 |
| Distance learning/video conferencing | 2.4 | 4.7 |

*Notes:*
*General Notes:* For resources available at the worksite or used for instructional purposes. Based on a sample survey conducted in the spring of 1996.

*Source: Statistical Abstract of the United States 1998*, No. 284; <http://wwwcensusgov/prod/3/98pubs/98statab/sasec4pdf>. Underlying data from National Education Association, Washington, DC, *Status of the American Public School Teacher, 1995-1996* (copyright).

## F4-4. Availability and Use of Selected Teaching Resources, by Size of School System: 1996, in Percent

| Resources | School System Size, Less than 3,000 | School System Size, 3,000 to 24,999 | School System Size, 25,000 or More |
|---|---|---|---|
| **RESOURCE AVAILABLE** | | | |
| Personal computers | 85.5 | 86.8 | 76.7 |
| Computers with CD-ROM drive | 60.5 | 60.9 | 51.1 |
| Networked computers | 48.6 | 46.0 | 39.1 |
| Computers with modems | 39.4 | 37.0 | 36.4 |
| VCR | 94.7 | 92.2 | 92.1 |
| Television monitor | 84.9 | 85.1 | 86.2 |
| Hypermedia or multimedia software | 40.0 | 40.4 | 38.9 |
| Standard software | 73.7 | 72.5 | 66.6 |
| Specialized instructional software | 60.6 | 53.7 | 56.3 |
| Online services/networks | 40.4 | 35.0 | 30.1 |
| Instructional laser/video disks | 32.6 | 40.0 | 37.7 |
| Instructional videotapes | 81.3 | 81.2 | 75.4 |
| Distance learning/video conferencing | 14.2 | 9.7 | 10.4 |
| **RESOURCE USED** | | | |
| Personal computers | 63.3 | 63.8 | 53.1 |
| Computers with CD-ROM drive | 33.2 | 30.8 | 22.9 |
| Networked computers | 27.1 | 24.1 | 20.1 |
| Computers with modems | 12.8 | 13.2 | 12.2 |
| VCR | 74.6 | 73.8 | 67.3 |
| Television monitor | 64.3 | 64.9 | 60.5 |
| Hypermedia or multimedia software | 18.8 | 21.9 | 17.8 |
| Standard software | 43.8 | 46.0 | 41.8 |
| Specialized instructional software | 42.2 | 36.8 | 37.0 |
| Online services/networks | 9.4 | 9.3 | 7.7 |
| Instructional laser/video disks | 13.5 | 17.7 | 16.1 |
| Instructional videotapes | 65.9 | 64.0 | 56.6 |
| Distance learning/video conferencing | 3.2 | 2.5 | 2.8 |

*Note:*
*General Notes:* For resources available at the worksite or used for instructional purposes. Based on a sample survey conducted in the spring of 1996.

*Source: Statistical Abstract of the United States 1998*, No. 284; <http://wwwcensusgov/prod/3/98pubs/98statab/sasec4pdf>. Underlying data from National Education Association, Washington, DC, *Status of the American Public School Teacher, 1995-1996* (copyright).

## F5. INSTITUTIONS OF HIGHER EDUCATION

### F5-1. Institutions of Higher Education, Tuition and Fees, Totals: 1985–1997, in Dollars

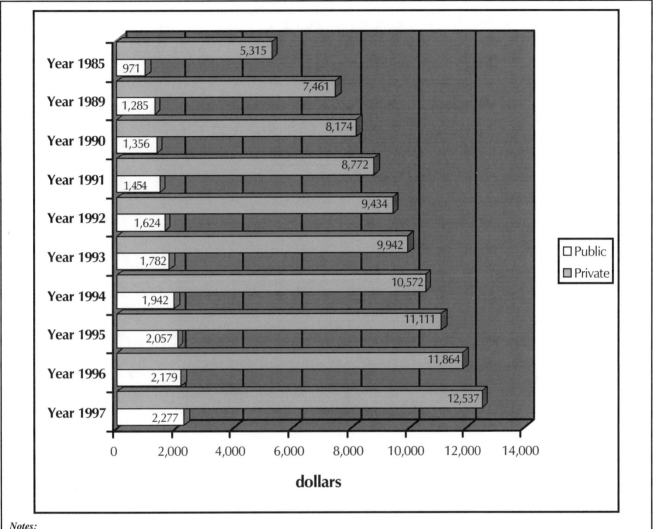

*Notes:*

1997 data are preliminary.

*General Notes:* Estimated. For the entire academic year ending in year shown. Figures are average charges per full-time equivalent student. Room and board are based on full-time students.

*Source: Statistical Abstract of the United States 1998*, No. 312; <http://www.census gov/prod/3/98pubs/98statab/sasec4.pdf>. Underlying data from U.S. National Center for Education Statistics, *Digest of Education Statistics,* annual.

## F5-2. Institutions of Higher Education, Dormitory Charges, Totals: 1985–1997, in Dollars

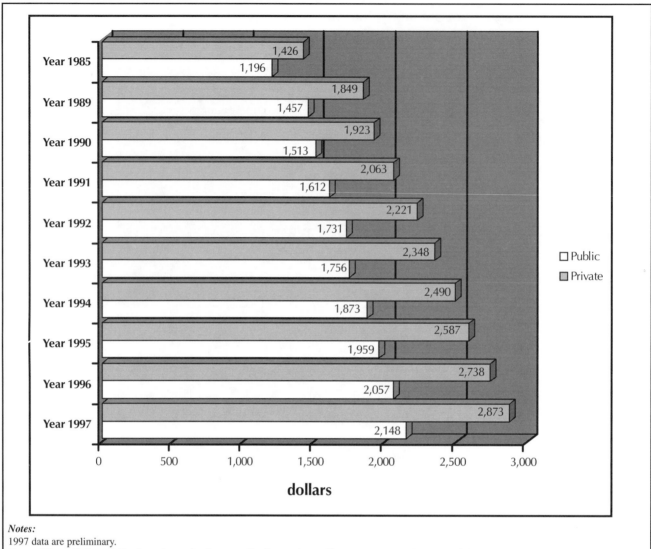

*Notes:*
1997 data are preliminary.
*General Notes:* Estimated. For the entire academic year ending in year shown. Figures are average charges per full-time equivalent student. Room and board are based on full-time students.

*Source: Statistical Abstract of the United States 1998*, No. 312; <http://www.census gov/prod/3/98pubs/98statab/sasec4.pdf>. Underlying data from U.S. National Center for Education Statistics, *Digest of Education Statistics,* annual.

**F5-3. Institutions of Higher Education, Board Rates, Totals: 1985–1997, in Dollars**

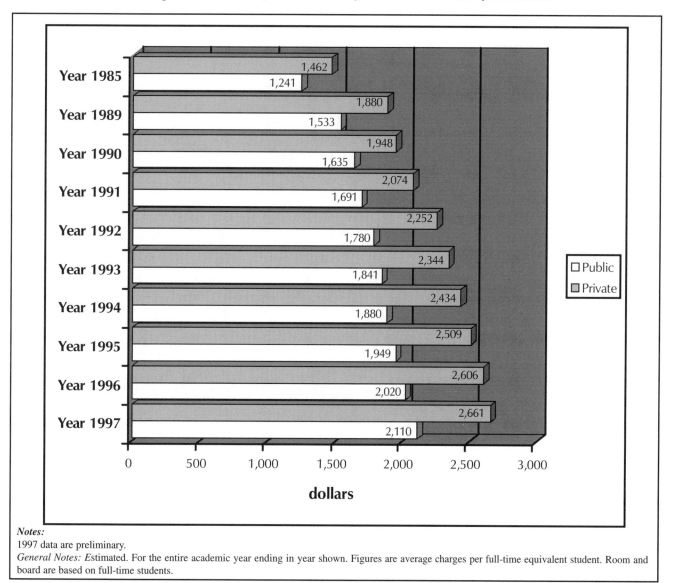

*Notes:*
1997 data are preliminary.
*General Notes: E*stimated. For the entire academic year ending in year shown. Figures are average charges per full-time equivalent student. Room and board are based on full-time students.

*Source: Statistical Abstract of the United States 1998*, No. 312; <http://www.census gov/prod/3/98pubs/98statab/sasec4.pdf>. Underlying data from U.S. National Center for Education Statistics, *Digest of Education Statistics*, annual.

## F5-4. Institutions of Higher Education, Tuition and Fees: 1985–1997, in Dollars

| Academic Control and Year | Tuition and required fees 2-year colleges | Tuition and required fees 4-year colleges | Tuition and required fees Over 4-year colleges |
|---|---|---|---|
| **Public:** | | | |
| 1985 | 584 | 1,386 | 1,117 |
| 1989 | 730 | 1,846 | 1,515 |
| 1990 | 756 | 2,035 | 1,608 |
| 1991 | 824 | 2,159 | 1,707 |
| 1992 | 937 | 2,410 | 1,933 |
| 1993 | 1,025 | 2,604 | 2,192 |
| 1994 | 1,125 | 2,820 | 2,360 |
| 1995 | 1,192 | 2,977 | 2,499 |
| 1996 | 1,239 | 3,151 | 2,660 |
| 1997[1] | 1,283 | 3,321 | 2,778 |
| **Private:** | | | |
| 1985 | 3,485 | 6,843 | 5,135 |
| 1989 | 4,817 | 9,451 | 7,172 |
| 1990 | 5,196 | 10,348 | 7,778 |
| 1991 | 5,570 | 11,379 | 8,389 |
| 1992 | 5,752 | 12,192 | 9,053 |
| 1993 | 6,059 | 13,055 | 9,533 |
| 1994 | 6,370 | 13,874 | 10,100 |
| 1995 | 6,914 | 14,537 | 10,653 |
| 1996 | 7,094 | 15,605 | 11,297 |
| 1997[1] | 7,190 | 16,531 | 11,911 |

*Notes:*
1. Preliminary.
General Notes: Estimated. For the entire academic year ending in year shown. Figures are average charges per full-time equivalent student. Room and board are based on full-time students.

*Source: Statistical Abstract of the United States 1998*, No. 312; <http://www.census gov/prod/3/98pubs/98statab/sasec4.pdf>. Underlying data from U.S. National Center for Education Statistics, *Digest of Education Statistics,* annual.

## F5-5. Institutions of Higher Education, Dormitory Charges: 1985–1997, in Dollars

| Academic Control and Year | Dormitory charges 2-year colleges | Dormitory charges 4-year colleges | Dormitory charges Over 4-year colleges |
|---|---|---|---|
| **Public:** | | | |
| 1985 | 921 | 1,237 | 1,200 |
| 1989 | 965 | 1,483 | 1,506 |
| 1990 | 962 | 1,561 | 1,554 |
| 1991 | 1,050 | 1,658 | 1,655 |
| 1992 | 1,074 | 1,789 | 1,782 |
| 1993 | 1,106 | 1,856 | 1,787 |
| 1994 | 1,190 | 1,897 | 1,958 |
| 1995 | 1,232 | 1,992 | 2,044 |
| 1996 | 1,297 | 2,104 | 2,133 |
| 1997[1] | 1,346 | 2,189 | 2,228 |
| **Private:** | | | |
| 1985 | 1,424 | 1,753 | 1,309 |
| 1989 | 1,540 | 2,353 | 1,686 |
| 1990 | 1,663 | 2,411 | 1,774 |
| 1991 | 1,744 | 2,654 | 1,889 |
| 1992 | 1,789 | 2,860 | 2,038 |
| 1993 | 1,970 | 3,018 | 2,151 |
| 1994 | 2,067 | 3,277 | 2,261 |
| 1995 | 2,233 | 3,469 | 2,347 |
| 1996 | 2,371 | 3,680 | 2,473 |
| 1997[1] | 2,513 | 3,820 | 2,597 |

*Notes:*
1. Preliminary.
*General Notes:* Estimated. For the entire academic year ending in year shown. Figures are average charges per full-time equivalent student. Room and board are based on full-time students.

*Source: Statistical Abstract of the United States 1998*, No. 312; <http://www.census gov/prod/3/98pubs/98statab/sasec4.pdf>. Underlying data from U.S. National Center for Education Statistics, *Digest of Education Statistics,* annual.

## F5-6. Institutions of Higher Education, Board Rates: 1985–1997, in Dollars

| Academic Control and Year | Board rates 2-year colleges | Board rates 4-year colleges | Board rates Over 4-year colleges |
|---|---|---|---|
| **Public:** | | | |
| 1985 | 1,302 | 1,276 | 1,201 |
| 1989 | 1,488 | 1,576 | 1,504 |
| 1990 | 1,581 | 1,728 | 1,561 |
| 1991 | 1,594 | 1,767 | 1,641 |
| 1992 | 1,612 | 1,852 | 1,745 |
| 1993 | 1,668 | 1,982 | 1,761 |
| 1994 | 1,681 | 1,993 | 1,828 |
| 1995 | 1,712 | 2,108 | 1,866 |
| 1996 | 1,681 | 2,192 | 1,937 |
| 1997[1] | 1,782 | 2,283 | 2,023 |
| **Private:** | | | |
| 1985 | 1,294 | 1,647 | 1,405 |
| 1989 | 1,609 | 2,269 | 1,762 |
| 1990 | 1,811 | 2,339 | 1,823 |
| 1991 | 1,989 | 2,470 | 1,943 |
| 1992 | 2,090 | 2,727 | 2,098 |
| 1993 | 1,875 | 2,825 | 2,197 |
| 1994 | 1,970 | 2,946 | 2,278 |
| 1995 | 2,023 | 3,035 | 2,362 |
| 1996 | 2,098 | 3,218 | 2,429 |
| 1997[1] | 2,186 | 3,140 | 2,518 |

*Notes:*
1. Preliminary.
Beginning in 1988, rates reflect 20 meals per week, rather than meals served 7 days a week
*General Notes:* Estimated. For the entire academic year ending in year shown. Figures are average charges per full-time equivalent student. Room and board are based on full-time students.

*Source: Statistical Abstract of the United States 1998*, No. 312; <http://www.census gov/prod/3/98pubs/98statab/sasec4.pdf>. Underlying data from U.S. National Center for Education Statistics, *Digest of Education Statistics,* annual.

## F6. INTERNET ACCESS AND USAGE

**F6-1. Internet Access and Usage, and Online Service Usage, Share of Population with Any Online Internet Usage: 1998, as of Spring**

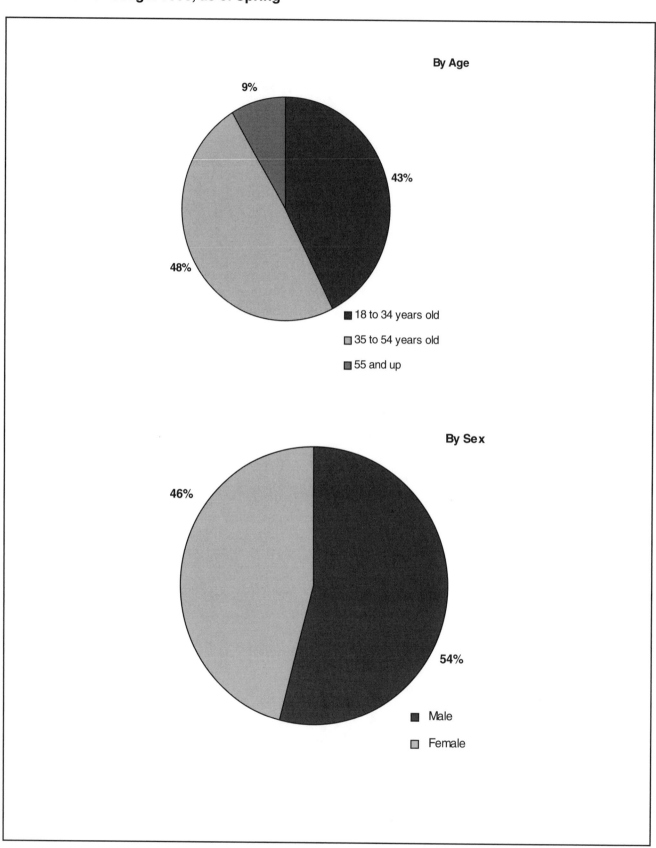

**F6-1. Internet Access and Usage, and Online Service Usage, Share of Population with Any Online Internet Usage: 1998, as of Spring *(continued)***

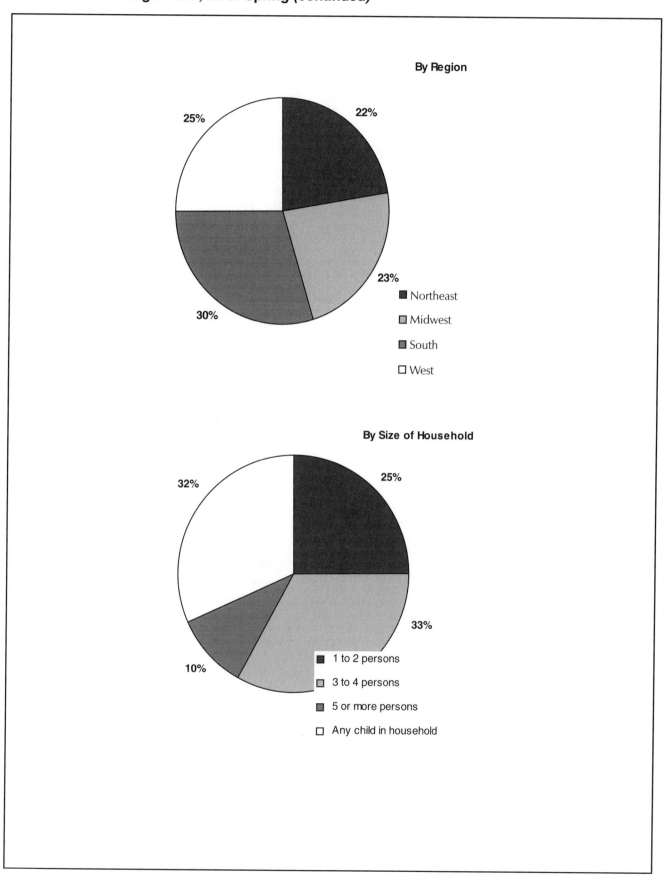

**F6-1. Internet Access and Usage, and Online Service Usage, Share of Population with Any Online Internet Usage: 1998, as of Spring *(continued)***

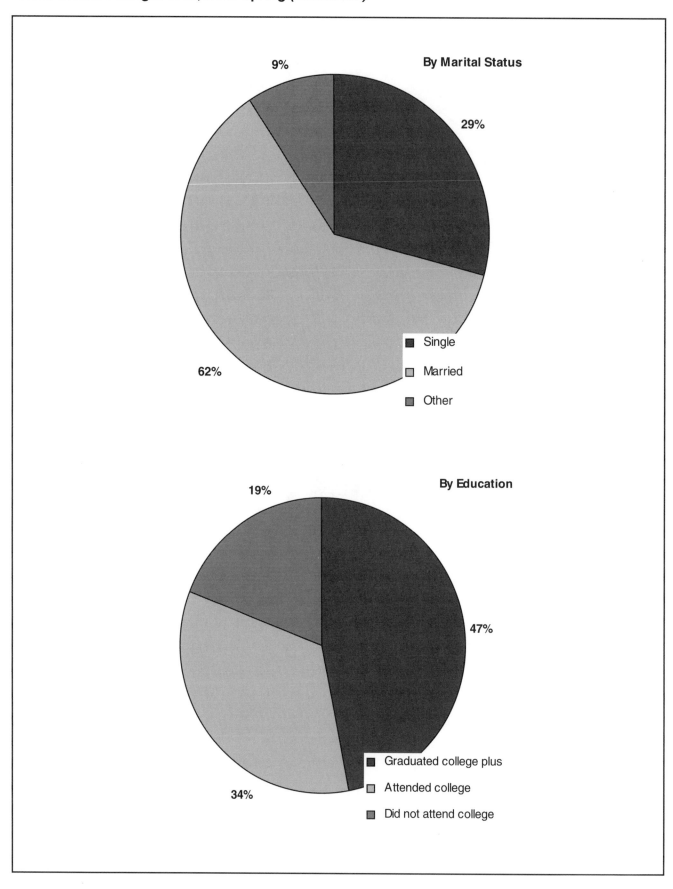

**F6-1. Internet Access and Usage, and Online Service Usage, Share of Population with Any Online Internet Usage: 1998, as of Spring *(continued)***

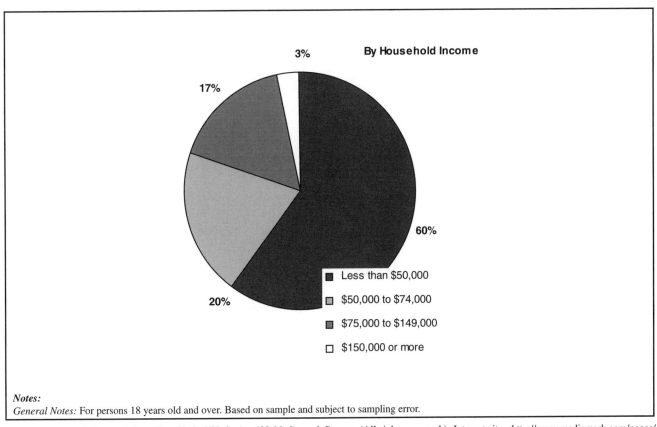

*Notes:*
*General Notes:* For persons 18 years old and over. Based on sample and subject to sampling error.

*Source:* Mediamark Research Inc., New York, NY, *Spring '98 Mediamark Reports* (All rights reserved.). Internet site <http://www.mediamark.com/pages/freedata.htm> .

## F6-2. Internet Access and Usage, and Online Service Usage, Total and by Age, Sex, and Region: 1998, as of Spring *(continued in F6-3)*

| ITEM | Total adults | Any online/ Internet usage | Have Internet access: At home or work | Have Internet access: Home only | Have Internet access: Work only |
|---|---|---|---|---|---|
| Total adults (1,000) * | 195,192 | 44,873 | 62,273 | 37,047 | 29,791 |
| **PERCENT DISTRIBUTION** | | | | | |
| **Age:** | | | | | |
| 18 to 34 years old | 33.7 | 42.6 | 40.9 | 35.9 | 33.7 |
| 35 to 54 years old | 39.0 | 48.8 | 48.2 | 53.2 | 57.2 |
| 55 years old and over | 27.3 | 8.6 | 10.8 | 10.8 | 9.1 |
| **Sex:** | | | | | |
| Male | 47.9 | 53.9 | 51.7 | 52.5 | 55.7 |
| Female | 52.1 | 46.1 | 48.3 | 47.5 | 44.3 |
| **Census region:** | | | | | |
| Northeast | 20.1 | 22.4 | 22.8 | 23.8 | 22.4 |
| Midwest | 23.3 | 22.5 | 23.1 | 21.6 | 23.6 |
| South | 35.0 | 29.9 | 30.0 | 29.2 | 29.9 |
| West | 21.6 | 25.2 | 24.0 | 25.3 | 24.1 |

*Notes:*
* Includes other labor force status and occupations, not shown separately.
*General Notes:* For persons 18 years old and over. Based on sample and subject to sampling error.

*Source:* Mediamark Research Inc., New York, NY, *Spring '98 Mediamark Reports* (All rights reserved.). Internet site <http://www.mediamark.com/pages/freedata.htm> .

## F6-3. Internet Access and Usage, and Online Service Usage, Total and by Age, Sex, and Region: 1998, as of Spring *(continued from previous table)*

| ITEM | Total adults | Used the Internet in the last 30 days: At home or work | Used the Internet in the last 30 days: At home only | Used the Internet in the last 30 days: At work only | Used any online service in the last 30 days |
|---|---|---|---|---|---|
| Total adults (1,000) * | 195,192 | 43,643 | 27,595 | 20,395 | 34,227 |
| **PERCENT DISTRIBUTION** | | | | | |
| **Age:** | | | | | |
| 18 to 34 years old | 33.7 | 42.8 | 37.0 | 35.5 | 42.2 |
| 35 to 54 years old | 39.0 | 48.8 | 53.6 | 57.2 | 49.2 |
| 55 years old and over | 27.3 | 8.4 | 9.4 | 7.3 | 8.6 |
| **Sex:** | | | | | |
| Male | 47.9 | 54.3 | 55.9 | 58.4 | 53.8 |
| Female | 52.1 | 45.7 | 44.1 | 41.6 | 46.2 |
| **Census region:** | | | | | |
| Northeast | 20.1 | 22.5 | 23.3 | 22.4 | 23.5 |
| Midwest | 23.3 | 22.8 | 21.3 | 22.5 | 21.1 |
| South | 35.0 | 29.7 | 29.7 | 30.0 | 31.5 |
| West | 21.6 | 25.0 | 25.6 | 25.1 | 23.9 |

*Notes:*
* Includes other labor force status and occupations, not shown separately.
*General Notes:* For persons 18 years old and over. Based on sample and subject to sampling error.

*Source:* Mediamark Research Inc., New York, NY, *Spring '98 Mediamark Reports* (All rights reserved.). Internet site <http://www.mediamark.com/pages/freedata.htm> .

## F6-4. Internet Access and Usage, and Online Service Usage, by Household, Marriage, and Employment Characteristics: 1998, as of Spring *(continued in F6-5)*

| ITEM | Total adults | Any online/ Internet usage | Have Internet access: At home or work | Have Internet access: Home only | Have Internet access: Work only |
|------|-------------|---------------|------------------|-----------------|----------------|
| **PERCENT DISTRIBUTION** | | | | | |
| **Household size:** | | | | | |
| 1 to 2 persons | 45.3 | 36.9 | 35.8 | 31.6 | 39.8 |
| 3 to 4 persons | 39.3 | 47.9 | 48.1 | 50.8 | 46.1 |
| 5 or more persons | 15.4 | 15.3 | 16.1 | 17.7 | 14.0 |
| Any child in household | 41.7 | 46.9 | 47.4 | 50.4 | 48.3 |
| **Marital status:** | | | | | |
| Single | 23.1 | 29.3 | 27.9 | 23.4 | 20.7 |
| Married | 57.6 | 61.4 | 61.6 | 68.0 | 67.5 |
| Other | 19.3 | 9.3 | 10.5 | 8.6 | 11.7 |
| **Educational attainment:** | | | | | |
| Graduated college plus | 21.7 | 46.9 | 41.8 | 45.8 | 54.7 |
| Attended college | 26.4 | 33.9 | 34.5 | 32.3 | 28.6 |
| Did not attend college | 51.9 | 19.2 | 23.7 | 21.9 | 16.7 |
| Employed full time | 55.1 | 73.8 | 71.5 | 70.8 | 92.1 |
| Employed part time | 10.2 | 12.0 | 12.6 | 13.3 | 7.7 |
| **Occupation:** | | | | | |
| Professional | 10.0 | 23.4 | 20.3 | 21.9 | 28.4 |
| Exec./manager/administrator | 9.3 | 19.1 | 17.8 | 18.9 | 26.1 |
| Clerical/sales/technical | 19.0 | 27.3 | 27.4 | 25.8 | 32.5 |
| Precision/crafts/repair | 7.2 | 4.6 | 5.2 | 5.1 | 4.5 |
| **Household income:** | | | | | |
| Less than $50,000 | 60.0 | 31.8 | 34.3 | 27.6 | 24.5 |
| $50,000 to $74,000 | 20.3 | 28.2 | 28.3 | 29.0 | 29.4 |
| $75,000 to $149,000 | 16.5 | 32.5 | 30.2 | 34.3 | 37.9 |
| $150,000 or more | 3.1 | 7.5 | 7.1 | 9.2 | 8.2 |

*Notes:*
*General Notes:* For persons 18 years old and over. Based on sample and subject to sampling error.

*Source:* Mediamark Research Inc., New York, NY, *Spring '98 Mediamark Reports* (All rights reserved.). Internet site <http://www.mediamark.com/pages/freedata.htm> .

## F6-5. Internet Access and Usage, and Online Service Usage, by Household, Marriage, and Employment Characteristics: 1998, as of Spring *(continued from previous table)*

| ITEM | Total adults | Used the Internet in the last 30 days: At home or work | Used the Internet in the last 30 days: At home only | Used the Internet in the last 30 days: At work only | Used any online service in the last 30 days |
|---|---|---|---|---|---|
| **PERCENT DISTRIBUTION** | | | | | |
| **Household size:** | | | | | |
| 1 to 2 persons | 45.3 | 37.0 | 34.4 | 39.6 | 36.5 |
| 3 to 4 persons | 39.3 | 47.7 | 49.6 | 46.6 | 48.4 |
| 5 or more persons | 15.4 | 15.3 | 16.0 | 13.8 | 15.1 |
| Any child in household | 41.7 | 46.8 | 49.3 | 47.8 | 47.3 |
| **Marital status:** | | | | | |
| Single | 23.1 | 29.4 | 24.0 | 22.7 | 28.8 |
| Married | 57.6 | 61.4 | 68.0 | 66.7 | 61.9 |
| Other | 19.3 | 9.2 | 8.1 | 10.6 | 9.3 |
| **Educational attainment:** | | | | | |
| Graduated college plus | 21.7 | 47.4 | 49.4 | 60.0 | 45.9 |
| Attended college | 26.4 | 33.6 | 31.8 | 27.0 | 34.7 |
| Did not attend college | 51.9 | 19.1 | 18.8 | 13.0 | 19.4 |
| Employed full time | 55.1 | 74.1 | 73.4 | 92.1 | 73.7 |
| Employed part time | 10.2 | 12.0 | 12.1 | 7.0 | 11.8 |
| **Occupation:** | | | | | |
| Professional | 10.0 | 23.8 | 23.8 | 31.4 | 22.9 |
| Exec./manager/administrator | 9.3 | 19.2 | 20.2 | 28.4 | 18.7 |
| Clerical/sales/technical | 19.0 | 27.2 | 25.8 | 30.0 | 27.7 |
| Precision/crafts/repair | 7.2 | 4.6 | 5.0 | 3.1 | 4.7 |
| **Household income:** | | | | | |
| Less than $50,000 | 60.0 | 31.6 | 26.9 | 21.9 | 30.7 |
| $50,000 to $74,000 | 20.3 | 28.2 | 28.4 | 28.9 | 28.3 |
| $75,000 to $149,000 | 16.5 | 32.7 | 35.5 | 40.3 | 33.0 |
| $150,000 or more | 3.1 | 7.5 | 9.2 | 8.9 | 8.0 |

*General Notes:* For persons 18 years old and over. Based on sample and subject to sampling error.

*Source:* Mediamark Research Inc., New York, NY, *Spring '98 Mediamark Reports* (All rights reserved.). Internet site <http://www.mediamark.com/pages/freedata.htm> .

## F7. SELECTED HEALTH SERVICES, ESTIMATED RECEIPTS AND GROWTH IN RECEIPTS

### F7-1. Selected Health Services (SIC 80)—Estimated Receipts for Taxable Firms: 1988–1992, in Millions of Dollars

| code | 1987 SIC  kind of business | 1988 | 1989 | 1990 | 1991 | 1992 |
|------|---------------------------|------|------|------|------|------|
| 80 | Health services | 221,741 | 241,558 | 271,212 | 293,907 | 321,653 |
| 801 | Offices and clinics of doctors of medicine | 108,835 | 117,213 | 128,871 | 138,576 | 151,824 |
| 802 | Offices and clinics of dentists | 27,325 | 29,297 | 31,502 | 33,279 | 36,939 |
| 803 | Offices and clinics of doctors of osteopathy | 2,661 | 2,833 | 3,254 | 3,584 | 4,008 |
| 804 | Offices and clinics of other health practitioners | 16,239 | 17,084 | 20,139 | 21,449 | 23,893 |
| 8041 | Offices and clinics of chiropractors | 4,510 | 5,005 | 5,467 | 5,647 | 6,555 |
| 8042 | Offices and clinics of optometrists | 4,133 | 4,296 | 4,799 | 5,028 | 5,333 |
| 8043 | Offices and clinics of podiatrists | (NA) | (NA) | 1,811 | 1,957 | 2,102 |
| 805 | Nursing and personal care facilities | 22,735 | 25,753 | 30,162 | 32,862 | 34,743 |
| 806 | Hospitals[1] | 22,108 | 23,495 | 26,487 | 28,807 | 31,083 |
| 8062 | General medical and surgical hospitals[1] | (NA) | (NA) | 20,442 | 22,220 | 24,162 |
| 8063 | Psychiatric hospitals[1] | (NA) | (NA) | 4,129 | 4,402 | 4,396 |
| 8069 | Specialty hospitals, except psychiatric[1] | (NA) | (NA) | 1,916 | 2,185 | 2,525 |
| 807 | Medical and dental laboratories | 8,921 | 10,336 | 12,033 | 13,567 | 15,172 |
| 8071 | Medical laboratories | 7,171 | 8,470 | 9,996 | 11,458 | 12,882 |
| 8072 | Dental laboratories | 1,750 | 1,866 | 2,037 | 2,109 | 2,290 |
| 808 | Home health care services | 4,589 | 5,595 | 7,556 | 9,129 | 11,208 |
| 809 | Miscellaneous health and allied services, n.e.c | 8,328 | 9,952 | 11,208 | 12,654 | 12,783 |
| 8092 | Kidney dialysis centers | (NA) | (NA) | 1,451 | 1,717 | 2,140 |
| 8093 | Specialty outpatient facilities, n.e.c | (NA) | (NA) | 5,326 | 6,508 | 6,476 |

*Notes:*
(NA) Not available.
1. Estimates are obtained from a sample of employer firms only.
SIC = Standard Industrial Classification
*General Notes:* Unless otherwise noted, estimates are obtained from a sample of employer and nonemployer firms. For selected SIC's (801, 802, 805, 806, 808, and 809), estimates are for taxable firms only. Firms in all other kinds of business were considered by definition to be subject to Federal income tax. Estimates are not adjusted for price changes. Group totals may include kinds of business not shown separately.

*Source:* U.S. Department of Commerce, Bureau of the Census, *Service Annual Survey: 1997* and *Current Population Reports,* Series P25-1127 and 1095; Table 7.1; <http://www.census.gov/svsd/sasann/view/alltab.pdf>.

### F7-2. Selected Health Services (SIC 80)—Estimated Receipts for Taxable Firms: 1993–1997, in Millions of Dollars

| code | 1987 SIC kind of business | 1993 | 1994 | 1995 | 1996 | 1997 |
|------|---------------------------|------|------|------|------|------|
| 80 | Health services | 335,108 | 351,419 | 376,279 | 398,353 | 421,317 |
| 801 | Offices and clinics of doctors of medicine | 154,242 | 159,616 | 167,969 | 172,926 | 179,718 |
| 802 | Offices and clinics of dentists | 38,946 | 41,663 | 44,909 | 47,411 | 50,979 |
| 803 | Offices and clinics of doctors of osteopathy | 4,159 | 4,354 | 4,698 | 4,749 | 4,952 |
| 804 | Offices and clinics of other health practitioners | 25,367 | 25,891 | 27,357 | 28,409 | 29,850 |
| 8041 | Offices and clinics of chiropractors | 6,936 | 6,757 | 6,742 | 7,003 | 7,259 |
| 8042 | Offices and clinics of optometrists | 5,715 | 6,021 | 6,113 | 6,330 | 6,491 |
| 8043 | Offices and clinics of podiatrists | 2,156 | 2,190 | 2,388 | 2,443 | 2,397 |
| 805 | Nursing and personal care facilities | 36,172 | 37,320 | 41,135 | 44,282 | 46,944 |
| 806 | Hospitals[1] | 33,331 | 35,143 | 38,417 | 44,669 | 50,154 |
| 8062 | General medical and surgical hospitals[1] | 26,683 | 27,993 | 30,704 | 36,496 | 40,920 |
| 8063 | Psychiatric hospitals[1] | 3,730 | 3,764 | 3,847 | 3,508 | 3,877 |
| 8069 | Specialty hospitals, except psychiatric[1] | 2,918 | 3,386 | 3,866 | 4,665 | 5,357 |
| 807 | Medical and dental laboratories | 15,066 | 15,427 | 15,524 | 16,054 | 16,523 |
| 8071 | Medical laboratories | 12,735 | 13,007 | 12,909 | 13,277 | 13,713 |
| 8072 | Dental laboratories | 2,331 | 2,420 | 2,615 | 2,777 | 2,810 |
| 808 | Home health care services | 13,178 | 15,394 | 17,987 | 19,556 | 19,248 |
| 809 | Miscellaneous health and allied services, n.e.c | 14,647 | 16,611 | 18,283 | 20,297 | 22,949 |
| 8092 | Kidney dialysis centers | 2,468 | 2,898 | 3,259 | 3,391 | 3,723 |
| 8093 | Specialty outpatient facilities, n.e.c | 6,999 | 7,965 | 8,616 | 9,500 | 10,619 |

*Notes:*
(NA) Not available.
1. Estimates are obtained from a sample of employer firms only.
SIC = Standard Industrial Classification
*General Notes:* Unless otherwise noted, estimates are obtained from a sample of employer and nonemployer firms. For selected SIC's (801, 802, 805, 806, 808, and 809), estimates are for taxable firms only. Firms in all other kinds of business were considered by definition to be subject to Federal income tax. Estimates are not adjusted for price changes. Group totals may include kinds of business not shown separately.

*Source:* U.S. Department of Commerce, Bureau of the Census, *Service Annual Survey: 1997* and *Current Population Reports,* Series P25-1127 and 1095; Table 7.1; <http://www.census.gov/svsd/sasann/view/alltab.pdf>.

## F7-3. Selected Health Services (SIC 80)—Estimated Year-to-Year Percent Change in Receipts for Taxable Firms: 1988–1992

| code | 1987 SIC kind of business | 1988/1987 | 1989/1988 | 1990/1989 | 1991/1990 | 1992/1991 |
|------|---------------------------|-----------|-----------|-----------|-----------|-----------|
| 80 | Health services | 13 | 8.9 | 12.3 | 8.4 | 9.4 |
| 801 | Offices and clinics of doctors of medicine | 12.6 | 7.7 | 9.9 | 7.5 | 9.6 |
| 802 | Offices and clinics of dentists | 8.2 | 7.2 | 7.5 | 5.6 | 11 |
| 803 | Offices and clinics of doctors of osteopathy | 16.7 | 6.5 | 14.9 | 10.1 | 11.8 |
| 804 | Offices and clinics of other health practitioners | 19 | 5.2 | 17.9 | 6.5 | 11.4 |
| 8041 | Offices and clinics of chiropractors | 21.7 | 11 | 9.2 | 3.3 | 16.1 |
| 8042 | Offices and clinics of optometrists | 10.1 | 3.9 | 11.7 | 4.8 | 6.1 |
| 8043 | Offices and clinics of podiatrists | (NA) | (NA) | (NA) | 8.1 | 7.4 |
| 805 | Nursing and personal care facilities | 10.5 | 13.3 | 17.1 | 9 | 5.7 |
| 806 | Hospitals[1] | 12.1 | 6.3 | 12.7 | 8.8 | 7.9 |
| 8062 | General medical and surgical hospitals[1] | (NA) | (NA) | (NA) | 8.7 | 8.7 |
| 8063 | Psychiatric hospitals[1] | (NA) | (NA) | (NA) | 6.6 | –0.1 |
| 8069 | Specialty hospitals, except psychiatric[1] | (NA) | (NA) | (NA) | 14 | 15.6 |
| 807 | Medical and dental laboratories | 19.1 | 15.9 | 16.4 | 12.7 | 11.8 |
| 8071 | Medical laboratories | 26.2 | 18.1 | 18 | 14.6 | 12.4 |
| 8072 | Dental laboratories | –3.3 | 6.6 | 9.2 | 3.5 | 8.6 |
| 808 | Home health care services | 29.3 | 21.9 | 35 | 20.8 | 22.8 |
| 809 | Miscellaneous health and allied services, n.e.c | 18.9 | 19.5 | 12.6 | 12.9 | 1 |
| 8092 | Kidney dialysis centers | (NA) | (NA) | (NA) | 18.3 | 24.6 |
| 8093 | Specialty outpatient facilities, n.e.c | (NA) | (NA) | (NA) | 222 | –0.5 |

*Notes:*
(NA) Not available.
1. Estimates are obtained from a sample of employer firms only.
SIC = Standard Industrial Classification
*General Notes:* Data for 1996 have been revised to reflect the use of 1996 administrative receipts for nonemployer firms. Unless otherwise noted, estimates are obtained from a sample of employer and nonemployer firms. For selected SIC's (801, 802, 805, 806, 808, and 809), estimates are for taxable firms only. Estimates are not adjusted for price changes. Group totals may include kinds of business not shown separately.

*Source:* U.S. Department of Commerce, Bureau of the Census, *Service Annual Survey: 1997* and *Current Population Reports,* Series P25-1127 and 1095; Table 7.2; <http://www.census.gov/svsd/sasann/view/alltab.pdf>.

## F7-4. Selected Health Services (SIC 80)—Estimated Year-to-Year Percent Change in Receipts for Taxable Firms: 1993–1997

| code | 1987 SIC kind of business | 1993/1992 | 1994/1993 | 1995/1994 | 1996/1995 | 1997/1996 |
|------|---------------------------|-----------|-----------|-----------|-----------|-----------|
| 80 | Health services | 4.2 | 4.9 | 7.1 | 5.9 | 5.8 |
| 801 | Offices and clinics of doctors of medicine | 1.6 | 3.5 | 5.2 | 3.0 | 3.9 |
| 802 | Offices and clinics of dentists | 5.4 | 7.0 | 7.8 | 5.6 | 7.5 |
| 803 | Offices and clinics of doctors of osteopathy | 3.8 | 4.7 | 7.9 | 1.1 | 4.3 |
| 804 | Offices and clinics of other health practitioners | 6.2 | 2.1 | 5.7 | 3.8 | 5.1 |
| 8041 | Offices and clinics of chiropractors | 5.8 | −2.6 | −0.2 | 3.9 | 3.7 |
| 8042 | Offices and clinics of optometrists | 7.2 | 5.4 | 1.5 | 3.5 | 2.5 |
| 8043 | Offices and clinics of podiatrists | 2.6 | 1.6 | 9.0 | 2.3 | −1.9 |
| 805 | Nursing and personal care facilities | 4.1 | 3.2 | 10.2 | 7.7 | 6.0 |
| 806 | Hospitals[1] | 7.2 | 5.4 | 9.3 | 16.3 | 12.3 |
| 8062 | General medical and surgical hospitals[1] | 10.4 | 4.9 | 9.7 | 18.9 | 12.1 |
| 8063 | Psychiatric hospitals[1] | −15.2 | 0.9 | 2.2 | −8.8 | 10.5 |
| 8069 | Specialty hospitals, except psychiatric[1] | 15.6 | 16.0 | 14.2 | 20.7 | 14.8 |
| 807 | Medical and dental laboratories | −0.7 | 2.4 | 0.6 | 3.4 | 2.9 |
| 8071 | Medical laboratories | −1.1 | 2.1 | −0.8 | 2.9 | 3.3 |
| 8072 | Dental laboratories | 1.8 | 3.8 | 8.1 | 6.2 | 1.2 |
| 808 | Home health care services | 17.6 | 16.8 | 16.8 | 8.7 | −1.6 |
| 809 | Miscellaneous health and allied services, n.e.c | 14.6 | 13.4 | 10.1 | 11.0 | 13.1 |
| 8092 | Kidney dialysis centers | 15.3 | 17.4 | 12.5 | 4.1 | 9.8 |
| 8093 | Specialty outpatient facilities, n.e.c | 8.1 | 13.8 | 8.2 | 10.3 | 11.8 |

*Notes:*
(NA) Not available.
1. Estimates are obtained from a sample of employer firms only.
SIC = Standard Industrial Classification
*General Notes:* Data for 1996 have been revised to reflect the use of 1996 administrative receipts for nonemployer firms. Unless otherwise noted, estimates are obtained from a sample of employer and nonemployer firms. For selected SIC's (801, 802, 805, 806, 808, and 809), estimates are for taxable firms only. Estimates are not adjusted for price changes. Group totals may include kinds of business not shown separately.

*Source:* U.S. Department of Commerce, Bureau of the Census, *Service Annual Survey: 1997* and *Current Population Reports,* Series P25-1127 and 1095; Table 7.2; <http://www.census.gov/svsd/sasann/view/alltab.pdf>.

## F8. NATIONAL HEALTH EXPENDITURES, BY OBJECT

### F8-1. National Health Expenditures, by Object, Totals: 1990–1996, in Billions of Dollars

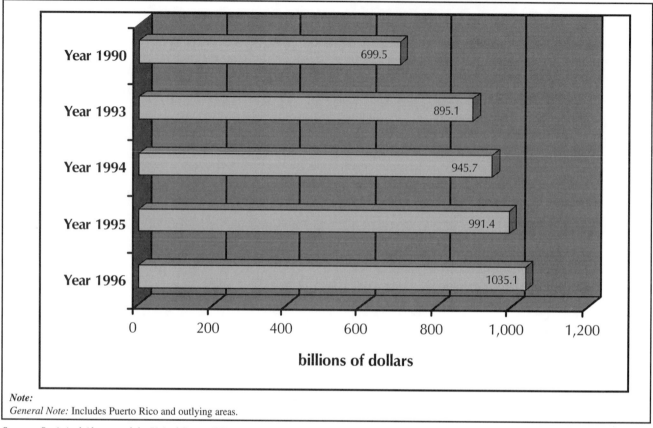

Note:

General Note: Includes Puerto Rico and outlying areas.

Source: Statistical Abstract of the United States 1998, No. 165; <http://www.census.gov/statab/freq/98s0165.txt>. Underlying data from U.S. Health Care Financing Administration, Health Care Financing Review, fall 1997; <http://www.hcfa.gov/stats/stats.htm>.

## F8-2. National Health Expenditures, by Object: 1990–1996, in Billions of Dollars

| OBJECT OF EXPENDITURE | 1990 | 1993 | 1994 | 1995 | 1996 |
|---|---|---|---|---|---|
| **Total** | **699.5** | **895.1** | **945.7** | **991.4** | **1035.1** |
| **Spent by** | | | | | |
| Consumers | 383.0 | 466.9 | 480.5 | 493.6 | 508.5 |
|   Out-of-pocket | 144.4 | 163.6 | 164.8 | 166.7 | 171.2 |
|   Private insurance | 238.6 | 303.3 | 315.6 | 326.9 | 337.3 |
| Government | 284.4 | 389.0 | 423.9 | 455.2 | 483.1 |
| Other[1] | 32.1 | 39.2 | 41.3 | 42.6 | 43.5 |
| | | | | | |
| **Spent for** | | | | | |
| Health services and supplies | 675.0 | 866.1 | 915.2 | 960.7 | 1003.6 |
|   Personal health care expenses | 614.7 | 787.0 | 828.5 | 869.0 | 907.2 |
|     Hospital care | 256.4 | 323.0 | 335.7 | 346.7 | 358.5 |
|     Physician services | 146.3 | 183.6 | 190.4 | 196.4 | 202.1 |
|     Dental services | 31.6 | 39.1 | 41.7 | 44.7 | 47.6 |
|     Other professional services[2] | 34.7 | 46.3 | 50.3 | 54.3 | 58.0 |
|     Home health care | 13.1 | 22.9 | 25.6 | 28.4 | 30.2 |
|     Drugs/other medical nondurables | 59.9 | 75.6 | 79.5 | 84.9 | 91.4 |
|     Vision products/other med. Durables[3] | 10.5 | 12.3 | 12.5 | 13.1 | 13.3 |
|     Nursing home care | 50.9 | 66.3 | 70.9 | 75.2 | 78.5 |
|     Other health services | 11.2 | 18.0 | 21.9 | 25.3 | 27.6 |
|   Net cost of insurance and admin.[4] | 40.7 | 53.8 | 58.2 | 60.1 | 60.9 |
|   Government public health activities | 19.6 | 25.3 | 28.5 | 31.5 | 35.5 |
| Medical research[5] | 12.2 | 14.5 | 15.9 | 16.7 | 17.0 |
| Medical facilities construction | 12.3 | 14.5 | 14.6 | 14.0 | 14.5 |

*Notes:*

1. Includes nonpatient revenues, privately funded construction, and industrial inplant.

2. Includes services of registered and practical nurses in private duty, podiatrists, optometrists, physical therapists, clinical psychologists, chiropractors, naturopaths, and Christian Science practitioners.

3. Includes expenditures for eyeglasses, hearing aids, orthopedic appliances, artificial limbs, crutches, wheelchairs, etc.

4. Includes administrative expenses of federally financed health programs.

5. Research and development expenditures of drug companies and other manufacturers and providers of medical equipment and supplies are excluded from research expenditures, but are included in the expenditure class in which the product falls.

*General Note:* Includes Puerto Rico and outlying areas.

*Source: Statistical Abstract of the United States 1998*, No. 165; <http://www.census.gov/statab/freq/98s0165.txt>. Underlying data from U.S. Health Care Financing Administration, *Health Care Financing Review,* fall 1997; <http://www.hcfa.gov/stats/stats.htm>.

## F9. HEALTH SERVICES AND SUPPLIES—PER CAPITA CONSUMER EXPENDITURES, BY OBJECT

**F9-1. Health Services and Supplies—Per Capita Consumer Expenditures, by Object, Totals: 1980–1996, in Dollars**

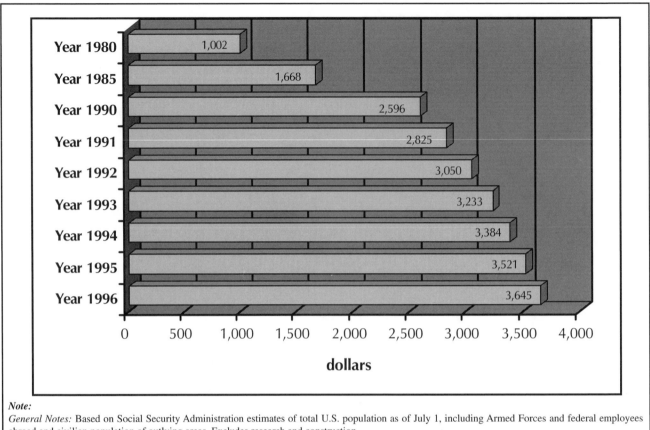

**Note:**
*General Notes:* Based on Social Security Administration estimates of total U.S. population as of July 1, including Armed Forces and federal employees abroad and civilian population of outlying areas. Excludes research and construction.

*Source: Statistical Abstract of the United States 1998,* No. 166; <http://www.census.gov/prod/3/98pubs/98statab/sasec3.pdf>. Underlying data from U.S. Health Care Financing Administration, *Health Care Financing Review,* fall 1997.

## F9-2. Health Services and Supplies—Per Capita Consumer Expenditures, by Object: 1980–1991, in Dollars (except percent.)

| OBJECT OF EXPENDITURE | 1980 | 1985 | 1990 | 1991 |
|---|---|---|---|---|
| Total, national | 1,002 | 1,668 | 2,596 | 2,825 |
|   Annual percent change[1] | 13.9 | 9.3 | 11.1 | 8.8 |
| Hospital care | 437 | 681 | 986 | 1,075 |
| Physicians' services | 192 | 338 | 563 | 618 |
| Dentists' services | 57 | 88 | 121 | 127 |
| Other professional services[2] | 27 | 67 | 133 | 146 |
| Home health care | 10 | 23 | 50 | 61 |
| Drugs and other medical nondurables | 92 | 150 | 230 | 250 |
| Vision products and other medical durables[2] | 16 | 27 | 40 | 43 |
| Nursing home care | 75 | 124 | 196 | 218 |
| Other health services | 17 | 25 | 43 | 52 |
| Net cost of insurance and administration[2] | 50 | 98 | 157 | 156 |
| Government public health activities | 29 | 47 | 75 | 82 |
|   Total, private consumer[3] | 553 | 945 | 1,473 | 1,565 |
| Hospital care | 178 | 274 | 404 | 422 |
| Physicians' services | 135 | 234 | 381 | 421 |
| Dentists' services | 54 | 85 | 117 | 122 |
| Other professional services[2] | 19 | 50 | 99 | 106 |
| Home health care | 4 | 8 | 23 | 26 |
| Drugs and other medical nondurables | 85 | 137 | 205 | 220 |
| Vision products and other medical durables[2] | 13 | 21 | 29 | 29 |
| Nursing home care | 32 | 58 | 92 | 97 |
| Net cost of insurance | 33 | 76 | 123 | 122 |

*Notes:*
1. Change from immediate prior year.
2. Includes services of registered and practical nurses in private duty, podiatrists, optometrists, physical therapists, clinical psychologists, chiropractors, naturopaths, and Christian Science practitioners.
3. Represents out-of-pocket payments and private health insurance.
*General Notes:* Based on Social Security Administration estimates of total U.S. population as of July 1, including Armed Forces and federal employees abroad and civilian population of outlying areas. Excludes research and construction.

*Source: Statistical Abstract of the United States 1998*, No. 166; <http://www.census.gov/prod/3/98pubs/98statab/sasec3.pdf>. Underlying data from U.S. Health Care Financing Administration, *Health Care Financing Review,* fall 1997.

## F9-3. Health Services and Supplies—Per Capita Consumer Expenditures, by Object: 1992–1996, in Dollars (except percent)

| OBJECT OF EXPENDITURE | 1992 | 1993 | 1994 | 1995 | 1996 |
|---|---|---|---|---|---|
| Total, national | 3,050 | 3,233 | 3,384 | 3,521 | 3,645 |
| Annual percent change[1] | 8 | 6 | 4.7 | 4 | 3.5 |
| Hospital care | 1,151 | 1,206 | 1,241 | 1,270 | 1,302 |
| Physicians' services | 663 | 685 | 704 | 720 | 734 |
| Dentists' services | 140 | 146 | 154 | 164 | 173 |
| Other professional services[2] | 159 | 173 | 186 | 199 | 211 |
| Home health care | 74 | 86 | 97 | 105 | 110 |
| Drugs and other medical nondurables | 268 | 282 | 294 | 311 | 332 |
| Vision products and other medical durables[2] | 45 | 46 | 46 | 48 | 48 |
| Nursing home care | 235 | 248 | 262 | 276 | 285 |
| Other health services | 58 | 67 | 81 | 93 | 100 |
| Net cost of insurance and administration[2] | 170 | 201 | 215 | 220 | 221 |
| Government public health activities | 88 | 95 | 105 | 116 | 129 |
| Total, private consumer[3] | 1,666 | 1,743 | 1,777 | 1,809 | 1,847 |
| Hospital care | 436 | 451 | 446 | 444 | 445 |
| Physicians' services | 454 | 466 | 473 | 472 | 477 |
| Dentists' services | 134 | 138 | 146 | 156 | 164 |
| Other professional services[2] | 115 | 124 | 132 | 140 | 148 |
| Home health care | 30 | 33 | 35 | 34 | 33 |
| Drugs and other medical nondurables | 237 | 247 | 256 | 268 | 284 |
| Vision products and other medical durables[2] | 30 | 30 | 29 | 28 | 27 |
| Nursing home care | 99 | 98 | 101 | 105 | 104 |
| Net cost of insurance | 132 | 156 | 162 | 162 | 163 |

*Notes:*
1. Change from immediate prior year.
2. Includes services of registered and practical nurses in private duty, podiatrists, optometrists, physical therapists, clinical psychologists, chiropractors, naturopaths, and Christian Science practitioners.
3. Represents out-of-pocket payments and private health insurance.
General Notes: Based on Social Security Administration estimates of total U.S. population as of July 1, including Armed Forces and federal employees abroad and civilian population of outlying areas. Excludes research and construction.

*Source: Statistical Abstract of the United States 1998*, No. 166; <http://www.census.gov/prod/3/98pubs/98statab/sasec3.pdf>. Underlying data from U.S. Health Care Financing Administration, *Health Care Financing Review*, fall 1997.

## F10. LIFE INSURANCE PURCHASES IN THE UNITED STATES

### F10-1. Life Insurance Purchases in the United States—Number: 1980–1996

| | Number of Policies Purchased (in thousands) | | | |
|---|---|---|---|---|
| Year | Total | Ordinary | Group | Industrial |
| 1980 | 29,007 | 14,750 | 11,379 | 2,878 |
| 1985 | 33,880 | 17,104 | 16,243 | 533 |
| 1990 | 28,791 | 14,066 | 14,592 | 133 |
| 1991 | 29,813 | 13,471 | 16,230 | 112 |
| 1992 | 28,382 | 13,350 | 14,930 | 102 |
| 1993 | 31,238 | 13,574 | 17,574 | 90 |
| 1994 | 31,955 | 13,780 | 18,061 | 114 |
| 1995 | 31,485 | 13,268 | 18,105 | 112 |
| 1996 | 29,908 | 12,246 | 17,575 | 87 |

*Note:*
*General Notes:* Excludes revivals, increases, dividend additions, and reinsurance acquired. Includes long-term credit insurance (life insurance on loans of more than 10 years' duration).

*Source: Statistical Abstract of the United States 1998*, No 853; <http://wwwcensusgov/prod/3/98pubs/98statab/sasec16pdf>. Underlying data from American Council of Life Insurance, Washington, DC, *Life Insurance Fact Book*, annual (copyright).

## F10-2. Life Insurance Purchases in the United States—Value of Amount Purchased: 1980–1996

| | Amount Purchased (billion dollars) | | | |
|---|---|---|---|---|
| Year | Total | Ordinary | Group | Industrial |
| 1980 | 573 | 386 | 183 | 4 |
| 1985 | 1231[1] | 911 | 320[1] | 1 |
| 1990 | 1,529 | 1,070 | 459 | (Z) |
| 1991 | 1616[2] | 1,042 | 574[2] | (Z) |
| 1992 | 1,489 | 1,048 | 441 | (Z) |
| 1993 | 1,678 | 1,101 | 577 | (Z) |
| 1994 | 1,657 | 1,107 | 550 | (Z) |
| 1995 | 1,600 | 1,101 | 499 | (Z) |
| 1996 | 1,700 | 1,118 | 581 | (Z) |

*Notes:*
Z Less than $500 million.
1. Includes Federal Employees' Group Life Insurance: $11 billion in 1985.
2. Includes Servicemen's Group Life Insurance: $167 billion in 1991.
General Notes: Excludes revivals, increases, dividend additions, and reinsurance acquired Includes long-term credit insurance (life insurance on loans of more than 10 years' duration).

*Source: Statistical Abstract of the United States 1998*, No 853; <http://wwwcensusgov/prod/3/98pubs/98statab/sasec16pdf>. Underlying data from American Council of Life Insurance, Washington, DC, *Life Insurance Fact Book,* annual (copyright).

## F11. AUTOMOBILE INSURANCE—AVERAGE EXPENDITURES PER INSURED VEHICLE

### F11-1. Automobile Insurance—Average Expenditures per Insured Vehicle, Totals: 1994–1996, in Dollars

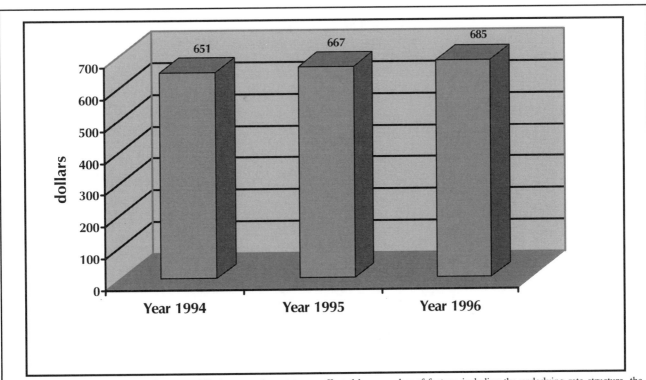

*Notes:* The average expenditures for automobile insurance in a state are affected by a number of factors, including the underlying rate structure, the coverages purchased, the deductibles and limits selected, the type of vehicles insured, and the distribution of driver characteristics.

*Source: Statistical Abstract of the United States 1998*, No 851; <http://wwwcensusgov/prod/3/98pubs/98statab/sasec16pdf>L. Underlying data from National Association of Insurance Commissioners, Kansas City, MO, *State Average Expenditures and Premiums for Personal Automobile Insurance,* annual (copyright).

## F11-2. Automobile Insurance—Average Expenditures per Insured Vehicle, by State: 1994–1996, in Dollars

| STATE | 1994 | 1995 | 1996 |
|---|---|---|---|
| Alabama | 524 | 549 | 578 |
| Alaska | 720 | 730 | 751 |
| Arizona | 731 | 727 | 785 |
| Arkansas | 507 | 500 | 558 |
| California | 791 | 794 | 791 |
| Colorado | 721 | 722 | 751 |
| Connecticut | 863 | 881 | 899 |
| Delaware | 776 | 784 | 806 |
| District of Columbia | 924 | 959 | 993 |
| Florida | 656 | 739 | 783 |
| Georgia | 564 | 597 | 627 |
| Hawaii | 962 | 963 | 959 |
| Idaho | 445 | 447 | 465 |
| Illinois | 587 | 612 | 638 |
| Indiana | 529 | 542 | 548 |
| Iowa | 422 | 429 | 445 |
| Kansas | 459 | 474 | 495 |
| Kentucky | 526 | 555 | 581 |
| Louisiana | 767 | 788 | 802 |
| Maine | 471 | 472 | 470 |
| Maryland | 712 | 732 | 759 |
| Massachusetts | 938 | 898 | 833 |
| Michigan | 665 | 645 | 697 |
| Minnesota | 620 | 628 | 654 |
| Mississippi | 557 | 579 | 604 |
| Missouri | 549 | 573 | 599 |
| Montana | 460 | 468 | 479 |
| Nebraska | 436 | 452 | 475 |
| Nevada | 748 | 759 | 803 |
| New Hampshire | 617 | 609 | 612 |
| New Jersey | 964 | 1,013 | 1,099 |
| New Mexico | 628 | 639 | 660 |
| New York | 870 | 906 | 960 |
| North Carolina | 462 | 501 | 518 |
| North Dakota | 368 | 381 | 402 |
| Ohio | 517 | 531 | 553 |
| Oklahoma | 503 | 526 | 545 |
| Oregon | 566 | 565 | 585 |
| Pennsylvania | 657 | 667 | 687 |
| Rhode Island | 861 | 870 | 870 |
| South Carolina | 582 | 582 | 602 |
| South Dakota | 396 | 428 | 448 |
| Tennessee | 500 | 519 | 557 |
| Texas | 714 | 711 | 726 |
| Utah | 540 | 547 | 581 |
| Vermont | 503 | 512 | 514 |
| Virginia | 515 | 553 | 550 |
| Washington | 654 | 650 | 666 |
| West Virginia | 619 | 646 | 671 |
| Wisconsin | 496 | 506 | 533 |
| Wyoming | 422 | 433 | 452 |

*Notes:* The average expenditures for automobile insurance in a state are affected by a number of factors, including the underlying rate structure, the coverages purchased, the deductibles and limits selected, the type of vehicles insured, and the distribution of driver characteristics.

*Source: Statistical Abstract of the United States 1998*, No 851; <http://wwwcensusgov/prod/3/98pubs/98statab/sasec16pdf>. Underlying data from National Association of Insurance Commissioners, Kansas City, MO, *State Average Expenditures and Premiums for Personal Automobile Insurance,* annual (copyright).

# G. Consumption—Travel, Leisure, and Other Non-Essentials

## GENERAL OVERVIEW

This section details the more discretionary aspect of individual consumption in the United States. It explores travel and leisure time activity, such as entertainment and sports, along with spending on charity and philanthropy.

The data presented here offer the user a highly detailed account of non-essential spending in the United States. The data are presented across a wide variety of variables, including such features as age, income level, and regional and state-by-state comparisons. This exploration of travel, leisure, and other non-essential consumption patterns rounds out the picture of the U.S. consumer painted in this volume.

## EXPLANATION OF INDICATORS

**G1. Travel by U.S. Residents:** The first grouping (two charts and two tables) presents detailed information on amount of travel in the United States. The first two charts present a time series (1985 to 1997) across two variables: total trips and person trips (the number of individual trips taken alone or with other parties). The two tables that follow break down the yearly totals into business, pleasure, and vacation trips, allowing users to gain a broad understanding of travel trends in recent years.

**G2. Characteristics of Trips:** The two tables that follow, one on travel for business and one on travel for pleasure, present various characteristics of business and pleasure trips, including such elements as average household members on trip and renting a car while traveling. These data are presented for selected years across a 13-year period (1985 to 1997).

**G3. Domestic Travel Expenditures, by State:** The next table presents expenditures on travel on a state-by-state basis. Presenting a snapshot at mid-decade (1995), the data help to illustrate regional trends in travel spending.

**G4. Media Usage and Consumer Spending:** The next grouping—two sets of one chart and two tables each—presents the amount of usage and spending from 1990 to 1998 across various media categories, including television, radio, newspapers, and books. The first set covers media usage in terms of average hours per person per year and the next set includes media spending in the same terms. The data in these sets allow users to explore the extent to which the U.S. consumer relies on media for entertainment, communications, and other purposes, and the exact types of media that occupy the most time and command the most of the average consumer's budget.

**G5. Books, Quantity Sold, and Expenditure:** The next two charts, each coupled with a table, show the volume of consumer book consumption across a 15-year span, from 1982 to 1996, both in terms of number of units purchased and amount of money spent. The charts show the total units and dollars and the tables break down the totals into various categories of book publishing, such as trade, reference, textbooks, etc.

**G6. Book Purchasing by Adults—Total, Mass Market, Trade, and Hardcover:** The next two tables show the percentage of purchases in each category—mass market, trade, and hardcover—against the total. Two years, 1991 and 1996, are shown, allowing the user to make comparisons over the short-term time span. Each category is analyzed according to a set of variables that includes age, size of household, and income level, among others.

**G7. Newspapers—Number and Circulation:** The next two tables show the number and circulation of daily and Sunday newspapers, by state. They present a snapshot of the most recent year available, 1997. The daily newspaper table also shows circulation per capita, which helps the user to compare daily consumption of newspapers across regional boundaries in terms of the population.

**G8. Expenditures per Consumer Unit for Entertainment and Reading:** The next two charts and two tables present data on expenses relating to entertainment and reading for an 11-year time span, from 1985 to 1995. The two charts present summary totals on a year-by-year basis of both spending on entertainment and on reading, and the next two tables present detailed analysis of those categories across several variables such as age, ethnicity, regional location, and household size.

**G9. Profile of Consumer Expenditures for Sound Recordings:** The next chart and table outline patterns of purchasing for sound recordings for selected years in the eight-year time span from 1990 to 1997. The chart presents summary totals for each year, and several variables, such as age, gender, and type of retail outlet, are analyzed on a year-by-year basis in the table.

**G10. Recent Trends in Dolls, Toys, and Games:** The next two tables present data on other forms of entertainment including dolls, toys, and games for an eight-year time span from 1991 to 1997. They offer information on total sales according to product classification and industry classification.

**G11. Motion Pictures and Amusement and Recreation Services—Estimated Receipts:** The next group—two charts and four tables—presents sales receipts for the 10-year time span from 1988 to 1997 for motion pictures and amusement services. The charts show the yearly totals for both motion pictures and amusement/recreation services. The tables show both aggregate and per capita figures, and detail the sales receipts for various specific types of entertainment in the two general categories.

**G12. Amusement Parks—Estimated Receipts by Source:** The next two tables present greater detail concerning the sources of revenue, and by implication, spending, at amusement parks. The tables chart the five-year time span, from 1993 to 1997, and break down the sales receipts into admission fees, beverages, etc. The first table shows dollar amounts, and the second table represents the share of total amusement park revenue coming from each source.

**G13. Selected Recreational Activities:** The next tables present details concerning various types of recreational activity—including motion pictures as well as sports—for selected years from 1975 to 1996. The tables

present the yearly activity in terms of several variables such as number of participants, number of establishments, and dollar value of expenditures. The 22-year time span helps the user to analyze long-term trends in these selected recreation categories.

**G14. Selected Spectator Sports:** The next four tables show data on attendance, number of teams or participants, and players' salaries in various spectator sports from baseball and football to rodeo and greyhound racing. Covering a 12-year period from 1985 to 1996, the details help users to analyze the trends in recent years regarding not just attendance but structure and expenditures in the most popular spectator sports.

**G15. Participation in Selected Sports Activities:** The next three tables present a snapshot of participation in a wide variety of sports activities for 1996. The first shows the total participation level for each type of activity, and then shows totals by gender; the next table shows participation by age level; and the third table shows participation by income level. These three sets of variables help the user to analyze the factors that contribute to different levels of participation, and by implication, consumption regarding various sport activities.

**G16. Household Pet Ownership:** The next table presents a variety of data concerning pet ownership in the U.S. The data offer a snapshot of a recent year, 1996, and cover categories such as number of households owning pets, percent of all households owning pets, average number of pets owned, and percent of households owning pets according to household income. Further, the above variables are broken down by type of pet, offering the user extensive detail on this area of discretionary household consumption.

**G17. Charity and Philanthropy:** The next group of four tables presents details concerning spending on charity. The first two tables show the average dollar amount and percent of household income contributed from 1991 to 1995; they also present data according to the age of the respondent. The next two tables show trends in philanthropy over a 17-year period from 1980 to 1996. They detail the sources of funds—individuals, foundations, corporations, and charitable bequests—and show how those funds are allocated to specific areas of endeavor, including activities such as religion, education, and the arts.

## G1. TRAVEL BY U.S. RESIDENTS

## G1-1. Travel by U.S. Residents—Summary: 1985–1997, in Millions

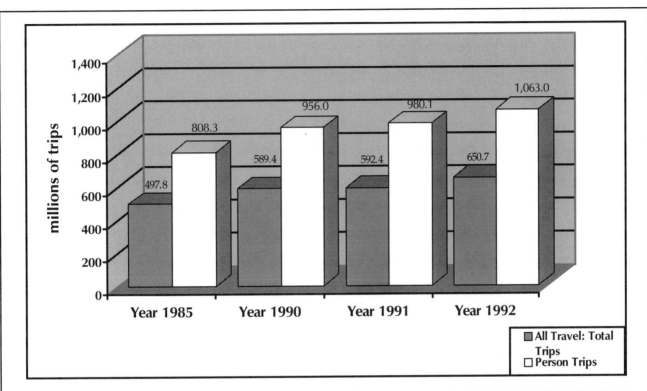

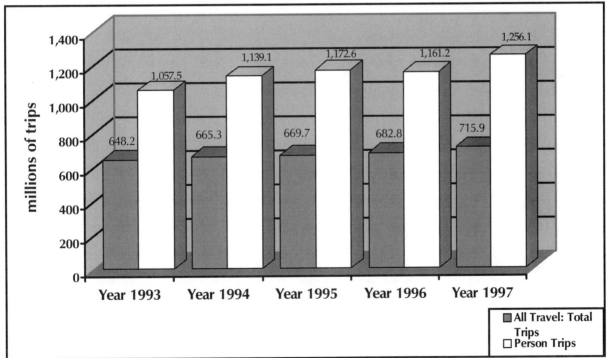

**Notes:**

*General Notes:* Represents trips to places 100 miles or more from home by one or more household members traveling together. Based on a monthly telephone survey of 1,500 U.S. adults. The next two tables present year-to-year detail concerning the kind of travel completed: business, pleasure, and vacation. Total travel may include other trips, not shown separately.

*Source: Statistical Abstract of the United States 1998*, No. 450;<http://www.census.gov/prod/3/98pubs/98statab/sasec7.pdf>. Underlying data from Travel Industry Association of America, Washington, DC, *National Travel Survey*, annual, (copyright).

## G1-2. Travel by U.S. Residents—Summary: 1985–1992, in Millions (except party size)

| TYPE OF TRIP | 1985 | 1990 | 1991 | 1992 |
|---|---|---|---|---|
| All travel: Total trips * | 497.8 | 589.4 | 592.4 | 650.7 |
| Person trips | 808.3 | 956 | 980.1 | 1,063.00 |
| Party size | 1.6 | 1.6 | 1.7 | 1.6 |
| | | | | |
| Business travel: Total trips | 156.6 | 182.8 | 176.9 | 210.8 |
| Person trips | 196.1 | 221.8 | 224 | 278 |
| Party size | 1.3 | 1.2 | 1.3 | 1.3 |
| | | | | |
| Pleasure travel: Total trips | 301.2 | 361.1 | 364.3 | 411.7 |
| Person trips | 539.5 | 649.4 | 666.6 | 736.4 |
| Party size | 1.8 | 1.8 | 1.8 | 1.8 |
| | | | | |
| Vacation travel: Total trips | 264.5 | 328.7 | 327.7 | 352.8 |
| Person trips | 487.8 | 591.6 | 605.3 | 637.1 |
| Party size | 1.8 | 1.8 | 1.9 | 1.8 |

*Notes:*
\* Includes other trips, not shown separately.
*General Notes:* Represents trips to places 100 miles or more from home by one or more household members traveling together. Based on a monthly telephone survey of 1,500 U.S. adults.

*Source: Statistical Abstract of the United States 1998*, No. 450; <http://www.census.gov/prod/3/98pubs/98statab/sasec7.pdf>. Underlying data from Travel Industry Association of America, Washington, DC, *National Travel Survey*, annual, (copyright).

## G1-3. Travel by U.S. Residents—Summary: 1993–1997, in Millions (except party size)

| TYPE OF TRIP | 1993 | 1994 | 1995 | 1996 | 1997 |
|---|---|---|---|---|---|
| All travel: Total trips * | 648.2 | 665.3 | 669.7 | 682.8 | 715.9 |
| Person trips | 1,057.50 | 1,139.10 | 1,172.60 | 1,161.20 | 1,256.10 |
| Party size | 1.6 | 1.7 | 1.8 | 1.7 | 1.8 |
| | | | | | |
| Business travel: Total trips | 210.4 | 193.2 | 207.8 | 192.8 | 207.4 |
| Person trips | 275.4 | 246.7 | 275.2 | 251.2 | 275.5 |
| Party size | 1.3 | 1.3 | 1.3 | 1.3 | 1.3 |
| | | | | | |
| Pleasure travel: Total trips | 413.4 | 434.3 | 413 | 432.5 | 443.2 |
| Person trips | 740 | 781.2 | 809.5 | 807.8 | 862.4 |
| Party size | 1.8 | 1.8 | 1.9 | 1.9 | 1.9 |
| | | | | | |
| Vacation travel: Total trips | 352.2 | 343.4 | 349.7 | 375.5 | 388.6 |
| Person trips | 633.2 | 664.6 | 680.4 | 706.1 | 751.8 |
| Party size | 1.8 | 1.9 | 1.9 | 1.9 | 1.9 |

*Notes:*
\* Includes other trips, not shown separately.
*General Notes:* Represents trips to places 100 miles or more from home by one or more household members traveling together. Based on a monthly telephone survey of 1,500 U.S. adults.

*Source: Statistical Abstract of the United States 1998*, No. 450; <http://www.census.gov/prod/3/98pubs/98statab/sasec7.pdf>. Underlying data from Travel Industry Association of America, Washington, DC, *National Travel Survey*, annual, (copyright).

# G2. CHARACTERISTICS OF TRIPS

## G2-1. Characteristics of Business Trips: 1985–1997

| CHARACTERISTIC | Unit | 1985 | 1990 | 1995 | 1997 |
|---|---|---|---|---|---|
| Total trips | Millions | 156.6 | 182.8 | 207.8 | 207.4 |
| Average household members on trip | Number | 1.3 | 1.2 | 1.3 | 1.3 |
| Average nights per trip * | Nights | 3.6 | 3.7 | 3.1 | 3.2 |
| Average miles per trip** | Miles | 1,180 | 1,020 | 1,022 | 1,128 |
| Traveled primarily by auto/truck/RV/ rental car | Percent | 51 | 58 | 63 | 60 |
| Traveled primarily by air | Percent | 44 | 37 | 35 | 38 |
| Used a rental car while on trip | Percent | 20 | 14 | 22 | 25 |
| Stayed in a hotel while on trip. | Percent | 62 | 71 | 66 | 65 |
| Used a travel agent | Percent | 28 | 21 | 24 | 27 |
| Also a vacation trip | Percent | 13 | 17 | 14 | 18 |
| Male travelers | Percent | 67 | 71 | 74 | 70 |
| Female travelers | Percent | 33 | 29 | 26 | 30 |
| Household income : | | | | | |
| Less than $40,000 | Percent | 58 | 42 | 25 | 25 |
| $40,000 or more | Percent | 42 | 56 | 75 | 75 |

*Notes:*
* Includes no overnight stays.
** United States only.
*** Recreational vehicle.
*General Notes:* Represents trips to places 100 miles or more from home by one or more household members traveling together. Based on a monthly telephone survey of 1,500 U.S. adults.

*Source: Statistical Abstract of the United States 1998,* No. 451; <http://www.census.gov/prod/3/98pubs/98statab/sasec7.pdf>. Underlying data from Travel Industry Association of America, Washington, DC, *National Travel Survey,* annual, (copyright).

## G2-2. Characteristics of Pleasure Trips: 1985–1997

| CHARACTERISTIC | Unit | 1985 | 1990 | 1995 | 1997 |
|---|---|---|---|---|---|
| Total trips | Millions | 301.2 | 361.1 | 413.0 | 443.2 |
| Average household members on trip | Number | 1.8 | 1.8 | 1.9 | 1.9 |
| Average nights per trip * | Nights | 5.6 | 4.4 | 3.8 | 3.8 |
| Average miles per trip** | Miles | 1,010 | 867 | 781 | 901 |
| Traveled primarily by auto/truck/RV/ rental car | Percent | 73 | 77 | 84 | 80 |
| Traveled primarily by air | Percent | 21 | 18 | 13 | 16 |
| Used a rental car while on trip | Percent | 6 | 7 | 8 | 9 |
| Stayed in a hotel while on trip. | Percent | 39 | 37 | 39 | 39 |
| Used a travel agent | Percent | 13 | 12 | 9 | 11 |
| Also a vacation trip | Percent | 80 | 82 | 74 | 74 |
| Male travelers | Percent | 48 | 49 | 53 | 53 |
| Female travelers | Percent | 52 | 51 | 47 | 47 |
| Household income : | | | | | |
| Less than $40,000 | Percent | 73 | 63 | 47 | 42 |
| $40,000 or more | Percent | 27 | 38 | 53 | 58 |

*Notes:*
* Includes no overnight stays.
** United States only.
*** Recreational vehicle.
*General Notes:* Represents trips to places 100 miles or more from home by one or more household members traveling together. Based on a monthly telephone survey of 1,500 U.S. adults.

*Source: Statistical Abstract of the United States 1998,* No. 451; <http://www.census.gov/prod/3/98pubs/98statab/sasec7.pdf>. Underlying data from Travel Industry Association of America, Washington, DC, *National Travel Survey,* annual, (copyright).

## G3. DOMESTIC TRAVEL EXPENDITURES, BY STATE

### G3-1. Domestic Travel Expenditures, by State: 1995

| State | Total (in million dollars) | Share of total (in percent) | Rank |
|---|---|---|---|
| United States | 360,314 | 100.0 | (X) |
| Alabama | 4,092 | 1.0 | 28 |
| Alaska | 1,157 | 0.3 | 46 |
| Arizona | 6,333 | 1.8 | 19 |
| Arkansas | 3,078 | 0.7 | 34 |
| California | 46,672 | 13.8 | 1 |
| Colorado | 6,707 | 1.7 | 17 |
| Connecticut | 3,810 | 1.0 | 30 |
| Delaware | 886 | 0.2 | 50 |
| Dist. of Columbia | 3,245 | 1.2 | 31 |
| Florida | 30,879 | 10.2 | 2 |
| Georgia | 10,457 | 2.7 | 9 |
| Hawaii | 6,434 | 3.1 | 18 |
| Idaho | 1,650 | 0.4 | 41 |
| Illinois | 15,852 | 4.1 | 5 |
| Indiana | 4,634 | 1.2 | 26 |
| Iowa | 3,172 | 0.8 | 33 |
| Kansas | 2,729 | 0.7 | 38 |
| Kentucky | 4,034 | 1.0 | 29 |
| Louisiana | 6,059 | 1.6 | 21 |
| Maine | 1,600 | 0.4 | 42 |
| Maryland | 5,667 | 1.4 | 22 |
| Massachusetts | 8,031 | 2.3 | 14 |
| Michigan | 8,396 | 2.1 | 13 |
| Minnesota | 4,931 | 1.2 | 24 |
| Mississippi | 3,185 | 0.8 | 32 |
| Missouri | 6,989 | 1.7 | 16 |
| Hawaii | 1,546 | 0.4 | 43 |
| Nebraska | 2,058 | 0.5 | 39 |
| Nevada | 15,006 | 4.0 | 6 |
| New Hampshire | 1,676 | 0.4 | 40 |
| New Jersey | 11,708 | 2.9 | 7 |
| New Mexico | 2,931 | 0.7 | 37 |
| New York | 21,647 | 7.0 | 4 |
| North Carolina | 9,056 | 2.2 | 12 |
| North Dakota | 897 | 0.2 | 49 |
| Ohio | 9,641 | 2.4 | 11 |
| Oklahoma | 3,015 | 0.7 | 36 |
| Oregon | 4,263 | 1.1 | 27 |
| Pennsylvania | 11,186 | 2.9 | 8 |
| Rhode Island | 744 | 0.2 | 51 |
| South Carolina | 5,366 | 1.4 | 23 |
| South Dakota | 909 | 0.2 | 48 |
| Tennessee | 7,679 | 1.9 | 15 |
| Texas | 22,562 | 6.1 | 3 |
| Utah | 3,046 | 0.8 | 35 |
| Vermont | 1,136 | 0.3 | 47 |
| Virginia | 9,996 | 2.5 | 10 |
| Washington | 6,060 | 1.7 | 20 |
| West Virginia | 1,467 | 0.4 | 44 |
| Wisconsin | 4,809 | 1.2 | 25 |
| Wyoming | 1,232 | 0.3 | 45 |

*Notes:*
(X) Not applicable.
*General Notes:* Represents U.S. spending on domestic overnight trips and day trips of 100 miles or more away from home. Excludes spending by foreign visitors and by U.S. residents in U.S. territories and abroad.

*Source: Statistical Abstract of the United States 1998*, No. 453; <http://www.census.gov/prod/3/98pubs/98statab/sasec7.pdf>. Underlying data from Travel Industry Association of America, Washington, DC, *Impact of Travel on State Economies,* 1995 (copyright).

## G4. MEDIA USAGE AND CONSUMER SPENDING

### G4-1. Media Usage: 1990–1998 (projected)

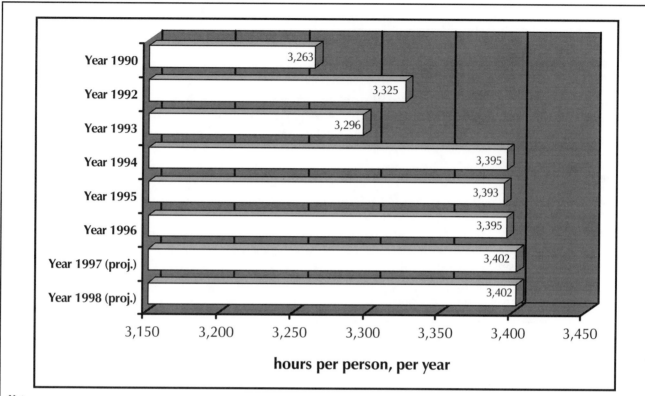

**hours per person, per year**

*Notes:*

*General Notes:* Estimates of time spent were derived using rating data for television and radio, survey research and consumer purchase data for recorded music, newspapers, magazines, books, home video, admissions for movies, and consumer online/Internet access services. Adults 18 and older except for recorded music, movies in theaters, and video games where estimates include persons 12 years and older.

*Source:* Veronis, Suhler & Associates Inc, New York, NY, *Veronis, Suhler & Associates Communications Industry Forecast*, annual, 1998 (copyright).

## G4-2. Media Usage: 1990–1994

| ITEM | 1990 | 1992 | 1993 | 1994 |
|---|---|---|---|---|
| **HOURS PER PERSON PER YEAR** | | | | |
| Total | 3,263 | 3,324 | 3,295 | 3,393 |
| Television | 1,470 | 1,510 | 1,535 | 1,560 |
| Broadcast TV | 1,120 | 1,073 | 1,082 | 1,091 |
| Network stations[1] | 780 | 914 | 920 | 919 |
| Independent stations | 340 | 159 | 162 | 172 |
| Subscription video services | 350 | 437 | 453 | 469 |
| Basic networks[2] | 260 | 359 | 375 | 388 |
| Premium channels | 90 | 78 | 78 | 81 |
| Radio | 1,135 | 1,150 | 1,082 | 1,102 |
| Recorded music | 235 | 233 | 248 | 294 |
| Daily newspapers | 175 | 172 | 170 | 169 |
| Consumer books | 95 | 100 | 99 | 102 |
| Consumer magazines | 90 | 85 | 85 | 84 |
| Home video[3] | 38 | 42 | 43 | 45 |
| Movies in theaters | 12 | 11 | 12 | 12 |
| Home video games | 12 | 19 | 19 | 22 |
| Consumer online Internet access | 1 | 2 | 2 | 3 |

*Notes:*
1. Affiliates of the Fox network are counted as network affiliates for part of 1991 and all latter years, but as independent stations in earlier years. Beginning in 1995, includes UPN and WB affiliates.
2. Includes TBS beginning in 1992.
3. Playback of prerecorded tapes only.
*General Notes:* Estimates of time spent were derived using rating data for television and radio, survey research and consumer purchase data for recorded music, newspapers, magazines, books, home video, admissions for movies, and consumer online/Internet access services. Adults 18 and older except for recorded music, movies in theaters, and video games where estimates include persons 12 years and older.

*Source:* Veronis, Suhler & Associates Inc, New York, NY, *Veronis, Suhler & Associates Communications Industry Forecast*, annual, 1998 (copyright).

## G4-3. Media Usage: 1995–1998 (projected)

| ITEM | 1995 | 1996 | 1997 | 1998 |
|---|---|---|---|---|
| **HOURS PER PERSON PER YEAR** | | | | |
| Total | 3,391 | 3,393 | 3,368 | 3,368 |
| Television | 1,575 | 1,567 | 1,561 | 1,560 |
| Broadcast TV | 1,019 | 980 | 926 | 882 |
| Network stations[1] | 836 | 803 | 748 | 704 |
| Independent stations | 183 | 177 | 178 | 178 |
| Subscription video services | 556 | 587 | 635 | 678 |
| Basic networks[2] | 468 | 498 | 537 | 580 |
| Premium channels | 88 | 89 | 98 | 98 |
| Radio | 1,091 | 1,091 | 1,082 | 1,075 |
| Recorded music | 289 | 289 | 265 | 260 |
| Daily newspapers | 165 | 161 | 159 | 157 |
| Consumer books | 99 | 99 | 92 | 95 |
| Consumer magazines | 84 | 83 | 82 | 82 |
| Home video[3] | 45 | 49 | 50 | 52 |
| Movies in theaters | 12 | 12 | 13 | 13 |
| Home video games | 24 | 26 | 36 | 39 |
| Consumer online Internet access | 7 | 16 | 28 | 35 |

*Notes:*
1. Affiliates of the Fox network are counted as network affiliates for part of 1991 and all latter years, but as independent stations in earlier years. Beginning in 1995, includes UPN and WB affiliates.
2. Includes TBS beginning in 1992.
3. Playback of prerecorded tapes only.
*General Notes:* Estimates of time spent were derived using rating data for television and radio, survey research and consumer purchase data for recorded music, newspapers, magazines, books, home video, admissions for movies, and consumer online/Internet access services. Adults 18 and older except for recorded music, movies in theaters, and video games where estimates include persons 12 years and older.

*Source:* Veronis, Suhler & Associates Inc, New York, NY, *Veronis, Suhler & Associates Communications Industry Forecast*, annual, 1998 (copyright).

## G4-4. Consumer Spending on Media: 1990–1998 (projected)

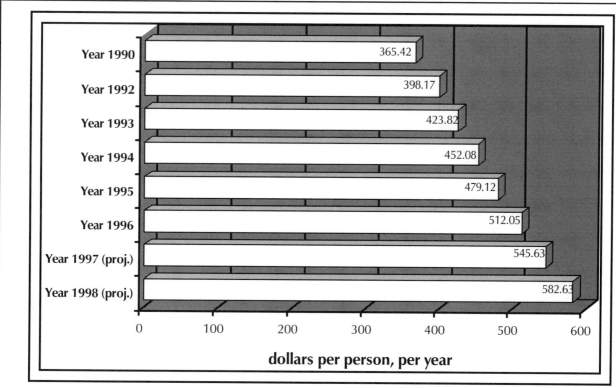

Notes:

*General Notes:* Estimates of time spent were derived using rating data for television and radio, survey research and consumer purchase data for recorded music, newspapers, magazines, books, home video, admissions for movies, and consumer online/Internet access services. Adults 18 and older except for recorded music, movies in theaters, and video games where estimates include persons 12 years and older.

*Source: Statistical Abstract of the United States 1998*, No. 914; <http://wwwcensusgov/prod/3/98pubs/98statab/sasec18pdf>. Underlying data from Veronis, Suhler & Associates Inc, New York, NY, *Communications Industry Report*, annual (copyright).

## G4-5. Consumer Spending on Media: 1990–1994

| ITEM | 1990 | 1992 | 1993 | 1994 |
|---|---|---|---|---|
| **CONSUMER SPENDING PER PERSON PER YEAR (dol.)** | | | | |
| Total | 365.42 | 398.17 | 423.82 | 452.08 |
| Television | 87.90 | 101.39 | 109.02 | 110.89 |
| Broadcast TV | (-) | (-) | (-) | (-) |
| Subscription video services | 87.90 | 101.39 | 109.02 | 110.89 |
| Radio | (-) | (-) | (-) | (-) |
| Recorded music | 36.64 | 43.05 | 47.42 | 56.35 |
| Daily newspapers | 47.55 | 48.54 | 48.25 | 49.12 |
| Consumer books | 63.90 | 71.39 | 75.28 | 80.28 |
| Consumer magazines | 33.14 | 34.26 | 35.27 | 36.36 |
| Home video[3] | 56.35 | 59.25 | 64.17 | 68.96 |
| Movies in theaters | 24.40 | 23.24 | 24.33 | 25.20 |
| Home video games | 12.39 | 11.51 | 12.56 | 13.15 |
| Consumer on-line Internet access | 2.93 | 4.39 | 5.35 | 7.44 |
| Educational software | 0.22 | 1.14 | 2.17 | 4.34 |

*Notes:

(-) Represents zero.

3. Playback of prerecorded tapes only

*General Notes:* Estimates of time spent were derived using rating data for television and radio, survey research and consumer purchase data for recorded music, newspapers, magazines, books, home video, admissions for movies, and consumer online/Internet access services. Adults 18 and older except for recorded music, movies in theaters, and video games where estimates include persons 12 years and older.

*Only notes that apply to this table are cited.

*Source: Statistical Abstract of the United States 1998*, No. 914; <http://wwwcensusgov/prod/3/98pubs/98statab/sasec18pdf>. Underlying data from Veronis, Suhler & Associates Inc, New York, NY, *Communications Industry Report*, annual (copyright).

## G4-6. Consumer Spending on Media: 1995–1998 (projected)

| ITEM | 1995 | 1996 | 1997, proj. | 1998, proj. |
|---|---|---|---|---|
| **CONSUMER SPENDING PER PERSON PER YEAR (dol.)** | | | | |
| Total | 479.12 | 512.05 | 545.63 | 582.63 |
| Television | 125.54 | 140.37 | 155.70 | 168.75 |
| Broadcast TV | (-) | (-) | (-) | (-) |
| Subscription video services | 125.54 | 140.37 | 155.70 | 168.75 |
| Radio | (-) | (-) | (-) | (-) |
| Recorded music | 56.93 | 57.33 | 59.21 | 61.54 |
| Daily newspapers | 50.08 | 50.95 | 51.59 | 52.62 |
| Consumer books | 81.39 | 82.98 | 84.67 | 88.09 |
| Consumer magazines | 36.10 | 36.63 | 37.22 | 37.92 |
| Home video[3] | 70.99 | 77.43 | 82.51 | 88.79 |
| Movies in theaters | 25.39 | 27.04 | 26.39 | 26.62 |
| Home video games | 13.34 | 14.92 | 16.86 | 18.59 |
| Consumer on-line Internet access | 15.03 | 20.01 | 27.23 | 35.30 |
| Educational software | 4.34 | 4.38 | 4.26 | 4.43 |

*Notes:*
(-) Represents zero.
3. Playback of prerecorded tapes only
*General Notes:* Estimates of time spent were derived using rating data for television and radio, survey research and consumer purchase data for recorded music, newspapers, magazines, books, home video, admissions for movies, and consumer online/Internet access services. Adults 18 and older except for recorded music, movies in theaters, and video games where estimates include persons 12 years and older.
*Only notes that apply to this table are cited.

*Source: Statistical Abstract of the United States 1998*, No. 914; <http://wwwcensusgov/prod/3/98pubs/98statab/sasec18pdf>. Underlying data from Veronis, Suhler & Associates Inc, New York, NY, *Communications Industry Report*, annual (copyright).

## G5. BOOKS, QUANTITY SOLD AND EXPENDITURE

## G5-1. Books, Quantity Sold, Totals: 1982–1996, in Millions of Units

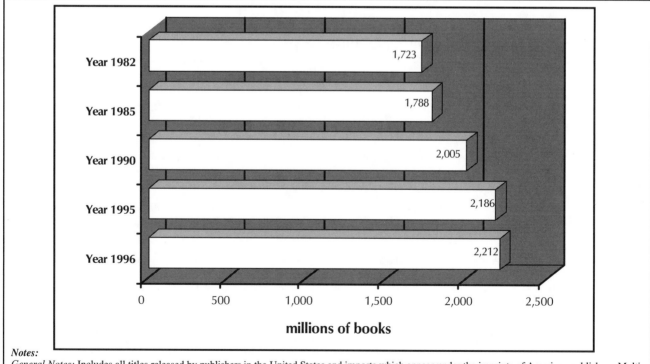

*Notes:*
*General Notes:* Includes all titles released by publishers in the United States and imports which appear under the imprints of American publishers. Multi-volume sets, such as encyclopedias, are counted as one unit.

*Source: Statistical Abstract of the United States 1998*, No. 428; <http://www.census.gov/prod/3/98pubs/98statab/sasec7.pdf>. Underlying data from Book Industry Study Group, Inc, New York, NY, *Book Industry Trends,* 1997, annual (copyright).

## G5-2. Books, Quantity Sold: 1982–1996, in Millions of Units

| Type of publication and market area | 1982 | 1985 | 1990 | 1995 | 1996 |
|---|---|---|---|---|---|
| Total * | 1,723 | 1,788 | 2,005 | 2,186 | 2,212 |
| Hardbound, total | 646 | 694 | 824 | 827 | 837 |
| Softbound, total | 1,077 | 1,094 | 1,181 | 1,359 | 1,375 |
| Trade | 459 | 553 | 705 | 813 | 819 |
| Adult | 315 | 360 | 403 | 465 | 440 |
| Juvenile | 144 | 193 | 301 | 348 | 379 |
| Religious | 144 | 134 | 130 | 148 | 155 |
| Professional | 106 | 110 | 131 | 146 | 144 |
| Bookclubs | 133 | 130 | 108 | 123 | 132 |
| Elhi text | 233 | 234 | 209 | 237 | 245 |
| College text | 115 | 110 | 137 | 142 | 150 |
| Mail order publications | 134 | 121 | 138 | 92 | 93 |
| Mass market paperbacks-racksized | 382 | 382 | 433 | 470 | 458 |
| General retailers | 756 | 829 | 1,010 | 1,145 | 1,153 |
| College stores | 224 | 225 | 255 | 274 | 275 |
| Libraries and institutions ** | 80 | 80 | 88 | 97 | 96 |
| Schools ** | 262 | 260 | 244 | 273 | 281 |
| Direct to consumers | 319 | 300 | 304 | 289 | 299 |
| Other | 82 | 94 | 104 | 108 | 108 |

*Notes:*
* Types of publications include university press publications and subscription reference works, not shown separately.
** Elhi libraries included in schools.
*General Notes:* Includes all titles released by publishers in the United States and imports which appear under the imprints of American publishers. Multi-volume sets, such as encyclopedias, are counted as one unit.

*Source: Statistical Abstract of the United States 1998*, No. 428; <http://www.census.gov/prod/3/98pubs/98statab/sasec7.pdf>. Underlying data from Book Industry Study Group, Inc, New York, NY, *Book Industry Trends*, 1997, annual (copyright).

## G5-3. Books, Consumer Expenditures, Totals: 1982–1996, in Millions of Dollars

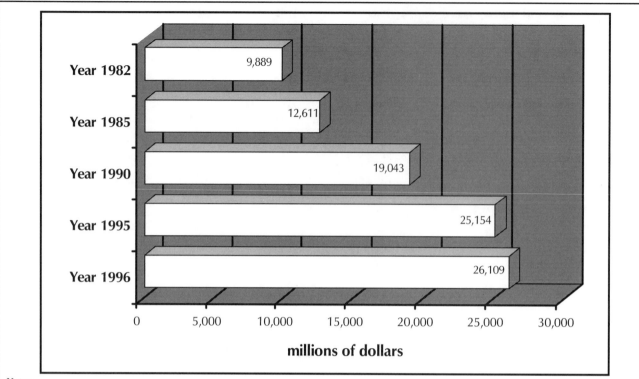

**Notes:**

*General Notes:* Includes all titles released by publishers in the United States and imports which appear under the imprints of American publishers. Multi-volume sets, such as encyclopedias, are counted as one unit.

*Source: Statistical Abstract of the United States 1998,* No. 428; <http://www.census.gov/prod/3/98pubs/98statab/sasec7.pdf>. Underlying data from Book Industry Study Group, Inc, New York, NY, *Book Industry Trends,* 1997, annual (copyright).

## G5-4. Books, Consumer Expenditures: 1982–1996, in Millions of Dollars

| Type of publication and market area | 1982 | 1985 | 1990 | 1995 | 1996 |
|---|---|---|---|---|---|
| Total * | 9,889 | 12,611 | 19,043 | 25,154 | 26,109 |
| Hardbound, total | 6,190 | 7,969 | 11,789 | 15,011 | 15,468 |
| Softbound, total | 3,699 | 4,642 | 7,254 | 10,143 | 10,641 |
| Trade | 2,484 | 3,660 | 6,498 | 9,340 | 9,474 |
| Adult | 2,028 | 2,871 | 4,777 | 7,060 | 6,925 |
| Juvenile | 456 | 789 | 1,721 | 2,280 | 2,549 |
| Religious | 706 | 926 | 1,362 | 1,792 | 1,909 |
| Professional | 1,630 | 2,043 | 2,957 | 4,153 | 4,288 |
| Bookclubs | 510 | 582 | 705 | 949 | 1,061 |
| Elhi text | 1,067 | 1,415 | 1,948 | 2,384 | 2,522 |
| College text | 1,388 | 1,575 | 2,319 | 2,708 | 2,920 |
| Mail order publications | 581 | 650 | 752 | 578 | 599 |
| Mass market paperbacks-racksized | 1,102 | 1,244 | 1,775 | 2,322 | 2,374 |
| General retailers | 3,743 | 5,103 | 8,465 | 11,888 | 12,211 |
| College stores | 1,910 | 2,309 | 3,403 | 4,311 | 4,528 |
| Libraries and institutions ** | 888 | 1,090 | 1,592 | 2,111 | 2,169 |
| Schools ** | 1,313 | 1,685 | 2,365 | 2,896 | 3,060 |
| Direct to consumers | 1,889 | 2,214 | 2,901 | 3,544 | 3,745 |
| Other | 146 | 210 | 316 | 404 | 396 |

**Notes:**

\* Types of publications include university press publications and subscription reference works, not shown separately.

\*\* Elhi libraries included in schools.

*General Notes:* Includes all titles released by publishers in the United States and imports which appear under the imprints of American publishers. Multi-volume sets, such as encyclopedias, are counted as one unit.

*Source: Statistical Abstract of the United States 1998,* No. 428; <http://www.census.gov/prod/3/98pubs/98statab/sasec7.pdf>. Underlying data from Book Industry Study Group, Inc, New York, NY, *Book Industry Trends,* 1997, annual (copyright).

# G6. BOOK PURCHASING BY ADULTS—TOTAL, MASS MARKET, TRADE, AND HARDCOVER

## G6-1. Book Purchasing by Adults, Total and Mass Market: 1991 and 1996, in Percent

| CHARACTERISTIC | TOTAL | TOTAL | MASS MARKET* | MASS MARKET* |
|---|---|---|---|---|
| | **1991** | **1996** | **1991** | **1996** |
| **Total** | 100.0 | 100.0 | 100.0 | 100.0 |
| **Age of purchaser:** | | | | |
| Under 25 years old | 4.3 | 3.9 | 3.7 | 3.6 |
| 25 to 34 years old | 18.8 | 15.7 | 13.9 | 13.7 |
| 35 to 44 years old | 23.7 | 25.9 | 22.8 | 22.1 |
| 45 to 54 years old | 22.4 | 22.3 | 26.0 | 21.5 |
| 55 to 64 years old | 15.6 | 15.6 | 15.8 | 16.5 |
| 65 years old and over | 15.2 | 16.6 | 17.8 | 22.6 |
| **Household income:** | | | | |
| Under $30,000 | 37.1 | 32.7 | 41.7 | 40.9 |
| $30,000 to 49,999 | 27.2 | 23.8 | 27.3 | 22.4 |
| $50,000 to 59,999 | 11.0 | 7.9 | 9.8 | 6.9 |
| $60,000 to 69,999 | 6.9 | 9.1 | 7.0 | 7.9 |
| $70,000 and over | 17.8 | 26.5 | 14.2 | 21.9 |
| **Household size:** | | | | |
| Singles | 20.8 | 18.7 | 17.7 | 20.1 |
| Families with no children | 40.4 | 43.4 | 42.3 | 42.1 |
| Families with children | 38.8 | 37.9 | 40.0 | 37.8 |
| **Age of reader:** | | | | |
| Under 25 years old | 7.3 | 6.9 | 5.2 | 5.1 |
| 25 to 34 years old | 18.7 | 16.6 | 14.1 | 14.2 |
| 35 to 44 years old | 22.9 | 24.8 | 22.3 | 21.6 |
| 45 to 54 years old | 20.8 | 20.2 | 24.9 | 20.0 |
| 55 to 64 years old | 14.9 | 14.4 | 15.9 | 16.9 |
| 65 years old and over | 15.4 | 17.1 | 17.6 | 22.2 |
| **Category of book:** | | | | |
| Popular fiction | 54.9 | 50.9 | 93.0 | 93.6 |
| General nonfiction | 10.3 | 9.4 | 3.6 | 2.7 |
| Cooking/crafts | 10.2 | 10.2 | 0.4 | 0.4 |
| Other | 24.6 | 29.5 | 3.0 | 3.3 |
| **Sales outlet:** | | | | |
| Independent | 32.5 | 18.6 | 26.5 | 11.3 |
| Chain book store | 22.0 | 25.6 | 17.2 | 22.0 |
| Book clubs | 16.6 | 18.0 | 17.8 | 18.7 |
| Other *** | 28.9 | 37.8 | 38.5 | 48.0 |

*Notes:*
* "Pocket size" books sold primarily through magazine and news outlets, supermarkets, variety stores, etc.
*** Includes mail order, price clubs, discount stores, food/drug stores, used book stores, and other outlets.
*General Notes:* Excludes books purchased for or by children under age 13. Based on a survey of 16,000 households conducted over 12 months ending in December of year shown.

*Source: Statistical Abstract of the United States 1998*, No. 429; <http://www.census.gov/prod/3/98pubs/98statab/sasec7.pdf>. Underlying data from Book Industry Study Group, Inc, New York, NY, *Consumer Research Study on Book Purchasing*, annual (copyright).

## G6-2. Book Purchasing by Adults, Trade and Hardcover: 1991 and 1996, in Percent

| CHARACTERISTIC | TRADE ** 1991 | TRADE ** 1996 | HARDCOVER 1991 | HARDCOVER 1996 |
|---|---|---|---|---|
| **Total** | 100.0 | 100.0 | 100.0 | 100.0 |
| **Age of purchaser:** | | | | |
| Under 25 years old | 5.2 | 4.4 | 4.4 | 3.6 |
| 25 to 34 years old | 25.4 | 17.9 | 19.6 | 14.8 |
| 35 to 44 years old | 25.2 | 29.7 | 23.7 | 26.5 |
| 45 to 54 years old | 18.5 | 21.9 | 20.5 | 23.7 |
| 55 to 64 years old | 13.9 | 14.1 | 17.2 | 16.0 |
| 65 years old and over | 11.8 | 12.0 | 14.6 | 15.4 |
| **Household income:** | | | | |
| Under $30,000 | 32.6 | 28.3 | 34.1 | 27.6 |
| $30,000 to 49,999 | 27.7 | 24.6 | 26.5 | 24.6 |
| $50,000 to 59,999 | 12.3 | 8.4 | 11.5 | 8.3 |
| $60,000 to 69,999 | 7.2 | 9.9 | 6.3 | 9.6 |
| $70,000 and over | 20.2 | 28.8 | 21.6 | 29.9 |
| **Household size:** | | | | |
| Singles | 24.1 | 17.8 | 22.8 | 18.1 |
| Families with no children | 38.0 | 43.2 | 39.7 | 45.1 |
| Families with children | 37.9 | 39.0 | 37.5 | 36.8 |
| **Age of reader:** | | | | |
| Under 25 years old | 10.1 | 9.2 | 7.7 | 6.3 |
| 25 to 34 years old | 24.7 | 19.2 | 20.2 | 16.2 |
| 35 to 44 years old | 24.0 | 28.0 | 22.7 | 25.2 |
| 45 to 54 years old | 16.5 | 19.6 | 18.4 | 21.6 |
| 55 to 64 years old | 12.7 | 11.8 | 15.6 | 14.3 |
| 65 years old and over | 12.0 | 12.2 | 15.6 | 16.4 |
| **Category of book:** | | | | |
| Popular fiction | 14.9 | 14.5 | 31.8 | 40.4 |
| General nonfiction | 15.6 | 12.2 | 16.5 | 14.4 |
| Cooking/crafts | 20.6 | 16.9 | 18.2 | 14.3 |
| Other | 48.9 | 56.4 | 33.5 | 30.9 |
| **Sales outlet:** | | | | |
| Independent | 44.9 | 27.6 | 29.0 | 17.2 |
| Chain book store | 27.4 | 27.6 | 25.2 | 27.7 |
| Book clubs | 9.5 | 13.6 | 22.6 | 22.0 |
| Other *** | 18.2 | 31.2 | 23.2 | 33.1 |

*Notes:*
** All paperbound books, except mass market.
*** Includes mail order, price clubs, discount stores, food/drug stores, used book stores, and other outlets.
*General Notes:* Excludes books purchased for or by children under age 13. Based on a survey of 16,000 households conducted over 12 months ending in December of year shown.

*Source: Statistical Abstract of the United States 1998*, No. 429; <http://www.census.gov/prod/3/98pubs/98statab/sasec7.pdf>. Underlying data from Book Industry Study Group, Inc, New York, NY, *Consumer Research Study on Book Purchasing*, annual (copyright).

## G7. NEWSPAPERS—NUMBER AND CIRCULATION

### G7-1. Daily Newspapers—Number and Circulation, by State: 1997

| State | Daily newspapers, number | Daily newspapers, circulation[1], net paid in 1,000s | Daily newspapers, circulation[1], per capita[2] |
|---|---|---|---|
| United States | 1,509 | 56,728 | 0.21 |
| Alabama | 24 | 678 | 0.15 |
| Alaska | 7 | 112 | 0.18 |
| Arizona | 16 | 767 | 0.16 |
| Arkansas | 31 | 473 | 0.18 |
| California | 95 | 6,118 | 0.19 |
| Colorado | 30 | 1,074 | 0.26 |
| Connecticut | 18 | 769 | 0.23 |
| Delaware | 2 | 147 | 0.19 |
| Dist. of Columbia | 2 | 877 | 1.64 |
| Florida | 42 | 3,013 | 0.20 |
| Georgia | 34 | 1,045 | 0.13 |
| Hawaii | 6 | 226 | 0.18 |
| Idaho | 12 | 219 | 0.17 |
| Illinois | 68 | 2,390 | 0.20 |
| Indiana | 70 | 1,366 | 0.23 |
| Iowa | 38 | 649 | 0.22 |
| Kansas | 47 | 464 | 0.18 |
| Kentucky | 23 | 624 | 0.16 |
| Louisiana | 26 | 734 | 0.16 |
| Maine | 7 | 248 | 0.20 |
| Maryland | 14 | 614 | 0.12 |
| Massachusetts | 33 | 1,726 | 0.28 |
| Michigan | 49 | 1,792 | 0.18 |
| Minnesota | 25 | 901 | 0.19 |
| Mississippi | 23 | 393 | 0.14 |
| Missouri | 45 | 986 | 0.18 |
| Hawaii | 11 | 188 | 0.20 |
| Nebraska | 16 | 452 | 0.27 |
| Nevada | 9 | 302 | 0.17 |
| New Hampshire | 12 | 235 | 0.20 |
| New Jersey | 19 | 1,422 | 0.17 |
| New Mexico | 18 | 295 | 0.16 |
| New York | 68 | 6,491 | 0.35 |
| North Carolina | 47 | 1,362 | 0.17 |
| North Dakota | 10 | 177 | 0.27 |
| Ohio | 84 | 2,528 | 0.22 |
| Oklahoma | 44 | 671 | 0.20 |
| Oregon | 19 | 690 | 0.21 |
| Pennsylvania | 86 | 2,869 | 0.23 |
| Rhode Island | 6 | 237 | 0.24 |
| South Carolina | 15 | 634 | 0.16 |
| South Dakota | 11 | 161 | 0.21 |
| Tennessee | 27 | 888 | 0.16 |
| Texas | 88 | 2,965 | 0.15 |
| Utah | 6 | 322 | 0.15 |
| Vermont | 8 | 126 | 0.21 |
| Virginia | 28 | 2,692 | 0.39 |
| Washington | 24 | 1,181 | 0.20 |
| West Virginia | 22 | 381 | 0.20 |
| Wisconsin | 35 | 965 | 0.18 |
| Wyoming | 9 | 89 | 0.18 |

*Notes:*
1. Circulation figures based on the principal community served by a newspaper which is not necessarily the same location as the publisher's office.
2. Per capita based on estimated resident population as of July 1.
*General Notes:* Number of newspapers as of February 1 the following year. Circulation as of September 30 of the year shown. For English language newspapers only. New York, Massachusetts, and Virginia Sunday newspapers include national circulation.

*Source: Statistical Abstract of the United States 1998*, No. 936; <http://www.census.gov/prod/3/98pubs/98statab/sasec18.pdf>. Underlying data from Editor & Publisher Co, New York, NY, *Editor & Publisher International Year Book,* annual (copyright).

## G7-2. Sunday Newspapers—Number and Circulation, by State: 1997

| State | Sunday newspaper, number | Sunday newspaper, net paid circulation in 1,000s |
|---|---|---|
| United States | 903 | 60,484 |
| Alabama | 20 | 749 |
| Alaska | 5 | 132 |
| Arizona | 11 | 910 |
| Arkansas | 18 | 532 |
| California | 61 | 6,247 |
| Colorado | 16 | 1,294 |
| Connecticut | 12 | 851 |
| Delaware | 2 | 171 |
| Dist. of Columbia | 2 | 1,161 |
| Florida | 36 | 3,875 |
| Georgia | 25 | 1,338 |
| Hawaii | 5 | 258 |
| Idaho | 8 | 237 |
| Illinois | 31 | 2,546 |
| Indiana | 21 | 1,299 |
| Iowa | 11 | 667 |
| Kansas | 15 | 425 |
| Kentucky | 14 | 683 |
| Louisiana | 21 | 827 |
| Maine | 4 | 203 |
| Maryland | 8 | 890 |
| Massachusetts | 14 | 1,658 |
| Michigan | 26 | 2,086 |
| Minnesota | 14 | 1,153 |
| Mississippi | 18 | 403 |
| Missouri | 23 | 1,289 |
| Hawaii | 7 | 196 |
| Nebraska | 6 | 434 |
| Nevada | 4 | 325 |
| New Hampshire | 8 | 251 |
| New Jersey | 16 | 1,718 |
| New Mexico | 13 | 297 |
| New York | 45 | 5,475 |
| North Carolina | 36 | 1,500 |
| North Dakota | 7 | 181 |
| Ohio | 38 | 2,776 |
| Oklahoma | 37 | 813 |
| Oregon | 10 | 711 |
| Pennsylvania | 41 | 3,258 |
| Rhode Island | 3 | 273 |
| South Carolina | 14 | 750 |
| South Dakota | 4 | 134 |
| Tennessee | 16 | 1,077 |
| Texas | 85 | 4,000 |
| Utah | 6 | 365 |
| Vermont | 3 | 102 |
| Virginia | 15 | 1,142 |
| Washington | 16 | 1,275 |
| West Virginia | 11 | 381 |
| Wisconsin | 17 | 1,101 |
| Wyoming | 4 | 65 |

*Notes:*

1. Circulation figures based on the principal community served by a newspaper which is not necessarily the same location as the publisher's office.
*General Notes:* Number of newspapers as of February 1 the following year. Circulation as of September 30 of the year shown. For English language newspapers only. New York, Massachusetts, and Virginia Sunday newspapers include national circulation.

*Source: Statistical Abstract of the United States 1998*, No. 936; <http://www.census.gov/prod/3/98pubs/98statab/sasec18.pdf>. Underlying data from Editor & Publisher Co, New York, NY, *Editor & Publisher International Year Book,* annual (copyright).

## G8. EXPENDITURES PER CONSUMER UNIT FOR ENTERTAINMENT AND READING

**G8-1. Expenditures per Consumer Unit for Entertainment and Reading, Average Annual Figures: 1985–1995, in Dollars (except as indicated)**

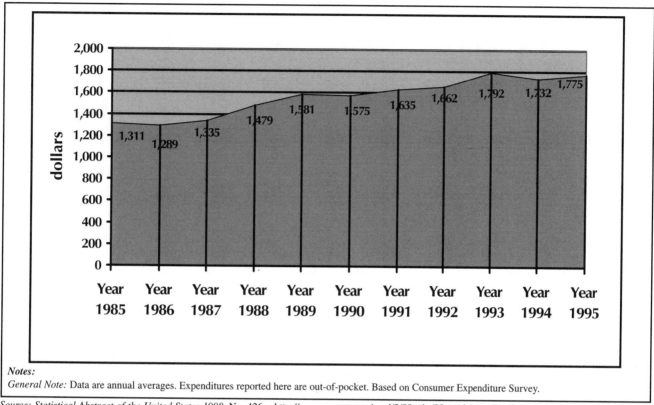

*Notes:*
*General Note:* Data are annual averages. Expenditures reported here are out-of-pocket. Based on Consumer Expenditure Survey.

*Source: Statistical Abstract of the United States 1998*, No. 426; <http://www.census.gov/prod/3/98pubs/98statab/sasec7.pdf. Underlying statistics from U.S. Bureau of Labor Statistics, *Consumer Expenditure Survey,* annual.

## G8-2. Expenditures per Consumer Unit for Entertainment and Reading, Percent of Total Expenditure: 1985–1995 (except as indicated)

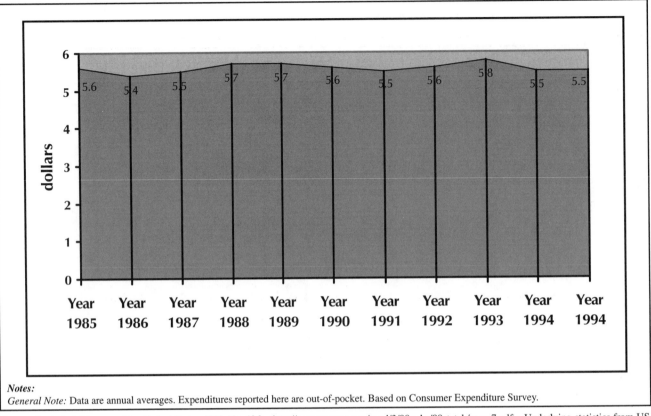

*Notes:*
*General Note:* Data are annual averages. Expenditures reported here are out-of-pocket. Based on Consumer Expenditure Survey.

*Source: Statistical Abstract of the United States 1998*, No. 426; <http://www.census.gov/prod/3/98pubs/98statab/sasec7.pdf>. Underlying statistics from US Bureau of Labor Statistics, *Consumer Expenditure Survey,* annual.

## G8-3. Expenditures per Consumer Unit for Entertainment and Reading: 1985–1995, in Dollars (except as indicated)

| Year | Total | Fees and Admission | Entertainment Television, Radio and Sound Equipment | Other Equipment and Services * | Reading |
|------|-------|--------------------|----------------------------------------------------|-------------------------------|---------|
| 1985 | 1,170 | 320 | 371 | 479 | 141 |
| 1986 | 1,149 | 308 | 371 | 470 | 140 |
| 1987 | 1,193 | 323 | 379 | 491 | 142 |
| 1988 | 1,329 | 353 | 416 | 560 | 150 |
| 1989 | 1,424 | 377 | 429 | 618 | 157 |
| 1990 | 1,422 | 371 | 454 | 597 | 153 |
| 1991 | 1,472 | 378 | 468 | 627 | 163 |
| 1992 | 1,500 | 379 | 492 | 629 | 162 |
| 1993 | 1,626 | 414 | 590 | 621 | 166 |
| 1994 | 1,567 | 439 | 533 | 595 | 165 |
| 1995 | 1,612 | 433 | 542 | 637 | 163 |

*Notes:*
* Other equipment and services includes pets, toys, and playground equipment; sports, exercise, and photographic equipment; and recreational vehicles
*General Note:* Data are annual averages. Expenditures reported here are out-of-pocket. Based on *Consumer Expenditure Survey.*

*Source: Statistical Abstract of the United States 1998*, No. 426; <http://www.census.gov/prod/3/98pubs/98statab/sasec7.pdf>. Underlying statistics from U.S. Bureau of Labor Statistics, *Consumer Expenditure Survey,* annual.

## G8-4. Expenditures per Consumer Unit for Entertainment and Reading, by Characteristic: 1985–1995, in Dollars (except as indicated)

| | Total | Fees and Admission | Entertainment Television, Radio and Sound Equipment | Other Equipment and Services * | Reading |
|---|---|---|---|---|---|
| **Age of reference person:** | | | | | |
| Under 25 years old | 1,081 | 225 | 456 | 400 | 71 |
| 25 to 34 years old | 1,682 | 394 | 580 | 708 | 134 |
| 35 to 44 years old | 1,951 | 531 | 657 | 763 | 173 |
| 45 to 54 years old | 2,138 | 585 | 664 | 889 | 199 |
| 55 to 64 years old | 1,577 | 418 | 492 | 666 | 188 |
| 65 to 74 years old | 1,156 | 377 | 397 | 382 | 180 |
| 75 years old and over | 652 | 223 | 260 | 170 | 138 |
| **Origin of reference person:** | | | | | |
| Hispanic | 1,060 | 231 | 459 | 369 | 74 |
| Non-Hispanic | 1,659 | 450 | 549 | 660 | 170 |
| Black | 935 | 147 | 516 | 273 | 73 |
| Other | 1,747 | 487 | 553 | 708 | 182 |
| **Region of residence:** | | | | | |
| Northeast | 1,544 | 429 | 520 | 595 | 186 |
| Midwest | 1,602 | 419 | 572 | 612 | 170 |
| South | 1,459 | 373 | 514 | 572 | 135 |
| West | 1,939 | 552 | 570 | 816 | 177 |
| **Size of consumer unit:** | | | | | |
| One person | 992 | 265 | 367 | 360 | 120 |
| Two or more persons | 1,856 | 499 | 611 | 747 | 179 |
| Two persons | 1,667 | 459 | 516 | 693 | 187 |
| Three persons | 1,834 | 452 | 618 | 764 | 176 |
| Four persons | 2,187 | 650 | 739 | 797 | 189 |
| Five persons plus | 1,986 | 476 | 701 | 809 | 146 |

*Notes:*

\* Other equipment and services includes pets, toys, and playground equipment; sports, exercise, and photographic equipment; and recreational vehicles

*General Note:* Data are annual averages. Expenditures reported here are out-of-pocket. Based on Consumer Expenditure Survey.

*Source: Statistical Abstract of the United States 1998*, No. 426; <http://www.census.gov/prod/3/98pubs/98statab/sasec7.pdf>. Underlying statistics from U.S. Bureau of Labor Statistics, *Consumer Expenditure Survey,* annual.

## G9. PROFILE OF CONSUMER EXPENDITURES FOR SOUND RECORDINGS

### G9-1. Profile of Consumer Expenditures for Sound Recordings: 1990–1997, in Millions of Dollars

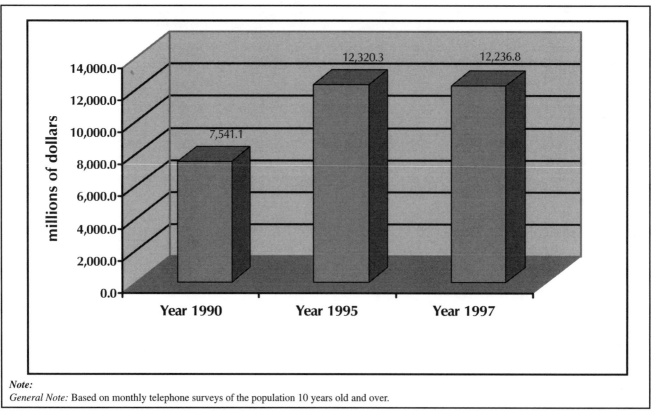

*Note:*
*General Note:* Based on monthly telephone surveys of the population 10 years old and over.

*Source: Statistical Abstract of the United States 1998*, No. 430; <http://www.census.gov/prod/3/98pubs/98statab/sasec7.pdf>. Underlying data from Recording Industry Association of America, Inc, Washington, DC, *1997 Consumer Profile.*

## G9-2. Profile of Consumer Expenditures for Sound Recordings: 1990–1997, in Percent (except total value)

| ITEM | 1990 | 1995 | 1997 |
|---|---|---|---|
| **Total value (mil dol)** | **7541.1** | **12320.3** | **12236.8** |
| **PERCENT DISTRIBUTION *** | | | |
| **Age:** | | | |
| 10 to 14 years | 7.6 | 8.0 | 8.9 |
| 15 to 19 years | 18.3 | 17.1 | 16.8 |
| 20 to 24 years | 16.5 | 15.3 | 13.8 |
| 25 to 29 years | 14.6 | 12.3 | 11.7 |
| 30 to 34 years | 13.2 | 12.1 | 11.0 |
| 35 to 39 years | 10.2 | 10.8 | 11.6 |
| 40 to 44 years | 7.8 | 7.5 | 8.8 |
| 45 years and over | 11.1 | 16.1 | 16.5 |
| **Sex:** | | | |
| Male | 54.4 | 53.0 | 48.6 |
| Female | 45.6 | 47.0 | 51.4 |
| **Sales outlet:** | | | |
| Record store | 69.8 | 52.0 | 51.8 |
| Other store | 18.5 | 28.2 | 31.9 |
| Music club | 8.9 | 14.3 | 11.6 |
| Mail order | 2.5 | 4.0 | 2.7 |
| Internet | (NA) | (NA) | 0.3 |
| **Music type:**** | | | |
| Rock | 36.1 | 33.5 | 32.5 |
| Country | 9.6 | 16.7 | 14.4 |
| R&B | 11.6 | 11.3 | 11.2 |
| Pop | 13.7 | 10.1 | 9.4 |
| Rap | 8.5 | 6.7 | 10.1 |
| Classical | 3.1 | 2.9 | 2.8 |
| Jazz | 4.8 | 3.0 | 2.8 |
| Oldies | 0.8 | 1.0 | 0.8 |
| Gospel | 2.5 | 3.1 | 4.5 |
| Soundtracks | 0.8 | 0.9 | 1.2 |
| New age | 1.1 | 0.7 | 0.8 |
| Children's | 0.5 | 0.5 | 0.9 |
| Other | 5.6 | 7.0 | 5.7 |

*Notes:*
(NA) Not available.
* Percent distributions exclude nonresponses and responses of "don't know."
** As classified by respondent.
*General Note:* Based on monthly telephone surveys of the population 10 years old and over.

*Source: Statistical Abstract of the United States 1998*, No. 430; <http://www.census.gov/prod/3/98pubs/98statab/sasec7.pdf>. Underlying data from Recording Industry Association of America, Inc, Washington, DC, *1997 Consumer Profile.*

## G10. RECENT TRENDS IN DOLLS, TOYS, AND GAMES

### G10-1. Recent Trends in Dolls, Toys, and Games (SIC 3942, 3944): 1991–1993

| ITEM | Unit | 1991 | 1992 | 1993 |
|------|------|------|------|------|
| **INDUSTRY DATA** | | | | |
| Value of shipments[1] | Million dollars | 4,494 | 4,542 | 4,968 |
| 3942 Dolls and stuffed toys | Million dollars | 438 | 251 | 273 |
| 3944 Games and toys | Million dollars | 4,056 | 4,291 | 4,696 |
| Value of shipments (1992 dollars) | Million dollars | 4,570 | 4,542 | 4,954 |
| 3942 Dolls and stuffed toys | Million dollars | 445 | 251 | 268 |
| 3944 Games and toys | Million dollars | 4,126 | 4,291 | 4,686 |
| Total employment | 1,000 | 32.4 | 35.5 | 39 |
| 3942 Dolls and stuffed toys | 1,000 | 5 | 3.6 | 4.2 |
| 3944 Games and toys | 1,000 | 27.4 | 31.9 | 34.8 |
| Production workers | 1,000 | 22.9 | 26.8 | 28.8 |
| 3942 Dolls and stuffed toys | 1,000 | 3.7 | 2.8 | 3.1 |
| 3944 Games and toys | 1,000 | 19.2 | 24 | 25.7 |
| Average hourly earnings | Dollars | 8.56 | 8.43 | 9.03 |
| 3942 Dolls and stuffed toys | Dollars | 9.09 | 6.88 | 6.73 |
| 3944 Games and toys | Dollars | 8.48 | 8.6 | 9.31 |
| Capital expenditures | Million dollars | 107 | 146 | 142 |
| 3942 Dolls and stuffed toys | Million dollars | 11.8 | 3 | 2.7 |
| 3944 Games and toys | Million dollars | 95.4 | 143 | 139 |
| **PRODUCT DATA** | | | | |
| Value of shipments[2] | Million dollars | 3,840 | 3,983 | 4,248 |
| 3942 Dolls and stuffed toys | Million dollars | 399 | 291 | 294 |
| 3944 Games and toys | Million dollars | 3,440 | 3,693 | 3,955 |
| Value of shipments (1992 dollars) | Million dollars | 3,905 | 3,983 | 4,235 |
| 3942 Dolls and stuffed toys | Million dollars | 405 | 291 | 289 |
| 3944 Games and toys | Million dollars | 3,500 | 3,693 | 3,947 |
| Value of imports | Million dollars | 5,752 | 7,111 | 7,897 |
| 3942 Dolls and stuffed toys | Million dollars | 1,466 | 1,661 | 1,687 |
| 3944 Games and toys | Million dollars | 4,286 | 5,450 | 6,210 |
| Value of exports | Million dollars | 568 | 720 | 744 |
| 3942 Dolls and stuffed toys | Million dollars | 39.3 | 54.5 | 45.1 |
| 3944 Games and toys | Million dollars | 529 | 665 | 698 |

*Notes:*
SIC = Standard Industrial Classification
1. Value of all products and services sold by establishments in the dolls, toys, and games industry.
2. Value of products classified in the dolls, toys, and games industry produced by all industries.

*Source: Statistical Abstract of the United States 1998*, No. 1486; <http://www.census.gov/prod/3/98pubs/98statab/sasec31.pdf>. Underlying data from U.S. Department of Commerce, Bureau of the Census, International Trade Administration (ITA).

## G10-2. Recent Trends in Dolls, Toys, and Games (SIC 3942, 3944): 1994–1997

| ITEM | Unit | 1994 | 1995 | 1996 | 1997 |
|---|---|---|---|---|---|
| **INDUSTRY DATA** | | | | | |
| Value of shipments[1] | Million dollars | 4,550 | 5,092 | 4,867 | (NA) |
|    3942 Dolls and stuffed toys | Million dollars | 239 | 227 | 253 | (NA) |
|    3944 Games and toys | Million dollars | 4,311 | 4,866 | 4,614 | (NA) |
| Value of shipments (1992 dollars) | Million dollars | 4,510 | 4,967 | 4,708 | (NA) |
|    3942 Dolls and stuffed toys | Million dollars | 234 | 220 | 246 | (NA) |
|    3944 Games and toys | Million dollars | 4,276 | 4,747 | 4,462 | (NA) |
| Total employment | 1,000 | 35.3 | 38.7 | 36.8 | (NA) |
|    3942 Dolls and stuffed toys | 1,000 | 3.2 | 2.9 | 3.5 | (NA) |
|    3944 Games and toys | 1,000 | 32.1 | 35.8 | 33.3 | (NA) |
| Production workers | 1,000 | 27.5 | 30 | 28.5 | (NA) |
|    3942 Dolls and stuffed toys | 1,000 | 2.5 | 2.2 | 2.6 | (NA) |
|    3944 Games and toys | 1,000 | 25 | 27.8 | 25.9 | (NA) |
| Average hourly earnings | Dollar | 9.31 | 9.58 | 9.59 | (NA) |
|    3942 Dolls and stuffed toys | Dollar | 7.66 | 7.45 | 7.74 | (NA) |
|    3944 Games and toys | Dollar | 9.45 | 9.73 | 9.76 | (NA) |
| Capital expenditures | Million dollars | 140 | 138 | 142 | (NA) |
|    3942 Dolls and stuffed toys | Million dollars | 1.7 | 1.8 | 1 | (NA) |
|    3944 Games and toys | Million dollars | 139 | 136 | 141 | (NA) |
| **PRODUCT DATA** | | | | | |
| Value of shipments[2] | Million dollars | 4,170 | 4,495 | 4,154 | (NA) |
|    3942 Dolls and stuffed toys | Million dollars | 290 | 241 | 265 | (NA) |
|    3944 Games and toys | Million dollars | 3,880 | 4,254 | 3,890 | (NA) |
| Value of shipments (1992 dollars) | Million dollars | 4,132 | 4,384 | 4,019 | (NA) |
|    3942 Dolls and stuffed toys | Million dollars | 283 | 234 | 257 | (NA) |
|    3944 Games and toys | Million dollars | 3,849 | 4,150 | 3,762 | (NA) |
| Value of imports | Million dollars | 7,445 | 8,041 | 9,523 | 12,063 |
|    3942 Dolls and stuffed toys | Million dollars | 1,711 | 2,034 | 2,464 | 3,578 |
|    3944 Games and toys | Million dollars | 5,734 | 6,008 | 7,059 | 8,484 |
| Value of exports | Million dollars | 867 | 916 | 898 | 973 |
|    3942 Dolls and stuffed toys | Million dollars | 56.1 | 59 | 54.5 | 62.6 |
|    3944 Games and toys | Million dollars | 811 | 857 | 844 | 910 |

*Notes:*
SIC = Standard Industrial Classification
(NA) Not available.
1. Value of all products and services sold by establishments in the dolls, toys, and games industry.
2. Value of products classified in the dolls, toys, and games industry produced by all industries.

*Source: Statistical Abstract of the United States 1998*, No. 1486; <http://www.census.gov/prod/3/98pubs/98statab/sasec31.pdf>. Underlying data from U.S. Department of Commerce, Bureau of the Census, International Trade Administration (ITA).

## G11. MOTION PICTURES AND AMUSEMENT AND RECREATION SERVICES—ESTIMATED RECEIPTS

### G11-1. Motion Pictures and Amusement and Recreation Services—Estimated Receipts, Totals: 1988–1997, in Millions of Dollars

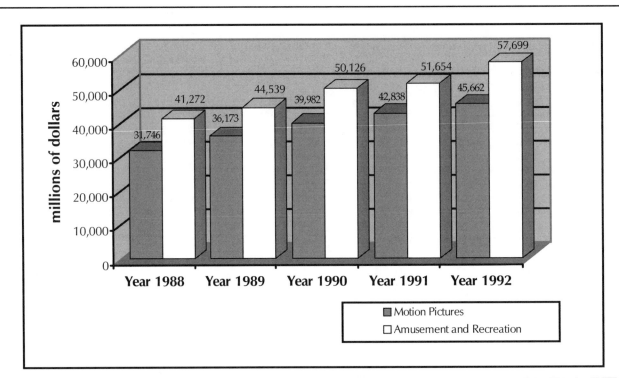

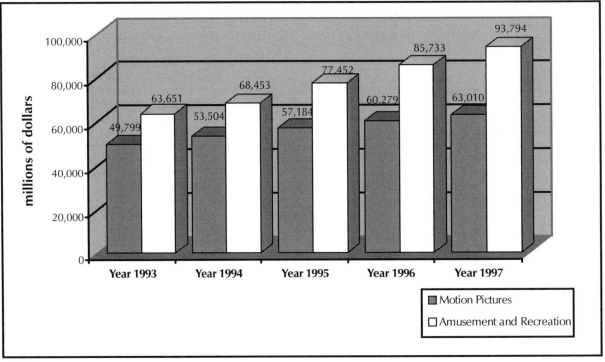

**Notes:**
*General Notes:* Data for 1996 have been revised to reflect the use of 1996 administrative receipts for nonemployer firms. Estimates are for employer and nonemployer firms. For selected SIC's (792, 799, 7991 and 7997), estimates are for taxable firms only. Estimates are not adjusted for price changes. Group totals may include kinds of business not shown separately.

*Source:* U.S. Bureau of the Census, Current Business Reports, *Service Annual Survey: 1996,* BS/96; Table 6.1; <http://www.census.gov/svsd/sasann/view/alltab.pdf>.

## G11-2. Motion Pictures (SIC 78) and Amusement and Recreation Services (SIC 79)—Estimated Receipts: 1988–1992, in Millions of Dollars

| code | 1987 SIC kind of business | 1988 | 1989 | 1990 | 1991 | 1992 |
|------|---------------------------|------|------|------|------|------|
| 78 | **Motion pictures** | 31,746 | 36,173 | 39,982 | 42,838 | 45,662 |
| 781, 782 | Motion picture production, distribution, and allied services | 23,426 | 26,415 | 28,888 | 31,590 | 34,288 |
| 783 | Motion picture theaters | 4,585 | 5,408 | 6,088 | 6,213 | 5,879 |
| 784 | Video tape rental | 3,735 | 4,350 | 5,006 | 5,035 | 5,495 |
| 79 | **Amusement and recreation services** | 41,272 | 44,539 | 50,126 | 51,654 | 57,699 |
| 792 | Theatrical producers (except motion picture), bands, orchestras, and entertainers | 8,555 | 8,447 | 10,735 | 11,694 | 13,054 |
| 793 | Bowling centers | 2,712 | 2,788 | 2,800 | 2,747 | 2,915 |
| 794 | Commercial sports | 6,808 | 7,571 | 8,636 | 8,597 | 9,010 |
| 7941 | Professional sports clubs and promoters | 2,519 | 3,046 | 3,702 | 3,719 | 3,978 |
| 7948 | Racing, including track operation | 4,289 | 4,525 | 4,934 | 4,878 | 5,032 |
| 799 | Miscellaneous amusement and recreation services | 22,401 | 25,032 | 27,329 | 27,954 | 31,936 |
| 7991 | Physical fitness facilities | 3,177 | 3,379 | 3,623 | 3,449 | 4,135 |
| 7992 | Public golf courses | 1,593 | 1,790 | 2,254 | 2,386 | 2,609 |
| 7993 | Coin-operated amusement devices | 1,904 | 1,933 | 2,146 | 2,301 | 2,566 |
| 7996 | Amusement parks | 4,017 | 4,562 | 4,922 | 4,820 | 5,366 |
| 7997 | Membership sports and recreation clubs | 4,239 | 4,457 | 4,825 | 5,151 | 5,397 |

*Notes:*
SIC = Standard Industrial Classification
*General Notes:* Data for 1996 have been revised to reflect the use of 1996 administrative receipts for nonemployer firms. Estimates are for employer and nonemployer firms. For selected SIC's (792, 799, 7991 and 7997), estimates are for taxable firms only. Estimates are not adjusted for price changes. Group totals may include kinds of business not shown separately.

*Source:* U.S. Bureau of the Census, Current Business Reports, *Service Annual Survey: 1996*, BS/96; Table 6.1; <http://www.census.gov/svsd/sasann/view/alltab.pdf>.

## G11-3. Motion Pictures (SIC 78) and Amusement and Recreation Services (SIC 79)—Estimated Receipts: 1993–1997, in Millions of Dollars

| code | 1987 SIC kind of business | 1993 | 1994 | 1995 | 1996 | 1997 |
|------|---------------------------|------|------|------|------|------|
| 78 | **Motion pictures** | 49,799 | 53,504 | 57,184 | 60,279 | 63,010 |
| 781, 782 | Motion picture production, distribution, and allied services | 37,653 | 40,256 | 43,264 | 46,274 | 48,216 |
| 783 | Motion picture theaters | 5,977 | 6,233 | 6,530 | 7,044 | 7,589 |
| 784 | Video tape rental | 6,169 | 7,015 | 7,390 | 6,961 | 7,204 |
| 79 | **Amusement and recreation services** | 63,651 | 68,453 | 77,452 | 85,733 | 93,794 |
| 791 | Dance studios, schools, and halls | 880 | 906 | 947 | 1,046 | 1,075 |
| 792 | Theatrical producers (except motion picture), bands, orchestras, and entertainers | 15,408 | 16,050 | 17,479 | 19,597 | 21,655 |
| 793 | Bowling centers | 2,724 | 2,709 | 2,681 | 2,751 | 2,765 |
| 794 | Commercial sports | 9,870 | 11,090 | 13,056 | 14,589 | 16,669 |
| 7941 | Professional sports clubs and promoters | 5,056 | 6,138 | 7,695 | 8,841 | 10,034 |
| 7948 | Racing, including track operation | 4,814 | 4,952 | 5,360 | 5,748 | 6,635 |
| 799 | Miscellaneous amusement and recreation services | 34,769 | 37,698 | 43,290 | 47,748 | 51,631 |
| 7991 | Physical fitness facilities | 3,961 | 4,033 | 4,412 | 4,975 | 5,713 |
| 7992 | Public golf courses | 2,828 | 3,059 | 3,584 | 3,979 | 4,290 |
| 7993 | Coin-operated amusement devices | 2,763 | 2,965 | 3,254 | 3,491 | 3,651 |
| 7996 | Amusement parks | 5,641 | 5,858 | 6,298 | 6,777 | 7,312 |
| 7997 | Membership sports and recreation clubs | 5,965 | 6,379 | 6,765 | 7,427 | 7657 |

*Notes:*
SIC = Standard Industrial Classification
*General Notes:* Data for 1996 have been revised to reflect the use of 1996 administrative receipts for nonemployer firms. Estimates are for employer and nonemployer firms. For selected SIC's (792, 799, 7991 and 7997), estimates are for taxable firms only. Estimates are not adjusted for price changes. Group totals may include kinds of business not shown separately.

*Source:* U.S. Bureau of the Census, Current Business Reports, *Service Annual Survey: 1996*, BS/96; Table 6.1; <http://www.census.gov/svsd/sasann/view/alltab.pdf>.

## G11-4. Selected Motion Pictures (SIC 78) and Amusement and Recreation Services (SIC 79)—Estimated per Capita Receipts: 1988–1992, in Whole Dollars

| code | 1987 SIC kind of business | 1988 | 1989 | 1990 | 1991 | 1992 |
|------|---------------------------|------|------|------|------|------|
| **Motion Pictures** | | | | | | |
| 783 | Motion picture theaters | 19 | 22 | 25 | 25 | 23 |
| 784 | Video tape rental | 15 | 18 | 20 | 20 | 22 |
| **Amusement and Recreation Services** | | | | | | |
| 793 | Bowling centers | 11 | 11 | 11 | 11 | 12 |
| 7991 | Physical fitness facilities | 13 | 14 | 15 | 14 | 16 |
| 7992 | Public golf courses | 7 | 7 | 9 | 10 | 10 |
| 7993 | Coin-operated amusement devices | 8 | 8 | 9 | 9 | 10 |
| 7996 | Amusement parks | 17 | 19 | 20 | 19 | 21 |

*Notes:*
SIC = Standard Industrial Classification
*General Note:* Estimates are for employer and nonemployer firms. Estimates are not adjusted for price changes. Data for 1996 have been revised to reflect the use of 1996 administrative receipts for nonemployer firms.

*Source:* U.S. Department of Commerce, Bureau of the Census: *Service Annual Survey: 1997* and *Current Population Reports,* Series P25-1127 and 1095; Table 6.5; <http://www.census.gov/svsd/sasann/view/alltab.pdf>.

## G11-5. Selected Motion Pictures (SIC 78) and Amusement and Recreation Services (SIC 79)—Estimated per Capita Receipts: 1993–1997, in Whole Dollars

| code | 1987 SIC kind of business | 1993 | 1994 | 1995 | 1996 | 1997 |
|------|---------------------------|------|------|------|------|------|
| **Motion Pictures** | | | | | | |
| 783 | Motion picture theaters | 23 | 24 | 25 | 26 | 28 |
| 784 | Video tape rental | 24 | 27 | 28 | 26 | 27 |
| **Amusement and Recreation Services** | | | | | | |
| 793 | Bowling centers | 11 | 10 | 10 | 10 | 10 |
| 7991 | Physical fitness facilities | 15 | 16 | 17 | 19 | 21 |
| 7992 | Public golf courses | 11 | 12 | 14 | 15 | 16 |
| 7993 | Coin-operated amusement devices | 11 | 11 | 12 | 13 | 14 |
| 7996 | Amusement parks | 22 | 23 | 24 | 26 | 27 |

*Notes:*
SIC = Standard Industrial Classification
*General Note:* Estimates are for employer and nonemployer firms. Estimates are not adjusted for price changes. Data for 1996 have been revised to reflect the use of 1996 administrative receipts for nonemployer firms.

*Source:* U.S. Department of Commerce, Bureau of the Census: *Service Annual Survey: 1997* and *Current Population Reports,* Series P25-1127 and 1095; Table 6.5; <http://www.census.gov/svsd/sasann/view/alltab.pdf>.

## G12.  AMUSEMENT PARKS—ESTIMATED RECEIPTS BY SOURCE

### G12-1. Amusement Parks (SIC 7996)—Estimated Receipts, by Source: 1993–1997, in Millions of Dollars

| Sources of receipts | 1993 | 1994 | 1995 | 1996 | 1997 |
|---|---|---|---|---|---|
| Total | 5,583 | 5,799 | 6,237 | 6,709 | 7,239 |
| Admissions | 3,009 | 3,112 | 3,404 | 3,685 | 3,948 |
| Sales of food, refreshments, and alcoholic beverages . | 1,066 | 1,074 | 1,148 | 1,202 | 1,277 |
| Sales of other merchandise | 1,110 | 1,097 | 1,186 | 1,261 | 1,293 |
| All other | 398 | 516 | 499 | 561 | 721 |

*Notes:*
SIC = Standard Industrial Classification
*General Notes:* Estimates are for employer firms only. Detail may not add to total due to rounding. Estimates are not adjusted for price changes.

*Source:* U.S. Bureau of the Census, Current Business Reports, *Service Annual Survey: 1996*, BS/96; Table 6.3; <http://www.census.gov/svsd/sasann/view/alltab.pdf>.

### G12-2. Amusement Parks (SIC 7996)— Estimated Sources of Receipts as a Percent of Total Dollar Volume: 1993–1997

| Sources of receipts | 1993 | 1994 | 1995 | 1996 | 1997 |
|---|---|---|---|---|---|
| Total | 100 | 100 | 100 | 100 | 100 |
| Admissions | 53.9 | 53.7 | 54.6 | 54.9 | 54.5 |
| Sales of food, refreshments, and alcoholic beverages | 19.1 | 18.5 | 18.4 | 17.9 | 17.6 |
| Sales of other merchandise | 19.9 | 18.9 | 19.0 | 18.8 | 17.9 |
| All other | 7.1 | 8.9 | 8.0 | 8.4 | 10.0 |

*Notes:*
SIC = Standard Industrial Classification
General Notes: Estimates are for employer firms only. Detail may not add to total due to rounding. Estimates are not adjusted for price changes.

*Source:* U.S. Bureau of the Census, Current Business Reports, *Service Annual Survey: 1996*, BS/96; Table 6.4; <http://www.census.gov/svsd/sasann/view/alltab.pdf>.

## G13. SELECTED RECREATIONAL ACTIVITIES

### G13-1. Selected Recreational Activities: 1975–1990

| ACTIVITY | Unit | 1975 | 1980 | 1985 | 1990 |
|---|---|---|---|---|---|
| **Softball, amateur:** | | | | | |
| Total participants | Million | 26 | 30 | 41 | 41 |
|   Youth participants | 1,000 | 450 | 650 | 712 | 1,100 |
|   Adult teams | 1,000 | 66 | 110 | 152 | 188 |
|   Youth teams | 1,000 | 9 | 18 | 31 | 46 |
| **Golfers (one round or more)** | 1,000 | 13,036 | 15,112 | 17,520 | 27,800 |
| Golf rounds played | 1,000 | 308,562 | 357,701 | 414,777 | 502,000 |
| Golf facilities | Number | 11,370 | 12,005 | 12,346 | 12,846 |
|   Classification: | | | | | |
|    Private | Number | 4,770 | 4,839 | 4,861 | 4,810 |
|    Daily fee | Number | 5,014 | 5,372 | 5,573 | 6,024 |
|    Municipal | Number | 1,586 | 1,794 | 1,912 | 2,012 |
| **Tennis:** | | | | | |
|   Players | 1,000 | 34,000 | (NA) | 13,000 | 21,000 |
|   Courts | 1,000 | 130 | (NA) | 220 | 220 |
|    Indoor | 1,000 | 8 | (NA) | 14 | 14 |
| **Tenpin bowling:** | | | | | |
|   Participants, total | Million | 62.5 | 72 | 67 | 71 |
|    Male | Million | 29.9 | 34 | 32 | 35.4 |
|    Female | Million | 32.6 | 38 | 35 | 35.6 |
|   Establishments | Number | 8,577 | 8,591 | 8,275 | 7,611 |
|   Lanes | 1,000 | 141 | 154 | 155 | 148 |
|   Membership, total | 1,000 | 8,751 | 9,664 | 8,064 | 6,588 |
|   American Bowling Congress | 1,000 | 4,300 | 4,688 | 3,657 | 3,036 |
|   Women's Bowling Congress | 1,000 | 3,692 | 4,187 | 3,714 | 2,859 |
|   Young American Bowling Alliance | 1,000 | 759 | 789 | 693 | 693 |
| **Motion picture theaters** | 1,000 | 15 | 18 | 21 | 24 |
|   Four-wall | 1,000 | 11 | 14 | 18 | 23 |
|   Drive-in | 1,000 | 4 | 4 | 3 | 1 |
|   Receipts, box office | Mil dol | 2,115 | 2,749 | 3,749 | 5,022 |
|   Admission, average price | Dollars | 2.05 | 2.69 | 3.55 | 4.23 |
|   Attendance | Million | 1,033 | 1,022 | 1,056 | 1,187 |
| **Boating:** | | | | | |
|   Recreational boats owned | 1,000 | (NA) | 11,832 | 13,778 | 15,987 |
|   Retail expenditures on boating | Mil dol | 4,800 | 7,370 | 13,284 | 13,731 |
|   Retail units purchased: | | | | | |
|    Total all boats | 1,000 | (NA) | 570 | 637 | 504 |
|    Outboard boats | 1,000 | (NA) | 290 | 305 | 227 |
|    Inboard boats | 1,000 | (NA) | 8 | 17 | 15 |
|    Sterndrive boats | 1,000 | (NA) | 56 | 115 | 97 |
|    Jet boats | 1,000 | (NA) | 69 | 34 | 19 |
|    Canoes | 1,000 | (NA) | 105 | 79 | 75 |
|    Personal watercraft | 1,000 | (NA) | 21 | 50 | 42 |
|   Boat trailers | 1,000 | (NA) | 176 | 192 | 165 |
|   Outboard motors | 1,000 | (NA) | 315 | 392 | 352 |
|   Sterndrive and inboard engines | 1,000 | (NA) | 88 | 155 | 134 |

*Notes:*
(NA) Not available.

*Source: Statistical Abstract of the United States 1998, No. 437; <http://www.census.gov/prod/3/98pubs/98statab/sasec7.pdf>.*

## G13-2. Selected Recreational Activities: 1993–1996

| ACTIVITY | Unit | 1993 | 1994 | 1995 | 1996 |
|---|---|---|---|---|---|
| **Softball, amateur:** | | | | | |
| Total participants | Million | 42 | 42 | 42 | 42 |
| Youth participants | 1,000 | 1,208 | 1,209 | 1,350 | 1,416 |
| Adult teams | 1,000 | 200 | 196 | 187 | 184 |
| Youth teams | 1,000 | 62 | 68 | 74 | 79 |
| **Golfers (one round or more)** | 1,000 | 24,600 | 24,300 | 25,000 | 24,737 |
| Golf rounds played | 1,000 | 498,600 | 464,800 | 490,200 | 477,400 |
| Golf facilities | Number | 13,439 | 13,683 | 14,074 | 14,341 |
| Classification: | | | | | |
| Private | Number | 4,492 | 4,367 | 4,324 | 4,306 |
| Daily fee | Number | 6,803 | 7,126 | 7,491 | 7,729 |
| Municipal | Number | 2,144 | 2,190 | 2,259 | 2,306 |
| **Tennis:** | | | | | |
| Players | 1,000 | 21,500 | 16,500 | 17,820 | 19,499 |
| Courts | 1,000 | 230 | 240 | 240 | 245 |
| Indoor | 1,000 | 14 | 15 | 15 | 15 |
| **Tenpin bowling:** | | | | | |
| Participants, total | Million | 79 | 79 | 79 | 91 |
| Male | Million | 36.3 | 36.3 | 36.3 | 41.8 |
| Female | Million | 42.6 | 42.6 | 42.6 | 49.2 |
| Establishments | Number | 7,250 | 7,183 | 7,049 | 6,880 |
| Lanes | 1,000 | 143 | 142 | 139 | 136 |
| Membership, total | 1,000 | 5,599 | 5,201 | 4,925 | 4,662 |
| American Bowling Congress | 1,000 | 2,576 | 2,455 | 2,370 | 2,261 |
| Women's Bowling Congress | 1,000 | 2,403 | 2,191 | 2,036 | 1,917 |
| Young American Bowling Alliance | 1,000 | 620 | 555 | 519 | 484 |
| **Motion picture theaters** | 1,000 | 26 | 26 | 28 | 30 |
| Four-wall | 1,000 | 25 | 26 | 27 | 29 |
| Drive-in | 1,000 | 1 | (Z) | 1 | 1 |
| Receipts, box office | Mil dol | 5,154 | 5,396 | 5,494 | 5,912 |
| Admission, average price | Dollars | 4.14 | 4.18 | 4.35 | 4.42 |
| Attendance | Million | 1,244 | 1,292 | 1,263 | 1,339 |
| **Boating:** | | | | | |
| Recreational boats owned | 1,000 | 16,212 | 16,239 | 15,375 | 15,830 |
| Retail expenditures on boating | Mil dol | 11,254 | 14,071 | 17,226 | 17,753 |
| Retail units purchased: | | | | | |
| Total all boats | 1,000 | 487 | 563 | 649 | 619 |
| Outboard boats | 1,000 | 205 | 220 | 231 | 215 |
| Inboard boats | 1,000 | 10 | 11 | 12 | 11 |
| Sterndrive boats | 1,000 | 75 | 90 | 94 | 95 |
| Jet boats | 1,000 | (NA) | (NA) | 15 | 14 |
| Canoes | 1,000 | 90 | 100 | 98 | 93 |
| Personal watercraft | 1,000 | 107 | 142 | 200 | 191 |
| Boat trailers | 1,000 | 163 | 176 | 207 | 194 |
| Outboard motors | 1,000 | 283 | 308 | 317 | 308 |
| Sterndrive and inboard engines | 1,000 | 95 | 114 | 120 | 120 |

*Notes:*
(NA) Not available.
(Z) Fewer than 500.

*Source: Statistical Abstract of the United States 1998*, No. 437; <http://www.census.gov/prod/3/98pubs/98statab/sasec7.pdf>.

# G14. SELECTED SPECTATOR SPORTS

## G14-1. Selected Spectator Sports: 1985–1992

| SPORT | Unit | 1985 | 1987 | 1990 | 1992 |
|---|---|---|---|---|---|
| **Baseball, major leagues:** | | | | | |
| Attendance | 1,000 | 47,742 | 53,182 | 55,512 | 56,852 |
|   Regular season | 1,000 | 46,824 | 52,011 | 54,824 | 55,873 |
|     National League | 1,000 | 22,292 | 24,734 | 24,492 | 24,113 |
|     American League | 1,000 | 24,532 | 27,277 | 30,332 | 31,760 |
|   Playoffs | 1,000 | 591 | 784 | 479 | 668 |
|   World Series | 1,000 | 327 | 387 | 209 | 311 |
| Players' salaries: | | | | | |
|   Average | $1,000 | 371 | 412 | 598 | 1,029 |
| **Basketball:** | | | | | |
| NCAA—Men's college: | | | | | |
|   Teams | Number | 753 | 760 | 767 | 813 |
|   Attendance | 1,000 | 26,584 | 26,798 | 28,741 | 29,378 |
| NCAA—Women's college: | | | | | |
|   Teams | Number | 746 | 756 | 782 | 815 |
|   Attendance | 1,000 | 2,072 | 2,156 | 2,777 | 3,397 |
| Pro: | | | | | |
|   Teams | Number | 23 | 23 | 27 | 27 |
|   Attendance, total | 1,000 | 11,534 | 13,190 | 18,586 | 18,609 |
|     Regular season | 1,000 | 10,506 | 12,065 | 17,369 | 17,367 |
|     Average per game | Number | 11,141 | 12,795 | 15,690 | 15,689 |
| Players' salaries: | | | | | |
|   Average | $1,000 | 325 | 440 | 817 | 1,202 |
| **Football:** | | | | | |
| NCAA College: | | | | | |
|   Teams | Number | 509 | 507 | 533 | 552 |
|   Attendance | 1,000 | 34,952 | 35,008 | 35,330 | 35,225 |
| National Football League: | | | | | |
|   Teams | Number | 28 | 28 | 28 | 28 |
|   Attendance, total | 1,000 | 14,058 | 15,180 | 17,666 | 17,784 |
|     Regular season | 1,000 | 13,345 | 11,406 | 13,960 | 13,829 |
|     Average per game | Number | 59,567 | 54,315 | 62,321 | 61,736 |
|     Postseason games | 1,000 | 711 | 656 | 848 | 815 |
| Players' salaries: | | | | | |
|   Average | $1,000 | 194 | 203 | 352 | 645 |
|   Median base salary | $1,000 | 140 | 175 | 236 | 325 |

*Notes:*
(NA) Not available.

*Source: Statistical Abstract of the United States 1998*, No. 436; <http://www.census.gov/prod/3/98pubs/98statab/sasec7.pdf>. Underlying data from The National League of Professional Baseball Clubs, New York, NY; *National League Green Book*; The American League of Professional Baseball Clubs, New York, NY; *American League Red Book;* Major League Baseball Players Association, New York, NY.; National Collegiate Athletic Assn., Overland Park, KS.; National Basketball Assn., New York, NY.; National Football League, New York, NY.; National Football League Players Association, Washington, DC.; National Hockey League, Montreal, Quebec.; Association of Racing Commissioners International, Inc., Lexington, KY.; Professional Rodeo Cowboys Association, Colorado Springs, CO.

## G14-2. Selected Spectator Sports: 1985–1992 *(continued from previous table)*

| SPORT | Unit | 1985 | 1987 | 1990 | 1992 |
|---|---|---|---|---|---|
| **National Hockey League:** | | | | | |
| Regular season attendance | 1,000 | 11,621 | 12,118 | 12,344 | 13,917 |
| Playoffs attendance | 1,000 | 1,153 | 1,337 | 1,442 | 1,346 |
| **Horseracing:** | | | | | |
| Racing days | Number | 13,745 | 14,208 | 13,841 | 13,644 |
| Attendance | 1,000 | 73,346 | 70,105 | 63,803 | 49,275 |
| Pari-mutuel turnover | Mil dol | 12,222 | 13,122 | 7,162 | 14,078 |
| Revenue to government | Mil dol | 625 | 608 | 624 | 491 |
| **Greyhound racing:** | | | | | |
| Total performances | Number | 9,590 | 11,156 | 14,915 | 17,528 |
| Attendance | 1,000 | 23,853 | 26,215 | 28,660 | 28,003 |
| Pari-mutuel turnover | Mil dol | 2,702 | 3,193 | 3,422 | 3,306 |
| Revenue to government | Mil dol | 201 | 221 | 235 | 204 |
| **Jai alai:** | | | | | |
| Total performances | Number | 2,736 | 2,906 | 3,620 | 3,288 |
| Games played | Number | 32,260 | 38,476 | (NA) | 45,067 |
| Attendance | 1,000 | 4,722 | 6,816 | 5,329 | 4,634 |
| Total handle | Mil dol | 664 | 707.5 | 545.5 | 425.9 |
| Revenue to government | Mil dol | 50 | 51 | 39 | 30 |
| **Professional rodeo:** | | | | | |
| Rodeos | Number | 617 | 637 | 754 | 770 |
| Performances | Number | 1,887 | 1,832 | 2,159 | 2,203 |
| Members | Number | 5,239 | 5,342 | 5,693 | 5,714 |
| Permit-holders (rookies) | Number | 2,534 | 2,746 | 3,290 | 2,857 |

*Note:*
(NA) Not available.

*Source: Statistical Abstract of the United States 1998*, No. 436; <http://www.census.gov/prod/3/98pubs/98statab/sasec7.pdf>. Underlying data from The National League of Professional Baseball Clubs, New York, NY; *National League Green Book;* The American League of Professional Baseball Clubs, New York, NY; *American League Red Book*; Major League Baseball Players Association, New York, NY.; National Collegiate Athletic Assn., Overland Park, KS.; National Basketball Assn., New York, NY.; National Football League, New York, NY.; National Football League Players Association, Washington, DC.; National Hockey League, Montreal, Quebec.; Association of Racing Commissioners International, Inc., Lexington, KY.; Professional Rodeo Cowboys Association, Colorado Springs, CO.

## G14-3. Selected Spectator Sports: 1993–1996

| SPORT | Unit | 1993 | 1994 | 1995 | 1996 |
|---|---|---|---|---|---|
| **Baseball, major leagues:** | | | | | |
| Attendance | 1,000 | 71,237 | 50,010 | 51,288 | 61,665 |
| Regular season | 1,000 | 70,257 | 50,010 | 50,469 | 60,097 |
| National League | 1,000 | 36,924 | 25,808 | 25,110 | 30,379 |
| American League | 1,000 | 33,333 | 24,202 | 25,359 | 29,718 |
| Playoffs | 1,000 | 636 | (X) | 533 | 1,300 |
| World Series | 1,000 | 344 | (X) | 286 | 268 |
| **Players' salaries:** | | | | | |
| Average | $1,000 | 1,076 | 1,168 | 1,111 | 1,120 |
| **Basketball:** | | | | | |
| **NCAA—Men's college:** | | | | | |
| Teams | Number | 831 | 858 | 868 | 866 |
| Attendance | 1,000 | 28,527 | 28,390 | 28,548 | 28,225 |
| **NCAA—Women's college:** | | | | | |
| Teams | Number | 746 | 859 | 864 | 874 |
| Attendance | 1,000 | 4,193 | 4,557 | 4,962 | 5,234 |
| **Pro:** | | | | | |
| Teams | Number | 27 | 27 | 27 | 29 |
| Attendance, total | 1,000 | 19,120 | 19,350 | 19,883 | 21,797 |
| Regular season | 1,000 | 17,778 | 17,984 | 18,516 | 20,513 |
| Average per game | Number | 16,060 | 16,246 | 16,727 | 17,253 |
| **Players' salaries:** | | | | | |
| Average | $1,000 | 1,348 | 1,700 | 1,900 | 2,100 |
| **Football:** | | | | | |
| **NCAA College:** | | | | | |
| Teams | Number | 560 | 568 | 565 | 566 |
| Attendance | 1,000 | 34,871 | 36,460 | 35,638 | 36,083 |
| **National Football League:** | | | | | |
| Teams | Number | 28 | (NA) | (NA) | (NA) |
| Attendance, total | 1,000 | 14,772 | (NA) | (NA) | (NA) |
| Regular season | 1,000 | 13,967 | (NA) | (NA) | (NA) |
| Average per game | Number | 62,352 | (NA) | (NA) | (NA) |
| Postseason games | 1,000 | 805 | (NA) | (NA) | (NA) |
| **Players' salaries:** | | | | | |
| Average | $1,000 | 683 | 637 | 714 | (NA) |
| Median base salary | $1,000 | 330 | 325 | 335 | (NA) |

*Notes:*
(NA) Not available.
(X) Not applicable.

*Source: Statistical Abstract of the United States 1998*, No. 436; <http://www.census.gov/prod/3/98pubs/98statab/sasec7.pdf>. Underlying data from The National League of Professional Baseball Clubs, New York, NY; *National League Green Book*; The American League of Professional Baseball Clubs, New York, NY; *American League Red Book;* Major League Baseball Players Association, New York, NY.; National Collegiate Athletic Assn., Overland Park, KS.; National Basketball Assn., New York, NY.; National Football League, New York, NY.; National Football League Players Association, Washington, DC.; National Hockey League, Montreal, Quebec.; Association of Racing Commissioners International, Inc., Lexington, KY.; Professional Rodeo Cowboys Association, Colorado Springs, CO.

## G14-4. Selected Spectator Sports: 1993–1996 *(continued from previous table)*

| SPORT | Unit | 1993 | 1994 | 1995 | 1996 |
|---|---|---|---|---|---|
| **National Hockey League:** | | | | | |
| Regular season attendance | 1,000 | 15,714 | (NA) | 15,658 | 16,237 |
| Playoffs attendance | 1,000 | 1,440 | (NA) | 1,447 | 1,423 |
| **Horseracing:** | | | | | |
| Racing days | Number | 13,237 | 13,082 | 13,243 | 12,457 |
| Attendance | 1,000 | 45,688 | 42,065 | 38,934 | 43,367 |
| Pari-mutuel turnover | Mil dol | 13,718 | 14,143 | 14,592 | 14,902 |
| Revenue to government | Mil dol | 472 | 452 | 456 | 444 |
| **Greyhound racing:** | | | | | |
| Total performances | Number | 17,976 | 17,035 | 16,110 | 15,151 |
| Attendance | 1,000 | (NA) | (NA) | (NA) | (NA) |
| Pari-mutuel turnover | Mil dol | 3,255 | 2,948 | 2,730 | 2,433 |
| Revenue to government | Mil dol | 195 | 183 | 157 | 139 |
| **Jai alai:** | | | | | |
| Total performances | Number | 3,200 | 3,146 | 2,748 | 2,542 |
| Games played | Number | 43,056 | 42,607 | 37,052 | 34,346 |
| Attendance | 1,000 | 4,194 | 3,684 | 3,208 | (NA) |
| Total handle | Mil dol | 384.2 | 330.7 | 296.4 | 273.4 |
| Revenue to government | Mil dol | 27 | 22 | 13 | 12 |
| **Professional rodeo:** | | | | | |
| Rodeos | Number | 791 | 782 | 739 | 742 |
| Performances | Number | 2,269 | 2,245 | 2,217 | 2,229 |
| Members | Number | 5,760 | 6,415 | 6,894 | 7,084 |
| Permit-holders (rookies) | Number | 2,888 | 3,346 | 3,835 | 4,141 |

*Notes:*
(NA) Not available.

*Source: Statistical Abstract of the United States 1998*, No. 436; <http://www.census.gov/prod/3/98pubs/98statab/sasec7.pdf>. Underlying data from The National League of Professional Baseball Clubs, New York, NY; *National League Green Book*; The American League of Professional Baseball Clubs, New York, NY; *American League Red Book;* Major League Baseball Players Association, New York, NY.; National Collegiate Athletic Assn., Overland Park, KS.; National Basketball Assn., New York, NY.; National Football League, New York, NY.; National Football League Players Association, Washington, DC.; National Hockey League, Montreal, Quebec.; Association of Racing Commissioners International, Inc., Lexington, KY.; Professional Rodeo Cowboys Association, Colorado Springs, CO.

## G15. PARTICIPATION IN SELECTED SPORTS ACTIVITIES

### G15-1. Participation in Selected Sports Activities, Total and by Gender: 1996, in Thousands, except Rank

|  | All persons, Number | All persons, Rank | Sex, Male | Sex, Female |
|---|---|---|---|---|
| Total | 237,745 | (X) | 115,443 | 122,301 |
| Number participated in— |  |  |  |  |
| Aerobic excercising * | 24,119 | 11 | 5,314 | 18,805 |
| Backpacking ** | 11,469 | 22 | 7,240 | 4,229 |
| Badminton | 6,084 | 28 | 2,909 | 3,175 |
| Baseball | 14,823 | 18 | 11,610 | 3,213 |
| Basketball | 33,281 | 9 | 22,375 | 10,906 |
| Bicycle riding* | 53,342 | 3 | 28,595 | 24,747 |
| Billiards | 34,477 | 8 | 21,841 | 12,636 |
| Bowling | 42,895 | 6 | 22,579 | 20,316 |
| Calisthenics * | 10,064 | 25 | 5,023 | 5,041 |
| Camping*** | 44,695 | 5 | 24,102 | 20,593 |
| Exercise walking* | 73,307 | 1 | 26,666 | 46,641 |
| Exercising with equipment* | 47,823 | 4 | 22,200 | 25,622 |
| Fishing— fresh water | 40,208 | 7 | 27,160 | 13,048 |
| Fishing— salt water | 11,045 | 23 | 7,926 | 3,119 |
| Football— tackle | 8,953 | 27 | 7,969 | 983 |
| Football— touch | 11,645 | 20 | 9,603 | 2,042 |
| Golf | 23,082 | 12 | 18,219 | 4,863 |
| Hiking | 26,457 | 10 | 14,465 | 11,992 |
| Hunting with firearms | 19,251 | 15 | 16,317 | 2,933 |
| Martial arts | 4,673 | 30 | 3,286 | 1,387 |
| Racquetball | 5,582 | 29 | 3,768 | 1,814 |
| Running/ jogging* | 22,239 | 13 | 12,320 | 9,919 |
| Skiing— alpine/ downhill | 10,466 | 24 | 6,277 | 4,188 |
| Skiing— cross country | 3,385 | 31 | 1,820 | 1,566 |
| Soccer | 13,876 | 19 | 8,626 | 5,251 |
| Softball | 19,873 | 14 | 10,837 | 9,035 |
| Swimming * | 60,223 | 2 | 29,145 | 31,078 |
| Table tennis | 9,542 | 26 | 5,907 | 3,635 |
| Target shooting | 15,695 | 17 | 11,097 | 4,598 |
| Tennis | 11,485 | 21 | 6,381 | 5,105 |
| Volleyball | 18,535 | 16 | 8,970 | 9,565 |

*Notes:*
(X) Not applicable.
* Participant engaged in activity at least six times in the year.
** Includes wilderness camping.
*** Vacation/overnight.
*General Notes:* For persons seven years of age or older. Except as indicated, a participant plays a sport more than once in the year on a sampling of 15,000 households. *Sports Participation in 1996*: Series I and Travel 1998.

*Source: Statistical Abstract of the United States 1998*, No 438; <http://www.census.gov/prod/3/98pubs/98statab/sasec7.pdf>.  Underlying data from National Sporting Goods Association, Mt Prospect, IL, *Sports Participation in 1996*.

## G15-2. Participation in Selected Sports Activities, by Age Category: 1996, in Thousands

| | Age, 7-11 years | Age, 12-17 years | Age, 18-24 years | Age, 25-34 years | Age, 35-44 years | Age, 45-54 years | Age, 55-64 years | 65 years and older |
|---|---|---|---|---|---|---|---|---|
| Total | 19,177 | 22,701 | 24,615 | 40,373 | 43,312 | 32,333 | 21,360 | 33,873 |
| Number participated in— | | | | | | | | |
| Aerobic excercising * | 757 | 1,981 | 4,067 | 6,168 | 5,206 | 2,982 | 1,371 | 1,587 |
| Backpacking ** | 1,229 | 2,008 | 2,002 | 2,725 | 2,065 | 986 | 332 | 122 |
| Badminton | 987 | 1,398 | 820 | 1,018 | 1,230 | 411 | 149 | 72 |
| Baseball | 4,529 | 4,144 | 1,465 | 1,874 | 1,764 | 520 | 200 | 327 |
| Basketball | 6,424 | 9,157 | 4,665 | 6,112 | 4,717 | 1,281 | 418 | 506 |
| Bicycle riding* | 11,774 | 10,397 | 4,973 | 8,495 | 8,409 | 4,317 | 2,469 | 2,508 |
| Billiards | 2,044 | 3,924 | 7,611 | 9,912 | 6,774 | 2,737 | 910 | 567 |
| Bowling | 5,239 | 6,744 | 7,006 | 9,185 | 7,760 | 3,571 | 1,537 | 1,853 |
| Calisthenics * | 1,307 | 2,132 | 1,056 | 2,007 | 1,777 | 1,016 | 320 | 449 |
| Camping*** | 5,594 | 6,200 | 5,306 | 9,186 | 9,374 | 4,610 | 2,493 | 1,932 |
| Exercise walking* | 2,701 | 3,522 | 7,104 | 13,151 | 14,827 | 12,499 | 8,433 | 11,070 |
| Exercising with equipment* | 664 | 4,066 | 6,625 | 11,482 | 10,521 | 6,970 | 3,918 | 3,576 |
| Fishing— fresh water | 4,302 | 4,393 | 5,087 | 7,869 | 8,210 | 5,146 | 2,844 | 2,356 |
| Fishing— salt water | 787 | 979 | 1,212 | 2,089 | 2,575 | 1,626 | 909 | 867 |
| Football— tackle | 1,639 | 3,472 | 1,786 | 1,170 | 568 | 98 | 46 | 174 |
| Football— touch | 2,252 | 3,772 | 1,768 | 2,166 | 1,251 | 253 | 50 | 133 |
| Golf | 834 | 1,952 | 2,410 | 5,376 | 5,036 | 3,457 | 1,860 | 2,157 |
| Hiking | 3,009 | 3,261 | 3,166 | 5,885 | 5,812 | 3,230 | 1,169 | 926 |
| Hunting with firearms | 642 | 1,861 | 2,704 | 4,862 | 4,269 | 2,503 | 1,238 | 1,171 |
| Martial arts | 1,239 | 929 | 635 | 768 | 630 | 340 | 56 | 76 |
| Racquetball | 351 | 522 | 1,169 | 1,804 | 1,014 | 529 | 79 | 114 |
| Running/ jogging* | 2,005 | 4,739 | 4,113 | 4,714 | 3,864 | 1,727 | 613 | 464 |
| Skiing— alpine/ downhill | 777 | 1,618 | 1,849 | 2,370 | 2,237 | 1,049 | 469 | 97 |
| Skiing— cross country | 209 | 341 | 392 | 665 | 825 | 597 | 183 | 174 |
| Soccer | 4,420 | 4,063 | 1,599 | 1,729 | 1,325 | 358 | 98 | 284 |
| Softball | 3,605 | 4,274 | 2,301 | 4,513 | 3,221 | 1,196 | 350 | 413 |
| Swimming * | 10,465 | 10,517 | 7,141 | 10,286 | 10,300 | 5,460 | 2,881 | 3,172 |
| Table tennis | 1,261 | 2,354 | 1,174 | 1,725 | 1,854 | 677 | 292 | 205 |
| Target shooting | 869 | 1,645 | 2,037 | 3,788 | 3,370 | 1,969 | 1,032 | 985 |
| Tennis | 1,196 | 2,081 | 2,156 | 2,631 | 1,893 | 850 | 325 | 354 |
| Volleyball | 1,460 | 4,721 | 3,471 | 4,534 | 2,945 | 934 | 256 | 215 |

*Notes:*
\* Participant engaged in activity at least six times in the year.
\*\* Includes wilderness camping.
\*\*\* Vacation/overnight.
*General Notes:* For persons 7 years of age or older. Except as indicated, a participant plays a sport more than once in the year on a sampling of 15,000 households. *Sports Participation in 1996*: Series I and Travel 1998.

*Source: Statistical Abstract of the United States 1998*, No. 438; <http://www.census.gov/prod/3/98pubs/98statab/sasec7.pdf>. Underlying data from National Sporting Goods Association, Mt Prospect, IL, *Sports Participation in 1996*.

## G15-3. Participation in Selected Sports Activities, by Household Income: 1996, in Thousands

| | Household Income (in dollars), | | | | | |
| | Under 15,000 | 15,000 to 24,999 | 25,000 to 34,999 | 35,000 to 49,999 | 50,000 to 74,999 | 75,000 and over |
|---|---|---|---|---|---|---|
| Total | 43,372 | 36,377 | 35,382 | 42,878 | 50,791 | 28,944 |
| Number participated in— | | | | | | |
| Aerobic exercising * | 3,117 | 3,024 | 3,462 | 4,619 | 5,739 | 4,159 |
| Backpacking ** | 1,825 | 1,990 | 1,539 | 2,107 | 2,309 | 1,698 |
| Badminton | 866 | 710 | 1,054 | 1,259 | 1,415 | 780 |
| Baseball | 1,851 | 1,736 | 2,318 | 2,948 | 3,875 | 2,095 |
| Basketball | 4,296 | 4,660 | 4,825 | 6,886 | 7,908 | 4,706 |
| Bicycle riding* | 7,802 | 6,775 | 7,883 | 10,287 | 12,575 | 8,020 |
| Billiards | 5,432 | 5,290 | 5,054 | 7,118 | 7,160 | 4,422 |
| Bowling | 5,542 | 6,150 | 6,515 | 8,636 | 10,648 | 5,404 |
| Calisthenics * | 1,116 | 1,045 | 1,438 | 2,047 | 2,523 | 1,894 |
| Camping*** | 6,214 | 6,907 | 7,039 | 9,323 | 10,691 | 4,521 |
| Exercise walking* | 12,821 | 10,945 | 10,464 | 13,534 | 15,846 | 9,698 |
| Exercising with equipment* | 5,525 | 5,788 | 6,711 | 8,904 | 12,372 | 8,522 |
| Fishing— fresh water | 6,653 | 6,229 | 6,346 | 7,746 | 9,031 | 4,203 |
| Fishing— salt water | 1,501 | 1,341 | 1,219 | 2,049 | 3,115 | 1,820 |
| Football— tackle | 1,569 | 1,624 | 1,286 | 1,723 | 1,825 | 925 |
| Football— touch | 1,893 | 1,676 | 1,757 | 2,137 | 2,981 | 1,202 |
| Golf | 1,575 | 2,069 | 2,641 | 4,233 | 7,119 | 5,444 |
| Hiking | 3,960 | 3,429 | 3,729 | 4,753 | 6,164 | 4,423 |
| Hunting with firearms | 2,662 | 2,960 | 3,160 | 4,329 | 4,151 | 1,989 |
| Martial arts | 755 | 625 | 736 | 794 | 1,084 | 679 |
| Racquetball | 517 | 809 | 695 | 1,015 | 1,569 | 976 |
| Running/ jogging* | 2,847 | 3,121 | 2,940 | 4,139 | 5,455 | 3,737 |
| Skiing— alpine/ downhill | 726 | 992 | 801 | 1,597 | 2,979 | 3,370 |
| Skiing— cross country | 249 | 310 | 327 | 752 | 976 | 772 |
| Soccer | 1,658 | 1,430 | 2,244 | 2,760 | 3,521 | 2,264 |
| Softball | 2,750 | 2,659 | 2,886 | 4,175 | 5,024 | 2,379 |
| Swimming * | 7,944 | 7,482 | 8,181 | 11,115 | 15,859 | 9,643 |
| Table tennis | 1,136 | 1,165 | 1,178 | 1,680 | 2,600 | 1,783 |
| Target shooting | 2,416 | 2,528 | 2,507 | 3,141 | 3,244 | 1,859 |
| Tennis | 1,057 | 1,214 | 1,484 | 2,420 | 2,719 | 2,591 |
| Volleyball | 2,694 | 2,282 | 2,760 | 3,771 | 4,458 | 2,571 |

*Notes:*

\* Participant engaged in activity at least six times in the year.

\*\* Includes wilderness camping.

\*\*\* Vacation/overnight.

*General Notes:* For persons seven years of age or older. Except as indicated, a participant plays a sport more than once in the year on a sampling of 15,000 households. *Sports Participation in 1996:*Series I and Travel 1998.

*Source: Statistical Abstract of the United States 1998*, No. 438; <http://www.census.gov/prod/3/98pubs/98statab/sasec7.pdf>. Underlying data from National Sporting Goods Association, Mt Prospect, IL, *Sports Participation in 1996.*

# G16. HOUSEHOLD PET OWNERSHIP

## G16-1. Household Pet Ownership: 1996

| ITEM | Unit | Dog | Cat | Pet Bird | Horse |
|---|---|---|---|---|---|
| Households owning companion pets * | Million | 31.2 | 27.0 | 4.6 | 1.5 |
| Percent of all households | Percent | 31.6 | 27.3 | 4.6 | 1.5 |
| Average number owned | Number | 1.7 | 2.2 | 2.7 | 2.7 |
| Total companion pet population * | Million | 52.9 | 59.1 | 12.6 | 4.0 |
| Households obtaining veterinary care ** | Percent | 88.7 | 72.9 | 15.8 | 66.3 |
| Average visits per household per year | Number | 2.6 | 1.9 | 0.2 | 2.3 |
| Average annual costs per household | Dollars | 186.8 | 112.24 | 10.95 | 226.26 |
| Total expenditures | Mil dol | 5,828 | 3,030 | 50 | 339 |
| PERCENT DISTRIBUTION OF HOUSEHOLDS OWNING PETS Annual household income: | | | | | |
| Under $12,500 | Percent | 12.7 | 13.9 | 17.3 | 9.5 |
| $12,500 to $24,999 | Percent | 19.1 | 19.7 | 20.9 | 20.3 |
| $25,000 to $39,999 | Percent | 21.6 | 21.5 | 22.0 | 21.8 |
| $40,000 to $59,999 | Percent | 21.5 | 21.2 | 17.5 | 23.1 |
| $60,000 and over | Percent | 25.2 | 23.7 | 22.3 | 25.4 |
| Family size: | | | | | |
| One person | Percent | 13.2 | 16.8 | 12.7 | 12.1 |
| Two persons | Percent | 31.0 | 32.6 | 27.9 | 29.1 |
| Three persons | Percent | 21.4 | 20.6 | 20.4 | 22.0 |
| Four or more persons | Percent | 34.5 | 29.9 | 38.9 | 36.7 |

*Notes:*
\* As of December.
\*\* During 1996.
*General Note:* Based on a sample survey of 80,000 households in 1996.

*Source: Statistical Abstract of the United States 1998*, No. 431; :<http//www.census.gov/prod/3/98pubs/98statab/sasec7.pdf>. Underlying data from American Veterinary Medical Association, Schaumburg, IL, *U.S. Pet Ownership and Demographics Sourcebook,* 1997, (copyright).

# G17. CHARITY AND PHILANTHROPY

## G17-1. Charity Contributions—Average Dollar Amount and Percent of Household Income, by Year (1991–1995) and by Age of Respondent

| Year and age | All contributing households, average amount (dollars) | All contributing households, percent of household income | Contributors and volunteers, average amount (dollars) | Contributors and volunteers, percent of household income |
|---|---|---|---|---|
| 1991 | 899 | 2.2 | 1,155 | 2.6 |
| 1993 | 880 | 2.1 | 1,193 | 2.6 |
| 1995, total | 1,017 | 2.2 | 1,279 | 2.6 |
| 18-24 years | 287 | 0.7 | 344 | 0.7 |
| 25-34 years | 743 | 1.6 | 922 | 2 |
| 35-44 years | 1,342 | 2.6 | 1,653 | 3 |
| 45-54 years | 955 | 1.8 | 1,142 | 2.1 |
| 55-64 years | 1,791 | 3.6 | 2,473 | 4.5 |
| 65-74 years | 980 | 2.8 | 1,125 | 3 |
| 75 years and over | 839 | 3.7 | 1,078 | 5 |

**Notes:** Estimates cover households' contribution activity for the year and are based on respondents' replies as to contribution and volunteer activity of household. Volunteers are persons who worked in some way to help others for no monetary pay during the previous year.

*Source: Statistical Abstract of the United States 1998*, No. 639; <http://www.census.gov/prod/3/98pubs/98statab/sasec12.pdf>.

## G17-2. Charity Contributions—Average Dollar Amount and Percent of Household Income, by Household Income, 1995

| Year and age | All contributing households, average amount (dollars) | All contributing households, percent of household income | Contributors and volunteers, average amount (dollars) | Contributors and volunteers, percent of household income |
|---|---|---|---|---|
| **1995** | | | | |
| Under $10,000 | 295 | 4.3 | (B) | (B) |
| $10,000-$19,999 | 425 | 2.8 | 444 | 2.9 |
| $20,000-$29,999 | 578 | 2.3 | 658 | 2.6 |
| $30,000-$39,999 | 722 | 2.1 | 928 | 2.7 |
| $40,000-$49,999 | 576 | 1.3 | 677 | 1.5 |
| $50,000-$59,999 | 1,001 | 1.8 | 1,142 | 2.1 |
| $60,000-$74,999 | 1,301 | 1.9 | 1,443 | 2.1 |
| $75,000-$99,999 | 1,582 | 1.8 | 1,682 | 2 |
| $100,000 and over | 3,379 | 3.4 | 4,195 | 4.2 |

*Notes:*
(B) Base too small to meet statistical standards for reliability.
*General Notes:* Estimates cover households' contribution activity for the year and are based on respondents' replies as to contribution and volunteer activity of household. Volunteers are persons who worked in some way to help others for no monetary pay during the previous year.

*Source: Statistical Abstract of the United States 1998*, No. 639; <http://www.census.gov/prod/3/98pubs/98statab/sasec12.pdf>.

## G17-3. Private Philanthropy Funds, by Source and Allocation: 1980–1990, in Billions of Dollars

| SOURCE AND ALLOCATION | 1980 | 1985 | 1987 | 1988 | 1989 | 1990 |
|---|---|---|---|---|---|---|
| Total funds | 48.6 | 73.0 | 90.0 | 98.1 | 106.7 | 111.5 |
| Individuals | 40.7 | 58.7 | 72.3 | 80.1 | 87.8 | 91.2 |
| Foundations | 2.8 | 4.9 | 5.9 | 6.2 | 6.6 | 7.2 |
| Corporations | 2.3 | 4.6 | 5.2 | 5.3 | 5.5 | 5.5 |
| Charitable bequests | 2.9 | 4.8 | 6.6 | 6.6 | 7.0 | 7.6 |
| Allocation: | | | | | | |
| Religion | 22.2 | 38.2 | 43.5 | 45.2 | 47.8 | 49.8 |
| Health | 5.3 | 7.7 | 9.2 | 9.6 | 9.9 | 9.9 |
| Education | 5.0 | 8.2 | 9.8 | 10.2 | 11.0 | 12.4 |
| Human service | 4.9 | 8.5 | 9.8 | 10.5 | 11.4 | 11.8 |
| Arts, culture and humanities | 3.2 | 5.1 | 6.3 | 6.8 | 7.5 | 7.9 |
| Public/societal benefit | 1.5 | 2.2 | 2.9 | 3.2 | 3.8 | 4.9 |
| Environment/wildlife | (1) | (1) | 2.1 | 2.4 | 2.0 | 2.6 |
| International | (1) | (1) | 0.9 | 1.0 | 1.2 | 1.5 |
| Unclassified | 6.6 | 3.1 | 5.4 | 5.4 | 7.8 | 6.8 |
| Gifts to foundations | (1) | (1) | (1) | 3.9 | 4.4 | 3.8 |

*Notes:*
(1) Included in "Unclassified."
*General Notes:* Estimates for sources of funds based on U.S. Internal Revenue Service reports of individual charitable deductions, household surveys of giving by Independent Sector, and, for 1980 and 1985, an econometric model. For corporate giving, data are those prepared by the Council for Aid to Education. Data about foundation donations are based upon surveys of foundations and data provided by the Foundation Center. Estimates of the allocation of funds were derived from surveys of nonprofits conducted by source and other groups.

*Source: Statistical Abstract of the United States 1998*, No. 641; <http://wwwcensusgov/prod/3/98pubs/98statab/sasec12pdf>. Underlying data from AAFRC Trust for Philanthropy, New York, NY, *Giving USA*, annual, (copyright).

## G17-4. Private Philanthropy Funds, by Source and Allocation: 1991–1996, in Billions of Dollars

| SOURCE AND ALLOCATION | 1991 | 1992 | 1993 | 1994 | 1995 | 1996 |
|---|---|---|---|---|---|---|
| Total funds | 117.2 | 121.1 | 126.5 | 129.3 | 140.5 | 150.7 |
| Individuals | 96.1 | 98.4 | 102.1 | 103.8 | 112.2 | 119.9 |
| Foundations | 7.7 | 8.6 | 9.5 | 9.7 | 10.6 | 11.8 |
| Corporations | 5.6 | 5.9 | 6.3 | 7.0 | 7.9 | 8.5 |
| Charitable bequests | 7.8 | 8.2 | 8.5 | 8.8 | 9.8 | 10.5 |
| Allocation: | | | | | | |
| Religion | 53.9 | 54.9 | 56.3 | 60.2 | 66.3 | 69.4 |
| Health | 9.7 | 10.2 | 10.8 | 11.5 | 12.6 | 13.9 |
| Education | 13.5 | 14.3 | 15.4 | 16.6 | 17.6 | 18.8 |
| Human service | 11.1 | 11.6 | 12.5 | 11.7 | 11.7 | 12.2 |
| Arts, culture and humanities | 8.8 | 9.3 | 9.6 | 9.7 | 10 | 10.9 |
| Public/societal benefit | 4.9 | 5.1 | 5.4 | 6.1 | 7.1 | 7.6 |
| Environment/wildlife | 2.9 | 3.1 | 3.2 | 3.5 | 4.0 | 4.0 |
| International | 1.8 | 1.7 | 1.9 | 2.2 | 2.1 | 2.0 |
| Unclassified | 6.2 | 5.9 | 5.1 | 1.4 | 1.7 | 3.6 |
| Gifts to foundations | 4.5 | 5.0 | 6.3 | 6.3 | 7.5 | 8.3 |

*Notes:*

*General Notes*: Estimates for sources of funds based on US Internal Revenue Service reports of individual charitable deductions, household surveys of giving by Independent Sector, and, for 1980 and 1985, an econometric model. For corporate giving, data are those prepared by the Council for Aid to Education. Data about foundation donations are based upon surveys of foundations and data provided by the Foundation Center. Estimates of the allocation of funds were derived from surveys of nonprofits conducted by source and other groups.

*Source: Statistical Abstract of the United States 1998*, No. 641; <http://wwwcensusgov/prod/3/98pubs/98statab/sasec12pdf>. Underlying data from AAFRC Trust for Philanthropy, New York, NY, *Giving USA*, annual, (copyright).

# H. The Role of Government

## GENERAL OVERVIEW

This chapter details the way that governments—at the federal and state levels—affect the generation of wealth and consumption in the United States. Included is a sampling of data, covering a broad range of statistics and policy instruments that represent government's various roles. The details cover such items as receipts, outlays, and balance sheets, along with federal loans to small businesses and savings instruments that help to finance government activity.

## EXPLANATION OF INDICATORS

**H1. Federal Budget:** The first table and three charts that follow it present data on the federal budget since World War II (1945 to 1998). The table shows total receipts against outlays on a year-by-year basis, along with the surplus or deficit for each year. The charts represent outlays as a percent of GDP; this allows the user to understand the extent to which federal government consumption has changed in relationship to the overall material capacity of the economy.

**H2. Federal Receipts, by Source:** The next two tables present detail on federal receipts from 1980 to 1998. Included is information on where government receipts come from including such categories as taxes, federal alcohol funds, and federal highway trust funds. This allows the user to understand the sectors of the economy that generate income for government consumption.

**H3. Federal Budget Outlays:** The next two tables present broad categories of government spending including defense, human resources, physical resources, and net interest payments from 1980 to 1998. They provide the user with a broad analysis of the federal government's consumption of resources.

**H4. Gross Federal Debt:** The next table and following three charts include data summarizing the changing nature of the gross federal debt over the long term, from 1945 to 1998. The table shows the structure of the debt including the amount held by the public, and the charts show the debt as a percent of the total GDP, which is a benchmark indicator that helps to analyze the capacity of our economy to carry the debt.

**H5. Small Business Administration (SBA) Loans to Small Businesses:** The next two tables present data on the federal government's loan program to small businesses. The tables represent the information on total loans and the share of the SBA program that goes to minority-owned firms across a mid-range time span (1980 to 1996). The SBA is an important federal policy instrument geared toward encouraging growth in the small business community, which is considered integral to the financial health and wealth of the country.

**H6. Social Welfare Expenditures Under Public Programs:** The next four tables, followed by three charts, present information on government moneys spent, at both federal and state/local level, on programs that support personal income and welfare. Presented across a mid-range timeframe, from 1980 to 1994, the data will help users analyze an arena of government involvement geared toward maintaining and supporting standardized levels of income and welfare.

**H7. State Governments—Sources of General Revenue:** The remaining tables and charts detail the way in which state governments fund their budgets and finance their expenditures. They represent the public component of income and wealth at the state level, and show how the wealth and consumption of governments derive from the constituencies they serve.

## H1. FEDERAL BUDGET

## H1-1. Federal Budget—Summary: 1945–1998, in Millions of Dollars, for Fiscal Years ending in Year Shown

| Year | Receipts | Outlays | Surplus or Deficit (-) |
|---|---|---|---|
| 1945 | 45,159 | 92,712 | -47,553 |
| 1950 | 39,443 | 42,562 | -3,119 |
| 1955 | 65,451 | 68,444 | -2,993 |
| 1960 | 92,492 | 92,191 | 301 |
| 1965 | 116,817 | 118,228 | -1,411 |
| 1970 | 192,807 | 195,649 | -2,842 |
| 1975 | 279,090 | 332,332 | -53,242 |
| 1980 | 517,112 | 590,947 | -73,835 |
| 1981 | 599,272 | 678,249 | -78,976 |
| 1982 | 617,766 | 745,755 | -127,989 |
| 1983 | 600,562 | 808,380 | -207,818 |
| 1984 | 666,486 | 851,874 | -185,388 |
| 1985 | 734,088 | 946,423 | -212,334 |
| 1986 | 769,215 | 990,460 | -221,245 |
| 1987 | 854,353 | 1,004,122 | -149,769 |
| 1988 | 909,303 | 1,064,489 | -155,187 |
| 1989 | 991,190 | 1,143,671 | -152,481 |
| 1990 | 1,031,969 | 1,253,163 | -221,194 |
| 1991 | 1,055,041 | 1,324,400 | -269,359 |
| 1992 | 1,091,279 | 1,381,681 | -290,402 |
| 1993 | 1,154,401 | 1,409,414 | -255,013 |
| 1994 | 1,258,627 | 1,461,731 | -203,104 |
| 1995 | 1,351,830 | 1,515,729 | -163,899 |
| 1996 | 1,453,062 | 1,560,512 | -107,450 |
| 1997 | 1,579,292 | 1,601,235 | -21,943 |
| 1998, est. | 1,657,858 | 1,667,815 | -9,957 |

*Notes:*
NA Not available.
The Balanced Budget and Emergency Deficit Control Act of 1985 put all the previously off-budget federal entities into the budget and moved Social Security off-budget. Minus sign (-) indicates deficit or decrease.

*Source: Statistical Abstract of the United States 1998*, No. 537; <http://www.census.gov/prod/3/98pubs/98statab/sasec10.pdf>. Underlying data from U.S. Office of Management and Budget, *Historical Tables,* annual.

**H1-2. Federal Budget—Outlays as Percent of GDP: 1945–1998, for Fiscal Years ending in Year Shown**

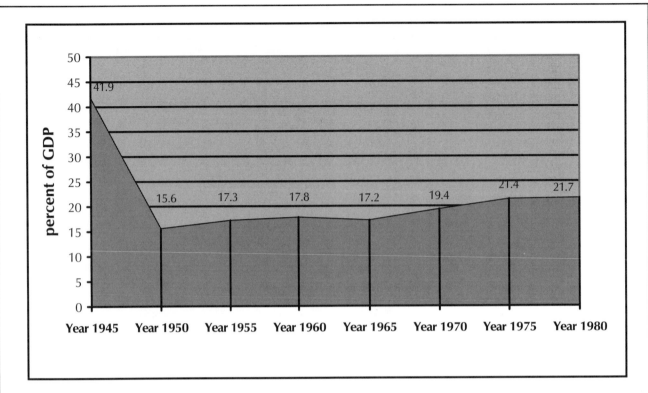

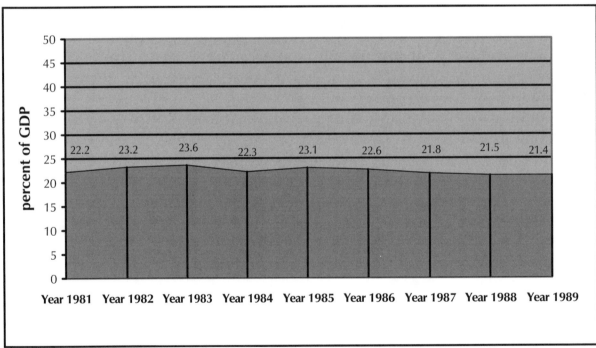

**H1-2. Federal Budget—Outlays as Percent of GDP: 1945–1998, for Fiscal Years ending in Year Shown *(continued)***

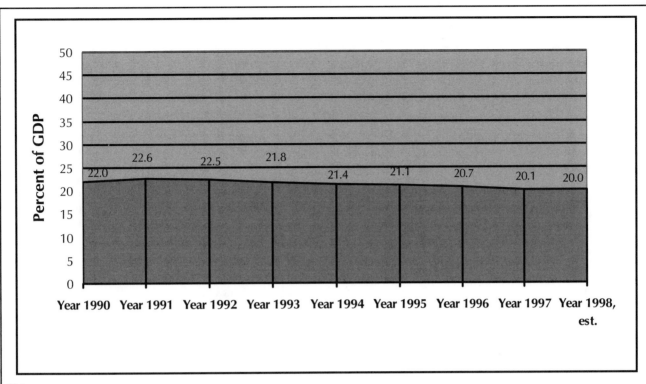

*Notes:*
The Balanced Budget and Emergency Deficit Control Act of 1985 put all the previously off-budget federal entities into the budget and moved Social Security off-budget. Minus sign (-) indicates deficit or decrease.

*Source: Statistical Abstract of the United States 1998*, No. 537; <http://www.census.gov/prod/3/98pubs/98statab/sasec10.pdf>. Underlying data from U.S. Office of Management and Budget, *Historical Tables*, annual.

## H2. FEDERAL RECEIPTS, BY SOURCE

### H2-1. Federal Receipts, by Source: 1980–1990, in Millions of Dollars, for Fiscal Years ending in Year Shown

| SOURCE | 1980 | 1985 | 1990 |
|---|---|---|---|
| **Total receipts[1]** | **517,112** | **734,088** | **1,031,969** |
| Individual income taxes | 244,069 | 334,531 | 466,884 |
| Corporation income taxes | 64,600 | 61,331 | 93,507 |
| Social insurance and retirement receipts | 157,803 | 265,163 | 380,047 |
| Excise taxes | 24,329 | 35,992 | 35,345 |
| Social insurance and retirement receipts[1] | 157,803 | 265,163 | 380,047 |
| Employment and general retirement | 138,748 | 234,646 | 353,891 |
| Unemployment insurance | 15,336 | 25,758 | 21,635 |
| **Federal funds:** | | | |
| Alcohol | 5,601 | 5,562 | 5,695 |
| Tobacco | 2,443 | 4,779 | 4,081 |
| Telephone | (NA) | 2,147 | 2,995 |
| Ozone depleting chemicals/products | (NA) | (NA) | 360 |
| Transportation fuels | (NA) | (NA) | (NA) |
| **Trust funds:** | | | |
| Highway | 6,620 | 13,015 | 13,867 |
| Airport and airway | 1,874 | 2,851 | 3,700 |
| Black lung disability | 272 | 581 | 665 |
| Inland waterway | (NA) | 40 | 63 |
| Hazardous substance superfund | (NA) | 273 | 818 |
| Post-closure liability (hazardous waste) | (NA) | 7 | -1 |
| Oil spill liability | (NA) | (NA) | 143 |
| Aquatic resources | (NA) | 126 | 218 |
| Leaking underground storage tank | (NA) | (NA) | 122 |
| Vaccine injury compensation | (NA) | (NA) | 159 |

*Notes:*

NA Not available.

1. Totals reflect interfund and intragovernmental transactions and/or other functions, not shown separately.

*General Notes:* Receipts reflect collections. Covers both federal funds and trust funds; see text, Section 10. Excludes government-sponsored but privately-owned corporations, Federal Reserve System, District of Columbia government, and money held in suspense as deposit funds.

*Source: Statistical Abstract of the United States 1998*, No. 539; <http://www.census.gov/prod/3/98pubs/98statab/sasec10.pdf>. Underlying data from U.S. Office of Management and Budget, *Historical Tables,* annual.

## H2-2. Federal Receipts, by Source: 1995–1998, in Millions of Dollars, for Fiscal Years ending in Year Shown

| SOURCE | 1995 | 1996 | 1997 | 1998, est. |
|---|---|---|---|---|
| **Total receipts**[1] | **1,351,830** | **1,453,062** | **1,579,292** | **1,657,858** |
| Individual income taxes | 590,244 | 656,417 | 737,466 | 767,768 |
| Corporation income taxes | 157,004 | 171,824 | 182,293 | 190,842 |
| Social insurance and retirement receipts | 484,473 | 509,414 | 539,371 | 571,374 |
| Excise taxes | 57,484 | 54,014 | 56,924 | 55,540 |
| Social insurance and retirement receipts[1] | 484,473 | 509,414 | 539,371 | 571,374 |
| Employment and general retirement | 451,045 | 476,361 | 506,751 | 538,124 |
| Unemployment insurance | 28,878 | 28,584 | 28,202 | 28,922 |
| **Federal funds:** | | | | |
| Alcohol | 7,216 | 7,220 | 7,257 | 7,251 |
| Tobacco | 5,878 | 5,795 | 5,873 | 5,926 |
| Telephone | 3,794 | 4,234 | 4,543 | 4,864 |
| Ozone depleting chemicals/products | 616 | 320 | 130 | 55 |
| Transportation fuels | 8,491 | 7,468 | 7,107 | 442 |
| **Trust funds:** | | | | |
| Highway | 22,611 | 24,651 | 23,867 | 26,063 |
| Airport and airway | 5,534 | 2,369 | 4,007 | 7,975 |
| Black lung disability | 608 | 614 | 614 | 640 |
| Inland waterway | 103 | 108 | 96 | 116 |
| Hazardous substance superfund | 867 | 313 | 71 | 101 |
| Post-closure liability (hazardous waste) | 7 | -1 | (NA) | (NA) |
| Oil spill liability | 211 | 34 | 1 | 46 |
| Aquatic resources | 306 | 315 | 316 | 281 |
| Leaking underground storage tanks | 165 | 48 | -2 | 140 |
| Vaccine injury compensation | 138 | 115 | 123 | 111 |

*Notes:*
NA Not available.
1. Totals reflect interfund and intragovernmental transactions and/or other functions, not shown separately.
*General Notes:* Receipts reflect collections. Covers both federal funds and trust funds; see text, Section 10. Excludes government-sponsored but privately-owned corporations, Federal Reserve System, District of Columbia government, and money held in suspense as deposit funds.

*Source: Statistical Abstract of the United States 1998*, No. 539; <http://www.census.gov/prod/3/98pubs/98statab/sasec10.pdf>. Underlying data from U.S. Office of Management and Budget, *Historical Tables*, annual.

## H3. FEDERAL BUDGET OUTLAYS

## H3-1. Federal Budget Outlays—Defense, Human and Physical Resources, and Net Interest Payments: 1980–1993, in Millions of Dollars, for Fiscal Years ending in Year Shown

| OUTLAYS | 1980 | 1985 | 1990 | 1993 |
|---|---|---|---|---|
| Federal outlays, total | 590,947 | 946,423 | 1,253,163 | 1,409,414 |
| National defense | 133,995 | 252,748 | 299,331 | 291,086 |
| Human resources | 313,374 | 471,822 | 619,329 | 827,535 |
| Physical resources | 65,985 | 56,821 | 126,004 | 46,762 |
| Net interest | 52,538 | 129,504 | 184,221 | 198,811 |
| Undistributed offsetting receipts | -19,942 | -32,698 | -36,615 | -37,386 |

*Note:*
Minus sign (-) indicates offsets

*Source: Statistical Abstract of the United States 1998*, No. 538; http://www.census.gov/prod/3/98pubs/98statab/sasec10.pdf. Underlying data from U. S. Office of Management and Budget, *Historical Tables,* annual.

## H3-2. Federal Budget Outlays—Defense, Human and Physical Resources, and Net Interest Payments: 1994–1998, in MIllions of Dollars, for Fiscal Years ending in Year Shown

| OUTLAYS | 1994 | 1995 | 1996 | 1997 | 1998, est. |
|---|---|---|---|---|---|
| Federal outlays, total | 1,461,731 | 1,515,729 | 1,560,512 | 1,601,235 | 1,667,815 |
| National defense | 281,642 | 272,066 | 265,748 | 270,473 | 264,112 |
| Human resources | 869,414 | 923,765 | 958,254 | 1,002,323 | 1,048,983 |
| Physical resources | 70,575 | 59,197 | 64,236 | 60,000 | 81,087 |
| Net interest | 202,957 | 232,169 | 241,090 | 244,013 | 242,694 |
| Undistributed offsetting receipts | -37,772 | -44,455 | -37,620 | -49,973 | -46,366 |

*Notes:*
Minus sign (-) indicates offsets.

*Source: Statistical Abstract of the United States 1998,* No. 538; <http://www.census.gov/prod/3/98pubs/98statab/sasec10.pdf>. Underlying data from U.S. Office of Management and Budget, *Historical Tables,* annual.

## H4. GROSS FEDERAL DEBT

## H4-1. Federal Budget—Summary, Gross Federal Debt: 1945–1998, in Millions of Dollars, for Fiscal Years ending in Year Shown

| Year | Total | Federal Gov't Account | Held by the public, Total | Held by the public, Federal Reserve Board |
|---|---|---|---|---|
| 1945 | 260,123 | 24,941 | 235,182 | 21,792 |
| 1950 | 256,853 | 37,830 | 219,023 | 18,331 |
| 1955 | 274,366 | 47,751 | 226,616 | 23,607 |
| 1960 | 290,525 | 53,686 | 236,840 | 26,523 |
| 1965 | 322,318 | 61,540 | 260,778 | 39,100 |
| 1970 | 380,921 | 97,723 | 283,198 | 57,714 |
| 1975 | 541,925 | 147,225 | 394,700 | 84,993 |
| 1980 | 909,050 | 199,212 | 709,838 | 120,846 |
| 1981 | 994,845 | 209,507 | 785,338 | 124,466 |
| 1982 | 1,137,345 | 217,560 | 919,785 | 134,497 |
| 1983 | 1,371,710 | 240,114 | 1,131,596 | 155,527 |
| 1984 | 1,564,657 | 264,159 | 1,300,498 | 155,122 |
| 1985 | 1,817,521 | 317,612 | 1,499,908 | 169,806 |
| 1986 | 2,120,629 | 383,919 | 1,736,709 | 190,855 |
| 1987 | 2,346,125 | 457,444 | 1,888,680 | 212,040 |
| 1988 | 2,601,307 | 550,507 | 2,050,799 | 229,218 |
| 1989 | 2,868,039 | 678,157 | 2,189,882 | 220,088 |
| 1990 | 3,206,564 | 795,841 | 2,410,722 | 234,410 |
| 1991 | 3,598,498 | 910,362 | 2,688,137 | 258,591 |
| 1992 | 4,002,136 | 1,003,302 | 2,998,834 | 296,397 |
| 1993 | 4,351,416 | 1,103,945 | 3,247,471 | 325,653 |
| 1994 | 4,643,705 | 1,211,588 | 3,432,117 | 355,150 |
| 1995 | 4,921,018 | 1,317,645 | 3,603,373 | 374,114 |
| 1996 | 5,181,934 | 1,448,967 | 3,732,968 | 390,924 |
| 1997 | 5,369,707 | 1,598,559 | 3,771,148 | 424,507 |
| 1998, est. | 5,543,589 | 1,746,773 | 3,796,816 | (NA) |

*Notes:*
NA Not available.
*General Notes:*
The Balanced Budget and Emergency Deficit Control Act of 1985 put all the previously off-budget federal entities into the budget and moved Social Security off-budget. Minus sign (-) indicates deficit or decrease.

*Source: Statistical Abstract of the United States 1998,* No. 537; <http://www.census.gov/prod/3/98pubs/98statab/sasec10.pdf>. Underlying data from U.S. Office of Management and Budget, *Historical Tables,* annual.

**H4-2. Federal Budget—Summary, Gross Federal Debt as Percent of GDP: 1945–1998, in Millions of Dollars, except percent, for Fiscal Years ending in Year Shown**

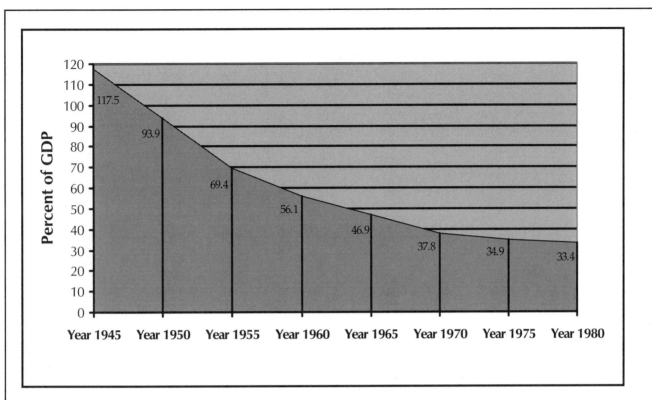

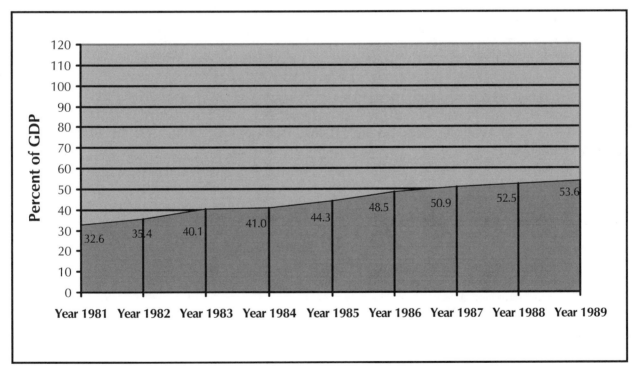

**H4-2. Federal Budget—Summary, Gross Federal Debt as Percent of GDP: 1945–1998, in Millions of Dollars, except percent, for Fiscal Years ending in Year Shown** *(continued)*

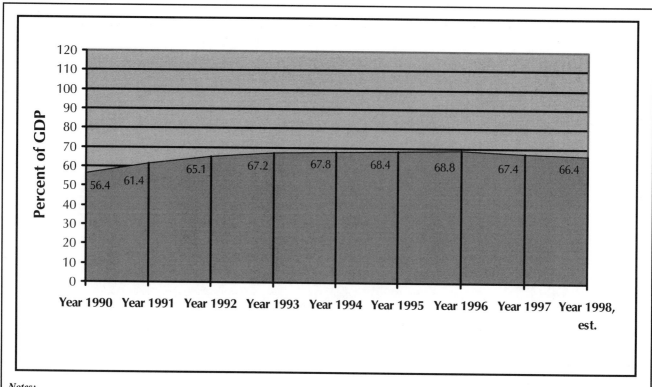

*Notes:*

*General Notes:* The Balanced Budget and Emergency Deficit Control Act of 1985 put all the previously off-budget federal entities into the budget and moved Social Security off-budget. Minus sign (-) indicates deficit or decrease.

*Source: Statistical Abstract of the United States 1998*, No. 537; <http://www.census.gov/prod/3/98pubs/98statab/sasec10.pdf>. Underlying data from U.S. Office of Management and Budget, *Historical Tables,* annual.

## H5. SMALL BUSINESS ADMINISTRATION (SBA) LOANS TO SMALL BUSINESSES

### H5-1. Small Business Administration Loans to Small Businesses: 1980–1991, for Fiscal Years ending in Year Shown

| LOANS APPROVED | Unit | 1980 | 1985 | 1989 | 1990 | 1991 |
|---|---|---|---|---|---|---|
| Loans, all businesses | 1,000 | 31.7 | 19.3 | 17 | 18.8 | 20.6 |
| Loans, minority-owned businesses | 1,000 | 6 | 2.8 | 2.4 | 2.4 | 3.1 |
| Percent of all business loans | Percent | 19 | 15 | 14 | 13 | 15 |
| Value of total loans[1] | Mil dol | 3,858 | 3,217 | 3,490 | 4,354 | 4,861 |
| Minority business loans[2] | Mil dol | 470 | 324 | 385 | 473 | 764 |

*Notes:*

1. Includes both SBA and bank portions of loans.
2. SBA direct loans and guaranteed portion of bank loans only.

*General Notes:*

A small business must be independently owned and operated, must not be dominant in its particular industry, and must meet standards set by the Small Business Administration as to its annual receipts or number of employees. Loans include both direct and guaranteed loans to small business establishments. Does not include Disaster Assistance Loans.

*Source: Statistical Abstract of the United States 1998*, No. 882; <http://wwwcensusgov/prod/3/98pubs/98statab/sasec17pdf>. Underlying data from U.S. Small Business Administration, *Management Information Summary*, unpublished data.

## H5-2. Small Business Administration Loans to Small Businesses: 1992–1996, for Fiscal Years ending in Year Shown

| LOANS APPROVED | Unit | 1992 | 1993 | 1994 | 1995 | 1996 |
|---|---|---|---|---|---|---|
| Loans, all businesses | 1,000 | 26.4 | 29.4 | 40.4 | 60.1 | 52.7 |
| Loans, minority-owned businesses | 1,000 | 3.9 | 4.5 | 6.8 | 10.4 | 9.1 |
| Percent of all business loans | Percent | 15 | 15 | 18 | 19 | 19 |
| Value of total loans[1] | Mil dol | 6,596 | 7,591 | 9,527 | 9,854 | 10,177 |
| Minority business loans[2] | Mil dol | 1,033 | 1,178 | 1,754 | 1,885 | 2,124 |

*Notes:*
1. Includes both SBA and bank portions of loans.
2. SBA direct loans and guaranteed portion of bank loans only.
*General Notes:* A small business must be independently owned and operated, must not be dominant in its particular industry, and must meet standards set by the Small Business Administration as to its annual receipts or number of employees. Loans include both direct and guaranteed loans to small business establishments. Does not include Disaster Assistance Loans.

*Source: Statistical Abstract of the United States 1998*, No. 882; <http://wwwcensusgov/prod/3/98pubs/98statab/sasec17pdf>. Underlying data from U.S. Small Business Administration, *Management Information Summary*, unpublished data.

## H6. SOCIAL WELFARE EXPENDITURES UNDER PUBLIC PROGRAMS

## H6-1. Social Welfare Expenditures Under Public Programs: 1980–1994, in Billions of Dollars (except percent) for Fiscal Years ending in Year Shown

| Year | Social insurance | Public aid | Health and medical programs[1] | Veterans programs |
|---|---|---|---|---|
| **Total:** | | | | |
| 1980 | 230 | 73 | 27 | 21 |
| 1985 | 370 | 98 | 39 | 27 |
| 1990 | 514 | 147 | 61 | 31 |
| 1991 | 561 | 181 | 66 | 33 |
| 1992 | 619 | 208 | 70 | 36 |
| 1993 | 659 | 221 | 75 | 36 |
| 1994 | 684 | 238 | 79 | 38 |
| **Federal:** | | | | |
| 1980 | 191 | 49 | 13 | 21 |
| 1985 | 310 | 63 | 18 | 27 |
| 1990 | 422 | 93 | 27 | 30 |
| 1991 | 454 | 113 | 30 | 32 |
| 1992 | 496 | 139 | 32 | 35 |
| 1993 | 534 | 152 | 33 | 36 |
| 1994 | 557 | 163 | 35 | 37 |
| **State and local:** | | | | |
| 1980 | 39 | 23 | 14 | (Z) |
| 1985 | 59 | 35 | 21 | (Z) |
| 1990 | 92 | 54 | 34 | (Z) |
| 1991 | 108 | 68 | 36 | 1 |
| 1992 | 123 | 69 | 38 | 1 |
| 1993 | 125 | 69 | 42 | 1 |
| 1994 | 126 | 75 | 45 | 1 |
| **Percent federal:** | | | | |
| 1980 | 83 | 68 | 47 | 99 |
| 1985 | 84 | 64 | 46 | 99 |
| 1990 | 82 | 63 | 44 | 98 |
| 1992 | 80 | 67 | 45 | 98 |
| 1993 | 81 | 69 | 44 | 98 |
| 1994 | 82 | 68 | 44 | 98 |

*Notes:*
(Z) Less than $500 million.
1. Excludes program parts of social insurance, public aid, veterans, and other social welfare.
*General Notes:* Represents outlays from trust funds (mostly social insurance funds built up by earmarked contributions from insured persons, their employers, or both) and budgetary outlays from general revenues. Includes administrative expenditures, capital outlay, and some expenditures and payments outside the United States.

*Source: Statistical Abstract of the United States 1998*, No. 599; <http://www.census.gov/prod/3/98pubs/98statab/sasec12.pdf>. Underlying data from U.S. Social Security Administration, *Social Security Bulletin*, Vol. 60, No. 3, 1997; and unpublished data.

## H6-2. Social Welfare Expenditures Under Public Programs, Per Capita: 1980–1994, in Dollars, for Fiscal Years ending in Year Shown

| Year | Social insurance | Public aid | Health and medical programs[1] | Veterans programs |
|------|------------------|------------|-------------------------------|-------------------|
| **Current dollars[3]** | | | | |
| 1980 | 990 | 314 | 118 | 92 |
| 1985 | 1,516 | 405 | 161 | 111 |
| 1990 | 2,017 | 579 | 243 | 120 |
| 1992 | 2,377 | 801 | 270 | 133 |
| 1993 | 2,523 | 849 | 287 | 137 |
| 1994 | 2,591 | 905 | 301 | 141 |
| **Constant (1994) dollars[3,4]** | | | | |
| 1980 | 1,723 | 547 | 205 | 160 |
| 1985 | 2,032 | 543 | 217 | 148 |
| 1990 | 2,265 | 650 | 273 | 135 |
| 1992 | 2,498 | 842 | 284 | 140 |
| 1993 | 2,585 | 869 | 294 | 141 |
| 1994 | 2,591 | 905 | 301 | 141 |

*Notes:*
1. Excludes program parts of social insurance, public aid, veterans, and other social welfare.
3. Excludes payments within foreign countries for education, veterans, OASDHI, and civil service retirement.
4. Constant dollar figures are based on implicit price deflators for personal consumption expenditures published by U.S. Bureau of Economic Analysis in *Survey of Current Business.*
*Only notes that apply to this table are cited.
*General Notes:* Represents outlays from trust funds (mostly social insurance funds built up by earmarked contributions from insured persons, their employers, or both) and budgetary outlays from general revenues. Includes administrative expenditures, capital outlay, and some expenditures and payments outside the United States.

*Source: Statistical Abstract of the United States 1998,* No. 599;  <http://www.census.gov/prod/3/98pubs/98statab/sasec12.pdf>.Underlying data from U.S. Social Security Administration, *Social Security Bulletin,* Vol. 60, No. 3, 1997; and unpublished data.

## H6-3. Social Welfare Expenditures Under Public Programs: 1980–1994, in Billions of Dollars, except percent, for Fiscal Years ending in Year Shown

| Year | Education | Housing | Other social welfare | All health and medical care[2] |
|------|-----------|---------|----------------------|--------------------------------|
| **Total:** | | | | |
| 1980 | 121 | 7 | 14 | 100 |
| 1985 | 172 | 13 | 14 | 171 |
| 1990 | 258 | 19 | 18 | 274 |
| 1991 | 277 | 22 | 20 | 314 |
| 1992 | 292 | 21 | 22 | 353 |
| 1993 | 332 | 20 | 23 | 382 |
| 1994 | 344 | 28 | 25 | 408 |
| **Federal:** | | | | |
| 1980 | 13 | 6 | 9 | 69 |
| 1985 | 14 | 11 | 8 | 122 |
| 1990 | 18 | 17 | 9 | 190 |
| 1991 | 19 | 19 | 10 | 214 |
| 1992 | 20 | 18 | 11 | 250 |
| 1993 | 20 | 18 | 11 | 275 |
| 1994 | 24 | 25 | 12 | 295 |
| **State and local:** | | | | |
| 1980 | 108 | 1 | 5 | 31 |
| 1985 | 158 | 2 | 6 | 49 |
| 1990 | 240 | 3 | 9 | 84 |
| 1991 | 258 | 3 | 10 | 100 |
| 1992 | 272 | 3 | 11 | 103 |
| 1993 | 311 | 2 | 12 | 107 |
| 1994 | 320 | 2 | 13 | 113 |

## H6-3. Social Welfare Expenditures Under Public Programs: 1980–1994, in Billions of Dollars, except percent, for Fiscal Years ending in Year Shown *(continued)*

| Year | Education | Housing | Other social welfare | All health and medical care[2] |
|------|-----------|---------|----------------------|--------------------------------|
| **Percent federal:** | | | | |
| 1980 | 11 | 91 | 65 | 69 |
| 1985 | 8 | 88 | 56 | 71 |
| 1990 | 7 | 85 | 50 | 69 |
| 1992 | 7 | 87 | 50 | 71 |
| 1993 | 6 | 91 | 48 | 72 |
| 1994 | 7 | 92 | 48 | 72 |

*Notes:*
2. Combines "Health and medical programs" with medical services included in social insurance, public aid, veterans, vocational rehabilitation, and anti-poverty programs.
General Notes: Represents outlays from trust funds (mostly social insurance funds built up by earmarked contributions from insured persons, their employers, or both) and budgetary outlays from general revenues. Includes administrative expenditures, capital outlay, and some expenditures and payments outside the United States.
*Only notes that apply to this table are cited.

*Source: Statistical Abstract of the United States 1998*, No. 599; <http://www.census.gov/prod/3/98pubs/98statab/sasec12.pdf>.Underlying data from U.S. Social Security Administration, *Social Security Bulletin*, Vol. 60, No. 3, 1997; and unpublished data.

## H6-4. Social Welfare Expenditures Under Public Programs: 1980–1994, in Dollars, for Fiscal Years ending in Year Shown

| Year | Education | Housing | Other social welfare | All health and medical care[2] |
|------|-----------|---------|----------------------|--------------------------------|
| **Current dollars[3]** | | | | |
| 1980 | 523 | 30 | 59 | 434 |
| 1985 | 708 | 52 | 56 | 705 |
| 1990 | 1,018 | 77 | 71 | 1,081 |
| 1992 | 1,126 | 79 | 83 | 1,359 |
| 1993 | 1,274 | 76 | 87 | 1,466 |
| 1994 | 1,308 | 102 | 94 | 1,551 |
| **Constant (1994) dollars[3,4]** | | | | |
| 1980 | 911 | 52 | 102 | 746 |
| 1985 | 950 | 70 | 75 | 942 |
| 1990 | 1,143 | 86 | 79 | 1,214 |
| 1992 | 1,183 | 85 | 87 | 1,428 |
| 1993 | 1,305 | 78 | 89 | 1,501 |
| 1994 | 1,308 | 102 | 94 | 1,551 |

*Notes:*
2. Combines "Health and medical programs" with medical services included in social insurance, public aid, veterans, vocational rehabilitation, and anti-poverty programs.
3. Excludes payments within foreign countries for education, veterans, OASDHI, and civil service retirement
4. Constant dollar figures are based on implicit price deflators for personal consumption expenditures published by US Bureau of Economic Analysis in Survey of Current Business.
General Notes: Represents outlays from trust funds (mostly social insurance funds built up by earmarked contributions from insured persons, their employers, or both) and budgetary outlays from general revenues. Includes administrative expenditures, capital outlay, and some expenditures and payments outside the United States.
*Only notes that apply to this table are cited.

*Source: Statistical Abstract of the United States 1998*, No. 599; <http://www.census.gov/prod/3/98pubs/98statab/sasec12.pdf>.Underlying data from U.S. Social Security Administration, *Social Security Bulletin*, Vol. 60, No. 3, 1997; and unpublished data.

## H6-5. Social Welfare Expenditures under Public Programs, Totals: 1980–1994, for Fiscal Years ending in Year Shown

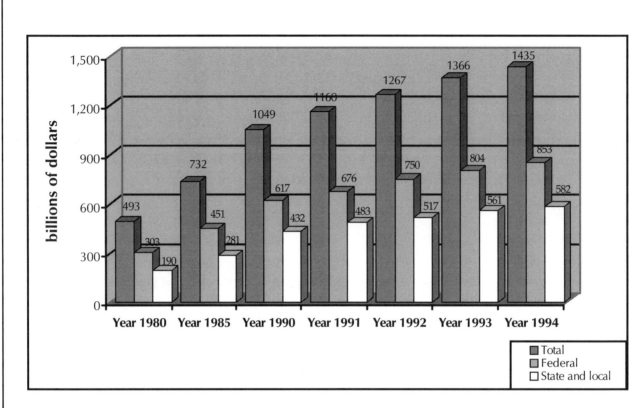

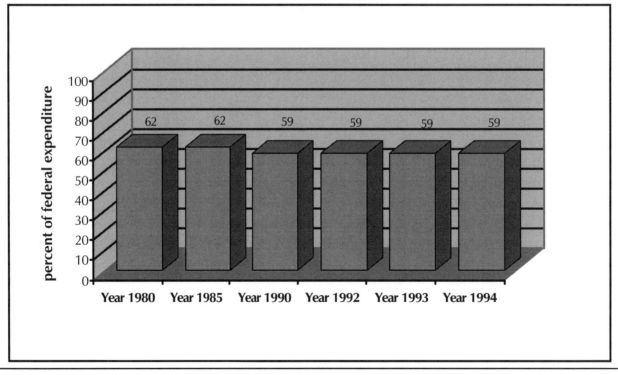

**H6-5. Social Welfare Expenditures Under Public Programs, Totals: 1980–1994, for Fiscal Years ending in Year Shown** *(continued)*

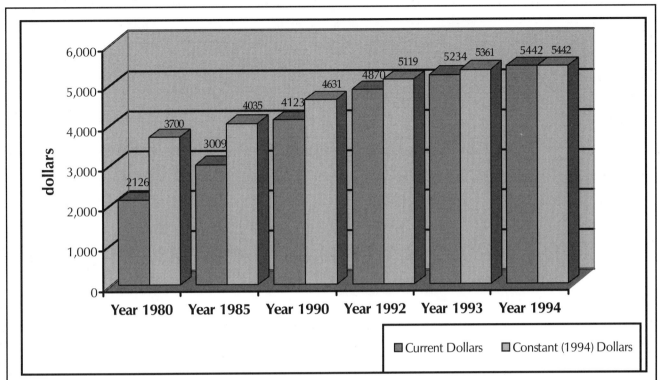

**Notes:**

*General Notes:* Represents outlays from trust funds (mostly social insurance funds built up by earmarked contributions from insured persons, their employers, or both) and budgetary outlays from general revenues. Includes administrative expenditures, capital outlay, and some expenditures and payments outside the United States.

*Source: Statistical Abstract of the United States 1998*, No. 599; <http://www.census.gov/prod/3/98pubs/98statab/sasec12.pdf>. Underlying data from U.S. Social Security Administration, *Social Security Bulletin*, Vol. 60, No. 3, 1997; and unpublished data.

## H7. STATE GOVERNMENTS—SOURCES OF GENERAL REVENUE

### H7-1. State Governments—Revenue, by State: 1996, in Millions of Dollars (except as noted)

| | Total revenue[1] | General revenue, total | General revenue, per capita[2] total (dollars) | General revenue, per capita[2], rank |
|---|---|---|---|---|
| **United States** | **966,298** | **770,006** | **2,910** | **X** |
| Alabama | 12,741 | 10,894 | 2,541 | 40 |
| Alaska | 8,254 | 6,819 | 11,272 | 1 |
| Arizona | 12,594 | 10,867 | 2,451 | 45 |
| Arkansas | 8,653 | 7,023 | 2,802 | 25 |
| California | 123,342 | 98,185 | 3,082 | 21 |
| Colorado | 11,866 | 9,461 | 2,479 | 43 |
| Connecticut | 14,349 | 12,357 | 3,782 | 6 |
| Delaware | 3,619 | 3,303 | 4,565 | 2 |
| Florida | 41,680 | 32,994 | 2,288 | 49 |
| Georgia | 22,409 | 18,345 | 2,501 | 41 |
| Hawaii | 6,383 | 5,379 | 4,547 | 3 |
| Idaho | 4,384 | 3,305 | 2,783 | 27 |
| Illinois | 36,991 | 30,306 | 2,559 | 38 |
| Indiana | 16,550 | 15,065 | 2,585 | 37 |
| Iowa | 9,245 | 8,133 | 2,856 | 24 |
| Kansas | 7,864 | 6,892 | 2,672 | 34 |
| Kentucky | 13,788 | 11,571 | 2,981 | 22 |
| Louisiana | 14,296 | 11,833 | 2,726 | 33 |
| Maine | 4,267 | 3,836 | 3,097 | 20 |
| Maryland | 16,041 | 14,011 | 2,769 | 28 |
| Massachusetts | 25,197 | 22,845 | 3,754 | 7 |
| Michigan | 38,047 | 32,129 | 3,302 | 14 |
| Minnesota | 20,525 | 16,192 | 3,483 | 9 |
| Mississippi | 8,865 | 7,461 | 2,752 | 30 |
| Missouri | 17,051 | 13,022 | 2,428 | 46 |
| Montana | 3,476 | 2,831 | 3,229 | 15 |
| Nebraska | 4,999 | 4,536 | 2,751 | 31 |
| Nevada | 5,997 | 4,146 | 2,590 | 36 |
| New Hampshire | 3,561 | 2,706 | 2,333 | 48 |
| New Jersey | 35,857 | 26,615 | 3,326 | 12 |
| New Mexico | 8,129 | 6,318 | 3,692 | 8 |
| New York | 94,277 | 71,219 | 3,927 | 5 |
| North Carolina | 23,387 | 20,047 | 2,743 | 32 |
| North Dakota | 2,569 | 2,144 | 3,337 | 11 |
| Ohio | 43,823 | 29,467 | 2,640 | 35 |
| Oklahoma | 10,609 | 8,156 | 2,475 | 44 |
| Oregon | 15,432 | 9,958 | 3,115 | 19 |
| Pennsylvania | 42,796 | 33,512 | 2,783 | 26 |
| Rhode Island | 4,271 | 3,346 | 3,385 | 10 |
| South Carolina | 12,602 | 10,261 | 2,761 | 29 |
| South Dakota | 2,284 | 1,886 | 2,557 | 39 |
| Tennessee | 14,749 | 12,510 | 2,357 | 47 |
| Texas | 51,118 | 42,616 | 2,232 | 50 |
| Utah | 6,773 | 5,831 | 2,890 | 23 |
| Vermont | 2,146 | 1,950 | 3,325 | 13 |
| Virginia | 20,072 | 16,617 | 2,493 | 42 |
| Washington | 24,790 | 17,195 | 3,115 | 18 |
| West Virginia | 6,866 | 5,836 | 3,206 | 16 |
| Wisconsin | 24,365 | 16,071 | 3,123 | 17 |
| Wyoming | 2,348 | 2,004 | 4,175 | 4 |

*Notes:*
1. Includes items not shown separately.
2. Based on estimated resident population as of July 1.

*Source: Statistical Abstract of the United States 1998*, No. 515; <http://www.census.gov/prod/3/98pubs/98statab/sasec9.pdf>. Underlying data from U.S. Bureau of the Census; <http://www.census.gov/govs/www/state.html> .

**H7-2. State Governments—Sources of General Revenue, Taxation by State: 1996, in Millions of Dollars (except as noted)**

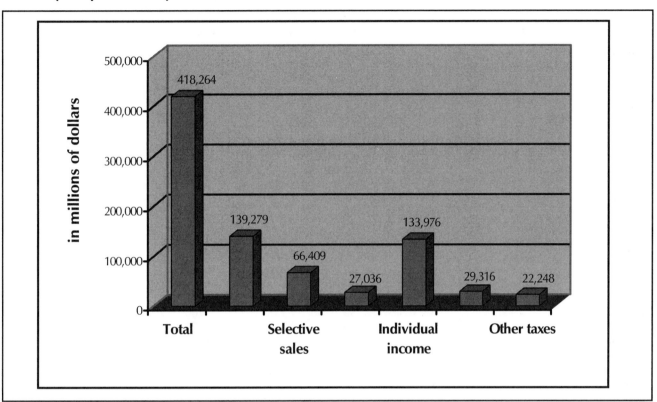

*Source: Statistical Abstract of the United States 1998*, No. 515; <http://www.census.gov/prod/3/98pubs/98statab/sasec9.pdf>. Underlying data from U.S. Bureau of the Census; <http://www.census.gov/govs/www/statehtml>.

## H7-3. State Governments—Sources of General Revenue, Taxation by State: 1996, in Millions of Dollars (except as noted)

| | Total | General sales | Selective sales[1] | License taxes | Individual income | Corporation net income | Other taxes |
|---|---|---|---|---|---|---|---|
| **United States** | **418,264** | **139,279** | **66,409** | **27,036** | **133,976** | **29,316** | **22,248** |
| Alabama | 5,258 | 1,439 | 1,335 | 423 | 1,578 | 218 | 265 |
| Alaska | 1,519 | (X) | 99 | 79 | (X) | 326 | 1,015 |
| Arizona | 6,409 | 2,720 | 938 | 391 | 1,494 | 448 | 418 |
| Arkansas | 3,709 | 1,376 | 564 | 216 | 1,162 | 229 | 162 |
| California | 57,747 | 18,980 | 5,113 | 3,035 | 20,760 | 5,831 | 4,028 |
| Colorado | 4,820 | 1,322 | 716 | 256 | 2,274 | 206 | 47 |
| Connecticut | 7,830 | 2,445 | 1,487 | 331 | 2,614 | 641 | 311 |
| Delaware | 1,688 | (X) | 253 | 533 | 632 | 166 | 105 |
| Florida | 19,699 | 11,429 | 3,812 | 1,315 | (X) | 1,008 | 2,136 |
| Georgia | 10,292 | 3,824 | 962 | 420 | 4,244 | 719 | 123 |
| Hawaii | 3,079 | 1,432 | 473 | 85 | 1,000 | 66 | 24 |
| Idaho | 1,857 | 600 | 252 | 156 | 655 | 153 | 41 |
| Illinois | 17,277 | 5,057 | 3,428 | 952 | 5,781 | 1,621 | 437 |
| Indiana | 8,437 | 2,868 | 894 | 202 | 3,478 | 894 | 102 |
| Iowa | 4,441 | 1,456 | 691 | 414 | 1,588 | 203 | 88 |
| Kansas | 3,979 | 1,401 | 530 | 203 | 1,377 | 255 | 213 |
| Kentucky | 6,489 | 1,784 | 1,282 | 381 | 2,075 | 285 | 683 |
| Louisiana | 4,906 | 1,622 | 937 | 418 | 1,160 | 328 | 441 |
| Maine | 1,897 | 658 | 278 | 114 | 709 | 71 | 66 |
| Maryland | 8,167 | 2,000 | 1,555 | 358 | 3,485 | 331 | 439 |
| Massachusetts | 12,455 | 2,610 | 1,278 | 398 | 6,707 | 1,228 | 235 |
| Michigan | 19,129 | 6,587 | 1,738 | 982 | 5,868 | 2,190 | 1,764 |
| Minnesota | 10,243 | 2,900 | 1,592 | 769 | 4,136 | 703 | 142 |
| Mississippi | 3,861 | 1,832 | 770 | 247 | 742 | 202 | 67 |
| Missouri | 7,210 | 2,465 | 986 | 516 | 2,741 | 426 | 76 |
| Montana | 1,256 | (X) | 269 | 148 | 383 | 76 | 380 |
| Nebraska | 2,369 | 815 | 410 | 158 | 840 | 127 | 20 |
| Nevada | 2,889 | 1,572 | 863 | 313 | (X) | (X) | 141 |
| New Hampshire | 837 | (X) | 429 | 108 | 52 | 180 | 69 |
| New Jersey | 14,385 | 4,318 | 3,045 | 753 | 4,734 | 1,155 | 379 |
| New Mexico | 3,061 | 1,284 | 452 | 165 | 643 | 163 | 354 |
| New York | 34,150 | 6,963 | 4,950 | 974 | 17,399 | 2,730 | 1,134 |
| North Carolina | 11,882 | 2,971 | 2,173 | 733 | 4,929 | 939 | 137 |
| North Dakota | 985 | 282 | 278 | 78 | 152 | 74 | 122 |
| Ohio | 15,649 | 4,991 | 2,613 | 1,219 | 5,903 | 807 | 116 |
| Oklahoma | 4,618 | 1,210 | 660 | 658 | 1,512 | 164 | 413 |
| Oregon | 4,416 | (X) | 591 | 581 | 2,823 | 300 | 120 |
| Pennsylvania | 18,295 | 5,701 | 3,056 | 1,809 | 5,214 | 1,504 | 1,010 |
| Rhode Island | 1,549 | 465 | 313 | 80 | 581 | 87 | 23 |
| South Carolina | 5,113 | 1,919 | 684 | 389 | 1,813 | 251 | 56 |
| South Dakota | 730 | 383 | 189 | 90 | (X) | 38 | 29 |
| Tennessee | 6,185 | 3,537 | 1,207 | 610 | 114 | 534 | 182 |
| Texas | 21,271 | 10,811 | 6,424 | 3,048 | (X) | (X) | 988 |
| Utah | 2,914 | 1,170 | 300 | 99 | 1,139 | 177 | 29 |
| Vermont | 841 | 183 | 221 | 72 | 281 | 45 | 40 |
| Virginia | 8,900 | 1,996 | 1,593 | 419 | 4,301 | 363 | 229 |
| Washington | 10,586 | 6,182 | 1,685 | 493 | (X) | (X) | 2,226 |
| West Virginia | 2,771 | 797 | 655 | 156 | 751 | 235 | 177 |
| Wisconsin | 9,586 | 2,708 | 1,322 | 614 | 4,151 | 621 | 170 |
| Wyoming | 626 | 211 | 63 | 74 | (X) | (X) | 278 |

*Notes:*
(X) Not Applicable
1. Special tax rate on specific items.

*Source: Statistical Abstract of the United States 1998*, No. 515; <http://www.census.gov/prod/3/98pubs/98statab/sasec9.pdf>. Underlying data from U.S. Bureau of the Census; <http://wwwcensusgov/govs/www/statehtml>.

## H7-4. State Governments—Sources of General Revenue, Intergovernmental and Miscellaneous, by State: 1996, in Millions of Dollars (except as noted)

| | Intergovernmental revenue | | | Charges and miscellaneous | | |
| | Total | From Federal Government | From Local Governments | Total | Current Charges | Misc. General Revenue |
|---|---|---|---|---|---|---|
| **United States** | **221,469** | **208,100** | **13,370** | **130,273** | **67,145** | **63,128** |
| Alabama | 3,347 | 3,301 | 46 | 2,290 | 1,641 | 649 |
| Alaska | 1,017 | 1,012 | 5 | 4,283 | 294 | 3,988 |
| Arizona | 3,105 | 2,767 | 338 | 1,352 | 666 | 686 |
| Arkansas | 2,163 | 2,156 | 7 | 1,152 | 736 | 415 |
| California | 29,087 | 26,731 | 2,356 | 11,351 | 6,743 | 4,609 |
| Colorado | 2,746 | 2,726 | 20 | 1,895 | 1,071 | 824 |
| Connecticut | 2,734 | 2,729 | 5 | 1,793 | 845 | 948 |
| Delaware | 662 | 633 | 29 | 952 | 466 | 487 |
| Florida | 8,493 | 8,171 | 322 | 4,801 | 1,818 | 2,983 |
| Georgia | 5,420 | 5,319 | 101 | 2,633 | 1,425 | 1,207 |
| Hawaii | 1,228 | 1,220 | 8 | 1,072 | 756 | 316 |
| Idaho | 850 | 844 | 7 | 597 | 280 | 318 |
| Illinois | 8,394 | 7,873 | 521 | 4,635 | 1,891 | 2,744 |
| Indiana | 3,750 | 3,625 | 125 | 2,878 | 1,678 | 1,200 |
| Iowa | 2,139 | 2,057 | 82 | 1,554 | 979 | 574 |
| Kansas | 1,694 | 1,658 | 37 | 1,219 | 729 | 490 |
| Kentucky | 3,152 | 3,141 | 11 | 1,929 | 1,085 | 844 |
| Louisiana | 4,111 | 4,084 | 26 | 2,816 | 1,621 | 1,195 |
| Maine | 1,245 | 1,242 | 3 | 694 | 287 | 407 |
| Maryland | 3,240 | 3,126 | 114 | 2,605 | 1,318 | 1,286 |
| Massachusetts | 5,827 | 5,354 | 474 | 4,562 | 1,814 | 2,748 |
| Michigan | 7,760 | 7,313 | 447 | 5,240 | 3,200 | 2,040 |
| Minnesota | 3,620 | 3,461 | 159 | 2,330 | 1,325 | 1,005 |
| Mississippi | 2,696 | 2,608 | 88 | 904 | 675 | 229 |
| Missouri | 3,711 | 3,690 | 20 | 2,101 | 1,103 | 998 |
| Montana | 991 | 977 | 15 | 583 | 250 | 334 |
| Nebraska | 1,190 | 1,164 | 26 | 977 | 640 | 337 |
| Nevada | 804 | 764 | 40 | 452 | 254 | 199 |
| New Hampshire | 1,011 | 862 | 149 | 858 | 372 | 486 |
| New Jersey | 6,663 | 6,424 | 240 | 5,567 | 2,529 | 3,038 |
| New Mexico | 1,794 | 1,749 | 45 | 1,464 | 599 | 865 |
| New York | 27,668 | 22,373 | 5,296 | 9,401 | 3,941 | 5,460 |
| North Carolina | 5,758 | 5,300 | 458 | 2,407 | 1,525 | 882 |
| North Dakota | 660 | 631 | 29 | 499 | 361 | 138 |
| Ohio | 8,726 | 8,485 | 241 | 5,091 | 2,882 | 2,209 |
| Oklahoma | 2,197 | 2,119 | 78 | 1,341 | 934 | 407 |
| Oregon | 3,334 | 3,267 | 67 | 2,208 | 1,141 | 1,067 |
| Pennsylvania | 9,151 | 9,063 | 88 | 6,066 | 3,512 | 2,554 |
| Rhode Island | 1,110 | 1,053 | 57 | 686 | 253 | 433 |
| South Carolina | 3,187 | 3,062 | 125 | 1,961 | 1,414 | 547 |
| South Dakota | 695 | 687 | 8 | 461 | 181 | 280 |
| Tennessee | 4,726 | 4,689 | 38 | 1,599 | 1,133 | 466 |
| Texas | 13,077 | 12,612 | 465 | 8,268 | 3,344 | 4,924 |
| Utah | 1,757 | 1,712 | 45 | 1,160 | 826 | 335 |
| Vermont | 650 | 647 | 4 | 459 | 286 | 173 |
| Virginia | 3,515 | 3,377 | 138 | 4,201 | 2,483 | 1,719 |
| Washington | 3,891 | 3,834 | 56 | 2,718 | 1,685 | 1,034 |
| West Virginia | 2,094 | 2,079 | 15 | 971 | 555 | 416 |
| Wisconsin | 3,860 | 3,578 | 282 | 2,626 | 1,505 | 1,121 |
| Wyoming | 768 | 753 | 15 | 610 | 95 | 515 |

*Source: Statistical Abstract of the United States 1998*, No. 515; <http://www.census.gov/prod/3/98pubs/98statab/sasec9.pdf>. Underlying data from U.S. Bureau of the Census; <http://www.census.gov/govs/www/state.html>.

## H7-5. State Governments—Sources of General Revenue; Utility, Liquor, and Insurance Trust Revenue: 1996, in Millions of Dollars (except as noted)

| | Utility revenue | Liquor store revenue | Insurance trust revenue |
|---|---|---|---|
| **United States** | **3,919** | **3,160** | **189,213** |
| Alabama | (X) | 136 | 1,710 |
| Alaska | 17 | (X) | 1,418 |
| Arizona | 21 | (X) | 1,706 |
| Arkansas | (X) | (X) | 1,630 |
| California | 143 | (X) | 25,014 |
| Colorado | (X) | (X) | 2,405 |
| Connecticut | 21 | (X) | 1,972 |
| Delaware | 7 | (X) | 309 |
| Florida | 5 | (X) | 8,681 |
| Georgia | (X) | (X) | 4,064 |
| Hawaii | (X) | (X) | 1,004 |
| Idaho | (X) | 47 | 1,032 |
| Illinois | (X) | (X) | 6,684 |
| Indiana | (X) | (X) | 1,485 |
| Iowa | (X) | 87 | 1,024 |
| Kansas | (X) | (X) | 973 |
| Kentucky | (X) | (X) | 2,218 |
| Louisiana | (X) | (X) | 2,463 |
| Maine | (X) | 70 | 361 |
| Maryland | 89 | (X) | 1,941 |
| Massachusetts | 69 | (X) | 2,283 |
| Michigan | (X) | 475 | 5,443 |
| Minnesota | (X) | (X) | 4,333 |
| Mississippi | (X) | 134 | 1,269 |
| Missouri | (X) | (X) | 4,029 |
| Montana | (X) | 39 | 606 |
| Nebraska | (X) | (X) | 463 |
| Nevada | 46 | (X) | 1,806 |
| New Hampshire | (-) | 223 | 632 |
| New Jersey | 447 | (X) | 8,796 |
| New Mexico | (X) | (X) | 1,811 |
| New York | 2,156 | (X) | 20,902 |
| North Carolina | (X) | (X) | 3,340 |
| North Dakota | (X) | (X) | 424 |
| Ohio | (X) | 373 | 13,983 |
| Oklahoma | 246 | (X) | 2,207 |
| Oregon | (X) | 184 | 5,290 |
| Pennsylvania | (X) | 693 | 8,592 |
| Rhode Island | 8 | (X) | 917 |
| South Carolina | 644 | (X) | 1,697 |
| South Dakota | (X) | (X) | 397 |
| Tennessee | (X) | (X) | 2,239 |
| Texas | (X) | (X) | 8,502 |
| Utah | (X) | 88 | 854 |
| Vermont | (X) | 28 | 168 |
| Virginia | (X) | 249 | 3,206 |
| Washington | (X) | 254 | 7,341 |
| West Virginia | (-) | 45 | 985 |
| Wisconsin | (X) | (X) | 8,294 |
| Wyoming | (X) | 34 | 310 |

*Notes:*
(-) Represents or rounds to zero
(X) Not applicable.

*Source: Statistical Abstract of the United States 1998*, No. 515; <http://www.census.gov/prod/3/98pubs/98statab/sasec9.pdf>. Underlying data from U.S. Bureau of the Census; <http://www.census.gov/govs/www/state.html>.

# Appendix: International Perspective

The following tables present the Gross Domestic Product (GDP) of countries across the world: the first in alphabetical order and the next in order of highest to lowest GDP. This information is included here to provide an international touchstone for the United States. Included here are 178 countries for which the World Bank collects data. Excluded are countries such as Iraq and Bosnia, whose societies are not open or whose economies are not stable enough to obtain meaningful data.

**Gross Domestic Product: 1997, in millions of U.S. dollars (in alphabetical order)**

| Ranking | | |
|---|---|---|
| 126 | Albania | 2,460 |
| 50 | Algeria | 47,072 |
| 88 | Angola | 7,662 |
| 156 | Antigua and Barbuda | 502 |
| 17 | Argentina | 325,012 |
| 140 | Armenia | 1,626 |
| 14 | Australia | 394,509 |
| 22 | Austria | 206,303 |
| 112 | Azerbaijan | 4,399 |
| 117 | Bahamas, The | 3,750 |
| 98 | Bahrain | 6,097 |
| 53 | Bangladesh | 41,419 |
| 139 | Barbados | 1,743 |
| 60 | Belarus | 22,462 |
| 19 | Belgium | 242,550 |
| 153 | Belize | 649 |
| 131 | Benin | 2,141 |
| 161 | Bhutan | 383 |
| 87 | Bolivia | 7,977 |
| 105 | Botswana | 5,070 |
| 8 | Brazil | 820,381 |
| 102 | Brunei | 5,271 |
| 80 | Bulgaria | 10,085 |
| 127 | Burkina Faso | 2,395 |
| 147 | Burundi | 957 |
| 121 | Cambodia | 3,044 |
| 83 | Cameroon | 9,115 |
| 9 | Canada | 609,778 |
| 159 | Cape Verde | 425 |
| 146 | Central African Republic | 1,019 |
| 141 | Chad | 1,603 |
| 41 | Chile | 77,082 |
| 37 | Colombia | 95,745 |
| 173 | Comoros | 194 |
| 97 | Congo, Dem. Rep. | 6,101 |
| 128 | Congo, Rep. | 2,298 |
| 82 | Costa Rica | 9,521 |
| 76 | Cote d'Ivoire | 10,251 |

## Gross Domestic Product: 1997, in millions of U.S. dollars (in alphabetical order) *(continued)*

| Ranking | | |
|---|---|---|
| 63 | Croatia | 19,081 |
| 86 | Cyprus | 8,204 |
| 49 | Czech Republic | 52,035 |
| 25 | Denmark | 170,152 |
| 157 | Djibouti | 500 |
| 170 | Dominica | 243 |
| 72 | Dominican Republic | 15,039 |
| 67 | Ecuador | 18,138 |
| 42 | Egypt, Arab Rep. | 75,605 |
| 75 | El Salvador | 11,264 |
| 158 | Equatorial Guinea | 487 |
| 152 | Eritrea | 655 |
| 107 | Estonia | 4,821 |
| 96 | Ethiopia | 6,381 |
| 132 | Fiji | 2,101 |
| 32 | Finland | 119,867 |
| 4 | France | 1,391,712 |
| 104 | Gabon | 5,153 |
| 160 | Gambia, The | 407 |
| 103 | Georgia | 5,216 |
| 3 | Germany | 2,097,225 |
| 94 | Ghana | 6,884 |
| 31 | Greece | 122,946 |
| 144 | Greenland | 1,252 |
| 165 | Grenada | 295 |
| 69 | Guatemala | 17,772 |
| 115 | Guinea | 3,888 |
| 167 | Guinea-Bissau | 266 |
| 151 | Guyana | 782 |
| 122 | Haiti | 2,815 |
| 110 | Honduras | 4,491 |
| 24 | Hong Kong, China | 171,401 |
| 51 | Hungary | 45,725 |
| 91 | Iceland | 7,296 |
| 16 | India | 359,718 |
| 21 | Indonesia | 214,995 |
| 38 | Iran, Islamic Rep. | 89,979 |
| 43 | Ireland | 74,989 |
| 35 | Israel | 98,081 |
| 6 | Italy | 1,145,558 |
| 114 | Jamaica | 4,135 |
| 2 | Japan | 4,190,264 |
| 92 | Jordan | 7,015 |
| 61 | Kazakhstan | 22,165 |
| 77 | Kenya | 10,240 |
| 177 | Kiribati | 55 |
| 12 | Korea, Rep. | 442,543 |
| 57 | Kuwait | 30,373 |
| 129 | Kyrgyz Republic | 2,243 |
| 138 | Lao PDR | 1,753 |
| 101 | Latvia | 5,352 |
| 73 | Lebanon | 14,962 |
| 148 | Lesotho | 950 |
| 81 | Lithuania | 9,585 |
| 70 | Luxembourg | 16,969 |
| 90 | Macao | 7,542 |
| 130 | Macedonia, FYR | 2,208 |
| 118 | Madagascar | 3,546 |

## Gross Domestic Product: 1997, in millions of U.S. dollars (in alphabetical order)

| Ranking | | |
|---|---|---|
| 125 | Malawi | 2,519 |
| 34 | Malaysia | 98,473 |
| 163 | Maldives | 342 |
| 124 | Mali | 2,532 |
| 119 | Malta | 3,323 |
| 176 | Marshall Islands | 97 |
| 145 | Mauritania | 1,097 |
| 113 | Mauritius | 4,398 |
| 13 | Mexico | 402,963 |
| 171 | Micronesia, Fed. Sts. | 213 |
| 133 | Moldova | 2,075 |
| 149 | Mongolia | 862 |
| 55 | Morocco | 33,514 |
| 123 | Mozambique | 2,753 |
| 120 | Namibia | 3,280 |
| 106 | Nepal | 4,929 |
| 15 | Netherlands | 360,513 |
| 44 | New Zealand | 64,761 |
| 135 | Nicaragua | 1,971 |
| 137 | Niger | 1,855 |
| 48 | Nigeria | 52,153 |
| 27 | Norway | 153,437 |
| 74 | Oman | 12,102 |
| 46 | Pakistan | 61,667 |
| 175 | Palau | 145 |
| 85 | Panama | 8,244 |
| 108 | Papua New Guinea | 4,639 |
| 79 | Paraguay | 10,180 |
| 45 | Peru | 63,849 |
| 40 | Philippines | 82,157 |
| 29 | Poland | 135,659 |
| 33 | Portugal | 102,135 |
| 52 | Puerto Rico | 42,364 |
| 89 | Qatar | 7,612 |
| 56 | Romania | 32,070 |
| 11 | Russian Federation | 489,608 |
| 136 | Rwanda | 1,863 |
| 172 | Samoa | 194 |
| 178 | Sao Tome and Principe | 44 |
| 28 | Saudi Arabia | 140,374 |
| 109 | Senegal | 4,542 |
| 155 | Seychelles | 539 |
| 150 | Sierra Leone | 823 |
| 36 | Singapore | 96,319 |
| 62 | Slovak Republic | 19,461 |
| 66 | Slovenia | 18,201 |
| 162 | Solomon Islands | 374 |
| 30 | South Africa | 129,094 |
| 10 | Spain | 532,047 |
| 71 | Sri Lanka | 15,093 |
| 169 | St. Kitts and Nevis | 247 |
| 154 | St. Lucia | 598 |
| 166 | St. Vincent and the Grenadines | 275 |
| 78 | Sudan | 10,224 |
| 164 | Suriname | 335 |
| 143 | Swaziland | 1,313 |
| 20 | Sweden | 227,785 |
| 18 | Switzerland | 255,497 |

## Gross Domestic Product: 1997, in millions of U.S. dollars (in alphabetical order)

| Ranking | | |
|---|---|---|
| 68 | Syrian Arab Republic | 17,899 |
| 134 | Tajikistan | 1,990 |
| 93 | Tanzania | 6,920 |
| 26 | Thailand | 153,909 |
| 142 | Togo | 1,475 |
| 174 | Tonga | 187 |
| 99 | Trinidad and Tobago | 5,894 |
| 64 | Tunisia | 18,937 |
| 23 | Turkey | 189,878 |
| 111 | Turkmenistan | 4,399 |
| 95 | Uganda | 6,582 |
| 47 | Ukraine | 59,756 |
| 54 | United Arab Emirates | 39,107 |
| 5 | United Kingdom | 1,288,252 |
| 1 | United States | 7,834,036 |
| 65 | Uruguay | 18,891 |
| 58 | Uzbekistan | 25,047 |
| 168 | Vanuatu | 252 |
| 39 | Venezuela | 87,480 |
| 59 | Vietnam | 24,848 |
| 100 | Yemen, Rep. | 5,656 |
| 116 | Zambia | 3,865 |
| 84 | Zimbabwe | 8,906 |

## Gross Domestic Product: 1997, in millions of U.S. dollars (in GDP order, highest to lowest)

| Ranking | | |
|---|---|---|
| 1 | United States | 7,834,036 |
| 2 | Japan | 4,190,264 |
| 3 | Germany | 2,097,225 |
| 4 | France | 1,391,712 |
| 5 | United Kingdom | 1,288,252 |
| 6 | Italy | 1,145,558 |
| 7 | China | 901,981 |
| 8 | Brazil | 820,381 |
| 9 | Canada | 609,778 |
| 10 | Spain | 532,047 |
| 11 | Russian Federation | 489,608 |
| 12 | Korea, Rep. | 442,543 |
| 13 | Mexico | 402,963 |
| 14 | Australia | 394,509 |
| 15 | Netherlands | 360,513 |
| 16 | India | 359,718 |
| 17 | Argentina | 325,012 |
| 18 | Switzerland | 255,497 |
| 19 | Belgium | 242,550 |
| 20 | Sweden | 227,785 |
| 21 | Indonesia | 214,995 |
| 22 | Austria | 206,303 |
| 23 | Turkey | 189,878 |
| 24 | Hong Kong, China | 171,401 |
| 25 | Denmark | 170,152 |
| 26 | Thailand | 153,909 |
| 27 | Norway | 153,437 |
| 28 | Saudi Arabia | 140,374 |

# Gross Domestic Product: 1997, in millions of U.S. dollars (in GDP order, highest to lowest)

| Ranking | | |
|---|---|---|
| 29 | Poland | 135,659 |
| 30 | South Africa | 129,094 |
| 31 | Greece | 122,946 |
| 32 | Finland | 119,867 |
| 33 | Portugal | 102,135 |
| 34 | Malaysia | 98,473 |
| 35 | Israel | 98,081 |
| 36 | Singapore | 96,319 |
| 37 | Colombia | 95,745 |
| 38 | Iran, Islamic Rep. | 89,979 |
| 39 | Venezuela | 87,480 |
| 40 | Philippines | 82,157 |
| 41 | Chile | 77,082 |
| 42 | Egypt, Arab Rep. | 75,605 |
| 43 | Ireland | 74,989 |
| 44 | New Zealand | 64,761 |
| 45 | Peru | 63,849 |
| 46 | Pakistan | 61,667 |
| 47 | Ukraine | 59,756 |
| 48 | Nigeria | 52,153 |
| 49 | Czech Republic | 52,035 |
| 50 | Algeria | 47,072 |
| 51 | Hungary | 45,725 |
| 52 | Puerto Rico | 42,364 |
| 53 | Bangladesh | 41,419 |
| 54 | United Arab Emirates | 39,107 |
| 55 | Morocco | 33,514 |
| 56 | Romania | 32,070 |
| 57 | Kuwait | 30,373 |
| 58 | Uzbekistan | 25,047 |
| 59 | Vietnam | 24,848 |
| 60 | Belarus | 22,462 |
| 61 | Kazakhstan | 22,165 |
| 62 | Slovak Republic | 19,461 |
| 63 | Croatia | 19,081 |
| 64 | Tunisia | 18,937 |
| 65 | Uruguay | 18,891 |
| 66 | Slovenia | 18,201 |
| 67 | Ecuador | 18,138 |
| 68 | Syrian Arab Republic | 17,899 |
| 69 | Guatemala | 17,772 |
| 70 | Luxembourg | 16,969 |
| 71 | Sri Lanka | 15,093 |
| 72 | Dominican Republic | 15,039 |
| 73 | Lebanon | 14,962 |
| 74 | Oman | 12,102 |
| 75 | El Salvador | 11,264 |
| 76 | Cote d'Ivoire | 10,251 |
| 77 | Kenya | 10,240 |
| 78 | Sudan | 10,224 |
| 79 | Paraguay | 10,180 |
| 80 | Bulgaria | 10,085 |
| 81 | Lithuania | 9,585 |
| 82 | Costa Rica | 9,521 |
| 83 | Cameroon | 9,115 |
| 84 | Zimbabwe | 8,906 |
| 85 | Panama | 8,244 |
| 86 | Cyprus | 8,204 |

## Gross Domestic Product: 1997, in millions of U.S. dollars (in GDP order, highest to lowest)

| Ranking | | |
|---|---|---|
| 87 | Bolivia | 7,977 |
| 88 | Angola | 7,662 |
| 89 | Qatar | 7,612 |
| 90 | Macao | 7,542 |
| 91 | Iceland | 7,296 |
| 92 | Jordan | 7,015 |
| 93 | Tanzania | 6,920 |
| 94 | Ghana | 6,884 |
| 95 | Uganda | 6,582 |
| 96 | Ethiopia | 6,381 |
| 97 | Congo, Dem. Rep. | 6,101 |
| 98 | Bahrain | 6,097 |
| 99 | Trinidad and Tobago | 5,894 |
| 100 | Yemen, Rep. | 5,656 |
| 101 | Latvia | 5,352 |
| 102 | Brunei | 5,271 |
| 103 | Georgia | 5,216 |
| 104 | Gabon | 5,153 |
| 105 | Botswana | 5,070 |
| 106 | Nepal | 4,929 |
| 107 | Estonia | 4,821 |
| 108 | Papua New Guinea | 4,639 |
| 109 | Senegal | 4,542 |
| 110 | Honduras | 4,491 |
| 111 | Turkmenistan | 4,399 |
| 112 | Azerbaijan | 4,399 |
| 113 | Mauritius | 4,398 |
| 114 | Jamaica | 4,135 |
| 115 | Guinea | 3,888 |
| 116 | Zambia | 3,865 |
| 117 | Bahamas, The | 3,750 |
| 118 | Madagascar | 3,546 |
| 119 | Malta | 3,323 |
| 120 | Namibia | 3,280 |
| 121 | Cambodia | 3,044 |
| 122 | Haiti | 2,815 |
| 123 | Mozambique | 2,753 |
| 124 | Mali | 2,532 |
| 125 | Malawi | 2,519 |
| 126 | Albania | 2,460 |
| 127 | Burkina Faso | 2,395 |
| 128 | Congo, Rep. | 2,298 |
| 129 | Kyrgyz Republic | 2,243 |
| 130 | Macedonia, FYR | 2,208 |
| 131 | Benin | 2,141 |
| 132 | Fiji | 2,101 |
| 133 | Moldova | 2,075 |
| 134 | Tajikistan | 1,990 |
| 135 | Nicaragua | 1,971 |
| 136 | Rwanda | 1,863 |
| 137 | Niger | 1,855 |
| 138 | Lao PDR | 1,753 |
| 139 | Barbados | 1,743 |
| 140 | Armenia | 1,626 |
| 141 | Chad | 1,603 |
| 142 | Togo | 1,475 |
| 143 | Swaziland | 1,313 |
| 144 | Greenland | 1,252 |

# Gross Domestic Product: 1997, in millions of U.S. dollars (in GDP order, highest to lowest)

| Ranking | | |
|---|---|---|
| 145 | Mauritania | 1,097 |
| 146 | Central African Republic | 1,019 |
| 147 | Burundi | 957 |
| 148 | Lesotho | 950 |
| 149 | Mongolia | 862 |
| 150 | Sierra Leone | 823 |
| 151 | Guyana | 782 |
| 152 | Eritrea | 655 |
| 153 | Belize | 649 |
| 154 | St. Lucia | 598 |
| 155 | Seychelles | 539 |
| 156 | Antigua and Barbuda | 502 |
| 157 | Djibouti | 500 |
| 158 | Equatorial Guinea | 487 |
| 159 | Cape Verde | 425 |
| 160 | Gambia, The | 407 |
| 161 | Bhutan | 383 |
| 162 | Solomon Islands | 374 |
| 163 | Maldives | 342 |
| 164 | Suriname | 335 |
| 165 | Grenada | 295 |
| 166 | St. Vincent and the Grenadines | 275 |
| 167 | Guinea-Bissau | 266 |
| 168 | Vanuatu | 252 |
| 169 | St. Kitts and Nevis | 247 |
| 170 | Dominica | 243 |
| 171 | Micronesia, Fed. Sts. | 213 |
| 172 | Samoa | 194 |
| 173 | Comoros | 194 |
| 174 | Tonga | 187 |
| 175 | Palau | 145 |
| 176 | Marshall Islands | 97 |
| 177 | Kiribati | 55 |
| 178 | Sao Tome and Principe | 44 |

# Index

## by Virgil Diodato

Acreage in farms, 94–96
Admissions expenditures, for entertainment, 232–33
Admissions receipts
    at amusement parks, 241
    at motion picture theaters, 242
Advertising firms, receipts of, 182
Affiliates of multinationals, foreign, 91–92, 93
Age
    book purchasing by, 227–28
    charity contributions by, 251
    of child, and expenditures on, 120
    consumer-unit expenditures by, 118–19, 233
    degree earned by, 51, 53
    household income and, 26, 29, 66
    Internet access and usage by, 198, 202
    nonfinancial family assets by, 75
    participation in sports by, 249
    percent distribution of expenditures by, 235
    personal earnings by, 51, 53
Agriculture. See Farms
Alcoholic beverages
    consumption of, 135–36
    expenditures on, 105
    expenditures on, by age of householder, 118
    expenditures on, by race and Hispanic origin, 117
    expenditures on, by region, 107
    expenditures on, by size of consumer unit, 109
Amusement and recreation services, receipts of, 238–40
Amusement parks, receipts of, 240, 241
Apparel, consumer-unit expenditures on, 105
    by age of householder, 119
    by race and Hispanic origin, 117
    by region, 108
    by size of consumer unit, 110
    by type of household unit, 113, 115
Apparel, family expenditures per child on, 120
Apparel, personal consumption expenditures on, 99, 101
Apparel, trends in, 162–65. See also Footwear
Appliances. See Household appliances
Asset-size class, corporate, 83–85
Assets, corporate, 80
    by asset-size class, 83–84
    by industry, 80–82, 83–84, 92–93
    of multinationals, 92–93
    profits and, by industry, 89

Assets, family, 75–76
Attendance (at school), and expenditures per pupil, 187, 188
Attendance (at spectator sports), 244–47
Automobile insurance, expenditures on, 213–14

Balance sheet data. See Assets; Liabilities
Baseball, as spectator sport, 244, 246
Basketball, as spectator sport, 244, 246
Beverages, 135–36. See also Food
Blacks. See Race and Hispanic origin
Board rates, in higher education, 195, 197
Boating, participation in, 242–43
Books. See also Reading
    hours of usage of, 222
    by purchaser characteristics, 227–28
    quantity sold, 224
    quantity sold, by type of book, 225
    by sales outlet, 227–28
    spending on, 223–24
    types of, 225, 227–28
Bowling centers, receipts of, 239–40
Bowling, participation in, 242–43, 248–50
Breakfast cereals. See also Flour and cereal products; Food
    consumption of, 126
    consumption of, by subcategories, 129, 132
Budget, federal. See Government, federal
Buildings. See Construction; Construction contracts; Homeownership rates; Housing units started
Buildings services firms, receipts of, 183
Business services, consumption of, 181–85
Business trips, 218, 219
Businesses. See Corporations; Farms; Multinational companies; Nonfarm proprietorships; Partnerships; Public companies

Calcium (nutrient), availability for consumption of, 141
Caloric sweeteners
    consumption of, 126
    consumption of, by subcategories, 129, 132
Carbohydrates, availability for consumption of, 137
Carotenes, availability for consumption of, 139
Cereal products. See Breakfast cereals; Flour and cereal products
Charity contributions, 251–52. See also Philanthropy funds, private

Child care, family expenditures per child on, 120

Children. *See also* Age; Pupils
consumer-unit expenditures and, 111–15
family expenditures on, 120
household book purchasing and, 227–28
household income and, 65
household Internet usage and, 199

Cholesterol, availability for consumption of, 138

Cleaners, recent trends in, 175–76

Clothing. *See* Apparel

Collection firms, receipts of, 182

College degree
Internet access and usage by, 200, 203–04
personal earnings by, 50–53

Compensation, 92–93. *See also* Earnings, personal; Income, personal; Pay

Computer services firms, receipts of, 185

Computers, personal. *See also* Microcomputer software sales
households using, by family income, 171, 173
households using, by region, 170
as teaching resources, 190–92

Construction. *See also* Construction contracts; Homeownership rates; Housing units started
new, private, value of, 144, 146
new, public, value of, 145, 147
new, total, value of, 143, 145

Construction contracts. *See also* Construction; Housing units started
floor space of, by class of construction, 151–52
value of, by class of construction, 151–52

Consumer durable goods, net stock of, 12–13

Consumer unit size, 109–11, 233. *See also* Households, size of

Consumer units, expenditures of. *See* Expenditures, consumer-unit

Consumption. *See also* Expenditures
of beverages, 135–36
of business services, 181–85
of construction goods, 143–52
of education services, elementary and secondary, 186–89
of education services, higher, 193–97
of energy, 153–61
of fixed capital, 71
of food commodities, 123–32
of health services, 205–12
of health supplies, 209, 211–12
of insurance services, 212–14
of Internet and online services, 198–204
for leisure and non-essentials, 221–51
macronutrient availability for, 137–42
of material goods, 121–76
of microcomputer software, 174
overview of, 97–120
of personal services, 179–81
of services, 177–214, 238–40
of teaching resources, 190–92
for travel, 217–20
trends in apparel/footwear and, 162–67
trends in household appliances and, 168–73
trends in soap/cleaners/toilet goods and, 175–76

Contributions, charity, by household income, 251–52

Contributions, consumer-unit expenditures on
by age of householder, 119
by race and Hispanic origin, 118
by region, 108
by size of consumer unit, 111
by type of household unit, 113, 115

Copper (nutrient), availability for consumption of, 142

Corporations. *See also* Multinational companies; Partnerships; Public companies
assets of, 80–82, 83–84
deductions of, 80–82, 83–84
dividends of, 85
liabilities of, 80–82
net income of, 80–82, 83–84
profits of, 85–87
receipts of, 79–82, 83–85
receipts of, changes in, 83
returns to, 80–82, 83–84
taxes on, 78, 85–87, 269–70

Corporations, farm, 94–95

Corporations, industrial, largest
earnings of, by industry, 90
profits of, by industry, 89
return to investors of, by industry, 90

Countries of the world, GDP for, 273–79

Credit reporting firms, receipts of, 182

Dairy products. *See also* Food
consumption of, 124
consumption of, by subcategories, 128, 131

Data processing services firms, receipts of, 185

Debt to capital, 88–89

Deductions, corporate
by asset-size class, 83–84
by industry, 80–82, 83–84

Defense, national, 3–9, 259–60

Deficits, federal budget, 255

Degree earned
Internet access and usage by, 200, 203–04
personal earnings by, 50–53

Dental laboratories, receipts of, 205–07

Dental services, expenditures for, 209, 211–12

Disposition, of personal income, 32–34. *See also* Income, personal, disposable

Dividend income, personal, 25, 32, 33

Dividends, corporate, 85

Dolls, recent trends in, 236–37

Dormitory charges, in higher education, 194, 196

Drugs, expenditures for, 209, 211–12

Durable goods, consumer, net stock of, 12–13

Earnings per share
 by industry, 90
 by industry, growth of, 88–89
 in largest companies, 88–89
Earnings, personal. *See also* Employee compensation;
  Income, personal; Pay
 by age, 51, 53
 in dolls/toys/games industry, 236–37
 in footwear industry, 166–67
 by highest degree earned, 50–53
 in household appliances industry, 169
 projected, by states, 49
 by race and Hispanic origin, 51, 53
 by sex (gender), 26, 51, 53
 in soap/cleaners/toilet goods industry, 175–76
 for spectator sport players, 244, 246
Education, consumer-unit expenditures on
 by age of householder, 119
 by race and Hispanic origin, 118
 by region, 108
 by size of consumer unit, 110
 by type of household unit, 113, 115
Education, elementary and secondary
 expenditures of, 186–87
 expenditures of, by state, 188
 receipts of, 186
 receipts of, by source, 187, 189
 teaching resource, availability and use of, 190–92
Education, family expenditures per child on, 120
Education, government expenditures on, 264–65
Education, higher
 board rates in, 195, 197
 dormitory charges in, 194, 196
 tuition and fees in, 193, 196
Education, personal consumption expenditures on, 100, 102
Educational attainment
 Internet access and usage by, 200, 203–04
 personal earnings by, 50–53
Educational software, spending on, 223–24
Employee compensation, 92–93. *See also* Earnings, personal; Income, personal; Pay
Employment
 in dolls/toys/games industry, 236–37
 in footwear industry, 166–67
 in household appliances industry, 169
 by multinationals, 92–93
 in soap/cleaners/toilet goods industry, 175–76
Energy
 consumption of, 153
 consumption of, by end-use sector, 158–59
 consumption of, by state, 157
 consumption of, by type of fuel, 155–56, 160–61
 exports of, 154, 155–56
 imports of, 154, 155–56
 production of, 153, 155–56
Entertainment, consumer-unit expenditures on, 231. *See also*
  Leisure and other non-essentials

 by age of householder, 119
 by percent of total expenditures, 232
 by race and Hispanic origin, 118
 by region, 108
 by size of consumer unit, 110
 by type of expense, 232
 by type of household unit, 113, 115
Entertainment, personal consumption expenditures on, 100,
  102. *See also* Leisure and other non-essentials
Equipment rental and leasing firms, receipts of, 184
Expenditures, capital
 in footwear industry, 166–67
 in household appliances industry, 169
 in soap/cleaners/toilet goods industry, 175–76
Expenditures, consumer. *See also* Consumption
 for health services and supplies, 209–12
 for media, 223–24
 for travel, 220
Expenditures, consumer-unit, 104. *See also* Consumption
 by age of householder, 118–19
 by expenditure type, 105–15, 117–19
 by household unit type, 111–15
 by race and Hispanic origin, 116–18
 by region, 106, 107–08
 by size of unit, 109–11
 units surveyed, 103
Expenditures, government. *See also* Consumption
 for education, 264–65
 for health/medical programs, 263–65
 for health services and supplies, 209
 for housing, 264–65
 for public aid, 263–64
 for social insurance, 263–64
 for social welfare, 263–67
 for veterans programs, 263–64
Expenditures, of elementary and secondary education, 186–
  87
Expenditures, personal consumption. *See also* Consumption
 in GDP, 3–9
 income and, 33, 39
 totals, in constant (1992) dollars, 101
 totals, in current dollars, 99
 by type, in constant (1992) dollars, 101–02
 by type, in current dollars, 99–100
Expenditures, types of
 by age of householder, 118–19
 of all consumer units, annual, 105–19
 children and, 120
 personal consumption and, 99–102
 by race and Hispanic origin, 116–18
 by region, 107–08
 by size of consumer unit, 109–11
 by type of household unit, 112–15
Exports
 of apparel, 163–65
 of cleaners, 175–76

Exports *(continued)*
    of dolls, 236–37
    of energy, 154–56
    of footwear, 166–67
    of games, 236–37
    in GDP, in constant (1992) dollars, 7–9
    in GDP, in current dollars, 3–6
    of household appliances, 168–69
    by multinationals, 93
    of soaps, 175–76
    of toilet goods, 175–76
    of toys, 236–37

Families, types of, 63, 65–66. *See also* Households, type of
Family assets. *See* Assets, family
Family farms, 94–95
Family income. *See* Income, family
Family size, pet ownership by, 251. *See also* Households, size of
Farms, 94–96
Fats and oils
    consumption of, 125
    consumption of, by subcategories, 128, 131
Fats, availability for consumption of, 138
Federal government. *See* Government, federal
Fee expenditures, for entertainment, 232–33
Financial assets, increases in, 71–72
Financial institutions, types of
    401(k) plans managed by, 73
    IRAs held by, 73
Fish and shellfish. *See also* Food
    consumption of, 123
    consumption of, by subcategories, 127, 130
    retail prices of, 133–34
Fixed capital, consumption of, 71
Fixed reproducible tangible wealth, net stock of, 11–13
Floor space, and construction contracts, 151–52
Flour and cereal products. *See also* Breakfast cereals; Food
    consumption of, 125
    consumption of, by subcategories, 129, 132
    retail prices of, 133–34
Flow of funds accounts, 71–72
Folate, availability for consumption of, 140
Food, consumer-unit expenditures on, 105
    by age of householder, 118
    by race and Hispanic origin, 117
    by region, 107
    by size of consumer unit, 109
    by type of household unit, 112, 114
Food, consumption of. *See also* Macronutrients
    by major groups, 123–26
    by subcategories, 127–32
Food energy, availability for consumption of, 137
Food, family expenditures on per child, 120
Food, personal consumption expenditures on, 99, 101
Food, retail prices of, 133–34
Food, sales of, at amusement parks, 241

Football, as spectator sport, 244, 246
Footwear, recent trends in, 166–67. *See also* Apparel
Foreign affiliates, of multinationals, 91–92, 93
Foreign direct investment, 14–15
Foreign travel, personal consumption expenditures on, 100, 102. *See also* Transportation
401(k) plans, 73–74
Fruits, retail prices of, 133–34. *See also* Food
Fuel, 155–56, 160–61. *See also* Energy
Furniture, 12. *See also* Household operations

Games, recent trends in, 236–37. *See also* Video games
GDP. *See* Gross domestic product
Gender. *See* Sex (gender)
Geographic regions. *See* Regions; States
GNP. *See* Gross national product
Golf courses, receipts of, 239–40
Golf, participation in, 242–43, 248–50
Goods and services, consumption of. *See* Consumption
Government
    expenditures for health services and supplies, 209
    expenditures for social welfare, 263–67
    investment by, 70
    savings by, 70
Government, federal
    budget, and gross federal debt, 260–62
    budget, outlays, and GDP, 256–57
    budget, outlays, by categories, 259–60
    budget, summary of, 255
    education receipts from, 187, 189
    expenditures and GDP, 3–9
    expenditures for defense, 3–9, 259–60
    expenditures for education, 264–65
    expenditures for health/medical programs, 263–65
    expenditures for housing, 264–65
    expenditures for human resources, 259–60
    expenditures for interest, 259–60
    expenditures for physical resources, 259–60
    expenditures for public aid, 263
    expenditures for social insurance, 263
    expenditures for social welfare programs, 266
    expenditures for veterans programs, 263
    gross federal debt, 260
    gross federal debt, as percent of GDP, 261–62
    investment and GDP, 3–9
    receipts, 255, 258–59. *See also* Income, national
    SBA loans, 262–63
    tangible wealth, net stock of fixed reproducible, 12–13
    trust funds, 258–59
Government, local
    education receipts from, 187, 189
    expenditures and GDP, 3–9
    expenditures for education, 264
    expenditures for health/medical programs, 263–64
    expenditures for housing, 264
    expenditures for public aid, 263
    expenditures for social insurance, 263

expenditures for social welfare programs, 266
expenditures for veterans programs, 263
investment and GDP, 3–9
tangible wealth, net stock of fixed reproducible, 12–13
Government, state. *See also* States
  education receipts from, 187, 189
  expenditures and GDP, 3–9
  expenditures for education, 264
  expenditures for health/medical programs, 263–64
  expenditures for housing, 264
  expenditures for public aid, 263
  expenditures for social insurance, 263
  expenditures for social welfare programs, 266
  expenditures for veterans programs, 263
  investment and GDP, 3–9
  revenue, 268
  revenue, sources of, 269–72
  tangible wealth, net stock of fixed reproducible, 12–13
  taxation, 269–70
Greyhound racing, as spectator sport, 245, 247
Gross domestic product (GDP)
  per capita, 2
  components of, 3–9
  in constant (1992) dollars, 7–9
  by country, 273–79
  in current dollars, 2–6
  federal budget debt as percent of, 261–62
  federal budget outlays as percent of, 256–57
  GNP and, 2, 10–11
  income, saving, and, 10–11
  international data on, 273–79
Gross national product (GNP)
  per capita, 2
  GDP and, 2, 10–11
  income, saving, and, 10–11
Gross product, of multinationals, 90–92
Gross state product
  in constant (1987) dollars, 17
  in constant (1992) dollars, 19, 21
  in current dollars, 18, 20
  population and, 16
  projections of, 17

Health care, consumer-unit expenditures on, 105
  by age of householder, 119
  by race and Hispanic origin, 118
  by region, 108
  by size of consumer unit, 110
  by type of household unit, 113, 115
Health care, family expenditures per child on, 120
Health care, personal expenditures on, 100, 102, 209, 211–12
Health insurance, 209, 211–12
Health/medical programs, government expenditures on, 263–65
Health services, consumption of, 205–12
Health services firms, receipts of, 205, 206–07

Health supplies, consumption of, 209, 211–12
High school degree, and personal earnings, 50–51
Higher education. *See* Education, higher
Hispanic origin. *See* Race and Hispanic origin
Hockey, as spectator sport, 245, 247
Home health care, expenditures for, 209, 211–12
Home health care services, receipts of, 205–07
Homeownership rates, 149, 150. *See also* Housing units started
Horseracing, as spectator sport, 245, 247
Hospital care, expenditures for, 209, 211–12
Hospital services, receipts of, 205–07
Household appliances
  exports and imports of, 168–69
  industry and product data on, 168–69
  use of, by family income, 171–73
  use of, by region, 170
Household income. *See* Income, household
Household office equipment, use of, 170–71
Household operations, consumer-unit expenditures on
  by age of householder, 119
  by race and Hispanic origin, 117
  by region, 107
  by size of consumer unit, 110
  by type of household unit, 112, 115
Household operations, personal consumption expenditures on, 99, 101
Households
  charity contributions by, 251–52
  pet ownership by, 251
  size of, 66. *See also* Consumer unit size
  size of, book purchasing by, 227–28
  size of, Internet access and usage by, 199, 203–04
  types of, expenditures by, 111–15
  types of, income for, 26–27, 65
Housing
  family expenditures per child on, 120
  government expenditures on, 264–65
  personal consumption expenditures on, 99, 101
Housing, consumer-unit expenditures on, 105
  by age of householder, 119
  by race and Hispanic origin, 117
  by region, 107
  by size of consumer unit, 110
  by type of household unit, 112, 115
Housing units started, 147, 148. *See also* Construction; Construction contracts; Homeownership rates
Human resources, in federal budget, 259–60

Imports
  of apparel, 163–65
  of cleaners, 175–76
  of dolls, 236–37
  of energy, 154–56
  of footwear, 166–67
  of games, 236–37
  of household appliances, 168–69

Imports *(continued)*
  by multinationals, 93
  of soaps, 175–76
  of toilet goods, 175–76
  of toys, 236–37
Income, corporate. *See also* Revenue, corporate
  by asset-size class, 83–84
  by industry, 80–82, 83–84
Income, family, 53–65, 67–68
  expenditure per child and, 120
  household appliances used by, 171–73
  household office equipment used by, 171
  nonfinancial family assets and, 75
  personal computers used by, 171, 173
  by race and Hispanic origin, 60, 61
  by sex (gender), 63, 65
  by state, for 4-person families, 53–59
  by type of family, 63, 65
Income, household, 26–31, 65–69
  by age, 26, 29, 66
  book purchasing by, 227–28
  charity contributions by, 252
  children and, 65
  by household size, 66
  by household type, 26–27, 65
  Internet access and usage by, 201, 203–04
  marital status and, 26, 68–69
  measures of, selected, 68–69
  by nativity, 26
  participation in sports by, 250
  pet ownership by, 251
  by race and Hispanic origin, 26, 28, 66–68
  by region, 26, 30
  by residence area, 26, 31
  by sex (gender), 26–27
  travel by, 219
Income levels
  household income and, 66–68
  race and Hispanic origin and, 66–68
Income, national, 10–11. *See also* Government, federal
Income, personal, 24–25, 32–53. *See also* Earnings,
      personal; Employee compensation; Pay
  per capita, 26, 39
  per capita, in constant (1992) dollars, 42–43, 45
  per capita, in current dollars, 39–41, 44
  components of, 25, 32–33
  disposable, 10–11, 33–34
  disposable, and saving, 71–72
  disposable, per capita, 39, 44–45
  disposition of, 32–34
  GDP, GNP, and, 10–11
  percent change of, 36–37
  projections of, 38
  saving and, 10–11, 33–34, 71–72
  by state, 34–38, 40–45
  totals for, 24

Income taxes, 269–70. *See also* Taxes
Individual retirement accounts (IRAs), 73
Industry, type of
  asset-size class and, 83–85
  assets by, 80–82, 83–84, 92–93
  debt to capital by, 88–89
  deductions by, 80–82, 83–84
  earnings per share by, 88–89, 90
  employee compensation by, 92–93
  employment by, 92–93
  gross product by, 90–92
  largest industrial corporations and, 89–90
  largest public companies and, 87–89
  liabilities by, 80–82
  multinationals and, 90–93
  net income by, 80–82, 83–84
  profitability by, 87
  profits by, 87, 89
  receipts of, 80–82, 83–84
  return to investors by, 90
  returns by, 80–82, 83–84
  sales by, 92–93
  sales growth by, 88
Insurance
  automobile, 213, 214
  health, 209, 211–12
  life, 212, 213
  social, 263–64
Insurance, consumer-unit expenditures on, 105, 106
  by age of householder, 119
  by race and Hispanic origin, 118
  by region, 108
  by size of consumer unit, 111
  by type of household unit, 113, 115
Insurance trust revenue, for states, 272
Interest, in federal budget, 259–60
Interest income, personal, 25, 32, 33
International GDP data, 273–79
Internet access and usage
  by access site, 202–03
  by age, 198, 202
  by educational attainment, 200, 203–04
  hours of, 222
  by household income, 201, 203–04
  by marital status, 200, 203–04
  by occupation, 203–04
  by recency of use, 202, 204
  by region, 199, 202
  by sex (gender), 198, 202
  by size of household, 199, 203–04
  spending on, 223–24
Investment
  foreign, 14–15, 70
  in 401(k) plans, 74
  government, 3–9, 70
  private, 70

saving and, 69–72
in tangible assets, 71–72
IRAs (individual retirement accounts), 73
Iron (nutrient), availability for consumption of, 142

Jai alai, as spectator sport, 245, 247

Labor force status. *See* Work status
Laboratories, medical and dental, receipts of, 205–07
Largest enterprises, 87–90
Legal services firms, receipts of, 185
Leisure and other non-essentials, 221–51. *See also* Entertainment; Travel
Liabilities
    corporate, 80–82
    individual saving and, 71–72
License taxes, 269–70
Life insurance, 212–13
Liquor store revenue, for states, 272
Local government. *See* Government, local

Macronutrients, availability for consumption of, 137–42
Magazines
    hours of usage of, 222
    spending on, 223–24
Magnesium (nutrient), availability for consumption of, 141
Mailing services firms, receipts of, 183
Manufacturing, average pay in, 48
Marital status
    consumer-unit expenditure and, 111–12
    family income and, 63, 65
    household income and, 65–66
    Internet access and usage and, 200, 203–04
Material goods, consumption of. *See* Consumption
Meat, red. *See* Red meat
Media. *See also* Books; Reading
    spending on, 223–24
    use of, by hours, 221–22
Medical care. *See* Health care
Medical durables, expenditures for, 209, 211–12
Medical facilities construction, 144–47, 209
Medical laboratories, receipts of, 205–07
Medical research, expenditures on, 209
Medical services. *See* Health services
Medicines. *See* Drugs
Men's and boys' apparel, trends in, 165. *See also* Apparel
Men's footwear, trends in, 166–67
Microcomputer software sales, 174. *See also* Computers, personal
Minerals and vitamins, availability for consumption of, 139–42
Motion picture industry, receipts of, 238, 239–40
Motion picture theaters
    attendance for, 242–43
    hours of usage of, 222
    spending on, 223–24
Motor vehicles, 12. *See also* Automobile insurance
Movies. *See* Motion picture theaters; Videos

Multinational companies. *See also* Corporations; Public companies
    assets of, by industry, 92–93
    employee compensation in, by industry, 92–93
    employment in, by industry, 92–93
    exports by, 93
    foreign affiliates of, 91–92, 93
    gross product of, by industry, 90–92
    imports of, 93
    sales of, by industry, 92–93
    U.S. parents of, 90–91, 92
Music, expenditures for recordings of, 235

Nativity, and household income, 26
Net national product, income, and savings, 10–11
Newspapers
    hours of usage of, 222
    number and circulation of, 229–30
    spending on, 223–24
Niacin, availability for consumption of, 140
Nonalcoholic beverages, consumption of, 135–36
Nonfarm proprietorships, 78, 79
Nonresidential buildings
    construction contracts for, 151–52
    new construction of, 144–47
Nursing care facilities, receipts of, 205–07
Nursing home care, expenditures for, 209, 211–12
Nutrients. *See* Food; Macronutrients

Occupation, type of, and Internet access and usage, 203–04
Office equipment, used by households, 170–71
Oil (fuel). *See* Energy
Oils (food). *See* Fats and oils
Online services. *See* Internet access and usage
Outlays, and federal budget, 255–57

Parent companies, of multinationals, 90–91, 92
Partnerships
    farm, 94–95
    receipts of, 79
    tax returns of, 78
Pay. *See also* Earnings, personal; Employee compensation; Income, personal
    in private industry, 47–48
    by state, 46–48
Pensions, consumer-unit expenditures on, 105, 106
    by age of householder, 119
    by race and Hispanic origin, 118
    by region, 108
    by size of consumer unit, 111
    by type of household unit, 113, 115
Personal care, consumer-unit expenditures on
    by age of householder, 119
    by race and Hispanic origin, 118
    by region, 108
    by size of consumer unit, 110
    by type of household unit, 113, 115

Personal care facilities, receipts of, 205–07
Personal care, personal consumption expenditures on, 99, 101
Personal computers. *See* Computers, personal
Personal consumption expenditures. *See* Expenditures, personal consumption
Personal income. *See* Income, personal
Personal services, consumption of, 179–81
Personnel supply services firms, receipts of, 184
Pet ownership, 251
Philanthropy funds, private, 252–53. *See also* Charity contributions
Phosphorus (nutrient), availability for consumption of, 141
Physical resources, in federal budget, 259–60
Physician services, expenditures for, 209, 211–12
Place of residence. *See* Residence
Pleasure trips, 218, 219
Population, and gross state product, 16
Potassium (nutrient), availability for consumption of, 142
Poultry products. *See also* Food
    consumption of, 124
    consumption of, by subcategories, 127, 130
    retail prices of, 133–34
Poverty rate, and household income, 68–69
Prices, retail, of food items, 133–34
Private capital, net stock of fixed, 94
Private construction, new, value of, 144, 146
Private domestic investment, and GDP, 3–9
Private education, higher, 193–97
Private tangible wealth, net stock of fixed reproducible, 12–13
Privately owned housing units started, 147, 148
Production, of energy, 153, 155–56
Profitability, corporate, 87
Profits, corporate, 85–86
    by industry, 87, 89
Projections
    of earnings, by state, 49
    of 401(k) plan assets, 73
    of gross state product, 17
    of personal income, by state, 38
Proprietors' income, 25, 32, 33
Proprietorships, nonfarm, 78, 79
Proteins, availability for consumption of, 137
Public aid, government expenditures on, 263–64
Public companies, largest. *See also* Corporations; Multinational companies
    debt to capital of, by industry, 88–89
    earnings growth of, by industry, 88–89
    profitability of, by industry, 87
    sales growth of, by industry, 88
Public construction, new, value of, 145, 147
Public education
    elementary and secondary, 186–92
    higher, 193–97

Public health services, expenditures on, 209
Pupils, expenditures per, 187, 188

Race and Hispanic origin
    consumer-unit expenditures by, 116–18
    degree earned and, 51, 53
    earnings, personal, by, 51, 53
    entertainment expenditures by, 233
    income, family, by, 60–61
    income, household, by, 26, 28, 66–68
    income, personal, by, 26
    reading expenditures by, 233
    teaching resources by, 191
Radio
    hours of usage of, 222
    spending on, 223–24, 232–33
Reading, consumer-unit expenditures on, 231–32. *See also* Books; Education
Receipts. *See also* Revenue; Sales
    for amusement and recreation services, 238–40
    for amusement parks, 240, 241
    for bowling centers, 239–40
    for business services, 182–85
    for corporations, 79
    for corporations, by asset-size class, 83–85
    for corporations, by industry, 80–84
    for corporations, changes in, 83
    for elementary and secondary education, 186, 187, 189
    for federal government, 255, 258–59
    for golf courses, 239–40
    for health services, 205–07
    for motion picture theaters, 242
    for nonfarm proprietorships, 79
    for partnerships, 79
    for personal services, 179–81
Recorded music. *See also* Sound recordings
    expenditures on sound equipment for, 232–33
    hours of usage of, 222
    households with equipment for, 170–71
    spending on, 223–24
Recreation. *See* Amusement and recreation services; Entertainment; Sports
Red meat. *See also* Food
    consumption of, 123
    consumption of, by subcategories, 127, 130
    retail prices of, 133–34
Regions
    consumer-unit expenditures by, 107–08
    entertainment expenditures by, 233
    household appliances used by, 170
    household income by, 26, 30
    household office equipment used by, 170
    Internet access and usage by, 199, 202
    personal computers used by, 170
    reading expenditures by, 233

Religious and welfare activities, personal consumption expenditures on, 100, 102

Rental income, personal, 25, 32, 33

Reproduction services firms, receipts of, 183

Residence (inside/outside metropolitan areas), and household income, 26, 31

Residential buildings. *See also* Housing
  construction contracts for, 151–52
  housing units started, 147–48
  new construction of, 144–47

Retail trade, average pay in, 48

Return to investors, by industry, 90

Returns, corporate
  by asset-size class, 83–84
  by industry, 80–82, 83–84

Revenue. *See also* Income; Receipts
  corporate, 89
  of state governments, 268–72

Riboflavin, availability for consumption of, 140

Rodeos, as spectator sport, 245, 247

Room and board, in higher education. *See* Board rates; Dormitory charges

Salary. *See* Earnings, personal; Employee compensation; Income, personal; Pay; Wage and salary disbursements

Sales. *See also* Receipts
  at amusement parks, 241
  of books, 224–25, 227–28
  by industry type, 92–93
  by multinationals, 92–93

Sales growth, 88

Sales outlets
  for books, 227–28
  for sound recordings, 235

Sales taxes, 269–70. *See also* Taxes

Saving
  in 401(k) plans, 73–74
  government, 70
  gross, 69–70
  individual, composition of, 71–72
  in IRAs, 73
  personal, 70
  personal, and GDP/GNP, 10–11
  personal, and income, 10–11, 33–34, 71–72
  private, 70

SBA (Small Business Administration) loans, 262–63

School system size, and teaching resources, 192. *See also* Education

Seafood. *See* Fish and shellfish

Services and goods, consumption of. *See* Consumption

Sex (gender)
  degree earned by, 51, 53
  family income by, 63, 65
  household income by, 26–27, 65–66
  Internet access and usage by, 198, 202
  participation in sports by, 248
  personal earnings by, 26, 51, 53

sound recordings and, 235
  teaching resources by, 190
  travel by, 219

Shellfish. *See* Fish and shellfish

Shelter. *See* Housing

Small Business Administration (SBA) loans, 262–63

Soaps, recent trends in, 175–76

Social insurance, government expenditures on, 263–64

Social Security, consumer-unit expenditures on, 105, 106
  by age of householder, 119
  by race and Hispanic origin, 118
  by region, 108
  by size of consumer unit, 111
  by type of household unit, 113, 115

Social welfare programs, government expenditures on, 263–67

Softball, participation in, 242–43, 248–50

Software
  sales of, 174
  spending on, 223–24

Sound recordings, expenditures on, 234–35. *See also* Recorded music

Spectator sports. *See* Sports, spectator

Spending. *See* Expenditures

Sports
  participation in, 242–43
  participation in, by age, 249
  participation in, by household income, 250
  participation in, by sex (gender), 248
  participation in, ranking of, 248
  spectator, attendance at, 244–47
  spectator, number of teams/performances in, 244–47
  spectator, players' salaries in, 244, 246

States. *See also* Government, state
  automobile insurance expenditures by, 214
  earnings, projected, by, 49
  education expenditures by, 188
  education receipts by, 189
  energy consumption by, 155, 159, 161
  foreign direct investment in, 14–15
  gross state product of, 16–21
  homeownership rates by, 150
  housing units started by, 148
  income, family, by, 53–59
  income, personal, by, 34–38, 40–45
  insurance trust revenue by, 272
  liquor store revenue by, 272
  newspaper number and circulation by, 229–30
  pay by, 46–48
  revenue sources by, 270–72
  state revenue by, 268
  taxation by, 270
  travel expenditures by, 220
  utility revenue by, 272

Stenographic services firms, receipts of, 183

Stockholder's equity, and profits, 89

Surpluses, federal budget, 255
Sweeteners. *See* Caloric sweeteners

Tangible assets, investment in, 71–72
Tax returns, business, 78
Taxes, corporate
 profits, pre- and after, 85–86, 87
 profits tax liability and, 85
 by state, 269–70
Taxes, personal
 expenditures on, by age of householder, 119
 expenditures on, by race and Hispanic origin, 118
 expenditures on, by region, 108
 expenditures on, by size of consumer unit, 111
 expenditures on, by type of household unit, 113, 115
Taxes, state revenue from, 269–70
Teaching resources, 190–92. *See also* Education
Television
 hours of usage of, 222
 households with, 170–71
 spending on, 223–24, 232–33
Tennis, participation in, 242–43, 248–50
Tenure (owning/renting), and nonfinancial family assets, 75–76
Textiles. *See* Apparel
Thiamin, availability for consumption of, 140
Tobacco products, consumer-unit expenditures on, 105, 106
 by age of householder, 119
 by race and Hispanic origin, 118
 by region, 108
 by size of consumer unit, 111
 by type of household unit, 113, 115
Tobacco products, personal consumption expenditures on, 99, 101
Toilet goods, recent trends in, 175–76
Toys, recent trends in, 236–37
Trade. *See* Exports; Imports
Transfer payments
 by persons, 33
 to persons, 25, 32, 33
Transportation, consumer-unit expenditures on, 105. *See also* Travel
 by age of householder, 119
 by race and Hispanic origin, 118
 by region, 108
 by size of consumer unit, 110
 by type of household unit, 113, 115

Transportation, family expenditures per child on, 120. *See also* Travel
Transportation, personal consumption expenditures on, 100, 102. *See also* Travel
Travel. *See also* Transportation
 characteristics of, 219
 expenditures on, 220
 foreign, 100, 102
 by number of trips, 217
 by type of trip, 218
Trust funds, and federal government, 258–59
Tuition and fees, in higher education, 193, 196

Utilities. *See* Housing
Utility revenue, for states, 272

Vegetables, retail prices of, 133–34. *See also* Food
Veterans, government expenditures on, 263–64
Video games
 hours of usage of, 222
 spending on, 223–24
Videos
 hours of usage of, 222
 households with equipment for, 170–71
 rental of, receipts for, 239, 240
 spending on, 223–24
Vision products, expenditures for, 209, 211–12
Vitamins and minerals, availability for consumption of, 139–42

Wage and salary disbursements, 25, 32, 33. *See also* Earnings, personal; Employee compensation; Income, personal; Pay
Welfare activities. *See* Religious and welfare activities
Welfare programs, social, government expenditures on, 263–67
Whites. *See* Race and Hispanic origin
Women's footwear, trends in, 166–67
Women's outerwear, trends in, 163–64. *See also* Apparel
Work status
 nonfinancial family assets and, 75–76
 of wife, and family income, 63, 65

Zinc (nutrient), availability for consumption of, 142